4.4BSD
User's Reference Manual
(URM)

Now in its twentieth year, the USENIX Association, the UNIX and Advanced Computing Systems professional and technical organization, is a not-for-profit membership association of individuals and institutions with an interest in UNIX and UNIX-like systems, and, by extension, C++, X windows, and other advanced tools and technologies.

USENIX and its members are dedicated to:

- fostering innovation and communicating research and technological developments,
- sharing ideas and experience relevant to UNIX, UNIX-related, and advanced computing systems, and
- providing a neutral forum for the exercise of critical thought and airing of technical issues.

USENIX publishes a journal (**Computing Systems**), a newsletter (*;login:*), Proceedings from its frequent Conferences and Symposia, and a Book Series.

SAGE, The Systems Administrators Guild, a Special Technical Group with the USENIX Association, is dedicated to the advancement of system administration as a profession.

SAGE brings together systems managers and administrators to:

- propagate knowledge of good professional practice,
- recruit talented individuals to the profession,
- recognize individuals who attain professional excellence,
- foster technical development and share solutions to technical problems, and
- communicate in an organized voice with users, management, and vendors on system administration topics.

4.4BSD
User's Reference Manual
(URM)

Berkeley Software Distribution
April, 1994

Computer Systems Research Group
University of California at Berkeley

A USENIX Association Book
O'Reilly & Associates, Inc.
103 Morris Street, Suite A
Sebastopol, CA 94572

The Institute of Electrical and Electronics Engineers and the American National Standards Committee X3, on Information Processing Systems have given us permission to reprint portions of their documentation.

In the following statement, the phrase ''this text'' refers to portions of the system documentation.

''Portions of this text are reprinted and reproduced in electronic form in 4.4BSD from IEEE Std 1003.1-1988, IEEE Standard Portable Operating System Interface for Computer Environments (POSIX), copyright 1988 by the Institute of Electrical and Electronics Engineers, Inc. In the event of any discrepancy between these versions and the original IEEE Standard, the original IEEE Standard is the referee document.''

In the following statement, the phrase ''This material'' refers to portions of the system documentation.

''This material is reproduced with permission from American National Standards Committee X3, on Information Processing Systems. Computer and Business Equipment Manufacturers Association (CBEMA), 311 First St., NW, Suite 500, Washington, DC 20001-2178. The developmental work of Programming Language C was completed by the X3J11 Technical Committee.''

Manual pages adb.1, bc.1, compact.1, crypt.1, dc.1, deroff.1, ed.1, expr.1, graph.1, ld.1, learn.1, m4.1, plot.1, ptx.1, spell.1, spline.1, struct.1, tar.1, units.1, uucp.1, uux.1, ching.6, eqnchar.7, man.7, ms.7, and term.7 are copyright 1979, AT&T Bell Laboratories, Incorporated. Holders of UNIX^{TM}/32V, System III, or System V software licenses are permitted to copy these documents, or any portion of them, as necessary for licensed use of the software, provided this copyright notice and statement of permission are included.

The views and conclusions contained in this manual are those of the authors and should not be interpreted as representing official policies, either expressed or implied, of the Regents of the University of California.

This book was printed and bound in the United States of America.
Distributed by O'Reilly & Associates, Inc.

[recycle logo]   This book is printed on acid-free paper with 50% recycled content, 10-13% post-consumer waste. O'Reilly & Associates is committed to using paper with the highest recycled content available consistent with high quality.

ISBN: 1-56592-075-9

Contents

The Computer Systems Research Group
1979 – 1993

CSRG Technical Staff

Jim Bloom
Keith Bostic
Ralph Campbell
Kevin Dunlap
William N. Joy
Michael J. Karels
Samuel J. Leffler
Marshall Kirk McKusick
Miriam Amos Nihart
Keith Sklower
Marc Teitelbaum
Michael Toy

CSRG Administration and Support

Robert Fabry
Domenico Ferrari
Susan L. Graham
Bob Henry
Anne Hughes
Bob Kridle
David Mosher
Pauline Schwartz
Mark Seiden
Jean Wood

Organizations that funded the CSRG with grants, gifts, personnel, and/or hardware.

Center for Advanced Aviation System Development, The MITRE Corp.
Compaq Computer Corporation
Cray Research Inc.
Department of Defense Advance Research Projects Agency (DARPA)
Digital Equipment Corporation
The Hewlett-Packard Company
NASA Ames Research Center
The National Science Foundation
The Open Software Foundation
UUNET Technologies Inc.

The following are people and organizations that provided a large subsystem for the BSD releases.

ANSI C library	Chris Torek
ANSI C prototypes	Donn Seeley and John Kohl
Autoconfiguration	Robert Elz
C library documentation	American National Standards Committee X3
CCI 6/32 support	Computer Consoles Inc.
DEC 3000/5000 support	Ralph Campbell
Disklabels	Symmetric Computer Systems
Documentation	Cynthia Livingston and The USENIX Association
Franz Lisp	Richard Fateman, John Foderaro, Keith Sklower, Kevin Layer
GCC, GDB	The Free Software Foundation
Groff	James Clark (The FSF)
HP300 support	Jeff Forys, Mike Hibler, Jay Lepreau, Donn Seeley and the Systems Programming Group; University of Utah Computer Science Department
ISODE	Marshall Rose
Ingres	Mike Stonebraker, Gene Wong, and the Berkeley Ingres Research Group
Intel 386/486 support	Bill Jolitz and TeleMuse
Job control	Jim Kulp
Kerberos	Project Athena and MIT
Kernel support	Bill Shannon and Sun Microsystems Inc.
LFS	Margo Seltzer, Mendel Rosenblum, Carl Staelin
MIPS support	Trent Hein
Math library	K.C. Ng, Zhishun Alex Liu, S. McDonald, P. Tang and W. Kahan
NFS	Rick Macklem
NFS automounter	Jan-Simon Pendry
Network device drivers	Micom-Interlan and Excelan
Omron Luna support	Akito Fujita and Shigeto Mochida
Quotas	Robert Elz
RPC support	Sun Microsystems Inc.
Shared library support	Rob Gingell and Sun Microsystems Inc.
Sony News 3400 support	Kazumasa Utashiro
Sparc I/II support	Computer Systems Engineering Group, Lawrence Berkeley Laboratory
Stackable file systems	John Heidemann
Stdio	Chris Torek
System documentation	The Institute of Electrical and Electronics Engineers, Inc.
TCP/IP	Rob Gurwitz and Bolt Beranek and Newman Inc.
Timezone support	Arthur David Olson
Transport/Network OSI layers	IBM Corporation and the University of Wisconsin
Kernel XNS assistance	William Nesheim, J. Q. Johnson, Chris Torek, and James O'Toole
User level XNS	Cornell University
VAX 3000 support	Mt. Xinu and Tom Ferrin
VAX BI support	Chris Torek
VAX device support	Digital Equipment Corporation and Helge Skrivervik
Versatec printer/plotter support	University of Toronto
Virtual memory implementation	Avadis Tevanian, Jr., Michael Wayne Young, and the Carnegie-Mellon University Mach project
X25	University of British Columbia

The following are people and organizations that provided a specific item, program, library routine or program maintenance for the BSD system. (Their contribution may not be part of the final 4.4BSD release.)

386 device drivers	Carnegie-Mellon University Mach project
386 device drivers	Don Ahn, Sean Fagan and Tim Tucker
HCX device drivers	Harris Corporation
Kernel enhancements	Robert Elz, Peter Ivanov, Ian Johnstone, Piers Lauder,
	John Lions, Tim Long, Chris Maltby, Greg Rose and John Wainwright
ISO-9660 filesystem	Pace Willisson, Atsushi Murai

adventure(6)	Don Woods	log(3)	Peter McIlroy
adventure(6)	Jim Gillogly	look(1)	David Hitz
adventure(6)	Will Crowther	ls(1)	Elan Amir
apply(1)	Rob Pike	ls(1)	Michael Fischbein
apply(1)	Jan-Simon Pendry	lsearch(3)	Roger L. Snyder
ar(1)	Hugh A. Smith	m4(1)	Ozan Yigit
arithmetic(6)	Eamonn McManus	mail(1)	Kurt Schoens
arp(8)	Sun Microsystems Inc.	make(1)	Adam de Boor
at(1)	Steve Wall	me(7)	Eric Allman
atc(6)	Ed James	mergesort(3)	Peter McIlroy
awk(1)	Arnold Robbins	mh(1)	Marshall Rose
awk(1)	David Trueman	mh(1)	The Rand Corporation
backgammon(6)	Alan Char	mille(6)	Ken Arnold
banner(1)	Mark Horton	mknod(8)	Kevin Fall
battlestar(6)	David Riggle	monop(6)	Ken Arnold
bcd(6)	Steve Hayman	more(1)	Eric Shienbrood
bdes(1)	Matt Bishop	more(1)	Mark Nudleman
berknet(1)	Eric Schmidt	mountd(8)	Herb Hasler
bib(1)	Dain Samples	mprof(1)	Ben Zorn
bib(1)	Gary M. Levin	msgs(1)	David Wasley
bib(1)	Timothy A. Budd	multicast	Stephen Deering
bitstring(3)	Paul Vixie	mv(1)	Ken Smith
boggle(6)	Barry Brachman	named/bind(8)	Douglas Terry
bpf(4)	Steven McCanne	named/bind(8)	Kevin Dunlap
btree(3)	Mike Olson	news(1)	Rick Adams (and a cast of thousands)
byte-range locking	Scooter Morris	nm(1)	Hans Huebner
caesar(6)	John Eldridge	pascal(1)	Kirk McKusick
caesar(6)	Stan King	pascal(1)	Peter Kessler
cal(1)	Kim Letkeman	paste(1)	Adam S. Moskowitz
cat(1)	Kevin Fall	patch(1)	Larry Wall
chess(6)	Stuart Cracraft (The FSF)	pax(1)	Keith Muller
ching(6)	Guy Harris	phantasia(6)	C. Robertson
cksum(1)	James W. Williams	phantasia(6)	Edward A. Estes
clri(8)	Rich $alz	ping(8)	Mike Muuss
col(1)	Michael Rendell	pom(6)	Keith E. Brandt
comm(1)	Case Larsen	pr(1)	Keith Muller
compact(1)	Colin L. McMaster	primes(6)	Landon Curt Noll
compress(1)	James A. Woods	qsort(3)	Doug McIlroy
compress(1)	Joseph Orost	qsort(3)	Earl Cohen
compress(1)	Spencer Thomas	qsort(3)	Jon Bentley
courier(1)	Eric Cooper	quad(3)	Chris Torek
cp(1)	David Hitz	quiz(6)	Jim R. Oldroyd
cpio(1)	AT&T	quiz(6)	Keith Gabryelski
crypt(3)	Tom Truscott	radixsort(3)	Dan Bernstein
csh(1)	Christos Zoulas	radixsort(3)	Peter McIlroy
csh(1)	Len Shar	rain(6)	Eric P. Scott
curses(3)	Elan Amir	ranlib(1)	Hugh A. Smith
curses(3)	Ken Arnold	rcs(1)	Walter F. Tichy
cut(1)	Adam S. Moskowitz	rdist(1)	Michael Cooper
cut(1)	Marciano Pitargue	regex(3)	Henry Spencer
dbx(1)	Mark Linton	robots(6)	Ken Arnold
dd(1)	Keith Muller	rogue(6)	Timothy C. Stoehr
dd(1)	Lance Visser	rs(1)	John Kunze
des(1)	Jim Gillogly	sail(6)	David Riggle
des(1)	Phil Karn	sail(6)	Edward Wang
des(1)	Richard Outerbridge	sccs(1)	Eric Allman

dipress(1)	Xerox Corporation	scsiformat(1)	Lawrence Berkeley Laboratory
disklabel(8)	Symmetric Computer Systems	sdb(1)	Howard Katseff
du(1)	Chris Newcomb	sed(1)	Diomidis Spinellis
dungeon(6)	R.M. Supnik	sendmail(8)	Eric Allman
ed(1)	Rodney Ruddock	setmode(3)	Dave Borman
emacs(1)	Richard Stallman	sh(1)	Kenneth Almquist
erf(3)	Peter McIlroy, K.C. Ng	slattach(8)	Rick Adams
error(1)	Robert R. Henry	slip(8)	Rick Adams
ex(1)	Mark Horton	spms(1)	Peter J. Nicklin
factor(6)	Landon Curt Noll	strtod(3)	David M. Gay
file(1)	Ian Darwin	swab(3)	Jeffrey Mogul
find(1)	Cimarron Taylor	sysconf(3)	Sean Eric Fagan
finger(1)	Tony Nardo	sysline(1)	J.K. Foderaro
fish(6)	Muffy Barkocy	syslog(3)	Eric Allman
fmt(1)	Kurt Schoens	systat(1)	Bill Reeves
fnmatch(3)	Guido van Rossum	systat(1)	Robert Elz
fold(1)	Kevin Ruddy	tail(1)	Edward Sze-Tyan Wang
fortune(6)	Ken Arnold	talk(1)	Clem Cole
fpr(1)	Robert Corbett	talk(1)	Kipp Hickman
fsdb(8)	Computer Consoles Inc.	talk(1)	Peter Moore
fsplit(1)	Asa Romberger	telnet(1)	Dave Borman
fsplit(1)	Jerry Berkman	telnet(1)	Paul Borman
gcc/groff integration	UUNET Technologies, Inc.	termcap(5)	John A. Kunze
gcore(1)	Eric Cooper	termcap(5)	Mark Horton
getcap(3)	Casey Leedom	test(1)	Kenneth Almquist
glob(3)	Guido van Rossum	tetris(6)	Chris Torek
gprof(1)	Peter Kessler	tetris(6)	Darren F. Provine
gprof(1)	Robert R. Henry	timed(8)	Riccardo Gusella
hack(6)	Andries Brouwer (and a cast of thousands)	timed(8)	Stefano Zatti
hangman(6)	Ken Arnold	tn3270(1)	Gregory Minshall
hash(3)	Margo Seltzer	tr(1)	Igor Belchinskiy
heapsort(3)	Elmer Yglesias	traceroute(8)	Van Jacobson
heapsort(3)	Kevin Lew	trek(6)	Eric Allman
heapsort(3)	Ronnie Kon	tset(1)	Eric Allman
hunt(6)	Conrad Huang	tsort(1)	Michael Rendell
hunt(6)	Greg Couch	unifdef(1)	Dave Yost
icon(1)	Bill Mitchell	uniq(1)	Case Larsen
icon(1)	Ralph Griswold	uucpd(8)	Rick Adams
indent(1)	David Willcox	uudecode(1)	Mark Horton
indent(1)	Eric Schmidt	uuencode(1)	Mark Horton
indent(1)	James Gosling	uuq(1)	Lou Salkind
indent(1)	Sun Microsystems	uuq(1)	Rick Adams
init(1)	Donn Seeley	uusnap(8)	Randy King
j0(3)	Sun Microsystems, Inc.	uusnap(8)	Rick Adams
j1(3)	Sun Microsystems, Inc.	vacation(1)	Eric Allman
jn(3)	Sun Microsystems, Inc.	vi(1)	Steve Kirkendall
join(1)	David Goodenough	which(1)	Peter Kessler
join(1)	Michiro Hikida	who(1)	Michael Fischbein
join(1)	Steve Hayman	window(1)	Edward Wang
jot(1)	John Kunze	worm(6)	Michael Toy
jove(1)	Jonathon Payne	worms(6)	Eric P. Scott
kermit(1)	Columbia University	write(1)	Craig Leres
kvm(3)	Peter Shipley	write(1)	Jef Poskanzer
kvm(3)	Steven McCanne	wump(6)	Dave Taylor
lam(1)	John Kunze	X25/Ethernet	Univ. of Erlangen-Nuremberg
larn(6)	Noah Morgan	X25/LLC2	Dirk Husemann
lastcomm(1)	Len Edmondson	xargs(1)	John B. Roll Jr.
lex(1)	Vern Paxson	xneko(6)	Masayuki Koba
libm(3)	Peter McIlroy	XNSrouted(1)	Bill Nesheim
libm(3)	UUNET Technologies, Inc.	xroach(6)	J.T. Anderson
locate(1)	James A. Woods	yacc(1)	Robert Paul Corbett
lock(1)	Bob Toxen		

Preface

1. Introduction

The major new facilities available in the 4.4BSD release are a new virtual memory system, the addition of ISO/OSI networking support, a new virtual filesystem interface supporting filesystem stacking, a freely redistributable implementation of NFS, a log-structured filesystem, enhancement of the local filesystems to support files and filesystems that are up to 2^{63} bytes in size, enhanced security and system management support, and the conversion to and addition of the IEEE Std1003.1 ("POSIX") facilities and many of the IEEE Std1003.2 facilities. In addition, many new utilities and additions have been made to the C-library. The kernel sources have been reorganized to collect all machine-dependent files for each architecture under one directory, and most of the machine-independent code is now free of code conditional on specific machines. The user structure and process structure have been reorganized to eliminate the statically-mapped user structure and to make most of the process resources shareable by multiple processes. The system and include files have been converted to be compatible with ANSI C, including function prototypes for most of the exported functions. There are numerous other changes throughout the system.

2. Changes in the Kernel

This release includes several important structural kernel changes. The kernel uses a new internal system call convention; the use of global ("u-dot") variables for parameters and error returns has been eliminated, and interrupted system calls no longer abort using non-local goto's (longjmp's). A new sleep interface separates signal handling from scheduling priority, returning characteristic errors to abort or restart the current system call. This sleep call also passes a string describing the process state, which is used by the ps(1) program. The old sleep interface can be used only for non-interruptible sleeps.

Many data structures that were previously statically allocated are now allocated dynamically. These structures include mount entries, file entries, user open file descriptors, the process entries, the vnode table, the name cache, and the quota structures.

The 4.4BSD distribution adds support for several new architectures including SPARC-based Sparcstations 1 and 2, MIPS-based Decstation 3100 and 5000 and Sony NEWS, 68000-based Hewlett-Packard 9000/300 and Omron Luna, and 386-based Personal Computers. Both the HP300 and SPARC ports feature the ability to run binaries built for the native operating system (HP-UX or SunOS) by emulating their system calls. Though this native operating system compatibility was provided by the developers as needed for their purposes and is by no means complete, it is complete enough to run several non-trivial applications including those that require HP-UX or SunOS shared libraries. For example, the vendor supplied X11 server and windowing environment can be used on both the HP300 and SPARC.

2.1. Virtual memory changes

The new virtual memory implementation is derived from the MACH operating system developed at Carnegie-Mellon, and was ported to the BSD kernel at the University of Utah. The MACH virtual memory system call interface has been replaced with the "mmap"-based interface described in the "Berkeley Software Architecture Manual". The interface is similar to the interfaces shipped by several commercial vendors such as Sun, USL, and Convex Computer Corp. The integration of the new virtual memory is functionally complete, but, like most MACH-based virtual memory systems, still has serious performance problems under heavy memory load.

2.2. Networking additions and changes

The ISO/OSI Networking consists of a kernel implementation of transport class 4 (TP-4), connectionless networking protocol (CLNP), and 802.3-based link-level support (hardware-compatible with Ethernet*). We also

---

*Ethernet is a trademark of the Xerox Corporation.

include support for ISO Connection-Oriented Network Service, X.25, TP-0. The session and presentation layers are provided outside the kernel by the ISO development environment (ISODE). Included in this development environment are file transfer and management (FTAM), virtual terminals (VT), a directory services implementation (X.500), and miscellaneous other utilities.

Several important enhancements have been added to the TCP/IP protocols including TCP header prediction and serial line IP (SLIP) with header compression. The routing implementation has been completely rewritten to use a hierarchical routing tree with a mask per route to support the arbitrary levels of routing found in the ISO protocols. The routing table also stores and caches route characteristics to speed the adaptation of the throughput and congestion avoidance algorithms.

2.3. Additions and changes to filesystems

The 4.4BSD distribution contains most of the interfaces specified in the IEEE Std1003.1 system interface standard. Filesystem additions include IEEE Std1003.1 FIFOs, byte-range file locking, and saved user and group identifiers.

A new virtual filesystem interface has been added to the kernel to support multiple filesystems. In comparison with other interfaces, the Berkeley interface has been structured for more efficient support of filesystems that maintain state (such as the local filesystem). The interface has been extended with support for stackable filesystems done at UCLA. These extensions allow for filesystems to be layered on top of each other and allow new vnode operations to be added without requiring changes to existing filesystem implementations. For example, the umap filesystem is used to mount a sub-tree of an existing filesystem that uses a different set of uids and gids than the local system. Such a filesystem could be mounted from a remote site via NFS or it could be a filesystem on removable media brought from some foreign location that uses a different password file.

In addition to the local "fast filesystem", we have added an implementation of the network filesystem (NFS) that fully interoperates with the NFS shipped by Sun and its licensees. Because our NFS implementation was implemented using only the publicly available NFS specification, it does not require a license from Sun to use in source or binary form. By default it runs over UDP to be compatible with Sun's implementation. However, it can be configured on a per-mount basis to run over TCP. Using TCP allows it to be used quickly and efficiently through gateways and over long-haul networks. Using an extended protocol, it supports Leases to allow a limited callback mechanism that greatly reduces the network traffic necessary to maintain cache consistency between the server and its clients.

A new log-structured filesystem has been added that provides near disk-speed output and fast crash recovery. It is still experimental in the 4.4BSD release, so we do not recommend it for production use. We have also added a memory-based filesystem that runs in pageable memory, allowing large temporary filesystems without requiring dedicated physical memory.

The local "fast filesystem" has been enhanced to do clustering which allows large pieces of files to be allocated contiguously resulting in near doubling of filesystem throughput. The filesystem interface has been extended to allow files and filesystems to grow to 2^{63} bytes in size. The quota system has been rewritten to support both user and group quotas (simultaneously if desired). Quota expiration is based on time rather than the previous metric of number of logins over quota. This change makes quotas more useful on fileservers onto which users seldom login.

The system security has been greatly enhanced by the addition of additional file flags that permit a file to be marked as immutable or append only. Once set, these flags can only be cleared by the super-user when the system is running single user. To protect against indiscriminate reading or writing of kernel memory, all writing and most reading of kernel data structures must be done using a new "sysctl" interface. The information to be access is described through an extensible "Management Information Base" (MIB).

2.4. POSIX terminal driver changes

The biggest area of change is a new terminal driver. The terminal driver is similar to the System V terminal driver with the addition of the necessary extensions to get the functionality previously available in the 4.3BSD terminal driver. 4.4BSD also adds the IEEE Std1003.1 job control interface, which is similar to the 4.3BSD job control interface, but adds a security model that was missing in the 4.3BSD job control implementation. A new system call, *setsid*, creates a job-control session consisting of a single process group with one member, the caller, that becomes a session leader. Only a session leader may acquire a controlling terminal. This is done explicitly via a TIOCSCTTY *ioctl* call, not implicitly by an *open* call. The call fails if the terminal is in use.

For backward compatibility, both the old *ioctl* calls and old options to *stty* are emulated.

3. Changes to the utilities

There are several new tools and utilities included in this release. A new version of "make" allows much-simplified makefiles for the system software and allows compilation for multiple architectures from the same source tree (which may be mounted read-only). Notable additions to the libraries include functions to traverse a filesystem hierarchy, database interfaces to btree and hashing functions, a new, fast implementation of stdio and a radix sort function. The additions to the utility suite include greatly enhanced versions of programs that display system status information, implementations of various traditional tools described in the IEEE Std1003.2 standard, and many others.

We have been tracking the IEEE Std1003.2 shell and utility work and have included prototypes of many of the proposed utilities. Most of the traditional utilities have been replaced with implementations conformant to the POSIX standards. Almost the entire manual suite has been rewritten to reflect the POSIX defined interfaces. In rewriting this software, we have generally been rewarded with significant performance improvements. Most of the libraries and header files have been converted to be compliant with ANSI C. The system libraries and utilities all compile with either ANSI or traditional C.

The Kerberos (version 4) authentication software has been integrated into much of the system (including NFS) to provide the first real network authentication on BSD.

A new implementation of the *ex/vi* text editors is available in this release. It is intended as a bug-for-bug compatible version of the editors. It also has a few new features: 8-bit clean data, lines and files limited only by memory and disk space, split screens, tags stacks and left-right scrolling among them. *Nex/nvi* is not yet production quality; future versions of this software may be retrieved by anonymous ftp from ftp.cs.berkeley.edu, in the directory ucb/4bsd.

The *find* utility has two new options that are important to be aware of if you intend to use NFS. The "fstype" and "prune" options can be used together to prevent find from crossing NFS mount points.

3.1. Additions and changes to the libraries

The *curses* library has been largely rewritten. Important additional features include support for scrolling and *termios*.

An application front-end editing library, named libedit, has been added to the system.

A superset implementation of the SunOS kernel memory interface library, *libkvm*, has been integrated into the system.

Nearly the entire C-library has been rewritten. Some highlights of the changes to the 4.4BSD C-library:

- The newly added *fts* functions will do either physical or logical traversal of a file hierarchy as well as handle essentially infinite depth filesystems and filesystems with cycles. All the utilities in 4.4BSD that traverse file hierarchies have been converted to use *fts*. The conversion has always resulted in a significant performance gain, often of four or five to one in system time.

- The newly added *dbopen* functions are intended to be a family of database access methods. Currently, they consist of *hash*, an extensible, dynamic hashing scheme, *btree*, a sorted, balanced tree structure (B+tree's), and *recno*, a flat-file interface for fixed or variable length records referenced by logical record number. Each of the access methods stores associated key/data pairs and uses the same record oriented interface for access. Future versions of this software may be retrieved by anonymous ftp from ftp.cs.berkeley.edu, in the directory ucb/4bsd.

- The *qsort* function has been rewritten for additional performance. In addition, three new types of sorting functions, *heapsort*, *mergesort*, and *radixsort* have been added to the system. The *mergesort* function is optimized for data with pre-existing order, in which case it usually significantly outperforms *qsort*. The *radixsort* functions are variants of most-significant-byte radix sorting. They take time linear to the number of bytes to be sorted, usually significantly outperforming *qsort* on data that can be sorted in this fashion. An implementation of the POSIX 1003.2 standard *sort* based on *radixsort* is included in 4.4BSD.

- The floating point support in the C-library has been replaced and is now accurate.

- The C functions specified by both ANSI C, POSIX 1003.1 and 1003.2 are now part of the C-library. This includes support for file name matching, shell globbing and both basic and extended regular expressions.

- ANSI C multibyte and wide character support has been integrated. The rune functionality from the Bell Labs' Plan 9 system is provided as well.

- The *termcap* functions have been generalized and replaced with a general purpose interface named *getcap*.

- The *stdio* routines have been replaced, and are usually much faster. In addition, the *funopen* interface permits applications to provide their own I/O stream function support.

4. Acknowledgements

We were greatly assisted by the past employees of the Computer Systems Research Group: Mike Karels, Keith Sklower, and Marc Tietelbaum. Our distribution coordinator, Pauline Schwartz, has reliably managed the finances and the mechanics of shipping distributions for nearly the entire fourteen years of the group's existence. Without the help of lawyers Mary MacDonald, Joel Linzner, and Carla Shapiro, the 4.4BSD-Lite distribution would never have seen the light of day. Much help was provided by Chris Demetriou in getting bug fixes from NetBSD integrated back into the 4.4BSD-Lite distribution.

The vast majority of the 4.4BSD distribution comes from the numerous people in the UNIX community that provided their time and energy in creating the software contained in this release. We dedicate this distribution to them.

M. K. McKusick
K. Bostic

Preface to the 4.3 Berkeley distribution

This update to the 4.2 distribution of August 1983 provides substantially improved performance, reliability, and security, the addition of Xerox Network System (NS) to the set of networking domains, and partial support for the VAX 8600 and MICROVAXII.

We were greatly assisted by the DEC UNIX Engineering group who provided two full time employees, Miriam Amos and Kevin Dunlap, to work at Berkeley. They were responsible for developing and debugging the distributed domain based name server and integrating it into the mail system. Mt Xinu provided the bug list distribution service as well as donating their MICROVAXII port to 4.3BSD. Drivers for the MICROVAXII were done by Rick Macklem at the University of Guelph. Sam Leffler provided valuable assistance and advice with many projects. Keith Sklower coordinated with William Nesheim and J. Q. Johnson at Cornell, and Chris Torek and James O'Toole at the University of Maryland to do the Xerox Network Systems implementation. Robert Elz at the University of Melbourne contributed greatly to the performance work in the kernel. Donn Seeley and Jay Lepreau at the University of Utah relentlessly dealt with a myriad of details; Donn completed the unfinished performance work on Fortran 77 and fixed numerous C compiler bugs. Ralph Campbell handled innumerable questions and problem reports and had time left to write rdist. George Goble was invaluable in shaking out the bugs on his production systems long before we were confident enough to inflict it on our users. Bill Shannon at Sun Microsystems has been helpful in providing us with bug fixes and improvements. Tom Ferrin, in his capacity as Board Member of Usenix Association, handled the logistics of large-scale reproduction of the 4.2BSD and 4.3BSD manuals. Mark Seiden helped with the typesetting and indexing of the 4.3BSD manuals. Special mention goes to Bob Henry for keeping ucbvax running in spite of new and improved software and an ever increasing mail, news, and uucp load.

Numerous others contributed their time and energy in creating the user contributed software for the release. As always, we are grateful to the UNIX user community for encouragement and support.

Once again, the financial support of the Defense Advanced Research Projects Agency is gratefully acknowledged.

M. K. McKusick
M. J. Karels
J. M. Bloom

Preface to the 4.2 Berkeley distribution

This update to the 4.1 distribution of June 1981 provides support for the VAX 11/730, full networking and interprocess communication support, an entirely new file system, and many other new features. It is certainly the most ambitious release of software ever prepared here and represents many man-years of work. Bill Shannon (both at DEC and at Sun Microsystems) and Robert Elz of the University of Melbourne contributed greatly to this distribution through new device drivers and painful debugging episodes. Rob Gurwitz of BBN wrote the initial version of the code upon which the current networking support is based. Eric Allman of Britton-Lee donated countless hours to the mail system. Bill Croft (both at SRI and Sun Microsystems) aided in the debugging and development of the networking facilities. Dennis Ritchie of Bell Laboratories also contributed greatly to this distribution, providing valuable advise and guidance. Helge Skrivervik worked on the device drivers which enabled the distribution to be delivered with a TU58 console cassette and RX01 console floppy disk, and rewrote major portions of the standalone i/o system to support formatting of non-DEC peripherals.

Numerous others contributed their time and energy in organizing the user software for release, while many groups of people on campus suffered patiently through the low spots of development. As always, we are grateful to the UNIX user community for encouragement and support.

Once again, the financial support of the Defense Advanced Research Projects Agency is gratefully acknowledged.

S. J. Leffler
W. N. Joy
M. K. McKusick

Preface to the 4.1 Berkeley distribution

This update to the fourth distribution of November 1980 provides support for the VAX 11/750 and for the full interconnect architecture of the VAX 11/780. Robert Elz of the University of Melbourne contributed greatly to this distribution especially in the boot-time system configuration code; Bill Shannon of DEC supplied us with the implementation of DEC standard bad block handling. The research group at Bell Laboratories and DEC Merrimack provided us with access to 11/750's in order to debug its support.

Other individuals too numerous to mention provided us with bug reports, fixes and other enhancements which are reflected in the system. We are grateful to the UNIX user community for encouragement and support.

The financial support of the Defense Advanced Research Projects Agency in support of this work is gratefully acknowledged.

W. N. Joy
R. S. Fabry
K. Sklower

Preface to the Fourth Berkeley distribution

This manual reflects the Berkeley system mid-October, 1980. A large amount of tuning has been done in the system since the last release; we hope this provides as noticeable an improvement for you as it did for us. This release finds the system in transition; a number of facilities have been added in experimental versions (job control, resource limits) and the implementation of others is imminent (shared-segments, higher performance from the file system, etc.). Applications which use facilities that are in transition should be aware that some of the system calls and library routines will change in the near future. We have tried to be conscientious and make it very clear where this is likely.

A new group has been formed at Berkeley, to assume responsibility for the future development and support of a version of UNIX on the VAX. The group has received funding from the Defense Advanced Research Projects Agency (DARPA) to supply a standard version of the system to DARPA contractors. The same version of the system will be made available to other licensees of UNIX on the VAX for a duplication charge. We gratefully acknowledge the support of this contract.

We wish to acknowledge the contribution of a number of individuals to the the system.

We would especially like to thank Jim Kulp of IIASA, Laxenburg Austria and his colleagues, who first put job control facilities into UNIX; Eric Allman, Robert Henry, Peter Kessler and Kirk McKusick, who contributed major new pieces of software; Mark Horton, who contributed to the improvement of facilities and substantially improved the quality of our bit-mapped fonts, our hardware support staff: Bob Kridle, Anita Hirsch, Len Edmondson and Fred Archibald, who helped us to debug a number of new peripherals; Ken Arnold who did much of the leg-work in getting this version of the manual prepared, and did the final editing of sections 2-6, some special individuals within Bell Laboratories: Greg Chesson, Stuart Feldman, Dick Haight, Howard Katseff, Brian Kernighan, Tom London, John Reiser, Dennis Ritchie, Ken Thompson, and Peter Weinberger who helped out by answering questions; our excellent local DEC field service people, Kevin Althaus and Frank Chargois who kept our machine running virtually all the time, and fixed it quickly when things broke; and, Mike Accetta of Carnegie-Mellon University, Robert Elz of the University of Melbourne, George Goble of Purdue University, and David Kashtan of the Stanford Research Institute for their technical advice and support.

Special thanks to Bill Munson of DEC who helped by augmenting our computing facility and to Eric Allman for carefully proofreading the ''last'' draft of the manual and finding the bugs which we knew were there but couldn't see.

We dedicate this to the memory of David Sakrison, late chairman of our department, who gave his support to the establishment of our VAX computing facility, and to our department as a whole.

> W. N. Joy
> Ö. Babaoğlu
> R. S. Fabry
> K. Sklower

Preface to the Third Berkeley distribution

This manual reflects the state of the Berkeley system, December 1979. We would like to thank all the people at Berkeley who have contributed to the system, and particularly thank Prof. Richard Fateman for creating and administrating a hospitable environment, Mark Horton who helped prepare this manual, and Eric Allman, Bob Kridle, Juan Porcar and Richard Tuck for their contributions to the kernel.

The cooperation of Bell Laboratories in providing us with an early version of UNIX/32V is greatly appreciated. We would especially like to thank Dr. Charles Roberts of Bell Laboratories for helping us obtain this release, and acknowledge T. B. London, J. F. Reiser, K. Thompson, D. M. Ritchie, G. Chesson and H. P. Katseff for their advice and support.

> W. N. Joy
> Ö. Babaoğlu

Preface to the UNIX/32V distribution

The UNIX operating system for the VAX*-11 provides substantially the same facilities as the UNIX system for the PDP*-11.

We acknowledge the work of many who came before us, and particularly thank G. K. Swanson, W. M. Cardoza, D. K. Sharma, and J. F. Jarvis for assistance with the implementation for the VAX-11/780.

> T. B. London
> J. F. Reiser

Preface to the Seventh Edition

Although this Seventh Edition no longer bears their byline, Ken Thompson and Dennis Ritchie remain the fathers and preceptors of the UNIX time-sharing system. Many of the improvements here described bear their mark. Among many, many other people who have contributed to the further flowering of UNIX, we wish especially to acknowledge the contributions of A. V. Aho, S. R. Bourne, L. L. Cherry, G. L. Chesson, S. I. Feldman, C. B. Haley, R. C. Haight, S. C. Johnson, M. E. Lesk, T. L. Lyon, L. E. McMahon, R. Morris, R. Muha, D. A. Nowitz, L. Wehr, and P. J. Weinberger. We appreciate also the effective advice and criticism of T. A. Dolotta, A. G. Fraser, J. F. Maranzano, and J. R. Mashey; and we remember the important work of the late Joseph F. Ossanna.

> B. W. Kernighan
> M. D. McIlroy

---

*VAX and PDP are Trademarks of Digital Equipment Corporation.

Introduction

The documentation for 4.4BSD is in a format similar to the one used for the 4.2BSD and 4.3BSD manuals. It is divided into three sets; each set consists of one or more volumes. The abbreviations for the volume names are listed in square brackets; the abbreviations for the manual sections are listed in parenthesis.

I. User's Documents
    User's Reference Manual [URM]
        Commands (1)
        Games (6)
        Macro packages and language conventions (7)
    User's Supplementary Documents [USD]
        Getting Started
        Basic Utilities
        Communicating with the World
        Text Editing
        Document Preparation
        Amusements

II. Programmer's Documents
    Programmer's Reference Manual [PRM]
        System calls (2)
        Subroutines (3)
        Special files (4)
        File formats and conventions (5)
    Programmer's Supplementary Documents [PSD]
        Documents of Historic Interest
        Languages in common use
        Programming Tools
        Programming Libraries
        General Reference

III. System Manager's Manual [SMM]
        Maintenance commands (8)
        System Installation and Administration

References to individual documents are given as "volume:document", thus USD:1 refers to the first document in the "User's Supplementary Documents". References to manual pages are given as "*name*(section)" thus *sh*(1) refers to the shell manual entry in section 1.

The manual pages give descriptions of the features of the 4.4BSD system, as developed at the University of California at Berkeley. They do not attempt to provide perspective or tutorial information about the 4.4BSD operating system, its facilities, or its implementation. Various documents on those topics are contained in the "UNIX User's Supplementary Documents" (USD), the "UNIX Programmer's Supplementary Documents" (PSD), and "UNIX System Manager's Manual" (SMM). In particular, for an overview see "The UNIX Time-Sharing System" (PSD:1) by Ritchie and Thompson; for a tutorial see "UNIX for Beginners" (USD:1) by Kernighan, and for an guide to the new features of this latest version, see "Berkeley Software Architecture Manual (4.4 Edition)" (PSD:5).

Within the area it surveys, this volume attempts to be timely, complete and concise. Where the latter two objectives conflict, the obvious is often left unsaid in favor of brevity. It is intended that each program be described as it is, not as it should be. Inevitably, this means that various sections will soon be out of date.

Commands are programs intended to be invoked directly by the user, in contrast to subroutines, that are intended to be called by the user's programs. User commands are described in URM section 1. Commands generally reside in directory */bin* (for *bin* ary programs). Some programs also reside in */usr/bin,* to save space in */bin.* These directories are searched automatically by the command interpreters. Additional directories that may be of interest include */usr/ contrib/ bin,* which has contributed software */usr/ old/ bin,* which has old but sometimes still useful software and */usr/ local/ bin,* which contains software local to your site.

Games have been relegated to URM section 6 and */usr/ games,* to keep them from contaminating the more staid information of URM section 1.

Miscellaneous collection of information necessary for writing in various specialized languages such as character codes, macro packages for typesetting, etc is contained in URM section 7.

System calls are entries into the BSD kernel. The system call interface is identical to a C language procedure call; the equivalent C procedures are described in PRM section 2.

An assortment of subroutines is available; they are described in PRM section 3. The primary libraries in which they are kept are described in *intro*(3). The functions are described in terms of C.

PRM section 4 discusses the characteristics of each system "file" that refers to an I/O device. The names in this section refer to the HP300 device names for the hardware, instead of the names of the special files themselves.

The file formats and conventions (PRM section 5) documents the structure of particular kinds of files; for example, the form of the output of the loader and assembler is given. Excluded are files used by only one command, for example the assembler's intermediate files.

Commands and procedures intended for use primarily by the system administrator are described in SMM section 8. The files described here are almost all kept in the directory */ etc.* The system administration binaries reside in */ sbin,* and */ usr/ sbin.*

Each section consists of independent entries of a page or so each. The name of the entry is in the upper corners of its pages, together with the section number. Entries within each section are alphabetized. The page numbers of each entry start at 1; it is infeasible to number consecutively the pages of a document like this that is republished in many variant forms.

All entries are based on a common format; not all subsections always appear.

The *name* subsection lists the exact names of the commands and subroutines covered under the entry and gives a short description of their purpose.

The *synopsis* summarizes the use of the program being described. A few conventions are used, particularly in the Commands subsection:

Boldface words are considered literals, and are typed just as they appear.

Square brackets [ ] around an argument show that the argument is optional. When an argument is given as "name", it always refers to a file name.

Ellipses "..." are used to show that the previous argument-prototype may be repeated.

A final convention is used by the commands themselves. An argument beginning with a minus sign "−" usually means that it is an option-specifying argument, even if it appears in a position where a file name could appear. Therefore, it is unwise to have files whose names begin with "−".

The *description* subsection discusses in detail the subject at hand.

The *files* subsection gives the names of files that are built into the program.

A *see also* subsection gives pointers to related information.

A *diagnostics* subsection discusses the diagnostic indications that may be produced. Messages that are intended to be self-explanatory are not listed.

The *bugs* subsection gives known bugs and sometimes deficiencies. Occasionally the suggested fix is also described.

At the beginning of URM, PRM, and SSM is a List of Manual Pages, organized by section and alphabetically within each section, and a Permuted Index derived from that List. Within each index entry, the title of the writeup to which it refers is followed by the appropriate section number in parentheses. This fact is important because there is considerable name duplication among the sections, arising principally from commands that exist only to exercise a particular system call. Finally, there is a list of documents on the inside back cover of each volume.

HOW TO GET STARTED

This section sketches the basic information you need to get started on UNIX; how to log in and log out, how to communicate through your terminal, and how to run a program. See "UNIX for Beginners" in (USD:1) for a more complete introduction to the system.

Logging in. Almost any ASCII terminal capable of full duplex operation and generating the entire character set can be used. You must have a valid user name, which may be obtained from the system administration. If you will be accessing UNIX remotely, you will also need to obtain the telephone number for the system that you will be using.

After a data connection is established, the login procedure depends on what type of terminal you are using and local system conventions. If your terminal is directly connected to the computer, it generally runs at 9600 or 19200 baud. If you are using a modem running over a phone line, the terminal must be set at the speed appropriate for the modem you are using, typically 1200, 2400, or 9600 baud. The half/full duplex switch should always be set at full-duplex. (This switch will often have to be changed since many other systems require half-duplex).

When a connection is established, the system types "login:"; you type your user name, followed by the "return" key. If you have a password, the system asks for it and suppresses echo to the terminal so the password will not appear. After you have logged in, the "return", "new line", or "linefeed" keys will give exactly the same results. A message-of-the-day usually greets you before your first prompt.

If the system types out a few garbage characters after you have established a data connection (the "login:" message at the wrong speed), depress the "break" (or "interrupt") key. This is a speed-independent signal to UNIX that a different speed terminal is in use. The system then will type "login:," this time at another speed. Continue depressing the break key until "login:" appears clearly, then respond with your user name.

For all these terminals, it is important that you type your name in lower-case if possible; if you type upper-case letters, UNIX will assume that your terminal cannot generate lower-case letters and will translate all subsequent lower-case letters to upper case.

The evidence that you have successfully logged in is that a shell program will type a prompt ("$" or "%") to you. (The shells are described below under "How to run a program.")

For more information, consult *tset*(1), and *stty*(1), which tell how to adjust terminal behavior; *getty*(8) discusses the login sequence in more detail, and *tty*(4) discusses terminal I/O.

Logging out. There are three ways to log out:

By typing "logout" or an end-of-file indication (EOT character, control-D) to the shell. The shell will terminate and the "login:" message will appear again.

You can log in directly as another user by giving a *login*(1) command.

If worse comes to worse, you can simply hang up the phone; but beware – some machines may lack the necessary hardware to detect that the phone has been hung up. Ask your system administrator if this is a problem on your machine.

How to communicate through your terminal. When you type characters, a gnome deep in the system gathers your characters and saves them in a secret place. The characters will not be given to a program until you type a return (or newline), as described above in *Logging in.*

UNIX terminal I/O is full-duplex. It has full read-ahead, which means that you can type at any time, even while a program is typing at you. Of course, if you type during output, the printed output will have the input characters interspersed. However, whatever you type will be saved up and interpreted in correct sequence. There is a limit to the amount of read-ahead, but it is generous and not likely to be exceeded unless the system is in trouble. When the read-ahead limit is exceeded, the system throws away all the saved characters (or beeps, if your prompt was a "%").

The ˆU (control-U) character in typed input kills all the preceding characters in the line, so typing mistakes can be repaired on a single line. Also, the delete character (DEL) or sometimes the backspace character (control-H) erases the last character typed. *Tset*(1) or *stty*(1) can be used to change these defaults. Successive uses of delete (or backspace) erases characters back to, but not beyond, the beginning of the line. DEL and ˆU (control-U) can be transmitted to a program by preceding them with ˆV (control-V). (So, to erase ˆV (control-V), you need two deletes or backspaces).

An *interrupt signal* is sent to a program by typing ^C (control-C) or the "break" key which is not passed to programs. This signal generally causes whatever program you are running to terminate. It is typically used to stop a long printout that you do not want. However, programs can arrange either to ignore this signal altogether, or to be notified when it happens (instead of being terminated). The editor, for example, catches interrupts and stops what it is doing, instead of terminating, so that an interrupt can be used to halt an editor printout without losing the file being edited. The interrupt character can also be changed with *tset*(1) or *stty*(1).

It is also possible to suspend output temporarily using ^S (control-S) and later resume output with ^Q (control-Q). Output can be thrown away without interrupting the program by typing ^O (control-O); see *tty*(4).

The *quit* signal is generated by typing the ASCII FS character. (FS appears many places on different terminals, most commonly as control-\ or control-|.) It not only causes a running program to terminate but also generates a file with the core image of the terminated process. Quit is useful for debugging.

Besides adapting to the speed of the terminal, UNIX tries to be intelligent about whether you have a terminal with the newline function or whether it must be simulated with carriage-return and line-feed. In the latter case, all input carriage returns are turned to newline characters (the standard line delimiter) and both a carriage return and a line feed are echoed to the terminal. If you get into the wrong mode, the *reset*(1) command will rescue you. If the terminal does not appear to be echoing anything that you type, it may be stuck in "no-echo" or "raw" mode. Try typing "(control-J)reset(control-J)" to recover.

Tab characters are used freely in UNIX source programs. If your terminal does not have the tab function, you can arrange to have them turned into spaces during output, and echoed as spaces during input. The system assumes that tabs are set every eight columns. Again, the *tset*(1) or *stty*(1) command can be used to change these defaults. *Tset*(1) can be used to set the tab stops automatically when necessary.

How to run a program; the shells. When you have successfully logged in, a program called a shell is listening to your terminal. The shell reads typed-in lines, splits them up into a command name and arguments, and executes the command. A command is simply an executable program. The shell looks in several system directories to find the command. You can also place commands in your own directory and have the shell find them there. There is nothing special about system-provided commands except that they are kept in a directory where the shell can find them.

The command name is always the first word on an input line; it and its arguments are separated from one another by spaces.

When a program terminates, the shell will ordinarily regain control and type a prompt at you to show that it is ready for another command.

The shells have many other capabilities, that are described in detail in sections *sh*(1) and *csh*(1). If the shell prompts you with "$", then it is an instance of *sh*(1), the original UNIX shell. If it prompts with "%" then it is an instance of *csh*(1), a shell written at Berkeley. The shells are different for all but the most simple terminal usage. Most users at Berkeley choose *csh*(1) because of the *history* mechanism and the *alias* feature, that greatly enhance its power when used interactively. *Csh* also supports the job-control facilities; see *csh*(1) or the Csh introduction in USD:4 for details.

You can change from one shell to the other by using the *chpass*(1) command, which takes effect at your next login.

The current directory. UNIX has a file system arranged as a hierarchy of directories. When the system administrator gave you a user name, they also created a directory for you (ordinarily with the same name as your user name). When you log in, any file name you type is by default in this directory. Since you are the owner of this directory, you have full permission to read, write, alter, or destroy its contents. Permissions to have your will with other directories and files will have been granted or denied to you by their owners. As a matter of observed fact, few UNIX users protect their files from perusal by other users.

To change the current directory (but not the set of permissions you were endowed with at login) use *cd*(1).

Path names. To refer to files not in the current directory, you must use a path name. Full path names begin with "/", the name of the root directory of the whole file system. After the slash comes the name of each directory containing the next sub-directory (followed by a "/") until finally the file name is reached. For example, */var/tmp/filex* refers to the file *filex* in the directory *tmp*; *tmp* is itself a subdirectory of *var*; *var* springs directly from the root directory.

If your current directory has subdirectories, the path names of files therein begin with the name of the subdirectory with no prefixed "/".

A path name may be used anywhere a file name is required.

Important commands that modify the contents of files are *cp*(1), *mv*(1), and *rm*(1), which respectively copy, move (i.e. rename) and remove files. To find out the status of files or directories, use *ls*(1). See *mkdir*(1) for making directories and *rmdir*(1) for destroying them.

For a fuller discussion of the file system, see "A Fast File System for UNIX" (SMM:5) by McKusick, Joy, Leffler, and Fabry. It may also be useful to glance through PRM section 2, that discusses system calls, even if you do not intend to deal with the system at that level.

Writing a program. To enter the text of a source program into a UNIX file, use the standard display editor *vi*(1) or its WYSIWYG counterparts *jove*(1) and *emacs*(1). (The old standard editor *ed*(1) is also available.) The principle language in UNIX is provided by the C compiler *cc*(1). User contributed software in the latest release of the system supports the programming languages perl and C++. After the program text has been entered through the editor and written to a file, you can give the file to the appropriate language processor as an argument. The output of the language processor will be left on a file in the current directory named "a.out". If the output is precious, use *mv*(1) to move it to a less exposed name after successful compilation.

When you have finally gone through this entire process without provoking any diagnostics, the resulting program can be run by giving its name to the shell in response to the shell ("$" or "%") prompt.

Your programs can receive arguments from the command line just as system programs do, see "UNIX Programming - Second Edition" (PSD:4), or for a more terse description *execve*(2).

Text processing. Almost all text is entered through an editor such as *vi*(1), *jove*(1), or *emacs*(1). The commands most often used to write text on a terminal are: *cat*(1), *more*(1), and *nroff*(1).

The *cat*(1) command simply dumps ASCII text on the terminal, with no processing at all. *More*(1) is useful for preventing the output of a command from scrolling off the top of your screen. It is also well suited to perusing files. *Nroff*(1) is an elaborate text formatting program. Used naked, it requires careful forethought, but for ordinary documents it has been tamed; see *me*(7) and *ms*(7).

Groff(1) converts documents to postscript for output to a Laserwriter or Phototypesetter. It is similar to *nroff*(1), and often works from exactly the same source text. It was used to produce this manual.

Script(1) lets you keep a record of your session in a file, which can then be printed, mailed, etc. It provides the advantages of a hard-copy terminal even when using a display terminal.

Status inquiries. Various commands exist to provide you with useful information. *w*(1) prints a list of users currently logged in, and what they are doing. *date*(1) prints the current time and date. *ls*(1) will list the files in your directory or give summary information about particular files.

Surprises. Certain commands provide inter-user communication. Even if you do not plan to use them, it would be well to learn something about them, because someone else may aim them at you.

To communicate with another user currently logged in, *write*(1) or *talk*(1) is used; *mail*(1) will leave a message whose presence will be announced to another user when they next log in. The write-ups in the manual also suggest how to respond to the these commands if you are a target.

If you use *csh*(1) the key ˆZ (control-Z) will cause jobs to "stop". If this happens before you learn about it, you can simply continue by saying "fg" (for foreground) to bring the job back.

We hope that you will come to enjoy using the BSD system. Although it is very large and contains many commands, you can become very productive using only a small subset of them. As your needs expand to doing new tasks, you will almost always find that the system has the facilities that you need to accomplish them easily and quickly.

Most importantly, the source code to the BSD system is cheaply available to anyone that wants it. On many BSD systems, it can be found in the directory */usr/src*. You may simply want to find out how something works or fix some important bug without waiting months for your vendor to respond. It is also particularly useful if you want to grab another piece of code to bootstrap a new project. Provided that you retain the copyrights and acknowledgements at the top of each file, you are free to redistribute your work for fun or profit. Naturally, we hope that you will allow others to also redistribute your code, though you are not required to do so unless you use copyleft code (which is primarily found in the software contributed from the Free Software Foundation and is clearly identified).

Good luck and enjoy BSD.

List of Manual Pages

1. Commands and Application Programs

2. System Calls

3. C Library Subroutines

4. Special Files

5. File Formats

6. Games

7. Miscellaneous

8. System Maintenance

Permuted Index

Section 1

Commands
and
Application
Programs

1

NAME
intro – introduction to general commands (tools and utilities)

DESCRIPTION
Section one of the manual contains most of the commands which comprise the BSD user environment. Some of the commands included in section one are text editors, command shell interpreters, searching and sorting tools, file manipulation commands system status commands, remote file copy commands, mail commands, compilers and compiler tools, formatted output tools, and line printer commands.

All commands set a status value upon exit which may be tested to see if the command completed normally. The exit values and their meanings are explained in the individual manuals. Traditionally, the value 0 signifies successful completion of the command.

SEE ALSO
man(1) intro(2) intro(3) intro(3) intro(4) intro(8)

Tutorials in the *UNIX User's Manual Supplementary Documents*.

HISTORY
A **intro** manual appeared in Version 6 AT&T UNIX.

NAME

adb – debugger

SYNOPSIS

adb ⌊ –w⌋ ⌊ –k⌋ [–I*dir*] [*objfil* [*corfil*]]

DESCRIPTION

Adb is a general purpose debugging program. It may be used to examine files and to provide a controlled environment for the execution of UNIX programs.

Objfil is normally an executable program file, preferably containing a symbol table; if not then the symbolic features of adb cannot be used although the file can still be examined. The default for *objfil* is a.out. *Corfil* is assumed to be a core image file produced after executing *objfil*; the default for *corfil* is core

Requests to adb are read from the standard input and responses are to the standard output. If the –w flag is present then both *objfil* and *corfil* are created if necessary and opened for reading and writing so that files can be modified using adb.

The –k option makes adb do UNIX kernel memory mapping; it should be used when core is a UNIX crash dump or /dev/mem.

The –I option specifies a directory where files to be read with $< or $<< (see below) will be sought; the default is /usr/lib/adb.

Adb ignores QUIT; INTERRUPT causes return to the next adb command.

In general requests to adb are of the form

      [*address*] [, *count*] [command] [;]

If *address* is present then *dot* is set to *address*. Initially *dot* is set to 0. For most commands *count* specifies how many times the command will be executed. The default *count* is 1. *Address* and *count* are expressions.

The interpretation of an address depends on the context it is used in. If a subprocess is being debugged then addresses are interpreted in the usual way in the address space of the subprocess. If the operating system is being debugged, either post-mortem or using the special file /dev/mem to interactively examine and/or modify memory, the maps are set to map the kernel virtual addresses which start at 0x80000000 (on the VAX); see ADDRESSES below.

EXPRESSIONS

.   The value of *dot*.

+   The value of *dot* incremented by the current increment.

^   The value of *dot* decremented by the current increment.

"   The last *address* typed.

integer   A number. The prefixes 0o and 0O (zero oh) force interpretation in octal radix; the prefixes 0t and 0T force interpretation in decimal radix; the prefixes 0x and 0X force interpretation in hexadecimal radix. Thus 0o20 = 0t16 = 0x10 = sixteen. If no prefix appears, then the *default radix* is used; see the $d command. The default radix is initially hexadecimal. The hexadecimal digits are 0123456789abcdefABCDEF with the obvious values. Note that a hexadecimal number whose most significant digit would otherwise be an alphabetic character must have a 0x (or 0X) prefix (or a leading zero if the default radix is hexadecimal).

integer.fraction
> A 32 bit floating point number.

´cccc´
> The ASCII value of up to 4 characters. \ may be used to escape a ´.

< *name*
> The value of *name*, which is either a variable name or a register name. **Adb** maintains a number of variables (see VARIABLES below) named by single letters or digits. If *name* is a register name then the value of the register is obtained from the system header in `corfil`. The register names are those printed by the `$r` command.

symbol
> A *symbol* is a sequence of upper or lower case letters, underscores or digits, not starting with a digit. The backslash character \ may be used to escape other characters. The value of the *symbol* is taken from the symbol table in `objfil`. An initial _ will be prepended to *symbol* if needed.

_symbol
> In C, the 'true name' of an external symbol begins with _. It may be necessary to utter this name to distinguish it from internal or hidden variables of a program.

routine.name
> The address of the variable *name* in the specified C routine. Both *routine* and *name* are *symbols*. If *routine* is omitted, the currently active frame is used. (This form is currently broken; local variables can be examined only with dbx(1)). If *name* is omitted the value is the address of the most recently activated C stack frame corresponding to *routine* (this much works).

(*exp*)
> The value of the expression *exp*.

Monadic Operators

∗exp　The contents of the location addressed by *exp* in `corfil`.
@exp　The contents of the location addressed by *exp* in `objfil`.
−exp　Integer negation.
˜exp　Bitwise complement.
#exp　Logical negation.

Dyadic operators
Are left associative and are less binding than monadic operators.

e1+e2　Integer addition.
e1−e2　Integer subtraction.
e1∗e2　Integer multiplication.
e1%e2　Integer division.
e1&e2　Bitwise conjunction.
e1|e2　Bitwise disjunction.
e1#e2　*e1* rounded up to the next multiple of *e2*.

COMMANDS
Most commands consist of a verb followed by a modifier or list of modifiers. The following verbs are available. (The commands ? and / may be followed by ∗; see the ADDRESSES section for further details.)

?f
> Locations starting at *address* in `objfil` are printed according to the format *f*. *dot* is incremented by the sum of the increments for each format letter (q.v.).

/f
> Locations starting at *address* in `corfil` are printed according to the format *f* and *dot* is incremented as for ?.

=f
> The value of *address* itself is printed in the styles indicated by the format *f*. (For *i* format, zero values are assumed for the parts of the instruction that reference subsequent words.)

A *format* consists of one or more characters that specify a style of printing. Each format character may be preceded by a decimal integer that is a repeat count for the format character. While stepping through a format, *dot* is incremented by the amount given for each format letter. If no format is given then the last format is used. The format characters available are as follows. Note that a backslash (\ ) must be used to quote the three numeric formats.

1	*1*	Print 1 byte in the current radix (which may be either signed or unsigned; see the $d command).
2	*2*	Print 2 bytes in the current radix.
4	*4*	Print 4 bytes in the current radix.
v	*2*	Print 2 bytes in the signed variant of the current radix.
V	*4*	Print 4 bytes in the signed variant of the current radix.
o	*2*	Print 2 bytes in unsigned octal. All octal numbers output by adb are preceded by 0.
O	*4*	Print 4 bytes in unsigned octal.
q	*2*	Print 2 bytes in signed octal.
Q	*4*	Print 4 bytes in signed octal.
u	*2*	Print 2 bytes in unsigned decimal.
U	*4*	Print 4 bytes in long unsigned decimal.
d	*2*	Print 2 bytes in signed decimal.
D	*4*	Print 4 bytes in long signed decimal.
x	*2*	Print 2 bytes in unsigned hexadecimal.
X	*4*	Print 4 bytes in unsigned hexadecimal.
z	*2*	Print 2 bytes in signed hexadecimal.
Z	*4*	Print 4 bytes in signed hexadecimal.
f	*4*	Print 4 bytes as a floating point number.
F	*8*	Print 8 bytes as a double precision floating point number.
b	*1*	Print 1 byte in unsigned octal.
c	*1*	Print 1 byte as a character.
C	*1*	Print 1 byte as a character, using the standard escape convention where control characters are printed as '^x' and the delete character is printed as '^?'.
s	*n*	Print the addressed characters until a zero character is reached. *n* is the length of the string including its zero terminator.
S	*n*	Print a string using the '^x' escape convention (see *C* above). *n* is the length of the string including its zero terminator.
Y	*4*	Print 4 bytes in date format (see ctime(3)).
i	*n*	Print as machine instructions. *n* is the number of bytes occupied by the instruction. This style of printing causes the numeric variables 1, 2, ... to be set according to the offset parts of the arguments, if any, of the instruction (up to 6 on the VAX).
a	*0*	Print the value of *dot* in symbolic form. Symbols are checked to ensure that they have an appropriate type as indicated below.

       /   local or global data symbol
       ?   local or global text symbol
       =   local or global absolute symbol

p	*4*	Print the addressed value in symbolic form using the same rules for symbol lookup as **a**.
t	*0*	When preceded by an integer, tabs to the next appropriate tab stop. For example, 8t moves to the next 8-space tab stop.
r	*0*	Print a space.
n	*0*	Print a newline.
''..."'	*0*	
		Print the enclosed string.
^		*Dot* is decremented by the current increment. Nothing is printed.
+		*Dot* is incremented by 1. Nothing is printed.

1

–	*Dot* is decremented by 1. Nothing is printed.
newline	Repeat the previous command with a *count* of 1.

[?/]l *value mask*

Words starting at *dot* are masked with *mask* and compared with *value* until a match is found. If L is used then the match is for 4 bytes at a time instead of 2. If no match is found then *dot* is unchanged; otherwise *dot* is set to the matched location. If *mask* is omitted then all bits are compared.

[?/]w *value ...*

Write the 2-byte *value* into the addressed location. If the command is W, write 4 bytes. Odd addresses *are* allowed when writing to the subprocess address space.

[?/]m *bl el fl* **[?/]**

New values for (*bl, el, fl*) are recorded. If less than three expressions are given then the remaining map parameters are left unchanged. If the ? or / is followed by * then the second segment (*b2, e2, f2*) of the mapping is changed. If the list is terminated by ? or / then the file (*objfil* or *corfil* respectively) is used for subsequent requests. For example, '/m?' will cause / to refer to *objfil*.

> *name*　　　　*Dot* is assigned to the variable or register named.

!　　　　A shell (/bin/sh) is called to read the rest of the line following !.

$ *modifier*　　　　Miscellaneous commands. The available *modifiers* are:

    < *file*　　Read commands from *file*. If this command is executed in a file, further commands in the file are not seen. If *file* is omitted, the current input stream is terminated. If a *count* is given, and is zero, the command will be ignored. The value of the count will be placed in variable *9* before the first command in *file* is executed.

    << *file*　　Similar to < except it can be used in a file of commands without causing the file to be closed. Variable *9* is saved during the execution of this command, and restored when it completes. There is a (small) finite limit to the number of << files that can be open at once.

    > *file*　　Append output to the file *file*, which is created if it does not exist. If *file* is omitted, output is returned to the terminal.

    ? *file*　　Print process id, the signal which caused stoppage or termination, as well as the registers as $r. This is the default if *modifier* is omitted.

    r　　Print the general registers and the instruction addressed by pc. *Dot* is set to pc.

    b　　Print all breakpoints and their associated counts and commands.

    c　　C stack backtrace. If *address* is given then it is taken as the address of the current frame instead of the contents of the frame–pointer register. If C is used then the names and (32 bit) values of all automatic and static variables are printed for each active function (this is partially broken; the names are not now available). If *count* is given then only the first *count* frames are printed.

1

d   Set the default radix to *address* and report the new value. If no *address* is given, the default radix is not changed. The new radix must be between -16 (decimal) and 16 (decimal) and must not be 0, 1, or -1. A negative radix implies that numbers printed in that radix will be treated as signed; otherwise they are treated as unsigned. Note that *address* is interpreted in the (old) current radix. Thus "10$d" simply changes the default radix to unsigned. To make signed decimal the default radix, use "-0t10$d"

e   The names and values of external variables are printed.

w   Set the page width for output to *address* (default 80).

s   Set the limit for symbol matches to *address* (default 1024).

q   Exit from **adb**.

v   Print all non zero variables in octal.

m   Print the address map.

p   (*Kernel debugging*) Change the current kernel memory mapping to map the designated **user structure** to the address given by the symbol **_u**. The *address* argument is the address of the user's user page table entries.

:modifier   Manage a subprocess. Available modifiers are:

bc   Set breakpoint at *address*. The breakpoint is executed *count–1* times before causing a stop, after which it stops unconditionally. Each time the breakpoint is encountered the command *c* is executed. If this command is omitted or sets *dot* to zero, the breakpoint causes a stop immediately, regardless of any remaining count.

d   Delete breakpoint at *address*.

D   Delete all breakpoints.

r   Run `objfil` as a subprocess. If *address* is given explicitly then the program is entered at this point; otherwise the program is entered at its standard entry point. *count* specifies how many breakpoints are to be ignored before stopping. Arguments to the subprocess may be supplied on the same line as the command. An argument starting with < or > causes the standard input or output to be established for the command.

cs   The subprocess is continued with signal *s*; see `sigvec`(2). If *address* is given then the subprocess is continued at this address. If no signal is specified then the signal that caused the subprocess to stop is sent. Breakpoint skipping is the same as for **r**.

ss   As for **c** except that the subprocess is single stepped *count* times. If there is no current subprocess then `objfil` is run as a subprocess as for **r**. In this case no signal can be sent; the remainder of the line is treated as arguments to the subprocess.

k   The current subprocess, if any, is terminated.

VARIABLES

Adb provides a number of variables. Named variables are set initially by **adb** but are not used subsequently. Numbered variables are reserved for communication as follows.

0   The last value printed.

1

1   The last offset part of an instruction source. This continues up through at most 6 on the VAX. For a
         three-operand instruction, variable 2 is the second source offset and variable 3 the destination offset
         part.

9   The count on the last $< or $<< command.

On entry the following are set from the system header in the *corfil*. If *corfil* does not appear to be a
core file then these values are set from *objfil*.

b   The base address of the data segment.
d   The data segment size.
e   The entry point.
m   The 'magic' number (0407, 0410 or 0413).
s   The stack segment size.
t   The text segment size.

ADDRESSES
The address in a file associated with a written address is determined by a mapping associated with that file.
Each mapping is represented by two triples (*b1*, *e1*, *f1*) and (*b2*, *e2*, *f2*) and the *file address* corresponding
to a written *address* is calculated as follows.

$$b1 \leq address \leq e1 \rightarrow \text{file address=address+f1-b1, otherwise}$$

$$b2 \leq address \leq e2 \rightarrow \text{file address=address+f2-b2}$$

otherwise, the requested *address* is not legal. In some cases (e.g. for programs with separated I and D
space) the two segments for a file may overlap. If a **?** or **/** is followed by an ***** then only the second triple is
used.

The initial setting of both mappings is suitable for normal `a.out` and `core` files. If either file is not of the
kind expected then, for that file, *b1* is set to 0, *e1* is set to the maximum file size and *f1* is set to 0; in this way
the whole file can be examined with no address translation.

FILES
        a.out
        core

SEE ALSO
        cc(1), dbx(1), ptrace(2), a.out(5), core(5)

HISTORY
        Adb was first released with Version 7 AT&T UNIX. The version of **adb** this man page describes is descend-
        ed from the original.

DIAGNOSTICS
        'adb' when there is no current command or format. Comments about inaccessible files, syntax errors, ab-
        normal termination of commands, etc. Exit status is 0, unless last command failed or returned nonzero
        status.

BUGS
        Since no shell is invoked to interpret the arguments of the **:r** command, the customary wild-card and vari-
        able expansions cannot occur.

NAME

addftinfo – add information to troff font files for use with groff

SYNOPSIS

addftinfo [–*param value...*] *res unitwidth font*

DESCRIPTION

addftinfo reads a troff font file and adds some additional font-metric information that is used by the groff system. The font file with the information added is written on the standard output. The information added is guessed using some parametric information about the font and assumptions about the traditional troff names for characters. The main information added is the heights and depths of characters. The *res* and *unitwidth* arguments should be the same as the corresponding parameters in the DESC file; *font* is the name of the file describing the font; if *font* ends with **I** the font will be assumed to be italic.

OPTIONS

Each of the options changes one of the parameters that is used to derive the heights and depths. Like the existing quantities in the font file, each *value* is in inches/*res* for a font whose point size is *unitwidth*. *param* must be one of:

x-height
> The height of lowercase letters without ascenders such as x.

fig-height
> The height of figures (digits).

asc-height
> The height of characters with ascenders, such as b, d or l.

body-height
> The height of characters such as parentheses.

cap-height
> The height of uppercase letters such as A.

comma-depth
> The depth of a comma.

desc-depth
> The depth of characters with descenders, such as p,q, or y.

body-depth
> The depth of characters such as parentheses.

addftinfo makes no attempt to use the specified parameters to guess the unspecified parameters. If a parameter is not specified the default will be used. The defaults are chosen to have the reasonable values for a Times font.

SEE ALSO

font(5) **groff_font**(5), **groff**(1), **groff_char**(7)

1

NAME
afmtodit – create font files for use with groff –Tps

SYNOPSIS
afmtodit [–**ns**] [–**d***desc_file*] [–**e***enc_file*] [–**i***n*] [–**a***n*] *afm_file map_file font*

DESCRIPTION
afmtodit creates a font file for use with groff and **grops**. **afmtodit** is written in perl; you must have perl
version 3 installed in order to run **afmtodit**. *afm_file* is the AFM (Adobe Font Metric) file for the font.
map_file is a file that says which groff character names map onto each PostScript character name; this file
should contain a sequence of lines of the form

　　　　ps_char groff_char

where *ps_char* is the PostScript name of the character and *groff_char* is the groff name of the character (as
used in the groff font file.) The same *ps_char* can occur multiple times in the file; each *groff_char* must
occur at most once. *font* is the groff name of the font. If a PostScript character is in the encoding to be
used for the font but is not mentioned in *map_file* then **afmtodit** will put it in the groff font file as an
unnamed character, which can be accessed by the \N escape sequence in **troff**. The groff font file will be
output to a file called *font*.

If there is a downloadable font file for the font, it may be listed in the file
/usr/share/groff_font/devps/download; see **grops**(1).

If the –**i** option is used, **afmtodit** will automatically generate an italic correction, a left italic correction and
a subscript correction for each character (the significance of these parameters is explained in
groff_font(5)); these parameters may be specified for individual characters by adding to the *afm_file* lines
of the form:

　　　　italicCorrection *ps_char n*
　　　　leftItalicCorrection *ps_char n*
　　　　subscriptCorrection *ps_char n*

where *ps_char* is the PostScript name of the character, and *n* is the desired value of the corresponding
parameter in thousandths of an em. These parameters are normally needed only for italic (or oblique)
fonts.

OPTIONS
–n　　　Don't output a **ligatures** command for this font. Use this with constant-width fonts.

–s　　　The font is special. The effect of this option is to add the **special** command to the font file.

–d*desc_file*
　　　　The device description file is *desc_file* rather than the default **DESC**.

–e*enc_file*
　　　　The PostScript font should be reencoded to use the encoding described in enc_file. The format of
　　　　enc_file is described in **grops**(1).

–a*n*　　　Use *n* as the slant parameter in the font file; this is used by groff in the positioning of accents. By
　　　　default **afmtodit** uses the negative of the ItalicAngle specified in the afm file; with true italic fonts
　　　　it is sometimes desirable to use a slant that is less than this. If you find that characters from an
　　　　italic font have accents placed too far to the right over them, then use the –**a** option to give the
　　　　font a smaller slant.

–i*n*　　　Generate an italic correction for each character so that the character's width plus the character's
　　　　italic correction is equal to *n* thousandths of an em plus the amount by which the right edge of the
　　　　character's bounding is to the right of the character's origin. If this would result in a negative
　　　　italic correction, use a zero italic correction instead.

　　　　Also generate a subscript correction equal to the product of the tangent of the slant of the font and
　　　　four fifths of the x-height of the font. If this would result in a subscript correction greater than the
　　　　italic correction, use a subscript correction equal to the italic correction instead.

Also generate a left italic correction for each character equal to *n* thousandths of an em plus the amount by which the left edge of the character's bounding box is to the left of the character's origin. The left italic correction may be negative.

This option is normally needed only with italic (or oblique) fonts. The font files distributed with groff were created using an option of –**i50** for italic fonts.

FILES

/usr/share/groff_font/devps/DESC	Device desciption file.
/usr/share/groff_font/devps/*F*	Font description file for font *F*.
/usr/share/groff_font/devps/download	List of downloadable fonts.
/usr/share/groff_font/devps/text.enc	Encoding used for text fonts.
/usr/share/groff_font/devps/generate/textmap	
	Standard mapping.

SEE ALSO

        groff(1), **grops**(1), **groff_font**(5), **perl**(1)

1

NAME

ansitape – ANSI standard tape handler

SYNOPSIS

ansitape [key] [keyargs] [files]

DESCRIPTION

Ansitape reads and writes magnetic tapes written in ANSI standard format (called "Files-11" by DEC). Tapes written by *ansitape* are labeled with the first 6 characters of the machine name by default. Actions are controlled by the *key* argument. The *key* is a string of characters containing at most one function letter. Other arguments to the command are a tape label and file names specifying which files are to be written onto or extracted from the tape.

The function portion of the key is specified by one of the following letters:

r   The named files are written at the end of the tape. The **c** function implies this.

x   The named files are extracted from the tape. If no file argument is given, the entire contents of the tape is extracted. Note that if the tape has duplicated file names, only the last file of a given name can be extracted.

t   The names of the specified files are listed each time they occur on the tape. If no file argument is given, all files on the tape are listed.

c   Create a new tape; writing begins at the beginning of the tape instead of after the last file. This command implies **r.**

The following characters may be used in addition to the letter which selects the function desired.

f   This argument allows the selection of a different tape device. The next word in the keyargs list is taken to be the full name of a device to write the tape on. The default is /dev/rmt12.

n   The **n** option allows the user to specify as the next argument in the keyargs list, a control file containing the names of files to put on the tape. If the file name is '-', the control file will, instead, be read from standard input. The control file contains one line for each file to be placed on the tape. Each line has two names, the name of the file on the local machine, and the name it is to have when placed on the tape. This allows for more convenient flattening of hierarchies when placing them on tape. If the second name is omitted, the UNIX file name will be used on the tape also. This argument can only be used with the **r** and **c** functions.

l   The **l** option allows the user to specify the label to be placed on the tape. The next argument in the keyargs list is taken as the tape label, which will be space padded or truncated to six characters. This option is meaningless unless **c** is also specified.

v   Normally *ansitape* works relatively silently. The **v** (verbose) option causes it to type information about each file as it processes it.

b   The **b** option allows the user to select the blocksize to be used for the tape. By default, *ansitape* uses the maximum block size permitted by the ANSI standard, 2048. Some systems will permit a much larger block size, and if large files are being put on the tape it may be advantageous to do so. *Ansitape* will take the next argument of the keyargs list as the blocksize for the tape. Values below 18 or above 32k will be limited to that range. The standard scale factors b=512 and k=1024 are accepted.

F   The **F** flag allows *ansitape* to write ansi 'D' format fixed record length tapes. The next two keyargs must be the recordsize and blocksize to be used, with the same scale factors and range limits as for the **b** option. The files to be written by the **F** flag must be in fixed format on the unix end - all lines should be *EXACTLY* **recordsize** bytes long plus a terminating newline (which will be discarded). Note that this is exactly the same format produced by *ansitape* when reading an ansi 'D' format tape.

Ansitape will not copy directories, character or block special files, symbolic links, sockets, or binary executables. Attempts to put these on tape will result in warnings, and they will be skipped completely.

FILES

/dev/rmt12

DIAGNOSTICS

A warning message will be generated when a record exceeds the maximum record length and the affected file will be truncated.

BUGS

Ansitape quietly truncates names longer than 17 characters.

Multivolume tapes can be read (provided no files cross the volume boundary) but not written.

1

NAME

apply – apply a command to a set of arguments

SYNOPSIS

apply [−ac] [−#] *command argument* ...

DESCRIPTION

Apply runs the named *command* on each argument *argument* in turn.

Character sequences of the form ''%d'' in *command*, where ''d'' is a digit from 1 to 9, are replaced by the d´th following unused *argument*. In this case, the largest digit number of arguments are discarded for each execution of *command*.

The options are as follows:

−#   Normally arguments are taken singly; the optional number −# specifies the number of arguments to be passed to *command*. If the number is zero, *command* is run, without arguments, once for each *argument*.

      If any sequences of ''%d'' occur in command, the −n option is ignored.

−a c

      The use of the character ''%'' as a magic character may be changed with the −a option.

ENVIRONMENT VARIABLES

The following environment variable affects the execution of apply:

SHELL Pathname of shell to use. If this variable is not defined, the Bourne shell is used.

EXAMPLES

apply echo a*
         is similar to ls(1);
apply −2 cmp a1 b1 a2 b2 a3 b3
         compares the 'a' files to the 'b' files;
apply −0 who 1 2 3 4 5
         runs who(1) 5 times; and
apply ´ln %1 /usr/joe´ *
         links all files in the current directory to the directory /usr/joe.

Files

/bin/sh Default shell

AUTHOR

Rob Pike

BUGS

Shell metacharacters in *command* may have bizarre effects; it is best to enclose complicated commands in single quotes ('') .

HISTORY

The apply command appeared in 4.2BSD.

NAME

`apropos` – locate commands by keyword lookup

SYNOPSIS

`apropos` [−M *path*] [−m *path*] *keyword* ...

DESCRIPTION

`Apropos` shows which manual pages contain instances of any of the given *keyword(s)* in their title line. Each word is considered separately and case of letters is ignored. Words which are part of other words are considered; when looking for "compile", `apropos` will also list all instances of "compiler".

If the line output by `apropos` starts "`name(section)` ..." you can enter "`man section name`" to get its documentation.

The options are as follows:

−M   Override the list of standard directories `apropos` searches for a database named `whatis.db`. The supplied *path* must be a colon ":" separated list of directories. This search path may also be set using the environment variable `MANPATH`.

−m   Augment the list of standard directories `apropos` searches for its database. The supplied *path* must be a colon ":" separated list of directories. These directories will be searched before the standard directories, or the directories supplied with the −M option or the `MANPATH` environment variable.

ENVIRONMENT

`MANPATH` The standard search path used by man(1) may be overridden by specifying a path in the `MANPATH` environment variable. The format of the path is a colon ":" separated list of directories.

FILES

`whatis.db` name of the apropos database

SEE ALSO

man(1), whatis(1), whereis(1)

HISTORY

The `apropos` command appeared in 3.0BSD.

NAME

ar – create and maintain library archives

SYNOPSIS

ar -d [-Tv] archive file ...
ar -m [-Tv] archive file ...
ar -m [-abiTv] position archive file ...
ar -p [-Tv] archive [file ...]
ar -q [-cTv] archive file ...
ar -r [-cuTv] archive file ...
ar -r [-abciuTv] position archive file ...
ar -t [-Tv] archive [file ...]
ar -x [-ouTv] archive [file ...]

DESCRIPTION

The *ar* utility creates and maintains groups of files combined into an archive. Once an archive has been created, new files can be added and existing files can be extracted, deleted, or replaced.

Files are named in the archive by a single component, i.e., if a file referenced by a path containing a slash (''/'') is archived it will be named by the last component of that path. When matching paths listed on the command line against file names stored in the archive, only the last component of the path will be compared.

All informational and error messages use the path listed on the command line, if any was specified; otherwise the name in the archive is used. If multiple files in the archive have the same name, and paths are listed on the command line to ''select'' archive files for an operation, only the **first** file with a matching name will be selected.

The normal use of *ar* is for the creation and maintenance of libraries suitable for use with the loader (see *ld*(1)), although it is not restricted to this purpose. The options are as follows:

−a   A positioning modifier used with the options −r and −m. The files are entered or moved **after** the archive member *position*, which must be specified.

−b   A positioning modifier used with the options −r and −m. The files are entered or moved **before** the archive member *position*, which must be specified.

−c   Whenever an archive is created, an informational message to that effect is written to standard error. If the −c option is specified, *ar* creates the archive silently.

−d   Delete the specified archive files.

−i   Identical to the −b option.

−m   Move the specified archive files within the archive. If one of the options −a, −b or −i is specified, the files are moved before or after the *position* file in the archive. If none of those options are specified, the files are moved to the end of the archive.

−o   Set the access and modification times of extracted files to the modification time of the file when it was entered into the archive. This will fail if the user is not the owner of the extracted file or the super-user.

−p   Write the contents of the specified archive files to the standard output. If no files are specified, the contents of all the files in the archive are written in the order they appear in the archive.

−q   (Quickly) append the specified files to the archive. If the archive does not exist a new archive file is created. Much faster than the −r option, when creating a large archive piece-by-piece, as no checking is done to see if the files already exist in the archive.

−r   Replace or add the specified files to the archive. If the archive does not exist a new archive file is created. Files that replace existing files do not change the order of the files within the archive. New files are appended to the archive unless one of the options −a, −b or −i is specified.

1

-T   Select and/or name archive members using only the first fifteen characters of the archive member or command line file name. The historic archive format had sixteen bytes for the name, but some historic archiver and loader implementations were unable to handle names that used the entire space. This means that file names that are not unique in their first fifteen characters can subsequently be confused. A warning message is printed to the standard error output if any file names are truncated. (See *ar* (5) for more information.)

-t   List the specified files in the order in which they appear in the archive, each on a separate line. If no files are specified, all files in the archive are listed.

-u   Update files. When used with the -r option, files in the archive will be replaced only if the disk file has a newer modification time than the file in the archive. When used with the -x option, files in the archive will be extracted only if the archive file has a newer modification time than the file on disk.

-v   Provide verbose output. When used with the -d, -m, -q or -x options, *ar* gives a file-by-file description of the archive modification. This description consists of three, white-space separated fields: the option letter, a dash ("-") and the file name. When used with the -r option, *ar* displays the description as above, but the initial letter is an "a" if the file is added to the archive and an "r" if the file replaces a file already in the archive.

When used with the -p option, the name of each printed file, enclosed in less-than ("<") and greater-than (">") characters, is written to the standard output before the contents of the file; it is preceded by a single newline character, and followed by two newline characters.

When used with the -t option, *ar* displays an "ls -l" style listing of information about the members of the archive. This listing consists of eight, white-space separated fields: the file permissions (see *strmode*(3)), the decimal user and group ID's separated by a single slash ("/"), the file size (in bytes), the file modification time (in the *date*(1) format "%b %e %H:%M %Y"), and the name of the file.

-x   Extract the specified archive members into the files named by the command line arguments. If no members are specified, all the members of the archive are extracted into the current directory.

If the file does not exist, it is created; if it does exist, the owner and group will be unchanged. The file access and modification times are the time of the extraction (but see the -o option). The file permissions will be set to those of the file when it was entered into the archive; this will fail if the user is not the owner of the extracted file or the super-user.

The *ar* utility exits 0 on success, and >0 if an error occurs.

ENVIRONMENT
TMPDIR
     The pathname of the directory to use when creating temporary files.

FILES
/tmp   default temporary file directory

ar.XXXXXX   temporary file names

COMPATIBILITY
By default, *ar* writes archives that may be incompatible with historic archives, as the format used for storing archive members with names longer than fifteen characters has changed. This implementation of *ar* is backward compatible with previous versions of *ar* in that it can read and write (using the -T option) historic archives. The -T option is provided for compatibility only, and will be deleted in a future release. See *ar* (5) for more information.

STANDARDS
The *ar* utility is expected to offer a superset of the POSIX 1003.2 functionality.

SEE ALSO
      ld(1), ranlib(1), strmode(3), ar(5)

NAME

    at – schedule execution of commands 'at' a given time

SYNOPSIS

    at [−c] [−m] [−s] *time* [*day*] [*command_filc*]

DESCRIPTION

    At schedules execution of commands at the specified *time*. The commands may be given to **at** via the *command_file* or accepted from the standard input. **At** will pass these commands to the appropriate shell at the requested time. While awaiting execution, the jobs reside in a spool directory and may be examined by the atq(1) program.

    Options available:

    −c   *Command_file* contains csh(1) commands.

    −s   *Command_file* contains sh(1) commands.

    −m   Mail will be sent to the user after the job has been run. If errors occur during execution of the job, then a copy of the error diagnostics will be sent to the user. If no errors occur, then a short message is sent informing the user that no errors occurred.

    If a *command_file* is not specified, **at** prompts for commands from standard input until a '^D' is typed.

    The format of the spool file is as follows: a four line header that includes the owner of the job, the name of the job, the shell used to run the job, and whether mail will be sent after the job is executed. The header is followed by a **cd** command to the current directory and a **umask** command to set the modes on any files created by the job. **At** copies all relevant environment variables to the spool file. When the script is run, it uses the user and group ID of the creator of the spool file.

    The *time* is either a 24 hour military time *hhmm*, where *hh* is hour and *mm* is minutes, or the traditional 12 hour time with qualifying options:

            am, a   am
            pm, p   pm
            n   noon
            m   midnight

    The time can be abbreviated as shown below in EXAMPLES.

    A *day* of the week may be specified by the first two letters of its name. A week (7 days) may be specified by the argument *week*. If a month name is given, the following argument is expected to be the day (numeric).

ENVIRONMENT

    If a shell is not specified, the current environment variable SHELL is used.

EXAMPLES

    at 10p

        Execute at 10pm today, or tomorrow if 10pm has past. Use the shell found in the environment variable SHELL.

    at -c -m 1705 mo

        Execute at 5:05pm on Monday using csh(1) and send mail upon completion or termination of the job.

```
at -s -m 1200n week
```
Execute at noon one week from today, using sh(1) and send mail upon completion.

```
at -s 8a apr 1
```
Ideally this would be given late in March. The commands would be run at 8 am on April first, using the sh(1).

ERRORS
Errors must be collected via the −m option or by redirecting the standard output from inside the command_file.

FILES
/var/spool/at	spooling area
/var/spool/at/yy.ddd.hhhh.*	job file
/var/spool/at/past	directory where jobs are executed from
/var/spool/at/lasttimedone	last time atrun was run
/var/libexec/atrun	executor (run by cron(8))

SEE ALSO
atq(1), atrm(1), calendar(1), cron(8) sleep(1),

DIAGNOSTICS
Complains about various syntax errors and times out of range.

BUGS
The queueing mechanism /usr/libexec/atrun, is scheduled by cron(8). If it is run infrequently, a job may fall through the cracks.

There are known problems attempting to specify a time of 2400 hours to at.

If the system crashes, mail is not sent to the user informing them that the job was not completed.

Sometimes old spool files are not removed from the directory /var/spool/at/past. This is usually due to a system crash, and requires that they be removed by hand.

HISTORY
An at command appeared in Version 7 AT&T UNIX.

NAME

   atq – display the at(1) job queue

SYNOPSIS

   atq [−c] [−n] [name ...]

DESCRIPTION

   Atq displays the queue of jobs, created by the at(1) command, which are currently awaiting execution. With no flags, the queue is sorted in the order that the jobs will be executed.

   Options available are:

   −c   the queue is sorted by the time that the at command was given.

   −n   only the total number of files that are currently in the queue are printed.

   If a name(s) is provided, only those files belonging to that user(s) are displayed.

FILES

   /var/spool/at spool area

SEE ALSO

   at(1), atrm(1), cron(8)

HISTORY

   The atq command appeared in 4.3BSD.

1

NAME
    atrm – remove jobs spooled by at(1)

SYNOPSIS
    atrm [−f] [−i] [−] [[job #][name ...]]

DESCRIPTION
    Atrm removes jobs that were created with the at(1) command.

    Options available are:

    −f   all information regarding the removal of the specified jobs is suppressed.

    −i   atrm asks if a job should be removed; a response of 'y' causes the job to be removed.

    −   all jobs belonging to the person invoking atrm are removed.

    If a job number(s) is specified, atrm attempts to remove only that job number(s).

    If a user(s) name is specified, all jobs belonging to that user(s) are removed. This form of invoking atrm is useful only to the super-user.

FILES
    /usr/spool/at spool area

SEE ALSO
    at(1), atq(1), cron(8)

HISTORY
    The atrm command appeared in 4.3BSD.

NAME

awk – pattern scanning and processing language

SYNOPSIS

awk [POSIX or GNU style options] –**f** *program-file* [– –] file ...

awk [POSIX or GNU style options] [– –] *program-text* file ...

DESCRIPTION

Gawk is the GNU Project's implementation of the AWK programming language. In the 4.4BSD distribution, it is installed as *awk*. It conforms to the definition of the language in the POSIX 1003.2 Command Language And Utilities Standard. This version in turn is based on the description in *The AWK Programming Language*, by Aho, Kernighan, and Weinberger, with the additional features defined in the System V Release 4 version of UNIX *awk*. *Gawk* also provides some GNU-specific extensions.

The command line consists of options to *gawk* itself, the AWK program text (if not supplied via the –**f** or ––**file** options), and values to be made available in the **ARGC** and **ARGV** pre-defined AWK variables.

OPTIONS

Gawk options may be either the traditional POSIX one letter options, or the GNU style long options. POSIX style options start with a single ''–'', while GNU long options start with ''––''. GNU style long options are provided for both GNU-specific features and for POSIX mandated features. Other implementations of the AWK language are likely to only accept the traditional one letter options.

Following the POSIX standard, *gawk*-specific options are supplied via arguments to the –**W** option. Multiple –**W** options may be supplied, or multiple arguments may be supplied together if they are separated by commas, or enclosed in quotes and separated by white space. Case is ignored in arguments to the –**W** option. Each –**W** option has a corresponding GNU style long option, as detailed below.

Gawk accepts the following options.

–**F** *fs*

––**field-separator=***fs*

> Use *fs* for the input field separator (the value of the **FS** predefined variable).

–**v** *var*=*val*

––**assign=***var*=*val*

> Assign the value *val*, to the variable *var*, before execution of the program begins. Such variable values are available to the **BEGIN** block of an AWK program.

–**f** *program-file*

––**file=***program-file*

> Read the AWK program source from the file *program-file*, instead of from the first command line argument. Multiple –**f** (or ––**file**) options may be used.

–**W compat**

––**compat**   Run in *compatibility* mode. In compatibility mode, *gawk* behaves identically to UNIX *awk*; none of the GNU-specific extensions are recognized. See **GNU EXTENSIONS**, below, for more information.

–**W copyleft**

–**W copyright**

––**copyleft**

––**copyright** Print the short version of the GNU copyright information message on the standard error output.

–**W help**

–**W usage**

––**help**

––**usage**   Print a relatively short summary of the available options on the standard error output.

1

−W lint

−−lint   Provide warnings about constructs that are dubious or non-portable to other AWK implementations.

−W posix

−−posix   This turns on *compatibility* mode, with the following additional restrictions:

- **\x** escape sequences are not recognized.

- The synonym **func** for the keyword **function** is not recognized.

- The operators ****** and ****=** cannot be used in place of ^ and ^=.

−W source=*program-text*

−−source=*program-text*

Use *program-text* as AWK program source code. This option allows the easy intermixing of library functions (used via the **−f** and **−−file** options) with source code entered on the command line. It is intended primarily for medium to large size AWK programs used in shell scripts.

The **−W source=** form of this option uses the rest of the command line argument for *program-text*; no other options to **−W** will be recognized in the same argument.

−W version

−−version   Print version information for this particular copy of *gawk* on the standard error output. This is useful mainly for knowing if the current copy of *gawk* on your system is up to date with respect to whatever the Free Software Foundation is distributing.

Signal the end of options. This is useful to allow further arguments to the AWK program itself to start with a ''−''. This is mainly for consistency with the argument parsing convention used by most other POSIX programs.

Any other options are flagged as illegal, but are otherwise ignored.

AWK PROGRAM EXECUTION

An AWK program consists of a sequence of pattern-action statements and optional function definitions.

> *pattern* { *action statements* }
> **function** *name(parameter list)* { *statements* }

Gawk first reads the program source from the *program-file*(s) if specified, or from the first non-option argument on the command line. The **−f** option may be used multiple times on the command line. *Gawk* will read the program text as if all the *program-file*s had been concatenated together. This is useful for building libraries of AWK functions, without having to include them in each new AWK program that uses them. To use a library function in a file from a program typed in on the command line, specify **/dev/tty** as one of the *program-file*s, type your program, and end it with a ^**D** (control-d).

The environment variable **AWKPATH** specifies a search path to use when finding source files named with the **−f** option. If this variable does not exist, the default path is **".:/usr/lib/awk:/usr/local/lib/awk"**. If a file name given to the **−f** option contains a ''/'' character, no path search is performed.

Gawk executes AWK programs in the following order. First, *gawk* compiles the program into an internal form. Next, all variable assignments specified via the **−v** option are performed. Then, *gawk* executes the code in the **BEGIN** block(s) (if any), and then proceeds to read each file named in the **ARGV** array. If there are no files named on the command line, *gawk* reads the standard input.

If a filename on the command line has the form *var=val* it is treated as a variable assignment. The variable *var* will be assigned the value *val*. (This happens after any **BEGIN** block(s) have been run.) Command line variable assignment is most useful for dynamically assigning values to the variables AWK uses to control how input is broken into fields and records. It is also useful for controlling state if multiple passes are needed over a single data file.

1

If the value of a particular element of **ARGV** is empty (""), *gawk* skips over it.

For each line in the input, *gawk* tests to see if it matches any *pattern* in the AWK program. For each pattern that the line matches, the associated *action* is executed. The patterns are tested in the order they occur in the program.

Finally, after all the input is exhausted, *gawk* executes the code in the **END** block(s) (if any).

VARIABLES AND FIELDS

AWK variables are dynamic; they come into existence when they are first used. Their values are either floating-point numbers or strings, or both, depending upon how they are used. AWK also has one dimensional arrays; multiply dimensioned arrays may be simulated. Several pre-defined variables are set as a program runs; these will be described as needed and summarized below.

Fields

As each input line is read, *gawk* splits the line into *fields*, using the value of the **FS** variable as the field separator. If **FS** is a single character, fields are separated by that character. Otherwise, **FS** is expected to be a full regular expression. In the special case that **FS** is a single blank, fields are separated by runs of blanks and/or tabs. Note that the value of **IGNORECASE** (see below) will also affect how fields are split when **FS** is a regular expression.

If the **FIELDWIDTHS** variable is set to a space separated list of numbers, each field is expected to have fixed width, and *gawk* will split up the record using the specified widths. The value of **FS** is ignored. Assigning a new value to **FS** overrides the use of **FIELDWIDTHS**, and restores the default behavior.

Each field in the input line may be referenced by its position, **$1, $2,** and so on. **$0** is the whole line. The value of a field may be assigned to as well. Fields need not be referenced by constants:

> **n = 5**
> **print $n**

prints the fifth field in the input line. The variable **NF** is set to the total number of fields in the input line.

References to non-existent fields (i.e., fields after **$NF**) produce the null-string. However, assigning to a non-existent field (e.g., **$(NF+2) = 5**) will increase the value of **NF**, create any intervening fields with the null string as their value, and cause the value of **$0** to be recomputed, with the fields being separated by the value of **OFS**.

Built-in Variables

AWK's built-in variables are:

ARGC	The number of command line arguments (does not include options to *gawk*, or the program source).
ARGIND	The index in **ARGV** of the current file being processed.
ARGV	Array of command line arguments. The array is indexed from 0 to **ARGC** – 1. Dynamically changing the contents of **ARGV** can control the files used for data.
CONVFMT	The conversion format for numbers, "%.6g", by default.
ENVIRON	An array containing the values of the current environment. The array is indexed by the environment variables, each element being the value of that variable (e.g., **ENVIRON["HOME"]** might be **/u/arnold**). Changing this array does not affect the environment seen by programs which *gawk* spawns via redirection or the **system()** function. (This may change in a future version of *gawk*.)
ERRNO	If a system error occurs either doing a redirection for **getline**, during a read for **getline**, or during a **close**, then **ERRNO** will contain a string describing the error.

FIELDWIDTHS   A white-space separated list of fieldwidths. When set, *gawk* parses the input into fields of fixed width, instead of using the value of the **FS** variable as the field separator. The fixed field width facility is still experimental; expect the semantics to change as *gawk* evolves over time.

FILENAME   The name of the current input file. If no files are specified on the command line, the value of **FILENAME** is ''–''.

FNR   The input record number in the current input file.

FS   The input field separator, a blank by default.

IGNORECASE   Controls the case-sensitivity of all regular expression operations. If **IGNORECASE** has a non-zero value, then pattern matching in rules, field splitting with **FS**, regular expression matching with ~ and !~, and the **gsub()**, **index()**, **match()**, **split()**, and **sub()** predefined functions will all ignore case when doing regular expression operations. Thus, if **IGNORECASE** is not equal to zero, **/aB/** matches all of the strings **"ab"**, **"aB"**, **"Ab"**, and **"AB"**. As with all AWK variables, the initial value of **IGNORECASE** is zero, so all regular expression operations are normally case-sensitive.

NF   The number of fields in the current input record.

NR   The total number of input records seen so far.

OFMT   The output format for numbers, **"%.6g"**, by default.

OFS   The output field separator, a blank by default.

ORS   The output record separator, a newline by default.

RS   The input record separator, a newline by default. **RS** is exceptional in that only the first character of its string value is used for separating records. (This will probably change in a future release of *gawk*.) If **RS** is set to the null string, then records are separated by blank lines. When **RS** is set to the null string, then the newline character always acts as a field separator, in addition to whatever value **FS** may have.

RSTART   The index of the first character matched by **match()**; 0 if no match.

RLENGTH   The length of the string matched by **match()**; −1 if no match.

SUBSEP   The character used to separate multiple subscripts in array elements, **"\034"** by default.

Arrays

Arrays are subscripted with an expression between square brackets ([and]). If the expression is an expression list (*expr*, *expr* ...) then the array subscript is a string consisting of the concatenation of the (string) value of each expression, separated by the value of the **SUBSEP** variable. This facility is used to simulate multiply dimensioned arrays. For example:

> **i = "A" ; j = "B" ; k = "C"**
> **x[i, j, k] = "hello, world\n"**

assigns the string **"hello, world\n"** to the element of the array **x** which is indexed by the string **"A\034B\034C"**. All arrays in AWK are associative, i.e., indexed by string values.

The special operator **in** may be used in an **if** or **while** statement to see if an array has an index consisting of a particular value.

> **if (val in array)**
> > **print array[val]**

If the array has multiple subscripts, use **(i, j) in array**.

The **in** construct may also be used in a **for** loop to iterate over all the elements of an array.

An element may be deleted from an array using the **delete** statement.

Variable Typing And Conversion

Variables and fields may be (floating point) numbers, or strings, or both. How the value of a variable is interpreted depends upon its context. If used in a numeric expression, it will be treated as a number, if used as a string it will be treated as a string.

To force a variable to be treated as a number, add 0 to it; to force it to be treated as a string, concatenate it with the null string.

When a string must be converted to a number, the conversion is accomplished using *atof*(3). A number is converted to a string by using the value of **CONVFMT** as a format string for *sprintf*(3), with the numeric value of the variable as the argument. However, even though all numbers in AWK are floating-point, integral values are *always* converted as integers. Thus, given

> **CONVFMT = " %2.2f"**
> **a = 12**
> **b = a " "**

the variable **b** has a value of **"12"** and not **"12.00"**.

Gawk performs comparisons as follows: If two variables are numeric, they are compared numerically. If one value is numeric and the other has a string value that is a ''numeric string,'' then comparisons are also done numerically. Otherwise, the numeric value is converted to a string and a string comparison is performed. Two strings are compared, of course, as strings. According to the POSIX standard, even if two strings are numeric strings, a numeric comparison is performed. However, this is clearly incorrect, and *gawk* does not do this.

Uninitialized variables have the numeric value 0 and the string value '''' (the null, or empty, string).

PATTERNS AND ACTIONS

AWK is a line oriented language. The pattern comes first, and then the action. Action statements are enclosed in **{** and **}**. Either the pattern may be missing, or the action may be missing, but, of course, not both. If the pattern is missing, the action will be executed for every single line of input. A missing action is equivalent to

> **{ print }**

which prints the entire line.

Comments begin with the ''#'' character, and continue until the end of the line. Blank lines may be used to separate statements. Normally, a statement ends with a newline, however, this is not the case for lines ending in a '','', ''**{**'', ''**?**'', '':'', ''**&&**'', or ''**ll**''. Lines ending in **do** or **else** also have their statements automatically continued on the following line. In other cases, a line can be continued by ending it with a ''\'', in which case the newline will be ignored.

Multiple statements may be put on one line by separating them with a '';''. This applies to both the statements within the action part of a pattern-action pair (the usual case), and to the pattern-action statements themselves.

Patterns

AWK patterns may be one of the following:

> **BEGIN**
> **END**
> */regular expression/*
> *relational expression*
> *pattern* **&&** *pattern*
> *pattern* **||** *pattern*
> *pattern* **?** *pattern* **:** *pattern*
> *(pattern)*

      ! *pattern*
      pattern1 **,** *pattern2*

BEGIN and **END** are two special kinds of patterns which are not tested against the input. The action parts of all **BEGIN** patterns are merged as if all the statements had been written in a single **BEGIN** block. They are executed before any of the input is read. Similarly, all the **END** blocks are merged, and executed when all the input is exhausted (or when an **exit** statement is executed). **BEGIN** and **END** patterns cannot be combined with other patterns in pattern expressions. **BEGIN** and **END** patterns cannot have missing action parts.

For **/**regular expression**/** patterns, the associated statement is executed for each input line that matches the regular expression. Regular expressions are the same as those in *egrep*(1), and are summarized below.

A *relational expression* may use any of the operators defined below in the section on actions. These generally test whether certain fields match certain regular expressions.

The **&&**, **||**, and **!** operators are logical AND, logical OR, and logical NOT, respectively, as in C. They do short-circuit evaluation, also as in C, and are used for combining more primitive pattern expressions. As in most languages, parentheses may be used to change the order of evaluation.

The **?:** operator is like the same operator in C. If the first pattern is true then the pattern used for testing is the second pattern, otherwise it is the third. Only one of the second and third patterns is evaluated.

The *pattern1*, *pattern2* form of an expression is called a range pattern. It matches all input records starting with a line that matches *pattern1*, and continuing until a record that matches *pattern2*, inclusive. It does not combine with any other sort of pattern expression.

Regular Expressions

Regular expressions are the extended kind found in *egrep*. They are composed of characters as follows:

c	matches the non-metacharacter *c*.
c	matches the literal character *c*.
.	matches any character except newline.
^	matches the beginning of a line or a string.
$	matches the end of a line or a string.
[*abc...*]	character class, matches any of the characters *abc...*.
[^*abc...*]	negated character class, matches any character except *abc...* and newline.
r1|*r2*	alternation: matches either *r1* or *r2*.
r1r2	concatenation: matches *r1*, and then *r2*.
r+	matches one or more *r*'s.
r∗	matches zero or more *r*'s.
r?	matches zero or one *r*'s.
(*r*)	grouping: matches *r*.

The escape sequences that are valid in string constants (see below) are also legal in regular expressions.

Actions

Action statements are enclosed in braces, **{** and **}**. Action statements consist of the usual assignment, conditional, and looping statements found in most languages. The operators, control statements, and input/output statements available are patterned after those in C.

Operators

The operators in AWK, in order of increasing precedence, are

= += −=

*= /= %= ^=   Assignment. Both absolute assignment (*var = value*) and operator-assignment (the other forms) are supported.

?:   The C conditional expression. This has the form *expr1* **?** *expr2* **:** *expr3*. If *expr1* is true, the value of the expression is *expr2*, otherwise it is *expr3*. Only one of *expr2* and *expr3* is evaluated.

‖   Logical OR.

&&   Logical AND.

˜ !˜   Regular expression match, negated match. **NOTE:** Do not use a constant regular expression (**/foo/**) on the left-hand side of a ˜ or !˜. Only use one on the right-hand side. The expression **/foo/** ˜ *exp* has the same meaning as ((**$0** ˜ **/foo/**) ˜ *exp*). This is usually *not* what was intended.

< >
<= >=
!= ==   The regular relational operators.

blank   String concatenation.

+ −   Addition and subtraction.

* / %   Multiplication, division, and modulus.

+ − !   Unary plus, unary minus, and logical negation.

^   Exponentiation (** may also be used, and **= for the assignment operator).

++ −−   Increment and decrement, both prefix and postfix.

$ Field reference.

Control Statements

The control statements are as follows:

> **if** (*condition*) *statement* [**else** *statement*]
> **while** (*condition*) *statement*
> **do** *statement* **while** (*condition*)
> **for** (*expr1*; *expr2*; *expr3*) *statement*
> **for** (*var* **in** *array*) *statement*
> **break**
> **continue**
> **delete** *array*[*index*]
> **exit** [*expression*]
> { *statements* }

I/O Statements

The input/output statements are as follows:

close(*filename*)   Close file (or pipe, see below).

getline   Set **$0** from next input record; set **NF**, **NR**, **FNR**.

getline <*file*   Set **$0** from next record of *file*; set **NF**.

getline *var*   Set *var* from next input record; set **NF**, **FNR**.

getline *var* <*file*   Set *var* from next record of *file*.

1

next   Stop processing the current input record. The next input record is read and processing starts over with the first pattern in the AWK program. If the end of the input data is reached, the **END** block(s), if any, are executed.

next file   Stop processing the current input file. The next input record read comes from the next input file. **FILENAME** is updated, **FNR** is reset to 1, and processing starts over with the first pattern in the AWK program. If the end of the input data is reached, the **END** block(s), if any, are executed.

print   Prints the current record.

print *expr-list*   Prints expressions.

print *expr-list >file* Prints expressions on *file*.

printf *fmt, expr-list* Format and print.

printf *fmt, expr-list >file*
                         Format and print on *file*.

system(*cmd-line*)   Execute the command *cmd-line*, and return the exit status. (This may not be available on non-POSIX systems.)

Other input/output redirections are also allowed. For **print** and **printf**, *>>file* appends output to the *file*, while | *command* writes on a pipe. In a similar fashion, *command* | **getline** pipes into **getline**. **Getline** will return 0 on end of file, and −1 on an error.

The *printf* Statement

The AWK versions of the **printf** statement and **sprintf**() function (see below) accept the following conversion specification formats:

%c   An ASCII character. If the argument used for **%c** is numeric, it is treated as a character and printed. Otherwise, the argument is assumed to be a string, and the only first character of that string is printed.

%d   A decimal number (the integer part).

%i   Just like **%d**.

%e   A floating point number of the form [−]d.ddddddE[+−]dd.

%f   A floating point number of the form [−]ddd.dddddd.

%g   Use **e** or **f** conversion, whichever is shorter, with nonsignificant zeros suppressed.

%o   An unsigned octal number (again, an integer).

%s   A character string.

%x   An unsigned hexadecimal number (an integer).

%X   Like **%x**, but using **ABCDEF** instead of **abcdef**.

%%   A single % character; no argument is converted.

There are optional, additional parameters that may lie between the % and the control letter:

−   The expression should be left-justified within its field.

width   The field should be padded to this width. If the number has a leading zero, then the field will be padded with zeros. Otherwise it is padded with blanks.

.prec   A number indicating the maximum width of strings or digits to the right of the decimal point.

The dynamic *width* and *prec* capabilities of the ANSI C **printf**() routines are supported. A * in place of either the **width** or **prec** specifications will cause their values to be taken from the argument list to **printf** or **sprintf**().

Special File Names

When doing I/O redirection from either **print** or **printf** into a file, or via **getline** from a file, *gawk* recognizes certain special filenames internally. These filenames allow access to open file descriptors inherited from *gawk*'s parent process (usually the shell). Other special filenames provide access information about the running **gawk** process. The filenames are:

/dev/pid　　Reading this file returns the process ID of the current process, in decimal, terminated with a newline.

/dev/ppid　　Reading this file returns the parent process ID of the current process, in decimal, terminated with a newline.

/dev/pgrpid

　　　　　　Reading this file returns the process group ID of the current process, in decimal, terminated with a newline.

/dev/user　　Reading this file returns a single record terminated with a newline. The fields are separated with blanks. **$1** is the value of the *getuid*(2) system call, **$2** is the value of the *geteuid*(2) system call, **$3** is the value of the *getgid*(2) system call, and **$4** is the value of the *getegid*(2) system call. If there are any additional fields, they are the group IDs returned by *getgroups*(2). (Multiple groups may not be supported on all systems.)

/dev/stdin　　The standard input.

/dev/stdout　The standard output.

/dev/stderr　The standard error output.

/dev/fd/*n*　　The file associated with the open file descriptor *n*.

These are particularly useful for error messages. For example:

　　　　print "You blew it!" > "/dev/stderr"

whereas you would otherwise have to use

　　　　print "You blew it!" | "cat 1>&2"

These file names may also be used on the command line to name data files.

Numeric Functions

AWK has the following pre-defined arithmetic functions:

atan2(*y***, ***x***)**　　returns the arctangent of *y*/*x* in radians.

cos(*expr***)**　　returns the cosine in radians.

exp(*expr***)**　　the exponential function.

int(*expr***)**　　truncates to integer.

log(*expr***)**　　the natural logarithm function.

rand()　　returns a random number between 0 and 1.

sin(*expr***)**　　returns the sine in radians.

sqrt(*expr***)**　　the square root function.

srand(*expr***)**　use *expr* as a new seed for the random number generator. If no *expr* is provided, the time of day will be used. The return value is the previous seed for the random number generator.

String Functions

AWK has the following pre-defined string functions:

1

gsub(*r, s, t*)	for each substring matching the regular expression *r* in the string *t*, substitute the string *s*, and return the number of substitutions. If *t* is not supplied, use **$0**.
index(*s, t*)	returns the index of the string *t* in the string *s*, or 0 if *t* is not present.
length(*s*)	returns the length of the string *s*, or the length of **$0** if *s* is not supplied.
match(*s, r*)	returns the position in *s* where the regular expression *r* occurs, or 0 if *r* is not present, and sets the values of **RSTART** and **RLENGTH**.
split(*s, a, r*)	splits the string *s* into the array *a* on the regular expression *r*, and returns the number of fields. If *r* is omitted, **FS** is used.
sprintf(*fmt, expr-list*)	prints *expr-list* according to *fmt*, and returns the resulting string.
sub(*r, s, t*)	just like **gsub**(), but only the first matching substring is replaced.
substr(*s, i, n*)	returns the *n*-character substring of *s* starting at *i*. If *n* is omitted, the rest of *s* is used.
tolower(*str*)	returns a copy of the string *str*, with all the upper-case characters in *str* translated to their corresponding lower-case counterparts. Non-alphabetic characters are left unchanged.
toupper(*str*)	returns a copy of the string *str*, with all the lower-case characters in *str* translated to their corresponding upper-case counterparts. Non-alphabetic characters are left unchanged.

Time Functions

Since one of the primary uses of AWK programs is processing log files that contain time stamp information, *gawk* provides the following two functions for obtaining time stamps and formatting them.

systime() returns the current time of day as the number of seconds since the Epoch (Midnight UTC, January 1, 1970 on POSIX systems).

strftime(*format, timestamp*)

    formats *timestamp* according to the specification in *format*. The *timestamp* should be of the same form as returned by **systime**(). If *timestamp* is missing, the current time of day is used. See the specification for the **strftime**() function in ANSI C for the format conversions that are guaranteed to be available. A public-domain version of *strftime*(3) and a man page for it are shipped with *gawk*; if that version was used to build *gawk*, then all of the conversions described in that man page are available to *gawk*.

String Constants

String constants in AWK are sequences of characters enclosed between double quotes ("). Within strings, certain *escape sequences* are recognized, as in C. These are:

**** A literal backslash.

\a The "alert" character; usually the ASCII BEL character.

\b backspace.

\f form-feed.

\n newline.

\r carriage return.

\t horizontal tab.

\v vertical tab.

\x*hex digits*

    The character represented by the string of hexadecimal digits following the **\x**. As in ANSI C, all following hexadecimal digits are considered part of the escape sequence. (This feature should tell us something about language design by committee.) E.g., "\x1B" is the ASCII ESC (escape) character.

\ddd The character represented by the 1-, 2-, or 3-digit sequence of octal digits. E.g. "\033" is the ASCII ESC (escape) character.

\c The literal character *c*.

The escape sequences may also be used inside constant regular expressions (e.g., /[\t\f\n\r\v]/ matches whitespace characters).

FUNCTIONS

Functions in AWK are defined as follows:

function *name(parameter list)* **{** *statements* **}**

Functions are executed when called from within the action parts of regular pattern-action statements. Actual parameters supplied in the function call are used to instantiate the formal parameters declared in the function. Arrays are passed by reference, other variables are passed by value.

Since functions were not originally part of the AWK language, the provision for local variables is rather clumsy: they are declared as extra parameters in the parameter list. The convention is to separate local variables from real parameters by extra spaces in the parameter list. For example:

function f(p, q,   a, b) { # a & b are local
**   ..... }**

/abc/   { ... ; f(1, 2) ; ... }

The left parenthesis in a function call is required to immediately follow the function name, without any intervening white space. This is to avoid a syntactic ambiguity with the concatenation operator. This restriction does not apply to the built-in functions listed above.

Functions may call each other and may be recursive. Function parameters used as local variables are initialized to the null string and the number zero upon function invocation.

The word **func** may be used in place of **function**.

EXAMPLES

Print and sort the login names of all users:

BEGIN { FS = ":" }
**   { print $1 | "sort" }**

Count lines in a file:

**   { nlines++ }**
END   { print nlines }

Precede each line by its number in the file:

{ print FNR, $0 }

Concatenate and line number (a variation on a theme):

{ print NR, $0 }

SEE ALSO

egrep(1)

The AWK Programming Language, Alfred V. Aho, Brian W. Kernighan, Peter J. Weinberger, Addison-Wesley, 1988. ISBN 0-201-07981-X.

The GAWK Manual, Edition 0.15, published by the Free Software Foundation, 1993.

POSIX COMPATIBILITY

A primary goal for *gawk* is compatibility with the POSIX standard, as well as with the latest version of UNIX *awk*. To this end, *gawk* incorporates the following user visible features which are not described in the AWK book, but are part of *awk* in System V Release 4, and are in the POSIX standard.

The −v option for assigning variables before program execution starts is new. The book indicates that command line variable assignment happens when *awk* would otherwise open the argument as a file, which is after the **BEGIN** block is executed. However, in earlier implementations, when such an assignment appeared before any file names, the assignment would happen *before* the **BEGIN** block was run. Applications came to depend on this "feature." When *awk* was changed to match its documentation, this option was added to accomodate applications that depended upon the old behavior. (This feature was agreed upon by both the AT&T and GNU developers.)

The −W option for implementation specific features is from the POSIX standard.

When processing arguments, *gawk* uses the special option "−−" to signal the end of arguments, and warns about, but otherwise ignores, undefined options.

The AWK book does not define the return value of **srand()**. The System V Release 4 version of UNIX *awk* (and the POSIX standard) has it return the seed it was using, to allow keeping track of random number sequences. Therefore **srand()** in *gawk* also returns its current seed.

Other new features are: The use of multiple −f options (from MKS *awk*); the **ENVIRON** array; the \a, and \v escape sequences (done originally in *gawk* and fed back into AT&T's version); the **tolower()** and **toupper()** built-in functions (from AT&T); and the ANSI C conversion specifications in **printf** (done first in AT&T's version).

GNU EXTENSIONS

Gawk has some extensions to POSIX *awk*. They are described in this section. All the extensions described here can be disabled by invoking *gawk* with the −W **compat** option.

The following features of *gawk* are not available in POSIX *awk*.

- The \x escape sequence.

- The **systime()** and **strftime()** functions.

- The special file names available for I/O redirection are not recognized.

- The **ARGIND** and **ERRNO** variables are not special.

- The **IGNORECASE** variable and its side-effects are not available.

- The **FIELDWIDTHS** variable and fixed width field splitting.

- No path search is performed for files named via the −f option. Therefore the **AWKPATH** environment variable is not special.

- The use of **next file** to abandon processing of the current input file.

The AWK book does not define the return value of the **close()** function. *Gawk*'s **close()** returns the value from *fclose*(3), or *pclose*(3), when closing a file or pipe, respectively.

When *gawk* is invoked with the −W **compat** option, if the *fs* argument to the −F option is "t", then **FS** will be set to the tab character. Since this is a rather ugly special case, it is not the default behavior. This behavior also does not occur if −W **posix** has been specified.

HISTORICAL FEATURES

There are two features of historical AWK implementations that *gawk* supports. First, it is possible to call the **length()** built-in function not only with no argument, but even without parentheses! Thus,

        a = length

is the same as either of

    a = length()
    a = length($0)

This feature is marked as ''deprecated'' in the POSIX standard, and *gawk* will issue a warning about its use if **−W lint** is specified on the command line.

The other feature is the use of the **continue** statement outside the body of a **while, for,** or **do** loop. Traditional AWK implementations have treated such usage as equivalent to the **next** statement. *Gawk* will support this usage if **−W posix** has not been specified.

BUGS

The **−F** option is not necessary given the command line variable assignment feature; it remains only for backwards compatibility.

If your system actually has support for **/dev/fd** and the associated **/dev/stdin, /dev/stdout,** and **/dev/stderr** files, you may get different output from *gawk* than you would get on a system without those files. When *gawk* interprets these files internally, it synchronizes output to the standard output with output to **/dev/stdout,** while on a system with those files, the output is actually to different open files. Caveat Emptor.

VERSION INFORMATION

This man page documents *gawk*, version 2.15.

Starting with the 2.15 version of *gawk*, the **−c, −V, −C, −a,** and **−e** options of the 2.11 version are no longer recognized.

AUTHORS

The original version of UNIX *awk* was designed and implemented by Alfred Aho, Peter Weinberger, and Brian Kernighan of AT&T Bell Labs. Brian Kernighan continues to maintain and enhance it.

Paul Rubin and Jay Fenlason, of the Free Software Foundation, wrote *gawk*, to be compatible with the original version of *awk* distributed in Seventh Edition UNIX. John Woods contributed a number of bug fixes. David Trueman, with contributions from Arnold Robbins, made *gawk* compatible with the new version of UNIX *awk*.

The initial DOS port was done by Conrad Kwok and Scott Garfinkle. Scott Deifik is the current DOS maintainer. Pat Rankin did the port to VMS, and Michal Jaegermann did the port to the Atari ST.

ACKNOWLEDGEMENTS

Brian Kernighan of Bell Labs provided valuable assistance during testing and debugging. We thank him.

1

NAME

basename, **dirname** – return filename or directory portion of pathname

SYNOPSIS

basename *string* [*suffix*]
dirname *string*

DESCRIPTION

Basename deletes any prefix ending with the last slash '/' character present in *string*, and a *suffix*, if given. The resulting filename is written to the standard output. If *string* ends in the slash character, '/', or is the same as the *suffix* argument, a newline is output. A non-existent suffix is ignored.

Dirname deletes the filename portion, beginning with the last slash '/' character to the end of *string*, and writes the result to the standard output.

EXAMPLES

The following line sets the shell variable FOO to /usr/bin.

        FOO='dirname /usr/bin/trail'

Both the **basename** and **dirname** exit 0 on success, and >0 if an error occurs.

SEE ALSO

csh(1) sh(1)

STANDARDS

The **basename** and **dirname** functions are expected to be POSIX 1003.2 compatible.

1

NAME
bc – arbitrary-precision arithmetic language and calculator

SYNOPSIS
bc [−c] [−l] *file* . . .

DESCRIPTION
Bc is an interactive processor for a language which resembles C but provides unlimited precision arithmetic. It takes input from any files given, then reads the standard input.

Options available:

−l   allow specification of an arbitrary precision math library.

−c   Bc is actually a preprocessor for *dc* 1, which it invokes automatically, unless the −c compile only option is present. Here, the *dc* input is sent to the standard output instead.

The syntax for bc programs is as follows; L means letter a-z, E means expression, S means statement.

Comments
are enclosed in /* and */.

Names
simple variables: L
array elements: L [E]
The words 'ibase', 'obase', and 'scale'

Other operands
arbitrarily long numbers with optional sign and decimal point.
(E)
sqrt (E)
length (E)   number of significant decimal digits
scale (E)   number of digits right of decimal point
L (E , ... , E)

Operators
+ − * / % ^ (% is remainder; ^ is power)
++ −−   (prefix and postfix; apply to names)
== <= >= != < >
= += −= *= /= %= ^=

Statements
E
{ S ; ... ; S }
if (E) S
while (E) S
for (E ; E ; E) S
null statement
break
quit

1

Function definitions
```
define L ( L ,..., L ) {
        auto L, ... , L
        S; ... S
        return ( E )
}
```

Functions in −1 math library

s(x)	sine
c(x)	cosine
e(x)	exponential
l(x)	log
a(x)	arctangent
j(n,x)	Bessel function

All function arguments are passed by value.

The value of a statement that is an expression is printed unless the main operator is an assignment. Either semicolons or newlines may separate statements. Assignment to *scale* influences the number of digits to be retained on arithmetic operations in the manner of dc(1). Assignments to *ibase* or *obase* set the input and output number radix respectively.

The same letter may be used as an array, a function, and a simple variable simultaneously. All variables are global to the program. 'Auto' variables are pushed down during function calls. When using arrays as function arguments or defining them as automatic variables, empty square brackets must follow the array name.

For example

```
scale = 20
define e(x){
        auto a, b, c, i, s
        a = 1
        b = 1
        s = 1
        for(i=1; 1==1; i++){
                a = a*x
                b = b*i
                c = a/b
                if(c == 0) return(s)
                s = s+c
        }
}
```

defines a function to compute an approximate value of the exponential function and

```
for(i=1; i<=10; i++) e(i)
```

prints approximate values of the exponential function of the first ten integers.

FILES
dc(1)   Desk calculator proper.

SEE ALSO

dc(1)

L. L. Cherry, and R. Morris, *BC – An arbitrary precision desk-calculator language.*

HISTORY

The bc command appeared in Version 6 AT&T UNIX.

BUGS

No &&, ||, or ! operators.

For statement must have all three E's.

Quit is interpreted when read, not when executed.

1

NAME

    bdes – encrypt/decrypt using the Data Encryption Standard

SYNOPSIS

    bdes [–abdp] [–F N] [–f N] [–k key]
            [–m N] [–o N] [–v vector]

DESCRIPTION

Bdes implements all DES modes of operation described in FIPS PUB 81, including alternative cipher feed-back mode and both authentication modes. *Bdes* reads from the standard input and writes to the standard output. By default, the input is encrypted using cipher block chaining mode. Using the same key for encryption and decryption preserves plain text.

All modes but the electronic code book mode require an initialization vector; if none is supplied, the zero vector is used. If no *key* is specified on the command line, the user is prompted for one (see *getpass*(3) for more details).

The options are as follows:

–a   The key and initialization vector strings are to be taken as ASCII, suppressing the special interpre-tation given to leading "0X", "0x", "0B", and "0b" characters. This flag applies to *both* the key and initialization vector.

–b   Use electronic code book mode.

–d   Decrypt the input.

–F   Use *N*-bit alternative cipher feedback mode. Currently *N* must be a multiple of 7 between 7 and 56 inclusive (this does not conform to the alternative CFB mode specification).

–f   Use *N*-bit cipher feedback mode. Currently *N* must be a multiple of 8 between 8 and 64 inclusive (this does not conform to the standard CFB mode specification).

–k   Use *key* as the cryptographic key.

–m   Compute a message authentication code (MAC) of *N* bits on the input. The value of *N* must be between 1 and 64 inclusive; if *N* is not a multiple of 8, enough 0 bits will be added to pad the MAC length to the nearest multiple of 8. Only the MAC is output. MACs are only available in cipher block chaining mode or in cipher feedback mode.

–o   Use *N*-bit output feedback mode. Currently *N* must be a multiple of 8 between 8 and 64 inclusive (this does not conform to the OFB mode specification).

–p   Disable the resetting of the parity bit. This flag forces the parity bit of the key to be used as typed, rather than making each character be of odd parity. It is used only if the key is given in ASCII.

–v   Set the initialization vector to *vector*; the vector is interpreted in the same way as the key. The vector is ignored in electronic codebook mode.

The key and initialization vector are taken as sequences of ASCII characters which are then mapped into their bit representations. If either begins with "0X" or "0x", that one is taken as a sequence of hexade-cimal digits indicating the bit pattern; if either begins with "0B" or "0b", that one is taken as a sequence of binary digits indicating the bit pattern. In either case, only the leading 64 bits of the key or initialization vector are used, and if fewer than 64 bits are provided, enough 0 bits are appended to pad the key to 64 bits.

According to the DES standard, the low-order bit of each character in the key string is deleted. Since most ASCII representations set the high-order bit to 0, simply deleting the low-order bit effectively reduces the size of the key space from 2^{56} to 2^{48} keys. To prevent this, the high-order bit must be a function depending in part upon the low-order bit; so, the high-order bit is set to whatever value gives odd parity. This preserves the key space size. Note this resetting of the parity bit is *not* done if the key is given in binary or hex, and can be disabled for ASCII keys as well.

The DES is considered a very strong cryptosystem, and other than table lookup attacks, key search attacks, and Hellman's time-memory tradeoff (all of which are very expensive and time-consuming), no cryptanalytic methods for breaking the DES are known in the open literature. No doubt the choice of keys and key security are the most vulnerable aspect of *bdes*.

IMPLEMENTATION NOTES

For implementors wishing to write software compatible with this program, the following notes are provided. This software is believed to be compatible with the implementation of the data encryption standard distributed by Sun Microsystems, Inc.

In the ECB and CBC modes, plaintext is encrypted in units of 64 bits (8 bytes, also called a block). To ensure that the plaintext file is encrypted correctly, *bdes* will (internally) append from 1 to 8 bytes, the last byte containing an integer stating how many bytes of that final block are from the plaintext file, and encrypt the resulting block. Hence, when decrypting, the last block may contain from 0 to 7 characters present in the plaintext file, and the last byte tells how many. Note that if during decryption the last byte of the file does not contain an integer between 0 and 7, either the file has been corrupted or an incorrect key has been given. A similar mechanism is used for the OFB and CFB modes, except that those simply require the length of the input to be a multiple of the mode size, and the final byte contains an integer between 0 and one less than the number of bytes being used as the mode. (This was another reason that the mode size must be a multiple of 8 for those modes.)

Unlike Sun's implementation, unused bytes of that last block are not filled with random data, but instead contain what was in those byte positions in the preceding block. This is quicker and more portable, and does not weaken the encryption significantly.

If the key is entered in ASCII, the parity bits of the key characters are set so that each key character is of odd parity. Unlike Sun's implementation, it is possible to enter binary or hexadecimal keys on the command line, and if this is done, the parity bits are *not* reset. This allows testing using arbitrary bit patterns as keys.

The Sun implementation always uses an initialization vector of 0 (that is, all zeroes). By default, *bdes* does too, but this may be changed from the command line.

SEE ALSO

crypt(1), crypt(3), getpass(3)

Data Encryption Standard, Federal Information Processing Standard #46, National Bureau of Standards, U.S. Department of Commerce, Washington DC (Jan. 1977)

DES Modes of Operation, Federal Information Processing Standard #81, National Bureau of Standards, U.S. Department of Commerce Washington DC (Dec. 1980)

Dorothy Denning, *Cryptography and Data Security*, Addison-Wesley Publishing Co., Reading, MA ©1982.

Matt Bishop, *Implementation Notes on bdes(1)*, Technical Report PCS-TR-91-158, Department of Mathematics and Computer Science, Dartmouth College, Hanover, NH 03755 (Apr. 1991).

DISCLAIMER

THIS SOFTWARE IS PROVIDED BY THE REGENTS AND CONTRIBUTORS ''AS IS'' AND ANY EXPRESS OR IMPLIED WARRANTIES, INCLUDING, BUT NOT LIMITED TO, THE IMPLIED WARRANTIES OF MERCHANTABILITY AND FITNESS FOR A PARTICULAR PURPOSE ARE DISCLAIMED. IN NO EVENT SHALL THE REGENTS OR CONTRIBUTORS BE LIABLE FOR ANY DIRECT, INDIRECT, INCIDENTAL, SPECIAL, EXEMPLARY, OR CONSEQUENTIAL DAMAGES (INCLUDING, BUT NOT LIMITED TO, PROCUREMENT OF SUBSTITUTE GOODS OR SERVICES; LOSS OF USE, DATA, OR PROFITS; OR BUSINESS INTERRUPTION) HOWEVER CAUSED AND ON ANY THEORY OF LIABILITY, WHETHER IN CONTRACT, STRICT LIABILITY, OR TORT (INCLUDING NEGLIGENCE OR OTHERWISE) ARISING IN ANY WAY

1

OUT OF THE USE OF THIS SOFTWARE, EVEN IF ADVISED OF THE POSSIBILITY OF
SUCH DAMAGE.

BUGS

There is a controversy raging over whether the DES will still be secure in a few years. The advent of
special-purpose hardware could reduce the cost of any of the methods of attack named above so that they
are no longer computationally infeasible.

As the key or key schedule is stored in memory, the encryption can be compromised if memory is readable.
Additionally, programs which display programs' arguments may compromise the key and initialization
vector, if they are specified on the command line. To avoid this *bdes* overwrites its arguments, however,
the obvious race cannot currently be avoided.

Certain specific keys should be avoided because they introduce potential weaknesses; these keys, called the
weak and *semiweak* keys, are (in hex notation, where p is either 0 or 1, and P is either e or f):

0x0p0p0p0p0p0p0p0p	0x0p1P0p1P0p0P0p0P
0x0pep0pep0pfp0pfp	0x0pfP0pfP0pfP0pfP
0x1P0p1P0p0P0p0P0p	0x1P1P1P1P0P0P0P0P
0x1Pep1Pep0Pfp0Pfp	0x1PfP1PfP0PfP0PfP
0xep0pep0pfp0pfp0p	0xep1Pep1pfp0Pfp0P
0xepepepepepepepep	0xepfPepfPfpfPfpfP
0xfP0pfP0pfP0pfP0p	0xfP1PfP1PfP0PfP0P
0xfPepfPepfPepfPep	0xfPfPfPfPfPfPfPfP

This is inherent in the DES algorithm (see Moore and Simmons, Cycle structure of the DES with weak and
semi-weak keys, *Advances in Cryptology – Crypto '86 Proceedings* , Springer-Verlag New York, ©1987,
pp. 9-32.)

1

NAME

bib, listrefs, bibinc, bib2tib – bibliographic formatter

SYNOPSIS

bib [options] ...
listrefs [options] ...
bibinc [options] ...

DESCRIPTION

Bib is a preprocessor for *nroff* or *troff*(1) that formats citations and bibliographies. The input files (standard input default) are copied to the standard output, except for text between [. and .] pairs, which are assumed to be keywords for searching a bibliographic database. If a matching reference is found a citation is generated replacing the text. References are collected, optionally sorted, and written out at a location specified by the user. Citation and reference formats are controlled by the –t option.

Reference databases are created using the *invert* utility.

The following options are available. Note that standard format styles (see the –t option) set options automatically. Thus if a standard format style is used the user need not indicate any further options for most documents.

–aa   reduce authors first names to abbreviations.

–ar*num*   reverse the first *num* author's names. If a number is not given all authors names are reversed.

–ax   print authors last names in Caps-Small Caps style. For example Budd becomes BUDD. This style is used by certain ACM publications.

–c*str*   build citations according to the template *str*. See the reference format designers guide for more information on templates.

–d   changes the default search directory for style files, include files, etc. and changes the value of the macro BMACLIB for bib, and of the macro l] used to find the troff macro definition file bmac.std. Defaults to /usr/new/lib/bmac. If you have your own private copies of all the necessary files, using this option is the easiest way to specify them.

–ea   reduce editors' first names to abbreviations.

–ex   print editors' last names in Caps-Small Caps style (see –ax option).

–er*num*   reverse the first *num* editors' names. If a number is not given all editors' names are reversed.

–f   instead of collecting references, dump each reference immediately following the line on which the citation is placed (used for footnoted references).

–i *file*

–i*file*   process the indicated file, such as a file of definitions. (see technical report for a description of file format).

–h   replace citations to three or more adjacent reference items with a hyphenated string (eg 2,3,4,5 becomes 2-5). This option implies the –o option.

–n*str*   turn off indicated options. *str* must be composed of the letters afhosx.

–o   contiguous citations are ordered according the the reference list before being printed (default).

–p *file*

–p*file*   instead of searching the file INDEX, search the indicated reference files before searching the system file. *files* is a comma separated list of inverted indices, created using the *invert* utility.

1

−s*str*	sort references according to the template *str*.
−t *type*	
−t*type*	use the standard macros and switch settings for the indicated style to generate citations and references. There are a number of standard styles provided. In addition users can generate their own style macros. See the format designers guide for details.
−Tib	the abbreviations and macros used all use the TiB style of macro call in which the name is enclosed in vertical |bars|.
−Tibx	instead of processing the input files, write the file bib.m4.in containing m4(I) macro definitions that make converting from bib style to Tib style macros a little easier. Note that m4 does not allow ampersands in macro names: this file and all of the files to be converted will have to be changed by hand. The m4 macros will *only* identify words that bib would normally expand: they do no other conversions. After creating .bib.m4.in, run the scriptfile bib2tib passing it the names of the files you wish converted.

Listrefs formats an entire reference database file. Options to *listrefs* are the same as for *bib*.

Bibinc is an old hack tool for solving the problem of multiple define files for multiple styles. Some journal styles require that journal names be spelled out completely, while others allow abbreviated names. Two macro definition files are available that allow this multiplicity of style: bibinc.fullnames and bibinc.shortnames. A frequent source of error is updating one of these files, and forgetting to update the other. *Bibinc* allows a single file, say bibinc.names, to define both the long and the short versions of names, and from which the files bibinc.fullnames and bibinc.shortnames can easily be created. *Bibinc* can also be used to define macro files for the TiB bibliographic preprocessor.

Bib2tib will use the bib.m4.in file created with the -Tibx option to convert any files you specify into one using the TiB-style macro conventions. It is a simple script that does about 95% of the necessary grunge work to make this conversion, but be aware that the user will still need to eyeball the converted files for correctness. To make use of the facility, run a *bib* job with the -Tibx option: *bib* will not process the input files, but will create bib.m4.in instead, after gathering together all the definitions it can find. Then for each of your bibliographic database files, run *bibinc*.

Bib was designed initially for use with the −ms macros, and uses a couple of the −ms macros (.ip and .lp) in its macro definitions. To use it with the −me macros, prefix the file being sent to nroff/troff with the following macro definitions:

```
.de IP
.ip \$1 \$2
..
.de LP
.lp
..
```

A file "bibmac.me" containing these macro definitions may be found in /usr/new/lib/bmac.

FILES

INDEX	inverted index for reference database
/usr/dict/papers/INDEX	default system index
/usr/new/lib/bmac/bmac.*	formatting macro packages
/usr/new/lib/bmac/bibinc.names	input to *bibinc*
/usr/new/lib/bmac/tibmacs/*	for use with TiB-style |macros|
/usr/new/lib/bmac/bibmacs/*	for use with old bib-style macros
/usr/tmp/bibr*	scratch file for collecting references
/usr/tmp/bibp*	output of pass one of bib
bib.m4.in	macros for converting to TiB (see -Tibx above)

SEE ALSO

A UNIX Bibliographic Database Facility, Timothy A. Budd and Gary M. Levin, University of Arizona Technical Report 82-1, 1982. (includes format designers guide).

BIB – A Program for Formatting Bibliographies, Timothy A. Budd, a BSD UNIX document found in /usr/doc/usd/31.bib.

invert(1), troff(1)

1

1

NAME
biff – be notified if mail arrives and who it is from

SYNOPSIS
biff [**ny**]

DESCRIPTION
Biff informs the system whether you want to be notified when mail arrives during the current terminal session.

Options supported by **biff**:

n   Disables notification.

y   Enables notification.

When mail notification is enabled, the header and first few lines of the message will be printed on your screen whenever mail arrives. A "biff y" command is often included in the file .login or .profile to be executed at each login.

Biff operates asynchronously. For synchronous notification use the *MAIL* variable of sh(1) or the *mail* variable of csh(1).

SEE ALSO
csh(1), mail(1), sh(1), comsat(8)

HISTORY
The **biff** command appeared in 4.0BSD.

1

NAME
cal – displays a calendar

SYNOPSIS
cal [−jy] [*month* [*year*]]

DESCRIPTION
Cal displays a simple calendar. If arguments are not specified, the current month is displayed. The options are as follows:

−j   Display julian dates (days one-based, numbered from January 1).

−y   Display a calendar for the current year.

A single parameter specifies the year (1 - 9999) to be displayed; note the year must be fully specified: "cal 89" will *not* display a calendar for 1989. Two parameters denote the month (1 - 12) and year. If no parameters are specified, the current month's calendar is displayed.

A year starts on Jan 1.

The Gregorian Reformation is assumed to have occurred in 1752 on the 3rd of September. By this time, most countries had recognized the reformation (although a few did not recognize it until the early 1900's.) Ten days following that date were eliminated by the reformation, so the calendar for that month is a bit unusual.

HISTORY
A cal command appeared in Version 6 AT&T UNIX.

1

NAME

calendar – reminder service

SYNOPSIS

calendar [–a]

DESCRIPTION

Calendar checks the current directory for a file named calendar and displays lines that begin with either today's date or tomorrow's. On Fridays, events on Friday through Monday are displayed.

The following options are available:

–a   Process the "calendar" files of all users and mail the results to them. This requires super-user privileges.

Lines should begin with a month and day. They may be entered in almost any format, either numeric or as character strings. A single asterisk ("*") matches every month. A day without a month matches that day of every week. A month without a day matches the first of that month. Two numbers default to the month followed by the day. Lines with leading tabs default to the last entered date, allowing multiple line specifications for a single date. By convention, dates followed by an asterisk are not fixed, i.e., change from year to year.

The "calendar" file is preprocessed by cpp(1), allowing the inclusion of shared files such as company holidays or meetings. If the shared file is not referenced by a full pathname, cpp(1) searches in the current (or home) directory first, and then in the directory /usr/share/calendar. Empty lines and lines protected by the C commenting syntax (/* ... */) are ignored.

Some possible calendar entries:

> #include <calendar.usholiday>
> #include <calendar.birthday>
>
> 6/15   ... June 15 (if ambiguous, will default to month/day).
> Jun. 15   ... June 15.
> 15 June   ... June 15.
> Thursday   ... Every Thursday.
> June   ... Every June 1st.
> 15 *   ... 15th of every month.

FILES

The following default calendar files are provided:

calendar.birthday	Births and deaths of famous (and not-so-famous) people.
calendar.christian	Christian holidays. This calendar should be updated yearly by the local system administrator so that roving holidays are set correctly for the current year.
calendar.computer	Days of special significance to computer people.
calendar.history	Everything else, mostly U. S. historical events.
calendar.holiday	Other holidays, including the not-well-known, obscure, and *really* obscure.
calendar.judaic	Jewish holidays. This calendar should be updated yearly by the local system administrator so that roving holidays are set correctly for the current year.
calendar.music	Musical events, births, and deaths. Strongly oriented toward rock 'n' roll.
calendar.usholiday	U.S. holidays. This calendar should be updated yearly by the local system administrator so that roving holidays are set correctly for the current year.

SEE ALSO
　　at(1), cpp(1), cron(8) mail(1),

COMPATIBILITY
　　The `calendar` program previously selected lines which had the correct date anywhere in the line. This is no longer true, the date is only recognized when it occurs first on the line.

HISTORY
　　A `calendar` command appeared in Version 7 AT&T UNIX.

BUGS
　　`Calendar` doesn't handle events that move around from year to year, i.e., ''the last Monday in April''.

NAME

    cap_mkdb – create capability database

SYNOPSIS

    cap_mkdb [−v] [−f *outfile*] *file1* [*file2* ...]

DESCRIPTION

    Cap_mkdb builds a hashed database out of the getcap(3) logical database constructed by the concatenation of the specified files .

    The database is named by the basename of the first file argument and the string ''.db''. The getcap(3) routines can access the database in this form much more quickly than they can the original text file(s).

    The ''tc'' capabilities of the records are expanded before the record is stored into the database.

    The options as as follows:

    −f *outfile*
        Specify a different database basename.

    −v   Print out the number of capability records in the database.

FORMAT

    Each record is stored in the database using two different types of keys.

    The first type is a key which consists of the first capability of the record (not including the trailing colon ('':'')) with a data field consisting of a special byte followed by the rest of the record. The special byte is either a 0 or 1, where a 0 means that the record is okay, and a 1 means that there was a ''tc'' capability in the record that couldn't be expanded.

    The second type is a key which consists of one of the names from the first capability of the record with a data field consisting a special byte followed by the the first capability of the record. The special byte is a 2.

    In normal operation names are looked up in the database, resulting in a key/data pair of the second type. The data field of this key/data pair is used to look up a key/data pair of the first type which has the real data associated with the name.

RETURN VALUE

    The **cap_mkdb** utility exits 0 on success and >0 if an error occurs.

SEE ALSO

    dbopen(3), getcap(3), termcap(5)

1

NAME

cat – concatenate and print files

SYNOPSIS

cat [–benstuv] [–] [*file ...*]

DESCRIPTION

The cat utility reads files sequentially, writing them to the standard output. The *file* operands are processed in command line order. A single dash represents the standard input.

The options are as follows:

–b   Implies the –n option but doesn't number blank lines.

–e   Implies the –v option, and displays a dollar sign ('$') at the end of each line as well.

–n   Number the *output* lines, starting at 1.

–s   Squeeze multiple adjacent empty lines, causing the output to be single spaced.

–t   Implies the –v option, and displays tab characters as ('^I') as well.

–u   The –u option guarantees that the output is unbuffered.

–v   Displays non-printing characters so they are visible. Control characters print as '^X' for control-X; the delete character (octal 0177) prints as '^?' Non-ascii characters (with the high bit set) are printed as 'M-' (for meta) followed by the character for the low 7 bits.

The cat utility exits 0 on success, and >0 if an error occurs.

BUGS

Because of the shell language mechanism used to perform output redirection, the command "cat file1 file 2 > file1" will cause the original data in file1 to be destroyed!

SEE ALSO

head(1), more(1), pr(1), tail(1)

Rob Pike, "UNIX Style, or cat -v Considered Harmful", *USENIX Summer Conference Proceedings*, 1983.

HISTORY

A cat command appeared in Version 6 AT&T UNIX.

1

NAME

cc, g++ – GNU project C and C++ Compiler (v2 preliminary)

SYNOPSIS

cc [*option* | *filename*]...
g++ [*option* | *filename*]...

WARNING

The information in this man page is an extract from the full documentation of the GNU C compiler, and is limited to the meaning of the options. This man page is not kept up to date except when volunteers want to maintain it.

For complete and current documentation, refer to the Info file ' **gcc** ' or the manual *Using and Porting GNU CC (for version 2.0)*. Both are made from the Texinfo source file **gcc.texinfo**.

DESCRIPTION

The C and C++ compilers are integrated. Both process input files through one or more of four stages: preprocessing, compilation, assembly, and linking. Source filename suffixes identify the source language, but which name you use for the compiler governs default assumptions:

gcc   assumes preprocessed (**.i**) files are C and assumes C style linking.

g++   assumes preprocessed (**.i**) files are C++ and assumes C++ style linking.

Suffixes of source file names indicate the language and kind of processing to be done:

.c	C source; preprocess, compile, assemble
.C	C++ source; preprocess, compile, assemble
.cc	C++ source; preprocess, compile, assemble
.cxx	C++ source; preprocess, compile, assemble
.m	Objective-C source; preprocess, compile, assemble
.i	preprocessed C; compile, assemble
.ii	preprocessed C++; compile, assemble
.s	Assembler source; assemble
.S	Assembler source; preprocess, assemble
.h	Preprocessor file; not usually named on command line
??	Other (unrecognized) files passed to linker.

Common cases:

.o	Object file
.a	Archive file

Linking is always the last stage unless you use one of the **–c**, **–S**, or **–E** options to avoid it (or unless compilation errors stop the whole process). For the link stage, all **.o** files corresponding to source files, **–l** libraries, unrecognized filenames (including named **.o** object files and **.a** archives) are passed to the linker in command-line order.

OPTIONS

Options must be separate: ' **–dr** ' is quite different from ' **–d –r** '.

Most ' **–f** ' and ' **–W** ' options have two contrary forms: **–f***name* and **–fno–***name* (or **–W***name* and **–Wno–***name*). Only the non-default forms are shown here.

Here is a summary of all the options, grouped by type. Explanations are in the following sections.

1

Overall Options
–c –S –E –o *file* –pipe –v –x *language*

Language Options
–ansi –fall–virtual –fcond–mismatch –fdollars–in–identifiers –fenum–int–equiv –fno–asm
–fno–builtin –fno–strict–prototype –fsigned–bitfields –fsigned–char –fthis–is–variable
–funsigned–bitfields –funsigned–char –fwritable–strings –traditional –traditional–cpp –trigraphs

Warning Options
–fsyntax–only –pedantic –pedantic–errors –w –W –Wall –Waggregate–return –Wcast–align
–Wcast–qual –Wcomment –Wconversion –Wenum–clash –Werror –Wformat –Wid–clash–*len*
–Wimplicit –Winline –Wmissing–prototypes –Wparentheses –Wpointer–arith –Wreturn–type
–Wshadow –Wstrict–prototypes –Wswitch –Wtraditional –Wtrigraphs –Wuninitialized
–Wunused –Wwrite–strings

Debugging Options
–a –d*letters* –fpretend–float –g –gstabs –gdwarf –ggdb –gsdb –p –pg –save–temps

Optimization Options
–fcaller–saves –fcse–follow–jumps –fdelayed–branch –felide–constructors
–fexpensive–optimizations –ffloat–store –fforce–addr –fforce–mem –finline –finline–functions
–fkeep–inline–functions –fmemoize–lookups –fno–default–inline –fno–defer–pop
–fno–function–cse –fomit–frame–pointer –frerun–cse–after–loop –fschedule–insns
–fschedule–insns2 –fstrength–reduce –fthread–jumps –funroll–all–loops –funroll–loops –O –O2

Preprocessor Options
–C –dD –dM –dN –D*macro* [=*defn*] –E –H –i *file* –M –MD –MM –MMD –nostdinc –P
–U*macro* –undef

Linker Options
–l*library* –nostdlib –static

Directory Options
–B*prefix* –I*dir* –I– –L*dir*

Target Options
–b *machine* –V *version*

Machine Dependent Options
M680x0 Options
–m68000 –m68020 –m68881 –mbitfield –mc68000 –mc68020 –mfpa –mnobitfield –mrtd
–mshort –msoft–float
VAX Options
–mg –mgnu –munix
SPARC Options
–mfpu –mno–epilogue
Convex Options
–margcount –mc1 –mc2 –mnoargcount
AMD29K Options
–m29000 –m29050 –mbw –mdw –mkernel–registers –mlarge –mnbw –mnodw –msmall
–mstack–check –muser–registers
M88K Options
–mbig–pic –mcheck–zero–division –mhandle–large–shift –midentify–revision
–mno–check–zero–division –mno–ocs–debug–info –mno–ocs–frame–position
–mno–optimize–arg–area –mno–underscores –mocs–debug–info –mocs–frame–position
–moptimize–arg–area –mshort–data–*num* –msvr3 –msvr4 –mtrap–large–shift
–muse–div–instruction –mversion–03.00 –mwarn–passed–structs
RS6000 Options
–mfp–in–toc –mno–fop–in–toc

1

RT Options
−mcall−lib−mul −mfp−arg−in−fpregs −mfp−arg−in−gregs −mfull−fp−blocks −mhc−struct−return
−min−line−mul −mminimum−fp−blocks −mnohc−struct−return
MIPS Options
−mcpu=*cpu type* −mips2 −mips3 −mint64 −mlong64 −mlonglong128 −mmips−as −mgas
−mrnames −mno−rnames −mgpopt −mno−gpopt −mstats −mno−stats −mmemcpy −mno−memcpy
−mno−mips−tfile −mmips−tfile −msoft−float −mhard−float −mabicalls −mno−abicalls −mhalf−pic
−mno−half−pic −G *num*
i386 Options
−m486 −mno486 −msoft−float

Code Generation Options
+e*N* −fcall−saved−*reg* −fcall−used−*reg* −ffixed−*reg* −fno−common −fno−gnu−binutils
−fnonnull−objects −fpcc−struct−return −fpic −fPIC −fshared−data −fshort−enums −fshort−double
−fvolatile

OVERALL OPTIONS

−x *language*
Specify explicitly the *language* for the following input files (rather than choosing a default based on the file name suffix) . This option applies to all following input files until the next '−x' option. Possible values of *language* are 'c', '**objective−c**', '**c−header**', '**c++**', '**cpp−output**', '**assembler**', and '**assembler−with−cpp**'.

−x none
Turn off any specification of a language, so that subsequent files are handled according to their file name suffixes (as they are if '−x' has not been used at all).

If you want only some of the four stages (preprocess, compile, assemble, link), you can use '−x' (or filename suffixes) to tell **gcc** where to start, and one of the options '−c', '−S', or '−E' to say where **gcc** is to stop. Note that some combinations (for example, '−x **cpp−output** −E') instruct **gcc** to do nothing at all.

−c   Compile or assemble the source files, but do not link. The compiler output is an object file corresponding to each source file.

By default, GCC makes the object file name for a source file by replacing the suffix '.c', '.i', '.s', etc., with '.o'. Use −o to select another name.

GCC ignores any unrecognized input files (those that do not require compilation or assembly) with the −c option.

−S   Stop after the stage of compilation proper; do not assemble. The output is an assembler code file for each non-assembler input file specified.

By default, GCC makes the assembler file name for a source file by replacing the suffix '.c', '.i', etc., with '.s'. Use −o to select another name.

GCC ignores any input files that don't require compilation.

−E   Stop after the preprocessing stage; do not run the compiler proper. The output is preprocessed source code, which is sent to the standard output.

GCC ignores input files which don't require preprocessing.

−o *file*   Place output in file *file*. This applies to whatever sort of output GCC is producing, whether it be an executable file, an object file, an assembler file or preprocessed C code.

Since only one output file can be specified, it does not make sense to use '−o' when compiling more than one input file, unless you are producing an executable file as output.

If you do not specify '−o', the default is to put an executable file in '**a.out**', an object file for '*source.suffix*' in '*source*.o', its assembler file in '*source*.s', and all preprocessed C source on the standard output.

−v   Print (on the standard error output) the commands executed to run the stages of compilation. Also print the version number of the compiler driver program and of the preprocessor and the compiler proper.

−pipe   Use pipes rather than temporary files for communication between the various stages of compilation. This fails to work on some systems where the assembler cannot read from a pipe; but the GNU assembler has no trouble.

LANGUAGE OPTIONS

The following options control the dialect of C that the compiler accepts:

−ansi   *Support all ANSI standard C programs.*

This turns off certain features of GNU C that are incompatible with ANSI C, such as the **asm**, **inline** and **typeof** keywords, and predefined macros such as **unix** and **vax** that identify the type of system you are using. It also enables the undesirable and rarely used ANSI trigraph feature, and makes the preprocessor accept '**$**' as part of identifiers.

The alternate keywords **__asm__**, **__extension__**, **__inline__** and **__typeof__** continue to work despite '−**ansi**'. You would not want to use them in an ANSI C program, of course, but it is useful to put them in header files that might be included in compilations done with '−**ansi**'. Alternate predefined macros such as **__unix__** and **__vax__** are also available, with or without '−**ansi**'.

The '−**ansi**' option does not cause non-ANSI programs to be rejected gratuitously. For that, '−**pedantic**' is required in addition to '−**ansi**'.

The preprocessor predefines a macro **__STRICT_ANSI__** when you use the '−**ansi**' option. Some header files may notice this macro and refrain from declaring certain functions or defining certain macros that the ANSI standard doesn't call for; this is to avoid interfering with any programs that might use these names for other things.

−fno−asm
     Do not recognize **asm**, **inline** or **typeof** as a keyword. These words may then be used as identifiers. You can use **__asm__**, **__inline__** and **__typeof__** instead. '−**ansi**' implies '−**fno−asm**'.

−fno−builtin
     (Ignored for C++.) Don't recognize non-ANSI built-in functions. '−**ansi**' also has this effect. Currently, the only function affected is **alloca**.

−fno−strict−prototype
     (C++ only.) Consider the declaration **int foo ();**. In C++, this means that the function **foo** takes no arguments. In ANSI C, this is declared **int foo(void);**. With the flag '−**fno−strict−prototype**', declaring functions with no arguments is equivalent to declaring its argument list to be untyped, i.e., **int foo ();** is equivalent to saying **int foo (...);**.

−trigraphs
     Support ANSI C trigraphs. The '−**ansi**' option implies '−**trigraphs**'.

1

–traditional
> Attempt to support some aspects of traditional C compilers. For details, see the GNU C Manual; the duplicate list here has been deleted so that we won't get complaints when it is out of date.
>
> But one note about C++ programs only (not C). ' **–traditional** ' has one additional effect for C++: assignment to **this** is permitted. This is the same as the effect of ' **–fthis–is–variable** '.

–traditional–cpp
> Attempt to support some aspects of traditional C preprocessors. This includes the items that specifically mention the preprocessor above, but none of the other effects of ' **–traditional** '.

–fdollars–in–identifiers
> *(C++ only.)* Permit the use of ' **$** ' in identifiers. (For GNU C, this is the default, and you can forbid it with ' **–ansi** '.) Traditional C allowed the character ' **$** ' to form part of identifiers; by default, GNU C also allows this. However, ANSI C forbids ' **$** ' in identifiers, and GNU C++ also forbids it by default on most platforms (though on some platforms it's enabled by default for GNU C++ as well).

–fenum–int–equiv
> *(C++ only.)* Normally GNU C++ allows conversion of **enum** to **int**, but not the other way around. Use this option if you want GNU C++ to allow conversion of **int** to **enum** as well.

–fall–virtual
> *(C++ only.)* When you use the ' **–fall–virtual** ', all member functions (except for constructor functions and new/delete member operators) declared in the same class with a "method-call" operator method are treated as virtual functions of the given class. In effect, all of these methods become "implicitly virtual."
>
> This does *not* mean that all calls to these methods will be made through the internal table of virtual functions. There are some circumstances under which it is obvious that a call to a given virtual function can be made directly, and in these cases the calls still go direct.
>
> The effect of making all methods of a class with a declared ' **operator->()()** ' implicitly virtual using ' **–fall–virtual** ' extends also to all non-constructor methods of any class derived from such a class.

–fcond–mismatch
> Allow conditional expressions with mismatched types in the second and third arguments. The value of such an expression is void.

–fthis–is–variable
> *(C++ only.)* The incorporation of user-defined free store management into C++ has made assignment to **this** an anachronism. Therefore, by default GNU C++ treats the type of **this** in a member function of **class X** to be X ***const**. In other words, it is illegal to assign to **this** within a class member function. However, for backwards compatibility, you can invoke the old behavior by using ' **–fthis–is–variable** '.

–funsigned–char
> Let the type **char** be unsigned, like **unsigned char**.
>
> Each kind of machine has a default for what **char** should be. It is either like **unsigned char** by default or like **signed char** by default.
>
> Ideally, a portable program should always use **signed char** or **unsigned char** when it depends on the signedness of an object. But many programs have been written to use plain **char** and expect it to be signed, or expect it to be unsigned, depending on the machines they were written for. This option, and its inverse, let you make such a program work with the opposite default.

The type **char** is always a distinct type from each of **signed char** and **unsigned char**, even though its behavior is always just like one of those two.

−fsigned−char

Let the type **char** be signed, like **signed char**.

Note that this is equivalent to ' **−fno−unsigned−char** ', which is the negative form of ' **−funsigned−char** '. Likewise, ' **−fno−signed−char** ' is equivalent to ' **−funsigned−char** '.

−fsigned−bitfields

−funsigned−bitfields

−fno−signed−bitfields

−fno−unsigned−bitfields

These options control whether a bitfield is signed or unsigned, when declared with no explicit ' **signed** ' or ' **unsigned** ' qualifier. By default, such a bitfield is signed, because this is consistent: the basic integer types such as **int** are signed types.

However, when you specify ' **−traditional** ', bitfields are all unsigned no matter what.

−fwritable−strings

Store string constants in the writable data segment and don't uniquize them. This is for compatibility with old programs which assume they can write into string constants. ' **−traditional** ' also has this effect.

Writing into string constants is a very bad idea; "constants" should be constant.

PREPROCESSOR OPTIONS

These options control the C preprocessor, which is run on each C source file before actual compilation.

If you use the ' **−E** ' option, GCC does nothing except preprocessing. Some of these options make sense only together with ' **−E** ' because they cause the preprocessor output to be unsuitable for actual compilation.

−i *file*   Process *file* as input, discarding the resulting output, before processing the regular input file. Because the output generated from *file* is discarded, the only effect of ' **−i** *file* ' is to make the macros defined in *file* available for use in the main input. The preprocessor evaluates any ' **−D** ' and ' **−U** ' options on the command line before processing ' **−i** ' *file*.

−nostdinc

Do not search the standard system directories for header files. Only the directories you have specified with ' **−I** ' options (and the current directory, if appropriate) are searched.

By using both ' **−nostdinc** ' and ' **−I−** ', you can limit the include-file search file to only those directories you specify explicitly.

−undef   Do not predefine any nonstandard macros. (Including architecture flags).

−E   Run only the C preprocessor. Preprocess all the C source files specified and output the results to the standard output or to the specified output file.

−C   Tell the preprocessor not to discard comments. Used with the ' **−E** ' option.

−P   Tell the preprocessor not to generate ' **#line** ' commands. Used with the ' **−E** ' option.

−M   Tell the preprocessor to output a rule suitable for **make** describing the dependencies of each object file. For each source file, the preprocessor outputs one **make**-rule whose target is the object file name for that source file and whose dependencies are all the files ' **#include** 'd in it. This rule may be a single line or may be continued with '****newline if it is long. The list of rules is printed on the standard output instead of the preprocessed C program.
' **−M** ' implies ' **−E** '.

1

−MM   Like '−**M**' but the output mentions only the user header files included with '**#include** *file*"'. System header files included with '**#include** <*file*>' are omitted.

−MD   Like '−**M**' but the dependency information is written to files with names made by replacing '**.c**' with '**.d**' at the end of the input file names. This is in addition to compiling the file as specified—'−**MD**' does not inhibit ordinary compilation the way '−**M**' does.

The Mach utility '**md**' can be used to merge the '**.d**' files into a single dependency file suitable for using with the '**make**' command.

−MMD Like '−**MD**' except mention only user header files, not system header files.

−H   Print the name of each header file used, in addition to other normal activities.

−D*macro*

Define macro *macro* with the string '**1**' as its definition.

−D*macro=defn*

Define macro *macro* as *defn*. All instances of '−**D**' on the command line are processed before any '−**U**' or '−**i**' options.

−U*macro*

Undefine macro *macro*. '−**U**' options are evaluated after all '−**D**' options, but before any '−**i**' options.

−dM   Tell the preprocessor to output only a list of the macro definitions that are in effect at the end of preprocessing. Used with the '−**E**' option.

−dD   Tell the preprocessing to pass all macro definitions into the output, in their proper sequence in the rest of the output.

−dN   Like '−**dD**' except that the macro arguments and contents are omitted. Only '**#define** *name*' is included in the output.

LINKER OPTIONS

These options come into play when the compiler links object files into an executable output file. They are meaningless if the compiler is not doing a link step.

object-file-name

A file name that does not end in a special recognized suffix is considered to name an object file or library. (Object files are distinguished from libraries by the linker according to the file contents.) If GCC does a link step, these object files are used as input to the linker.

−l*library*

Use the library named *library* when linking.

The linker searches a standard list of directories for the library, which is actually a file named '**lib***library*.a'. The linker then uses this file as if it had been specified precisely by name.

The directories searched include several standard system directories plus any that you specify with '−**L**'.

Normally the files found this way are library files—archive files whose members are object files. The linker handles an archive file by scanning through it for members which define symbols that have so far been referenced but not defined. However, if the linker finds an ordinary object file rather than a library, the object file is linked in the usual fashion. The only difference between using an '−**l**' option and specifying a file name is that '−**l**' surrounds *library* with '**lib**' and '**.a**' and searches several directories.

−nostdlib

Don't use the standard system libraries and startup files when linking. Only the files you specify will be passed to the linker.

−static   On systems that support dynamic linking, this prevents linking with the shared libraries. On other systems, this option has no effect.

DIRECTORY OPTIONS

These options specify directories to search for header files, for libraries and for parts of the compiler:

−I*dir*   Append directory *dir* to the list of directories searched for include files.

−I−   Any directories you specify with '−I' options before the '−I−' option are searched only for the case of '**#include "***file***"** '; they are not searched for '**#include <***file***>** '.

If additional directories are specified with '−I' options after the '−I−', these directories are searched for all '**#include**' directives. (Ordinarily *all* '−I' directories are used this way.)

In addition, the '−I−' option inhibits the use of the current directory (where the current input file came from) as the first search directory for '**#include "***file***"** '. There is no way to override this effect of '−I−'. With '−I.' you can specify searching the directory which was current when the compiler was invoked. That is not exactly the same as what the preprocessor does by default, but it is often satisfactory.

'−I−' does not inhibit the use of the standard system directories for header files. Thus, '−I−' and '**−nostdinc**' are independent.

−L*dir*   Add directory *dir* to the list of directories to be searched for '−l'.

−B*prefix*

This option specifies where to find the executables, libraries and data files of the compiler itself.

The compiler driver program runs one or more of the subprograms '**cpp**', '**cc1**' (or, for C++, '**cc1plus**'), '**as**' and '**ld**'. It tries *prefix* as a prefix for each program it tries to run, both with and without '*machine/version/*'.

For each subprogram to be run, the compiler driver first tries the '−B' prefix, if any. If that name is not found, or if '−B' was not specified, the driver tries two standard prefixes, which are '**/usr/lib/gcc/**' and '**/usr/local/lib/gcc-lib/**'. If neither of those results in a file name that is found, the compiler driver searches for the unmodified program name, using the directories specified in your '**PATH**' environment variable.

The run-time support file '**libgcc.a**' is also searched for using the '−B' prefix, if needed. If it is not found there, the two standard prefixes above are tried, and that is all. The file is left out of the link if it is not found by those means. Most of the time, on most machines, '**libgcc.a**' is not actually necessary.

You can get a similar result from the environment variable **GCC_EXEC_PREFIX**; if it is defined, its value is used as a prefix in the same way. If both the '−B' option and the **GCC_EXEC_PREFIX** variable are present, the '−B' option is used first and the environment variable value second.

WARNING OPTIONS

Warnings are diagnostic messages that report constructions which are not inherently erroneous but which are risky or suggest there may have been an error.

These options control the amount and kinds of warnings produced by GNU CC:

−fsyntax−only

Check the code for syntax errors, but don't emit any output.

1

−w   Inhibit all warning messages.

−pedantic
> Issue all the warnings demanded by strict ANSI standard C; reject all programs that use forbidden extensions.

> Valid ANSI standard C programs should compile properly with or without this option (though a rare few will require ' **−ansi** '). However, without this option, certain GNU extensions and traditional C features are supported as well. With this option, they are rejected. There is no reason to *use* this option; it exists only to satisfy pedants.

> ' **−pedantic** ' does not cause warning messages for use of the alternate keywords whose names begin and end with ' __ '. Pedantic warnings are also disabled in the expression that follows **__extension__**. However, only system header files should use these escape routes; application programs should avoid them.

−pedantic−errors
> Like ' **−pedantic** ', except that errors are produced rather than warnings.

−W   Print extra warning messages for these events:

- A nonvolatile automatic variable might be changed by a call to **longjmp**. These warnings are possible only in optimizing compilation.

  > The compiler sees only the calls to **setjmp**. It cannot know where **longjmp** will be called; in fact, a signal handler could call it at any point in the code. As a result, you may get a warning even when there is in fact no problem because **longjmp** cannot in fact be called at the place which would cause a problem.

- A function can return either with or without a value. (Falling off the end of the function body is considered returning without a value.) For example, this function would evoke such a warning:

  ```
  foo (a)
  {
   if (a > 0)
     return a;
  }
  ```

  > Spurious warnings can occur because GNU CC does not realize that certain functions (including **abort** and **longjmp**) will never return.

- An expression-statement contains no side effects.

- An unsigned value is compared against zero with ' > ' or ' <= '.

−Wimplicit
> Warn whenever a function or parameter is implicitly declared.

−Wreturn−type
> Warn whenever a function is defined with a return-type that defaults to **int**. Also warn about any **return** statement with no return-value in a function whose return-type is not **void**.

−Wunused
> Warn whenever a local variable is unused aside from its declaration, whenever a function is declared static but never defined, and whenever a statement computes a result that is explicitly not used.

−Wswitch
> Warn whenever a **switch** statement has an index of enumeral type and lacks a **case** for one or

more of the named codes of that enumeration. (The presence of a **default** label prevents this warning.) **case** labels outside the enumeration range also provoke warnings when this option is used.

−Wcomment

Warn whenever a comment-start sequence ' **/∗** ' appears in a comment.

−Wtrigraphs

Warn if any trigraphs are encountered (assuming they are enabled).

−Wformat

Check calls to **printf** and **scanf**, etc., to make sure that the arguments supplied have types appropriate to the format string specified.

−Wuninitialized

An automatic variable is used without first being initialized.

These warnings are possible only in optimizing compilation, because they require data flow information that is computed only when optimizing. If you don't specify '−**O** ', you simply won't get these warnings.

These warnings occur only for variables that are candidates for register allocation. Therefore, they do not occur for a variable that is declared **volatile**, or whose address is taken, or whose size is other than 1, 2, 4 or 8 bytes. Also, they do not occur for structures, unions or arrays, even when they are in registers.

Note that there may be no warning about a variable that is used only to compute a value that itself is never used, because such computations may be deleted by data flow analysis before the warnings are printed.

These warnings are made optional because GNU CC is not smart enough to see all the reasons why the code might be correct despite appearing to have an error. Here is one example of how this can happen:

```
{
 int x;
 switch (y)
  {
  case 1: x = 1;
   break;
  case 2: x = 4;
   break;
  case 3: x = 5;
  }
 foo (x);
}
```

If the value of **y** is always 1, 2 or 3, then **x** is always initialized, but GNU CC doesn't know this. Here is another common case:

```
{
 int save_y;
```

1

```
        if (change_y) save_y = y, y = new_y;
        ...
        if (change_y) y = save_y;
        }
```

This has no bug because **save_y** is used only if it is set.

Some spurious warnings can be avoided if you declare as **volatile** all the functions you use that never return.

−Wparentheses
Warn if parentheses are omitted in certain contexts.

−Wall   All of the above ' −W ' options combined. These are all the options which pertain to usage that we recommend avoiding and that we believe are easy to avoid, even in conjunction with macros.

The remaining ' −W... ' options are not implied by ' −Wall ' because they warn about constructions that we consider reasonable to use, on occasion, in clean programs.

−Wtraditional
Warn about certain constructs that behave differently in traditional and ANSI C.

•   Macro arguments occurring within string constants in the macro body. These would substitute the argument in traditional C, but are part of the constant in ANSI C.

•   A function declared external in one block and then used after the end of the block.

•   A **switch** statement has an operand of type **long**.

−Wshadow
Warn whenever a local variable shadows another local variable.

−Wid−clash−_len_
Warn whenever two distinct identifiers match in the first _len_ characters. This may help you prepare a program that will compile with certain obsolete, brain-damaged compilers.

−Wpointer−arith
Warn about anything that depends on the "size of" a function type or of **void**. GNU C assigns these types a size of 1, for convenience in calculations with **void** ∗ pointers and pointers to functions.

−Wcast−qual
Warn whenever a pointer is cast so as to remove a type qualifier from the target type. For example, warn if a **const char** ∗ is cast to an ordinary **char** ∗.

−Wcast−align
Warn whenever a pointer is cast such that the required alignment of the target is increased. For example, warn if a **char** ∗ is cast to an **int** ∗ on machines where integers can only be accessed at two- or four-byte boundaries.

−Wwrite−strings
Give string constants the type **const char[**_length_**]** so that copying the address of one into a non-**const char** ∗ pointer will get a warning. These warnings will help you find at compile time code that can try to write into a string constant, but only if you have been very careful about using **const** in declarations and prototypes. Otherwise, it will just be a nuisance; this is why we did not make ' −Wall ' request these warnings.

−Wconversion
Warn if a prototype causes a type conversion that is different from what would happen to the same argument in the absence of a prototype. This includes conversions of fixed point to floating and

vice versa, and conversions changing the width or signedness of a fixed point argument except when the same as the default promotion.

−Waggregate−return
> Warn if any functions that return structures or unions are defined or called. (In languages where you can return an array, this also elicits a warning.)

−Wstrict−prototypes
> Warn if a function is declared or defined without specifying the argument types. (An old-style function definition is permitted without a warning if preceded by a declaration which specifies the argument types.)

−Wmissing−prototypes
> Warn if a global function is defined without a previous prototype declaration. This warning is issued even if the definition itself provides a prototype. The aim is to detect global functions that fail to be declared in header files.

−Wenum−clash
> *(C++ only.)* Warn when converting between different enumeration types.

−Woverloaded−virtual
> *(C++ only.)* In a derived class, the definitions of virtual functions must match the type signature of a virtual function declared in the base class. Use this option to request warnings when a derived class declares a function that may be an erroneous attempt to define a virtual function: that is, warn when a function with the same name as a virtual function in the base class, but with a type signature that doesn't match any virtual functions from the base class.

−Winline
> Warn if a function can not be inlined, and either it was declared as inline, or else the **−finline−functions** option was given.

−Werror
> Treat warnings as errors; abort compilation after any warning.

DEBUGGING OPTIONS

> GNU CC has various special options that are used for debugging either your program or GCC:

−g   Produce debugging information in the operating system's native format (for DBX or SDB or DWARF). GDB also can work with this debugging information. On most systems that use DBX format, ' **−g** ' enables use of extra debugging information that only GDB can use; if you want to control for certain whether to generate this information, use ' **−ggdb** ' or ' **−gdbx** '.

> Unlike most other C compilers, GNU CC allows you to use ' **−g** ' with ' **−O** '. The shortcuts taken by optimized code may occasionally produce surprising results: some variables you declared may not exist at all; flow of control may briefly move where you did not expect it; some statements may not be executed because they compute constant results or their values were already at hand; some statements may execute in different places because they were moved out of loops.

> Nevertheless it proves possible to debug optimized output. This makes it reasonable to use the optimizer for programs that might have bugs.

> The following options are useful when GNU CC is configured and compiled with the capability for more than one debugging format.

−ggdb   Produce debugging information in DBX format (if that is supported), including GDB extensions.

−gdbx   Produce debugging information in DBX format (if that is supported), without GDB extensions.

−gsdb   Produce debugging information in SDB format (if that is supported).

1

–gdwarf

Produce debugging information in DWARF format (if that is supported).

–g*level*
–ggdb*level*
–gdbx*level*
–gsdb*level*
–gdwarf*level*

Request debugging information and also use *level* to specify how much information. The default level is 2.

Level 1 produces minimal information, enough for making backtraces in parts of the program that you don't plan to debug. This includes descriptions of functions and external variables, but no information about local variables and no line numbers.

–p   Generate extra code to write profile information suitable for the analysis program **prof.**

–pg   Generate extra code to write profile information suitable for the analysis program **gprof.**

–a   Generate extra code to write profile information for basic blocks, which will record the number of times each basic block is executed. This data could be analyzed by a program like **tcov.** Note, however, that the format of the data is not what **tcov** expects. Eventually GNU **gprof** should be extended to process this data.

–d*letters*

Says to make debugging dumps during compilation at times specified by *letters.* This is used for debugging the compiler. The file names for most of the dumps are made by appending a word to the source file name (e.g., ' **foo.c.rtl** ' or ' **foo.c.jump** ').

–dM   Dump all macro definitions, at the end of preprocessing, and write no output.

–dN   Dump all macro names, at the end of preprocessing.

–dD   Dump all macro definitions, at the end of preprocessing, in addition to normal output.

–dy   Dump debugging information during parsing, to the standard error.

–dr   Dump after RTL generation, to ' *file*.rtl '.

–dx   Just generate RTL for a function instead of compiling it. Usually used with ' **r** '.

–dj   Dump after first jump optimization, to ' *file*.jump '.

–ds   Dump after CSE (including the jump optimization that sometimes follows CSE), to ' *file*.cse '.

–dL   Dump after loop optimization, to ' *file*.loop '.

–dt   Dump after the second CSE pass (including the jump optimization that sometimes follows CSE), to ' *file*.cse2 '.

–df   Dump after flow analysis, to ' *file*.flow '.

–dc   Dump after instruction combination, to ' *file*.combine '.

–dS   Dump after the first instruction scheduling pass, to ' *file*.sched '.

–dl   Dump after local register allocation, to ' *file*.lreg '.

–dg   Dump after global register allocation, to ' *file*.greg '.

–dR   Dump after the second instruction scheduling pass, to ' *file*.sched2 '.

–dJ   Dump after last jump optimization, to ' *file*.jump2 '.

–dd   Dump after delayed branch scheduling, to ' *file*.dbr '.

–dk   Dump after conversion from registers to stack, to ' *file*.stack '.

1

–dm   Print statistics on memory usage, at the end of the run, to the standard error.

–dp   Annotate the assembler output with a comment indicating which pattern and alternative was used.

–fpretend–float

When running a cross-compiler, pretend that the target machine uses the same floating point format as the host machine. This causes incorrect output of the actual floating constants, but the actual instruction sequence will probably be the same as GNU CC would make when running on the target machine.

–save–temps

Store the usual ''temporary'' intermediate files permanently; place them in the current directory and name them based on the source file. Thus, compiling ' **foo.c** ' with ' **–c –save–temps** ' would produce files ' **foo.cpp** ' and ' **foo.s** ', as well as ' **foo.o** '.

OPTIMIZATION OPTIONS

These options control various sorts of optimizations:

–O   Optimize. Optimizing compilation takes somewhat more time, and a lot more memory for a large function.

Without ' **–O** ', the compiler's goal is to reduce the cost of compilation and to make debugging produce the expected results. Statements are independent: if you stop the program with a breakpoint between statements, you can then assign a new value to any variable or change the program counter to any other statement in the function and get exactly the results you would expect from the source code.

Without ' **–O** ', only variables declared **register** are allocated in registers. The resulting compiled code is a little worse than produced by PCC without ' **–O** '.

With ' **–O** ', the compiler tries to reduce code size and execution time.

When you specify ' **–O** ', ' **–fthread–jumps** ' and ' **–fdelayed–branch** ' are turned on. On some machines other flags may also be turned on.

–O2   Highly optimize. As compared to ' **–O** ', this option will increase both compilation time and the performance of the generated code.

All ' **–f***flag* ' options that control optimization are turned on when you specify ' **–O2** ', except ' **–funroll–loops** ' and ' **–funroll–all–loops** '.

Options of the form ' **–f***flag* ' specify machine-independent flags. Most flags have both positive and negative forms; the negative form of ' **–ffoo** ' would be ' **–fno–foo** '. The following list shows only one form—the one which is not the default. You can figure out the other form by either removing ' **no–** ' or adding it.

–ffloat–store

Do not store floating point variables in registers. This prevents undesirable excess precision on machines such as the 68000 where the floating registers (of the 68881) keep more precision than a **double** is supposed to have.

For most programs, the excess precision does only good, but a few programs rely on the precise definition of IEEE floating point. Use ' **–ffloat–store** ' for such programs.

–fmemoize–lookups

–fsave–memoized

(C++ only.) These flags are used to get the compiler to compile programs faster using heuristics. They are not on by default since they are only effective about half the time. The other half of the time programs compile more slowly (and take more memory).

1

The first time the compiler must build a call to a member function (or reference to a data member), it must (1) determine whether the class implements member functions of that name; (2) resolve which member function to call (which involves figuring out what sorts of type conversions need to be made); and (3) check the visibility of the member function to the caller. All of this adds up to slower compilation. Normally, the second time a call is made to that member function (or reference to that data member), it must go through the same lengthy process again. This means that code like this

    cout << "This " << p << " has " << n << " legs.\n";

makes six passes through all three steps. By using a software cache, a ''hit'' significantly reduces this cost. Unfortunately, using the cache introduces another layer of mechanisms which must be implemented, and so incurs its own overhead. '−fmemoize−lookups' enables the software cache.

Because access privileges (visibility) to members and member functions may differ from one function context to the next, **g++** may need to flush the cache. With the '−fmemoize−lookups' flag, the cache is flushed after every function that is compiled. The '−fsave−memoized' flag enables the same software cache, but when the compiler determines that the context of the last function compiled would yield the same access privileges of the next function to compile, it preserves the cache. This is most helpful when defining many member functions for the same class: with the exception of member functions which are friends of other classes, each member function has exactly the same access privileges as every other, and the cache need not be flushed.

−fno−default−inline
> *(C++ only.)* If '−**fdefault−inline**' is enabled then member functions defined inside class scope are compiled inline by default; i.e., you don't need to add ' **inline** ' in front of the member function name. By popular demand, this option is now the default. To keep GNU C++ from inlining these member functions, specify '−**fno−default−inline**'.

−fno−defer−pop
> Always pop the arguments to each function call as soon as that function returns. For machines which must pop arguments after a function call, the compiler normally lets arguments accumulate on the stack for several function calls and pops them all at once.

−fforce−mem
> Force memory operands to be copied into registers before doing arithmetic on them. This may produce better code by making all memory references potential common subexpressions. When they are not common subexpressions, instruction combination should eliminate the separate register-load. I am interested in hearing about the difference this makes.

−fforce−addr
> Force memory address constants to be copied into registers before doing arithmetic on them. This may produce better code just as ' −**fforce−mem** ' may. I am interested in hearing about the difference this makes.

−fomit−frame−pointer
> Don't keep the frame pointer in a register for functions that don't need one. This avoids the instructions to save, set up and restore frame pointers; it also makes an extra register available in many functions. *It also makes debugging impossible on* most machines.
>
> On some machines, such as the Vax, this flag has no effect, because the standard calling sequence automatically handles the frame pointer and nothing is saved by pretending it doesn't exist. The machine-description macro **FRAME_POINTER_REQUIRED** controls whether a target machine supports this flag.

–finline Pay attention the **inline** keyword. Normally the negation of this option ‘ **–fno–inline** ’ is used to keep the compiler from expanding any functions inline. However, the opposite effect may be desirable when compiling with ‘ **–g** ’, since ‘ **–g** ’ normally turns off all inline function expansion.

–finline–functions

> Integrate all simple functions into their callers. The compiler heuristically decides which functions are simple enough to be worth integrating in this way.
>
> If all calls to a given function are integrated, and the function is declared **static**, then GCC normally does not output the function as assembler code in its own right.

–fcaller–saves

> Enable values to be allocated in registers that will be clobbered by function calls, by emitting extra instructions to save and restore the registers around such calls. Such allocation is done only when it seems to result in better code than would otherwise be produced.
>
> This option is enabled by default on certain machines, usually those which have no call-preserved registers to use instead.

–fkeep–inline–functions

> Even if all calls to a given function are integrated, and the function is declared **static**, nevertheless output a separate run-time callable version of the function.

–fno–function–cse

> Do not put function addresses in registers; make each instruction that calls a constant function contain the function's address explicitly.
>
> This option results in less efficient code, but some strange hacks that alter the assembler output may be confused by the optimizations performed when this option is not used.

The following options control specific optimizations. The ‘ **–O2** ’ option turns on all of these optimizations except ‘ **–funroll–loops** ’ and ‘ **–funroll–all–loops** ’.

The ‘ **–O** ’ option usually turns on the ‘ **–fthread–jumps** ’ and ‘ **–fdelayed–branch** ’ options, but specific machines may change the default optimizations.

You can use the following flags in the rare cases when "fine-tuning" of optimizations to be performed is desired.

–fstrength–reduce

> Perform the optimizations of loop strength reduction and elimination of iteration variables.

–fthread–jumps

> Perform optimizations where we check to see if a jump branches to a location where another comparison subsumed by the first is found. If so, the first branch is redirected to either the destination of the second branch or a point immediately following it, depending on whether the condition is known to be true or false.

–funroll–loops

> Perform the optimization of loop unrolling. This is only done for loops whose number of iterations can be determined at compile time or run time.

–funroll–all–loops

> Perform the optimization of loop unrolling. This is done for all loops. This usually makes programs run more slowly.

–fcse–follow–jumps

> In common subexpression elimination, scan through jump instructions in certain cases. This is not as powerful as completely global CSE, but not as slow either.

1

−frerun−cse−after−loop

    Re-run common subexpression elimination after loop optimizations has been performed.

−felide−constructors

    (C++ only.) Use this option to instruct the compiler to be smarter about when it can elide con-structors. Without this flag, GNU C++ and cfront both generate effectively the same code for:

    A foo ();
    A x (foo ()); // x initialized by 'foo ()', no ctor called
    A y = foo (); // call to 'foo ()' heads to temporary,
             // y is initialized from the temporary.

    Note the difference! With this flag, GNU C++ initializes '**y**' directly from the call to **foo** () without going through a temporary.

−fexpensive−optimizations

    Perform a number of minor optimizations that are relatively expensive.

−fdelayed−branch

    If supported for the target machine, attempt to reorder instructions to exploit instruction slots available after delayed branch instructions.

−fschedule−insns

    If supported for the target machine, attempt to reorder instructions to eliminate execution stalls due to required data being unavailable. This helps machines that have slow floating point or memory load instructions by allowing other instructions to be issued until the result of the load or floating point instruction is required.

−fschedule−insns2

    Similar to '**−fschedule−insns**', but requests an additional pass of instruction scheduling after re-gister allocation has been done. This is especially useful on machines with a relatively small number of registers and where memory load instructions take more than one cycle.

TARGET OPTIONS

    By default, GNU CC compiles code for the same type of machine that you are using. However, it can also be installed as a cross-compiler, to compile for some other type of machine. In fact, several different configurations of GNU CC, for different target machines, can be installed side by side. Then you specify which one to use with the '**−b**' option.

    In addition, older and newer versions of GNU CC can be installed side by side. One of them (probably the newest) will be the default, but you may sometimes wish to use another.

−b *machine*

    The argument *machine* specifies the target machine for compilation. This is useful when you have installed GNU CC as a cross-compiler.

    The value to use for *machine* is the same as was specified as the machine type when configuring GNU CC as a cross-compiler. For example, if a cross-compiler was configured with '**configure** i386v', meaning to compile for an 80386 running System V, then you would specify '**−b i386v**' to run that cross compiler.

    When you do not specify '**−b**', it normally means to compile for the same type of machine that you are using.

−V *version*

    The argument *version* specifies which version of GNU CC to run. This is useful when multiple versions are installed. For example, *version* might be '**2.0**', meaning to run GNU CC version 2.0.

1

The default version, when you do not specify '−V', is controlled by the way GNU CC is installed. Normally, it will be a version that is recommended for general use.

MACHINE DEPENDENT OPTIONS

Each of the target machine types can have its own special options, starting with '−m', to choose among various hardware models or configurations—for example, 68010 vs 68020, floating coprocessor or none. A single installed version of the compiler can compile for any model or configuration, according to the options specified.

These are the '−m' options defined for the 68000 series:

−m68020

−mc68020

Generate output for a 68020 (rather than a 68000). This is the default if you use the unmodified sources.

−m68000

−mc68000

Generate output for a 68000 (rather than a 68020).

−m68881

Generate output containing 68881 instructions for floating point. This is the default if you use the unmodified sources.

−mfpa Generate output containing Sun FPA instructions for floating point.

−msoft−float

Generate output containing library calls for floating point. *WARNING:* the requisite libraries are not part of GNU CC. Normally the facilities of the machine's usual C compiler are used, but this can't be done directly in cross-compilation. You must make your own arrangements to provide suitable library functions for cross-compilation.

−mshort

Consider type **int** to be 16 bits wide, like **short int**.

−mnobitfield

Do not use the bit-field instructions. '−m68000' implies '−mnobitfield'.

−mbitfield

Do use the bit-field instructions. '−m68020' implies '−mbitfield'. This is the default if you use the unmodified sources.

−mrtd   Use a different function-calling convention, in which functions that take a fixed number of arguments return with the **rtd** instruction, which pops their arguments while returning. This saves one instruction in the caller since there is no need to pop the arguments there.

This calling convention is incompatible with the one normally used on Unix, so you cannot use it if you need to call libraries compiled with the Unix compiler.

Also, you must provide function prototypes for all functions that take variable numbers of arguments (including **printf**); otherwise incorrect code will be generated for calls to those functions.

In addition, seriously incorrect code will result if you call a function with too many arguments. (Normally, extra arguments are harmlessly ignored.)

The **rtd** instruction is supported by the 68010 and 68020 processors, but not by the 68000.

These '−**m**' options are defined for the Vax:

−**munix** Do not output certain jump instructions (**aobleq** and so on) that the Unix assembler for the Vax cannot handle across long ranges.

−**mgnu** Do output those jump instructions, on the assumption that you will assemble with the GNU assembler.

−**mg** Output code for g-format floating point numbers instead of d-format.

These '−**m**' switches are supported on the Sparc:

−**mfpu** Generate output containing floating point instructions. This is the default if you use the unmodified sources.

−**mno−epilogue**
　　　Generate separate return instructions for **return** statements. This has both advantages and disadvantages; I don't recall what they are.

These '−**m**' options are defined for the Convex:

−**mc1** Generate output for a C1. This is the default when the compiler is configured for a C1.

−**mc2** Generate output for a C2. This is the default when the compiler is configured for a C2.

−**margcount**
　　　Generate code which puts an argument count in the word preceding each argument list. Some non-portable Convex and Vax programs need this word. (Debuggers don't, except for functions with variable-length argument lists; this information is in the symbol table.)

−**mnoargcount**
　　　Omit the argument count word. This is the default if you use the unmodified sources.

These '−**m**' options are defined for the AMD Am29000:

−**mdw** Generate code that assumes the DW bit is set, i.e., that byte and halfword operations are directly supported by the hardware. This is the default.

−**mnodw**
　　　Generate code that assumes the DW bit is not set.

−**mbw** Generate code that assumes the system supports byte and halfword write operations. This is the default.

−**mnbw** Generate code that assumes the systems does not support byte and halfword write operations. This implies '−**mnodw**'.

−**msmall**
　　　Use a small memory model that assumes that all function addresses are either within a single 256 KB segment or at an absolute address of less than 256K. This allows the **call** instruction to be used instead of a **const, consth, calli** sequence.

−**mlarge**
　　　Do not assume that the **call** instruction can be used; this is the default.

−**m29050**
　　　Generate code for the Am29050.

−**m29000**
　　　Generate code for the Am29000. This is the default.

−**mkernel−registers**
　　　Generate references to registers **gr64-gr95** instead of **gr96-gr127**. This option can be used when compiling kernel code that wants a set of global registers disjoint from that used by user-mode code.

Note that when this option is used, register names in '−f' flags must use the normal, user-mode, names.

−muser−registers

Use the normal set of global registers, **gr96-gr127**. This is the default.

−mstack−check

Insert a call to **__msp_check** after each stack adjustment. This is often used for kernel code.

These '−m' options are defined for Motorola 88K architectures:

−mbig−pic

Emit position-independent code, suitable for dynamic linking, even if branches need large displacements. Equivalent to the general-use option '−fPIC'. The general-use option '−fpic', by contrast, only emits valid 88k code if all branches involve small displacements. GCC does not emit position-independent code by default.

−midentify−revision

Include an **ident** directive in the assembler output recording the source file name, compiler name and version, timestamp, and compilation flags used.

−mno−underscores

In assembler output, emit symbol names without adding an underscore character at the beginning of each name. The default is to use an underscore as prefix on each name.

−mno−check−zero−division

−mcheck−zero−division

Early models of the 88K architecture had problems with division by zero; in particular, many of them didn't trap. Use these options to avoid including (or to include explicitly) additional code to detect division by zero and signal an exception. All GCC configurations for the 88K use '−mcheck−zero−division' by default.

−mocs−debug−info

−mno−ocs−debug−info

Include (or omit) additional debugging information (about registers used in each stack frame) as specified in the 88Open Object Compatibility Standard, "OCS". This extra information is not needed by GDB. The default for DG/UX, SVr4, and Delta 88 SVr3.2 is to include this information; other 88k configurations omit this information by default.

−mocs−frame−position

−mno−ocs−frame−position

Force (or do not require) register values to be stored in a particular place in stack frames, as specified in OCS. The DG/UX, Delta88 SVr3.2, and BCS configurations use '−mocs−frame−position'; other 88k configurations have the default '−mno−ocs−frame−position'.

−moptimize−arg−area

−mno−optimize−arg−area

Control how to store function arguments in stack frames. '−moptimize−arg−area' saves space, but may break some debuggers (not GDB). '−mno−optimize−arg−area' conforms better to standards. By default GCC does not optimize the argument area.

−mshort−data−*num*

num Generate smaller data references by making them relative to **r0**, which allows loading a value using a single instruction (rather than the usual two). You control which data references are affected by specifying *num* with this option. For example, if you specify '−**mshort−data−512**', then the data references affected are those involving displacements of less than 512 bytes. '−**mshort−data−***num*' is not effective for *num* greater than 64K.

1

−msvr4

−msvr3 Turn on ('−msvr4') or off ('−msvr3') compiler extensions related to System V release 4 (SVr4). This controls the following:

- Which variant of the assembler syntax to emit (which you can select independently using '−mversion03.00').

- '−msvr4' makes the C preprocessor recognize '#pragma weak'

- '−msvr4' makes GCC issue additional declaration directives used in SVr4.

'−msvr3' is the default for all m88K configurations except the SVr4 configuration.

−mtrap−large−shift

−mhandle−large−shift

> Include code to detect bit-shifts of more than 31 bits; respectively, trap such shifts or emit code to handle them properly. By default GCC makes no special provision for large bit shifts.

−muse−div−instruction

> Very early models of the 88K architecture didn't have a divide instruction, so GCC avoids that instruction by default. Use this option to specify that it's safe to use the divide instruction.

−mversion−03.00

> Use alternative assembler syntax for the assembler version corresponding to SVr4, but without enabling the other features triggered by '−svr4'. This is implied by '−svr4', is the default for the SVr4 configuration of GCC, and is permitted by the DG/UX configuration only if '−svr4' is also specified. The Delta 88 SVr3.2 configuration ignores this option.

−mwarn−passed−structs

> Warn when a function passes a struct as an argument or result. Structure-passing conventions have changed during the evolution of the C language, and are often the source of portability problems. By default, GCC issues no such warning.

These options are defined for the IBM RS6000:

−mfp−in−toc

−mno−fp−in−toc

> Control whether or not floating-point constants go in the Table of Contents (TOC), a table of all global variable and function addresses. By default GCC puts floating-point constants there; if the TOC overflows, '−mno−fp−in−toc' will reduce the size of the TOC, which may avoid the overflow.

These '−m' options are defined for the IBM RT PC:

−min−line−mul

> Use an in-line code sequence for integer multiplies. This is the default.

−mcall−lib−mul

> Call **lmul$$** for integer multiples.

−mfull−fp−blocks

> Generate full-size floating point data blocks, including the minimum amount of scratch space recommended by IBM. This is the default.

−mminimum−fp−blocks

> Do not include extra scratch space in floating point data blocks. This results in smaller code, but slower execution, since scratch space must be allocated dynamically.

−mfp−arg−in−fpregs

> Use a calling sequence incompatible with the IBM calling convention in which floating point ar-

guments are passed in floating point registers. Note that **varargs.h** and **stdargs.h** will not work with floating point operands if this option is specified.

−mfp−arg−in−gregs

Use the normal calling convention for floating point arguments. This is the default.

−mhc−struct−return

Return structures of more than one word in memory, rather than in a register. This provides compatibility with the MetaWare HighC (hc) compiler. Use '**−fpcc−struct−return**' for compatibility with the Portable C Compiler (pcc).

−mnohc−struct−return

Return some structures of more than one word in registers, when convenient. This is the default. For compatibility with the IBM-supplied compilers, use either '**−fpcc−struct−return**' or '**−mhc−struct−return**'.

These '**−m**' options are defined for the MIPS family of computers:

−mcpu=cpu-type

Assume the defaults for the machine type cpu-type when scheduling instructions. The default cpu-type is **default**, which picks the longest cycles times for any of the machines, in order that the code run at reasonable rates on all MIPS cpu's. Other choices for cpu-type are **r2000**, **r3000**, **r4000**, and **r6000**. While picking a specific cpu-type will schedule things appropriately for that particular chip, the compiler will not generate any code that does not meet level 1 of the MIPS ISA (instruction set architecture) without the **−mips2** or **−mips3** switches being used.

−mips2 Issue instructions from level 2 of the MIPS ISA (branch likely, square root instructions). The **−mcpu=r4000** or **−mcpu=r6000** switch must be used in conjunction with **−mips2**.

−mips3 Issue instructions from level 3 of the MIPS ISA (64 bit instructions). The **−mcpu=r4000** switch must be used in conjunction with **−mips2**.

−mint64

−mlong64

−mlonglong128

These options don't work at present.

−mmips−as

Generate code for the MIPS assembler, and invoke **mips−tfile** to add normal debug information. This is the default for all platforms except for the OSF/1 reference platform, using the OSF/rose object format. If any of the **−ggdb**, **−gstabs**, or **−gstabs+** switches are used, the **mips−tfile** program will encapsulate the stabs within MIPS ECOFF.

−mgas Generate code for the GNU assembler. This is the default on the OSF/1 reference platform, using the OSF/rose object format.

−mrnames

−mno−rnames

The **−mrnames** switch says to output code using the MIPS software names for the registers, instead of the hardware names (ie, **a0** instead of **$4**). The GNU assembler does not support the **−mrnames** switch, and the MIPS assembler will be instructed to run the MIPS C preprocessor over the source file. The **−mno−rnames** switch is default.

−mgpopt

−mno−gpopt

The **−mgpopt** switch says to write all of the data declarations before the instructions in the text section, to all the MIPS assembler to generate one word memory references instead of using two words for short global or static data items. This is on by default if optimization is selected.

1

−mstats

−mno−stats

>   For each non-inline function processed, the **−mstats** switch causes the compiler to emit one line to the standard error file to print statistics about the program (number of registers saved, stack size, etc.).

−mmemcpy

−mno−memcpy

>   The **−mmemcpy** switch makes all block moves call the appropriate string function (**memcpy** or **bcopy**) instead of possibly generating inline code.

−mmips−tfile

−mno−mips−tfile

>   The **−mno−mips−tfile** switch causes the compiler not postprocess the object file with the **mips−tfile** program, after the MIPS assembler has generated it to add debug support. If **mips−tfile** is not run, then no local variables will be available to the debugger. In addition, **stage2** and **stage3** objects will have the temporary file names passed to the assembler embedded in the object file, which means the objects will not compare the same.

−msoft−float

>   Generate output containing library calls for floating point. *WARNING:* the requisite libraries are not part of GNU CC. Normally the facilities of the machine's usual C compiler are used, but this can't be done directly in cross-compilation. You must make your own arrangements to provide suitable library functions for cross-compilation.

−mhard−float

>   Generate output containing floating point instructions. This is the default if you use the unmodified sources.

−mfp64

>   Assume that the **FR** bit in the status word is on, and that there are 32 64-bit floating point registers, instead of 32 32-bit floating point registers. You must also specify the **−mcpu=r4000** and **−mips3** switches.

−mfp32

>   Assume that there are 32 32-bit floating point registers. This is the default.

−mabicalls

>   The **−mabicalls** switch says to emit the **.abicalls**, **.cpload**, and **.cprestore** pseudo operations that some System V.4 ports use for position independent code.

−mhalf−pic

−mno−half−pic

>   The **−mhalf−pic** switch says to put pointers to extern references into the data section and load them up, rather than put the references in the text section. This option does not work at present. **−G***num* Put global and static items less than or equal to *num* bytes into the small data or bss sections instead of the normal data or bss section. This allows the assembler to emit one word memory reference instructions based on the global pointer (**gp** or **$28**), instead of the normal two words used. By default, *num* is 8 when the MIPS assembler is used, and 0 when the GNU assembler is used. The **−G***num* switch is also passed to the assembler and linker. All modules should be compiled with the same **−G***num* value.

CODE GENERATION OPTIONS

>   These machine-independent options control the interface conventions used in code generation.

>   Most of them begin with '−f'. These options have both positive and negative forms; the negative form of '**−f**foo' would be '**−f**no−foo'. In the table below, only one of the forms is listed—the one which is not the default. You can figure out the other form by either removing '**no−**' or adding it.

+e*N* (*C++ only.*) control whether virtual function definitions in classes are used to generate code, or only to define interfaces for their callers. These options are provided for compatibility with cfront 1.x usage; the recommended GNU C++ usage is to use **#pragma interface** and **#pragma implementation**, instead.

With ' **+e0** ', virtual function definitions in classes are declared extern; the declaration is used only as an interface specification, not to generate code for the virtual functions (in this compilation).

With ' **+e1** ', **g++** actually generates the code implementing virtual functions defined in the code, and makes them publicly visible.

−fnonnull−objects

(*C++ only.*) Normally, GNU C++ makes conservative assumptions about objects reached through references. For example, the compiler must check that ' **a** ' is not null in code like the following:

    obj &a = g ();
    a.f (2);

Checking that references of this sort have non-null values requires extra code, however, and it is unnecessary for many programs. You can use ' **−fnonnull−objects** ' to omit the checks for null, if your program doesn't require the default checking.

−fpcc−struct−return

Use the same convention for returning **struct** and **union** values that is used by the usual C compiler on your system. This convention is less efficient for small structures, and on many machines it fails to be reentrant; but it has the advantage of allowing intercallability between GCC-compiled code and PCC-compiled code.

−fshort−enums

Allocate to an **enum** type only as many bytes as it needs for the declared range of possible values. Specifically, the **enum** type will be equivalent to the smallest integer type which has enough room.

−fshort−double

Use the same size for **double** as for **float** .

−fshared−data

Requests that the data and non-**const** variables of this compilation be shared data rather than private data. The distinction makes sense only on certain operating systems, where shared data is shared between processes running the same program, while private data exists in one copy per process.

−fno−common

Allocate even uninitialized global variables in the bss section of the object file, rather than generating them as common blocks. This has the effect that if the same variable is declared (without **extern**) in two different compilations, you will get an error when you link them. The only reason this might be useful is if you wish to verify that the program will work on other systems which always work this way.

−fvolatile

Consider all memory references through pointers to be volatile.

−fpic If supported for the target machines, generate position-independent code, suitable for use in a shared library.

−fPIC If supported for the target machine, emit position-independent code, suitable for dynamic linking, even if branches need large displacements.

−ffixed−*reg*

Treat the register named *reg* as a fixed register; generated code should never refer to it (except perhaps as a stack pointer, frame pointer or in some other fixed role).

reg must be the name of a register. The register names accepted are machine-specific and are defined in the **REGISTER_NAMES** macro in the machine description macro file.

This flag does not have a negative form, because it specifies a three-way choice.

−fcall−used−*reg*

Treat the register named *reg* as an allocatable register that is clobbered by function calls. It may be allocated for temporaries or variables that do not live across a call. Functions compiled this way will not save and restore the register *reg*.

Use of this flag for a register that has a fixed pervasive role in the machine's execution model, such as the stack pointer or frame pointer, will produce disastrous results.

This flag does not have a negative form, because it specifies a three-way choice.

−fcall−saved−*reg*

Treat the register named *reg* as an allocatable register saved by functions. It may be allocated even for temporaries or variables that live across a call. Functions compiled this way will save and restore the register *reg* if they use it.

Use of this flag for a register that has a fixed pervasive role in the machine's execution model, such as the stack pointer or frame pointer, will produce disastrous results.

A different sort of disaster will result from the use of this flag for a register in which function values may be returned.

This flag does not have a negative form, because it specifies a three-way choice.

−fgnu−binutils

−fno−gnu−binutils

(C++ only.) ' **−fgnu−binutils** ' (the default for most, but not all, platforms) makes GNU C++ emit extra information for static initialization and finalization. This information has to be passed from the assembler to the GNU linker. Some assemblers won't pass this information; you must either use GNU **as** or specify the option '**−fno−gnu−binutils**'.

With '**−fno−gnu−binutils**', you must use the program **collect** (part of the GCC distribution) for linking.

PRAGMAS

Two '**#pragma**' directives are supported for GNU C++, to permit using the same header file for two purposes: as a definition of interfaces to a given object class, and as the full definition of the contents of that object class.

#pragma interface

(C++ only.) Use this directive in header files that define object classes, to save space in most of the object files that use those classes. Normally, local copies of certain information (backup copies of inline member functions, debugging information, and the internal tables that implement virtual functions) must be kept in each object file that includes class definitions. You can use this pragma to avoid such duplication. When a header file containing '**#pragma interface**' is included in a compilation, this auxiliary information will not be generated (unless the main input source file itself uses '**#pragma implementation**'). Instead, the object files will contain references to be resolved at link time.

#pragma implementation

#pragma implementation "*objects***.h"**

(C++ only.) Use this pragma in a main input file, when you want full output from included header

1

files to be generated (and made globally visible). The included header file, in turn, should use '**#pragma interface**'. Backup copies of inline member functions, debugging information, and the internal tables used to implement virtual functions are all generated in implementation files.

If you use '**#pragma implementation**' with no argument, it applies to an include file with the same basename as your source file; for example, in '**allclass.cc**', '**#pragma implementation**' by itself is equivalent to '**#pragma implementation "allclass.h"**'. Use the string argument if you want a single implementation file to include code from multiple header files.

There is no way to split up the contents of a single header file into multiple implementation files.

FILES

file.c	C source file
file.h	C header (preprocessor) file
file.i	preprocessed C source file
file.C	C++ source file
file.cc	C++ source file
file.cxx	C++ source file
file.m	Objective-C source file
file.s	assembly language file
file.o	object file
a.out	link edited output
TMPDIR/cc*	temporary files
LIBDIR/cpp	preprocessor
LIBDIR/cc1	compiler for C
LIBDIR/cc1plus	compiler for C++
LIBDIR/collect	linker front end needed on some machines
LIBDIR/libgcc.a	GCC subroutine library
/lib/crt[01n].o	start-up routine
LIBDIR/ccrt0	additional start-up routine for C++
/lib/libc.a	standard C library, see *intro*(3)
/usr/include	standard directory for **#include** files
LIBDIR/include	standard gcc directory for **#include** files
LIBDIR/g++−include	additional g++ directory for **#include**

LIBDIR is usually **/usr/local/lib/***machine*/*version*.
TMPDIR comes from the environment variable **TMPDIR** (default **/usr/tmp** if available, else **/tmp**).

SEE ALSO

cpp(1), as(1), ld(1), gdb(1), adb(1), dbx(1), sdb(1).
'**gcc**', '**cpp**', '**as**','**ld**', and '**gdb**' entries in **info**.
Using and Porting GNU CC (for version 2.0), Richard M. Stallman, November 1990; *The C Preprocessor*, Richard M. Stallman, July 1990; *Using GDB: A Guide to the GNU Source-Level Debugger*, Richard M. Stallman and Roland H. Pesch, December 1991; *Using as: the GNU Assembler*, Dean Elsner, Jay Fenlason & friends, March 1991; *gld: the GNU linker*, Steve Chamberlain and Roland Pesch, April 1991.

BUGS

Report bugs to **bug−gcc@prep.ai.mit.edu**. Bugs tend actually to be fixed if they can be isolated, so it is in your interest to report them in such a way that they can be easily reproduced.

COPYING

Copyright (c) 1991 Free Software Foundation, Inc.

Permission is granted to make and distribute verbatim copies of this manual provided the copyright notice and this permission notice are preserved on all copies.

1

Permission is granted to copy and distribute modified versions of this manual under the conditions for verbatim copying, provided that the entire resulting derived work is distributed under the terms of a permission notice identical to this one.

Permission is granted to copy and distribute translations of this manual into another language, under the above conditions for modified versions, except that this permission notice may be included in translations approved by the Free Software Foundation instead of in the original English.

AUTHORS

See the GNU CC Manual for the contributors to GNU CC.

1

NAME
cd – change working directory

SYNOPSIS
cd *directory*

DESCRIPTION
Directory is an absolute or relative pathname which becomes the new working directory. The interpretation of a relative pathname by cd depends on the CDPATH environment variable (see below).

ENVIRONMENT
The following environment variables affect the execution of cd:

CDPATH   If the *directory* operand does not begin with a slash (/) character, and the first component is not dot (.) or dot-dot (..), cd searches for the directory relative to each directory named in the CDPATH variable, in the order listed. The new working directory is set to the first matching directory found. An empty string in place of a directory pathname represents the current directory. If the new working directory was derived from CDPATH, it will be printed to the standard output.

HOME   If cd is invoked without arguments and the HOME environment variable exists and contains a directory name, that directory becomes the new working directory.

See csh(1) for more information on environment variables.

The cd utility exits 0 on success, and >0 if an error occurs.

SEE ALSO
csh(1), pwd(1), sh(1), chdir(2)

STANDARDS
The cd command is expected to be IEEE Std1003.2 (''POSIX'') compatible.

NAME

checknr – check nroff/troff files

SYNOPSIS

checknr [**–a** . *x1.y1.x2.y2. ... .xn.yn*] [**–c** . *x1.x2.x3 ... .xn*] [**–s**] [**–f**] *file*

DESCRIPTION

Checknr checks a list of nroff(1) or troff(1) input files for certain kinds of errors involving mismatched opening and closing delimiters and unknown commands. If no files are specified, **checknr** checks the standard input.

Options:

–a Add additional pairs of macros to the list of known macros. This must be followed by groups of six characters, each group defining a pair of macros. The six characters are a period, the first macro name, another period, and the second macro name. For example, to define a pair .BS and .ES, use '**–a.BS.ES**'

–c Define commands which would otherwise be complained about as undefined.

–f Request **checknr** to ignore '\f' font changes.

–s Ignore '\s' size changes.

Delimiters checked are:

1. Font changes using \fx ... \fP.

2. Size changes using \sx ... \s0.

3. Macros that come in open ... close forms, for example, the .TS and .TE macros which must always come in pairs.

Checknr is intended for use on documents that are prepared with **checknr** in mind, much the same as lint(1). It expects a certain document writing style for '\f' and '\s' commands, in that each \fx must be terminated with \fP and each \sx must be terminated with \s0. While it will work to directly go into the next font or explicitly specify the original font or point size, and many existing documents actually do this, such a practice will produce complaints from **checknr**. Since it is probably better to use the \fP and \s0 forms anyway, you should think of this as a contribution to your document preparation style.

Checknr knows about the ms(7) and me(7) macro packages.

SEE ALSO

nroff(1), troff(1), checkeq(1), ms(7), me(7)

DIAGNOSTICS

Complaints about unmatched delimiters. Complaints about unrecognized commands. Various complaints about the syntax of commands.

BUGS

There is no way to define a 1 character macro name using **–a**.

Does not correctly recognize certain reasonable constructs, such as conditionals.

HISTORY

The `checknr` command appeared in 4.0BSD.

NAME
   chflags – change file flags

SYNOPSIS
   chflags [−R [−H | −L | −P]] *flags file ...*

DESCRIPTION
   The chflags utility modifies the file flags of the listed files as specified by the *flags* operand.

   The options are as follows:

   −H   If the −R option is specified, symbolic links on the command line are followed. (Symbolic links en-
        countered in the tree traversal are not followed.)

   −L   If the −R option is specified, all symbolic links are followed.

   −P   If the −R option is specified, no symbolic links are followed.

   −R   Change the file flags for the file hierarchies rooted in the files instead of just the files themselves.

   Flags are a comma separated list of keywords. The following keywords are currently defined:

   ```
   dump    set the dump flag
   sappnd  set the system append-only flag (super-user only)
   schg    set the system immutable flag (super-user only)
   uappnd  set the user append-only flag (owner or super-user only)
   uchg    set the user immutable flag (owner or super-user only)
   ```

   Putting the letters ''no'' before an option causes the flag to be turned off. For example:

   ```
   nodump  the file should never be dumped
   ```

   Symbolic links do not have flags, so unless the −H or −L option is set, chflags on a symbolic link always
   succeeds and has no effect. The −H, −L and −P options are ignored unless the −R option is specified. In
   addition, these options override each other and the command's actions are determined by the last one
   specified.

   The chflags utility exits 0 on success, and >0 if an error occurs.

SEE ALSO
   chflags(2), stat(2), fts(3), symlink(7)

NAME

chgrp – change group

SYNOPSIS

chgrp [−R [−H | −L | −P]] [−f] *group files* ...

DESCRIPTION

The chgrp utility sets the group ID of the file named by each *file* operand to the *group* ID specified by the group operand.

Options:

−H   If the −R option is specified, symbolic links on the command line are followed. (Symbolic links encountered in the tree traversal are not followed.)

−L   If the −R option is specified, all symbolic links are followed.

−P   If the −R option is specified, no symbolic links are followed.

−R   Change the group ID for the file hierarchies rooted in the files instead of just the files themselves.

−f   The force option ignores errors, except for usage errors and doesn't query about strange modes (unless the user does not have proper permissions).

Symbolic links don't have groups, so unless the −H or −L option is set, **chgrp** on a symbolic link always succeeds and has no effect. The −H, −L and −P options are ignored unless the −R option is specified. In addition, these options override each other and the command's actions are determined by the last one specified.

The *group* operand can be either a group name from the group database, or a numeric group ID. If a group name is also a numeric group ID, the operand is used as a group name.

The user invoking **chgrp** must belong to the specified group and be the owner of the file, or be the superuser.

The **chgrp** utility exits 0 on success, and >0 if an error occurs.

COMPATIBILITY

Previous versions of the **chgrp** utility changed the group of symbolic links specified on the command line. In this system, symbolic links do not have groups.

FILES

/etc/group Group ID file

SEE ALSO

chown(2), group(5), passwd(5), fts(3), symlink(7), chown(8)

STANDARDS

The **chgrp** utility is expected to be POSIX 1003.2 compatible.

1

NAME
chkey – change your encryption key

SYNOPSIS
chkey

DESCRIPTION
chkey prompts the user for their login password, and uses it to encrypt a new encryption key for the user to be stored in the **publickey**(5) database.

SEE ALSO
keylogin(1), **publickey**(5), **keyserv**(8C), **newkey**(8)

NAME
chmod – change file modes

SYNOPSIS
chmod [–R [–H | –L | –P]] *mode file* ...

DESCRIPTION
The **chmod** utility modifies the file mode bits of the listed files as specified by the *mode* operand.

The options are as follows:

–H   If the –R option is specified, symbolic links on the command line are followed. (Symbolic links encountered in the tree traversal are not followed.)

–L   If the –R option is specified, all symbolic links are followed.

–P   If the –R option is specified, no symbolic links are followed.

–R   Change the modes of the file hierarchies rooted in the files instead of just the files themselves.

Symbolic links do not have modes, so unless the –H or –L option is set, **chmod** on a symbolic link always succeeds and has no effect. The –H, –L and –P options are ignored unless the –R option is specified. In addition, these options override each other and the command's actions are determined by the last one specified.

Only the owner of a file or the super-user is permitted to change the mode of a file.

The **chmod** utility exits 0 on success, and >0 if an error occurs.

MODES
Modes may be absolute or symbolic. An absolute mode is an octal number constructed by *or-ing* the following values:

4000	set-user-ID-on-execution
2000	set-group-ID-on-execution
1000	sticky bit, see chmod(2)
0400	read by owner
0200	write by owner
0100	execute (or search for directories) by owner
0070	read, write, execute/search by group
0007	read, write, execute/search by others

The read, write, and execute/search values for group and others are encoded as described for owner.

The symbolic mode is described by the following grammar:

```
mode            ::= clause [, clause ...]
clause          ::= [who ...] [action ...] last_action
action          ::= op [perm ...]
last_action     ::= op [perm ...]
who             ::= a | u | g | o
op              ::= + | - | =
perm            ::= r | s | t | w | x | X | u | g | o
```

The *who* symbols "u", "g", and "o" specify the user, group, and other parts of the mode bits, respectively. The *who* symbol "a" is equivalent to "ugo".

1

The *perm* symbols represent the portions of the mode bits as follows:

r The read bits.
s The set-user-ID-on-execution and set-group-ID-on-execution bits.
t The sticky bit.
w The write bits.
x The execute/search bits.
X The execute/search bits if the file is a directory or any of the execute/search bits are set in the original (unmodified) mode. Operations with the *perm* symbol "X" are only meaningful in conjunction with the *op* symbol "+", and are ignored in all other cases.
u The user permission bits in the mode of the original file.
g The group permission bits in the mode of the original file.
o The other permission bits in the mode of the original file.

The *op* symbols represent the operation performed, as follows:

+ If no value is supplied for *perm*, the "+" operation has no effect. If no value is supplied for *who*, each permission bit specified in *perm*, for which the corresponding bit in the file mode creation mask is clear, is set. Otherwise, the mode bits represented by the specified *who* and *perm* values are set.

− If no value is supplied for *perm*, the "−" operation has no effect. If no value is supplied for *who*, each permission bit specified in *perm*, for which the corresponding bit in the file mode creation mask is clear, is cleared. Otherwise, the mode bits represented by the specified *who* and *perm* values are cleared.

= The mode bits specified by the *who* value are cleared, or, if no who value is specified, the owner, group and other mode bits are cleared. Then, if no value is supplied for *who*, each permission bit specified in *perm*, for which the corresponding bit in the file mode creation mask is clear, is set. Otherwise, the mode bits represented by the specified *who* and *perm* values are set.

Each *clause* specifies one or more operations to be performed on the mode bits, and each operation is applied to the mode bits in the order specified.

Operations upon the other permissions only (specified by the symbol "o" by itself), in combination with the *perm* symbols "s" or "t", are ignored.

EXAMPLES

644   make a file readable by anyone and writable by the owner only.

go-w   deny write permission to group and others.

=rw,+X   set the read and write permissions to the usual defaults, but retain any execute permissions that are currently set.

+X   make a directory or file searchable/executable by everyone if it is already searchable/executable by anyone.

755
u=rwx,go=rx
u=rwx,go=u-w   make a file readable/executable by everyone and writable by the owner only.

go=   clear all mode bits for group and others.

g=u-w   set the group bits equal to the user bits, but clear the group write bit.

BUGS

There's no *perm* option for the naughty bits.

SEE ALSO

install(1), chmod(2), stat(2), umask(2), fts(3), setmode(3), symlink(7), chown(8)

STANDARDS

The chmod utility is expected to be POSIX 1003.2 compatible with the exception of the *perm* symbols ''t'' and ''X'' which are not included in that standard.

1

NAME
chpass – add or change user database information

SYNOPSIS
chpass [−a *list*] [−s *newshell*] [user]

DESCRIPTION
Chpass allows editing of the user database information associated with *user* or, by default, the current user. The information is formatted and supplied to an editor for changes.

Only the information that the user is allowed to change is displayed.

The options are as follows:

−a   The super-user is allowed to directly supply a user database entry, in the format specified by passwd(5), as an argument. This argument must be a colon (":") separated list of all the user database fields, although they may be empty.

−s   The −s option attempts to change the user's shell to *newshell*.

Possible display items are as follows:

Login:	user's login name
Password:	user's encrypted password
Uid:	user's login
Gid:	user's login group
Change:	password change time
Expire:	account expiration time
Class:	user's general classification
Home Directory:	user's home directory
Shell:	user's login shell
Full Name:	user's real name
Location:	user's normal location
Home Phone:	user's home phone
Office Phone:	user's office phone

The *login* field is the user name used to access the computer account.

The *password* field contains the encrypted form of the user's password.

The *uid* field is the number associated with the *login* field. Both of these fields should be unique across the system (and often across a group of systems) as they control file access.

While it is possible to have multiple entries with identical login names and/or identical user id's, it is usually a mistake to do so. Routines that manipulate these files will often return only one of the multiple entries, and that one by random selection.

The *group* field is the group that the user will be placed in at login. Since BSD supports multiple groups (see groups(1)) this field currently has little special meaning. This field may be filled in with either a number or a group name (see group(5)).

The *change* field is the date by which the password must be changed.

The *expire* field is the date on which the account expires.

Both the *change* and *expire* fields should be entered in the form "month day year" where *month* is the month name (the first three characters are sufficient), *day* is the day of the month, and *year* is the year.

The `class` field is currently unused. In the near future it will be a key to a `termcap(5)` style database of user attributes.

The user's `home directory` is the full UNIX path name where the user will be placed at login.

The `shell` field is the command interpreter the user prefers. If the `shell` field is empty, the Bourne shell, `/bin/sh`, is assumed. When altering a login shell, and not the super-user, the user may not change from a non-standard shell or to a non-standard shell. Non-standard is defined as a shell not found in `/etc/shells`.

The last four fields are for storing the user's `full name`, `office location`, and `home` and `work telephone` numbers.

Once the information has been verified, **chpass** uses pwd_mkdb(8) to update the user database.

ENVIRONMENT

The vi(1) editor will be used unless the environment variable EDITOR is set to an alternate editor. When the editor terminates, the information is re-read and used to update the user database itself. Only the user, or the super-user, may edit the information associated with the user.

FILES

`/etc/master.passwd`	The user database
`/etc/passwd`	A Version 7 format password file
`/etc/chpass.XXXXXX`	Temporary copy of the password file
`/etc/shells`	The list of approved shells

SEE ALSO

login(1), finger(1), passwd(1), getusershell(3), passwd(5), pwd_mkdb(8), vipw(8)

and Robert Morris, and Ken Thompson, *UNIX Password security*.

BUGS

User information should (and eventually will) be stored elsewhere.

HISTORY

The **chpass** command appeared in 4.3BSD–Reno.

1

NAME

ci – check in RCS revisions

SYNOPSIS

ci [*options*] *file* ...

DESCRIPTION

ci stores new revisions into RCS files. Each pathname matching an RCS suffix is taken to be an RCS file. All others are assumed to be working files containing new revisions. **ci** deposits the contents of each working file into the corresponding RCS file. If only a working file is given, **ci** tries to find the corresponding RCS file in an RCS subdirectory and then in the working file's directory. For more details, see FILE NAMING below.

For **ci** to work, the caller's login must be on the access list, except if the access list is empty or the caller is the superuser or the owner of the file. To append a new revision to an existing branch, the tip revision on that branch must be locked by the caller. Otherwise, only a new branch can be created. This restriction is not enforced for the owner of the file if non-strict locking is used (see **rcs**(1)). A lock held by someone else may be broken with the **rcs** command.

Unless the **–f** option is given, **ci** checks whether the revision to be deposited differs from the preceding one. If not, instead of creating a new revision **ci** reverts to the preceding one. To revert, ordinary **ci** removes the working file and any lock; **ci –l** keeps and **ci –u** removes any lock, and then they both generate a new working file much as if **co –l** or **co –u** had been applied to the preceding revision. When reverting, any **–n** and **–s** options apply to the preceding revision.

For each revision deposited, **ci** prompts for a log message. The log message should summarize the change and must be terminated by end-of-file or by a line containing **.** by itself. If several files are checked in **ci** asks whether to reuse the previous log message. If the standard input is not a terminal, **ci** suppresses the prompt and uses the same log message for all files. See also **–m**.

If the RCS file does not exist, **ci** creates it and deposits the contents of the working file as the initial revision (default number: **1.1**). The access list is initialized to empty. Instead of the log message, **ci** requests descriptive text (see **–t** below).

The number *rev* of the deposited revision can be given by any of the options **–f, –I, –k, –l, –M, –q, –r,** or **–u**. *rev* may be symbolic, numeric, or mixed. If *rev* is **$**, **ci** determines the revision number from keyword values in the working file.

If *rev* is a revision number, it must be higher than the latest one on the branch to which *rev* belongs, or must start a new branch.

If *rev* is a branch rather than a revision number, the new revision is appended to that branch. The level number is obtained by incrementing the tip revision number of that branch. If *rev* indicates a non-existing branch, that branch is created with the initial revision numbered *rev*.**1**.

If *rev* is omitted, **ci** tries to derive the new revision number from the caller's last lock. If the caller has locked the tip revision of a branch, the new revision is appended to that branch. The new revision number is obtained by incrementing the tip revision number. If the caller locked a non-tip revision, a new branch is started at that revision by incrementing the highest branch number at that revision. The default initial branch and level numbers are **1**.

If *rev* is omitted and the caller has no lock, but owns the file and locking is not set to *strict*, then the revision is appended to the default branch (normally the trunk; see the **–b** option of **rcs**(1)).

Exception: On the trunk, revisions can be appended to the end, but not inserted.

OPTIONS

–r[*rev*]   checks in a revision, releases the corresponding lock, and removes the working file. This is the default.

The −**r** option has an unusual meaning in **ci**. In other RCS commands, −**r** merely specifies a revision number, but in **ci** it also releases a lock and removes the working file. See −**u** for a tricky example.

−**l**[*rev*]   works like −**r**, except it performs an additional **co** −**l** for the deposited revision. Thus, the deposited revision is immediately checked out again and locked. This is useful for saving a revision although one wants to continue editing it after the checkin.

−**u**[*rev*]   works like −**l**, except that the deposited revision is not locked. This lets one read the working file immediately after checkin.

The −**l**, −**r**, and −**u** options are mutually exclusive and silently override each other. For example, **ci** −**u** −**r** is equivalent to **ci** −**r** because −**r** overrides −**u**.

−**f**[*rev*]   forces a deposit; the new revision is deposited even it is not different from the preceding one.

−**k**[*rev*]   searches the working file for keyword values to determine its revision number, creation date, state, and author (see **co**(1)), and assigns these values to the deposited revision, rather than computing them locally. It also generates a default login message noting the login of the caller and the actual checkin date. This option is useful for software distribution. A revision that is sent to several sites should be checked in with the −**k** option at these sites to preserve the original number, date, author, and state. The extracted keyword values and the default log message may be overridden with the options −**d**, −**m**, −**s**, −**w**, and any option that carries a revision number.

−**q**[*rev*]   quiet mode; diagnostic output is not printed. A revision that is not different from the preceding one is not deposited, unless −**f** is given.

−**I**[*rev*]   interactive mode; the user is prompted and questioned even if the standard input is not a terminal.

−**d**[*date*]

uses *date* for the checkin date and time. The *date* is specified in free format as explained in **co**(1). This is useful for lying about the checkin date, and for −**k** if no date is available. If *date* is empty, the working file's time of last modification is used.

−**M**[*rev*]

Set the modification time on any new working file to be the date of the retrieved revision. For example, **ci** −**d** −**M** −**u** *f* does not alter *f*'s modification time, even if *f*'s contents change due to keyword substitution. Use this option with care; it can confuse **make**(1).

−**m***msg*   uses the string *msg* as the log message for all revisions checked in.

−**n***name*

assigns the symbolic name *name* to the number of the checked-in revision. **ci** prints an error message if *name* is already assigned to another number.

−**N***name*

same as −**n**, except that it overrides a previous assignment of *name*.

−**s***state*   sets the state of the checked-in revision to the identifier *state*. The default state is **Exp**.

−**t***file*   writes descriptive text from the contents of the named *file* into the RCS file, deleting the existing text. The *file* may not begin with −.

−**t**−*string*

Write descriptive text from the *string* into the RCS file, deleting the existing text.

The −**t** option, in both its forms, has effect only during an initial checkin; it is silently ignored otherwise.

During the initial checkin, if −**t** is not given, **ci** obtains the text from standard input, terminated by end-of-file or by a line containing **.** by itself. The user is prompted for the text if interaction is possible; see −**I**.

1

For backward compatibility with older versions of RCS, a bare **−t** option is ignored.

−w*login*
> uses *login* for the author field of the deposited revision. Useful for lying about the author, and for **−k** if no author is available.

−V*n*   Emulate RCS version *n*. See **co**(1) for details.

−x*suffixes*
> specifies the suffixes for RCS files. A nonempty suffix matches any pathname ending in the suffix. An empty suffix matches any pathname of the form **RCS/***file* or *path***/RCS/***file*. The **−x** option can specify a list of suffixes separated by **/**. For example, **−x,v/** specifies two suffixes: **,v** and the empty suffix. If two or more suffixes are specified, they are tried in order when looking for an RCS file; the first one that works is used for that file. If no RCS file is found but an RCS file can be created, the suffixes are tried in order to determine the new RCS file's name. The default for *suffixes* is installation-dependent; normally it is **,v/** for hosts like Unix that permit commas in file names, and is empty (i.e. just the empty suffix) for other hosts.

FILE NAMING

Pairs of RCS files and working files may be specified in three ways (see also the example section).

1) Both the RCS file and the working file are given. The RCS pathname is of the form *path1* **/***workfileX* and the working pathname is of the form *path2* **/***workfile* where *path1* **/** and *path2* **/** are (possibly different or empty) paths, *workfile* is a filename, and *X* is an RCS suffix. If *X* is empty, *path1* **/** must be **RCS/** or must end in **/RCS/**.

2) Only the RCS file is given. Then the working file is created in the current directory and its name is derived from the name of the RCS file by removing *path1* **/** and the suffix *X*.

3) Only the working file is given. Then **ci** considers each RCS suffix *X* in turn, looking for an RCS file of the form *path2* **/RCS/***workfileX* or (if the former is not found and *X* is nonempty) *path2* **/***workfileX*.

If the RCS file is specified without a path in 1) and 2), **ci** looks for the RCS file first in the directory **./RCS** and then in the current directory.

ci reports an error if an attempt to open an RCS file fails for an unusual reason, even if the RCS file's pathname is just one of several possibilities. For example, to suppress use of RCS commands in a directory *d*, create a regular file named *d***/RCS** so that casual attempts to use RCS commands in *d* fail because *d***/RCS** is not a directory.

EXAMPLES

Suppose **,v** is an RCS suffix and the current directory contains a subdirectory **RCS** with an RCS file **io.c,v**. Then each of the following commands check in a copy of **io.c** into **RCS/io.c,v** as the latest revision, removing **io.c**.

>   ci io.c;   ci RCS/io.c,v;   ci io.c,v;
>   ci io.c RCS/io.c,v;   ci io.c io.c,v;
>   ci RCS/io.c,v io.c;   ci io.c,v io.c;

Suppose instead that the empty suffix is an RCS suffix and the current directory contains a subdirectory **RCS** with an RCS file **io.c**. The each of the following commands checks in a new revision.

>   ci io.c;   ci RCS/io.c;
>   ci io.c RCS/io.c;
>   ci RCS/io.c io.c;

FILE MODES

An RCS file created by **ci** inherits the read and execute permissions from the working file. If the RCS file exists already, **ci** preserves its read and execute permissions. **ci** always turns off all write permissions of RCS files.

FILES

Several temporary files may be created in the directory containing the working file, and also in the temporary directory (see **TMPDIR** under **ENVIRONMENT**). A semaphore file or files are created in the directory containing the RCS file. With a nonempty suffix, the semaphore names begin with the first character of the suffix; therefore, do not specify a suffix whose first character could be that of a working filename. With an empty suffix, the semaphore names end with _ so working filenames should not end in _.

ci never changes an RCS or working file. Normally, **ci** unlinks the file and creates a new one; but instead of breaking a chain of one or more symbolic links to an RCS file, it unlinks the destination file instead. Therefore, **ci** breaks any hard or symbolic links to any working file it changes; and hard links to RCS files are ineffective, but symbolic links to RCS files are preserved.

The effective user must be able to search and write the directory containing the RCS file. Normally, the real user must be able to read the RCS and working files and to search and write the directory containing the working file; however, some older hosts cannot easily switch between real and effective users, so on these hosts the effective user is used for all accesses. The effective user is the same as the real user unless your copies of **ci** and **co** have setuid privileges. As described in the next section, these privileges yield extra security if the effective user owns all RCS files and directories, and if only the effective user can write RCS directories.

Users can control access to RCS files by setting the permissions of the directory containing the files; only users with write access to the directory can use RCS commands to change its RCS files. For example, in hosts that allow a user to belong to several groups, one can make a group's RCS directories writable to that group only. This approach suffices for informal projects, but it means that any group member can arbitrarily change the group's RCS files, and can even remove them entirely. Hence more formal projects sometimes distinguish between an RCS administrator, who can change the RCS files at will, and other project members, who can check in new revisions but cannot otherwise change the RCS files.

SETUID USE

To prevent anybody but their RCS administrator from deleting revisions, a set of users can employ setuid privileges as follows.

- Check that the host supports RCS setuid use. Consult a trustworthy expert if there are any doubts. It is best if the **seteuid**() system call works as described in Posix 1003.1a Draft 5, because RCS can switch back and forth easily between real and effective users, even if the real user is **root**. If not, the second best is if the **setuid**() system call supports saved setuid (the {_POSIX_SAVED_IDS} behavior of Posix 1003.1-1990); this fails only if the real user is **root**. If RCS detects any failure in setuid, it quits immediately.

- Choose a user _A_ to serve as RCS administrator for the set of users. Only _A_ will be able to invoke the **rcs** command on the users' RCS files. _A_ should not be **root** or any other user with special powers. Mutually suspicious sets of users should use different administrators.

- Choose a path name _B_ that will be a directory of files to be executed by the users.

- Have _A_ set up _B_ to contain copies of **ci** and **co** that are setuid to _A_ by copying the commands from their standard installation directory _D_ as follows:

    mkdir _B_
    cp _D_/c[io] _B_
    chmod go−w,u+s _B_/c[io]

- Have each user prepend _B_ to their path as follows:

    PATH=_B_**:$PATH; export PATH** # ordinary shell
    set path=(_B_ **$path)** # C shell

- Have *A* create each RCS directory *R* with write access only to *A* as follows:

  mkdir *R*
  chmod go–w *R*

- If you want to let only certain users read the RCS files, put the users into a group *G*, and have *A* further protect the RCS directory as follows:

  chgrp *G* *R*
  chmod g–w,o–rwx *R*

- Have *A* copy old RCS files (if any) into *R*, to ensure that *A* owns them.

- An RCS file's access list limits who can check in and lock revisions. The default access list is empty, which grants checkin access to anyone who can read the RCS file. If you want limit checkin access, have *A* invoke **rcs –a** on the file; see **rcs**(1). In particular, **rcs –e –a***A* limits access to just *A*.

- Have *A* initialize any new RCS files with **rcs –i** before initial checkin, adding the –a option if you want to limit checkin access.

- Give setuid privileges only to **ci, co,** and **rcsclean**; do not give them to **rcs** or to any other command.

- Do not use other setuid commands to invoke RCS commands; setuid is trickier than you think!

ENVIRONMENT

RCSINIT

    options prepended to the argument list, separated by spaces. A backslash escapes spaces within an option. The **RCSINIT** options are prepended to the argument lists of most RCS commands. Useful **RCSINIT** options include –**q**, –**V**, and –**x**.

TMPDIR

    Name of the temporary directory. If not set, the environment variables **TMP** and **TEMP** are inspected instead and the first value found is taken; if none of them are set, a host-dependent default is used, typically **/tmp**.

DIAGNOSTICS

    For each revision, **ci** prints the RCS file, the working file, and the number of both the deposited and the preceding revision. The exit status is zero if and only if all operations were successful.

IDENTIFICATION

    Author: Walter F. Tichy.
    Revision Number: 5.9; Release Date: 1991/10/07.
    Copyright © 1982, 1988, 1989 by Walter F. Tichy.
    Copyright © 1990, 1991 by Paul Eggert.

SEE ALSO

    co(1), ident(1), make(1), rcs(1), rcsclean(1), rcsdiff(1), rcsintro(1), rcsmerge(1), rlog(1), rcsfile(5)
    Walter F. Tichy, RCS—A System for Version Control, *Software—Practice & Experience* **15**, 7 (July 1985), 637-654.

1

NAME

cksum – display file checksums and block counts

SYNOPSIS

cksum [−o [1 | 2]] [*file ...*]

DESCRIPTION

The cksum utility writes to the standard output three whitespace separated fields for each input file. These fields are a checksum CRC, the total number of octets in the file and the file name. If no file name is specified, the standard input is used and no file name is written.

The options are as follows:

−o   Use historic algorithms instead of the (superior) default one.

Algorithm 1 is the algorithm used by historic BSD systems as the sum(1) algorithm and by historic AT&T System V UNIX systems as the sum algorithm when using the −r option. This is a 16-bit checksum, with a right rotation before each addition; overflow is discarded.

Algorithm 2 is the algorithm used by historic AT&T System V UNIX systems as the default sum algorithm. This is a 32-bit checksum, and is defined as follows:

$$s = \text{sum of all bytes;}$$
$$r = s \ \% \ 2\char`^16 + (s \ \% \ 2\char`^32) \ / \ 2\char`^16;$$
$$\text{cksum} = (r \ \% \ 2\char`^16) + r \ / \ 2\char`^16;$$

Both algorithm 1 and 2 write to the standard output the same fields as the default algorithm except that the size of the file in bytes is replaced with the size of the file in blocks. For historic reasons, the block size is 1024 for algorithm 1 and 512 for algorithm 2. Partial blocks are rounded up.

The default CRC used is based on the polynomial used for CRC error checking in the networking standard ISO 8802-3: 1989 The CRC checksum encoding is defined by the generating polynomial:

$$G(x) = x\char`^32 + x\char`^26 + x\char`^23 + x\char`^22 + x\char`^16 + x\char`^12 +$$
$$x\char`^11 + x\char`^10 + x\char`^8 + x\char`^7 + x\char`^5 + x\char`^4 + x\char`^2 + x + 1$$

Mathematically, the CRC value corresponding to a given file is defined by the following procedure:

The *n* bits to be evaluated are considered to be the coefficients of a mod 2 polynomial M(x) of degree *n*−1. These *n* bits are the bits from the file, with the most significant bit being the most significant bit of the first octet of the file and the last bit being the least significant bit of the last octet, padded with zero bits (if necessary) to achieve an integral number of octets, followed by one or more octets representing the length of the file as a binary value, least significant octet first. The smallest number of octets capable of representing this integer are used.

M(x) is multiplied by x^32 (i.e., shifted left 32 bits) and divided by G(x) using mod 2 division, producing a remainder R(x) of degree <= 31.

The coefficients of R(x) are considered to be a 32-bit sequence.

The bit sequence is complemented and the result is the CRC.

The cksum utility exits 0 on success, and >0 if an error occurs.

SEE ALSO

The default calculation is identical to that given in pseudo-code in the following ACM article.

1

Dilip V. Sarwate, "Computation of Cyclic Redundancy Checks Via Table Lookup", *Communications of the ACM*, August 1988.

STANDARDS

The cksum utility is expected to be POSIX 1003.2 compatible.

HISTORY

The cksum utility appears in 4.4BSD.

1

NAME

cmp – compare two files

SYNOPSIS

cmp [−l | −s] *file1 file2* [*skip1* [*skip2*]]

DESCRIPTION

The cmp utility compares two files of any type and writes the results to the standard output. By default, cmp is silent if the files are the same; if they differ, the byte and line number at which the first difference occurred is reported.

Bytes and lines are numbered beginning with one.

The following options are available:

−l   Print the byte number (decimal) and the differing byte values (octal) for each difference.

−s   Print nothing for differing files; return exit status only.

The optional arguments *skip1* and *skip2* are the byte offsets from the beginning of *file1* and *file2*, respectively, where the comparison will begin. The offset is decimal by default, but may be expressed as an hexadecimal or octal value by preceding it with a leading ''0x'' or ''0''.

The cmp utility exits with one of the following values:

0   The files are identical.

1   The files are different; this includes the case where one file is identical to the first part of the other. In the latter case, if the −s option has not been specified, cmp writes to standard output that EOF was reached in the shorter file (before any differences were found).

>1   An error occurred.

SEE ALSO

diff(1), diff3(1)

STANDARDS

The cmp utility is expected to be IEEE Std1003.2 (''POSIX'') compatible.

1

NAME

co – check out RCS revisions

SYNOPSIS

co [*options*] *file* ...

DESCRIPTION

co retrieves a revision from each RCS file and stores it into the corresponding working file.

Pathnames matching an RCS suffix denote RCS files; all others denote working files. Names are paired as explained in **ci**(1).

Revisions of an RCS file may be checked out locked or unlocked. Locking a revision prevents overlapping updates. A revision checked out for reading or processing (e.g., compiling) need not be locked. A revision checked out for editing and later checkin must normally be locked. Checkout with locking fails if the revision to be checked out is currently locked by another user. (A lock may be broken with **rcs**(1).) Checkout with locking also requires the caller to be on the access list of the RCS file, unless he is the owner of the file or the superuser, or the access list is empty. Checkout without locking is not subject to accesslist restrictions, and is not affected by the presence of locks.

A revision is selected by options for revision or branch number, checkin date/time, author, or state. When the selection options are applied in combination, **co** retrieves the latest revision that satisfies all of them. If none of the selection options is specified, **co** retrieves the latest revision on the default branch (normally the trunk, see the **–b** option of **rcs**(1)). A revision or branch number may be attached to any of the options **–f**, **–I**, **–l**, **–M**, **–p**, **–q**, **–r**, or **–u**. The options **–d** (date), **–s** (state), and **–w** (author) retrieve from a single branch, the *selected* branch, which is either specified by one of **–f**, ..., **–u**, or the default branch.

A **co** command applied to an RCS file with no revisions creates a zero-length working file. **co** always performs keyword substitution (see below).

OPTIONS

–r[*rev*]   retrieves the latest revision whose number is less than or equal to *rev*. If *rev* indicates a branch rather than a revision, the latest revision on that branch is retrieved. If *rev* is omitted, the latest revision on the default branch (see the **–b** option of **rcs**(1)) is retrieved. If *rev* is **$**, **co** determines the revision number from keyword values in the working file. Otherwise, a revision is composed of one or more numeric or symbolic fields separated by periods. The numeric equivalent of a symbolic field is specified with the **–n** option of the commands **ci**(1) and **rcs**(1).

–l[*rev*]   same as **–r**, except that it also locks the retrieved revision for the caller.

–u[*rev*]   same as **–r**, except that it unlocks the retrieved revision if it was locked by the caller. If *rev* is omitted, **–u** retrieves the revision locked by the caller, if there is one; otherwise, it retrieves the latest revision on the default branch.

–f[*rev*]   forces the overwriting of the working file; useful in connection with **–q**. See also FILE MODES below.

–kkv   Generate keyword strings using the default form, e.g. **$Revision: 5.7 $** for the **Revision** keyword. A locker's name is inserted in the value of the **Header, Id,** and **Locker** keyword strings only as a file is being locked, i.e. by **ci –l** and **co –l**. This is the default.

–kkvl   Like **–kkv**, except that a locker's name is always inserted if the given revision is currently locked.

–kk   Generate only keyword names in keyword strings; omit their values. See KEYWORD SUBSTITUTION below. For example, for the **Revision** keyword, generate the string **$Revision$** instead of **$Revision: 5.7 $**. This option is useful to ignore differences due to keyword substitution when comparing different revisions of a file.

–ko   Generate the old keyword string, present in the working file just before it was checked in. For example, for the **Revision** keyword, generate the string **$Revision: 1.1 $** instead of **$Revision: 5.7 $** if that is how the string appeared when the file was checked in. This can be useful for binary file formats that cannot tolerate any changes to substrings that happen to take the form of keyword strings.

−kv   Generate only keyword values for keyword strings. For example, for the **Revision** keyword, generate the string **5.7** instead of **$Revision: 5.7 $**. This can help generate files in programming languages where it is hard to strip keyword delimiters like **$Revision: $** from a string. However, further keyword substitution cannot be performed once the keyword names are removed, so this option should be used with care. Because of this danger of losing keywords, this option cannot be combined with −l, and the owner write permission of the working file is turned off; to edit the file later, check it out again without −**kv**.

−p[*rev*]   prints the retrieved revision on the standard output rather than storing it in the working file. This option is useful when **co** is part of a pipe.

−q[*rev*]   quiet mode; diagnostics are not printed.

−I[*rev*]   interactive mode; the user is prompted and questioned even if the standard input is not a terminal.

−d*date*   retrieves the latest revision on the selected branch whose checkin date/time is less than or equal to *date*. The date and time may be given in free format. The time zone **LT** stands for local time; other common time zone names are understood. For example, the following *date*s are equivalent if local time is January 11, 1990, 8pm Pacific Standard Time, eight hours west of Coordinated Universal Time (UTC):

> **8:00 pm lt**
> **4:00 AM, Jan. 12, 1990**   note: default is UTC
> **1990/01/12 04:00:00**   RCS date format
> **Thu Jan 11 20:00:00 1990 LT**   output of **ctime**(3) + **LT**
> **Thu Jan 11 20:00:00 PST 1990**   output of **date**(1)
> **Fri Jan 12 04:00:00 GMT 1990**
> **Thu, 11 Jan 1990 20:00:00 −0800**
> **Fri-JST, 1990, 1pm Jan 12**
> **12-January-1990, 04:00-WET**

Most fields in the date and time may be defaulted. The default time zone is UTC. The other defaults are determined in the order year, month, day, hour, minute, and second (most to least significant). At least one of these fields must be provided. For omitted fields that are of higher significance than the highest provided field, the time zone's current values are assumed. For all other omitted fields, the lowest possible values are assumed. For example, the date **20, 10:30** defaults to 10:30:00 UTC of the 20th of the UTC time zone's current month and year. The date/time must be quoted if it contains spaces.

−M[*rev*]

Set the modification time on the new working file to be the date of the retrieved revision. Use this option with care; it can confuse **make**(1).

−s*state*   retrieves the latest revision on the selected branch whose state is set to *state*.

−w[*login*]

retrieves the latest revision on the selected branch which was checked in by the user with login name *login*. If the argument *login* is omitted, the caller's login is assumed.

−j*joinlist*

generates a new revision which is the join of the revisions on *joinlist*. This option is largely obsoleted by **rcsmerge**(1) but is retained for backwards compatibility.

The *joinlist* is a comma-separated list of pairs of the form *rev2* :*rev3*, where *rev2* and *rev3* are (symbolic or numeric) revision numbers. For the initial such pair, *rev1* denotes the revision selected by the above options −**f**, ..., −**w**. For all other pairs, *rev1* denotes the revision generated by the previous pair. (Thus, the output of one join becomes the input to the next.)

1

For each pair, **co** joins revisions *rev1* and *rev3* with respect to *rev2*. This means that all changes that transform *rev2* into *rev1* are applied to a copy of *rev3*. This is particularly useful if *rev1* and *rev3* are the ends of two branches that have *rev2* as a common ancestor. If *rev1* <*rev2*<*rev3* on the same branch, joining generates a new revision which is like *rev3*, but with all changes that lead from *rev1* to *rev2* undone. If changes from *rev2* to *rev1* overlap with changes from *rev2* to *rev3*, **co** reports overlaps as described in **merge**(1).

For the initial pair, *rev2* may be omitted. The default is the common ancestor. If any of the arguments indicate branches, the latest revisions on those branches are assumed. The options –**l** and –**u** lock or unlock *rev1*.

–**V***n*   Emulate RCS version *n*, where *n* may be **3**, **4**, or **5**. This may be useful when interchanging RCS files with others who are running older versions of RCS. To see which version of RCS your correspondents are running, have them invoke **rlog** on an RCS file; if none of the first few lines of output contain the string **branch:** it is version 3; if the dates' years have just two digits, it is version 4; otherwise, it is version 5. An RCS file generated while emulating version 3 will lose its default branch. An RCS revision generated while emulating version 4 or earlier will have a timestamp that is off by up to 13 hours. A revision extracted while emulating version 4 or earlier will contain dates of the form *yy/mm/dd* instead of *yyyy/mm/dd* and may also contain different white space in the substitution for **Log**.

–**x***suffixes*
        Use *suffixes* to characterize RCS files. See **ci**(1) for details.

KEYWORD SUBSTITUTION
Strings of the form $*keyword*$ and $*keyword*:...$ embedded in the text are replaced with strings of the form $*keyword*:*value*$ where *keyword* and *value* are pairs listed below. Keywords may be embedded in literal strings or comments to identify a revision.

Initially, the user enters strings of the form $*keyword*$. On checkout, **co** replaces these strings with strings of the form $*keyword*:*value*$. If a revision containing strings of the latter form is checked back in, the value fields will be replaced during the next checkout. Thus, the keyword values are automatically updated on checkout. This automatic substitution can be modified by the –**k** options.

Keywords and their corresponding values:

$Author$
        The login name of the user who checked in the revision.

$Date$ The date and time (UTC) the revision was checked in.

$Header$
        A standard header containing the full pathname of the RCS file, the revision number, the date (UTC), the author, the state, and the locker (if locked).

Id   Same as **$Header$**, except that the RCS filename is without a path.

$Locker$
        The login name of the user who locked the revision (empty if not locked).

Log   The log message supplied during checkin, preceded by a header containing the RCS filename, the revision number, the author, and the date (UTC). Existing log messages are *not* replaced. Instead, the new log message is inserted after **$Log:**...**$**. This is useful for accumulating a complete change log in a source file.

$RCSfile$
        The name of the RCS file without a path.

$Revision$
        The revision number assigned to the revision.

1

$Source$

The full pathname of the RCS file.

$State$ The state assigned to the revision with the −s option of **rcs**(1) or **ci**(1).

FILE MODES

The working file inherits the read and execute permissions from the RCS file. In addition, the owner write permission is turned on, unless −**kv** is set or the file is checked out unlocked and locking is set to strict (see **rcs**(1)).

If a file with the name of the working file exists already and has write permission, **co** aborts the checkout, asking beforehand if possible. If the existing working file is not writable or −**f** is given, the working file is deleted without asking.

FILES

co accesses files much as **ci**(1) does, except that it does not need to read the working file.

ENVIRONMENT

RCSINIT

options prepended to the argument list, separated by spaces. See **ci**(1) for details.

DIAGNOSTICS

The RCS pathname, the working pathname, and the revision number retrieved are written to the diagnostic output. The exit status is zero if and only if all operations were successful.

IDENTIFICATION

Author: Walter F. Tichy.
Revision Number: 5.7; Release Date: 1991/08/19.
Copyright © 1982, 1988, 1989 by Walter F. Tichy.
Copyright © 1990, 1991 by Paul Eggert.

SEE ALSO

ci(1), ctime(3), date(1), ident(1), make(1), rcs(1), rcsdiff(1), rcsintro(1), rcsmerge(1), rlog(1), rcsfile(5)
Walter F. Tichy, RCS—A System for Version Control, *Software—Practice & Experience* **15**, 7 (July 1985), 637-654.

LIMITS

Links to the RCS and working files are not preserved.

There is no way to selectively suppress the expansion of keywords, except by writing them differently. In nroff and troff, this is done by embedding the null-character **\&** into the keyword.

BUGS

The −**d** option sometimes gets confused, and accepts no date before 1970.

1

NAME

col – filter reverse line feeds from input

SYNOPSIS

col [–bfx] [–l *num*]

DESCRIPTION

Col filters out reverse (and half reverse) line feeds so that the output is in the correct order with only forward and half forward line feeds, and replaces white-space characters with tabs where possible. This can be useful in processing the output of nroff(1) and tbl(1).

Col reads from the standard input and writes to the standard output.

The options are as follows:

–b   Do not output any backspaces, printing only the last character written to each column position.

–f   Forward half line feeds are permitted (''fine'' mode). Normally characters printed on a half line boundary are printed on the following line.

–x   Output multiple spaces instead of tabs.

–l *num*   Buffer at least *num* lines in memory. By default, 128 lines are buffered.

The control sequences for carriage motion that col understands and their decimal values are listed in the following table:

ESC–7	reverse line feed (escape then 7)
ESC–8	half reverse line feed (escape then 8)
ESC–9	half forward line feed (escape then 9)
backspace	moves back one column (8); ignored in the first column
carriage return	(13)
newline	forward line feed (10); also does carriage return
shift in	shift to normal character set (15)
shift out	shift to alternate character set (14)
space	moves forward one column (32)
tab	moves forward to next tab stop (9)
vertical tab	reverse line feed (11)

All unrecognized control characters and escape sequences are discarded.

Col keeps track of the character set as characters are read and makes sure the character set is correct when they are output.

If the input attempts to back up to the last flushed line, col will display a warning message.

SEE ALSO

expand(1), nroff(1), tbl(1)

HISTORY

A col command appeared in Version 6 AT&T UNIX.

1

NAME

`colcrt` – filter nroff output for CRT previewing

SYNOPSIS

`colcrt` [–] [–2] [*file ...*]

DESCRIPTION

`Colcrt` provides virtual half-line and reverse line feed sequences for terminals without such capability, and on which overstriking is destructive. Half-line characters and underlining (changed to dashing '–') are placed on new lines in between the normal output lines.

Available options:

– Suppress all underlining. This option is especially useful for previewing *allboxed* tables from `tbl`(1).

–2 Causes all half-lines to be printed, effectively double spacing the output. Normally, a minimal space output format is used which will suppress empty lines. The program never suppresses two consecutive empty lines, however. The –2 option is useful for sending output to the line printer when the output contains superscripts and subscripts which would otherwise be invisible.

EXAMPLES

A typical use of `colcrt` would be

`tbl exum2.n | nroff –ms | colcrt – | more`

SEE ALSO

`nroff`(1), `troff`(1), `col`(1), `more`(1), `ul`(1)

BUGS

Should fold underlines onto blanks even with the ' – ' option so that a true underline character would show.

Can't back up more than 102 lines.

General overstriking is lost; as a special case ' | ' overstruck with '–' or underline becomes '+'.

Lines are trimmed to 132 characters.

Some provision should be made for processing superscripts and subscripts in documents which are already double-spaced.

HISTORY

The `colcrt` command appeared in 3.0BSD.

1

NAME
colrm – remove columns from a file

SYNOPSIS
colrm [*start* [*stop*]]

DESCRIPTION
Colrm removes selected columns from the lines of a file. A column is defined as a single character in a line. Input is read from the standard input. Output is written to the standard output.

If only the *start* column is specified, columns numbered less than the *start* column will be written. If both *start* and *stop* columns are specified, columns numbered less than the *start* column or greater than the *stop* column will be written. Column numbering starts with one, not zero.

Tab characters increment the column count to the next multiple of eight. Backspace characters decrement the column count by one.

SEE ALSO
awk(1), column(1), cut(1), paste(1)

HISTORY
The colrm command appeared in 3.0BSD.

NAME
>   column – columnate lists

SYNOPSIS
>   column [–tx] [–c *columns*] [–s *sep*] [*file* ...]

DESCRIPTION
>   The column utility formats its input into multiple columns. Rows are filled before columns. Input is taken
>   from *file* operands, or, by default, from the standard input. Empty lines are ignored.

>   The options are as follows:

>   –c   Output is formatted for a display *columns* wide.

>   –s   Specify a set of characters to be used to delimit columns for the –t option.

>   –t   Determine the number of columns the input contains and create a table. Columns are delimited with
>   whitespace, by default, or with the characters supplied using the –s option. Useful for pretty-
>   printing displays.

>   –x   Fill columns before filling rows.

>   Column exits 0 on success, >0 if an error occurred.

ENVIRONMENT
>   COLUMNS The environment variable COLUMNS is used to determine the size of the screen if no other infor-
>   mation is available.

EXAMPLES
>   (printf "PERM LINKS OWNER SIZE MONTH DAY HH:MM/YEAR NAME\n" ; \
>   ls -l | sed 1d) | column -t

SEE ALSO
>   colrm(1), ls(1), paste(1), sort(1)

HISTORY
>   The column command appeared in 4.3BSD–Reno.

1

NAME

comm – select or reject lines common to two files

SYNOPSIS

comm [–123] *file1 file2*

DESCRIPTION

The comm utility reads *file1* and *file2*, which should be sorted lexically, and produces three text columns as output: lines only in *file1*; lines only in *file2*; and lines in both files.

The filename ''-'' means the standard input.

The following options are available:

–1   Suppress printing of column 1.

–2   Suppress printing of column 2.

–3   Suppress printing of column 3.

Each column will have a number of tab characters prepended to it equal to the number of lower numbered columns that are being printed. For example, if column number two is being suppressed, lines printed in column number one will not have any tabs preceding them, and lines printed in column number three will have one.

Comm assumes that the files are lexically sorted; all characters participate in line comparisons.

Comm exits 0 on success, >0 if an error occurred.

SEE ALSO

cmp(1), diff(1), sort(1), uniq(1)

STANDARDS

The comm command is expected to be POSIX 1003.2 compatible.

1

NAME
compact, uncompact, ccat – compress and uncompress files, and cat them

SYNOPSIS
compact [−v] [name ...]
uncompact [−v] [name ...]
ccat [−v] [file ...]

DESCRIPTION
Compact compresses the named files using an adaptive Huffman code. If no file names are given, the standard input is compacted to the standard output. *Compact* operates as an on-line algorithm. Each time a byte is read, it is encoded immediately according to the current prefix code. This code is an optimal Huffman code for the set of frequencies seen so far. It is unnecessary to prepend a decoding tree to the compressed file since the encoder and the decoder start in the same state and stay synchronized. Furthermore, *compact* and *uncompact* can operate as filters. In particular,

> ... | compact | uncompact | ...

operates as a (very slow) no-op.

When an argument *file* is given, it is compacted and the resulting file is placed in *file.C; file* is unlinked. The first two bytes of the compacted file code the fact that the file is compacted. This code is used to prohibit recompaction.

The amount of compression to be expected depends on the type of file being compressed. Typical values of compression are: Text (38%), Pascal Source (43%), C Source (36%) and Binary (19%). These values are the percentages of file bytes reduced.

Uncompact restores the original file from a file compressed by *compact*. If no file names are given, the standard input is uncompacted to the standard output.

Ccat cats the original file from a file compressed by *compact,* without uncompressing the file (it is just a shell script which directs the uncompacted output to the standard output).

Compact, *uncompact*, and *ccat* normally do their work silently. If a −v flag is supplied, *compact* will report the compression percentage for each compacted file while *uncompact* and *ccat* will print out the name of each file as they're uncompacted.

RESTRICTION
The last segment of the filename must be short enough to allow space for the appended '.C'.

FILES
*.C   compacted file created by compact, removed by uncompact

SEE ALSO
Gallager, Robert G., 'Variations on a Theme of Huffman', *I.E.E.E. Transactions on Information Theory,* vol. IT-24, no. 6, November 1978, pp. 668 - 674.

AUTHOR
Colin L. Mc Master

1

NAME
compress, uncompress, zcat – compress and expand data

SYNOPSIS
compress [−cfv] [−b *bits*] [*file* ...]
uncompress [−cfv] [*file* ...]
zcat [*file* ...]

DESCRIPTION
Compress reduces the size of the named files using adaptive Lempel-Ziv coding. Each *file* is renamed to the same name plus the extension ".Z". As many of the modification time, access time, file flags, file mode, user ID, and group ID as allowed by permissions are retained in the new file. If compression would not reduce the size of a *file*, the file is ignored.

Uncompress restores the compressed files to their original form, renaming the files by deleting the ".Z" extension.

Zcat is an alias for "uncompress -c".

If renaming the files would cause files to be overwritten and the standard input device is a terminal, the user is prompted (on the standard error output) for confirmation. If prompting is not possible or confirmation is not received, the files are not overwritten.

If no files are specified, the standard input is compressed or uncompressed to the standard output. If either the input and output files are not regular files, the checks for reduction in size and file overwriting are not performed, the input file is not removed, and the attributes of the input file are not retained.

The options are as follows:

−b   Specify the *bits* code limit (see below).

−c   Compressed or uncompressed output is written to the standard output. No files are modified.

−f   Force compression of *file*, even if it is not actually reduced in size. Additionally, files are overwritten without prompting for confirmation.

−v   Print the percentage reduction of each file.

Compress uses a modified Lempel-Ziv algorithm. Common substrings in the file are first replaced by 9-bit codes 257 and up. When code 512 is reached, the algorithm switches to 10-bit codes and continues to use more bits until the limit specified by the −b flag is reached (the default is 16). *Bits* must be between 9 and 16.

After the *bits* limit is reached, compress periodically checks the compression ratio. If it is increasing, compress continues to use the existing code dictionary. However, if the compression ratio decreases, compress discards the table of substrings and rebuilds it from scratch. This allows the algorithm to adapt to the next "block" of the file.

The −b flag is omitted for *uncompress* since the *bits* parameter specified during compression is encoded within the output, along with a magic number to ensure that neither decompression of random data nor recompression of compressed data is attempted.

The amount of compression obtained depends on the size of the input, the number of *bits* per code, and the distribution of common substrings. Typically, text such as source code or English is reduced by 50–60%. Compression is generally much better than that achieved by Huffman coding (as used in the historical command pack), or adaptive Huffman coding (as used in the historical command compact), and takes less time to compute.

The **compress** utility exits 0 on success, and >0 if an error occurs.

SEE ALSO

Welch, Terry A., "A Technique for High Performance Data Compression", *IEEE Computer*, 17:6, pp. 8-19, June, 1984.

HISTORY

The **compress** command appeared in 4.3BSD.

1

NAME

cp – copy files

SYNOPSIS

cp [−R [−H | −L | −P]] [−fip] *source_file target_file*
cp [−R [−H | −L | −P]] [−fip] *source_file ... target_directory*

DESCRIPTION

In the first synopsis form, the **cp** utility copies the contents of the *source_file* to the *target_file*. In the second synopsis form, the contents of each named *source_file* is copied to the destination *target_directory*. The names of the files themselves are not changed. If **cp** detects an attempt to copy a file to itself, the copy will fail.

The following options are available:

−H   If the −R option is specified, symbolic links on the command line are followed. (Symbolic links encountered in the tree traversal are not followed.)

−L   If the −R option is specified, all symbolic links are followed.

−P   If the −R option is specified, no symbolic links are followed.

−R   If *source_file* designates a directory, **cp** copies the directory and the entire subtree connected at that point. This option also causes symbolic links to be copied, rather than indirected through, and for **cp** to create special files rather than copying them as normal files. Created directories have the same mode as the corresponding source directory, unmodified by the process' umask.

−f   For each existing destination pathname, remove it and create a new file, without prompting for confirmation regardless of its permissions. (The −i option is ignored if the −f option is specified.)

−i   Causes **cp** to write a prompt to the standard error output before copying a file that would overwrite an existing file. If the response from the standard input begins with the character 'y', the file copy is attempted.

−p   Causes **cp** to preserve in the copy as many of the modification time, access time, file flags, file mode, user ID, and group ID as allowed by permissions.

If the user ID and group ID cannot be preserved, no error message is displayed and the exit value is not altered.

If the source file has its set user ID bit on and the user ID cannot be preserved, the set user ID bit is not preserved in the copy's permissions. If the source file has its set group ID bit on and the group ID cannot be preserved, the set group ID bit is not preserved in the copy's permissions. If the source file has both its set user ID and set group ID bits on, and either the user ID or group ID cannot be preserved, neither the set user ID or set group ID bits are preserved in the copy's permissions.

For each destination file that already exists, its contents are overwritten if permissions allow, but its mode, user ID, and group ID are unchanged.

In the second synopsis form, *target_directory* must exist unless there is only one named *source_file* which is a directory and the −R flag is specified.

If the destination file does not exist, the mode of the source file is used as modified by the file mode creation mask (**umask**, see csh(1)). If the source file has its set user ID bit on, that bit is removed unless both the source file and the destination file are owned by the same user. If the source file has its set group ID bit on, that bit is removed unless both the source file and the destination file are in the same group and the user is a member of that group. If both the set user ID and set group ID bits are set, all of the above conditions must be fulfilled or both bits are removed.

Appropriate permissions are required for file creation or overwriting.

Symbolic links are always followed unless the −R flag is set, in which case symbolic links are not followed, by default. The −H or −L flags (in conjunction with the −R flag) cause symbolic links to be followed as described above. The −H, −L and −P options are ignored unless the −R option is specified. In addition, these options override each other and the command's actions are determined by the last one specified.

Cp exits 0 on success, >0 if an error occurred.

COMPATIBILITY

Historic versions of the cp utility had a −r option. This implementation supports that option, however, its use is strongly discouraged, as it does not correctly copy special files, symbolic links or fifo's.

SEE ALSO

mv(1), rcp(1), umask(2), fts(3), symlink(7)

HISTORY

The cp command is expected to be IEEE Std1003.2 ("POSIX") compatible.

1

NAME

cccp, cpp – the GNU C-compatible compiler preprocessor

SYNOPSIS

cccp   [–$] [–C] [–D*name*[=*definition*]] [–dD] [–dM] [–I *directory*] [–H] [–I–] [–imacros *file*]
       [–include *file*] [–lang–c] [–lang–c++] [–lang–objc] [–lang–objc++] [–lint] [–M] [–MD]
       [–MM] [–MMD] [–nostdinc] [–P] [–pedantic] [–pedantic–errors] [–trigraphs]
       [–U*name*] [–undef] [–Wtrigraphs] [–Wcomment] [–Wall] [–Wtraditional]
       [*infile*l–] [*outfile*l–]

DESCRIPTION

The C preprocessor is a *macro processor* that is used automatically by the C compiler to transform your program before actual compilation. It is called a macro processor because it allows you to define *macros*, which are brief abbreviations for longer constructs.

The C preprocessor provides four separate facilities that you can use as you see fit:

- Inclusion of header files. These are files of declarations that can be substituted into your program.

- Macro expansion. You can define *macros*, which are abbreviations for arbitrary fragments of C code, and then the C preprocessor will replace the macros with their definitions throughout the program.

- Conditional compilation. Using special preprocessor commands, you can include or exclude parts of the program according to various conditions.

- Line control. If you use a program to combine or rearrange source files into an intermediate file which is then compiled, you can use line control to inform the compiler of where each source line originally came from.

C preprocessors vary in some details. For a full explanation of the GNU C preprocessor, see the **info** file ' **cpp.info** ', or the manual *The C Preprocessor*. Both of these are built from the same documentation source file, ' **cpp.texinfo** '. The GNU C preprocessor provides a superset of the features of ANSI Standard C.

ANSI Standard C requires the rejection of many harmless constructs commonly used by today's C programs. Such incompatibility would be inconvenient for users, so the GNU C preprocessor is configured to accept these constructs by default. Strictly speaking, to get ANSI Standard C, you must use the options ' –trigraphs ', ' –undef ' and ' –pedantic ', but in practice the consequences of having strict ANSI Standard C make it undesirable to do this.

Most often when you use the C preprocessor you will not have to invoke it explicitly: the C compiler will do so automatically. However, the preprocessor is sometimes useful individually.

When you call the preprocessor individually, either name (**cpp** or **cccp**) will do—they are completely synonymous.

The C preprocessor expects two file names as arguments, *infile* and *outfile*. The preprocessor reads *infile* together with any other files it specifies with ' #include '. All the output generated by the combined input files is written in *outfile*.

Either *infile* or *outfile* may be ' – ', which as *infile* means to read from standard input and as *outfile* means to write to standard output. Also, if *outfile* or both file names are omitted, the standard output and standard input are used for the omitted file names.

1

OPTIONS

Here is a table of command options accepted by the C preprocessor. These options can also be given when compiling a C program; they are passed along automatically to the preprocessor when it is invoked by the compiler.

−P   Inhibit generation of ' **#** '-lines with line-number information in the output from the preprocessor. This might be useful when running the preprocessor on something that is not C code and will be sent to a program which might be confused by the ' **#** '-lines.

−C   Do not discard comments: pass them through to the output file. Comments appearing in arguments of a macro call will be copied to the output before the expansion of the macro call.

−trigraphs

Process ANSI standard trigraph sequences. These are three-character sequences, all starting with ' **??** ', that are defined by ANSI C to stand for single characters. For example, ' **??/** ' stands for '****', so ' '**??/n**' ' is a character constant for a newline. Strictly speaking, the GNU C preprocessor does not support all programs in ANSI Standard C unless ' **−trigraphs** ' is used, but if you ever notice the difference it will be with relief.

You don't want to know any more about trigraphs.

−pedantic

Issue warnings required by the ANSI C standard in certain cases such as when text other than a comment follows ' **#else** ' or ' **#endif** '.

−pedantic−errors

Like ' **−pedantic** ', except that errors are produced rather than warnings.

−Wtrigraphs

Warn if any trigraphs are encountered (assuming they are enabled).

−Wcomment

−Wcomments

Warn whenever a comment-start sequence ' **/*** ' appears in a comment. (Both forms have the same effect).

−Wall   Requests both ' **−Wtrigraphs** ' and ' **−Wcomment** ' (but not ' **−Wtraditional** ').

−Wtraditional

Warn about certain constructs that behave differently in traditional and ANSI C.

−I *directory*

Add the directory *directory* to the end of the list of directories to be searched for header files. This can be used to override a system header file, substituting your own version, since these directories are searched before the system header file directories. If you use more than one ' **−I** ' option, the directories are scanned in left-to-right order; the standard system directories come after.

−I−   Any directories specified with ' **−I** ' options before the ' **−I−** ' option are searched only for the case of ' **#include** *file*" '; they are not searched for ' **#include** *<file>* '.

If additional directories are specified with ' **−I** ' options after the ' **−I−** ', these directories are searched for all ' **#include** ' directives.

In addition, the ' **−I−** ' option inhibits the use of the current directory as the first search directory for ' **#include** *file*" '. Therefore, the current directory is searched only if it is requested explicitly with ' **−I.** '. Specifying both ' **−I−** ' and ' **−I.** ' allows you to control precisely which directories are searched before the current one and which are searched after.

1

−nostdinc
> Do not search the standard system directories for header files. Only the directories you have specified with ' −I ' options (and the current directory, if appropriate) are searched.

−D *name*
> Predefine *name* as a macro, with definition ' **1** '.

−D *name=definition*
> Predefine *name* as a macro, with definition *definition*. There are no restrictions on the contents of *definition*, but if you are invoking the preprocessor from a shell or shell-like program you may need to use the shell's quoting syntax to protect characters such as spaces that have a meaning in the shell syntax. If you use more than one ' −D ' for the same *name*, the rightmost definition takes effect.

−U *name*
> Do not predefine *name*. If both ' −U ' and ' −D ' are specified for one name, the ' −U ' beats the ' −D ' and the name is not predefined.

−undef Do not predefine any nonstandard macros.

−dM
> Instead of outputting the result of preprocessing, output a list of ' **#define** ' commands for all the macros defined during the execution of the preprocessor, including predefined macros. This gives you a way of finding out what is predefined in your version of the preprocessor; assuming you have no file ' **foo.h** ', the command

> touch foo.h; cpp −dM foo.h

> will show the values of any predefined macros.

−dD
> Like ' −dM ' except in two respects: it does *not* include the predefined macros, and it outputs *both* the ' **#define** ' commands and the result of preprocessing. Both kinds of output go to the standard output file.

−M
> Instead of outputting the result of preprocessing, output a rule suitable for **make** describing the dependencies of the main source file. The preprocessor outputs one **make** rule containing the object file name for that source file, a colon, and the names of all the included files. If there are many included files then the rule is split into several lines using ' '-newline.

> This feature is used in automatic updating of makefiles.

−MM
> Like ' −M ' but mention only the files included with ' **#include** "*file*" '. System header files included with ' **#include** <*file*> ' are omitted.

−MD
> Like ' −M ' but the dependency information is written to files with names made by replacing ' **.c** ' with ' **.d** ' at the end of the input file names. This is in addition to compiling the file as specified—' −MD ' does not inhibit ordinary compilation the way ' −M ' does.

> In Mach, you can use the utility **md** to merge the ' **.d** ' files into a single dependency file suitable for using with the ' **make** ' command.

−MMD Like ' −MD ' except mention only user header files, not system header files.

−H   Print the name of each header file used, in addition to other normal activities.

−imacros *file*
> Process *file* as input, discarding the resulting output, before processing the regular input file. Because the output generated from *file* is discarded, the only effect of ' −**imacros** *file* ' is to make the macros defined in *file* available for use in the main input. The preprocessor evaluates any ' −D ' and ' −U ' options on the command line before processing ' −**imacros** *file* ' .

–include *file*
>   Process *file* as input, and include all the resulting output, before processing the regular input file.

–lang-c

–lang-c++

–lang-objc

–lang-objc++
>   Specify the source language. ' **–lang-c++** ' makes the preprocessor handle C++ comment syntax, and includes extra default include directories for C++, and ' **–lang-objc** ' enables the Objective C ' **#import** ' directive. ' **–lang-c** ' explicitly turns off both of these extensions, and ' **–lang-objc++** ' enables both.

>   These options are generated by the compiler driver **gcc**, but not passed from the ' **gcc** ' command line.

–lint Look for commands to the program checker **lint** embedded in comments, and emit them preceded by ' **#pragma lint** '. For example, the comment ' **/* NOTREACHED */** ' becomes ' **#pragma lint** NOTREACHED '.

>   This option is available only when you call **cpp** directly; **gcc** will not pass it from its command line.

–$** Forbid the use of ' **$ ' in identifiers. This is required for ANSI conformance. **gcc** automatically supplies this option to the preprocessor if you specify ' **–ansi** ', but **gcc** doesn't recognize the ' **–$** ' option itself—to use it without the other effects of ' **–ansi** ', you must call the preprocessor directly.

SEE ALSO
>   ' **Cpp** ' entry in **info**; *The C Preprocessor*, Richard M. Stallman.
>   **gcc(1)**; ' **Gcc** ' entry in **info**; *Using and Porting GNU CC (for version 2.0)*, Richard M. Stallman.

COPYING

Copyright (c) 1991, 1992 Free Software Foundation, Inc.

Permission is granted to make and distribute verbatim copies of this manual provided the copyright notice and this permission notice are preserved on all copies.

Permission is granted to copy and distribute modified versions of this manual under the conditions for verbatim copying, provided that the entire resulting derived work is distributed under the terms of a permission notice identical to this one.

Permission is granted to copy and distribute translations of this manual into another language, under the above conditions for modified versions, except that this permission notice may be included in translations approved by the Free Software Foundation instead of in the original English.

1

NAME

crypt – encode/decode

SYNOPSIS

crypt [password]

DESCRIPTION

This interface is obsoleted by bdes(1).

Crypt reads from the standard input and writes on the standard output. The *password* is a key that selects a particular transformation. If no *password* is given, *crypt* demands a key from the terminal and turns off printing while the key is being typed in. *Crypt* encrypts and decrypts with the same key:

    crypt key <clear >cypher
    crypt key <cypher | pr

will print the clear.

Files encrypted by *crypt* are compatible with those treated by the editor *ed* in encryption mode.

The security of encrypted files depends on three factors: the fundamental method must be hard to solve; direct search of the key space must be infeasible; 'sneak paths' by which keys or cleartext can become visible must be minimized.

Crypt implements a one-rotor machine designed along the lines of the German Enigma, but with a 256-element rotor. Methods of attack on such machines are known, but not widely; moreover the amount of work required is likely to be large.

The transformation of a key into the internal settings of the machine is deliberately designed to be expensive, i.e. to take a substantial fraction of a second to compute. However, if keys are restricted to (say) three lower-case letters, then encrypted files can be read by expending only a substantial fraction of five minutes of machine time.

Since the key is an argument to the *crypt* command, it is potentially visible to users executing *ps*(1) or a derivative. To minimize this possibility, *crypt* takes care to destroy any record of the key immediately upon entry. No doubt the choice of keys and key security are the most vulnerable aspect of *crypt*.

FILES

/dev/tty for typed key

SEE ALSO

ed(1), crypt(3), makekey(8)

BUGS

There is no warranty of merchantability nor any warranty of fitness for a particular purpose nor any other warranty, either express or implied, as to the accuracy of the enclosed materials or as to their suitability for any particular purpose. Accordingly, Bell Telephone Laboratories assumes no responsibility for their use by the recipient. Further, Bell Laboratories assumes no obligation to furnish any assistance of any kind whatsoever, or to furnish any additional information or documentation.

1

NAME
     csh – a shell (command interpreter) with C-like syntax

SYNOPSIS
     csh [–bcefinstvVxX] [arg ...]
     csh [–l]

DESCRIPTION
     The **csh** is a command language interpreter incorporating a history mechanism (see **History**
     Substitutions), job control facilities (see **Jobs**), interactive file name and user name completion (see
     File Name Completion), and a C-like syntax. It is used both as an interactive login shell and a shell
     script command processor.

Argument list processing
     If the first argument (argument 0) to the shell is '', then this is a login shell. A login shell also can be
     specified by invoking the shell with the ' –l' flag as the only argument.

     The rest of the flag arguments are interpreted as follows:

     –b   This flag forces a "break" from option processing, causing any further shell arguments to be treated
             as non-option arguments. The remaining arguments will not be interpreted as shell options. This
             may be used to pass options to a shell script without confusion or possible subterfuge. The shell will
             not run a set-user ID script without this option.

     –c   Commands are read from the (single) following argument which must be present. Any remaining ar-
             guments are placed in *argv*.

     –e   The shell exits if any invoked command terminates abnormally or yields a non-zero exit status.

     –f   The shell will start faster, because it will neither search for nor execute commands from the file
             .cshrc in the invoker's home directory.

     –i   The shell is interactive and prompts for its top-level input, even if it appears not to be a terminal.
             Shells are interactive without this option if their inputs and outputs are terminals.

     –l   The shell is a login shell (only applicable if –l is the only flag specified).

     –n   Commands are parsed, but not executed. This aids in syntactic checking of shell scripts.

     –s   Command input is taken from the standard input.

     –t   A single line of input is read and executed. A '\' may be used to escape the newline at the end of
             this line and continue onto another line.

     –v   Causes the *verbose* variable to be set, with the effect that command input is echoed after history
             substitution.

     –x   Causes the *echo* variable to be set, so that commands are echoed immediately before execution.

     –V   Causes the *verbose* variable to be set even before .cshrc is executed.

     –X   Is to –x as –V is to –v.

     After processing of flag arguments, if arguments remain but none of the –c, –i, –s, or –t options were
     given, the first argument is taken as the name of a file of commands to be executed. The shell opens this file,
     and saves its name for possible resubstitution by '$0'. Since many systems use either the standard version 6
     or version 7 shells whose shell scripts are not compatible with this shell, the shell will execute such a 'stan-
     dard' shell if the first character of a script is not a '#', i.e., if the script does not start with a comment.

1

Remaining arguments initialize the variable `argv`.

An instance of **csh** begins by executing commands from the file `/etc/csh.cshrc` and, if this is a login shell, `/etc/csh.login`. It then executes commands from `.cshrc` in the *home* directory of the invoker, and, if this is a login shell, the file `.login` in the same location. It is typical for users on crt's to put the command "stty crt" in their `.login` file, and to also invoke `tset`(1) there.

In the normal case, the shell will begin reading commands from the terminal, prompting with '% '. Processing of arguments and the use of the shell to process files containing command scripts will be described later.

The shell repeatedly performs the following actions: a line of command input is read and broken into *words*. This sequence of words is placed on the command history list and parsed. Finally each command in the current line is executed.

When a login shell terminates it executes commands from the files `.logout` in the user's *home* directory and `/etc/csh.logout`.

Lexical structure

The shell splits input lines into words at blanks and tabs with the following exceptions. The characters '&' '|' ';' '<' '>' '(' ')' form separate words. If doubled in '&&', '||', '<<' or '>>' these pairs form single words. These parser metacharacters may be made part of other words, or prevented their special meaning, by preceding them with '\'. A newline preceded by a '\' is equivalent to a blank.

Strings enclosed in matched pairs of quotations, ' ', '`' or '"', form parts of a word; metacharacters in these strings, including blanks and tabs, do not form separate words. These quotations have semantics to be described later. Within pairs of '`' or '"' characters, a newline preceded by a '\' gives a true newline character.

When the shell's input is not a terminal, the character '#' introduces a comment that continues to the end of the input line. It is prevented this special meaning when preceded by '\' and in quotations using '`', '`', and '"'.

Commands

A simple command is a sequence of words, the first of which specifies the command to be executed. A simple command or a sequence of simple commands separated by '|' characters forms a pipeline. The output of each command in a pipeline is connected to the input of the next. Sequences of pipelines may be separated by ';', and are then executed sequentially. A sequence of pipelines may be executed without immediately waiting for it to terminate by following it with an '&'.

Any of the above may be placed in '(' ')' to form a simple command (that may be a component of a pipeline, etc.). It is also possible to separate pipelines with '||' or '&&' showing, as in the C language, that the second is to be executed only if the first fails or succeeds respectively. (See *Expressions*.)

Jobs

The shell associates a *job* with each pipeline. It keeps a table of current jobs, printed by the *jobs* command, and assigns them small integer numbers. When a job is started asynchronously with '&', the shell prints a line that looks like:

　　[1] 1234

showing that the job which was started asynchronously was job number 1 and had one (top-level) process, whose process id was 1234.

If you are running a job and wish to do something else you may hit the key `^Z` (control-Z) which sends a STOP signal to the current job. The shell will then normally show that the job has been 'Stopped', and print another prompt. You can then manipulate the state of this job, putting it in the *background* with the *bg* command, or run some other commands and eventually bring the job back into the foreground with the *foreground* command *fg*. A ^z takes effect immediately and is like an interrupt in that pending output and unread input are discarded when it is typed. There is another special key ^Y that does not generate a STOP signal until a program attempts to read(2) it. This request can usefully be typed ahead when you have prepared some commands for a job that you wish to stop after it has read them.

A job being run in the background will stop if it tries to read from the terminal. Background jobs are normally allowed to produce output, but this can be disabled by giving the command "stty tostop". If you set this tty option, then background jobs will stop when they try to produce output like they do when they try to read input.

There are several ways to refer to jobs in the shell. The character '%' introduces a job name. If you wish to refer to job number 1, you can name it as '%1'. Just naming a job brings it to the foreground; thus '%1' is a synonym for 'fg %1', bringing job number 1 back into the foreground. Similarly saying '%1 &' resumes job number 1 in the background. Jobs can also be named by prefixes of the string typed in to start them, if these prefixes are unambiguous, thus '%ex' would normally restart a suspended ex(1) job, if there were only one suspended job whose name began with the string 'ex'. It is also possible to say '%?string' which specifies a job whose text contains *string*, if there is only one such job.

The shell maintains a notion of the current and previous jobs. In output about jobs, the current job is marked with a '+' and the previous job with a '−'. The abbreviation '%+' refers to the current job and '%−' refers to the previous job. For close analogy with the syntax of the *history* mechanism (described below), '%%' is also a synonym for the current job.

The job control mechanism requires that the stty(1) option **new** be set. It is an artifact from a *new* implementation of the tty driver that allows generation of interrupt characters from the keyboard to tell jobs to stop. See stty(1) for details on setting options in the new tty driver.

Status reporting

This shell learns immediately whenever a process changes state. It normally informs you whenever a job becomes blocked so that no further progress is possible, but only just before it prints a prompt. This is done so that it does not otherwise disturb your work. If, however, you set the shell variable *notify*, the shell will notify you immediately of changes of status in background jobs. There is also a shell command *notify* that marks a single process so that its status changes will be immediately reported. By default *notify* marks the current process; simply say 'notify' after starting a background job to mark it.

When you try to leave the shell while jobs are stopped, you will be warned that 'You have stopped jobs.' You may use the *jobs* command to see what they are. If you do this or immediately try to exit again, the shell will not warn you a second time, and the suspended jobs will be terminated.

File Name Completion

When the file name completion feature is enabled by setting the shell variable *filec* (see **set**), **csh** will interactively complete file names and user names from unique prefixes, when they are input from the terminal followed by the escape character (the escape key, or control-[) For example, if the current directory looks like

```
DSC.OLD   bin        cmd       lib      xmpl.c
DSC.NEW   chaosnet   cmtest    mail     xmpl.o
bench     class      dev       mbox     xmpl.out
```

and the input is

```
% vi ch<escape>
```

1

csh will complete the prefix ''ch'' to the only matching file name ''chaosnet'', changing the input line to

%%   % vi chaosnet

However, given

%%   % vi D<escape>

csh will only expand the input to

%%   % vi DSC.

and will sound the terminal bell to indicate that the expansion is incomplete, since there are two file names matching the prefix ''D''.

If a partial file name is followed by the end-of-file character (usually control-D), then, instead of completing the name, csh will list all file names matching the prefix. For example, the input

%%   % vi D<control-D>

causes all files beginning with ''D'' to be listed:

DSC.NEW   DSC.OLD

while the input line remains unchanged.

The same system of escape and end-of-file can also be used to expand partial user names, if the word to be completed (or listed) begins with the character ''~''. For example, typing

%%   cd ~ro<escape>

may produce the expansion

%%   cd ~root

The use of the terminal bell to signal errors or multiple matches can be inhibited by setting the variable *nobeep*.

Normally, all files in the particular directory are candidates for name completion. Files with certain suffixes can be excluded from consideration by setting the variable *fignore* to the list of suffixes to be ignored. Thus, if *fignore* is set by the command

%%   % set fignore = (.o .out)

then typing

%%   % vi x<escape>

would result in the completion to

%%   % vi xmpl.c

ignoring the files "xmpl.o" and "xmpl.out". However, if the only completion possible requires not ignoring these suffixes, then they are not ignored. In addition, *fignore* does not affect the listing of file names by control-D. All files are listed regardless of their suffixes.

Substitutions

We now describe the various transformations the shell performs on the input in the order in which they occur.

History substitutions

History substitutions place words from previous command input as portions of new commands, making it easy to repeat commands, repeat arguments of a previous command in the current command, or fix spelling mistakes in the previous command with little typing and a high degree of confidence. History substitutions begin with the character '!' and may begin *anywhere* in the input stream (with the proviso that they do not nest.) This '!' may be preceded by a '\' to prevent its special meaning; for convenience, an '!' is passed unchanged when it is followed by a blank, tab, newline, '=' or '('. (History substitutions also occur when an input line begins with '↑'. This special abbreviation will be described later.) Any input line that contains history substitution is echoed on the terminal before it is executed as it could have been typed without history substitution.

Commands input from the terminal that consist of one or more words are saved on the history list. The history substitutions reintroduce sequences of words from these saved commands into the input stream. The size of the history list is controlled by the *history* variable; the previous command is always retained, regardless of the value of the history variable. Commands are numbered sequentially from 1.

For definiteness, consider the following output from the *history* command:

```
 9   write michael
10   ex write.c
11   cat oldwrite.c
12   diff *write.c
```

The commands are shown with their event numbers. It is not usually necessary to use event numbers, but the current event number can be made part of the *prompt* by placing an '!' in the prompt string.

With the current event 13 we can refer to previous events by event number '!11', relatively as in '!−2' (referring to the same event), by a prefix of a command word as in '!d' for event 12 or '!wri' for event 9, or by a string contained in a word in the command as in '!?mic?' also referring to event 9. These forms, without further change, simply reintroduce the words of the specified events, each separated by a single blank. As a special case, '!!' refers to the previous command; thus '!!' alone is a *redo*.

To select words from an event we can follow the event specification by a ':' and a designator for the desired words. The words of an input line are numbered from 0, the first (usually command) word being 0, the second word (first argument) being 1, etc. The basic word designators are:

0	first (command) word
n	*n*'th argument
↑	first argument, i.e., '1'
$	last argument
%	word matched by (immediately preceding) ?*s*? search
x−y	range of words
−y	abbreviates '0−*y*˘
*	abbreviates '↑−$', or nothing if only 1 word in event
x*	abbreviates '*x*−$˘
x−	like '*x**˘ but omitting word '$'

The ':' separating the event specification from the word designator can be omitted if the argument selector begins with a '↑', '$', '*' '−' or '%'. After the optional word designator can be placed a sequence of modifiers, each preceded by a ':'. The following modifiers are defined:

h	Remove a trailing pathname component, leaving the head.
r	Remove a trailing '.xxx' component, leaving the root name.
e	Remove all but the extension '.xxx' part.
s/*l*/*r*/	
	Substitute *l* for *r*
t	Remove all leading pathname components, leaving the tail.

       &   Repeat the previous substitution.

       g   Apply the change once on each word, prefixing the above, e.g., 'g&'.

       a   Apply the change as many times as possible on a single word, prefixing the above. It can be used together with 'g' to apply a substitution globally.

       p   Print the new command line but do not execute it.

       q   Quote the substituted words, preventing further substitutions.

       x   Like q, but break into words at blanks, tabs and newlines.

Unless preceded by a 'g' the change is applied only to the first modifiable word. With substitutions, it is an error for no word to be applicable.

The left hand side of substitutions are not regular expressions in the sense of the editors, but instead strings. Any character may be used as the delimiter in place of '/'; a '\' quotes the delimiter into the l and r strings. The character '&' in the right hand side is replaced by the text from the left. A '\' also quotes '&'. A null l ('//') uses the previous string either from an l or from a contextual scan string s in '!?s\?'. The trailing delimiter in the substitution may be omitted if a newline follows immediately as may the trailing '?' in a contextual scan.

A history reference may be given without an event specification, e.g., '!$'. Here, the reference is to the previous command unless a previous history reference occurred on the same line in which case this form repeats the previous reference. Thus '!?foo?↑ !$' gives the first and last arguments from the command matching '?foo?'.

A special abbreviation of a history reference occurs when the first non-blank character of an input line is a '↑'. This is equivalent to '!:s↑' providing a convenient shorthand for substitutions on the text of the previous line. Thus '↑lb↑lib' fixes the spelling of 'lib' in the previous command. Finally, a history substitution may be surrounded with '{' and '}' if necessary to insulate it from the characters that follow. Thus, after 'ls −ld ~paul' we might do '!{l}a' to do 'ls −ld ~paula', while '!la' would look for a command starting with 'la'.

Quotations with ´ and "

The quotation of strings by '´' and '""' can be used to prevent all or some of the remaining substitutions. Strings enclosed in '´' are prevented any further interpretation. Strings enclosed in '""' may be expanded as described below.

In both cases the resulting text becomes (all or part of) a single word; only in one special case (see *Command Substitution* below) does a '""' quoted string yield parts of more than one word; '´' quoted strings never do.

Alias substitution

The shell maintains a list of aliases that can be established, displayed and modified by the *alias* and *unalias* commands. After a command line is scanned, it is parsed into distinct commands and the first word of each command, left-to-right, is checked to see if it has an alias. If it does, then the text that is the alias for that command is reread with the history mechanism available as though that command were the previous input line. The resulting words replace the command and argument list. If no reference is made to the history list, then the argument list is left unchanged.

Thus if the alias for 'ls' is 'ls −l' the command 'ls /usr' would map to 'ls −l /usr', the argument list here being undisturbed. Similarly if the alias for 'lookup' was 'grep !↑ /etc/passwd' then 'lookup bill' would map to 'grep bill /etc/passwd'.

If an alias is found, the word transformation of the input text is performed and the aliasing process begins again on the reformed input line. Looping is prevented if the first word of the new text is the same as the old by flagging it to prevent further aliasing. Other loops are detected and cause an error.

Note that the mechanism allows aliases to introduce parser metasyntax. Thus, we can 'alias print ´pr \!* | lpr´' to make a command that *pr*'s its arguments to the line printer.

1

Variable substitution

The shell maintains a set of variables, each of which has as value a list of zero or more words. Some of these variables are set by the shell or referred to by it. For instance, the *argv* variable is an image of the shell's argument list, and words of this variable's value are referred to in special ways.

The values of variables may be displayed and changed by using the *set* and *unset* commands. Of the variables referred to by the shell a number are toggles; the shell does not care what their value is, only whether they are set or not. For instance, the *verbose* variable is a toggle that causes command input to be echoed. The setting of this variable results from the −v command line option.

Other operations treat variables numerically. The '@' command permits numeric calculations to be performed and the result assigned to a variable. Variable values are, however, always represented as (zero or more) strings. For the purposes of numeric operations, the null string is considered to be zero, and the second and additional words of multiword values are ignored.

After the input line is aliased and parsed, and before each command is executed, variable substitution is performed keyed by '$' characters. This expansion can be prevented by preceding the '$' with a '\' except within ""s where it *always* occurs, and within ''s where it *never* occurs. Strings quoted by '`' are interpreted later (see **Command substitution** below) so '$' substitution does not occur there until later, if at all. A '$' is passed unchanged if followed by a blank, tab, or end-of-line.

Input/output redirections are recognized before variable expansion, and are variable expanded separately. Otherwise, the command name and entire argument list are expanded together. It is thus possible for the first (command) word (to this point) to generate more than one word, the first of which becomes the command name, and the rest of which become arguments.

Unless enclosed in '"' or given the ':q' modifier the results of variable substitution may eventually be command and filename substituted. Within '"', a variable whose value consists of multiple words expands to a (portion of) a single word, with the words of the variables value separated by blanks. When the ':q' modifier is applied to a substitution the variable will expand to multiple words with each word separated by a blank and quoted to prevent later command or filename substitution.

The following metasequences are provided for introducing variable values into the shell input. Except as noted, it is an error to reference a variable that is not set.

$name
${name}

> Are replaced by the words of the value of variable *name*, each separated by a blank. Braces insulate *name* from following characters that would otherwise be part of it. Shell variables have names consisting of up to 20 letters and digits starting with a letter. The underscore character is considered a letter. If *name* is not a shell variable, but is set in the environment, then that value is returned (but : modifiers and the other forms given below are not available here).

$name[selector]
${name[selector] }

> May be used to select only some of the words from the value of *name*. The selector is subjected to '$' substitution and may consist of a single number or two numbers separated by a '−'. The first word of a variables value is numbered '1'. If the first number of a range is omitted it defaults to '1'. If the last number of a range is omitted it defaults to '$#name'. The selector '*' selects all words. It is not an error for a range to be empty if the second argument is omitted or in range.

1

$#name
${#name}
   Gives the number of words in the variable. This is useful for later use in a '$argv[selector]'.
$0 Substitutes the name of the file from which command input is being read. An error occurs if the name is not known.
$number
${number}
   Equivalent to '$argv[number]'.
$* Equivalent to '$argv[*]'. The modifiers ':e', ':h', ':t', ':r', ':q' and ':x' may be applied to the substitutions above as may ':gh', ':gt' and ':gr'. If braces '{' '}' appear in the command form then the modifiers must appear within the braces. The current implementation allows only one ':' modifier on each '$' expansion.

The following substitutions may not be modified with ':' modifiers.

$?name
${?name}
   Substitutes the string '1' if name is set, '0' if it is not.
$?0 Substitutes '1' if the current input filename is known, '0' if it is not.
$$ Substitute the (decimal) process number of the (parent) shell.
$! Substitute the (decimal) process number of the last background process started by this shell.
$< Substitutes a line from the standard input, with no further interpretation. It can be used to read from the keyboard in a shell script.

Command and filename substitution

The remaining substitutions, command and filename substitution, are applied selectively to the arguments of builtin commands. By selectively, we mean that portions of expressions which are not evaluated are not subjected to these expansions. For commands that are not internal to the shell, the command name is substituted separately from the argument list. This occurs very late, after input-output redirection is performed, and in a child of the main shell.

Command substitution

Command substitution is shown by a command enclosed in '`'. The output from such a command is normally broken into separate words at blanks, tabs and newlines, with null words being discarded; this text then replaces the original string. Within '""'s, only newlines force new words; blanks and tabs are preserved.

In any case, the single final newline does not force a new word. Note that it is thus possible for a command substitution to yield only part of a word, even if the command outputs a complete line.

Filename substitution

If a word contains any of the characters '*', '?', '[' or '{' or begins with the character '~', then that word is a candidate for filename substitution, also known as 'globbing'. This word is then regarded as a pattern, and replaced with an alphabetically sorted list of file names that match the pattern. In a list of words specifying filename substitution it is an error for no pattern to match an existing file name, but it is not required for each pattern to match. Only the metacharacters '*', '?' and '[' imply pattern matching, the characters '~' and '{' being more akin to abbreviations.

In matching filenames, the character '.' at the beginning of a filename or immediately following a '/', as well as the character '/' must be matched explicitly. The character '*' matches any string of characters, including the null string. The character '?' matches any single character. The sequence '[...]' matches any one of the characters enclosed. Within '[...]', a pair of characters separated by '−' matches any character lexically between the two (inclusive).

The character '~' at the beginning of a filename refers to home directories. Standing alone, i.e., '~' it expands to the invokers home directory as reflected in the value of the variable *home*. When followed by a name consisting of letters, digits and '−' characters, the shell searches for a user with that name and substitutes their home directory; thus '~ken' might expand to '/usr/ken' and '~ken/chmach' to '/usr/ken/chmach'. If the character '~' is followed by a character other than a letter or '/' or does not appear at the beginning of a word, it is left undisturbed.

The metanotation 'a{b,c,d}e' is a shorthand for 'abe ace ade'. Left to right order is preserved, with results of matches being sorted separately at a low level to preserve this order. This construct may be nested. Thus, '~source/s1/{oldls,ls}.c' expands to '/usr/source/s1/oldls.c /usr/source/s1/ls.c' without chance of error if the home directory for 'source' is '/usr/source'. Similarly '../{memo,*box}' might expand to '../memo ../box ../mbox'. (Note that 'memo' was not sorted with the results of the match to '*box'.) As a special case '{', '}' and '{}' are passed undisturbed.

Input/output

The standard input and the standard output of a command may be redirected with the following syntax:

< name Open file *name* (which is first variable, command and filename expanded) as the standard input.

<< word

Read the shell input up to a line that is identical to *word*. *Word* is not subjected to variable, filename or command substitution, and each input line is compared to *word* before any substitutions are done on the input line. Unless a quoting '\', '""', '' or '~' appears in *word*, variable and command substitution is performed on the intervening lines, allowing '\' to quote '$', '\' and '~'. Commands that are substituted have all blanks, tabs, and newlines preserved, except for the final newline which is dropped. The resultant text is placed in an anonymous temporary file that is given to the command as its standard input.

> name
>! name
>& name
>&! name

The file *name* is used as the standard output. If the file does not exist then it is created; if the file exists, it is truncated; its previous contents are lost.

If the variable *noclobber* is set, then the file must not exist or be a character special file (e.g., a terminal or '/dev/null') or an error results. This helps prevent accidental destruction of files. Here, the '!' forms can be used to suppress this check.

The forms involving '&' route the standard error output into the specified file as well as the standard output. *Name* is expanded in the same way as '<' input filenames are.

>> name
>>& name
>>! name
>>&! name

Uses file *name* as the standard output; like '>' but places output at the end of the file. If the variable *noclobber* is set, then it is an error for the file not to exist unless one of the '!' forms is given. Otherwise similar to '>'.

A command receives the environment in which the shell was invoked as modified by the input-output parameters and the presence of the command in a pipeline. Thus, unlike some previous shells, commands run from a file of shell commands have no access to the text of the commands by default; instead they receive the original standard input of the shell. The '<<' mechanism should be used to present inline data. This permits shell command scripts to function as components of pipelines and allows the shell to block read its input. Note that the default standard input for a command run detached is *not* modified to be the empty file

1

/dev/null; instead the standard input remains as the original standard input of the shell. If this is a terminal and if the process attempts to read from the terminal, then the process will block and the user will be notified (see Jobs above).

The standard error output may be directed through a pipe with the standard output. Simply use the form '|&' instead of just '|'.

Expressions

Several of the builtin commands (to be described later) take expressions, in which the operators are similar to those of C, with the same precedence. These expressions appear in the *@, exit, if,* and *while* commands. The following operators are available:

$$|| \ \&\& \ | \uparrow \ \& \ == \ != \ =\tilde{} \ !\tilde{} \ <= \ >= < \ >< \ << \ >> \ + - * \ / \ \% \ ! \ \tilde{} \ (\ )$$

Here the precedence increases to the right, '==' '!=' '=~' and '!~', '<=' '>=' '<' and '>', '<<' and '>>', '+' and '−', '*' '/' and '%' being, in groups, at the same level. The '==' '!=' '=~' and '!~' operators compare their arguments as strings; all others operate on numbers. The operators '=~' and '!~' are like '!=' and '==' except that the right hand side is a *pattern* (containing, e.g., '*'s, '?'s and instances of '[...]') against which the left hand operand is matched. This reduces the need for use of the *switch* statement in shell scripts when all that is really needed is pattern matching.

Strings that begin with '0' are considered octal numbers. Null or missing arguments are considered '0'. The result of all expressions are strings, which represent decimal numbers. It is important to note that no two components of an expression can appear in the same word; except when adjacent to components of expressions that are syntactically significant to the parser ('&' '|' '<' '>' '(' ')'), they should be surrounded by spaces.

Also available in expressions as primitive operands are command executions enclosed in '{' and '}' and file enquiries of the form −1 *name* where 1 is one of:

r	read access
w	write access
x	execute access
e	existence
o	ownership
z	zero size
f	plain file
d	directory

The specified name is command and filename expanded and then tested to see if it has the specified relationship to the real user. If the file does not exist or is inaccessible then all enquiries return false, i.e., '0'. Command executions succeed, returning true, i.e., '1', if the command exits with status 0, otherwise they fail, returning false, i.e., '0'. If more detailed status information is required then the command should be executed outside an expression and the variable *status* examined.

Control flow

The shell contains several commands that can be used to regulate the flow of control in command files (shell scripts) and (in limited but useful ways) from terminal input. These commands all operate by forcing the shell to reread or skip in its input and, because of the implementation, restrict the placement of some of the commands.

The **foreach, switch,** and **while** statements, as well as the **if-then-else** form of the **if** statement require that the major keywords appear in a single simple command on an input line as shown below.

If the shell's input is not seekable, the shell buffers up input whenever a loop is being read and performs seeks in this internal buffer to accomplish the rereading implied by the loop. (To the extent that this allows, backward goto's will succeed on non-seekable inputs.)

1

Builtin commands

Builtin commands are executed within the shell. If a builtin command occurs as any component of a pipeline except the last then it is executed in a subshell.

alias
alias *name*
alias *name wordlist*
>   The first form prints all aliases. The second form prints the alias for name. The final form assigns the specified *wordlist* as the alias of *name*; *wordlist* is command and filename substituted. *Name* is not allowed to be *alias* or *unalias*.

alloc Shows the amount of dynamic memory acquired, broken down into used and free memory. With an argument shows the number of free and used blocks in each size category. The categories start at size 8 and double at each step. This command's output may vary across system types, since systems other than the VAX may use a different memory allocator.

bg
bg *%job* ...
>   Puts the current or specified jobs into the background, continuing them if they were stopped.

break Causes execution to resume after the **end** of the nearest enclosing **foreach** or **while**. The remaining commands on the current line are executed. Multi-level breaks are thus possible by writing them all on one line.

breaksw
>   Causes a break from a **switch**, resuming after the **endsw**.

case *label*:
>   A label in a **switch** statement as discussed below.

cd
cd *name*
chdir
chdir *name*
>   Change the shell's working directory to directory *name*. If no argument is given then change to the home directory of the user. If *name* is not found as a subdirectory of the current directory (and does not begin with '/', './' or '../'), then each component of the variable **cdpath** is checked to see if it has a subdirectory *name*. Finally, if all else fails but *name* is a shell variable whose value begins with '/', then this is tried to see if it is a directory.

continue
>   Continue execution of the nearest enclosing **while** or **foreach**. The rest of the commands on the current line are executed.

default:
>   Labels the default case in a **switch** statement. The default should come after all **case** labels.

dirs Prints the directory stack; the top of the stack is at the left, the first directory in the stack being the current directory.

echo *wordlist*
echo **-n** *wordlist*
>   The specified words are written to the shell's standard output, separated by spaces, and terminated with a newline unless the **-n** option is specified.

1

else
end
endif
endsw See the description of the **foreach, if, switch,** and **while** statements below.

eval *arg ...*
> (As in sh(1).) The arguments are read as input to the shell and the resulting command(s) executed in the context of the current shell. This is usually used to execute commands generated as the result of command or variable substitution, since parsing occurs before these substitutions. See tset(1) for an example of using **eval.**

exec *command*
> The specified command is executed in place of the current shell.

exit
exit *(expr)*
> The shell exits either with the value of the **status** variable (first form) or with the value of the specified **expr** (second form).

fg
fg %*job ...*
> Brings the current or specified jobs into the foreground, continuing them if they were stopped.

foreach *name (wordlist)*
...
end   The variable **name** is successively set to each member of **wordlist** and the sequence of commands between this command and the matching **end** are executed. (Both **foreach** and **end** must appear alone on separate lines.) The builtin command **continue** may be used to continue the loop prematurely and the builtin command **break** to terminate it prematurely. When this command is read from the terminal, the loop is read once prompting with '?' before any statements in the loop are executed. If you make a mistake typing in a loop at the terminal you can rub it out.

glob *wordlist*
> Like **echo** but no '\' escapes are recognized and words are delimited by null characters in the output. Useful for programs that wish to use the shell to filename expand a list of words.

goto *word*
> The specified **word** is filename and command expanded to yield a string of the form 'label'. The shell rewinds its input as much as possible and searches for a line of the form 'label:' possibly preceded by blanks or tabs. Execution continues after the specified line.

hashstat
> Print a statistics line showing how effective the internal hash table has been at locating commands (and avoiding **exec**'s). An **exec** is attempted for each component of the *path* where the hash function indicates a possible hit, and in each component that does not begin with a '/'.

history
history *n*
history −**r** *n*
history −**h** *n*
> Displays the history event list; if *n* is given only the *n* most recent events are printed. The −**r** option reverses the order of printout to be most recent first instead of oldest first. The −**h** option causes the history list to be printed without leading numbers. This format produces files suitable for sourcing using the −h option to **source.**

if (*expr*) command
> If the specified expression evaluates true, then the single *command* with arguments is exe-
> cuted. Variable substitution on *command* happens early, at the same time it does for the
> rest of the **if** command. *Command* must be a simple command, not a pipeline, a command
> list, or a parenthesized command list. Input/output redirection occurs even if *expr* is false,
> i.e., when command is **not** executed (this is a bug).

if (*expr*) **then**
...
else if (*expr2*) **then**
...
else
...
endif If the specified *expr* is true then the commands up to the first **else** are executed; other-
> wise if *expr2* is true then the commands up to the second **else** are executed, etc. Any
> number of **else-if** pairs are possible; only one **endif** is needed. The **else** part is like-
> wise optional. (The words **else** and **endif** must appear at the beginning of input lines;
> the **if** must appear alone on its input line or after an **else**.)

jobs
jobs **−l**
> Lists the active jobs; the **−l** option lists process id's in addition to the normal information.

kill %*job*
kill *pid*
kill **−sig** *pid* ...
kill **−l**
> Sends either the TERM (terminate) signal or the specified signal to the specified jobs or
> processes. Signals are either given by number or by names (as given in
> /usr/include/signal.h, stripped of the prefix "SIG"). The signal names are listed
> by "kill −l". There is no default, just saying 'kill' does not send a signal to the current job.
> If the signal being sent is TERM (terminate) or HUP (hangup), then the job or process will
> be sent a CONT (continue) signal as well.

limit
limit *resource*
limit *resource maximum-use*
limit **−h**
limit **−h** *resource*
limit **−h** *resource maximum-use*
> Limits the consumption by the current process and each process it creates to not individually
> exceed *maximum-use* on the specified *resource*. If no *maximum-use* is given, then
> the current limit is printed; if no *resource* is given, then all limitations are given. If the
> **−h** flag is given, the hard limits are used instead of the current limits. The hard limits im-
> pose a ceiling on the values of the current limits. Only the super-user may raise the hard
> limits, but a user may lower or raise the current limits within the legal range.

> Resources controllable currently include *cputime* (the maximum number of cpu-seconds
> to be used by each process), *filesize* (the largest single file that can be created),
> *datasize* (the maximum growth of the data+stack region via sbrk(2) beyond the end of
> the program text), *stacksize* (the maximum size of the automatically-extended stack re-
> gion), and *coredumpsize* (the size of the largest core dump that will be created). (.bp

> The *maximum-use* may be given as a (floating point or integer) number followed by a
> scale factor. For all limits other than *cputime* the default scale is 'k' or 'kilobytes' (1024
> bytes); a scale factor of 'm' or 'megabytes' may also be used. For *cputime* the default

scale is 'seconds'; a scale factor of 'm' for minutes or 'h' for hours, or a time of the form 'mm:ss' giving minutes and seconds also may be used.

For both *resource* names and scale factors, unambiguous prefixes of the names suffice.

login   Terminate a login shell, replacing it with an instance of `/bin/login`. This is one way to log off, included for compatibility with `sh(1)`.

logout
Terminate a login shell. Especially useful if **ignoreeof** is set.

nice
nice *+number*
nice *command*
nice *+number command*
The first form sets the scheduling priority for this shell to 4. The second form sets the priority to the given *number*. The final two forms run command at priority 4 and *number* respectively. The greater the number, the less cpu the process will get. The super-user may specify negative priority by using 'nice −number ...'. *Command* is always executed in a sub-shell, and the restrictions placed on commands in simple **if** statements apply.

nohup
nohup *command*
The first form can be used in shell scripts to cause hangups to be ignored for the remainder of the script. The second form causes the specified command to be run with hangups ignored. All processes detached with '&' are effectively **nohup**´ed.

notify
notify *%job ...*
Causes the shell to notify the user asynchronously when the status of the current or specified jobs change; normally notification is presented before a prompt. This is automatic if the shell variable **notify** is set.

onintr
onintr −
onintr *label*
Control the action of the shell on interrupts. The first form restores the default action of the shell on interrupts which is to terminate shell scripts or to return to the terminal command input level. The second form 'onintr −' causes all interrupts to be ignored. The final form causes the shell to execute a 'goto label' when an interrupt is received or a child process terminates because it was interrupted.

In any case, if the shell is running detached and interrupts are being ignored, all forms of **onintr** have no meaning and interrupts continue to be ignored by the shell and all invoked commands. Finally **onintr** statements are ignored in the system startup files where interrupts are disabled (/etc/csh.cshrc, /etc/csh.login).

popd
popd *+n*
Pops the directory stack, returning to the new top directory. With an argument `+ n´ discards the *n*´th entry in the stack. The members of the directory stack are numbered from the top starting at 0.

1

pushd
pushd *name*
pushd *n*
> With no arguments, **pushd** exchanges the top two elements of the directory stack. Given a *name* argument, **pushd** changes to the new directory (ala **cd**) and pushes the old current working directory (as in **csw**) onto the directory stack. With a numeric argument, **pushd** rotates the *n*´th argument of the directory stack around to be the top element and changes to it. The members of the directory stack are numbered from the top starting at 0.

rehash
> Causes the internal hash table of the contents of the directories in the **path** variable to be recomputed. This is needed if new commands are added to directories in the **path** while you are logged in. This should only be necessary if you add commands to one of your own directories, or if a systems programmer changes the contents of a system directory.

repeat *count command*
> The specified *command* which is subject to the same restrictions as the *command* in the one line **if** statement above, is executed *count* times. I/O redirections occur exactly once, even if *count* is 0.

set
set *name*
set *name*=word
set *name[index]*=word
set *name*=(wordlist)
> The first form of the command shows the value of all shell variables. Variables that have other than a single word as their value print as a parenthesized word list. The second form sets *name* to the null string. The third form sets *name* to the single *word*. The fourth form sets the *index*'th component of *name* to *word*; this component must already exist. The final form sets *name* to the list of words in *wordlist*. The value is always command and filename expanded.
>
> These arguments may be repeated to set multiple values in a single set command. Note however, that variable expansion happens for all arguments before any setting occurs.

setenv
setenv *name*
setenv *name value*
> The first form lists all current environment variables. It is equivalent to printenv(1). The last form sets the value of environment variable *name* to be *value*, a single string. The second form sets *name* to an empty string. The most commonly used environment variables USER, TERM, and PATH are automatically imported to and exported from the **csh** variables *user*, *term*, and *path*; there is no need to use **setenv** for these.

shift
shift *variable*
> The members of **argv** are shifted to the left, discarding **argv**[1]. It is an error for **argv** not to be set or to have less than one word as value. The second form performs the same function on the specified variable.

source *name*
source –**h** *name*
> The shell reads commands from *name*. **Source** commands may be nested; if they are nested too deeply the shell may run out of file descriptors. An error in a **source** at any level terminates all nested **source** commands. Normally input during **source** commands is not

placed on the history list; the −h option causes the commands to be placed on the history list without being executed.

stop
stop *%job ...*
> Stops the current or specified jobs that are executing in the background.

suspend
> Causes the shell to stop in its tracks, much as if it had been sent a stop signal with ^z. This is most often used to stop shells started by su(1).

switch *(string)*
case *str1*:
> ...
> **breaksw**
> ...
default:
> ...
> **breaksw**
endsw Each case label is successively matched against the specified *string* which is first command and filename expanded. The file metacharacters '*', '?' and '[...]' may be used in the case labels, which are variable expanded. If none of the labels match before the 'default' label is found, then the execution begins after the default label. Each case label and the default label must appear at the beginning of a line. The command **breaksw** causes execution to continue after the **endsw**. Otherwise control may fall through case labels and the default label as in C. If no label matches and there is no default, execution continues after the **endsw**.

time
time *command*
> With no argument, a summary of time used by this shell and its children is printed. If arguments are given the specified simple command is timed and a time summary as described under the **time** variable is printed. If necessary, an extra shell is created to print the time statistic when the command completes.

umask
umask *value*
> The file creation mask is displayed (first form) or set to the specified value (second form). The mask is given in octal. Common values for the mask are 002 giving all access to the group and read and execute access to others or 022 giving all access except write access for users in the group or others.

unalias *pattern*
> All aliases whose names match the specified pattern are discarded. Thus all aliases are removed by 'unalias *'. It is not an error for nothing to be **unaliased**.

unhash
> Use of the internal hash table to speed location of executed programs is disabled.

unlimit
unlimit *resource*
unlimit −h
unlimit −h *resource*
> Removes the limitation on *resource*. If no *resource* is specified, then all *resource* limitations are removed. If −h is given, the corresponding hard limits are removed. Only the super-user may do this.

unset *pattern*
>All variables whose names match the specified pattern are removed. Thus all variables are removed by 'unset *'; this has noticeably distasteful side-effects. It is not an error for nothing to be **unset**.

unsetenv *pattern*
>Removes all variables whose name match the specified pattern from the environment. See also the **setenv** command above and printenv(1).

wait   Wait for all background jobs. If the shell is interactive, then an interrupt can disrupt the wait. After the interrupt, the shell prints names and job numbers of all jobs known to be outstanding.

which *command*
>Displays the resolved command that will be executed by the shell.

while *(expr)*
...
end   While the specified expression evaluates non-zero, the commands between the **while** and the matching **end** are evaluated. **Break** and **continue** may be used to terminate or continue the loop prematurely. (The **while** and **end** must appear alone on their input lines.) Prompting occurs here the first time through the loop as for the **foreach** statement if the input is a terminal.

%_job_   Brings the specified job into the foreground.

%_job_ **&**
>Continues the specified job in the background.

@
@_name_= expr
@_name[index]_= expr
>The first form prints the values of all the shell variables. The second form sets the specified *name* to the value of *expr*. If the expression contains '<', '>', '&' or '|' then at least this part of the expression must be placed within '(' ')'. The third form assigns the value of *expr* to the *index*'th argument of *name*. Both *name* and its *index*'th component must already exist.

The operators '*=', '+=', etc are available as in C. The space separating the name from the assignment operator is optional. Spaces are, however, mandatory in separating components of *expr* which would otherwise be single words.

Special postfix '++' and '--' operators increment and decrement *name* respectively, i.e., '@ i++'.

Pre-defined and environment variables
The following variables have special meaning to the shell. Of these, *argv, cwd, home, path, prompt, shell* and *status* are always set by the shell. Except for *cwd* and *status*, this setting occurs only at initialization; these variables will not then be modified unless done explicitly by the user.

The shell copies the environment variable USER into the variable *user*, TERM into *term*, and HOME into *home*, and copies these back into the environment whenever the normal shell variables are reset. The environment variable PATH is likewise handled; it is not necessary to worry about its setting other than in the file *.cshrc* as inferior **csh** processes will import the definition of *path* from the environment, and re-export it if you then change it.

1

argv   Set to the arguments to the shell, it is from this variable that positional parameters are substituted, i.e., '$1' is replaced by '$argv[1]', etc.

cdpath   Gives a list of alternate directories searched to find subdirectories in *chdir* commands.

cwd   The full pathname of the current directory.

echo   Set when the −x command line option is given. Causes each command and its arguments to be echoed just before it is executed. For non-builtin commands all expansions occur before echoing. Builtin commands are echoed before command and filename substitution, since these substitutions are then done selectively.

filec   Enable file name completion.

histchars Can be given a string value to change the characters used in history substitution. The first character of its value is used as the history substitution character, replacing the default character '!'. The second character of its value replaces the character '↑' in quick substitutions.

histfile   Can be set to the pathname where history is going to be saved/restored.

history   Can be given a numeric value to control the size of the history list. Any command that has been referenced in this many events will not be discarded. Too large values of *history* may run the shell out of memory. The last executed command is always saved on the history list.

home   The home directory of the invoker, initialized from the environment. The filename expansion of '~' refers to this variable.

ignoreeof If set the shell ignores end-of-file from input devices which are terminals. This prevents shells from accidentally being killed by control-D's.

mail   The files where the shell checks for mail. This checking is done after each command completion that will result in a prompt, if a specified interval has elapsed. The shell says 'You have new mail.' if the file exists with an access time not greater than its modify time.

               If the first word of the value of *mail* is numeric it specifies a different mail checking interval, in seconds, than the default, which is 10 minutes.

               If multiple mail files are specified, then the shell says 'New mail in *name*' when there is mail in the file *name*.

noclobber As described in the section on input/output, restrictions are placed on output redirection to insure that files are not accidentally destroyed, and that '>>' redirections refer to existing files.

noglob   If set, filename expansion is inhibited. This inhibition is most useful in shell scripts that are not dealing with filenames, or after a list of filenames has been obtained and further expansions are not desirable.

nonomatch If set, it is not an error for a filename expansion to not match any existing files; instead the primitive pattern is returned. It is still an error for the primitive pattern to be malformed, i.e., 'echo [' still gives an error.

notify   If set, the shell notifies asynchronously of job completions; the default is to present job completions just before printing a prompt.

path   Each word of the path variable specifies a directory in which commands are to be sought for execution. A null word specifies the current directory. If there is no *path* variable then only full path names will execute. The usual search path is '.', '/bin' and '/usr/bin', but this may vary from system to system. For the super-user the default search path is '/etc', '/bin' and '/usr/bin'. A shell that is given neither the −c nor the −t option will normally hash the contents of the directories in the *path* variable after reading `.cshrc`, and each time the *path* variable is reset. If new commands are added to these directories while the shell is active, it may be necessary to do a **rehash** or the commands may not be found.

prompt   The string that is printed before each command is read from an interactive terminal input. If a '!' appears in the string it will be replaced by the current event number unless a preceding '\' is given. Default is '% ', or '# ' for the super user.

savehist   Is given a numeric value to control the number of entries of the history list that are saved in ˜/.history when the user logs out. Any command that has been referenced in this many events will be saved. During start up the shell sources ˜/.history into the history list enabling history to be saved across logins. Too large values of *savehist* will slow down the shell during start up. If *savehist* is just set, the shell will use the value of *history*.

shell   The file in which the shell resides. This variable is used in forking shells to interpret files that have execute bits set, but which are not executable by the system. (See the description of Non-builtin Command Execution below.) Initialized to the (system-dependent) home of the shell.

status   The status returned by the last command. If it terminated abnormally, then 0200 is added to the status. Builtin commands that fail return exit status '1', all other builtin commands set status to '0'.

time   Controls automatic timing of commands. If set, then any command that takes more than this many cpu seconds will cause a line giving user, system, and real times and a utilization percentage which is the ratio of user plus system times to real time to be printed when it terminates.

verbose   Set by the −v command line option, causes the words of each command to be printed after history substitution.

Non-builtin command execution

When a command to be executed is found to not be a builtin command the shell attempts to execute the command via execve(2). Each word in the variable *path* names a directory from which the shell will attempt to execute the command. If it is given neither a −c nor a −t option, the shell will hash the names in these directories into an internal table so that it will only try an **exec** in a directory if there is a possibility that the command resides there. This shortcut greatly speeds command location when many directories are present in the search path. If this mechanism has been turned off (via **unhash**), or if the shell was given a −c or −t argument, and in any case for each directory component of *path* that does not begin with a '/', the shell concatenates with the given command name to form a path name of a file which it then attempts to execute.

Parenthesized commands are always executed in a subshell. Thus

     `(cd; pwd); pwd`

prints the *home* directory; leaving you where you were (printing this after the home directory), while

     `cd; pwd`

leaves you in the *home* directory. Parenthesized commands are most often used to prevent **chdir** from affecting the current shell.

If the file has execute permissions but is not an executable binary to the system, then it is assumed to be a file containing shell commands and a new shell is spawned to read it.

If there is an **alias** for **shell** then the words of the alias will be prepended to the argument list to form the shell command. The first word of the **alias** should be the full path name of the shell (e.g., '$shell'). Note that this is a special, late occurring, case of **alias** substitution, and only allows words to be prepended to the argument list without change.

1

Signal handling

The shell normally ignores *quit* signals. Jobs running detached (either by **&** or the **bg** or **%... &** commands) are immune to signals generated from the keyboard, including hangups. Other signals have the values which the shell inherited from its parent. The shell's handling of interrupts and terminate signals in shell scripts can be controlled by **onintr**. Login shells catch the *terminate* signal; otherwise this signal is passed on to children from the state in the shell's parent. Interrupts are not allowed when a login shell is reading the file .logout.

AUTHOR

William Joy. Job control and directory stack features first implemented by J.E. Kulp of IIASA, Laxenburg, Austria, with different syntax than that used now. File name completion code written by Ken Greer, HP Labs. Eight-bit implementation Christos S. Zoulas, Cornell University.

FILES

~/.cshrc	Read at beginning of execution by each shell.
~/.login	Read by login shell, after '.cshrc' at login.
~/.logout	Read by login shell, at logout.
/bin/sh	Standard shell, for shell scripts not starting with a '#'.
/tmp/sh*	Temporary file for '<<'.
/etc/passwd	Source of home directories for '~name'.

LIMITATIONS

Word lengths – Words can be no longer than 1024 characters. The system limits argument lists to 10240 characters. The number of arguments to a command that involves filename expansion is limited to 1/6'th the number of characters allowed in an argument list. Command substitutions may substitute no more characters than are allowed in an argument list. To detect looping, the shell restricts the number of **alias** substitutions on a single line to 20.

SEE ALSO

sh(1), access(2), execve(2), fork(2), killpg(2), pipe(2), sigvec(2), umask(2), setrlimit(2), wait(2), tty(4), a.out(5), environ(7), introduction to the C shell

HISTORY

Csh appeared in 3BSD. It was a first implementation of a command language interpreter incorporating a history mechanism (see History Substitutions), job control facilities (see Jobs), interactive file name and user name completion (see File Name Completion), and a C-like syntax. There are now many shells that also have these mechanisms, plus a few more (and maybe some bugs too), which are available through the usenet.

BUGS

When a command is restarted from a stop, the shell prints the directory it started in if this is different from the current directory; this can be misleading (i.e., wrong) as the job may have changed directories internally.

Shell builtin functions are not stoppable/restartable. Command sequences of the form 'a ; b ; c' are also not handled gracefully when stopping is attempted. If you suspend 'b', the shell will immediately execute 'c'. This is especially noticeable if this expansion results from an *alias*. It suffices to place the sequence of commands in ()'s to force it to a subshell, i.e., '(a ; b ; c)'.

Control over tty output after processes are started is primitive; perhaps this will inspire someone to work on a good virtual terminal interface. In a virtual terminal interface much more interesting things could be done with output control.

Alias substitution is most often used to clumsily simulate shell procedures; shell procedures should be provided instead of aliases.

Commands within loops, prompted for by '?', are not placed on the `history` list. Control structure should be parsed instead of being recognized as built-in commands. This would allow control commands to be placed anywhere, to be combined with 'l', and to be used with '&' and ';' metasyntax.

It should be possible to use the ':' modifiers on the output of command substitutions.

The way the `filec` facility is implemented is ugly and expensive.

1

NAME

    ctags – create a tags file

SYNOPSIS

    ctags [**−BFadtuwvx**] [**−f** *tagsfile*] *name* . . .

DESCRIPTION

    Ctags makes a tags file for ex(1) from the specified C, Pascal, Fortran, YACC, lex, and lisp sources. A tags file gives the locations of specified objects in a group of files. Each line of the tags file contains the object name, the file in which it is defined, and a search pattern for the object definition, separated by whitespace. Using the *tags* file, ex(1) can quickly locate these object definitions. Depending upon the options provided to **ctags**, objects will consist of subroutines, typedefs, defines, structs, enums and unions.

    −B   use backward searching patterns (?...?).

    −F   use forward searching patterns (/.../) (the default).

    −a   append to *tags* file.

    −d   create tags for #defines that don't take arguments; #defines that take arguments are tagged automatically.

    −f   Places the tag descriptions in a file called *tagsfile*. The default behaviour is to place them in a file called *tags*.

    −t   create tags for typedefs, structs, unions, and enums.

    −u   update the specified files in the *tags* file, that is, all references to them are deleted, and the new values are appended to the file. (Beware: this option is implemented in a way which is rather slow; it is usually faster to simply rebuild the *tags* file.)

    −v   An index of the form expected by vgrind(1) is produced on the standard output. This listing contains the object name, file name, and page number (assuming 64 line pages). Since the output will be sorted into lexicographic order, it may be desired to run the output through sort(1). Sample use:

```
ctags −v files | sort −f > index
vgrind −x index
```

    −w   suppress warning diagnostics.

    −x   **ctags** produces a list of object names, the line number and file name on which each is defined, as well as the text of that line and prints this on the standard output. This is a simple index which can be printed out as an off-line readable function index.

    Files whose names end in **.c** or **.h** are assumed to be C source files and are searched for C style routine and macro definitions. Files whose names end in **.y** are assumed to be YACC source files. Files whose names end in **.l** are assumed to be lisp files if their first non-blank character is ';', '(', or '[', otherwise, they are treated as lex files. Other files are first examined to see if they contain any Pascal or Fortran routine definitions, and, if not, are searched for C style definitions.

    The tag main is treated specially in C programs. The tag formed is created by prepending *M* to the name of the file, with the trailing **.c** and any leading pathname components removed. This makes use of **ctags** practical in directories with more than one program.

    Yacc and lex files each have a special tag. *Yyparse* is the start of the second section of the yacc file, and *yylex* is the start of the second section of the lex file.

1

FILES
tags default output tags file

DIAGNOSTICS
Ctags exits with a value of 1 if an error occurred, 0 otherwise. Duplicate objects are not considered errors.

SEE ALSO
ex(1), vi(1)

BUGS
Recognition of **functions, subroutines** and **procedures** for FORTRAN and Pascal is done is a very simpleminded way. No attempt is made to deal with block structure; if you have two Pascal procedures in different blocks with the same name you lose. Ctags doesn't understand about Pascal types.

The method of deciding whether to look for C, Pascal or FORTRAN functions is a hack.

Ctags relies on the input being well formed, and any syntactical errors will completely confuse it. It also finds some legal syntax confusing; for example, since it doesn't understand #ifdef's (incidentally, that's a feature, not a bug), any code with unbalanced braces inside #ifdef's will cause it to become somewhat disoriented. In a similar fashion, multiple line changes within a definition will cause it to enter the last line of the object, rather than the first, as the searching pattern. The last line of multiple line typedef's will similarly be noted.

HISTORY
The ctags command appeared in 3.0BSD.

1

NAME
cut – select portions of each line of a file

SYNOPSIS
cut **–c** *list file* ...
cut **–f** *list* [**–d** *string*] [**–s**] *file* ...

DESCRIPTION
The **cut** utility selects portions of each line (as specified by *list*) from each *file* (or the standard input by default), and writes them to the standard output. The items specified by *list* can be in terms of column position or in terms of fields delimited by a special character. Column numbering starts from 1.

List is a comma or whitespace separated set of increasing numbers and/or number ranges. Number ranges consist of a number, a dash (–), and a second number and select the fields or columns from the first number to the second, inclusive. Numbers or number ranges may be preceded by a dash, which selects all fields or columns from 1 to the first number. Numbers or number ranges may be followed by a dash, which selects all fields or columns from the last number to the end of the line. Numbers and number ranges may be repeated, overlapping, and in any order. It is not an error to select fields or columns not present in the input line.

The options are as follows:

–c *list*   The *list* specifies character positions.

–d *string*
           Use the first character of *string* as the field delimiter character instead of the tab character.

–f *list*   The *list* specifies fields, delimited in the input by a single tab character. Output fields are separated by a single tab character.

–s   Suppresses lines with no field delimiter characters. Unless specified, lines with no delimiters are passed through unmodified.

Cut exits 0 on success, 1 if an error occurred.

SEE ALSO
paste(1)

STANDARDS
The **cut** utility is expected to conform to IEEE Std1003.2 (''POSIX'').

NAME

`date` – display or set date and time

SYNOPSIS

`date` [`−d` *dst*] [`−r` *seconds*] [`−t` *minutes_west*] [`−nu`] [`+format`]
    [[yy[mm[dd[hh]]]]mm[.ss]]

DESCRIPTION

`Date` displays the current date and time when invoked without arguments. Providing arguments will format the date and time in a user-defined way or set the date. Only the superuser may set the date.

The options are as follows:

`−d`   Set the kernel's value for daylight savings time. If *dst* is non-zero, future calls to `gettimeof-day(2)` will return a non-zero tz_dsttime.

`−n`   The utility `timed(8)` is used to synchronize the clocks on groups of machines. By default, if `timed` is running, `date` will set the time on all of the machines in the local group. The `−n` option stops `date` from setting the time for other than the current machine.

`−r`   Print out the date and time in *seconds* from the Epoch.

`−t`   Set the kernel's value for minutes west of GMT. *Minutes_west* specifies the number of minutes returned in tz_minuteswest by future calls to `gettimeofday(2)`.

`−u`   Display or set the date in UCT (universal) time.

An operand with a leading plus ("+") sign signals a user-defined format string which specifies the format in which to display the date and time. The format string may contain any of the conversion specifications described in the `strftime(3)` manual page, as well as any arbitrary text. The format string for the default display is:

    ``''%a %b %e %H:%M:%S %Z n''``.

If an operand does not have a leading plus sign, it is interpreted as a value for setting the system's notion of the current date and time. The canonical representation for setting the date and time is:

yy   Year in abbreviated form (.e.g 89 for 1989).
mm   Numeric month. A number from 1 to 12.
dd   Day, a number from 1 to 31.
hh   Hour, a number from 0 to 23.
mm   Minutes, a number from 0 to 59.
.ss   Seconds, a number from 0 to 61 (59 plus a a maximum of two leap seconds).

Everything but the minutes is optional.

Time changes for Daylight Saving and Standard time and leap seconds and years are handled automatically.

EXAMPLES

The command:

```
date ''+DATE: %m/%d/%y%nTIME: %H:%M:0n''
```

will display:

```
DATE: 11/21/87
TIME: 13:36:16
```

1

The command:

     date 8506131627

sets the date to "June 13, 1985, 4:27 PM".

The command:

     date 1432

sets the time to 2:32 PM, without modifying the date.

ENVIRONMENTAL VARIABLES
The following environment variables affect the execution of **date**:

TZ
  The timezone to use when displaying dates. See environ(7) for more information.

FILES
  /var/log/wtmp   A record of date resets and time changes.
  /var/log/messages A record of the user setting the time.

SEE ALSO
  gettimeofday(2), strftime(3), utmp(5), timed(8)

  R. Gusella, and S. Zatti, *TSP: The Time Synchronization Protocol for UNIX 4.3BSD.*

DIAGNOSTICS
  Exit status is 0 on success, 1 if unable to set the date, and 2 if able to set the local date, but unable to set it globally.

  Occasionally, when timed synchronizes the time on many hosts, the setting of a new time value may require more than a few seconds. On these occasions, **date** prints: Network time being set. The message Communication error with timed occurs when the communication between **date** and timed fails.

BUGS
  The system attempts to keep the date in a format closely compatible with VMS. VMS, however, uses local time (rather than GMT) and does not understand daylight-savings time. Thus, if you use both UNIX and VMS, VMS will be running on GMT.

STANDARDS
  The **date** command is expected to be compatible with IEEE Std1003.2 ("POSIX").

1

NAME

dc – desk calculator

SYNOPSIS

dc [file]

DESCRIPTION

Dc is an arbitrary precision arithmetic package. Ordinarily it operates on decimal integers, but one may specify an input base, output base, and a number of fractional digits to be maintained. The overall structure of dc is a stacking (reverse Polish) calculator. If an argument is given, input is taken from that file until its end, then from the standard input. The following constructions are recognized:

number

> The value of the number is pushed on the stack. A number is an unbroken string of the digits 0-9. It may be preceded by an underscore _ to input a negative number. Numbers may contain decimal points.

+ – / * % ^

> The top two values on the stack are added (+), subtracted (–), multiplied (*), divided (/), remaindered (%), or exponentiated (^). The two entries are popped off the stack; the result is pushed on the stack in their place. Any fractional part of an exponent is ignored.

s*x*

> The top of the stack is popped and stored into a register named *x*, where *x* may be any character. If the s is capitalized, *x* is treated as a stack and the value is pushed on it.

l*x*

> The value in register *x* is pushed on the stack. The register *x* is not altered. All registers start with zero value. If the *l* is capitalized, register *x* is treated as a stack and its top value is popped onto the main stack.

d

> The top value on the stack is duplicated.

p

> The top value on the stack is printed. The top value remains unchanged. *P* interprets the top of the stack as an ascii string, removes it, and prints it.

f

> All values on the stack and in registers are printed.

q

> exits the program. If executing a string, the recursion level is popped by two. If *q* is capitalized, the top value on the stack is popped and the string execution level is popped by that value.

x

> treats the top element of the stack as a character string and executes it as a string of dc commands.

X

> replaces the number on the top of the stack with its scale factor.

[...]

> puts the bracketed ascii string onto the top of the stack.

⟨ *x* ⟩ *x* = *x*

> The top two elements of the stack are popped and compared. Register *x* is executed if they obey the stated relation.

v

> replaces the top element on the stack by its square root. Any existing fractional part of the argument is taken into account, but otherwise the scale factor is ignored.

!

> interprets the rest of the line as a UNIX command.

c

> All values on the stack are popped.

1

i   The top value on the stack is popped and used as the number radix for further input. I pushes the input base on the top of the stack.

o   The top value on the stack is popped and used as the number radix for further output.

O   pushes the output base on the top of the stack.

k   the top of the stack is popped, and that value is used as a non-negative scale factor: the appropriate number of places are printed on output, and maintained during multiplication, division, and exponentiation. The interaction of scale factor, input base, and output base will be reasonable if all are changed together.

z   The stack level is pushed onto the stack.

Z   replaces the number on the top of the stack with its length.

?   A line of input is taken from the input source (usually the terminal) and executed.

; :   are used by bc for array operations.

An example which prints the first ten values of n!:

```
[la1+dsa*pla10>y]sy
0sa1
1yx
```

SEE ALSO
bc(1), which is a preprocessor for dc providing infix notation and a C-like syntax which implements functions and reasonable control structures for programs.

HISTORY
The dc command appeared in Version 6 AT&T UNIX.

DIAGNOSTICS
x is unimplemented
    where x is an octal number.

stack empty
    for not enough elements on the stack to do what was asked.

Out of space
    when the free list is exhausted (too many digits).

Out of headers
    for too many numbers being kept around.

Out of pushdown
    for too many items on the stack.

Nesting Depth
    for too many levels of nested execution.

1

NAME

dd – convert and copy a file

SYNOPSIS

dd [operands ...]

DESCRIPTION

The **dd** utility copies the standard input to the standard output. Input data is read and written in 512-byte blocks. If input reads are short, input from multiple reads are aggregated to form the output block. When finished, **dd** displays the number of complete and partial input and output blocks and truncated input records to the standard error output.

The following operands are available:

bs=n Set both input and output block size, superseding the **ibs** and **obs** operands. If no conversion values other than **noerror, notrunc** or **sync** are specified, then each input block is copied to the output as a single block without any aggregation of short blocks.

cbs=n Set the conversion record size to n bytes. The conversion record size is required by the record oriented conversion values.

count=n Copy only n input blocks.

files=n Copy n input files before terminating. This operand is only applicable when the input device is a tape.

ibs=n Set the input block size to n bytes instead of the default 512.

if=$file$ Read input from $file$ instead of the standard input.

obs=n Set the output block size to n bytes instead of the default 512.

of=$file$ Write output to $file$ instead of the standard output. Any regular output file is truncated unless the **notrunc** conversion value is specified. If an initial portion of the output file is skipped (see the **seek** operand) the output file is truncated at that point.

seek=n Seek n blocks from the beginning of the output before copying. On non-tape devices, a lseek(2) operation is used. Otherwise, existing blocks are read and the data discarded. If the user does not have read permission for the tape, it is positioned using the tape ioctl(2) function calls. If the seek operation is past the end of file, space from the current end of file to the specified offset is filled with blocks of NUL bytes.

skip=n Skip n blocks from the beginning of the input before copying. On input which supports seeks, a lseek(2) operation is used. Otherwise, input data is read and discarded. For pipes, the correct number of bytes is read. For all other devices, the correct number of blocks is read without distinguishing between a partial or complete block being read.

conv= value[, value ...]

Where **value** is one of the symbols from the following list.

1

`ascii, oldascii`
>   The same as the **unblock** value except that characters are translated from ECBDIC
>   to ASCII before the records are converted. (These values imply **unblock** if the
>   operand **cbs** is also specified.) There are two conversion maps for ASCII. The value
>   **ascii** specifies the recommended one which is compatible with System V. The
>   value **oldascii** specifies the one used in historic AT&T and pre-4.3BSD-reno sys-
>   tems.

`block`   Treats the input as a sequence of newline or end-of-file terminated variable length
>   records independent of input and output block boundaries. Any trailing newline
>   character is discarded. Each input record is converted to a fixed length output record
>   where the length is specified by the **cbs** operand. Input records shorter than the
>   conversion record size are padded with spaces. Input records longer than the conver-
>   sion record size are truncated. The number of truncated input records, if any, are re-
>   ported to the standard error output at the completion of the copy.

`ebcdic, ibm, oldebcdic, oldibm`
>   The same as the **block** value except that characters are translated from ASCII to
>   EBCDIC after the records are converted. (These values imply **block** if the operand
>   **cbs** is also specified.) There are four conversion maps for EBCDIC. The value
>   **ebcdic** specifies the recommended one which is compatible with AT&T System V
>   UNIX. The value **ibm** is a slightly different mapping, which is compatible with the
>   AT&T System V UNIX **ibm** value. The values **oldebcdic** and **oldibm** are maps
>   used in historic AT&T and pre-4.3BSD-reno systems.

`lcase`   Transform uppercase characters into lowercase characters.

`noerror` Do not stop processing on an input error. When an input error occurs, a diagnostic
>   message followed by the current input and output block counts will be written to the
>   standard error output in the same format as the standard completion message. If the
>   **sync** conversion is also specified, any missing input data will be replaced with NUL
>   bytes (or with spaces if a block oriented conversion value was specified) and pro-
>   cessed as a normal input buffer. If the **sync** conversion is not specified, the input
>   block is omitted from the output. On input files which are not tapes or pipes, the file
>   offset will be positioned past the block in which the error occurred using lseek(2).

`notrunc` Do not truncate the output file. This will preserve any blocks in the output file not
>   explicitly written by **dd**. The **notrunc** value is not supported for tapes.

`osync`   Pad the final output block to the full output block size. If the input file is not a multi-
>   ple of the output block size after conversion, this conversion forces the final output
>   block to be the same size as preceding blocks for use on devices that require regular-
>   ly sized blocks to be written. This option is incompatible with use of the **bs**=*n* block
>   size specification.

`swab`   Swap every pair of input bytes. If an input buffer has an odd number of bytes, the
>   last byte will be ignored during swapping.

`sync`   Pad every input block to the input buffer size. Spaces are used for pad bytes if a
>   block oriented conversion value is specified, otherwise NUL bytes are used.

`ucase`   Transform lowercase characters into uppercase characters.

`unblock` Treats the input as a sequence of fixed length records independent of input and output
>   block boundaries. The length of the input records is specified by the **cbs** operand.
>   Any trailing space characters are discarded and a newline character is appended.

Where sizes are specified, a decimal number of bytes is expected. If the number ends with a ''b'', ''k'', ''m'' or ''w'', the number is multiplied by 512, 1024 (1K), 1048576 (1M) or the number of bytes in an integer, respectively. Two or more numbers may be separated by an ''x'' to indicate a product.

When finished, dd displays the number of complete and partial input and output blocks, truncated input records and odd-length byte-swapping blocks to the standard error output. A partial input block is one where less than the input block size was read. A partial output block is one where less than the output block size was written. Partial output blocks to tape devices are considered fatal errors. Otherwise, the rest of the block will be written. Partial output blocks to character devices will produce a warning message. A truncated input block is one where a variable length record oriented conversion value was specified and the input line was too long to fit in the conversion record or was not newline terminated.

Normally, data resulting from input or conversion or both are aggregated into output blocks of the specified size. After the end of input is reached, any remaining output is written as a block. This means that the final output block may be shorter than the output block size.

If dd receives a SIGINFO (see the ''status'' argument for stty(1)) signal, the current input and output block counts will be written to the standard error output in the same format as the standard completion message. If dd receives a SIGINT signal, the current input and output block counts will be written to the standard error output in the same format as the standard completion message and dd will exit.

The dd utility exits 0 on success and >0 if an error occurred.

SEE ALSO

   cp(1), mt(1), tr(1)

STANDARDS

   The dd utility is expected to be a superset of the IEEE Std1003.2 (''POSIX'') standard. The **files** operand and the **ascii**, **ebcdic**, **ibm**, **oldascii**, **oldebcdic** and **oldibm** values are extensions to the POSIX standard.

NAME

deroff – remove nroff, troff, tbl and eqn constructs

SYNOPSIS

deroff [**–w**] *file ...*

DESCRIPTION

Deroff reads each file in sequence and removes all nroff(1) and troff(1) command lines, backslash constructions, macro definitions, eqn(1) constructs (between '.EQ' and '.EN' lines or between delimiters), and table descriptions and writes the remainder on the standard output. **Deroff** follows chains of included files ('.so' and '.nx' commands); if a file has already been included, a '.so' is ignored and a '.nx' terminates execution. If no input file is given, **deroff** reads from the standard input.

If the **–w** flag is given, the output is a word list, one 'word' (string of letters, digits, and apostrophes, beginning with a letter; apostrophes are removed) per line, and all other characters ignored. Otherwise, the output follows the original, with the deletions mentioned above.

SEE ALSO

troff(1), eqn(1), tbl(1)

HISTORY

Deroff appeared in Version 7 AT&T Unix.

BUGS

Deroff is not a complete troff(1) interpreter, so it can be confused by subtle constructs. Most errors result in too much rather than too little output.

1

NAME
df – display free disk space

SYNOPSIS
df [−in] [−t *type*] [*file* | *filesystem* ...]

DESCRIPTION
Df displays statistics about the amount of free disk space on the specified *filesystem* or on the filesystem of which *file* is a part. Values are displayed in 512-byte per block block counts. If neither a file or a filesystem operand is specified, statistics for all mounted filesystems are displayed (subject to the −t option below).

The following options are available:

−i   Include statistics on the number of free inodes.

−n   Print out the previously obtained statistics from the filesystems. This option should be used if it is possible that one or more filesystems are in a state such that they will not be able to provide statistics without a long delay. When this option is specified, df will not request new statistics from the filesystems, but will respond with the possibly stale statistics that were previously obtained.

−t   Only print out statistics for filesystems of the specified types. The recognized types are: ufs, nfs, mfs, lfs, msdos, fdesc, portal, kernfs, procfs, afs and isofs. along with the aggregates: all (the default), local (ufs, mfs, lfs, msdos, isofs), and misc (fdesc, portal, kernfs, procfs). The string ''no'' may be prepending to a type to get its complement (e.g. ''nonfs'' to get non-NFS filesystems). The first −t option overrides the default, additional such options will add to (or subtract from) the current set of types; e.g. either ''df -t ufs -t lfs'' or ''df -t local -t nomfs'' will display statistics for UFS and LFS filesystems.

ENVIRONMENTAL VARIABLES
BLOCKSIZE   If the environmental variable BLOCKSIZE is set, the block counts will be displayed in units of that size block.

BUGS
The −n and −t flags are ignored if a file or filesystem is specified.

SEE ALSO
quota(1), statfs(2), fstatfs(2), getfsstat(2), getmntinfo(3), fstab(5), mount(8), quot(8)

HISTORY
A df command appeared in Version 6 AT&T UNIX.

1

NAME
diction, explain – print wordy sentences; thesaurus for diction

SYNOPSIS
diction [–f *pfile*] [–ml] [–mm] [–n] *file* ...
explain

DESCRIPTION
Diction finds all sentences in a document that contain phrases from a data base of bad or wordy diction. Each phrase is bracketed with '[ ]'. Because **diction** runs deroff(1) before looking at the text, formatting header files should be included as part of the input.

–f *pfile*.
> Use *pfile* as a pattern file in addition to the default file.

–ml causes deroff(1) to skip lists, should be used if the document contains many lists of non-sentences.

–mm The default macro package, –ms, may be overridden with the flag –mm.

–n Suppress usage of default file.

Explain is an interactive thesaurus for the phrases found by diction.

SEE ALSO
deroff(1)

BUGS
Use of non-standard formatting macros may cause incorrect sentence breaks. In particular, **diction** doesn't grok –me.

HISTORY
The **diction** command appeared in 4BSD.

NAME
diff – differential file and directory comparator

SYNOPSIS
diff [–**cefhn**] [–**biwt**] *file1 file2*
diff [–**D***string*] [–**biw**] *file1 file2*
diff [–**l**] [–**r**] [–**s**] [–**cefhn**] [–**biwt**] [–**S***name*] *dir1 dir2*

DESCRIPTION
The **diff** utility compares the contents of *file1* and *file2* and writes to the standard output the list of changes necessary to convert one file into the other. No output is produced if the files are identical.

Output options (mutually exclusive):

–**c**   produces a diff with lines of context. The default is to present 3 lines of context and may be changed, e.g., to 10, by –**c10**. With –**c** the output format is modified slightly: the output beginning with identification of the files involved and their creation dates and then each change is separated by a line with a dozen *'s. The lines removed from *file1* are marked with '– '; those added to *file2* are marked '+ '. Lines which are changed from one file to the other are marked in both files with '! '. Changes which lie within <context> lines of each other are grouped together on output. (This is a change from the previous "diff -c" but the resulting output is usually much easier to interpret.)

–**e**   produces output in a form suitable as input for the editor utility, ed(1), which can then be used to convert file1 into file2.

Extra commands are added to the output when comparing directories with –**e**, so that the result is a sh(1) script for converting text files which are common to the two directories from their state in *dir1* to their state in *dir2*.

–**f**   identical output to that of the –**e** flag, but in reverse order. It cannot be digested by ed(1).

–**h**   Invokes an alternate algorithm which can handle files of very long lengths. There is a trade off. The algorithm can only deal with changes which are clearly delimited and brief. Long sections of changes and overlaps will confuse it.

–**n**   produces a script similar to that of –**e**, but in the opposite order and with a count of changed lines on each insert or delete command. This is the form used by rcsdiff(1).

–**D***string*
        creates a merged version of *file1* and *file2* on the standard output, with C preprocessor controls included so that a compilation of the result without defining *string* is equivalent to compiling *file1*, while defining *string* will yield *file2*.

Comparison options:

–**b**   causes trailing blanks (spaces and tabs) to be ignored, and other strings of blanks to compare equal.

–**i**   ignores the case of letters. E.g., "A" will compare equal to "a".

–**t**   will expand tabs in output lines. Normal or –**c** output adds character(s) to the front of each line which may screw up the indentation of the original source lines and make the output listing difficult to interpret. This option will preserve the original source's indentation.

–**w**   is similar to –**b** but causes whitespace (blanks and tabs) to be totally ignored. E.g., "if (a == b)" will compare equal to "if(a==b)".

Directory comparison options:

−l   long output format; each text file `diff`'d is piped through `pr`(1) to paginate it, other differences are remembered and summarized after all text file differences are reported.

−r   causes application of `diff` recursively to common subdirectories encountered.

−s   causes `diff` to report files which are the same, which are otherwise not mentioned.

−S*name*
      re-starts a directory `diff` in the middle beginning with file *name*.

If both arguments are directories, `diff` sorts the contents of the directories by name, and then runs the regular file `diff` algorithm, producing a change list, on text files which are different. Binary files which differ, common subdirectories, and files which appear in only one directory are described as such.

If only one of *file1* and *file2* is a directory, `diff` is applied to the non-directory file and the file contained in the directory file with a filename that is the same as the last component of the non-directory file.

If either *file1* or *file2* is '−', the standard input is used in its place.

Output Style

The default (without −e, −c, or −n options) output contains lines of these forms, where *XX*, *YY*, *ZZ*, *QQ* are line numbers respective of file order.

XXa*YY*	At (the end of) line *XX* of *file1*, append the contents of line *YY* of *file2* to make them equal.
XXa*YY*,*ZZ*	Same as above, but append the range of lines, *YY* through *ZZ* of *file2* to line *XX* of file1.
XXd*YY*	At line *XX* delete the line. The value *YY* tells to which line the change would bring *file1* in line with *file1*.
XX,*YY*d*ZZ*	Delete the range of lines *XX* through *YY* in *file1*.
XXc*YY*	Change the line *XX* in *file1* to the line *YY* in *file2*.
XX,*YY*c*ZZ*	Replace the range of specified lines with the line *ZZ*.
XX,*YY*c*ZZ*,*QQ*	Replace the range *XX*,YY from *file1* with the range *ZZ*,*QQ* from *file2*.

These lines resemble ed(1) subcommands to convert *file1* into *file2*. The line numbers before the action letters pertain to *file1*; those after pertain to *file2*. Thus, by exchanging **a** for **d** and reading the line in reverse order, one can also determine how to convert *file2* into *file1*. As in ed(1), identical pairs (where num1 = num2) are abbreviated as a single number.

ENVIRONMENT

TMPDIR If the environment variable `TMPDIR` exists, `diff` will use the directory specified by `TMPDIR` as the temporary directory.

FILES

```
/tmp/d?????
/usr/bin/diffh   Alternate algorithm version (used by option −h).
/usr/bin/diff    for directory diffs
/usr/bin/pr      used by the −l option.
```

SEE ALSO

cmp(1), cc(1), comm(1), ed(1), diff3(1)

DIAGNOSTICS

The diff utility exits with one of the following values:

0   No differences were found.
1   Differences were found.
>1   An error occurred.

BUGS

The −f and −e options do not provide special handling for lines on which the first and only character is ''.''. This can cause problems for ed(1).

When comparing directories with the −b, −w or −i options specified, diff first compares the files ala *cmp*, and then decides to run the diff algorithm if they are not equal. This may cause a small amount of spurious output if the files then turn out to be identical because the only differences are insignificant white space or case differences.

HISTORY

A diff command appeared in Version 6 AT&T UNIX.

1

NAME
diff3 – 3-way differential file comparison

SYNOPSIS
diff3 [−exEX3] *file1 file2 file3*

DESCRIPTION
The diff3 utility compares the contents of three different versions of a file, *file1*, *file2* and *file3*, writing the result to the standard output. The options describe different methods of merging and purging the separate versions into a new file. Diff3 is used by RCS(1) to merge specific versions or create new versions.

Options are:

−e   Produces output in a form suitable as an input script for the ed(1) utility. The script may then be used to merge differences common between all three files and differences specific to file1 and file3. In other words, the −e option ignores differences specific to file1 and file2, and those specific to file2 and file3. It is useful for backing out changes specific to file2 only.

−x   Produces an output script suitable for ed(1) with changes specific only to all three versions.

−3   Produces an output script suitable for ed(1) with changes specific only to file3.

−E, −X Similar to −e and −x, respectively, but treat overlapping changes (i.e., changes that would be noted with ==== in the normal listing) differently. The overlapping lines from both files will be inserted by the edit script, bracketed by "<<<<<<" and ">>>>>>" lines.

The −E option is used by RCS merge(1) to insure that overlapping changes in the merged files are preserved and brought to someone's attention.

For example, suppose lines 7-8 are changed in both file1 and file2. Applying the edit script generated by the command

```
diff3 -E file1 file2 file3
```

to file1 results in the file:

```
lines 1-6
of file1
<<<<<<< file1
lines 7-8
of file1
=======
lines 7-8
of file3
>>>>>>> file3
rest of file1
```

The default output of diff3 makes notation of the differences between all files, and those differences specific to each pair of files. The changes are described by the commands necessary for ed(1) to create the desired target from the different versions. See diff(1) for a description of the commands.

====   The lines beneath this notation are ranges of lines which are different between all files.

====*n* The lines beneath this notation are ranges of lines which are exclusively different in file *n*.

FILES

    `/tmp/d3?????`　　　temporary files.
    `/usr/bin/diff3`　the executable.

SEE ALSO

    `diff`(1) `ed`(1) `rcs`(1)

BUGS

    The −e option cannot catch and change lines which have '.' as the first and only character on the line. The resulting script will fail on that line as '.' is an `ed`(1) editing command.

HISTORY

    A `diff3` command appeared in Version 7 AT&T UNIX.

1

NAME
dig – send domain name query packets to name servers

SYNOPSIS
dig [@*server*] *domain* [*<query-type>*] [*<query-class>*] [+*<query-option>*] [−*<dig-option>*] [*%comment*]

DESCRIPTION
Dig (domain information groper) is a flexible command line tool which can be used to gather information from the Domain Name System servers. *Dig* has two modes: simple interactive mode which makes a single query, and batch which executes a query for each in a list of several query lines. All query options are accessible from the command line.

The usual simple use of *dig* will take the form:

        dig @server domain query-type query-class

where:

server   may be either a domain name or a dot-notation Internet address. If this optional field is omitted, *dig* will attempt to use the default name server for your machine.

   Note: If a domain name is specified, this will be resolved using the domain name system resolver (i.e., BIND). If your system does not support DNS, you may *have* to specify a dot-notation address. Alternatively, if there is a server at your disposal somewhere, all that is required is that /etc/resolv.conf be present and indicate where the default name servers reside, so that *server* itself can be resolved. See *resolver*(5) for information on /etc/resolv.conf. (WARNING: Changing /etc/resolv.conf will affect the standard resolver library and potentially several programs which use it.) As an option, the user may set the environment variable LOCALRES to name a file which is to be used instead of /etc/resolv.conf (LOCALRES is specific to the *dig* resolver and not referenced by the standard resolver). If the LOCALRES variable is not set or the file is not readable then /etc/resolv.conf will be used.

domain   is the domain name for which you are requesting information. See OPTIONS [-x] for convenient way to specify inverse address query.

query-type
        is the type of information (DNS query type) that you are requesting. If omitted, the default is "a" (T_A = address). The following types are recognized:

        a   T_A   network address
        any   T_ANY   all/any information about specified domain
        mx   T_MX   mail exchanger for the domain
        ns   T_NS   name servers
        soa   T_SOA   zone of authority record
        hinfo   T_HINFO   host information
        axfr   T_AXFR   zone transfer
                             (must ask an authoritative server)
        txt   T_TXT   arbitrary number of strings

        (See RFC 1035 for the complete list.)

query-class
        is the network class requested in the query. If omitted, the default is "in" (C_IN = Internet). The following classes are recognized:

        in   C_IN   Internet class domain
        any   C_ANY   all/any class information

1

(See RFC 1035 for the complete list.)

Note: "Any" can be used to specify a class and/or a type of query. *Dig* will parse the first occurrence of "any" to mean query-type = T_ANY. To specify query-class = C_ANY you must either specify "any" twice, or set query-class using "–c" option (see below).

OTHER OPTIONS

%ignored-comment

"%" is used to included an argument that is simply not parsed. This may be useful if running *dig* in batch mode. Instead of resolving every @server-domain-name in a list of queries, you can avoid the overhead of doing so, and still have the domain name on the command line as a reference. Example:

dig @128.9.0.32 %venera.isi.edu mx isi.edu

–<dig option>

"–" is used to specify an option which effects the operation of *dig*. The following options are currently available (although not guaranteed to be useful):

–x *dot-notation-address*

Convenient form to specify inverse address mapping. Instead of "dig 32.0.9.128.in-addr.arpa" one can simply "dig -x 128.9.0.32".

–f *file*   File for *dig* batch mode. The file contains a list of query specifications (*dig* command lines) which are to be executed successively. Lines beginning with ';', '#', or '\n' are ignored. Other options may still appear on command line, and will be in effect for each batch query.

–T *time*   Time in seconds between start of successive queries when running in batch mode. Can be used to keep two or more batch *dig* commands running roughly in sync. Default is zero.

–p *port*   Port number. Query a name server listening to a non-standard port number. Default is 53.

–P[*ping-string*]

After query returns, execute a *ping*(8) command for response time comparison. This rather unelegantly makes a call to the shell. The last three lines of statistics is printed for the command:

ping –s server_name 56 3

If the optional "ping string" is present, it replaces "ping –s" in the shell command.

–t *query-type*

Specify type of query. May specify either an integer value to be included in the type field or use the abbreviated mnemonic as discussed above (i.e., mx = T_MX).

–c *query-class*

Specify class of query. May specify either an integer value to be included in the class field or use the abbreviated mnemonic as discussed above (i.e., in = C_IN).

–envsav

This flag specifies that the *dig* environment (defaults, print options, etc.), after all of the arguments are parsed, should be saved to a file to become the default environment. Useful if you do not like the standard set of defaults and do not desire to include a large number of options each time *dig* is used. The environment consists of resolver state variable flags, timeout, and retries as well as the flags detailing *dig* output (see below). If the shell environment variable LOCALDEF is set to the name of a file, this is where the default *dig* environment is saved. If not, the file "DiG.env" is created in the current working directory.

1

Note: LOCALDEF is specific to the *dig* resolver, and will not affect operation of the standard resolver library.

Each time *dig* is executed, it looks for "./DiG.env" or the file specified by the shell environment variable LOCALDEF. If such file exists and is readable, then the environment is restored from this file before any arguments are parsed.

−envset This flag only affects batch query runs. When "−envset" is specified on a line in a *dig* batch file, the *dig* environment after the arguments are parsed, becomes the default environment for the duration of the batch file, or until the next line which specifies "−envset".

−[no]stick

This flag only affects batch query runs. It specifies that the *dig* environment (as read initially or set by "−envset" switch) is to be restored before each query (line) in a *dig* batch file. The default "−nostick" means that the *dig* environment does not stick, hence options specified on a single line in a *dig* batch file will remain in effect for subsequent lines (i.e. they are not restored to the "sticky" default).

+<query option>

"+" is used to specify an option to be changed in the query packet or to change *dig* output specifics. Many of these are the same parameters accepted by *nslookup*(1). If an option requires a parameter, the form is as follows:

+keyword[=value]

Most keywords can be abbreviated. Parsing of the "+" options is very simplistic — a value must not be separated from its keyword by white space. The following keywords are currently available:

Keyword	Abbrev.	Meaning [default]
[no]debug	(deb)	turn on/off debugging mode [deb]
[no]d2		turn on/off extra debugging mode [nod2]
[no]recurse	(rec)	use/don't use recursive lookup [rec]
retry=#	(ret)	set number of retries to # [4]
time=#	(ti)	set timeout length to # seconds [4]
[no]ko		keep open option (implies vc) [noko]
[no]vc		use/don't use virtual circuit [novc]
[no]defname	(def)	use/don't use default domain name [def]
[no]search	(sea)	use/don't use domain search list [sea]
domain=NAME	(do)	set default domain name to NAME
[no]ignore	(i)	ignore/don't ignore trunc. errors [noi]
[no]primary	(pr)	use/don't use primary server [nopr]
[no]aaonly	(aa)	authoritative query only flag [noaa]
[no]sort	(sor)	sort resource records [nosor]
[no]cmd		echo parsed arguments [cmd]
[no]stats	(st)	print query statistics [st]
[no]Header	(H)	print basic header [H]
[no]header	(he)	print header flags [he]
[no]ttlid	(tt)	print TTLs [tt]
[no]cl		print class info [nocl]
[no]qr		print outgoing query [noqr]
[no]reply	(rep)	print reply [rep]

[no]ques	(qu)	print question section [qu]
[no]answer	(an)	print answer section [an]
[no]author	(au)	print authoritative section [au]
[no]addit	(ad)	print additional section [ad]
pfdef		set to default print flags
pfmin		set to minimal default print flags
pfset=#		set print flags to #
		(# can be hex/octal/decimal)
pfand=#		bitwise and print flags with #
pfor=#		bitwise or print flags with #

The retry and time options affect the retransmission strategy used by resolver library when sending datagram queries. The algorithm is as follows:

```
for i = 0 to retry - 1
    for j = 1 to num_servers
            send_query
            wait((time * (2**i)) / num_servers)
    end
end
```

(Note: *dig* always uses a value of 1 for num_servers.)

DETAILS

Dig once required a slightly modified version of the BIND *resolver*(3) library. BIND's resolver has (as of BIND 4.9) been augmented to work properly with *Dig*. Essentially, *Dig* is a straight-forward (albeit not pretty) effort of parsing arguments and setting appropriate parameters. *Dig* uses resolver routines res_init(), res_mkquery(), res_send() as well as accessing _res structure.

FILES

/etc/resolv.conf   initial domain name and name server
                        addresses

ENVIRONMENT

LOCALRES   file to use in place of /etc/resolv.conf
LOCALDEF   default environment file

AUTHOR

Steve Hotz hotz@isi.edu

ACKNOWLEDGMENTS

Dig uses functions from *nslookup*(1) authored by Andrew Cherenson.

BUGS

Dig has a serious case of "creeping featurism" -- the result of considering several potential uses during it's development. It would probably benefit from a rigorous diet. Similarly, the print flags and granularity of the items they specify make evident their rather ad hoc genesis.

Dig does not consistently exit nicely (with appropriate status) when a problem occurs somewhere in the resolver (NOTE: most of the common exit cases are handled). This is particularly annoying when running in batch mode. If it exits abnormally (and is not caught), the entire batch aborts; when such an event is trapped, *dig* simply continues with the next query.

SEE ALSO

named(8), resolver(3), resolver(5), nslookup(1)

1

NAME

du – display disk usage statistics

SYNOPSIS

du [−H | −L | −P] [−a | −s] [−x] [*file ...*]

DESCRIPTION

The du utility displays the file system block usage for each file argument and for each directory in the file hierarchy rooted in each directory argument. If no file is specified, the block usage of the hierarchy rooted in the current directory is displayed. The number of blocks are in the same units as that returned by the stat(2) system call, i.e. 512-byte blocks. Partial numbers of blocks are rounded up.

The options are as follows:

−H   Symbolic links on the command line are followed. (Symbolic links encountered in the tree traversal are not followed.)

−L   All symbolic links are followed.

−P   No symbolic links are followed.

−a   Display an entry for each file in the file hierarchy.

−s   Display only the grand total for the specified files.

−x   Filesystem mount points are not traversed.

Du counts the storage used by symbolic links and not the files they reference unless the −H or −L option is specified. If either the −H or −L options are specified, storage used by any symbolic links which are followed is not counted or displayed. The −H, −L and −P options override each other and the command's actions are determined by the last one specified.

Files having multiple hard links are counted (and displayed) a single time per du execution.

ENVIRONMENTAL VARIABLES

BLOCKSIZE If the environmental variable BLOCKSIZE is set, the block counts will be displayed in units of that size block.

SEE ALSO

df(1), fts(3), symlink(7), quot(8)

HISTORY

A du command appeared in Version 6 AT&T UNIX.

NAME

    echo – produce message in a shell script

SYNOPSIS

    echo [–n | –e] *args...*

DESCRIPTION

    Echo prints its arguments on the standard output, separated by spaces. Unless the –n option is present, a
newline is output following the arguments. The –e option causes echo to treat the escape sequences specially, as described in the following paragraph. The –e option is the default, and is provided solely for compatibility with other systems. Only one of the options –n and –e may be given.

    If any of the following sequences of characters is encountered during output, the sequence is not output. In-
stead, the specified action is performed:

    \b   A backspace character is output.

    \c   Subsequent output is suppressed. This is normally used at the end of the last argument to suppress
the trailing newline that echo would otherwise output.

    \f   Output a form feed.

    \n   Output a newline character.

    \r   Output a carriage return.

    \t   Output a (horizontal) tab character.

    \v   Output a vertical tab.

    \0*digits*

            Output the character whose value is given by zero to three digits. If there are zero digits, a nul
character is output.

    \\   Output a backslash.

HINTS

    Remember that backslash is special to the shell and needs to be escaped. To output a message to standard
error, say

        message >&2

BUGS

    The octal character escape mechanism (\0*digits*) differs from the C language mechanism.

    There is no way to force echo to treat its arguments literally, rather than interpreting them as options and
escape sequences.

1

NAME
ed – line oriented text editor

SYNOPSIS
ed [**–p** *prompt-string*] [**–s**] [**–v**] [*filename*]

DESCRIPTION
Ed is a standard text editor.

Ed is a powerful line oriented editor. Although ex(1)/vi(1) have gained popularity, *ed* still maintains advantages over them. Most notable points are the *W* command (see below) (which is not part of ex(1)/vi(1)), the smaller executable size (you can often be editing before the others finish loading), and the better response when editing from slow terminals or across low baud data lines. *Ed* continues to be used by many system utilities.

OPTIONS
When a filename is present *ed* starts by simulating an *e* command (see below) If no filename is present *ed* starts with an empty buffer. The option **–p** allows for the setting of a prompt string in *ed*. The option **–s** suppresses the printing of explanatory output (from the commands *e*, *E*, *r*, *w*, *W* and *wq*; see below) and should be used with a script. The **–v** option will display a message of which mode (BSD or POSIX) *ed* as been set locally. This is useful for determining the described behavior below.

Ed performs all changes to a copy of the file which is contained in a **buffer**. For the changes to have an effect one of the write commands (*w*, *W*, *wq*, or *Wq*) must be issued.

The contents of the **buffer** can changed by issuing commands that are lead by zero, one, or two addresses. All commands are alphabetically listed below with their parameter structures if applicable; trailing structures not described with commands are regarded as erroneous. Commands that accept zero addresses regard the presence of any address as an error.

Ed works in two modes: command, and input. The two modes are exclusive of each other. While in command mode *ed* accepts commands that display, modify, or give information about the **buffer**. While in input mode *ed* accepts lines of text to be added to the **buffer**.

Addressing in *ed* specifies one or more lines contained in the **buffer**. For commands that expect at least one address, and none are given, default addresses will be used. Using addresses in *ed* involves understanding that during the execution of most *ed* commands that a *current line* (**current**) exists. **Current** (as a rule of thumb) is the location in the **buffer** that the last command issued affected; some commands do not affect **current**. Each command description (below) describes its affects on **current** as the affect will vary depending under which compile option (BSD or POSIX) *ed* was compiled under. Addresses can be divided into three cases: one address (**single address**), two addresses (an **address pair**), and special address forms.

For the first two cases an address is formed with the use of:

1.   A positive decimal integer (e.g. 123) indicating a line number in the buffer. Line number 1 is the first line in the buffer.

2.   The '.' character indicating the current line (**current**).

3.   The '$' character which indicates the last line in the buffer.

4.   A regular expression (RE) enclosed with '/'s as delimiters (i.e. /RE/). This causes a forward search to the first occurrence of the specified RE. The address will then become this line. The character sequence ∨ escapes the forwardslash from being a delimiter. The search will wrap from the bottom of the buffer to the top of the buffer if need be. *Ed* RE's are, outside of this document, now refered to as *basic regular expressions*. Basic regular expressions (BRE's), traditionally described in *ed(1)* are now fully described in regex(7). BRE's are, for the most part, the same as the old RE's - the name has changed and the expressions extended to meet POSIX 1003.2 specifications. (See the search command for more details.)

1

5.   A RE enclosed with '?'s as delimiters (i.e. ?RE?). This will cause a backward search to the first occurrence of the specified BRE. The address will then become this line. The character sequence \? escapes the questionmark from being a delimiter. The search will wrap from the top of the buffer to the bottom of the buffer if need be. (See the search command for more details.)

6.   A line previously marked by the 'k' command (see below). 'x addresses the line marked by the single lower-case letter 'x' (from the portable character set in the range a-z).

7.   An address of the form 1-6 followed by a '+' followed by an integer number, **n**, specifies the line to be addressed is **n** lines after the address of the form 1-6. If the address starts with a '+' then by default the addressed line is taken with respect to **current** (equivalent to '.'; form 2). If no integer number is given then 1 is added to the address. Hence, if more than one '+' is given in a sequence, with no integer number following, 1 is added to the address for each '+'. Therefore, +++ is eqivalent to +3, but +++1 is equivalent to +1.

8.   An address of the form 1-6 followed by a '−' followed by an integer number, **n**, specifies the line to be addressed is **n** lines before the address of the form 1-6. If the address starts with a '−' then by default the addressed line is taken with respect to **current** ('.'; form 1). If no integer number is given then 1 is subtracted from the address. Hence, if more than one '−' is given in a sequence, with no integer number following, 1 is subtracted from the address for each '−'. Therefore, —— is eqivalent to −3, but ——1 is equivalent to −1. For backward compatibility '^' is the equivalent to '−'.

9.   A ',' (comma) may be used to separate two addresses of the form 1-8 to create an **address pair**. The first address must occur no later in the buffer than the second address to be legal.

10. A ';' (semicolon) may be used to separate two addresses of the form 1-8 to create an **address pair**. With this form the second address is evaluated with respect to and after the first address has been evaluated. This is useful when addresses of the forms 2-8 are used. The first address must occur no later in the buffer than the second address to be legal.

NOTE: Addresses of the forms 7 and 8 cannot be followed by addresses of forms 2-6; it is an error.

The following are special address forms that cannot be combined with any of the address forms listed above. A ',' by itself represents the address pair '1,$'. Likewise '%' by itself represents the address pair '1,$'. A ';' by itself represents the address pair '.,$'.

The *ed* commands listed below default to the addresses prefixing the commands. Commands without default addresses accept zero addresses. The parentheses with the default addresses are not part of the address; they are used to show that the addresses are default.

Generally only one command appears on a line at a time. However, many of the commands may be suffixed by 'l', 'n', or 'p', in which case the current line is printed in the manner discussed below. These suffixes may be combined in any order.

(.)a
<text>
.

    Append text after the addressed line. A '.' in the first column followed immediately by a <newline> places *ed* back in command mode - the '.' is not included in the text. Line 0 is legal for this command; text will be placed at the top of the buffer. **Current** is the last line appended (or the addressed line if no text given).

(.,.)c
<text>
.

    Change text on the addressed line(s). The addressed lines are deleted before *ed* is placed in input mode. A '.' in the first column followed immediately by a <newline> places *ed* back in command mode - the '.' is not included in the text. **Current** is the new last line appended (or if no text is given the line after the addressed line deleted).

1

(.,.) d

Delete the addressed line(s) from the buffer. Deleted lines may be recovered with the undo command (*u*; see below). **Current** is the line after the last addressed line deleted.

e [filename]

Edit the new file 'filename'. The **buffer** is cleared and the new file is placed in the **buffer**. If the **buffer** has been modified since the last write command *ed* will issue a warning ('?'); a second issuing of the command will be obeyed regardless. The number of characters read is printed (unless -s is specified at startup). If 'filename' is missing, the remembered name is used. If 'filename' is lead by ! then it shall be interpreted as a shell command to be executed, from which the standard output will be placed into the buffer; 'filename' will be non-remembered. Undo will not restore the **buffer** to its state before the edit command. **Current** is the last line in the **buffer** ('$').

E [filename]

E works the same as *e* except if the buffer has been modified no warning is issued.

f [filename]

Print the **remembered filename**. If 'filename' is specified the **remembered filename** will be set to 'filename'. If 'filename' is lead by ! then it shall be interpreted as a shell command to be executed, from which the standard output will be used as the new remembered filename. **Current** is unchanged.

(1,$) g/regular expression/command list

The global command first marks all lines matching the regular expression. For each matching line, the command list is executed. At the start of each command list execution, **current** is set to equal that line; **current** may change as each command in the command list is executed for that line. The first command of the command list begins on the same line as the global command. Generally, in the command list one command occupies a line. Thus to have multiple commands in the command list it is necessary to escape the <newline> at the end of each line so that the global command does not interpret it as an indication that the command list entry has ended. The <newline> is escaped by proceeding it with a backslash ('\'). Similarly with the commands that set *ed* into input mode the <newlines> of the entered text need to be escaped. If the '.' used to end input mode is the last line of the command list the <newline> following the '.' need not be escaped, or the '.' may be omitted entirely. Commands in the command list can affect any line in the buffer. For the behaviour of each *ed* command within a command list refer to the information on the individual command, particularly *s* and *!*. The commands *g*, *G*, *v*, and *V*, and *!* are permitted in the command list, but should be used with caution. The command list defaults to *p* if left empty (i.e. g/RE/p). For the regular expression the delimiters can be any characters except for <space> and <newline>; delimiters within a regular expression can be escaped with a backslash preceding it.

(1,$) G/regular expression/

The interactive global command works similar to *g*. The first step is to mark every line which matches the given regular expression. For every line matched it will print this line, set **current** to this line, and accept one command (not including *a*, *c*, *i*, *g*, *G*, *v*, and *V*) for execution. The command can affect any line in the buffer. '%' by itself executes the last non-null command. A return by itself will act as a null command. **Current** will be set to the last line affected by the last successful command input. If no match or an input command error occurs **current** will be set to the last line searched by *G*. *G* can be prematurely ended by 'ctrl-C' (SIGINT). For the behaviour of each *ed* command within a command list refer to the information on the individual command, particularly *s* and *!*.

h

The help command displays a message explaining the most recent command error (indicated by '?'). **Current** is unchanged.

H

This toggles on or off the automatic display of messages explaining the most recent command error in place of '?'. **Current** is unchanged.

(.)i

<text>

.

The insert command places *ed* in input mode with the text being placed before the addressed line. Line 0 is invalid for this command. A '.' in the first column followed immediately by a return places *ed* back in command mode - the '.' is not included in the text. **Current** is the last line inserted. If no text is inserted then **current** is the addressed when *ed* is compiled for POSIX; compiled for BSD, **current** is the addressed line -1.

(.,.+1)j

The join command joins the addressed lines together to make one line. If no addresses are specified **current** and **current**+1 lines are joined. If one address only is given then no join is performed. **Current** becomes that line if *ed* has been compiled under the BSD option; if compiled under the POSIX option **current** is unchanged.

(.)kx

The mark command marks the addressed line with label **x**, where **x** is a lowercase letter from the portable character set (a-z). The address form '**x** will refer to this line (address form 6 above). **Current** is unchanged.

(.,.)l

The list command prints the addressed lines in an unambiguous way: non-graphic characters are printed in three-digit octal preceded by a \ unless they are one of the following in which case they will be printed as indicated in the brackets: backslash ('\\'), horizontal tab (\t), form feed (\f). return (\r), vertical tab (\v), and backspace (\b). Long lines will be broken based on the type of terminal currently in use and will likely be ragged at the right side if text and octal are mixed on the same line. **Current** is set to the last line printed. The *l* command may be placed on the same line after any command except (*e, E, f, q, Q, r, w, W,* or *!*).

(.,.)ma

The move command moves the addressed lines in the buffer to after the address **a**. Line 0 is valid as the address **a** for this command. **Current** is the location in the **buffer** of the last line moved.

(.,.)n

The number command prints the addressed lines preceding the text with the line number. The *n* command may be placed on the same line after any command except (*e, E, f, q, Q, r, w, W,* or *!*). **Current** is the last line printed.

(.,.)p

The print command prints the addressed lines. The *p* command may be placed on the same line after any command except (*e, E, f, q, Q, r, w, W,* or *!*). **Current** is the last line printed.

(.,.)P

This command is a synonym for *p* if *ed* has been compiled under the BSD option. If *ed* has been compiled under the POSIX option then the prompt is toggled on or off. **Current** is unchanged when compiled under the POSIX option. The default prompt is "*" if not specified with the –p option at startup. The prompt is initially off unless the –p option is specified.

q

The quit command causes *ed* to exit. If the entire **buffer** (1,$) has not been written since the last modification *ed* will issue a warning once ('?'); a second issuing of the command will be obeyed regardless.

Q

Q works the same as *q* except if the buffer has been modified no warning is issued.

1

($) r [filename]

The read command reads in the file 'filename' after the addressed line. If no 'filename' is specified then the **remembered filename** is used. Address 0 is valid for this command. If read is successful then the number of characters read is printed (unless the -s option is specified). If 'filename' is lead by ! then it shall be interpreted as a shell command to be executed, from which the standard output will be placed in the buffer; 'filename' will be non-remembered. **Current** is the last line read.

(., .) s/regular expression/**replacement**/**flags**

The substitute command searches for the regular expression in the addressed lines. On each line in which a match is found, matched strings are replaced by the **replacement** as specified by the **flags** (see below). If no **flags** appear, by default only the first occurrence of the matched string in each line is replaced. It is an error if no matches to the RE occur.

The delimiters may be any character except <space> or <newline>. The delimiter lead by a \ will escape it to be a literal in the RE or **replacement**.

An ampersand, '&', appearing in the replacement will equal the string matching the RE. The '&'s special meaning is supressable by leading it with a '\'. When '%' is the only replacement character in **replacement** the most recent replacement is used. The '%'s special meaning is supressable by leading it with a '\'.

The characters '\n' (where **n** is a digit 1-9) is replaced by the text matching the RE subexpression **n** (known as backreferencing). *S* may be used to break lines by including a <newline> in **replacement** preceeded by a backslash ('\') to escape it. **Replacement** can continue on the next line and can include another escaped <newline>.

The following extention should not be included in portable scripts. When spliting lines using *s* within the global commands (*g*, *G*, *v*, or *V*) the <newline> in the replacement string must be escaped by preceding it with '\\\' (three adjacent '\' s – the first '\' escapes the second '\' so that it is passed to *s* to escape the <newline> passed by the global command; the third '\' is to escape the <newline> so that the global command list continues). [N.B. Other *ed*'s do not allow line splitting within the global commands].

The **flags** may be any combination of:

count   in each addressed line replace the *count*–th matching occurrence.

g   in each addressed line replace all matching occurrences. When *count* and g are specified together inclusively replace in each addressed line all matches from the *count*–th match to the end of line.

l   write the line after replacement in the manner specified by the *l* command.

n   write the line after replacement in the manner specified by the *n* command.

p   write the line after replacement in the manner specified by the *p* command.

The following special form should not be included in portable scripts. This form is maintained for backward compatibility and is extended to dovetail into the above forms of s. *S* followed by *no* delimiters repeats the most recent substitute command on the addressed lines. *S* may be suffixed with the letters **r** (use the most recent RE rather than the last RE used with *s*), **p** (complement the setting of the any print command (l, n, p) suffix from the previous substitution), **g** (complement the setting of the *g* suffix) or **N** (negate the previous *count* flag). These modifying letters may be combined in any order (N.B. multiple use of the modifying letters may cause them to be interpreted as delimiters).

Current is set to the last line search (BSD) or where the last replacement occurred (POSIX).

(.,.) t **a**

The transcribe command copies the addressed lines in the **buffer** to after the address **a**. Address 0 is valid as the address **a** for this command. **Current** is the last line transcribed.

1

(. , .) u
> The undo command nullifies the most recent **buffer** modifying command. Buffer modifying commands undo works on are *a*, *c*, *d*, *g*, *G*, *i*, *j*, *m*, *r*, *s*, *t*, *u*, *v*, and *V*. Marks set by the *k* command will also be restored. All commands (including nested *g*, *G*, *v*, and *V* commands within the *g* or *v*) that undo works on are treated as a single buffer modification. **Current** is set to the line it addressed before the last buffer modification.

(1, $) v/regular expression/command list
> The global non-matching command performs as the *g* command does except that the command list is executed for every line that does not match the RE.

(1, $) V/regular expression/
> The interactive global non-matching command is the same as the *G* except that one command will be accepted as input with **current** initially set to every line that does not match the RE.

(1, $) w [filename]
> The write command writes the addressed lines to the file 'filename'. If no 'filename' is specified then the **remembered filename** is used. If no addresses are specified the whole **buffer** is written. If the command is successful, the number of characters written is printed (unless the -s option is specified). If 'filename' is lead by ! then it shall be interpreted as a shell command to be executed which will accept on its standard input the section of the buffer specified for writting. **Current** is unchanged.

(1, $) W [filename]
> *W* works as the *w* command does except the addressed contents of the **buffer** are appended to 'filename' (or the **remembered filename** if 'filename' is not specified). If 'filename' is lead by ! then *W* will act exactly as the *w* command. **Current** is unchanged.

(1, $) wq [filename]
> *wq* works as the *w* command does with the addition that *ed* exits immediately after the write is complete. **Current** is unchanged.

(1,$) Wq [filename]
> *Wq* works as the *W* command does with the addition that *ed* exits immediately after the appended write is complete. **Current** is unchanged.

(. +1) z   or,

(. +1) z**n**
> Scroll through the **buffer**. Starting from the addressed line (or **current**+1) print the next 22 (by default or **n**) lines. The **n** is a sticky value; it becomes the default number of lines printed for successive scrolls. **Current** is the last line printed.

($) = Print the number of lines in the **buffer**. If an address is provided (in the forms 1-8 above) then the line number for that line will be printed. **Current** is unchanged.

!<shell command>
> The command after the *!* is executed by *sh(1)* and the results are printed. A '!' is printed in the first column when execution has completed (unless the -s option has been specified). A '!' immediately after *!* repeats the last shell command. An unescaped '%' represents the remembered filename. Commands to *sh(1)* can have several lines by escaping the <newline> with a '\' immediately before it. The line continuation character for *sh(1)*, '\', can be included on a line provided that it is escaped by a '\' immediately before so that *ed* passes it literally to *sh(1)*: '\\'. It is implicit that for the command line that the *sh(1)* line continuation character is on that the <newline> will be escaped (e.g. '\\\<newline>'). This behavior can be used within global command lists. However, an additional '\' must be added so that the *!* command continuor is passed to *!* - it must occur immediately before the global command's continuor. Therefore, the *!* command continuation sequence in a global command list will appear as '\\\' (explanation as with *sfR*). *The line continuation character for sh(1) needs no additional escaping* (since it it not dependant on <newline> being adjacent) - hence, the sequence in a global command list with a line continuation will appear as '\\\\\<newline>'. **Current** is unchanged.

1

/regular expression/   or,

?regular expression?

> The search command searches forward, '/', (or backward, '?') through the **buffer** attempting to find a line that matches the RE. The search will wrap to the top (or bottom) of the **buffer** if necessary. Search returns the line number that the match occurs on - combined with the null command (see below) this causes the line to be printed. **Current** is the matching line.

(.+1, .+1) <newline>

> The null command is equivalent to asking for the line **current**+1 to be printed according to the *p* command. This is a useful command to quickly print the next couple of lines. If more than a couple of lines are needed the *z* command (see above) is much better to use. **Current** is the last line printed.

OTHER

If an interrupt signal (SIGINT) is sent, *ed* prints '?' and returns to command mode.

BSD command pairs (pp, ll, etc.) are permitted. Additionally any single print command may follow any of the non-I/O commands (I/O commands: e, E, f, r, w, W, wq, and !). This will cause the current line to be printed in the specified manner after the command has completed.

Previous limitations on the number of characters per line and per command list have been lifted; there is now no maximum. File name and path length is restricted to the maximum length that the current file system supports. The *undo* command now restores marks to affected lines. The temporary buffer method will vary dependent on the method selected at compile. Two methods work with a temporary file (stdio and db), while the third uses memory. The limit on the number of lines depends on the amount of memory.

FILES

/tmp/_bsd44_ed*

ed.hup: the buffer is written to this file in the current directory if possible and in the HOME directory is not (if the signal SIGHUP (hangup) is received).

SEE ALSO

B. W. Kernighan, *A Tutorial Introduction to the ED Text Editor*

B. W. Kernighan, *Advanced editing on UNIX*

ex(1), learn(1), regex(3), regex(7), sed(1), vi(1), POSIX 1003.2 (4.20)

AUTHOR

Rodney Ruddock

DIAGNOSTICS

'?name' for a file that is either inaccessible, does not exist, or is a directory. '?' for all other errors unless the help messages have been toggled on (with the H command) in which case a descriptive message will be printed.

EOF is treated as a newline during input so that characters after the last <newline> are included into the **buffer**; the message "<newline> added at end of line" is printed.

Ed Returns an exit status of 0 on successful completion. A value >0 is returned to indicate an *ed* error: 1 for a command line error, 2 for HUP signal received, 4 for an *ed* command error; these error values will be or'd together when appropriate.

NOTES

Regular expressions are now described on regex(7). *Ed* follows basic regular expressions (BRE's) as described on regex(7). BRE's, for the most part, are the same as previous *ed* RE's. The changes to the RE's are extensions for internationalization under POSIX 1003.2. Old scripts with RE's should work without modification.

Regular expression logic is very tight. If you believe a command with a regular expression in it has performed erroneously then a close reading of regex(7) is likely required.

Address '0' is legal only for those commands which explicitly state that it may be used; its use is illegal for all other commands.

The special form of substitute has been maintained for backward compatability and should not be used in scripts if they are to portable.

Help messages may appear ambiguous to beginners - particularly when BRE's form part of the command.

For backward compatability, when more addresses are provided than required by a command the one or two addresses closest to the command are used (depending on how may addresses the command accepts). Portable scripts should not rely on this feature.

For backward compatibility the option '-' is equivalent to the '-s' option at the startup of *ed*.

1

NAME

emacs – GNU project Emacs

SYNOPSIS

emacs [*command-line switches*] [*file ...*]

DESCRIPTION

GNU Emacs is a new version of *Emacs*, written by the author of the original (PDP-10) *Emacs*, Richard Stallman. Its user functionality encompasses everything other *Emacs* editors do, and it is easily extensible since its editing commands are written in Lisp.

Emacs has an extensive interactive help facility, but the facility assumes that you know how to manipulate *Emacs* windows and buffers. CTRL-h (backspace or CTRL-h) enters the Help facility. Help Tutorial (CTRL-h t) requests an interactive tutorial which can teach beginners the fundamentals of *Emacs* in a few minutes. Help Apropos (CTRL-h a) helps you find a command given its functionality, Help Character (CTRL-h c) describes a given character's effect, and Help Function (CTRL-h f) describes a given Lisp function specified by name.

Emacs's Undo can undo several steps of modification to your buffers, so it is easy to recover from editing mistakes.

GNU Emacs's many special packages handle mail reading (RMail) and sending (Mail), outline editing (Outline), compiling (Compile), running subshells within *Emacs* windows (Shell), running a Lisp read-eval-print loop (Lisp-Interaction-Mode), and automated psychotherapy (Doctor).

There is an extensive reference manual, but users of other Emacses should have little trouble adapting even without a copy. Users new to *Emacs* will be able to use basic features fairly rapidly by studying the tutorial and using the self-documentation features.

Emacs Options

The following options are of general interest:

file   Edit *file*.

+number Go to the line specified by *number* (do not insert a space between the "+" sign and the number).

–q   Do not load an init file.

–u *user*   Load *user's* init file.

–t *file*   Use specified *file* as the terminal instead of using stdin/stdout. This must be the first argument specified in the command line.

The following options are lisp-oriented (these options are processed in the order encountered):

–f *function*

Execute the lisp function *function*.

–l *file*   Load the lisp code in the file *file*.

The following options are useful when running *Emacs* as a batch editor:

–batch *commandfile*

Edit in batch mode using the commands found in *commandfile*. The editor will send messages to stdout. This option must be the first in the argument list.

–kill   Exit *Emacs* while in batch mode.

Using Emacs with X

Emacs has been tailored to work well with the X window system. If you run *Emacs* from under X windows, it will create its own X window to display in. You will probably want to start the editor as a background process so that you can continue using your original window.

Emacs can be started with the following X switches:

−rn *name*

    Specifies the program name which should be used when looking up defaults in the user's X resources. This must be the first option specified in the command line.

−wn *name*

    Specifies the name which should be assigned to the *Emacs* window.

−r   Display the *Emacs* window in reverse video.

−i   Use the "kitchen sink" bitmap icon when iconifying the *Emacs* window.

−font *font,* **−fn** *font*

    Set the *Emacs* window's font to that specified by *font.* You will find the various *X* fonts in the */usr/lib/X11/fonts* directory. Note that *Emacs* will only accept fixed width fonts. Under the X11 Release 4 font-naming conventions, any font with the value "m" or "c" in the eleventh field of the font name is a fixed width font. Furthermore, fonts whose name are of the form *width*x*height* are generally fixed width, as is the font *fixed.* See *xlsfonts*(1) for more information.

    When you specify a font, be sure to put a space between the switch and the font name.

−b *pixels*

    Set the *Emacs* window's border width to the number of pixels specified by *pixels.* Defaults to one pixel on each side of the window.

−ib *pixels*

    Set the window's internal border width to the number of pixels specified by *pixels.* Defaults to one pixel of padding on each side of the window.

−w *geometry,* **−geometry** *geometry*

    Set the *Emacs* window's width, height, and position as specified. The geometry specification is in the standard X format; see *X*(1) for more information. The width and height are specified in characters; the default is 80 by 24.

−fg *color*

    On color displays, sets the color of the text.

    See the file */usr/lib/X11/rgb.txt* for a list of valid color names.

−bg *color*

    On color displays, sets the color of the window's background.

−bd *color*

    On color displays, sets the color of the window's border.

−cr *color*

    On color displays, sets the color of the window's text cursor.

−ms *color*

    On color displays, sets the color of the window's mouse cursor.

−d *displayname,* **−display** *displayname*

    Create the *Emacs* window on the display specified by *displayname.* Must be the first option specified in the command line.

−nw   Tells *Emacs* not to use its special interface to X. If you use this switch when invoking *Emacs* from an *xterm*(1) window, display is done in that window. This must be the first option specified in the command line.

You can set *X* default values for your *Emacs* windows in your *.Xresources* file (see *xrdb*(1)). Use the following format:

　　　emacs.keyword:value

where *value* specifies the default value of *keyword*. *Emacs* lets you set default values for the following keywords:

font (class **Font**)
　　　Sets the window's text font.

reverseVideo (class **ReverseVideo**)
　　　If *reverseVideo's* value is set to *on,* the window will be displayed in reverse video.

bitmapIcon (class **BitmapIcon**)
　　　If *bitmapIcon's* value is set to *on,* the window will iconify into the "kitchen sink."

borderWidth (class **BorderWidth**)
　　　Sets the window's border width in pixels.

internalBorder (class **BorderWidth**)
　　　Sets the window's internal border width in pixels.

foreground (class **Foreground**)
　　　For color displays, sets the window's text color.

background (class **Background**)
　　　For color displays, sets the window's background color.

borderColor (class **BorderColor**)
　　　For color displays, sets the color of the window's border.

cursorColor (class **Foreground**)
　　　For color displays, sets the color of the window's text cursor.

pointerColor (class **Foreground**)
　　　For color displays, sets the color of the window's mouse cursor.

geometry (class **Geometry**)
　　　Sets the geometry of the *Emacs* window (as described above).

title (class **Title**)
　　　Sets the title of the *Emacs* window.

iconName (class **Title**)
　　　Sets the icon name for the *Emacs* window icon.

If you try to set color values while using a black and white display, the window's characteristics will default as follows: the foreground color will be set to black, the background color will be set to white, the border color will be set to grey, and the text and mouse cursors will be set to black.

Using the Mouse

The following lists the mouse button bindings for the *Emacs* window under X11.

MOUSE BUTTON	FUNCTION
left	Set point.
middle	Paste text.
right	Cut text into X cut buffer.
SHIFT-middle	Cut text into X cut buffer.
SHIFT-right	Paste text.
CTRL-middle	Cut text into X cut buffer and kill it.
CTRL-right	Select this window, then split it into two windows. Same as typing CTRL-x 2.
CTRL-SHIFT-left	X buffer menu--hold the buttons and keys down, wait for menu to appear, select buffer, and release. Move mouse out of menu and release to cancel.
CTRL-SHIFT-middle	X help menu--pop up index card menu for Emacs help.

1

CTRL-SHIFT-right   Select window with mouse, and delete all other windows. Same as typing CTRL-x 1.

MANUALS

You can order printed copies of the GNU Emacs Manual for $15.00/copy postpaid from the Free Software Foundation, which develops GNU software (contact them for quantity prices on the manual). Their address is:

> Free Software Foundation
> 675 Mass Ave.
> Cambridge, MA 02139

Your local Emacs maintainer might also have copies available. As with all software and publications from FSF, everyone is permitted to make and distribute copies of the Emacs manual. The TeX source to the manual is also included in the Emacs source distribution.

FILES

/usr/local/emacs/src - C source files and object files

/usr/local/emacs/lisp - Lisp source files and compiled files that define most editing commands. Some are preloaded; others are autoloaded from this directory when used.

/usr/local/emacs/man - sources for the Emacs reference manual.

/usr/local/emacs/etc - various programs that are used with GNU Emacs, and some files of information.

/usr/local/emacs/etc/DOC.* - contains the documentation strings for the Lisp primitives and preloaded Lisp functions of GNU Emacs. They are stored here to reduce the size of Emacs proper.

/usr/local/emacs/etc/DIFF discusses GNU Emacs vs. Twenex Emacs;
/usr/local/emacs/etc/CCADIFF discusses GNU Emacs vs. CCA Emacs;
/usr/local/emacs/etc/GOSDIFF discusses GNU Emacs vs. Gosling Emacs.
/usr/local/emacs/etc/SERVICE lists people offering various services to assist users of GNU Emacs, including education, troubleshooting, porting and customization.
These files also have information useful to anyone wishing to write programs in the Emacs Lisp extension language, which has not yet been fully documented.

/usr/local/emacs/info - files for the Info documentation browser (a subsystem of Emacs) to refer to. Currently not much of Unix is documented here, but the complete text of the Emacs reference manual is included in a convenient tree structured form.

/usr/local/emacs/lock - holds lock files that are made for all files being modified in Emacs, to prevent simultaneous modification of one file by two users.

/usr/local/emacs/cpp - the GNU cpp, needed for building Emacs on certain versions of Unix where the standard cpp cannot handle long names for macros.

/usr/local/emacs/shortnames - facilities for translating long names to short names in C code, needed for building Emacs on certain versions of Unix where the C compiler cannot handle long names for functions or variables.

/usr/lib/X11/rgb.txt - list of valid X color names.

BUGS

There is a mailing list, bug-gnu-emacs@prep.ai.mit.edu on the internet (ucbvax!prep.ai.mit.edu!bug-gnu-emacs on UUCPnet), for reporting Emacs bugs and fixes. But before reporting something as a bug, please try to be sure that it really is a bug, not a misunderstanding or a deliberate feature. We ask you to read the section "Reporting Emacs Bugs" near the end of the reference manual (or Info system) for hints on how and when to report bugs. Also, include the version number of the Emacs you are running in *every* bug report that you send in.

Do not expect a personal answer to a bug report. The purpose of reporting bugs is to get them fixed for everyone in the next release, if possible. For personal assistance, look in the SERVICE file (see above) for a list of people who offer it.

Please do not send anything but bug reports to this mailing list. Send requests to be added to mailing lists to the special list info-gnu-emacs-request@prep.ai.mit.edu (or the corresponding UUCP address). For more information about Emacs mailing lists, see the file /usr/local/emacs/etc/MAILINGLISTS. Bugs tend actually to be fixed if they can be isolated, so it is in your interest to report them in such a way that they can be easily reproduced.

Bugs that I know about are: shell will not work with programs running in Raw mode on some Unix versions.

UNRESTRICTIONS

Emacs is free; anyone may redistribute copies of *Emacs* to anyone under the terms stated in the *Emacs* General Public License, a copy of which accompanies each copy of *Emacs* and which also appears in the reference manual.

Copies of *Emacs* may sometimes be received packaged with distributions of Unix systems, but it is never included in the scope of any license covering those systems. Such inclusion violates the terms on which distribution is permitted. In fact, the primary purpose of the General Public License is to prohibit anyone from attaching any other restrictions to redistribution of *Emacs*.

Richard Stallman encourages you to improve and extend *Emacs,* and urges that you contribute your extensions to the GNU library. Eventually GNU (Gnu's Not Unix) will be a complete replacement for Berkeley Unix. Everyone will be able to use the GNU system for free.

SEE ALSO

X(1), xlsfonts(1), xterm(1), xrdb(1)

AUTHORS

Emacs was written by Richard Stallman and the Free Software Foundation. Joachim Martillo and Robert Krawitz added the X features.

NAME

    eqn – format equations for troff

SYNOPSIS

    eqn [**–rvCNR**] [**–d***cc*] [**–T***name*] [**–M***dir*] [**–f***F*] [**–s***n*] [**–p***n*] [**–m***n*] [*files* ...]

DESCRIPTION

    This manual page describes the GNU version of **eqn**, which is part of the groff document formatting system. **eqn** compiles descriptions of equations embedded within **troff** input files into commands that are understood by **troff**. Normally, it should be invoked using the **–e** option of **groff**. The syntax is quite compatible with Unix eqn. The output of GNU eqn cannot be processed with Unix troff; it must be processed with GNU troff. If no files are given on the command line, the standard input will be read. A filename of – will cause the standard input to be read.

    eqn searches for the file **eqnrc** using the path **@MACROPATH@**. If it exists, eqn will process it before the other input files. The **–R** option prevents this.

    GNU eqn does not provide the functionality of neqn: it does not support low-resolution, typewriter-like devices (although it may work adequately for very simple input).

OPTIONS

    –C   Recognize **.EQ** and **.EN** even when followed by a character other than space or newline.

    –N   Don't allow newlines within delimiters. This option allows **eqn** to recover better from missing closing delimiters.

    –v   Print the version number.

    –r   Only one size reduction.

    –m*n*   The minimum point-size is n. eqn will not reduce the size of subscripts or superscripts to a smaller size than n.

    –T*name*

           The output is for device *name*. The only effect of this is to define a macro *name* with a value of **1**. Typically **eqnrc** will use this to provide definitions appropriate for the output device. The default output device is **/usr/share/groff_font**.

    –M*dir*   Search *dir* for **eqnrc** before the default directories.

    –R   Don't load **eqnrc**.

    –f*F*   This is equivalent to a **gfont** *F* command.

    –s*n*   This is equivalent to a **gsize** *n* command. This option is deprecated. eqn will normally set equations at whatever the current point size is when the equation is encountered.

    –p*n*   This says that subscripts and superscripts should be n points smaller than the surrounding text. This option is deprecated. Normally eqn makes sets subscripts and superscripts at 70% of the size of the surrounding text.

USAGE

    Only the differences between GNU eqn and Unix eqn are described here.

    Most of the new features of GNU eqn are based on TEX. There are some references to the differences between TEX and GNU eqn below; these may safely be ignored if you do not know TEX.

Automatic spacing

    eqn gives each component of an equation a type, and adjusts the spacing between components using that type. Possible types are:

    ordinary   an ordinary character such as 1 or x;

    operator   a large operator such as Σ;

1

binary   a binary operator such as +;

relation   a relation such as =;

opening   a opening bracket such as (;

closing   a closing bracket such as);

punctuation   a punctutation character such as ,;

inner   a subformula contained within brackets;

suppress   spacing that suppresses automatic spacing adjustment.

Components of an equation get a type in one of two ways.

type *t e* This yields an equation component that contains *e* but that has type *t*, where *t* is one of the types
mentioned above. For example, **times** is defined as

> type "binary" \(mu

The name of the type doesn't have to be quoted, but quoting protects from macro expansion.

chartype *t text*

Unquoted groups of characters are split up into individual characters, and the type of each character is looked up; this changes the type that is stored for each character; it says that the characters in
text from now on have type *t*. For example,

> **chartype "punctuation"** .,;:

would make the characters .,;: have type punctuation whenever they subsequently appeared in an
equation. The type *t* can also be **letter** or **digit**; in these cases **chartype** changes the font type of
the characters. See the Fonts subsection.

New primitives

e1 **smallover** *e2*

This is similar to **over**; **smallover** reduces the size of *e1* and *e2*; it also puts less vertical space
between *e1* or *e2* and the fraction bar. The **over** primitive corresponds to the TEX **\over** primitive
in display styles; **smallover** corresponds to **\over** in non-display styles.

vcenter *e*

This vertically centers *e* about the math axis. The math axis is the vertical position about which
characters such as + and - are centered; also it is the vertical position used for the bar of fractions.
For example, **sum** is defined as

> { type "operator" vcenter size +5 \(*S }

e1 **accent** *e2*

This sets *e2* as an accent over *e1* . *e2* is assumed to be at the correct height for a lowercase letter;
e2 will be moved down according if *e1* is taller or shorter than a lowercase letter. For example,
hat is defined as

> accent { "^" }

dotdot, dot, tilde, vec and **dyad** are also defined using the **accent** primitive.

e1 **uaccent** *e2*

This sets *e2* as an accent under *e1* . *e2* is assumed to be at the correct height for a character
without a descender; *e2* will be moved down if *e1* has a descender. **utilde** is pre-defined using
uaccent as a tilde accent below the baseline.

split "*text*"

This has the same effect as simply

> *text*

but *text* is not subject to macro expansion because it is quoted; *text* will be split up and the spacing between individual characters will be adjusted.

nosplit *text*

This has the same effect as

  "*text***"**

but because *text* is not quoted it will be subject to macro expansion; *text* will not be split up and the spacing between individual characters will not be adjusted.

e **opprime**

This is a variant of **prime** that acts as an operator on *e*. It produces a different result from **prime** in a case such as **A opprime sub 1**: with **opprime** the **1** will be tucked under the prime as a subscript to the **A** (as is conventional in mathematical typesetting), whereas with **prime** the **1** will be a subscript to the prime character. The precedence of **opprime** is the same as that of **bar** and **under,** which is higher than that of everything except **accent** and **uaccent.** In unquoted text a **'** that is not the first character will be treated like **opprime.**

special *text e*

This constructs a new object from *e* using a **troff**(1) macro named *text*. When the macro is called, the string **0s** will contain the output for *e*, and the number registers **0w, 0h, 0d, 0skern** and **0skew** will contain the width, height, depth, subscript kern, and skew of *e*. (The *subscript kern* of an object says how much a subscript on that object should be tucked in; the *skew* of an object says how far to the right of the center of the object an accent over the object should be placed.) The macro must modify **0s** so that it will output the desired result with its origin at the current point, and increase the current horizontal position by the width of the object. The number registers must also be modified so that they correspond to the result.

For example, suppose you wanted a construct that 'cancels' an expression by drawing a diagonal line through it.

```
.EQ
define cancel 'special Ca'
.EN
.de Ca
.ds 0s \Z'\\*(0s'\v'\\n(0du'\D'l \\n(0wu -\\n(0hu-\\n(0du'\v'\\n(0hu'
..
```

Then you could cancel an expression *e* with **cancel {** *e* **}**

Here's a more complicated construct that draws a box round an expression:

```
.EQ
define box 'special Bx'
.EN
.de Bx
.ds 0s \Z'\h'1n'\\*(0s'\
\Z'\v'\\n(0du+1n'\D'l \\n(0wu+2n 0'\D'l 0 -\\n(0hu-\\n(0du-2n'\
\D'l -\\n(0wu-2n 0'\D'l 0 \\n(0hu+\\n(0du+2n''\h'\\n(0wu+2n'
.nr 0w +2n
.nr 0d +1n
.nr 0h +1n
..
```

Customization

The appearance of equations is controlled by a large number of parameters. These can be set using the **set** command.

1

set *p n*   This sets parameter *p* to value *n* ; *n* is an integer. For example,

        set x_height 45

says that **eqn** should assume an x height of 0.45 ems.

Possible parameters are as follows. Values are in units of hundredths of an em unless otherwise stated. These descriptions are intended to be expository rather than definitive.

minimum_size	**eqn** will not set anything at a smaller point-size than this. The value is in points.
fat_offset	The **fat** primitive emboldens an equation by overprinting two copies of the equation horizontally offset by this amount.
over_hang	A fraction bar will be longer by twice this amount than the maximum of the widths of the numerator and denominator; in other words, it will overhang the numerator and denominator by at least this amount.
accent_width	When **bar** or **under** is applied to a single character, the line will be this long. Normally, **bar** or **under** produces a line whose length is the width of the object to which it applies; in the case of a single character, this tends to produce a line that looks too long.
delimiter_factor	Extensible delimiters produced with the **left** and **right** primitives will have a combined height and depth of at least this many thousandths of twice the maximum amount by which the sub-equation that the delimiters enclose extends away from the axis.
delimiter_shortfall	Extensible delimiters produced with the **left** and **right** primitives will have a combined height and depth not less than the difference of twice the maximum amount by which the sub-equation that the delimiters enclose extends away from the axis and this amount.
null_delimiter_space	This much horizontal space is inserted on each side of a fraction.
script_space	The width of subscripts and superscripts is increased by this amount.
thin_space	This amount of space is automatically inserted after punctuation characters.
medium_space	This amount of space is automatically inserted on either side of binary operators.
thick_space	This amount of space is automatically inserted on either side of relations.
x_height	The height of lowercase letters without ascenders such as x.
axis_height	The height above the baseline of the center of characters such as + and −. It is important that this value is correct for the font you are using.
default_rule_thickness	This should set to the thickness of the \\(ru character, or the thickness of horizontal lines produced with the \\D escape sequence.
num1	The **over** command will shift up the numerator by at least this amount.
num2	The **smallover** command will shift up the numerator by at least this amount.
denom1	The **over** command will shift down the denominator by at least this amount.
denom2	The **smallover** command will shift down the denominator by at least this amount.

1

sup1	Normally superscripts will be shifted up by at least this amount.
sup2	Superscripts within superscripts or upper limits or numerators of **small-over** fractions will be shifted up by at least this amount. This is usually less than sup1.
sup3	Superscripts within denominators or square roots or subscripts or lower limits will be shifted up by at least this amount. This is usually less than sup2.
sub1	Subscripts will normally be shifted down by at least this amount.
sub2	When there is both a subscript and a superscript, the subscript will be shifted down by at least this amount.
sup_drop	The baseline of a superscript will be no more than this much amount below the top of the object on which the superscript is set.
sub_drop	The baseline of a subscript will be at least this much below the bottom of the object on which the subscript is set.
big_op_spacing1	The baseline of an upper limit will be at least this much above the top of the object on which the limit is set.
big_op_spacing2	The baseline of a lower limit will be at least this much below the bottom of the object on which the limit is set.
big_op_spacing3	The bottom of an upper limit will be at least this much above the top of the object on which the limit is set.
big_op_spacing4	The top of a lower limit will be at least this much below the bottom of the object on which the limit is set.
big_op_spacing5	This much vertical space will be added above and below limits.
baseline_sep	The baselines of the rows in a pile or matrix will normally be this far apart. In most cases this should be equal to the sum of **num1** and **denom1**.
shift_down	The midpoint between the top baseline and the bottom baseline in a matrix or pile will be shifted down by this much from the axis. In most cases this should be equal to **axis_height**.
column_sep	This much space will be added between columns in a matrix.
matrix_side_sep	This much space will be added at each side of a matrix.
draw_lines	If this is non-zero, lines will be drawn using the \D escape sequence, rather than with the \l escape sequence and the \(ru character.
body_height	The amount by which the height of the equation exceeds this will be added as extra space before the line containing the equation (using \x.) The default value is 85.
body_depth	The amount by which the depth of the equation exceeds this will be added as extra space after the line containing the equation (using \x.) The default value is 35.
nroff	If this is non-zero, then **ndefine** will behave like **define** and **tdefine** will be ignored, otherwise **tdefine** will behave like **define** and **ndefine** will be ignored. The default value is 0 (This is typically changed to 1 by the **eqnrc** file for the **ascii** and **latin1** devices.)

A more precise description of the role of many of these parameters can be found in Appendix H of *The TEXbook*.

1

Macros

Macros can take arguments. In a macro body, **$n** where *n* is between 1 and 9, will be replaced by the *n-th* argument if the macro is called with arguments; if there are fewer than *n* arguments, it will be replaced by nothing. A word containing a left parenthesis where the part of the word before the left parenthesis has been defined using the **define** command will be recognized as a macro call with arguments; characters following the left parenthesis up to a matching right parenthesis will be treated as comma-separated arguments; commas inside nested parentheses do not terminate an argument.

sdefine *name X anything X*

> This is like the **define** command, but *name* will not be recognized if called with arguments.

include "*file*"

> Include the contents of *file*. Lines of *file* beginning with **.EQ** or **.EN** will be ignored.

ifdef *name X anything X*

> If *name* has been defined by **define** (or has been automatically defined because *name* is the output device) process *anything*; otherwise ignore *anything*. *X* can be any character not appearing in *anything*.

Fonts

eqn normally uses at least two fonts to set an equation: an italic font for letters, and a roman font for everything else. The existing **gfont** command changes the font that is used as the italic font. By default this is **I**. The font that is used as the roman font can be changed using the new **grfont** command.

grfont *f* Set the roman font to *f*.

The **italic** primitive uses the current italic font set by **gfont**; the **roman** primitive uses the current roman font set by **grfont**. There is also a new **gbfont** command, which changes the font used by the **bold** primitive. If you only use the **roman**, **italic** and **bold** primitives to changes fonts within an equation, you can change all the fonts used by your equations just by using **gfont**, **grfont** and **gbfont** commands.

You can control which characters are treated as letters (and therefore set in italics) by using the **chartype** command described above. A type of **letter** will cause a character to be set in italic type. A type of **digit** will cause a character to be set in roman type.

FILES

> **/usr/share/tmac/eqnrc**   Initialization file.

BUGS

> Inline equations will be set at the point size that is current at the beginning of the input line.

SEE ALSO

> **groff**(1), **troff**(1), **groff_font**(5), *The TₑXbook*

NAME

`error` – analyze and disperse compiler error messages

SYNOPSIS

`error [ –n] [ –s] [ –q] [ –v] [ –t` *suffixlist*`] [ –I` *ignorefile*`] [name]`

DESCRIPTION

Error analyzes and optionally disperses the diagnostic error messages produced by a number of compilers and language processors to the source file and line where the errors occurred. It can replace the painful, traditional methods of scribbling abbreviations of errors on paper, and permits error messages and source code to be viewed simultaneously without machinations of multiple windows in a screen editor.

Options are:

–n   Do *not* touch any files; all error messages are sent to the standard output.

–q   The user is *queried* whether s/he wants to touch the file. A ''y'' or ''n'' to the question is necessary to continue. Absence of the –q option implies that all referenced files (except those referring to discarded error messages) are to be touched.

–v   After all files have been touched, overlay the visual editor `vi`(1) with it set up to edit all files touched, and positioned in the first touched file at the first error. If `vi`(1) can't be found, try `ex`(1) or `ed`(1) from standard places.

–t   Take the following argument as a suffix list. Files whose suffixes do not appear in the suffix list are not touched. The suffix list is dot separated, and ''*'' wildcards work. Thus the suffix list:

`.c.y.foo*.h`

allows **error** to touch files ending with ''.c'', ''.y'', ''.foo*'' and ''.y''.

–s   Print out *statistics* regarding the error categorization. Not too useful.

Error looks at the error messages, either from the specified file *name* or from the standard input, and attempts to determine which language processor produced each error message, determines the source file and line number to which the error message refers, determines if the error message is to be ignored or not, and inserts the (possibly slightly modified) error message into the source file as a comment on the line preceding to which the line the error message refers. Error messages which can't be categorized by language processor or content are not inserted into any file, but are sent to the standard output. **Error** touches source files only after all input has been read.

Error is intended to be run with its standard input connected via a pipe to the error message source. Some language processors put error messages on their standard error file; others put their messages on the standard output. Hence, both error sources should be piped together into **error**. For example, when using the `csh`(1) syntax,

`make –s lint | error –q –v`

will analyze all the error messages produced by whatever programs `make`(1) runs when making lint.

Error knows about the error messages produced by: `make`(1), `cc`(1), `cpp`(1), `ccom`(1), `as`(1), `ld`(1), `lint`(1), `pi`(1), `pc`(1), `f77`(1), and *DEC Western Research Modula–2*. **Error** knows a standard format for error messages produced by the language processors, so is sensitive to changes in these formats. For all languages except *Pascal*, error messages are restricted to be on one line. Some error messages refer to more than one line in more than one files; **error** will duplicate the error message and insert it at all of the places referenced.

1

Error will do one of six things with error messages.

synchronize Some language processors produce short errors describing which file it is processing. **Error** uses these to determine the file name for languages that don't include the file name in each error message. These synchronization messages are consumed entirely by **error**.

discard Error messages from lint(1) that refer to one of the two lint(1) libraries, /usr/libdata/lint/llib-lc and /usr/libdata/lint/llib-port are discarded, to prevent accidently touching these libraries. Again, these error messages are consumed entirely by **error**.

nullify Error messages from lint(1) can be nullified if they refer to a specific function, which is known to generate diagnostics which are not interesting. Nullified error messages are not inserted into the source file, but are written to the standard output. The names of functions to ignore are taken from either the file named .errorrc in the users's home directory, or from the file named by the −I option. If the file does not exist, no error messages are nullified. If the file does exist, there must be one function name per line.

not file specific
Error messages that can't be intuited are grouped together, and written to the standard output before any files are touched. They will not be inserted into any source file.

file specific Error message that refer to a specific file, but to no specific line, are written to the standard output when that file is touched.

true errors Error messages that can be intuited are candidates for insertion into the file to which they refer.

Only true error messages are candidates for inserting into the file they refer to. Other error messages are consumed entirely by **error** or are written to the standard output. **Error** inserts the error messages into the source file on the line preceding the line the language processor found in error. Each error message is turned into a one line comment for the language, and is internally flagged with the string ''###'' at the beginning of the error, and ''%%%'' at the end of the error. This makes pattern searching for errors easier with an editor, and allows the messages to be easily removed. In addition, each error message contains the source line number for the line the message refers to. A reasonably formatted source program can be recompiled with the error messages still in it, without having the error messages themselves cause future errors. For poorly formatted source programs in free format languages, such as C or Pascal, it is possible to insert a comment into another comment, which can wreak havoc with a future compilation. To avoid this, programs with comments and source on the same line should be formatted so that language statements appear before comments.

Error catches interrupt and terminate signals, and if in the insertion phase, will orderly terminate what it is doing.

FILES
~/.errorrc function names to ignore for lint(1) error messages
/dev/tty user's teletype

HISTORY
The **error** command appeared in 4.0BSD.

AUTHOR
Robert Henry

BUGS

Opens the teletype directly to do user querying.

Source files with links make a new copy of the file with only one link to it.

Changing a language processor's format of error messages may cause **error** to not understand the error message.

Error, since it is purely mechanical, will not filter out subsequent errors caused by 'floodgating' initiated by one syntactically trivial error. Humans are still much better at discarding these related errors.

Pascal error messages belong after the lines affected (error puts them before). The alignment of the '\' marking the point of error is also disturbed by **error**.

Error was designed for work on CRT's at reasonably high speed. It is less pleasant on slow speed terminals, and has never been used on hardcopy terminals.

1

NAME
expand, unexpand – expand tabs to spaces, and vice versa

SYNOPSIS
expand [*–tabstop*] [*–tab1,tab2,...,tabn*] *file ...*
unexpand [*–a*] *file ...*

DESCRIPTION
Expand processes the named files or the standard input writing the standard output with tabs changed into blanks. Backspace characters are preserved into the output and decrement the column count for tab calculations. Expand is useful for pre-processing character files (before sorting, looking at specific columns, etc.) that contain tabs.

If a single *tabstop* argument is given, then tabs are set *tabstop* spaces apart instead of the default 8. If multiple tabstops are given then the tabs are set at those specific columns.

Unexpand puts tabs back into the data from the standard input or the named files and writes the result on the standard output.

Option (with unexpand only):

–a   By default, only leading blanks and tabs are reconverted to maximal strings of tabs. If the –a option is given, then tabs are inserted whenever they would compress the resultant file by replacing two or more characters.

HISTORY
The expand command appeared in 3.0BSD.

1

NAME

expr – evaluate arguments as an expression

SYNOPSIS

expr arg ...

DESCRIPTION

The arguments are taken as an expression. After evaluation, the result is written on the standard output. Each token of the expression is a separate argument.

The operators and keywords are listed below. The list is in order of increasing precedence, with equal precedence operators grouped.

expr | expr

      yields the first *expr* if it is neither null nor '0', otherwise yields the second *expr*.

expr & expr

      yields the first *expr* if neither *expr* is null or '0', otherwise yields '0'.

expr relop expr

      where *relop is one of* < <= = != >= >, yields '1' if the indicated comparison is true, '0' if false. The comparison is numeric if both *expr* are integers, otherwise lexicographic.

expr + expr
expr – expr

      addition or subtraction of the arguments.

*expr * expr*
expr / expr
expr % expr

      multiplication, division, or remainder of the arguments.

expr : expr

      The matching operator compares the string first argument with the regular expression second argument; regular expression syntax is the same as that of *ed*(1). The \(...\) pattern symbols can be used to select a portion of the first argument. Otherwise, the matching operator yields the number of characters matched ('0' on failure).

(*expr*)   parentheses for grouping.

Examples:

To add 1 to the Shell variable *a*:

    a=`expr $a + 1`

To find the filename part (least significant part) of the pathname stored in variable *a*, which may or may not contain '/':

    expr $a : ´.*\(.*\)´ ´|´ $a

Note the quoted Shell metacharacters.

SEE ALSO

sh(1), test(1)

DIAGNOSTICS

Expr returns the following exit codes:

0	if the expression is neither null nor '0',
1	if the expression is null or '0',
2	for invalid expressions.

1

NAME

`false` – return false value

SYNOPSIS

`false`

DESCRIPTION

`False` is usually used in a Bourne shell script. It tests for the appropriate status "false" before running (or failing to run) a list of commands.

The `false` utility always exits with a value other than zero.

SEE ALSO

csh(1), sh(1), true(1)

STANDARDS

The `false` utility is expected to be IEEE Std1003.2 (''POSIX'') compatible.

NAME

file – identify file content

SYNOPSIS

file [**–h**] *file* ...

DESCRIPTION

File tests the specified files and attempts to classify them. If a file is a text file, it attempts to determine the type of text (e.g. csh(1) commands or C source code).

The options are as follows:

–h   If a symbolic link is specified, identify the file as a symbolic link. By default, symbolic links are only identified if they reference non-existent files.

COMPATIBILITY

Previous implementations of the **file** utility did not follow symbolic links by default.

BUGS

As many tests are used and **file** stops testing on the first successful one, it can often make mistakes.

HISTORY

A **file** command appeared in Version 6 AT&T UNIX.

NAME

find – walk a file hierarchy

SYNOPSIS

find [**–H** | **–L** | **–P**] [**–Xdx**] [**–f** *file*] [*file* ...] *expression*

DESCRIPTION

Find recursively descends the directory tree for each *file* listed, evaluating an *expression* (composed of the "primaries" and "operands" listed below) in terms of each file in the tree.

The options are as follows:

–H   The **–H** option causes the file information and file type (see stat(2)) returned for each symbolic link specified on the command line to be those of the file referenced by the link, not the link itself. If the referenced file does not exist, the file information and type will be for the link itself. File information of all symbolic links not on the command line is that of the link itself.

–L   The **–L** option causes the file information and file type (see stat(2)) returned for each symbolic link to be those of the file referenced by the link, not the link itself. If the referenced file does not exist, the file information and type will be for the link itself.

–P   The **–P** option causes the file information and file type (see stat(2)) returned for each symbolic link to be those of the link itself.

–X   The **–X** option is a modification to permit **find** to be safely used in conjunction with xargs(1). If a file name contains any of the delimiting characters used by xargs, a diagnostic message is displayed on standard error, and the file is skipped. The delimiting characters include single (" ' ") and double (" " ") quotes, backslash ("\"), space, tab and newline characters.

–d   The **–d** option causes **find** to perform a depth–first traversal, i.e. directories are visited in post–order and all entries in a directory will be acted on before the directory itself. By default, **find** visits directories in pre–order, i.e. before their contents. Note, the default is *not* a breadth–first traversal.

–f   The **–f** option specifies a file hierarchy for **find** to traverse. File hierarchies may also be specified as the operands immediately following the options.

–x   The **–x** option prevents **find** from descending into directories that have a device number different than that of the file from which the descent began.

PRIMARIES

-atime *n*

True if the difference between the file last access time and the time **find** was started, rounded up to the next full 24–hour period, is *n* 24–hour periods.

-ctime *n*

True if the difference between the time of last change of file status information and the time **find** was started, rounded up to the next full 24–hour period, is *n* 24–hour periods.

-exec *utility* [argument ...];

True if the program named *utility* returns a zero value as its exit status. Optional arguments may be passed to the utility. The expression must be terminated by a semicolon (";"). If the string "{}" appears anywhere in the utility name or the arguments it is replaced by the pathname of the current file. *Utility* will be executed from the directory from which **find** was executed.

-fstype *type*

    True if the file is contained in a file system of type *type*. Currently supported types are "local", "mfs", "nfs", "msdos", "rdonly" and "ufs". The types "local" and "rdonly" are not specific file system types. The former matches any file system physically mounted on the system where the **find** is being executed and the latter matches any file system which is mounted read-only.

-group *gname*

    True if the file belongs to the group *gname*. If *gname* is numeric and there is no such group name, then *gname* is treated as a group id.

-inum *n*

    True if the file has inode number *n*.

-links *n*

    True if the file has *n* links.

-ls   This primary always evaluates to true. The following information for the current file is written to standard output: its inode number, size in 512–byte blocks, file permissions, number of hard links, owner, group, size in bytes, last modification time, and pathname. If the file is a block or character special file, the major and minor numbers will be displayed instead of the size in bytes. If the file is a symbolic link, the pathname of the linked–to file will be displayed preceded by "–>". The format is identical to that produced by "ls –dgils".

-mtime *n*

    True if the difference between the file last modification time and the time **find** was started, rounded up to the next full 24–hour period, is *n* 24–hour periods.

-ok *utility*[argument ...];

    The **-ok** primary is identical to the **-exec** primary with the exception that **find** requests user affirmation for the execution of the utility by printing a message to the terminal and reading a response. If the response is other than "y" the command is not executed and the value of the *ok* expression is false.

-name *pattern*

    True if the last component of the pathname being examined matches *pattern*. Special shell pattern matching characters ("[", "]", "*", and "?") may be used as part of *pattern*. These characters may be matched explicitly by escaping them with a backslash ("\").

-newer *file*

    True if the current file has a more recent last modification time than *file*.

-nouser

    True if the file belongs to an unknown user.

-nogroup

    True if the file belongs to an unknown group.

-path *pattern*

    True if the pathname being examined matches *pattern*. Special shell pattern matching characters ("[", "]", "*", and "?") may be used as part of *pattern*. These characters may be matched explicitly by escaping them with a backslash ("\"). Slashes ("/") are treated as normal characters and do not have to be matched explicitly.

-perm [*–mode*]

    The *mode* may be either symbolic (see chmod(1)) or an octal number. If the mode is symbolic, a starting value of zero is assumed and the mode sets or clears permissions without regard to the process' file mode creation mask. If the mode is octal, only bits 07777 (S_ISUID | S_ISGID | S_ISTXT | S_IRWXU | S_IRWXG | S_IRWXO) of the file's mode bits participate in the comparis-

1

on. If the mode is preceded by a dash (''−''), this primary evaluates to true if at least all of the bits in the mode are set in the file's mode bits. If the mode is not preceded by a dash, this primary evaluates to true if the bits in the mode exactly match the file's mode bits. Note, the first character of a symbolic mode may not be a dash (''−'').

-print

This primary always evaluates to true. It prints the pathname of the current file to standard output. The expression is appended to the user specified expression if neither **-exec**, **-ls** or **-ok** is specified.

-prune

This primary always evaluates to true. It causes **find** to not descend into the current file. Note, the **-prune** primary has no effect if the **−d** option was specified.

-size *n*[*c*]

True if the file's size, rounded up, in 512–byte blocks is *n*. If *n* is followed by a ''c'', then the primary is true if the file's size is *n* bytes.

-type *t*

True if the file is of the specified type. Possible file types are as follows:

b	block special
c	character special
d	directory
f	regular file
l	symbolic link
p	FIFO
s	socket

-user *uname*

True if the file belongs to the user *uname*. If *uname* is numeric and there is no such user name, then *uname* is treated as a user id.

All primaries which take a numeric argument allow the number to be preceded by a plus sign (''+'') or a minus sign (''−''). A preceding plus sign means ''more than n'', a preceding minus sign means ''less than n'' and neither means ''exactly n'' .

OPERATORS

The primaries may be combined using the following operators. The operators are listed in order of decreasing precedence.

(*expression*) This evaluates to true if the parenthesized expression evaluates to true.

! *expression*   This is the unary NOT operator. It evaluates to true if the expression is false.

expression **-and** *expression*

expression *expression*

The **-and** operator is the logical AND operator. As it is implied by the juxtaposition of two expressions it does not have to be specified. The expression evaluates to true if both expressions are true. The second expression is not evaluated if the first expression is false.

expression **-or** *expression*

The **-or** operator is the logical OR operator. The expression evaluates to true if either the first or the second expression is true. The second expression is not evaluated if the first expression is true.

All operands and primaries must be separate arguments to **find**. Primaries which themselves take arguments expect each argument to be a separate argument to **find**.

EXAMPLES
The following examples are shown as given to the shell:

    find / \! -name *.c" -print"
Print out a list of all the files whose names do not end in ".c".

    find / -newer ttt -user wnj -print
Print out a list of all the files owned by user "wnj" that are newer than the file "ttt".

    find / \! \(-newer ttt -user wnj \) -print
Print out a list of all the files which are not both newer than "ttt" and owned by "wnj".

    find / \(-newer ttt -or -user wnj \) -print
Print out a list of all the files that are either owned by "wnj" or that are newer than "ttt".

SEE ALSO
chmod(1), locate(1), stat(2), fts(3), getgrent(3), getpwent(3), strmode(3), symlink(7)

STANDARDS
The **find** utility syntax is a superset of the syntax specified by the IEEE Std1003.2 ("POSIX") standard.

The −s and −X options and the -**inum** and -**ls** primaries are extensions to IEEE Std1003.2 ("POSIX").

Historically, the −d, −h and −x options were implemented using the primaries "−depth", "−follow", and "−xdev". These primaries always evaluated to true. As they were really global variables that took effect before the traversal began, some legal expressions could have unexpected results. An example is the expression "−print −o −depth". As −print always evaluates to true, the standard order of evaluation implies that −depth would never be evaluated. This is not the case.

The operator "-or" was implemented as "−o", and the operator "-and" was implemented as "−a".

Historic implementations of the **exec** and **ok** primaries did not replace the string "{}" in the utility name or the utility arguments if it had preceding or following non-whitespace characters. This version replaces it no matter where in the utility name or arguments it appears.

BUGS
The special characters used by **find** are also special characters to many shell programs. In particular, the characters "*", "[", "]", "?", "(", ")", "!", "\" and ";" may have to be escaped from the shell.

As there is no delimiter separating options and file names or file names and the *expression*, it is difficult to specify files named "-xdev" or "!". These problems are handled by the −f option and the getopt(3) "--" construct.

1

NAME

finger – user information lookup program

SYNOPSIS

finger [**-lmsp**] [*user* ...] [*user@host* ...]

DESCRIPTION

The **finger** displays information about the system users.

Options are:

-s   **Finger** displays the user's login name, real name, terminal name and write status (as a ''*'' before the terminal name if write permission is denied), idle time, login time, office location and office phone number.

    Idle time is in minutes if it is a single integer, hours and minutes if a '':'' is present, or days if a ''d'' is present. Login time is displayed as month, day, hours and minutes, unless more than six months ago, in which case the year is displayed rather than the hours and minutes.

    Unknown devices as well as nonexistent idle and login times are displayed as single asterisks.

-l   Produces a multi-line format displaying all of the information described for the −s option as well as the user's home directory, home phone number, login shell, and the contents of the files ''.forward'', ''.plan'' and ''.project'' from the user's home directory.

    If idle time is at least a minute and less than a day, it is presented in the form ''hh:mm''. Idle times greater than a day are presented as ''d day[s]hh:mm''.

    Phone numbers specified as eleven digits are printed as ''+N-NNN-NNN-NNNN''. Numbers specified as ten or seven digits are printed as the appropriate subset of that string. Numbers specified as five digits are printed as ''xN-NNNN''.

    If write permission is denied to the device, the phrase ''(messages off)'' is appended to the line containing the device name. One entry per user is displayed with the −l option; if a user is logged on multiple times, terminal information is repeated once per login.

-p   Prevents the −l option of **finger** from displaying the contents of the ''.forward'', ''.plan'' and ''.project'' files.

-m   Prevent matching of *user* names. *User* is usually a login name; however, matching will also be done on the users' real names, unless the −m option is supplied. All name matching performed by **finger** is case insensitive.

If no options are specified, **finger** defaults to the −l style output if operands are provided, otherwise to the −s style. Note that some fields may be missing, in either format, if information is not available for them.

If no arguments are specified, **finger** will print an entry for each user currently logged into the system.

Finger may be used to look up users on a remote machine. The format is to specify a *user* as ''user@host'', or ''@host'', where the default output format for the former is the −l style, and the default output format for the latter is the −s style. The −l option is the only option that may be passed to a remote machine.

FILES

/var/log/lastlog   last login data base

SEE ALSO

chpass(1), w(1), who(1),

HISTORY

The **finger** command appeared in 3.0BSD.

1

NAME

fmt – simple text formatter

SYNOPSIS

fmt [*goal* [*maximum*]] [name ...]

DESCRIPTION

Fmt is a simple text formatter which reads the concatenation of input files (or standard input if none are given) and produces on standard output a version of its input with lines as close to the *goal* length as possible without exceeding the maximum. The *goal* length defaults to 65 and the maximum to 75. The spacing at the beginning of the input lines is preserved in the output, as are blank lines and interword spacing.

Fmt is meant to format mail messages prior to sending, but may also be useful for other simple tasks. For instance, within visual mode of the ex(1) editor (e.g. vi(1)) the command

      ! } fmt

will reformat a paragraph, evening the lines.

SEE ALSO

nroff(1), mail(1)

HISTORY

The **fmt** command appeared in 3BSD.

BUGS

The program was designed to be simple and fast – for more complex operations, the standard text processors are likely to be more appropriate.

1

NAME

   fold – fold long lines for finite width output device

SYNOPSIS

   fold [–w *width*] *file* ...

DESCRIPTION

   Fold is a filter which folds the contents of the specified files, or the standard input if no files are specified, breaking the lines to have maximum of 80 characters.

   The options are as follows:

   –w   Specifies a line width to use instead of the default 80 characters. *Width* should be a multiple of 8 if tabs are present, or the tabs should be expanded using expand(1) before using fold.

SEE ALSO

   expand(1)

BUGS

   If underlining is present it may be messed up by folding.

1

NAME
fpr – print Fortran file

SYNOPSIS
fpr

DESCRIPTION
Fpr is a filter that transforms files formatted according to Fortran's carriage control conventions into files formatted according to UNIX line printer conventions.

Fpr copies its input onto its output, replacing the carriage control characters with characters that will produce the intended effects when printed using lpr(1). The first character of each line determines the vertical spacing as follows:

Blank	One line
0	Two lines
1	To first line of next page
+	No advance

A blank line is treated as if its first character is a blank. A blank that appears as a carriage control character is deleted. A zero is changed to a newline. A one is changed to a form feed. The effects of a "+" are simulated using backspaces.

EXAMPLES
```
a.out | fpr | lpr

fpr < f77.output | lpr
```

HISTORY
The **fpr** command appeared in 4.2BSD.

BUGS
Results are undefined for input lines longer than 170 characters.

NAME
from – print names of those who have sent mail

SYNOPSIS
from [−s *sender*] [−f *file*] [*user*]

DESCRIPTION
From prints out the mail header lines from the invoker's mailbox.

Options:

−f *file*   The supplied file is examined instead of the invoker's mailbox. If the −f option is used, the *user* argument should not be used.

−s *sender*
Only mail from addresses containing the supplied string are printed.

If *user* is given, the *user*'s mailbox, is examined instead of the invoker's own mailbox. (Privileges are required.)

FILES
/var/mail/*

SEE ALSO
biff(1), mail(1)

HISTORY
The from command appeared in 3.0BSD.

1

NAME

fsplit – split a multi-routine Fortran file into individual files

SYNOPSIS

fsplit [**–e** *efile*] ... [*file*]

DESCRIPTION

Fsplit takes as input either a file or standard input containing Fortran source code. It attempts to split the input into separate routine files of the form *name.f*, where *name* is the name of the program unit (e.g. function, subroutine, block data or program). The name for unnamed block data subprograms has the form *blkdtaNNN.f* where NNN is three digits and a file of this name does not already exist. For unnamed main programs the name has the form *mainNNN.f*. If there is an error in classifying a program unit, or if *name.f* already exists, the program unit will be put in a file of the form *zzzNNN.f* where *zzzNNN.f* does not already exist.

–e *efile* Normally each subprogram unit is split into a separate file. When the –e option is used, only the specified subprogram units are split into separate files. E.g.:

    fsplit -e readit -e doit prog.f

will split readit and doit into separate files.

DIAGNOSTICS

If names specified via the –e option are not found, a diagnostic is written to standard error.

HISTORY

The **fsplit** command appeared in 4.2BSD.

AUTHORS

Asa Romberger and Jerry Berkman

BUGS

Fsplit assumes the subprogram name is on the first noncomment line of the subprogram unit. Nonstandard source formats may confuse **fsplit**.

It is hard to use –e for unnamed main programs and block data subprograms since you must predict the created file name.

1

NAME
   fstat – file status

SYNOPSIS
   fstat [–fnv] [–M core] [–N system] [–p pid] [–u user] [filename...]

DESCRIPTION
   Fstat identifies open files. A file is considered open by a process if it was explicitly opened, is the working directory, root directory, active pure text, or kernel trace file for that process. If no options are specified, fstat reports on all open files in the system.

   Options:

   –f   Restrict examination to files open in the same filesystems as the named file arguments, or to the filesystem containing the current directory if there are no additional filename arguments. For example, to find all files open in the filesystem where the directory /usr/src resides, type "fstat -f /usr/src".

   –M   Extract values associated with the name list from the specified core instead of the default /dev/kmem.

   –N   Extract the name list from the specified system instead of the default /vmunix.

   –n   Numerical format. Print the device number (maj,min) of the filesystem the file resides in rather than the mount point name; for special files, print the device number that the special device refers to rather than the filename in /dev; and print the mode of the file in octal instead of symbolic form.

   –p   Report all files open by the specified process.

   –u   Report all files open by the specified user.

   –v   Verbose mode. Print error messages upon failures to locate particular system data structures rather than silently ignoring them. Most of these data structures are dynamically created or deleted and it is possible for them to disappear while fstat is running. This is normal and unavoidable since the rest of the system is running while fstat itself is running.

   filename ...
           Restrict reports to the specified files.

   The following fields are printed:

   USER   The username of the owner of the process (effective uid).

   CMD   The command name of the process.

   PID   The process id.

   FD   The file number in the per-process open file table or one of the following special names:

                   text   - pure text inode wd   - current working directory root   - root inode
                   tr   - kernel trace file

           If the file number is followed by an asterisk ("*"), the file is not an inode, but rather a socket, FIFO, or there is an error. In this case the remainder of the line doesn't correspond to the remaining headers -- the format of the line is described later under Sockets.

1

MOUNT   If the −n flag wasn't specified, this header is present and is the pathname that the filesystem the file resides in is mounted on.

DEV   If the −n flag is specified, this header is present and is the major/minor number of the device that this file resides in.

INUM   The inode number of the file.

MODE   The mode of the file. If the −n flag isn't specified, the mode is printed using a symbolic format (see strmode(3)); otherwise, the mode is printed as an octal number.

SZ│DV   If the file is not a character or block special, prints the size of the file in bytes. Otherwise, if the −n flag is not specified, prints the name of the special file as located in /dev. If that cannot be located, or the −n flag is specified, prints the major/minor device number that the special device refers to.

R/W   This column describes the access mode that the file allows. The letter ''r'' indicates open for reading; the letter ''w'' indicates open for writing. This field is useful when trying to find the processes that are preventing a filesystem from being down graded to read-only.

NAME   If filename arguments are specified and the −f flag is not, then this field is present and is the name associated with the given file. Normally the name cannot be determined since there is no mapping from an open file back to the directory entry that was used to open that file. Also, since different directory entries may reference the same file (via ln(2)), the name printed may not be the actual name that the process originally used to open that file.

SOCKETS

The formating of open sockets depends on the protocol domain. In all cases the first field is the domain name, the second field is the socket type (stream, dgram, etc), and the third is the socket flags field (in hex). The remaining fields are protocol dependent. For tcp, it is the address of the tcpcb, and for udp, the inpcb (socket pcb). For unix domain sockets, its the address of the socket pcb and the address of the connected pcb (if connected). Otherwise the protocol number and address of the socket itself are printed. The attempt is to make enough information available to permit further analysis without duplicating netstat(1).

For example, the addresses mentioned above are the addresses which the ''netstat -A'' command would print for tcp, udp, and unixdomain. Note that since pipes are implemented using sockets, a pipe appears as a connected unix domain stream socket. A unidirectional unix domain socket indicates the direction of flow with an arrow (''<-'' or ''->''), and a full duplex socket shows a double arrow (''<->'').

BUGS

Since fstat takes a snapshot of the system, it is only correct for a very short period of time.

SEE ALSO

netstat(1), nfsstat(1), ps(1), systat(1), vmstat(1), iostat(8), pstat(8)

HISTORY

The fstat command appeared in 4.3BSD–Tahoe.

NAME

ftp – ARPANET file transfer program

SYNOPSIS

ftp [–v] [–d] [–i] [–n] [–g] [host]

DESCRIPTION

Ftp is the user interface to the ARPANET standard File Transfer Protocol. The program allows a user to transfer files to and from a remote network site.

Options may be specified at the command line, or to the command interpreter.

–v   Verbose option forces ftp to show all responses from the remote server, as well as report on data transfer statistics.

–n   Restrains ftp from attempting "auto-login" upon initial connection. If auto-login is enabled, ftp will check the .netrc (see below) file in the user's home directory for an entry describing an account on the remote machine. If no entry exists, ftp will prompt for the remote machine login name (default is the user identity on the local machine), and, if necessary, prompt for a password and an account with which to login.

–i   Turns off interactive prompting during multiple file transfers.

–d   Enables debugging.

–g   Disables file name globbing.

The client host with which ftp is to communicate may be specified on the command line. If this is done, ftp will immediately attempt to establish a connection to an FTP server on that host; otherwise, ftp will enter its command interpreter and await instructions from the user. When ftp is awaiting commands from the user the prompt ftp> is provided to the user. The following commands are recognized by ftp:

! [command [args]]
        Invoke an interactive shell on the local machine. If there are arguments, the first is taken to be a command to execute directly, with the rest of the arguments as its arguments.

$ macro-name [args]
        Execute the macro macro-name that was defined with the macdef command. Arguments are passed to the macro unglobbed.

account [passwd]
        Supply a supplemental password required by a remote system for access to resources once a login has been successfully completed. If no argument is included, the user will be prompted for an account password in a non-echoing input mode.

append local-file [remote-file]
        Append a local file to a file on the remote machine. If remote-file is left unspecified, the local file name is used in naming the remote file after being altered by any ntrans or nmap setting. File transfer uses the current settings for type, format, mode, and structure.

ascii   Set the file transfer type to network ASCII. This is the default type.

bell   Arrange that a bell be sounded after each file transfer command is completed.

binary   Set the file transfer type to support binary image transfer.

bye   Terminate the FTP session with the remote server and exit **ftp**. An end of file will also terminate the session and exit.

case   Toggle remote computer file name case mapping during **mget** commands. When **case** is on (default is off), remote computer file names with all letters in upper case are written in the local directory with the letters mapped to lower case.

cd *remote-directory*
               Change the working directory on the remote machine to *remote-directory*.

cdup   Change the remote machine working directory to the parent of the current remote machine working directory.

chmod *mode file-name*
               Change the permission modes of the file *file-name* on the remote sytem to *mode*.

close   Terminate the FTP session with the remote server, and return to the command interpreter. Any defined macros are erased.

cr   Toggle carriage return stripping during ascii type file retrieval. Records are denoted by a carriage return/linefeed sequence during ascii type file transfer. When **cr** is on (the default), carriage returns are stripped from this sequence to conform with the UNIX single linefeed record delimiter. Records on non–Ux remote systems may contain single linefeeds; when an ascii type transfer is made, these linefeeds may be distinguished from a record delimiter only when **cr** is off.

delete *remote-file*
               Delete the file *remote-file* on the remote machine.

debug [*debug-value*]
               Toggle debugging mode. If an optional *debug-value* is specified it is used to set the debugging level. When debugging is on, **ftp** prints each command sent to the remote machine, preceded by the string —>

dir [*remote-directory*] [*local-file*]
               Print a listing of the directory contents in the directory, *remote-directory*, and, optionally, placing the output in *local-file*. If interactive prompting is on, **ftp** will prompt the user to verify that the last argument is indeed the target local file for receiving **dir** output. If no directory is specified, the current working directory on the remote machine is used. If no local file is specified, or *local-file* is −, output comes to the terminal.

disconnect
               A synonym for *close*.

form *format*
               Set the file transfer **form** to *format*. The default format is "file".

get *remote-file* [*local-file*]
               Retrieve the *remote-file* and store it on the local machine. If the local file name is not specified, it is given the same name it has on the remote machine, subject to alteration by the current **case**, **ntrans**, and **nmap** settings. The current settings for **type**, **form**, **mode**, and **structure** are used while transferring the file.

glob   Toggle filename expansion for **mdelete**, **mget** and **mput**. If globbing is turned off with **glob**, the file name arguments are taken literally and not expanded. Globbing for **mput** is done as in csh(1). For **mdelete** and **mget**, each remote file name is expanded separately on the remote machine and the lists are not merged. Expansion of a directory name is likely to be different from expansion of the name of an ordinary file: the exact result depends on the

1

       foreign operating system and ftp server, and can be previewed by doing `mls remote-files` — Note: **mget** and **mput** are not meant to transfer entire directory subtrees of files. That can be done by transferring a `tar(1)` archive of the subtree (in binary mode).

hash   Toggle hash-sign ("#") printing for each data block transferred. The size of a data block is 1024 bytes.

help [*command*]
      Print an informative message about the meaning of *command*. If no argument is given, **ftp** prints a list of the known commands.

idle [*seconds*]
      Set the inactivity timer on the remote server to *seconds* seconds. If *seconds* is omitted, the current inactivity timer is printed.

lcd [*directory*]
      Change the working directory on the local machine. If no *directory* is specified, the user's home directory is used.

ls [*remote-directory*] [*local-file*]
      Print a listing of the contents of a directory on the remote machine. The listing includes any system-dependent information that the server chooses to include; for example, most UNIX systems will produce output from the command 'ls −l'. (See also **nlist**.) If *remote-directory* is left unspecified, the current working directory is used. If interactive prompting is on, **ftp** will prompt the user to verify that the last argument is indeed the target local file for receiving **ls** output. If no local file is specified, or if *local-file* is '−', the output is sent to the terminal.

macdefNs *macro-name*
      Define a macro. Subsequent lines are stored as the macro *macro-name*; a null line (consecutive newline characters in a file or carriage returns from the terminal) terminates macro input mode. There is a limit of 16 macros and 4096 total characters in all defined macros. Macros remain defined until a **close** command is executed. The macro processor interprets '$' and '\' as special characters. A '$' followed by a number (or numbers) is replaced by the corresponding argument on the macro invocation command line. A '$' followed by an 'i' signals that macro processor that the executing macro is to be looped. On the first pass '$i' is replaced by the first argument on the macro invocation command line, on the second pass it is replaced by the second argument, and so on. A '\' followed by any character is replaced by that character. Use the '\' to prevent special treatment of the '$'.

mdelete [*remote-files*]
      Delete the *remote-files* on the remote machine.

mdir *remote-files local-file*
      Like **dir**, except multiple remote files may be specified. If interactive prompting is on, **ftp** will prompt the user to verify that the last argument is indeed the target local file for receiving **mdir** output.

mget *remote-files*
      Expand the *remote-files* on the remote machine and do a **get** for each file name thus produced. See **glob** for details on the filename expansion. Resulting file names will then be processed according to **case**, **ntrans**, and **nmap** settings. Files are transferred into the local working directory, which can be changed with `lcd directory`; new local directories can be created with `! mkdir directory`.

1

mkdir *directory-name*

Make a directory on the remote machine.

mls *remote-files local-file*

Like **nlist**, except multiple remote files may be specified, and the *local-file* must be specified. If interactive prompting is on, **ftp** will prompt the user to verify that the last argument is indeed the target local file for receiving **mls** output.

mode [*mode-name*]

Set the file transfer **mode** to *mode-name*. The default mode is "stream" mode.

modtime *file-name*

Show the last modification time of the file on the remote machine.

mput *local-files*

Expand wild cards in the list of local files given as arguments and do a **put** for each file in the resulting list. See **glob** for details of filename expansion. Resulting file names will then be processed according to **ntrans** and **nmap** settings.

newer *file-name*

Get the file only if the modification time of the remote file is more recent that the file on the current system. If the file does not exist on the current system, the remote file is considered **newer**. Otherwise, this command is identical to *get*.

nlist [*remote-directory*] [*local-file*]

Print a list of the files in a directory on the remote machine. If *remote-directory* is left unspecified, the current working directory is used. If interactive prompting is on, **ftp** will prompt the user to verify that the last argument is indeed the target local file for receiving **nlist** output. If no local file is specified, or if *local-file* is −, the output is sent to the terminal.

nmap [*inpattern outpattern*]

Set or unset the filename mapping mechanism. If no arguments are specified, the filename mapping mechanism is unset. If arguments are specified, remote filenames are mapped during **mput** commands and **put** commands issued without a specified remote target filename. If arguments are specified, local filenames are mapped during **mget** commands and **get** commands issued without a specified local target filename. This command is useful when connecting to a non–Ux remote computer with different file naming conventions or practices. The mapping follows the pattern set by *inpattern* and *outpattern*. [*Inpattern*] is a template for incoming filenames (which may have already been processed according to the **ntrans** and **case** settings). Variable templating is accomplished by including the sequences '$1', '$2', ..., '$9' in *inpattern*. Use '\' to prevent this special treatment of the '$' character. All other characters are treated literally, and are used to determine the **nmap** [*inpattern*] variable values. For example, given *inpattern* $1.$2 and the remote file name "mydata.data", $1 would have the value "mydata", and $2 would have the value "data". The *outpattern* determines the resulting mapped filename. The sequences '$1', '$2', ..., '$9' are replaced by any value resulting from the *inpattern* template. The sequence '$0' is replace by the original filename. Additionally, the sequence '[*seq1*, *seq2*]' is replaced by [*seq1*] if *seq1* is not a null string; otherwise it is replaced by *seq2*. For example, the command

            nmap $1.$2.$3 [$1,$2].[$2,file]

would yield the output filename "myfile.data" for input filenames "myfile.data" and "myfile.data.old", "myfile.file" for the input filename "myfile", and "myfile.myfile" for the input filename ".myfile". Spaces may be included in *outpattern*, as in the example: 'nmap $1 sed "s/ *$//" > $1' . Use the '\' character to prevent special treatment of the '$','[',']', and ',' characters.

ntrans [*inchars* [*outchars*]]

Set or unset the filename character translation mechanism. If no arguments are specified, the filename character translation mechanism is unset. If arguments are specified, characters in remote filenames are translated during **mput** commands and **put** commands issued without a specified remote target filename. If arguments are specified, characters in local filenames are translated during **mget** commands and **get** commands issued without a specified local target filename. This command is useful when connecting to a non–Ux remote computer with different file naming conventions or practices. Characters in a filename matching a character in *inchars* are replaced with the corresponding character in *outchars*. If the character's position in *inchars* is longer than the length of *outchars*, the character is deleted from the file name.

open *host* [*port*]

Establish a connection to the specified *host* FTP server. An optional port number may be supplied, in which case, **ftp** will attempt to contact an FTP server at that port. If the **auto-login** option is on (default), **ftp** will also attempt to automatically log the user in to the FTP server (see below).

prompt

Toggle interactive prompting. Interactive prompting occurs during multiple file transfers to allow the user to selectively retrieve or store files. If prompting is turned off (default is on), any **mget** or **mput** will transfer all files, and any **mdelete** will delete all files.

proxy *ftp-command*

Execute an ftp command on a secondary control connection. This command allows simultaneous connection to two remote ftp servers for transferring files between the two servers. The first **proxy** command should be an **open**, to establish the secondary control connection. Enter the command "proxy ?" to see other ftp commands executable on the secondary connection. The following commands behave differently when prefaced by **proxy**: **open** will not define new macros during the auto-login process, **close** will not erase existing macro definitions, **get** and **mget** transfer files from the host on the primary control connection to the host on the secondary control connection, and **put**, **mput**, and **append** transfer files from the host on the secondary control connection to the host on the primary control connection. Third party file transfers depend upon support of the ftp protocol PASV command by the server on the secondary control connection.

put *local-file* [*remote-file*]

Store a local file on the remote machine. If *remote-file* is left unspecified, the local file name is used after processing according to any **ntrans** or **nmap** settings in naming the remote file. File transfer uses the current settings for **type**, **format**, **mode**, and **structure**.

pwd

Print the name of the current working directory on the remote machine.

quit

A synonym for **bye**.

quote *arg1 arg2 ...*

The arguments specified are sent, verbatim, to the remote FTP server.

recv *remote-file* [*local-file*]

A synonym for get.

reget *remote-file* [*local-file*]

Reget acts like get, except that if *local-file* exists and is smaller than *remote-file*, *local-file* is presumed to be a partially transferred copy of *remote-file* and the

1

transfer is continued from the apparent point of failure. This command is useful when transferring very large files over networks that are prone to dropping connections.

remotehelp [*command-name*]
> Request help from the remote FTP server. If a *command-name* is specified it is supplied to the server as well.

remotestatus [*file-name*]
> With no arguments, show status of remote machine. If *file-name* is specified, show status of *file-name* on remote machine.

rename [*from*] [*to*]
> Rename the file *from* on the remote machine, to the file *to*.

reset   Clear reply queue. This command re-synchronizes command/reply sequencing with the remote ftp server. Resynchronization may be necessary following a violation of the ftp protocol by the remote server.

restart *marker*
> Restart the immediately following **get** or **put** at the indicated *marker*. On UNIX systems, marker is usually a byte offset into the file.

rmdir *directory-name*
> Delete a directory on the remote machine.

runique   Toggle storing of files on the local system with unique filenames. If a file already exists with a name equal to the target local filename for a **get** or **mget** command, a ".1" is appended to the name. If the resulting name matches another existing file, a ".2" is appended to the original name. If this process continues up to ".99", an error message is printed, and the transfer does not take place. The generated unique filename will be reported. Note that **runique** will not affect local files generated from a shell command (see below). The default value is off.

send *local-file* [*remote-file*]
> A synonym for put.

sendport   Toggle the use of PORT commands. By default, **ftp** will attempt to use a PORT command when establishing a connection for each data transfer. The use of PORT commands can prevent delays when performing multiple file transfers. If the PORT command fails, **ftp** will use the default data port. When the use of PORT commands is disabled, no attempt will be made to use PORT commands for each data transfer. This is useful for certain FTP implementations which do ignore PORT commands but, incorrectly, indicate they've been accepted.

site *arg1 arg2 ...*
> The arguments specified are sent, verbatim, to the remote FTP server as a SITE command.

size *file-name*
> Return size of *file-name* on remote machine.

status   Show the current status of **ftp**.

struct [*struct-name*]
> Set the file transfer *structure* to *struct-name*. By default "stream" structure is used.

sunique   Toggle storing of files on remote machine under unique file names. Remote ftp server must support ftp protocol STOU command for successful completion. The remote server will report unique name. Default value is off.

1

system   Show the type of operating system running on the remote machine.

tenex   Set the file transfer type to that needed to talk to TENEX machines.

trace   Toggle packet tracing.

type [*type-name*]
            Set the file transfer **type** to *type-name*. If no type is specified, the current type is printed.
            The default type is network ASCII.

umask [*newmask*]
            Set the default umask on the remote server to *newmask*. If *newmask* is omitted, the current
            umask is printed.

user *user-name* [*password*] [*account*]
            Identify yourself to the remote FTP server. If the *password* is not specified and the server re-
            quires it, **ftp** will prompt the user for it (after disabling local echo). If an *account* field is
            not specified, and the FTP server requires it, the user will be prompted for it. If an *account*
            field is specified, an account command will be relayed to the remote server after the login se-
            quence is completed if the remote server did not require it for logging in. Unless **ftp** is in-
            voked with "auto-login" disabled, this process is done automatically on initial connection to
            the FTP server.

verbose   Toggle verbose mode. In verbose mode, all responses from the FTP server are displayed to the
            user. In addition, if verbose is on, when a file transfer completes, statistics regarding the
            efficiency of the transfer are reported. By default, verbose is on.

? [*command*]
            A synonym for help.

Command arguments which have embedded spaces may be quoted with quote "" marks.

ABORTING A FILE TRANSFER
To abort a file transfer, use the terminal interrupt key (usually Ctrl-C). Sending transfers will be immediately halted. Receiving transfers will be halted by sending a ftp protocol ABOR command to the remote server,
and discarding any further data received. The speed at which this is accomplished depends upon the remote
server's support for ABOR processing. If the remote server does not support the ABOR command, an ftp>
prompt will not appear until the remote server has completed sending the requested file.

The terminal interrupt key sequence will be ignored when **ftp** has completed any local processing and is
awaiting a reply from the remote server. A long delay in this mode may result from the ABOR processing
described above, or from unexpected behavior by the remote server, including violations of the ftp protocol.
If the delay results from unexpected remote server behavior, the local **ftp** program must be killed by hand.

FILE NAMING CONVENTIONS
Files specified as arguments to **ftp** commands are processed according to the following rules.

1.   If the file name ' − ' is specified, the *stdin* (for reading) or *stdout* (for writing) is used.

2.   If the first character of the file name is 'l', the remainder of the argument is interpreted as a shell com-
     mand. **Ftp** then forks a shell, using popen(3) with the argument supplied, and reads (writes) from the
     stdout (stdin). If the shell command includes spaces, the argument must be quoted; e.g. "" ls -lt"". A
     particularly useful example of this mechanism is: "dir more".

3.   Failing the above checks, if "globbing" is enabled, local file names are expanded according to the rules
     used in the csh(1); c.f. the **glob** command. If the **ftp** command expects a single local file (.e.g.

put), only the first filename generated by the "globbing" operation is used.

4. For **mget** commands and **get** commands with unspecified local file names, the local filename is the remote filename, which may be altered by a **case**, **ntrans**, or **nmap** setting. The resulting filename may then be altered if **runique** is on.

5. For **mput** commands and **put** commands with unspecified remote file names, the remote filename is the local filename, which may be altered by a **ntrans** or **nmap** setting. The resulting filename may then be altered by the remote server if **sunique** is on.

FILE TRANSFER PARAMETERS

The FTP specification specifies many parameters which may affect a file transfer. The **type** may be one of "ascii", "image" (binary), "ebcdic", and "local byte size" (for PDP-10's and PDP-20's mostly). **Ftp** supports the ascii and image types of file transfer, plus local byte size 8 for **tenex** mode transfers.

Ftp supports only the default values for the remaining file transfer parameters: **mode**, **form**, and **struct**.

THE .netrc FILE

The .netrc file contains login and initialization information used by the auto-login process. It resides in the user's home directory. The following tokens are recognized; they may be separated by spaces, tabs, or new-lines:

machine *name*
> Identify a remote machine *name*. The auto-login process searches the .netrc file for a **machine** token that matches the remote machine specified on the **ftp** command line or as an **open** command argument. Once a match is made, the subsequent .netrc tokens are processed, stopping when the end of file is reached or another **machine** or a **default** token is encountered.

default This is the same as **machine** *name* except that **default** matches any name. There can be only one **default** token, and it must be after all **machine** tokens. This is normally used as:

> default login anonymous password user@site

> thereby giving the user *automatic* anonymous ftp login to machines not specified in .netrc. This can be overridden by using the −**n** flag to disable auto-login.

login *name*
> Identify a user on the remote machine. If this token is present, the auto-login process will initiate a login using the specified *name*.

password *string*
> Supply a password. If this token is present, the auto-login process will supply the specified string if the remote server requires a password as part of the login process. Note that if this token is present in the .netrc file for any user other than *anonymous*, **ftp** will abort the auto-login process if the .netrc is readable by anyone besides the user.

account *string*
> Supply an additional account password. If this token is present, the auto-login process will supply the specified string if the remote server requires an additional account password, or the auto-login process will initiate an ACCT command if it does not.

macdef *name*
> Define a macro. This token functions like the **ftp macdef** command functions. A macro is defined with the specified name; its contents begin with the next .netrc line and continue until a null line (consecutive new-line characters) is encountered. If a macro named **init** is defined, it is automatically executed as the last step in the auto-login process.

ENVIRONMENT

Ftp utilizes the following environment variables.

HOME   For default location of a .netrc file, if one exists.

SHELL   For default shell.

SEE ALSO

ftpd(8)

HISTORY

The ftp command appeared in 4.2BSD.

BUGS

Correct execution of many commands depends upon proper behavior by the remote server.

An error in the treatment of carriage returns in the 4.2BSD ascii-mode transfer code has been corrected. This correction may result in incorrect transfers of binary files to and from 4.2BSD servers using the ascii type. Avoid this problem by using the binary image type.

1

NAME

g++ – GNU project C++ Compiler (v2 preliminary)

SYNOPSIS

g++ [option | filename]...

DESCRIPTION

The C and C++ compilers are integrated; **g++** is a script to call **gcc with options to recognize C++. gcc** processes input files through one or more of four stages: preprocessing, compilation, assembly, and linking. This man page contains full descriptions for *only* C++ specific aspects of the compiler, though it also contains summaries of some general-purpose options. For a fuller explanation of the compiler, see **gcc(1)**.

C++ source files use one of the suffixes '**.C**', '**.cc**', or '**.cxx**'; preprocessed C++ files use the suffix '**.ii**'.

OPTIONS

There are many command-line options, including options to control details of optimization, warnings, and code generation, which are common to both **gcc** and **g++**. For full information on all options, see **gcc(1)**.

Options must be separate: '**−dr**' is quite different from '**−d −r** '.

Most '**−f**' and '**−W**' options have two contrary forms: **−f***name* and **−fno−***name* (or **−W***name* and **−Wno−***name*). Only the non-default forms are shown here.

−c   Compile or assemble the source files, but do not link. The compiler output is an object file corresponding to each source file.

−D*macro*
        Define macro *macro* with the string '**1**' as its definition.

−D*macro=defn*
        Define macro *macro* as *defn*.

−E   Stop after the preprocessing stage; do not run the compiler proper. The output is preprocessed source code, which is sent to the standard output.

+e*N*   control whether virtual function definitions in classes are used to generate code, or only to define interfaces for their callers. These options are provided for compatibility with cfront 1.x usage; the recommended GNU C++ usage is to use **#pragma interface** and **#pragma implementation**, instead.

        With '**+e0**', virtual function definitions in classes are declared extern; the declaration is used only as an interface specification, not to generate code for the virtual functions (in this compilation).

        With '**+e1**', **g++** actually generates the code implementing virtual functions defined in the code, and makes them publicly visible.

−fall−virtual
        When you use the '**−fall−virtual**', all member functions (except for constructor functions and new/delete member operators) declared in the same class with a "method-call" operator method are treated as virtual functions of the given class. In effect, all of these methods become "implicitly virtual."

        This does *not* mean that all calls to these methods will be made through the internal table of virtual functions. There are some circumstances under which it is obvious that a call to a given virtual function can be made directly, and in these cases the calls still go direct.

1

The effect of making all methods of a class with a declared '**operator->**()()' implicitly virtual using '**-fall-virtual**' extends also to all non-constructor methods of any class derived from such a class.

-fdollars-in-identifiers

Permit the use of '**$**' in identifiers. Traditional C allowed the character '**$**' to form part of identifiers; by default, GNU C also allows this. However, ANSI C forbids '**$**' in identifiers, and GNU C++ also forbids it by default on most platforms (though on some platforms it's enabled by default for GNU C++ as well).

-felide-constructors

Use this option to instruct the compiler to be smarter about when it can elide constructors. Without this flag, GNU C++ and cfront both generate effectively the same code for:

A foo ();
A x (foo ());   // x initialized by 'foo ()', no ctor called
A y = foo ();   // call to 'foo ()' heads to temporary,
        // y is initialized from the temporary.

Note the difference! With this flag, GNU C++ initializes '**y**' directly from the call to **foo** () without going through a temporary.

-fenum-int-equiv

Normally GNU C++ allows conversion of **enum** to **int**, but not the other way around. Use this option if you want GNU C++ to allow conversion of **int** to **enum** as well.

-fgnu-binutils

-fno-gnu-binutils

'**-fgnu-binutils**' (the default for most, but not all, platforms) makes GNU C++ emit extra information for static initialization and finalization. This information has to be passed from the assembler to the GNU linker. Some assemblers won't pass this information; you must either use GNU **as** or specify the option '**-fno-gnu-binutils**'.

With '**-fno-gnu-binutils**', you must use the program **collect** (part of the GCC distribution) for linking.

-fmemoize-lookups

-fsave-memoized

These flags are used to get the compiler to compile programs faster using heuristics. They are not on by default since they are only effective about half the time. The other half of the time programs compile more slowly (and take more memory).

The first time the compiler must build a call to a member function (or reference to a data member), it must (1) determine whether the class implements member functions of that name; (2) resolve which member function to call (which involves figuring out what sorts of type conversions need to be made); and (3) check the visibility of the member function to the caller. All of this adds up to slower compilation. Normally, the second time a call is made to that member function (or reference to that data member), it must go through the same lengthy process again. This means that code like this

cout << "This " << p << " has " << n << " legs.\n";

makes six passes through all three steps. By using a software cache, a "hit" significantly reduces this cost. Unfortunately, using the cache introduces another layer of mechanisms which must be implemented, and so incurs its own overhead. '**-fmemoize-lookups**' enables the software cache.

1

Because access privileges (visibility) to members and member functions may differ from one function context to the next, **g++** may need to flush the cache. With the '**–fmemoize–lookups**' flag, the cache is flushed after every function that is compiled. The '**–fsave–memoized**' flag enables the same software cache, but when the compiler determines that the context of the last function compiled would yield the same access privileges of the next function to compile, it preserves the cache. This is most helpful when defining many member functions for the same class: with the exception of member functions which are friends of other classes, each member function has exactly the same access privileges as every other, and the cache need not be flushed.

–fno–default–inline

If '**–fdefault–inline**' is enabled then member functions defined inside class scope are compiled inline by default; i.e., you don't need to add '**inline**' in front of the member function name. By popular demand, this option is now the default. To keep GNU C++ from inlining these member functions, specify '**–fno–default–inline**'.

–fno–strict–prototype

Consider the declaration **int foo ();**. In C++, this means that the function **foo** takes no arguments. In ANSI C, this is declared **int foo(void);**. With the flag '**–fno–strict–prototype**', declaring functions with no arguments is equivalent to declaring its argument list to be untyped, i.e., **int foo ();** is equivalent to saying **int foo (...);**.

–fnonnull–objects

Normally, GNU C++ makes conservative assumptions about objects reached through references. For example, the compiler must check that '**a**' is not null in code like the following:

    obj &a = g ();
    a.f (2);

Checking that references of this sort have non-null values requires extra code, however, and it is unnecessary for many programs. You can use '**–fnonnull–objects**' to omit the checks for null, if your program doesn't require the default checking.

–fthis–is–variable

The incorporation of user-defined free store management into C++ has made assignment to **this** an anachronism. Therefore, by default GNU C++ treats the type of **this** in a member function of **class X** to be **X *const**. In other words, it is illegal to assign to **this** within a class member function. However, for backwards compatibility, you can invoke the old behavior by using '**–fthis–is–variable**'.

–g   Produce debugging information in the operating system's native format (for DBX or SDB or DWARF). GDB also can work with this debugging information. On most systems that use DBX format, '**–g**' enables use of extra debugging information that only GDB can use.

    Unlike most other C compilers, GNU CC allows you to use '**–g**' with '**–O**'. The shortcuts taken by optimized code may occasionally produce surprising results: some variables you declared may not exist at all; flow of control may briefly move where you did not expect it; some statements may not be executed because they compute constant results or their values were already at hand; some statements may execute in different places because they were moved out of loops.

    Nevertheless it proves possible to debug optimized output. This makes it reasonable to use the optimizer for programs that might have bugs.

–I*dir*   Append directory *dir* to the list of directories searched for include files.

–L*dir*   Add directory *dir* to the list of directories to be searched for '**–l**'.

–l*library*

Use the library named *library* when linking. (C++ programs often require '**–lg++**' for successful linking.)

1

–O   Optimize. Optimizing compilation takes somewhat more time, and a lot more memory for a large function.

Without ' **–O** ', the compiler's goal is to reduce the cost of compilation and to make debugging produce the expected results. Statements are independent: if you stop the program with a breakpoint between statements, you can then assign a new value to any variable or change the program counter to any other statement in the function and get exactly the results you would expect from the source code.

Without ' **–O** ', only variables declared **register** are allocated in registers. The resulting compiled code is a little worse than produced by PCC without ' **–O** '.

With ' **–O** ', the compiler tries to reduce code size and execution time.

–o *file*   Place output in file *file*.

–S   Stop after the stage of compilation proper; do not assemble. The output is an assembler code file for each non-assembler input file specified.

–static On systems that support dynamic linking, this prevents linking with the shared libraries. On other systems, this option has no effect.

–traditional

Attempt to support some aspects of traditional C compilers.

Specifically, for both C and C++ programs:

- In the preprocessor, comments convert to nothing at all, rather than to a space. This allows traditional token concatenation.

- In the preprocessor, macro arguments are recognized within string constants in a macro definition (and their values are stringified, though without additional quote marks, when they appear in such a context). The preprocessor always considers a string constant to end at a newline.

- The preprocessor does not predefine the macro __**STDC**__ when you use ' **–traditional** ', but still predefines __**GNUC**__ (since the GNU extensions indicated by __**GNUC**__ are not affected by ' **–traditional** '). If you need to write header files that work differently depending on whether ' **–traditional** ' is in use, by testing both of these predefined macros you can distinguish four situations: GNU C, traditional GNU C, other ANSI C compilers, and other old C compilers.

- In the preprocessor, comments convert to nothing at all, rather than to a space. This allows traditional token concatenation.

- In the preprocessor, macro arguments are recognized within string constants in a macro definition (and their values are stringified, though without additional quote marks, when they appear in such a context). The preprocessor always considers a string constant to end at a newline.

- The preprocessor does not predefine the macro __**STDC**__ when you use ' **–traditional** ', but still predefines __**GNUC**__ (since the GNU extensions indicated by __**GNUC**__ are not affected by ' **–traditional** '). If you need to write header files that work differently depending on whether ' **–traditional** ' is in use, by testing both of these predefined macros you can distinguish four situations: GNU C, traditional GNU C, other ANSI C compilers, and other old C compilers.

- String ''constants'' are not necessarily constant; they are stored in writable space, and identical looking constants are allocated separately. (This is the same as the effect of ' **–fwritable–strings** '.)

For C++ programs only (not C), ' **–traditional** ' has one additional effect: assignment to **this** is permitted. This is the same as the effect of ' **–fthis–is–variable** '.

1

−U*macro*
  Undefine macro *macro*.

−**Wall** Issue warnings for conditions which pertain to usage that we recommend avoiding and that we
  believe is easy to avoid, even in conjunction with macros.

−**Wenum−clash**
  Warn when converting between different enumeration types.

−**Woverloaded−virtual**
  In a derived class, the definitions of virtual functions must match the type signature of a virtual
  function declared in the base class. Use this option to request warnings when a derived class
  declares a function that may be an erroneous attempt to define a virtual function: that is, warn
  when a function with the same name as a virtual function in the base class, but with a type signature that doesn't match any virtual functions from the base class.

−**w** Inhibit all warning messages.

PRAGMAS
  Two '**#pragma**' directives are supported for GNU C++, to permit using the same header file for two purposes: as a definition of interfaces to a given object class, and as the full definition of the contents of that
  object class.

#pragma interface
  Use this directive in header files that define object classes, to save space in most of the object files
  that use those classes. Normally, local copies of certain information (backup copies of inline
  member functions, debugging information, and the internal tables that implement virtual functions) must be kept in each object file that includes class definitions. You can use this pragma to
  avoid such duplication. When a header file containing '**#pragma interface**' is included in a
  compilation, this auxiliary information will not be generated (unless the main input source file
  itself uses '**#pragma implementation**'). Instead, the object files will contain references to be
  resolved at link time.

#pragma implementation

#pragma implementation "*objects*.h"
  Use this pragma in a main input file, when you want full output from included header files to be
  generated (and made globally visible). The included header file, in turn, should use '**#pragma
  interface**'. Backup copies of inline member functions, debugging information, and the internal
  tables used to implement virtual functions are all generated in implementation files.

  If you use '**#pragma implementation**' with no argument, it applies to an include file with the
  same basename as your source file; for example, in '**allclass.cc**', '**#pragma implementation**' by
  itself is equivalent to '**#pragma implementation "allclass.h"**'. Use the string argument if you
  want a single implementation file to include code from multiple header files.

  There is no way to split up the contents of a single header file into multiple implementation files.

FILES

file.h	C header (preprocessor) file
file.i	preprocessed C source file
file.C	C++ source file
file.cc	C++ source file
file.cxx	C++ source file
file.s	assembly language file
file.o	object file
a.out	link edited output
TMPDIR/cc*	temporary files
LIBDIR/cpp	preprocessor

LIBDIR/cc1plus	compiler
LIBDIR/collect	linker front end needed on some machines
LIBDIR/libgcc.a	GCC subroutine library
/lib/crt[01n].o	start-up routine
LIBDIR/ccrt0	additional start-up routine for C++
/lib/libc.a	standard C library, see *intro*(3)
/usr/include	standard directory for **#include** files
LIBDIR/include	standard gcc directory for **#include** files
LIBDIR/g++-include	additional g++ directory for **#include**

LIBDIR is usually **/usr/local/lib/***machine*/*version*.

TMPDIR comes from the environment variable **TMPDIR** (default **/usr/tmp** if available, else **/tmp**).

SEE ALSO

gcc(1), cpp(1), as(1), ld(1), gdb(1), adb(1), dbx(1), sdb(1).

' **gcc** ', ' **cpp** ', ' **as** ',' ld **'**, and ' **gdb** ' entries in **info**.

Using and Porting GNU CC (for version 2.0), Richard M. Stallman, November 1990; *The C Preprocessor*, Richard M. Stallman, July 1990; *Using GDB: A Guide to the GNU Source-Level Debugger*, Richard M. Stallman and Roland H. Pesch, December 1991; *Using as: the GNU Assembler*, Dean Elsner, Jay Fenlason & friends, March 1991; *gld: the GNU linker*, Steve Chamberlain and Roland Pesch, April 1991.

BUGS

Report bugs to **bug–g++@prep.ai.mit.edu**. Bugs tend actually to be fixed if they can be isolated, so it is in your interest to report them in such a way that they can be easily reproduced.

COPYING

Copyright (c) 1991 Free Software Foundation, Inc.

Permission is granted to make and distribute verbatim copies of this manual provided the copyright notice and this permission notice are preserved on all copies.

Permission is granted to copy and distribute modified versions of this manual under the conditions for verbatim copying, provided that the entire resulting derived work is distributed under the terms of a permission notice identical to this one.

Permission is granted to copy and distribute translations of this manual into another language, under the above conditions for modified versions, except that this permission notice may be included in translations approved by the Free Software Foundation instead of in the original English.

AUTHORS

See the GNU CC Manual for the contributors to GNU CC.

1

NAME

gcore – get core images of running process

SYNOPSIS

gcore [**–s**] [**–c** *core*] *exec pid*

DESCRIPTION

Gcore creates a core image of the specified process, suitable for use with gdb(1). By default, the core is written to the file "core.<pid>". Both the executable image, *exec*, and the process identifier, *pid*, must be given on the command line.

The options are:

–c   Write the core file to the specified file instead of "core.<pid>".

–s   Stop the process while gathering the core image, and resume it when done. This guarantees that the resulting core dump will be in a consistent state. The process is resumed even if it was already stopped. The same effect can be achieved manually with kill(1).

FILES

core.<pid>   The core image.

HISTORY

Gcore appeared in 4.2BSD.

BUGS

Context switches or paging activity that occur while **gcore** is running may cause the program to become confused. For best results, use -s to temporarily stop the target process.

Gcore is not compatible with the original 4.2BSD version. In particular, 4.4BSD requires the *exec* argument.

NAME

gdb – the GNU debugger

SYNOPSIS

gdb　　　[**−help**] [**−nx**] [**−q**] [**−batch**] [**−cd**=*dir*] [**−f**] [**−b** *bps*] [**−tty**=*dev*] [**−s** *symfile*] [**−e** *prog*]
　　　　　　[**−se** *prog*] [**−c** *core*] [**−x** *cmds*] [**−d** *dir*] [*prog*[*core* | *procID*]]

DESCRIPTION

The purpose of a debugger such as GDB is to allow you to see what is going on ''inside'' another program while it executes—or what another program was doing at the moment it crashed.

GDB can do four main kinds of things (plus other things in support of these) to help you catch bugs in the act:

- Start your program, specifying anything that might affect its behavior.

- Make your program stop on specified conditions.

- Examine what has happened, when your program has stopped.

- Change things in your program, so you can experiment with correcting the effects of one bug and go on to learn about another.

You can use GDB to debug programs written in C, C++, and Modula-2. Fortran support will be added when a GNU Fortran compiler is ready.

GDB is invoked with the shell command **gdb**. Once started, it reads commands from the terminal until you tell it to exit with the GDB command **quit**. You can get online help from **gdb** itself by using the command **help**.

You can run **gdb** with no arguments or options; but the most usual way to start GDB is with one argument or two, specifying an executable program as the argument:

gdb program

You can also start with both an executable program and a core file specified:

gdb program core

You can, instead, specify a process ID as a second argument, if you want to debug a running process:

gdb program 1234

would attach GDB to process **1234** (unless you also have a file named ' **1234** '; GDB does check for a core file first).

Here are some of the most frequently needed GDB commands:

break [*file*:]*function*
　　　　Set a breakpoint at *function* (in *file*).

1

run [*arglist*]
>   Start your program (with *arglist*, if specified).

bt   Backtrace: display the program stack.

print *expr*
>   Display the value of an expression.

c   Continue running your program (after stopping, e.g. at a breakpoint).

next   Execute next program line (after stopping); step *over* any function calls in the line.

step   Execute next program line (after stopping); step *into* any function calls in the line.

help [*name*]
>   Show information about GDB command *name*, or general information about using GDB.

quit   Exit from GDB.

For full details on GDB, see *Using GDB: A Guide to the GNU Source-Level Debugger*, by Richard M. Stallman and Roland H. Pesch. The same text is available online as the **gdb** entry in the **info** program.

OPTIONS

Any arguments other than options specify an executable file and core file (or process ID); that is, the first argument encountered with no associated option flag is equivalent to a ' **−se** ' option, and the second, if any, is equivalent to a ' **−c** ' option if it's the name of a file. Many options have both long and short forms; both are shown here. The long forms are also recognized if you truncate them, so long as enough of the option is present to be unambiguous. (If you prefer, you can flag option arguments with ' **+** ' rather than ' **−** ', though we illustrate the more usual convention.)

All the options and command line arguments you give are processed in sequential order. The order makes a difference when the ' **−x** ' option is used.

−help

−h   List all options, with brief explanations.

−symbols=*file*

−s *file*   Read symbol table from file *file*.

−exec=*file*

−e *file*   Use file *file* as the executable file to execute when appropriate, and for examining pure data in conjunction with a core dump.

−se=*file* Read symbol table from file *file* and use it as the executable file.

−core=*file*

−c *file*   Use file *file* as a core dump to examine.

−command=*file*

−x *file*   Execute GDB commands from file *file*.

−directory=*directory*

−d *directory*
>   Add *directory* to the path to search for source files.

−nx

−n   Do not execute commands from any ' **.gdbinit** ' initialization files. Normally, the commands in these files are executed after all the command options and arguments have been processed.

−quiet

−q   ''Quiet''. Do not print the introductory and copyright messages. These messages are also suppressed in batch mode.

−batch Run in batch mode. Exit with status **0** after processing all the command files specified with ' **−x** ' (and ' **.gdbinit** ', if not inhibited). Exit with nonzero status if an error occurs in executing the GDB commands in the command files.

Batch mode may be useful for running GDB as a filter, for example to download and run a program on another computer; in order to make this more useful, the message

Program exited normally.

(which is ordinarily issued whenever a program running under GDB control terminates) is not issued when running in batch mode.

−cd=*directory*
Run GDB using *directory* as its working directory, instead of the current directory.

−fullname

−f   Emacs sets this option when it runs GDB as a subprocess. It tells GDB to output the full file name and line number in a standard, recognizable fashion each time a stack frame is displayed (which includes each time the program stops). This recognizable format looks like two ' **32** ' characters, followed by the file name, line number and character position separated by colons, and a newline. The Emacs-to-GDB interface program uses the two ' **32** ' characters as a signal to display the source code for the frame.

−b *bps* Set the line speed (baud rate or bits per second) of any serial interface used by GDB for remote debugging.

−tty=*device*
Run using *device* for your program's standard input and output.

SEE ALSO
' **gdb** ' entry in **info**; *Using GDB: A Guide to the GNU Source-Level Debugger*, Richard M. Stallman and Roland H. Pesch, July 1991.

COPYING
Copyright (c) 1991 Free Software Foundation, Inc.

Permission is granted to make and distribute verbatim copies of this manual provided the copyright notice and this permission notice are preserved on all copies.

Permission is granted to copy and distribute modified versions of this manual under the conditions for verbatim copying, provided that the entire resulting derived work is distributed under the terms of a permission notice identical to this one.

Permission is granted to copy and distribute translations of this manual into another language, under the above conditions for modified versions, except that this permission notice may be included in translations approved by the Free Software Foundation instead of in the original English.

NAME

    gprof – display call graph profile data

SYNOPSIS

    gprof [options] [a.out [gmon.out ...]]

DESCRIPTION

    Gprof produces an execution profile of C, Pascal, or Fortran77 programs. The effect of called routines is incorporated in the profile of each caller. The profile data is taken from the call graph profile file (gmon.out default) which is created by programs that are compiled with the **−pg** option of cc(1), pc(1), and f77(1). The **−pg** option also links in versions of the library routines that are compiled for profiling. Gprof reads the given object file (the default is a.out) and establishes the relation between it's symbol table and the call graph profile from gmon.out. If more than one profile file is specified, the **gprof** output shows the sum of the profile information in the given profile files.

    Gprof calculates the amount of time spent in each routine. Next, these times are propagated along the edges of the call graph. Cycles are discovered, and calls into a cycle are made to share the time of the cycle. The first listing shows the functions sorted according to the time they represent including the time of their call graph descendents. Below each function entry is shown its (direct) call graph children, and how their times are propagated to this function. A similar display above the function shows how this function's time and the time of its descendents is propagated to its (direct) call graph parents.

    Cycles are also shown, with an entry for the cycle as a whole and a listing of the members of the cycle and their contributions to the time and call counts of the cycle.

    Second, a flat profile is given, similar to that provided by prof(1). This listing gives the total execution times, the call counts, the time in milleseconds the call spent in the routine itself, and the time in milleseconds the call spent in the routine itself including its descendents.

    Finally, an index of the function names is provided.

    The following options are available:

    −a   Suppresses the printing of statically declared functions. If this option is given, all relevant information about the static function (e.g., time samples, calls to other functions, calls from other functions) belongs to the function loaded just before the static function in the a.out file.

    −b   Suppresses the printing of a description of each field in the profile.

    −c   The static call graph of the program is discovered by a heuristic that examines the text space of the object file. Static-only parents or children are shown with call counts of 0.

    −C *count* Find a minimal set of arcs that can be broken to eliminate all cycles with *count* or more members. Caution: the algorithm used to break cycles is exponential, so using this option may cause **gprof** to run for a very long time.

    −e *name* Suppresses the printing of the graph profile entry for routine *name* and all its descendants (unless they have other ancestors that aren't suppressed). More than one **−e** option may be given. Only one *name* may be given with each **−e** option.

    −E *name* Suppresses the printing of the graph profile entry for routine *name* (and its descendants) as **−e**, above, and also excludes the time spent in *name* (and its descendants) from the total and percentage time computations. (For example, **−E** *mcount* **−E** *mcleanup* is the default.)

1

-**f** *name*   Prints the graph profile entry of only the specified routine *name* and its descendants. More than one −**f** option may be given. Only one *name* may be given with each −**f** option.

-**F** *name*   Prints the graph profile entry of only the routine *name* and its descendants (as −**f**, above) and also uses only the times of the printed routines in total time and percentage computations. More than one −**F** option may be given. Only one *name* may be given with each −**F** option. The −**F** option overrides the −**E** option.

-**k** *fromname toname*

    Will delete any arcs from routine *fromname* to routine *toname*. This can be used to break undesired cycles. More than one −**k** option may be given. Only one pair of routine names may be given with each −**k** option.

-**s**   A profile file gmon.sum is produced that represents the sum of the profile information in all the specified profile files. This summary profile file may be given to later executions of gprof (probably also with a −**s**) to accumulate profile data across several runs of an a.out file.

-**z**   Displays routines that have zero usage (as shown by call counts and accumulated time). This is useful with the −**c** option for discovering which routines were never called.

FILES
a.out   The namelist and text space.
gmon.out Dynamic call graph and profile.
gmon.sum Summarized dynamic call graph and profile.

SEE ALSO
monitor(3), profil(2), cc(1), prof(1)

S. Graham, P. Kessler, and M. McKusick, "An Execution Profiler for Modular Programs", *Software - Practice and Experience*, 13, pp. 671-685, 1983.

S. Graham, P. Kessler, and M. McKusick, "gprof: A Call Graph Execution Profiler", *Proceedings of the SIGPLAN '82 Symposium on Compiler Construction, SIGPLAN Notices*, 6, 17, pp. 120-126, June 1982.

HISTORY
The **gprof** profiler appeared in 4.2BSD.

BUGS
The granularity of the sampling is shown, but remains statistical at best. We assume that the time for each execution of a function can be expressed by the total time for the function divided by the number of times the function is called. Thus the time propagated along the call graph arcs to the function's parents is directly proportional to the number of times that arc is traversed.

Parents that are not themselves profiled will have the time of their profiled children propagated to them, but they will appear to be spontaneously invoked in the call graph listing, and will not have their time propagated further. Similarly, signal catchers, even though profiled, will appear to be spontaneous (although for more obscure reasons). Any profiled children of signal catchers should have their times propagated properly, unless the signal catcher was invoked during the execution of the profiling routine, in which case all is lost.

The profiled program must call exit(2) or return normally for the profiling information to be saved in the gmon.out file.

GRAPH (1)   BSD Reference Manual   GRAPH (1)

1

NAME

graph – draw a graph

SYNOPSIS

graph [option] . . .

DESCRIPTION

Graph with no options takes pairs of numbers from the standard input as abscissas and ordinates of a graph. Successive points are connected by straight lines. The graph is encoded on the standard output for display by the plot(1) filters.

If the coordinates of a point are followed by a nonnumeric string, that string is printed as a label beginning on the point. Labels may be surrounded with quotes "...", in which case they may be empty or contain blanks and numbers; labels never contain newlines.

The following options are recognized, each as a separate argument.

-a   Supply abscissas automatically (they are missing from the input); spacing is given by the next argument (default 1). A second optional argument is the starting point for automatic abscissas (default 0 or lower limit given by -x).

-b   Break (disconnect) the graph after each label in the input.

-c   Character string given by next argument is default label for each point.

-g   Next argument is grid style, 0 no grid, 1 frame with ticks, 2 full grid (default).

-l   Next argument is label for graph.

-m   Next argument is mode (style) of connecting lines: 0 disconnected, 1 connected (default). Some devices give distinguishable line styles for other small integers.

-s   Save screen, don't erase before plotting.

-x[l]   If l is present, x axis is logarithmic. Next 1 (or 2) arguments are lower (and upper) x limits. Third argument, if present, is grid spacing on x axis. Normally these quantities are determined automatically.

-y[l]   Similarly for y.

-h   Next argument is fraction of space for height.

-w   Similarly for width.

-r   Next argument is fraction of space to move right before plotting.

-u   Similarly to move up before plotting.

-t   Transpose horizontal and vertical axes. (Option -x now applies to the vertical axis.)

A legend indicating grid range is produced with a grid unless the -s option is present.

If a specified lower limit exceeds the upper limit, the axis is reversed.

SEE ALSO

spline(1), plot(1)

GRAPH (1)   BSD Reference Manual   GRAPH (1)

HISTORY

The `graph` command appeared in Version 6 AT&T UNIX.

BUGS

`Graph` stores all points internally and drops those for which there isn't room.

Segments that run out of bounds are dropped, not windowed.

Logarithmic axes may not be reversed.

1

NAME

grep – file pattern searcher

SYNOPSIS

grep [−bchilnosvw] [−e *pattern*] [*file* ...]
egrep [−bchilnosv] [−e *pattern*] [−f *pattern_file*] [*file* ...]
fgrep [−bchilnosvx] [−e *pattern*] [−f *pattern_file*] [*file* ...]

DESCRIPTION

The **grep** utilities search the given input files selecting lines which match one or more patterns; the type of patterns is controlled by the options specified. By default, a pattern matches an input line if any regular expression (RE) in the pattern matches the input line without its trailing <new-line>. A null RE matches every line. Each input line that matches at least one of the patterns is written to the standard output.

For simple patterns or ex(1) or ed(1) style regular expressions, the **grep** utility is used. The **egrep** utility can handle extended regular expressions and embedded <newline>s in patterns. The **fgrep** utility is quick but can handle only fixed strings. A fixed string is a string of characters, each character is matched only by itself. The pattern value can consist of multiple lines with embedded <newline>s. In this case, the <newline>s act as alternation characters, allowing any of the pattern lines to match a portion of the input.

The following options are available:

−b   The block number on the disk in which a matched pattern is located is displayed in front of the respective matched line.

−c   Only a count of selected lines is written to standard output.

−e *expression*
        Specify a pattern used during the search of the input. Multiple −e options can be used to specify multiple patterns; an input line is selected if it matches any of the specified patterns.

−f *pattern_file*
        The pattern is read from the file named by the pathname pattern_file. Trailing newlines in the pattern_file are ignored. (**Egrep** and **fgrep** only).

−h   Never print filename headers with output lines.

−i   The case of letters is ignored in making comparisons – that is, upper and lower case are considered identical.

−l   Only the names of files containing selected lines are written to standard output. Pathnames are listed once per file searched. If the standard input is searched, the pathname ' − ' is written.

−n   Each output line is preceded by its relative line number in the file; each file starting at line 1. The line number counter is reset for each file processed. This option is ignored if −c, −l, or −s is specified.

−o   Always print filename headers with output lines.

−s   Silent mode. Nothing is printed (except error messages). This is useful for checking the error status.

−v   Selected lines are those *not* matching the specified patterns.

1

−x   Only input lines selected against an entire fixed string or regular expression are considered to be
        matching lines. (**Fgrep** only).

−w   The expression is searched for as a word (as if surrounded by '\<' and '\>', see ex(1).) (**Grep**
        only)

If no file arguments are specified, the standard input is used.

The **grep** utility exits with one of the following values:

0   One or more lines were selected.
1   No lines were selected.
>1   An error occurred.

EXTENDED REGULAR EXPRESSIONS

The following characters are interpreted by **egrep**:

$ Align the match from the end of the line.
^   Align the match from the beginning of the line.
| Add another pattern (see example below).
?   Match 1 or less sequential repetitions of the pattern.
+   Match 1 or more sequential repetitions of the pattern.
*   Match 0 or more sequential repetitions of the pattern.
[]   Match any single character or range of characters enclosed in the brackets.
\   Escape special characters which have meaning to **egrep**, the set of {$,.,^,[,],|,?,+,*,(,)}.

EXAMPLES

To find all occurrences of the word patricia in a file:

        grep patricia myfile

To find all occurrences of the pattern . Pp at the beginning of a line:

        grep '^\.Pp'

The apostrophes assure the entire expression is evaluated by **grep** instead of by the users shell. The carat or
hat '^' means *from the beginning of a line*, and the '\' escapes the '.' which would otherwise match any
character.

A simple example of an extended regular expression:

        egrep '19|20|25' calendar

Peruses the file calendar looking for either 19, 20 or 25.

SEE ALSO

ed(1), ex(1), sed(1)

HISTORY

The **grep** command appeared in Version 6 AT&T UNIX.

BUGS

Lines are limited to 256 characters; longer lines are truncated.

NAME

grodvi – convert groff output to TeX dvi format

SYNOPSIS

grodvi [**−dv**] [**−w***n*] [**−F***dir*] [*files* ...]

DESCRIPTION

grodvi is a driver for **groff** that produces TeX dvi format. Normally it should be run by **groff −Tdvi**. This will run **troff −Tdvi**; it will also input the macros **/usr/share/tmac/tmac.dvi**; if the input is being preprocessed with eqn it will also input **/usr/share/groff_font/devdvi/eqnchar**.

The dvi file generated by **grodvi** can be printed by any correctly-written dvi driver. The troff drawing primitives are implemented using the tpic version 2 specials. If the driver does not support these, the \D commands will not produce any output.

There is an additional drawing command available:

\D'R *dh dv'*

Draw a rule (solid black rectangle), with one corner at the current position, and the diagonally opposite corner at the current position +(*dh,dv*). Afterwards the current position will be at the opposite corner. This produces a rule in the dvi file and so can be printed even with a driver that does not support the tpic specials unlike the other \D commands.

The groff command \X'*anything*' is translated into the same command in the dvi file as would be produced by **\special**{*anything*} in TeX; *anything may not contain a newline*.

Font files for **grodvi** can be created from tfm files using **tfmtodit**(1). The font description file should contain the following additional commands:

internalname *name*

The name of the tfm file (without the **.tfm** extension) is *name*.

checksum *n*   The checksum in the tfm file is *n*.

designsize *n*   The designsize in the tfm file is *n*.

These are automatically generated by **tfmtodit**.

In **troff** the \N escape sequence can be used to access characters by their position in the corresponding tfm file; all characters in the tfm file can be accessed this way.

OPTIONS

−d   Do not use tpic specials to implement drawing commands. Horizontal and vertical lines will be implemented by rules. Other drawing commands will be ignored.

−v   Print the version number.

−w*n*   Set the default line thickness to *n* thousandths of an em.

−F*dir*   Search directory *dir***/devdvi** for font and device description files.

FILES

/usr/share/groff_font/devdvi/DESC

Device description file.

/usr/share/groff_font/devdvi/ F

Font description file for font *F*.

/usr/share/tmac/tmac.dvi

Macros for use with **grodvi**.

BUGS

Dvi files produced by **grodvi** use a different resolution (57816 units per inch) to those produced by TeX. Incorrectly written drivers which assume the resolution used by TeX, rather than using the resolution specified in the dvi file will not work with grodvi.

1

When using the −**d** option with boxed tables, vertical and horizontal lines can sometimes protrude by one pixel. This is a consequence of the way TEX requires that the heights and widths of rules be rounded.

SEE ALSO
   tfmtodit(1), **groff**(1), **troff**(1), **eqn**(1), **groff_out**(5), **groff_font**(5), **groff_char**(7)

1

NAME

groff – front end for the groff document formatting system

SYNOPSIS

groff [**–tpeszaivhblCENRVXZ**] [**–w***name*] [**–W***name*] [**–m***name*] [**–F***dir*] [**–T***dev*] [**–ff***am*] [
–M*dir*] [**–d***cs*] [**–r***cn*] [**–n***num*] [**–o***list*] [**–P***arg*] [*files ...*]

DESCRIPTION

groff is a front-end to the groff document formatting system. Normally it runs the **troff** program and a
postprocessor appropriate for the selected device. Available devices are:

ps	For PostScript printers and previewers
dvi	For TeX dvi format
X75	For a 75 dpi X11 previewer
X100	For a 100dpi X11 previewer
ascii	For typewriter-like devices
latin1	For typewriter-like devices using the ISO Latin-1 character set.

The postprocessor to be used for a device is specified by the **postpro** command in the device description
file. This can be overridden with the **–X** option.

The default device is **/usr/share/groff_font**. It can optionally preprocess with any of **pic**, **eqn**, **tbl**, **refer**,
or **soelim**.

Options without an argument can be grouped behind a single **–**. A filename of **–** denotes the standard
input.

The **grog** command can be used to guess the correct groff command to use to format a file.

OPTIONS

–h	Print a help message.
–e	Preprocess with eqn.
–t	Preprocess with tbl.
–p	Preprocess with pic.
–s	Preprocess with soelim.
–R	Preprocess with refer. No mechanism is provided for passing arguments to **refer** because most refer options have equivalent commands which can be included in the file. See **refer**(1) for more details.
–v	Make programs run by **groff** print out their version number.
–V	Print the pipeline on stdout instead of executing it.
–z	Suppress output from **troff**. Only error messages will be printed.
–Z	Do not postprocess the output of **troff**. Normally **groff** will automatically run the appropriate postprocessor.
–P*arg*	Pass *arg* to the postprocessor. Each argument should be passed with a separate **–P** option. Note that **groff** does not prepend **–** to *arg* before passing it to the postprocessor.
–l	Send the output to a printer. The command used for this is specified by the **print** command in the device description file.
–L*arg*	Pass *arg* to the spooler. Each argument should be passed with a separate **–L** option. Note that **groff** does not prepend **–** to *arg* before passing it to the postprocessor.
–T*dev*	Prepare output for device *dev*. The default device is **/usr/share/groff_font**.

1

–X	Preview with **gxditview** instead of using the usual postprocessor. This is unlikely to produce good results except with **–Tps**.
–N	Don't allow newlines with eqn delimiters. This is the same as the –N option in **eqn**.

–a
–b
–i
–C
–E
–w_name_
–W_name_
–m_name_
–o_list_
–d_cs_
–r_cn_
–F_dir_
–M_dir_
–f_fam_
–n_num_   These are as described in **troff**(1).

ENVIRONMENT

GROFF_COMMAND_PREFIX
> If this is set X, then **groff** will run X**troff** instead of **troff**. This also applies to **tbl**, **pic**, **eqn**, **refer** and **soelim**. It does not apply to **grops**, **grodvi**, **grotty** and **gxditview**.

GROFF_TMAC_PATH
> A colon separated list of directories in which to search for macro files.

GROFF_TYPESETTER
> Default device.

GROFF_FONT_PATH
> A colon separated list of directories in which to search for the **dev**_name_ directory.

PATH   The search path for commands executed by **groff**.

GROFF_TMPDIR
> The directory in which temporary files will be created. If this is not set and **TMPDIR** is set, temporary files will be created in that directory. Otherwise temporary files will be created in **/tmp**. The **grops**(1) and **refer**(1) commands can create temporary files.

FILES

/usr/share/groff_font/dev_name_**/DESC**   Device description file for device _name_.

/usr/share/groff_font/dev_name_**/F**   Font file for font _F_ of device _name_.

AUTHOR
> James Clark <jjc@jclark.com>

BUGS
> Report bugs to bug-groff@prep.ai.mit.edu. Include a complete, self-contained example that will allow the bug to be reproduced, and say which version of groff you are using.

COPYRIGHT
> Copyright © 1989, 1990, 1991, 1992 Free Software Foundation, Inc.

> groff is free software; you can redistribute it and/or modify it under the terms of the GNU General Public License as published by the Free Software Foundation; either version 2, or (at your option) any later version.

groff is distributed in the hope that it will be useful, but WITHOUT ANY WARRANTY; without even the implied warranty of MERCHANTABILITY or FITNESS FOR A PARTICULAR PURPOSE. See the GNU General Public License for more details.

You should have received a copy of the GNU General Public License along with groff; see the file COPY-ING. If not, write to the Free Software Foundation, 675 Mass Ave, Cambridge, MA 02139, USA.

AVAILABILITY

The most recent released version of groff is always available for anonymous ftp from prep.ai.mit.edu (18.71.0.38) in the directory pub/gnu.

SEE ALSO

grog(1), troff(1), tbl(1), pic(1), eqn(1), soelim(1), refer(1), grops(1), grodvi(1), grotty(1), gxditview(1), groff_font(5), groff_out(5), groff_ms(7), groff_me(7), groff_char(7)

1

NAME

grog – guess options for groff command

SYNOPSIS

grog [*–option* ...] [*files* ...]

DESCRIPTION

grog reads *files* and guesses which of the **groff**(1) options **–e**, **–man**, **–me**, **–mm**, **–ms**, **–p**, **–s**, and **–t** are required for printing *files*, and prints the groff command including those options on the standard output. A filename of – is taken to refer to the standard input. If no files are specified the standard input will be read. Any specified options will be included in the printed command. No space is allowed between options and their arguments. For example,

        'grog –Tdvi paper.ms'

will guess the approriate command to print **paper.ms** and then run it after adding the **–Tdvi** option.

SEE ALSO

doctype(1), **groff**(1), **troff**(1), **tbl**(1), **pic**(1), **eqn**(1), **soelim**(1)

NAME

grops – PostScript driver for groff

SYNOPSIS

grops [–**glv**] [–**b**n] [–**c**n] [–**w**n] [–**F**dir] [files ...]

DESCRIPTION

grops translates the output of GNU **troff** to PostScript. Normally **grops** should be invoked by using the groff command with a –**Tps** option. If no files are given, **grops** will read the standard input. A filename of – will also cause **grops** to read the standard input. PostScript output is written to the standard output. When **grops** is run by **groff** options can be passed to **grops** using the **groff** –**P** option.

OPTIONS

–**b**n   Workaround broken spoolers and previewers. Normally **grops** produces output that conforms the Document Structuring Conventions version 3.0. Unfortunately some spoolers and previewers can't handle such output. The value of n controls what **grops** does to its output acceptable to such programs. A value of 0 will cause grops not to employ any workarounds. Add 1 if no **%%BeginDocumentSetup** and **%%EndDocumentSetup** comments should be generated; this is needed for early versions of TranScript that get confused by anything between the **%%EndProlog** comment and the first **%%Page** comment. Add 2 if lines in included files beginning with **%!** should be stripped out; this is needed for Sun's pageview previewer. Add 4 if **%%Page**, **%%Trailer** and **%%EndProlog** comments should be stripped out of included files; this is needed for spoolers that don't understand the **%%BeginDocument** and **%%EndDocument** comments. Add 8 if the first line of the PostScript output should be **%!PS-Adobe-2.0** rather than **%!PS-Adobe-3.0**; this is needed when using Sun's Newsprint with a printer that requires page reversal. The default value can be specified by a

          broken n

command in the DESC file. Otherwise the default value is 0.

–**c**n   Print n copies of each page.

–**g**   Guess the page length. This generates PostScript code that guesses the page length. The guess will be correct only if the imageable area is vertically centered on the page. This option allows you to generate documents that can be printed both on letter (8.5×11) paper and on A4 paper without change.

–**l**   Print the document in landscape format.

–**F**dir   Search the directory dir/**dev**name for font and device description files; name is the name of the device, usually **ps**.

–**w**n   Lines should be drawn using a thickness of n thousandths of an em.

–**v**   Print the version number.

USAGE

There are styles called **R**, **I**, **B**, and **BI** mounted at font positions 1 to 4. The fonts are grouped into families **A**, **BM**, **C**, **H**, **HN**, **N**, **P** and **T** having members in each of these styles:

AR   AvantGarde-Book

AI   AvantGarde-BookOblique

AB   AvantGarde-Demi

ABI   AvantGarde-DemiOblique

BMR   Bookman-Light

BMI   Bookman-LightItalic

BMB   Bookman-Demi

BMBI	Bookman-DemiItalic
CR	Courier
CI	Courier-Oblique
CB	Courier-Bold
CBI	Courier-BoldOblique
HR	Helvetica
HI	Helvetica-Oblique
HB	Helvetica-Bold
HBI	Helvetica-BoldOblique
HNR	Helvetica-Narrow
HNI	Helvetica-Narrow-Oblique
HNB	Helvetica-Narrow-Bold
HNBI	Helvetica-Narrow-BoldOblique
NR	NewCenturySchlbk-Roman
NI	NewCenturySchlbk-Italic
NB	NewCenturySchlbk-Bold
NBI	NewCenturySchlbk-BoldItalic
PR	Palatino-Roman
PI	Palatino-Italic
PB	Palatino-Bold
PBI	Palatino-BoldItalic
TR	Times-Roman
TI	Times-Italic
TB	Times-Bold
TBI	Times-BoldItalic

There is also the following font which is not a member of a family:

ZCMI   ZapfChancery-MediumItalic

There are also some special fonts called **SS** and **S**. Zapf Dingbats is available as **ZD** and a reversed version of ZapfDingbats (with symbols pointing in the opposite direction) is available as **ZDR**; most characters in these fonts are unnamed and must be accessed using \N.

grops understands various X commands produced using the \X escape sequence; **grops** will only interpret commands that begin with a **ps:** tag.

\X'ps: exec *code'*

This executes the arbitrary PostScript commands in *code*. The PostScript currentpoint will be set to the position of the \X command before executing *code*. The origin will be at the top left corner of the page, and y coordinates will increase down the page. A procedure **u** will be defined that converts groff units to the coordinate system in effect. For example,

    .nr x 1i
    \X'ps: exec \nx u 0 rlineto stroke'

will draw a horizontal line one inch long. *code* may make changes to the graphics state, but any changes will persist only to the end of the page. Any definitions will also persist only until the end of the page. If you use the **\Y** escape sequence with an argument that names a macro, *code* can extend over multiple lines. For example,

```
.nr x 1i
.de y
ps: exec
\nx u 0 rllneto
stroke
..
\Yy
```

is another way to draw a horizontal line one inch long.

\X'ps: file *name***'**

> This is the same as the **exec** command except that the PostScript code is read from file *name*.

\X'ps: def *code***'**

> Place a PostScript definition contained in *code* in the prologue. There should be at most one definition per **\X** command. Long definitions can be split over several **\X** commands; all the *code* arguments are simply joined together separated by newlines. The definitions are placed in a dictionary which is automatically pushed on the dictionary stack when an **exec** command is executed. If you use the **\Y** escape sequence with an argument that names a macro, *code* can extend over multiple lines.

\X'ps: mdef *n code***'**

> Like **def**, except that *code* may contain up to *n* definitions. **grops** needs to know how many definitions *code* contains so that it can create an appropriately sized PostScript dictionary to contain them.

\X'ps: import *file llx lly urx ury width* [*height*]**'**

> Import a PostScript graphic from *file*. The arguments *llx*, *lly*, *urx*, and *ury* give the bounding box of the graphic in the default PostScript coordinate system; they should all be integers; *llx* and *lly* are the x and y coordinates of the lower left corner of the graphic; *urx* and *ury* are the x and y coordinates of the upper right corner of the graphic; *width* and *height* are integers that give the desired width and height in groff units of the graphic. The graphic will be scaled so that it has this width and height and translated so that the lower left corner of the graphic is located at the position associated with **\X** command. If the height argument is omitted it will be scaled uniformly in the x and y directions so that it has the specified width. Note that the contents of the **\X** command are not interpreted by **troff**; so vertical space for the graphic is not automatically added, and the *width* and *height* arguments are not allowed to have attached scaling indicators. If the PostScript file complies with the Adobe Document Structuring Conventions and contains a **%%Bounding-Box** comment, then the bounding box can be automatically extracted from within groff by using the sy request to run the **psbb** command.

> The −**mps** macros (which are automatically loaded when **grops** is run by the groff command) include a **PSPIC** macro which allows a picture to be easily imported. This has the format

> > **.PSPIC** *file* [*width* [*height*

> *file* is the name of the file containing the illustration; *width* and *height* give the desired width and height of the graphic. The *width* and *height* arguments may have scaling indicators attached; the default scaling indicator is **i**. This macro will scale the graphic uniformly in the x and y directions so that it is no more than *width* wide and *height* high.

\X'ps: invis'
\X'ps: endinvis'

> No output will be generated for text and drawing commands that are bracketed with these **\X** commands. These commands are intended for use when output from **troff** will be previewed before being processed with **grops**; if the previewer is unable to display certain characters or other

constructs, then other substitute characters or constructs can be used for previewing by bracketing them with these \X commands.

For example, **gxditview** is not able to display a proper \(em character because the standard X11 fonts do not provide it; this problem can be overcome by executing the following request

> .char \(em \X'ps: invis'\
> \Z'\v'-.25m'\h'.05m'\D'l .9m 0'\h'.05m''\
> \X'ps: endinvis'\(em

In this case, **gxditview** will be unable to display the \(em character and will draw the line, whereas **grops** will print the \(em character and ignore the line.

The input to **grops** must be in the format output by **troff**(1). This is described in **groff_out**(1). In addition the device and font description files for the device used must meet certain requirements. The device and font description files supplied for **ps** device meet all these requirements. **afmtodit**(1) can be used to create font files from AFM files. The resolution must be an integer multiple of 72 times the **sizescale**. The **ps** device uses a resolution of 72000 and a sizescale of 1000. The device description file should contain a command

> **paperlength** *n*

which says that output should be generated which is suitable for printing on a page whose length is *n* machine units. Each font description file must contain a command

> **internalname** *psname*

which says that the PostScript name of the font is *psname*. It may also contain a command

> **encoding** *enc_file*

which says that the PostScript font should be reencoded using the encoding described in *enc_file*; this file should consist of a sequence of lines of the form:

> *pschar code*

where *pschar* is the PostScript name of the character, and *code* is its position in the encoding expressed as a decimal integer. The code for each character given in the font file must correspond to the code for the character in encoding file, or to the code in the default encoding for the font if the PostScript font is not to be reencoded. This code can be used with the \N escape sequence in **troff** to select the character, even if the character does not have a groff name. Every character in the font file must exist in the PostScript font, and the widths given in the font file must match the widths used in the PostScript font. **grops** will assume that a character with a groff name of **space** is blank (makes no marks on the page); it can make use of such a character to generate more efficient and compact PostScript output.

grops can automatically include the downloadable fonts necessary to print the document. Any downloadable fonts which should, when required, be included by **grops** must be listed in the file **/usr/share/groff_font/devps/download**; this should consist of lines of the form

> *font filename*

where *font* is the PostScript name of the font, and *filename* is the name of the file containing the font; lines beginning with # and blank lines are ignored; fields may be separated by tabs or spaces; *filename* will be searched for using the same mechanism that is used for groff font metric files. The **download** file itself will also be searched for using this mechanism.

If the file containing a downloadable font or imported document conforms to the Adobe Document Structuring Conventions, then **grops** will interpret any comments in the files sufficiently to ensure that its own output is conforming. It will also supply any needed font resources that are listed in the **download** file as well as any needed file resources. It is also able to handle inter-resource dependencies. For example, suppose that you have a downloadable font called Garamond, and also a downloadable font called Garamond-Outline which depends on Garamond (typically it would be defined to copy Garamond's font dictionary,

1

and change the PaintType), then it is necessary for Garamond to appear before Garamond-Outline in the PostScript document. **grops** will handle this automatically provided that the downloadable font file for Garamond-Outline indicates its dependence on Garamond by means of the Document Structuring Conventions, for example by beginning with the following lines

> **%!PS-Adobe-3.0 Resource-Font**
> **%%DocumentNeededResources: font Garamond**
> **%%EndComments**
> **%%IncludeResource: font Garamond**

In this case both Garamond and Garamond-Outline would need to be listed in the **download** file. A downloadable font should not include its own name in a **%%DocumentSuppliedResources** comment.

grops will not interpret **%%DocumentFonts** comments. The **%%DocumentNeededResources**, **%%DocumentSuppliedResources**, **%%IncludeResource**, **%%BeginResource** and **%%EndResource** comments (or possibly the old **%%DocumentNeededFonts**, **%%DocumentSuppliedFonts**, **%%IncludeFont**, **%%BeginFont** and **%%EndFont** comments) should be used.

FILES

/usr/share/groff_font/devps/DESC	Device description file.
/usr/share/groff_font/devps/F	Font description file for font *F*.
/usr/share/groff_font/devps/download	List of downloadable fonts.
/usr/share/groff_font/devps/text.enc	Encoding used for text fonts.
/usr/share/tmac/tmac.ps	Macros for use with **grops**; automatically loaded by **troffrc**
/usr/share/tmac/tmac.pspic	Definition of **PSPIC** macro, automatically loaded by **tmac.ps**.
/usr/share/tmac/tmac.psold	Macros to disable use of characters not present in older PostScript printers; automatically loaded by **tmac.ps**.
/usr/share/tmac/tmac.psnew	Macros to undo the effect of **tmac.psold**.
/tmp/grops*XXXXXX*	Temporary file.

SEE ALSO

afmtodit(1), **groff**(1), **troff**(1), **psbb**(1), **groff_out**(5), **groff_font**(5), **groff_char**(7)

NAME

grotty – groff driver for typewriter-like devices

SYNOPSIS

grotty [**–hfbuodBUv**] [*–Fdir*] [*files ...*]

DESCRIPTION

grotty translates the output of GNU **troff** into a form suitable for typewriter-like devices. Normally **grotty** should be invoked by using the **groff** command with a **–Tascii** or **–Tlatin1** option. If no files are given, **grotty** will read the standard input. A filename of – will also cause **grotty** to read the standard input. Output is written to the standard output.

Normally **grotty** prints a bold character *c* using the sequence '*c* BACKSPACE *c*' and an italic character *c* by the sequence '_ BACKSPACE *c*'. These sequences can be displayed on a terminal by piping through **ul**(1). Pagers such as **more**(1) or **less**(1) are also able to display these sequences. Use either **–B** or **–U** when piping into **less**(1); use **–b** when piping into **more**(1). There is no need to filter the output through **col**(1) since **grotty** never outputs reverse line feeds.

The font description file may contain a command

internalname *n*

where *n* is a decimal integer. If the 01 bit in *n* is set, then the font will be treated as an italic font; if the 02 bit is set, then it will be treated as a bold font. The code field in the font description field gives the code which will be used to output the character. This code can also be used in the \N escape sequence in **troff**.

OPTIONS

–Fdir   Search the directory *dir*/**dev***name* for font and device description files; *name* is the name of the device, usually **ascii** or **latin1**.

–h   Use horizontal tabs in the output. Tabs are assumed to be set every 8 columns.

–f   Use form feeds in the output. A form feed will be output at the end of each page that has no output on its last line.

–b   Suppress the use of overstriking for bold characters.

–u   Suppress the use of underlining for italic characters.

–B   Use only overstriking for bold-italic characters.

–U   Use only underlining for bold-italic characters.

–o   Suppress overstriking (other than for bold or underlined characters).

–d   Ignore all \D commands. Without this **grotty** will render \D'l...' commands that have at least one zero argument (and so are either horizontal or vertical) using –, | and + characters.

–v   Print the version number.

FILES

/usr/share/groff_font/devascii/DESC
Device description file for **ascii** device.

/usr/share/groff_font/devascii/ F
Font description file for font *F* of **ascii device.**

/usr/share/groff_font/devlatin1/DESC
Device description file for **latin1** device.

/usr/share/groff_font/devlatin1/ F
Font description file for font *F* of **latin1 device.**

/usr/share/tmac/tmac.tty
Macros for use with **grotty**.

/usr/share/tmac/tmac.tty-char
> Additional klugey character definitions for use with **grotty**.

BUGS
> **grotty** is intended only for simple documents.
>
> There is no support for fractional horizontal or vertical motions.
>
> There is no support for **\D** commands other than horizontal and vertical lines.
>
> Characters above the first line (ie with a vertical position of 0) cannot be printed.

SEE ALSO
> **groff**(1), **troff**(1), **groff_out**(5), **groff_font**(5), **groff_char**(7), **ul**(1), **more**(1), **less**(1)

1

NAME
>   **groups** – show group memberships

SYNOPSIS
>   **groups** [*user*]

DESCRIPTION
>   The **groups** utility has been obsoleted by the id(1) utility, and is equivalent to "**id** **–Gn** [*user*]". The command "**id** **–p**" is suggested for normal interactive use.
>
>   The **groups** utility displays the groups to which you (or the optionally specified user) belong.
>
>   The **groups** utility exits 0 on success, and >0 if an error occurs.

SEE ALSO
>   id(1)

NAME

    gzexe – compress executable files in place

SYNOPSIS

    gzexe [name ...]

DESCRIPTION

    The *gzexe* utility allows you to compress executables in place and have them automatically uncompress and execute when you run them (at a penalty in performance). For example if you execute "gzexe /bin/cat" it will create the following two files:

      -r-xr-xr-x 1 root bin   9644 Feb 11 11:16 /bin/cat

      -r-xr-xr-x 1 bin   bin 24576 Nov 23 13:21 /bin/cat˜

    /bin/cat˜ is the original file and /bin/cat is the self-uncompressing executable file. You can remove /bin/cat˜ once you are sure that /bin/cat works properly.

    This utility is most useful on systems with very small disks.

OPTIONS

    −d   Decompress the given executables instead of compressing them.

SEE ALSO

    gzip(1), znew(1), zmore(1), zcmp(1), zforce(1)

CAVEATS

    The compressed executable is a shell script. This may create some security holes. In particular, the compressed executable relies on the PATH environment variable to find *gzip* and some other utilities *(tail, chmod, ln, sleep).*

BUGS

    gzexe attempts to retain the original file attributes on the compressed executable, but you may have to fix them manually in some cases, using *chmod* or *chown.*

1

NAME

gzip, gunzip, zcat – compress or expand files

SYNOPSIS

gzip [**−acdfhlLnNrtvV19**] [**−S suffix**] [*name ...*]
gunzip [**−acfhlLnNrtvV**] [**−S suffix**] [*name ...*]
zcat [**−fhLV**] [*name ...*]

DESCRIPTION

Gzip reduces the size of the named files using Lempel-Ziv coding (LZ77). Whenever possible, each file is replaced by one with the extension **.gz,** while keeping the same ownership modes, access and modification times. (The default extension is **−gz** for VMS, **z** for MSDOS, OS/2 FAT, Windows NT FAT and Atari.) If no files are specified, or if a file name is "-", the standard input is compressed to the standard output. *Gzip* will only attempt to compress regular files. In particular, it will ignore symbolic links.

If the compressed file name is too long for its file system, *gzip* truncates it. *Gzip* attempts to truncate only the parts of the file name longer than 3 characters. (A part is delimited by dots.) If the name consists of small parts only, the longest parts are truncated. For example, if file names are limited to 14 characters, gzip.msdos.exe is compressed to gzi.msd.exe.gz. Names are not truncated on systems which do not have a limit on file name length.

By default, *gzip* keeps the original file name and timestamp in the compressed file. These are used when decompressing the file with the −N option. This is useful when the compressed file name was truncated or when the time stamp was not preserved after a file transfer.

Compressed files can be restored to their original form using *gzip -d* or *gunzip* or *zcat*. If the original name saved in the compressed file is not suitable for its file system, a new name is constructed from the original one to make it legal.

gunzip takes a list of files on its command line and replaces each file whose name ends with .gz, -gz, .z, -z, _z or .Z and which begins with the correct magic number with an uncompressed file without the original extension. *gunzip* also recognizes the special extensions **.tgz** and **.taz** as shorthands for **.tar.gz** and **.tar.Z** respectively. When compressing, *gzip* uses the **.tgz** extension if necessary instead of truncating a file with a **.tar** extension.

gunzip can currently decompress files created by *gzip, zip, compress, compress -H* or *pack*. The detection of the input format is automatic. When using the first two formats, *gunzip* checks a 32 bit CRC. For *pack*, *gunzip* checks the uncompressed length. The standard *compress* format was not designed to allow consistency checks. However *gunzip* is sometimes able to detect a bad .Z file. If you get an error when uncompressing a .Z file, do not assume that the .Z file is correct simply because the standard *uncompress* does not complain. This generally means that the standard *uncompress* does not check its input, and happily generates garbage output. The SCO compress -H format (lzh compression method) does not include a CRC but also allows some consistency checks.

Files created by *zip* can be uncompressed by gzip only if they have a single member compressed with the 'deflation' method. This feature is only intended to help conversion of tar.zip files to the tar.gz format. To extract zip files with several members, use *unzip* instead of *gunzip*.

zcat is identical to *gunzip* **−c.** (On some systems, *zcat* may be installed as *gzcat* to preserve the original link to *compress*.) *zcat* uncompresses either a list of files on the command line or its standard input and writes the uncompressed data on standard output. *zcat* will uncompress files that have the correct magic number whether they have a **.gz** suffix or not.

Gzip uses the Lempel-Ziv algorithm used in *zip* and PKZIP. The amount of compression obtained depends on the size of the input and the distribution of common substrings. Typically, text such as source code or English is reduced by 60–70%. Compression is generally much better than that achieved by LZW (as used in *compress*), Huffman coding (as used in *pack*), or adaptive Huffman coding (*compact*).

1

Compression is always performed, even if the compressed file is slightly larger than the original. The worst case expansion is a few bytes for the gzip file header, plus 5 bytes every 32K block, or an expansion ratio of 0.015% for large files. Note that the actual number of used disk blocks almost never increases. *gzip* preserves the mode, ownership and timestamps of files when compressing or decompressing.

OPTIONS

−a --ascii

Ascii text mode: convert end-of-lines using local conventions. This option is supported only on some non-Unix systems. For MSDOS, CR LF is converted to LF when compressing, and LF is converted to CR LF when decompressing.

−c --stdout --to-stdout

Write output on standard output; keep original files unchanged. If there are several input files, the output consists of a sequence of independently compressed members. To obtain better compression, concatenate all input files before compressing them.

−d --decompress --uncompress

Decompress.

−f --force

Force compression or decompression even if the file has multiple links or the corresponding file already exists, or if the compressed data is read from or written to a terminal. If the input data is not in a format recognized by *gzip,* and if the option --stdout is also given, copy the input data without change to the standard ouput: let *zcat* behave as *cat.* If −f is not given, and when not running in the background, *gzip* prompts to verify whether an existing file should be overwritten.

−h --help

Display a help screen and quit.

−l --list For each compressed file, list the following fields:

> compressed size: size of the compressed file
> uncompressed size: size of the uncompressed file
> ratio: compression ratio (0.0% if unknown)
> uncompressed_name: name of the uncompressed file

The uncompressed size is given as -1 for files not in gzip format, such as compressed .Z files. To get the uncompressed size for such a file, you can use:

> zcat file.Z | wc -c

In combination with the --verbose option, the following fields are also displayed:

> method: compression method
> crc: the 32-bit CRC of the uncompressed data
> date & time: time stamp for the uncompressed file

The compression methods currently supported are deflate, compress, lzh (SCO compress -H) and pack. The crc is given as ffffffff for a file not in gzip format.

With --name, the uncompressed name, date and time are those stored within the compress file if present.

With --verbose, the size totals and compression ratio for all files is also displayed, unless some sizes are unknown. With --quiet, the title and totals lines are not displayed.

1

−L --license

>   Display the *gzip* license and quit.

−n --no-name

>   When compressing, do not save the original file name and time stamp by default. (The original name is always saved if the name had to be truncated.) When decompressing, do not restore the original file name if present (remove only the *gzip* suffix from the compressed file name) and do not restore the original time stamp if present (copy it from the compressed file). This option is the default when decompressing.

−N --name

>   When compressing, always save the original file name and time stamp; this is the default. When decompressing, restore the original file name and time stamp if present. This option is useful on systems which have a limit on file name length or when the time stamp has been lost after a file transfer.

−q --quiet

>   Suppress all warnings.

−r --recursive

>   Travel the directory structure recursively. If any of the file names specified on the command line are directories, *gzip* will descend into the directory and compress all the files it finds there (or decompress them in the case of *gunzip*).

−S .suf --suffix .suf

>   Use suffix .suf instead of .gz. Any suffix can be given, but suffixes other than .z and .gz should be avoided to avoid confusion when files are transferred to other systems. A null suffix forces gunzip to try decompression on all given files regardless of suffix, as in:
>
>   gunzip -S "" *   (*.* for MSDOS)
>
>   Previous versions of gzip used the .z suffix. This was changed to avoid a conflict with *pack*(1).

−t --test

>   Test. Check the compressed file integrity.

−v --verbose

>   Verbose. Display the name and percentage reduction for each file compressed or decompressed.

−V --version

>   Version. Display the version number and compilation options then quit.

−# --fast --best

>   Regulate the speed of compression using the specified digit #, where −1 or —**fast** indicates the fastest compression method (less compression) and −9 or —**best** indicates the slowest compression method (best compression). The default compression level is −6 (that is, biased towards high compression at expense of speed).

ADVANCED USAGE

Multiple compressed files can be concatenated. In this case, *gunzip* will extract all members at once. For example:

    gzip -c file1 > foo.gz
    gzip -c file2 >> foo.gz

Then
    gunzip -c foo

is equivalent to

     cat file1 file2

In case of damage to one member of a .gz file, other members can still be recovered (if the damaged member is removed). However, you can get better compression by compressing all members at once:

     cat file1 file2 | gzip > foo.gz

compresses better than

     gzip -c file1 file2 > foo.gz

If you want to recompress concatenated files to get better compression, do:

     gzip -cd old.gz | gzip > new.gz

If a compressed file consists of several members, the uncompressed size and CRC reported by the --list option applies to the last member only. If you need the uncompressed size for all members, you can use:

     gzip -cd file.gz | wc -c

If you wish to create a single archive file with multiple members so that members can later be extracted independently, use an archiver such as tar or zip. GNU tar supports the -z option to invoke gzip transparently. gzip is designed as a complement to tar, not as a replacement.

ENVIRONMENT

The environment variable **GZIP** can hold a set of default options for *gzip*. These options are interpreted first and can be overwritten by explicit command line parameters. For example:
    for sh: GZIP="-8v --name"; export GZIP
    for csh: setenv GZIP "-8v --name"
    for MSDOS: set GZIP=-8v --name

On Vax/VMS, the name of the environment variable is GZIP_OPT, to avoid a conflict with the symbol set for invocation of the program.

SEE ALSO

znew(1), zcmp(1), zmore(1), zforce(1), gzexe(1), zip(1), unzip(1), compress(1), pack(1), compact(1)

DIAGNOSTICS

Exit status is normally 0; if an error occurs, exit status is 1. If a warning occurs, exit status is 2.

Usage: gzip [-cdfhlLnNrtvV19] [-S suffix] [file ...]
          Invalid options were specified on the command line.
file: not in gzip format
          The file specified to *gunzip* has not been compressed.
file: Corrupt input. Use zcat to recover some data.
          The compressed file has been damaged. The data up to the point of failure can be recovered using
                    zcat file > recover
file: compressed with *xx* bits, can only handle *yy* bits
          File was compressed (using LZW) by a program that could deal with more *bits* than the decompress code on this machine. Recompress the file with gzip, which compresses better and uses less memory.
file: already has .gz suffix -- no change
          The file is assumed to be already compressed. Rename the file and try again.

file already exists; do you wish to overwrite (y or n)?
> Respond "y" if you want the output file to be replaced; "n" if not.

gunzip: corrupt input
> A SIGSEGV violation was detected which usually means that the input file has been corrupted.

xx.x%
> Percentage of the input saved by compression. (Relevant only for −v and −l.)

-- not a regular file or directory: ignored
> When the input file is not a regular file or directory, (e.g. a symbolic link, socket, FIFO, device file), it is left unaltered.

-- has *xx* other links: unchanged
> The input file has links; it is left unchanged. See *ln*(1) for more information. Use the −f flag to force compression of multiply-linked files.

CAVEATS

When writing compressed data to a tape, it is generally necessary to pad the output with zeroes up to a block boundary. When the data is read and the whole block is passed to *gunzip* for decompression, *gunzip* detects that there is extra trailing garbage after the compressed data and emits a warning by default. You have to use the --quiet option to suppress the warning. This option can be set in the **GZIP** environment variable as in:
```
for sh:  GZIP="-q"  tar -xfz --block-compress /dev/rst0
for csh: (setenv GZIP -q; tar -xfz --block-compr /dev/rst0
```

In the above example, gzip is invoked implicitly by the -z option of GNU tar. Make sure that the same block size (-b option of tar) is used for reading and writing compressed data on tapes. (This example assumes you are using the GNU version of tar.)

BUGS

The --list option reports incorrect sizes if they exceed 2 gigabytes. The --list option reports sizes as -1 and crc as ffffffff if the compressed file is on a non seekable media.

In some rare cases, the --best option gives worse compression than the default compression level (-6). On some highly redundant files, *compress* compresses better than *gzip*.

1

NAME
   head – display first lines of a file

SYNOPSIS
   head [**–n** *count*] [*file ...*]

DESCRIPTION
   This filter displays the first *count* lines of each of the specified files, or of the standard input if no files are
   specified. If *count* is omitted it defaults to 10.

   If more than a single file is specified, each file is preceded by a header consisting of the string ''**==>** XXX
   <=='' where ''XXX'' is the name of the file.

   The **head** utility exits 0 on success, and >0 if an error occurs.

SEE ALSO
   tail(1)

HISTORY
   The **head** command appeared in 3.0BSD.

NAME

hexdump – ascii, decimal, hexadecimal, octal dump

SYNOPSIS

hexdump [–bcdovx] [–e *format_string*] [–f *format_file*] [–n *length*] [–s *skip*]
        file ...

DESCRIPTION

The hexdump utility is a filter which displays the specified files, or the standard input, if no files are specified, in a user specified format.

The options are as follows:

–b   *One-byte octal display.* Display the input offset in hexadecimal, followed by sixteen space-separated, three column, zero-filled, bytes of input data, in octal, per line.

–c   *One-byte character display.* Display the input offset in hexadecimal, followed by sixteen space-separated, three column, space-filled, characters of input data per line.

–d   *Two-byte decimal display.* Display the input offset in hexadecimal, followed by eight space-separated, five column, zero-filled, two-byte units of input data, in unsigned decimal, per line.

–e *format_string*
         Specify a format string to be used for displaying data.

–f *format_file*
         Specify a file that contains one or more newline separated format strings. Empty lines and lines whose first non-blank character is a hash mark (#) are ignored.

–n *length*
         Interpret only *length* bytes of input.

–o   *Two-byte octal display.* Display the input offset in hexadecimal, followed by eight space-separated, six column, zero-filled, two byte quantities of input data, in octal, per line.

–s *offset*
         Skip *offset* bytes from the beginning of the input. By default, *offset* is interpreted as a decimal number. With a leading **0x** or **0X**, *offset* is interpreted as a hexadecimal number, otherwise, with a leading **0**, *offset* is interpreted as an octal number. Appending the character **b**, **k**, or **m** to *offset* causes it to be interpreted as a multiple of 512, 1024, or 1048576, respectively.

–v   The **–v** option causes hexdump to display all input data. Without the **–v** option, any number of groups of output lines, which would be identical to the immediately preceding group of output lines (except for the input offsets), are replaced with a line comprised of a single asterisk.

–x   *Two-byte hexadecimal display.* Display the input offset in hexadecimal, followed by eight, space separated, four column, zero-filled, two-byte quantities of input data, in hexadecimal, per line.

For each input file, **hexdump** sequentially copies the input to standard output, transforming the data according to the format strings specified by the **–e** and **–f** options, in the order that they were specified.

Formats

A format string contains any number of format units, separated by whitespace. A format unit contains up to three items: an iteration count, a byte count, and a format.

The iteration count is an optional positive integer, which defaults to one. Each format is applied iteration count times.

The byte count is an optional positive integer. If specified it defines the number of bytes to be interpreted by each iteration of the format.

If an iteration count and/or a byte count is specified, a single slash must be placed after the iteration count and/or before the byte count to disambiguate them. Any whitespace before or after the slash is ignored.

The format is required and must be surrounded by double quote (" ") marks. It is interpreted as a fprintf-style format string (see fprintf(3)), with the following exceptions:

- An asterisk (*) may not be used as a field width or precision.

- A byte count or field precision *is* required for each "s" conversion character (unlike the fprintf(3) default which prints the entire string if the precision is unspecified).

- The conversion characters "h", "l", "n", "p" and "q" are not supported.

- The single character escape sequences described in the C standard are supported:

NUL	\0
\<alert character\>	\a
\<backspace\>	\b
\<form-feed\>	\f
\<newline\>	\n
\<carriage return\>	\r
\<tab\>	\t
\<vertical tab\>	\v

Hexdump also supports the the following additional conversion strings:

_a[dox]   Display the input offset, cumulative across input files, of the next byte to be displayed. The appended characters **d**, **o**, and **x** specify the display base as decimal, octal or hexadecimal respectively.

_A[dox]   Identical to the _a conversion string except that it is only performed once, when all of the input data has been processed.

_c   Output characters in the default character set. Nonprinting characters are displayed in three character, zero-padded octal, except for those representable by standard escape notation (see above), which are displayed as two character strings.

_p   Output characters in the default character set. Nonprinting characters are displayed as a single "•".

_u   Output US ASCII characters, with the exception that control characters are displayed using the following, lower-case, names. Characters greater than 0xff, hexadecimal, are displayed as hexadecimal strings.

000 nul	001 soh	002 stx	003 etx	004 eot	005 enq
006 ack	007 bel	008 bs	009 ht	00A lf	00B vt
00C ff	00D cr	00E so	00F si	010 dle	011 dc1
012 dc2	013 dc3	014 dc4	015 nak	016 syn	017 etb
018 can	019 em	01A sub	01B esc	01C fs	01D gs
01E rs	01F us	0FF del			

1

The default and supported byte counts for the conversion characters are as follows:

%_c, %_p, %_u, %c	One byte counts only.
%d, %i, %o, %u, %X, %x	Four byte default, one, two and four byte counts supported.
%E, %e, %f, %G, %g	Eight byte default, four byte counts supported.

The amount of data interpreted by each format string is the sum of the data required by each format unit, which is the iteration count times the byte count, or the iteration count times the number of bytes required by the format if the byte count is not specified.

The input is manipulated in ''blocks'', where a block is defined as the largest amount of data specified by any format string. Format strings interpreting less than an input block's worth of data, whose last format unit both interprets some number of bytes and does not have a specified iteration count, have the iteration count incremented until the entire input block has been processed or there is not enough data remaining in the block to satisfy the format string.

If, either as a result of user specification or hexdump modifying the iteration count as described above, an iteration count is greater than one, no trailing whitespace characters are output during the last iteration.

It is an error to specify a byte count as well as multiple conversion characters or strings unless all but one of the conversion characters or strings is _a or _A.

If, as a result of the specification of the −n option or end-of-file being reached, input data only partially satisfies a format string, the input block is zero-padded sufficiently to display all available data (i.e. any format units overlapping the end of data will display some number of the zero bytes).

Further output by such format strings is replaced by an equivalent number of spaces. An equivalent number of spaces is defined as the number of spaces output by an **s** conversion character with the same field width and precision as the original conversion character or conversion string but with any ''+'', '' '', ''#'' conversion flag characters removed, and referencing a NULL string.

If no format strings are specified, the default display is equivalent to specifying the −x option.

hexdump exits 0 on success and >0 if an error occurred.

EXAMPLES

Display the input in perusal format:

```
"%06.6_ao "   12/1 "%3_u "
"\t\t" "%_p "
"\n"
```

Implement the −x option:

```
"%07.7_Ax\n"
"%07.7_ax  " 8/2 "%04x " "\n"
```

SEE ALSO

adb(1)

NAME

    rhost – look up host names using domain server

SYNOPSIS

    rhost [-l] [-v] [-w] [-r] [-d] [-t querytype] [-a] host [server]

DESCRIPTION

    Host looks for information about Internet hosts. It gets this information from a set of interconnected servers that are spread across the country. By default, it simply converts between host names and Internet addresses. However with the -t or -a options, it can be used to find all of the information about this host that is maintained by the domain server.

    The arguments can be either host names or host numbers. The program first attempts to interpret them as host numbers. If this fails, it will treat them as host names. A host number consists of first decimal numbers separated by dots, e.g. 128.6.4.194 A host name consists of names separated by dots, e.g. topaz.rutgers.edu. Unless the name ends in a dot, the local domain is automatically tacked on the end. Thus a Rutgers user can say "host topaz", and it will actually look up "topaz.rutgers.edu". If this fails, the name is tried unchanged (in this case, "topaz"). This same convention is used for mail and other network utilities. The actual suffix to tack on the end is obtained by looking at the results of a "hostname" call, and using everything starting at the first dot. (See below for a description of how to customize the host name lookup.)

    The first argument is the host name you want to look up. If this is a number, an "inverse query" is done, i.e. the domain system looks in a separate set of databases used to convert numbers to names.

    The second argument is optional. It allows you to specify a particular server to query. If you don't specify this argument, the default server (normally the local machine) is used.

    If a name is specified, you may see output of three different kinds. Here is an example that shows all of them:

    % host sun4

    sun4.rutgers.edu is a nickname for ATHOS.RUTGERS.EDU

    ATHOS.RUTGERS.EDU has address 128.6.5.46

    ATHOS.RUTGERS.EDU has address 128.6.4.4

    ATHOS.RUTGERS.EDU mail is handled by ARAMIS.RUTGERS.EDU

    The user has typed the command "host sun4". The first line indicates that the name "sun4.rutgers.edu" is actually a nickname. The official host name is "ATHOS.RUTGERS.EDU'. The next two lines show the address. If a system has more than one network interface, there will be a separate address for each. The last line indicates that ATHOS.RUTGERS.EDU does not receive its own mail. Mail for it is taken by ARAMIS.RUTGERS.EDU. There may be more than one such line, since some systems have more than one other system that will handle mail for them. Technically, every system that can receive mail is supposed to have an entry of this kind. If the system receives its own mail, there should be an entry the mentions the system itself, for example "XXX mail is handled by XXX". However many systems that receive their own mail do not bother to mention that fact. If a system has a "mail is handled by" entry, but no address, this indicates that it is not really part of the Internet, but a system that is on the network will forward mail to it. Systems on Usenet, Bitnet, and a number of other networks have entries of this kind.

    There are a number of options that can be used before the host name. Most of these options are meaningful only to the staff who have to maintain the domain database.

    The option -w causes host to wait forever for a response. Normally it will time out after around a minute.

    The option -v causes printout to be in a "verbose" format. This is the official domain master file format, which is documented in the man page for "named". Without this option, output still follows this format in general terms, but some attempt is made to make it more intelligible to normal users. Without -v, "a", "mx", and "cname" records are written out as "has address", "mail is handled by", and "is a nickname for", and TTL and class fields are not shown.

1

The option -r causes recursion to be turned off in the request. This means that the name server will return only data it has in its own database. It will not ask other servers for more information.

The option -d turns on debugging. Network transactions are shown in detail.

The option -t allows you to specify a particular type of information to be looked up. The arguments are defined in the man page for "named". Currently supported types are a, ns, md, mf, cname, soa, mb, mg, mr, null, wks, ptr, hinfo, minfo, mx, uinfo, uid, gid, unspec, and the wildcard, which may be written as either "any" or "*". Types must be given in lower case. Note that the default is to look first for "a", and then "mx", except that if the verbose option is turned on, the default is only "a".

The option -a (for "all") is equivalent to "-v -t any".

The option -l causes a listing of a complete domain. E.g.
    host -l rutgers.edu
will give a listing of all hosts in the rutgers.edu domain. The -t option is used to filter what information is presented, as you would expect. The default is address information, which also include PTR and NS records. The command
    host -l -v -t any rutgers.edu
will give a complete download of the zone data for rutgers.edu, in the official master file format. (However the SOA record is listed twice, for arcane reasons.) NOTE: -l is implemented by doing a complete zone transfer and then filtering out the information the you have asked for. This command should be used only if it is absolutely necessary.

CUSTOMIZING HOST NAME LOOKUP

In general, if the name supplied by the user does not have any dots in it, a default domain is appended to the end. This domain can be defined in /etc/resolv.conf, but is normally derived by taking the local host-name after its first dot. The user can override this, and specify a different default domain, using the environment variable *LOCALDOMAIN*. In addition, the user can supply his own abbreviations for host names. They should be in a file consisting of one line per abbreviation. Each line contains an abbreviation, a space, and then the full host name. This file must be pointed to by an environment variable *HOS-TALIASES*, which is the name of the file.

See Also

named (8)

BUGS

Unexpected effects can happen when you type a name that is not part of the local domain. Please always keep in mind the fact that the local domain name is tacked onto the end of every name, unless it ends in a dot. Only if this fails is the name used unchanged.

The -l option only tries the first name server listed for the domain that you have requested. If this server is dead, you may need to specify a server manually. E.g. to get a listing of foo.edu, you could try "host -t ns foo.edu" to get a list of all the name servers for foo.edu, and then try "host -l foo.edu xxx" for all xxx on the list of name servers, until you find one that works.

1

NAME

>   **hostname** – set or print name of current host system

SYNOPSIS

>   **hostname** [−s] [*nameofhost*]

DESCRIPTION

>   **Hostname** prints the name of the current host. The super-user can set the hostname by supplying an argument; this is usually done in the network initialization script /etc/netstart, normally run at boot time.

>   Options:

>   **−s**   Trims off any domain information from the printed name.

SEE ALSO

>   gethostname(2)

HISTORY

>   The **hostname** command appeared in 4.2BSD.

NAME

id – return user identity

SYNOPSIS

id [*user*]
id −G [−n][*user*]
id −g [−nr][*user*]
id −p
id −u [−nr][*user*]

DESCRIPTION

The **id** utility displays the user and group names and numeric IDs, of the calling process, to the standard output. If the real and effective IDs are different, both are displayed, otherwise only the real ID is displayed.

If a *user* (login name or user ID) is specified, the user and group IDs of that user are displayed. In this case, the real and effective IDs are assumed to be the same.

The options are as follows:

−G   Display the different group IDs (effective, real and supplementary) as white-space separated numbers, in no particular order.

−g   Display the effective group ID as a number.

−n   Display the name of the user or group ID for the −G, −g and −u options instead of the number. If any of the ID numbers cannot be mapped into names, the number will be displayed as usual.

−p   Make the output human-readable. If the user name returned by getlogin(2) is different from the login name referenced by the user ID, the name returned by getlogin(2) is displayed, preceded by the keyword ''login''. The user ID as a name is displayed, preceded by the keyword ''uid''. If the effective user ID is different from the real user ID, the real user ID is displayed as a name, preceded by the keyword ''euid''. If the effective group ID is different from the real group ID, the real group ID is displayed as a name, preceded by the keyword ''rgid''. The list of groups to which the user belongs is then displayed as names, preceded by the keyword ''groups''. Each display is on a separate line.

−r   Display the real ID for the −g and −u options instead of the effective ID.

−u   Display the effective user ID as a number.

The **id** utility exits 0 on success, and >0 if an error occurs.

SEE ALSO

who(1)

STANDARDS

The **id** function is expected to conform to IEEE Std1003.2 (''POSIX'').

HISTORY

The historic groups(1) command is equivalent to ''id −Gn [*user*]''.

The historic whoami(1) command is equivalent to ''id −un''.

The **id** command first appeared in 4.4BSD.

1

NAME
ident – identify files

SYNOPSIS
ident [−q] [*file* ...]

DESCRIPTION
ident searches for all occurrences of the pattern $keyword:...$ in the named files or, if no file name appears, the standard input.

These patterns are normally inserted automatically by the RCS command **co**(1), but can also be inserted manually. The option **−q** suppresses the warning given if there are no patterns in a file.

ident works on text files as well as object files and dumps. For example, if the C program in **f.c** contains

  char rcsid[] = "$Id: f.c,v 5.0 1990/08/22 09:09:36 eggert Exp $";

and **f.c** is compiled into **f.o**, then the command

  ident f.c f.o

will output

  f.c:
   $Id: f.c,v 5.0 1990/08/22 09:09:36 eggert Exp $
  f.o:
   $Id: f.c,v 5.0 1990/08/22 09:09:36 eggert Exp $

IDENTIFICATION
Author: Walter F. Tichy.
Revision Number: 5.0; Release Date: 1990/08/22.
Copyright © 1982, 1988, 1989 by Walter F. Tichy.
Copyright © 1990 by Paul Eggert.

SEE ALSO
ci(1), co(1), rcs(1), rcsdiff(1), rcsintro(1), rcsmerge(1), rlog(1), rcsfile(5)
Walter F. Tichy, RCS—A System for Version Control, *Software—Practice & Experience* **15**, 7 (July 1985), 637-654.

1

NAME

indent – indent and format C program source

SYNOPSIS

indent [*input-file* [*output-file*]] [−bad | −nbad] [−bap | −nbap] [−bbb | −nbbb]
[−bc | −nbc] [−bl] [−br] [−c*n*] [−cd*n*] [−cdb | −ncdb] [−ce | −nce] [−ci*n*]
[−cli*n*] [−d*n*] [−di*n*] [−fc1 | −nfc1] [−i*n*] [−ip | −nip] [−l*n*] [−lc*n*] [−lp |
−nlp] [−npro] [−pcs | −npcs] [−psl | −npsl] [−sc | −nsc] [−sob | −nsob]
[−st] [−troff] [−v | −nv]

DESCRIPTION

Indent is a *C* program formatter. It reformats the *C* program in the *input-file* according to the switches. The switches which can be specified are described below. They may appear before or after the file names.

NOTE: If you only specify an *input-file*, the formatting is done 'in-place', that is, the formatted file is written back into *input-file* and a backup copy of *input-file* is written in the current directory. If *input-file* is named '/blah/blah/file', the backup file is named file.BAK.

If *output-file* is specified, **indent** checks to make sure it is different from *input-file*.

The options listed below control the formatting style imposed by **indent**.

−bad, −nbad   If −bad is specified, a blank line is forced after every block of declarations. Default: −nbad.

−bap, −nbap   If −bap is specified, a blank line is forced after every procedure body. Default: −nbap.

−bbb, −nbbb   If −bbb is specified, a blank line is forced before every block comment. Default: −nbbb.

−bc, −nbc   If −bc is specified, then a newline is forced after each comma in a declaration. −nbc turns off this option. The default is −bc.

−br, −bl   Specifying −bl lines up compound statements like this:

```
if (...)
{
  code
}
```

Specifying −br (the default) makes them look like this:

```
if (...) {
  code
}
```

−c −n   The column in which comments on code start. The default is 33.

−cd −n   The column in which comments on declarations start. The default is for these comments to start in the same column as those on code.

−cdb, −ncdb   Enables (disables) the placement of comment delimiters on blank lines. With this option enabled, comments look like this:

```
/*
 * this is a comment
 */
```

Rather than like this:

```
                /* this is a comment */
```

This only affects block comments, not comments to the right of code. The default is
–**cdb**.

–**ce**, –**nce**   Enables (disables) forcing 'else's to cuddle up to the immediately preceding '}'. The default is –**ce**.

–**ci**n   Sets the continuation indent to be *n*. Continuation lines will be indented that far from the beginning of the first line of the statement. Parenthesized expressions have extra indentation added to indicate the nesting, unless –**lp** is in effect. –**ci** defaults to the same value as –**i**.

–**cli**n   Causes case labels to be indented *n* tab stops to the right of the containing **switch** statement. –**cli0** –.5 causes case labels to be indented half a tab stop. The default is –**cli0**.

–**d**n   Controls the placement of comments which are not to the right of code. The default –**d1** means that such comments are placed one indentation level to the left of code. Specifying –**d0** lines up these comments with the code. See the section on comment indentation below.

–**di**n   Specifies the indentation, in character positions, from a declaration keyword to the following identifier. The default is –**di16**.

–**dj**, –**ndj**   –**dj** left justifies declarations. –**ndj** indents declarations the same as code. The default is –**ndj**.

–**ei**, –**nei**   Enables (disables) special **else-if** processing. If it's enabled, an **if** following an **else** will have the same indentation as the preceding **if** statement.

–**fc1**, –**nfc1** Enables (disables) the formatting of comments that start in column 1. Often, comments whose leading '/' is in column 1 have been carefully hand formatted by the programmer. In such cases, –**nfc1** should be used. The default is –**fc1**.

–**i**n   The number of spaces for one indentation level. The default is 4.

–**ip**, –**nip**   Enables (disables) the indentation of parameter declarations from the left margin. The default is –**ip**.

–**l**n   Maximum length of an output line. The default is 75.

–**lp**, –**nlp**   Lines up code surrounded by parenthesis in continuation lines. If a line has a left paren which is not closed on that line, then continuation lines will be lined up to start at the character position just after the left paren. For example, here is how a piece of continued code looks with –**nlp** in effect:

```
        p1 = first_procedure(second_procedure(p2, p3),
          third_procedure(p4,p5));
```

With –**lp** in effect (the default) the code looks somewhat clearer:

```
        p1 = first_procedure(second_procedure(p2, p3),
                             third_procedure(p4,p5));
```

1

Inserting two more newlines we get:

```
p1 = first_procedure(second_procedure(p2,
                                       p3),
                     third_procedure(p4
                                     p5));
```

−npro   Causes the profile files, '`./.indent.pro`' and '`~/.indent.pro`', to be ignored.

−pcs, −npcs If true (**−pcs**) all procedure calls will have a space inserted between the name and the '('. The default is **−npcs**.

−psl, −npsl If true (**−psl**) the names of procedures being defined are placed in column 1 – their types, if any, will be left on the previous lines. The default is **−psl**.

−sc, −nsc Enables (disables) the placement of asterisks ('*'s) at the left edge of all comments.

−sob, −nsob If **−sob** is specified, indent will swallow optional blank lines. You can use this to get rid of blank lines after declarations. Default: **−nsob**.

−st   Causes **indent** to take its input from stdin, and put its output to stdout.

−T*typename* Adds *typename* to the list of type keywords. Names accumulate: **−T** can be specified more than once. You need to specify all the typenames that appear in your program that are defined by **typedef** – nothing will be harmed if you miss a few, but the program won't be formatted as nicely as it should. This sounds like a painful thing to have to do, but it's really a symptom of a problem in C: **typedef** causes a syntactic change in the language and **indent** can't find all instances of **typedef**.

−troff   Causes **indent** to format the program for processing by troff(1). It will produce a fancy listing in much the same spirit as vgrind(1). If the output file is not specified, the default is standard output, rather than formatting in place.

−v, −nv   **−v** turns on 'verbose' mode; **−nv** turns it off. When in verbose mode, **indent** reports when it splits one line of input into two or more lines of output, and gives some size statistics at completion. The default is **−nv**.

You may set up your own 'profile' of defaults to **indent** by creating a file called `.indent.pro` in your login directory and/or the current directory and including whatever switches you like. A '.indent.pro' in the current directory takes precedence over the one in your login directory. If **indent** is run and a profile file exists, then it is read to set up the program's defaults. Switches on the command line, though, always override profile switches. The switches should be separated by spaces, tabs or newlines.

Comments

'*Box*' *comments*. **Indent** assumes that any comment with a dash or star immediately after the start of comment (that is, '/*−' or '/**') is a comment surrounded by a box of stars. Each line of such a comment is left unchanged, except that its indentation may be adjusted to account for the change in indentation of the first line of the comment.

Straight text. All other comments are treated as straight text. **Indent** fits as many words (separated by blanks, tabs, or newlines) on a line as possible. Blank lines break paragraphs.

Comment indentation

If a comment is on a line with code it is started in the 'comment column', which is set by the −c*n* command line parameter. Otherwise, the comment is started at *n* indentation levels less than where code is currently being placed, where *n* is specified by the −d*n* command line parameter. If the code on a line extends past the comment column, the comment starts further to the right, and the right margin may be automatically extended in extreme cases.

Preprocessor lines

In general, **indent** leaves preprocessor lines alone. The only reformatting that it will do is to straighten up trailing comments. It leaves embedded comments alone. Conditional compilation (`#ifdef...#endif`) is recognized and **indent** attempts to correctly compensate for the syntactic peculiarities introduced.

C syntax

Indent understands a substantial amount about the syntax of C, but it has a 'forgiving' parser. It attempts to cope with the usual sorts of incomplete and misformed syntax. In particular, the use of macros like:

```
#define forever for(;;)
```

is handled properly.

ENVIRONMENT

Indent uses the HOME environment variable.

FILES

`./.indent.pro` profile file
`~/.indent.pro` profile file

HISTORY

The **indent** command appeared in 4.2BSD.

BUGS

Indent has even more switches than `ls`(1).

A common mistake that often causes grief is typing:

```
indent *.c
```

to the shell in an attempt to indent all the C programs in a directory. This is probably a bug, not a feature.

1

NAME
indxbib – make inverted index for bibliographic databases

SYNOPSIS
indxbib [−vw] [−c*file*] [−d*dir*] [−f*file*] [−h*n*] [−i*string*] [−k*n*] [−l*n*] [−n*n*] [−o*file*] [−t*n*]
[*filename* ...]

DESCRIPTION
indxbib makes an inverted index for the bibliographic databases in *filename* ... for use with **refer**(1),
lookbib(1), and **lkbib**(1). The index will be named *filename*.i; the index is written to a temporary file
which is then renamed to this. If no filenames are given on the command line because the −f option has
been used, and no −o option is given, the index will be named **/usr/share/dict/papers/Ind.i**.

Bibliographic databases are divided into records by blank lines. Within a record, each fields starts with a
% character at the beginning of a line. Fields have a one letter name which follows the % character.

The values set by the −c, −n, −l and −t options are stored in the index; when the index is searched, keys
will be discarded and truncated in a manner appropriate to these options; the original keys will be used for
verifying that any record found using the index actually contains the keys. This means that a user of an
index need not know whether these options were used in the creation of the index, provided that not all the
keys to be searched for would have been discarded during indexing and that the user supplies at least the
part of each key that would have remained after being truncated during indexing. The value set by the −i
option is also stored in the index and will be used in verifying records found using the index.

OPTIONS
−v   Print the version number.

−w   Index whole files. Each file is a separate record.

−c*file*   Read the list of common words from *file* instead of **/usr/share/dict/papers/words**.

−d*dir*   Use *dir* as the pathname of the current working directory to store in the index, instead of the path
      printed by **pwd**(1). Usually *dir* will be a symbolic link that points to the directory printed by
      pwd(1).

−f*file*   Read the files to be indexed from *file*. If *file* is −, files will be read from the standard input. The
      −f option can be given at most once.

−i*string* Don't index the contents of fields whose names are in *string*. Initially *string* is **XYZ**.

−h*n*   Use the first prime greater than or equal to *n* for the size of the hash table. Larger values of *n* will
      usually make searching faster, but will make the index larger and **indxbib** use more memory. Ini-
      tially *n* is 997.

−k*n*   Use at most *n* keys per input record. Initially *n* is 100.

−l*n*   Discard keys that are shorter than *n*. Initially *n* is 3.

−n*n*   Discard the *n* most common words. Initially *n* is 100.

−o*basename*
      The index should be named *basename*.i.

−t*n*   Truncate keys to *n*. Initially *n* is 6.

FILES
filename.i   Index.

/usr/share/dict/papers/Ind.i
      Default index name.

/usr/share/dict/papers/words
      List of common words.

indxbib*XXXXXX*   Temporary file.

SEE ALSO
>   **refer**(1), **lkbib**(1), **lookbib**(1)

1

NAME

`install` – install binaries

SYNOPSIS

`install` [−cs] [−f *flags*] [−g *group*] [−m *mode*] [−o *owner*] *file1 file2*
`install` [−cs] [−f *flags*] [−g *group*] [−m *mode*] [−o *owner*] *file1 ... fileN*
        directory

DESCRIPTION

The file(s) are moved (or copied if the −c option is specified) to the target file or directory. If the destination is a directory, then the *file* is moved into *directory* with its original filename. If the target file already exists, it is overwritten if permissions allow.

−c   Copy the file. This flag turns off the default behavior of **install** where it deletes the original file after creating the target.

−f   Specify the target's file flags. (See chflags(1) for a list of possible flags and their meanings.)

−g   Specify a group.

−m   Specify an alternate mode. The default mode is set to rwxr-xr-x (0755). The specified mode may be either an octal or symbolic value; see chmod(1) for a description of possible mode values.

−o   Specify an owner.

−s   **Install** exec's the command strip(1) to strip binaries so that install can be portable over a large number of systems and binary types.

By default, **install** preserves all file flags, with the exception of the "nodump" flag.

The **install** utility attempts to prevent moving a file onto itself.

Installing /dev/null creates an empty file.

Upon successful completion a value of 0 is returned. Otherwise, a value of 1 is returned.

SEE ALSO

chflags(1), chgrp(1), chmod(1), cp(1), mv(1), strip(1), chown(8)

HISTORY

The **install** utility appeared in 4.2BSD.

1

NAME

invert, lookup – create and access an inverted index

SYNOPSIS

invert [option ...] file ...

lookup [option ...]

DESCRIPTION

Invert creates an inverted index to one or more files. *Lookup* retrieves records from files for which an inverted index exists. The inverted indices are intended for use with *bib*(1).

Invert creates one inverted index to all of its input files. The index must be stored in the current directory and may not be moved. Input files may be absolute path names or paths relative to the current directory. Each input file is viewed as a set of records; each record consists of non-blank lines; records are separated by blank lines.

Lookup retrieves records based on its input *(stdin)*. Each line of input is a retrieval request. All records that contain all of the keywords in the retrieval request are sent to *stdout*. If there are no matching references, "No references found." is sent to *stdout*. *Lookup* first searches in the user's private index (default INDEX) and then, if no references are found, in the system index (/usr/dict/papers/INDEX). The system index was produced using *invert* with the default options; in general, the user is advised to use the defaults.

Keywords are a sequence of non-white space characters with non-alphanumeric characters removed. Keywords must be at least two characters and are truncated (default length is 6). Some common words are ignored. Some lines of input are ignored for the purpose of collecting keywords.

The following options are available for *invert:*

−c *file*

−c*file*   File contains common words, one per line. Common words are not used as keys. (Default /usr/new/lib/bmac/common.)

−k *i*

−k*i*   Maximum number of keys kept per record. (Default 100)

−l *i*

−l*i*   Maximum length of keys. (Default 6)

−p *file*

−p*file*   File is the name of the private index file (output of *invert*). (Default is INDEX.) The index must be stored in the current directory. (Be careful of the second form. The shell will not know to expand the file name. E.g. −p˜/index won't work; use −p ˜/index.)

−s   Silent. Suppress statistics.

-%*str*   Ignore lines that begin with %x where x is in *str*. (Default is CNOPVX. See *bib*(1) for explanation of field names.)

Lookup has only the options **c**, **l**, and **p** with the same meanings as *bib*. In particular, the **p** option can be followed by a list of comma separated index files. These are searched in order from left to right until at least one reference is found.

FILES

INDEX   inverted index
/usr/tmp/invertxxxxxx   scratch file for invert
/usr/new/lib/bmac/common   default list of common words
/usr/dict/papers/INDEX default system index

SEE ALSO

A UNIX Bibliographic Database Facility, Timothy A. Budd and Gary M. Levin, University of Arizona Technical Report 82-1, 1982.

bib(1)

DIAGNOSTICS

Messages indicating trouble accessing files are sent on *stderr*. There is an explicit message on *stdout* from *lookup* if no references are found.

Invert produces a one line message of the form, %D documents   %D distinct keys   %D key occurrences. This can be suppressed with the −s option.

The message locate: first key (%s) matched too many refs indicates that the first key matched more references than could be stored in memory. The simple solution is to use a less frequently occurring key as the first key in the citation.

BUGS

No attempt is made to check the compatibility between an index and the files indexed. The user must create a new index whenever the files that are indexed are modified.

Attempting to invert a file containing unprintable characters can cause chaos.

NAME

join – relational database operator

SYNOPSIS

join [−a *file_number* | −v *file_number*] [−e *string*] [−j *file_number field*] [−o *list*] [−t *char*] [−1 *field*] [−2 *field*] *file1 file2*

DESCRIPTION

The join utility performs an "equality join" on the specified files and writes the result to the standard output. The "join field" is the field in each file by which the files are compared. The first field in each line is used by default. There is one line in the output for each pair of lines in *file1* and *file2* which have identical join fields. Each output line consists of the join field, the remaining fields from *file1* and then the remaining fields from *file2*.

The default field separators are tab and space characters. In this case, multiple tabs and spaces count as a single field separator, and leading tabs and spaces are ignored. The default output field separator is a single space character.

Many of the options use file and field numbers. Both file numbers and field numbers are 1 based, i.e. the first file on the command line is file number 1 and the first field is field number 1. The following options are available:

−a *file_number*
> In addition to the default output, produce a line for each unpairable line in file *file_number*.

−e *string*
> Replace empty output fields with *string*.

−o *list*   The −o option specifies the fields that will be output from each file for each line with matching join fields. Each element of *list* has the form file_number.field, where *file_number* is a file number and *field* is a field number. The elements of list must be either comma (",") or whitespace separated. (The latter requires quoting to protect it from the shell, or, a simpler approach is to use multiple −o options.)

−t *char*   Use character *char* as a field delimiter for both input and output. Every occurrence of *char* in a line is significant.

−v *file_number*
> Do not display the default output, but display a line for each unpairable line in file *file_number*. The options −v *1* and −v *2* may be specified at the same time.

−1 *field* Join on the *field*'th field of file 1.

−2 *field* Join on the *field*'th field of file 2.

When the default field delimiter characters are used, the files to be joined should be ordered in the collating sequence of sort(1), using the −b option, on the fields on which they are to be joined, otherwise join may not report all field matches. When the field delimiter characters are specified by the −t option, the collating sequence should be the same as sort without the −b option.

If one of the arguments *file1* or *file2* is "-", the standard input is used.

The join utility exits 0 on success, and >0 if an error occurs.

COMPATIBILITY

For compatibility with historic versions of **join**, the following options are available:

−a   In addition to the default output, produce a line for each unpairable line in both file 1 and file 2.

−j1 *field*
            Join on the *field*'th field of file 1.

−j2 *field*
            Join on the *field*'th field of file 2.

−j *field* Join on the *field*'th field of both file 1 and file 2.

−o *list* ...
            Historical implementations of **join** permitted multiple arguments to the −o option. These arguments were of the form ''file_number.field_number'' as described for the current −o option. This has obvious difficulties in the presence of files named ''1.2''.

These options are available only so historic shellscripts don't require modification and should not be used.

STANDARDS

The **join** command is expected to be IEEE Std1003.2 (''POSIX'') compatible.

SEE ALSO

awk(1), comm(1), paste(1), sort(1), uniq(1)

NAME

     jot – print sequential or random data

SYNOPSIS

     jot [options] [reps [begin [end [s]]]]

DESCRIPTION

     Jot is used to print out increasing, decreasing, random, or redundant data, usually numbers, one per line. The *options* are understood as follows.

     −r   Generate random data instead of sequential data, the default.

     −b word

          Just print *word* repetitively.

     −w word

          Print *word* with the generated data appended to it. Octal, hexadecimal, exponential, ASCII, zero padded, and right-adjusted representations are possible by using the appropriate *printf*(3) conversion specification inside *word*, in which case the data are inserted rather than appended.

     −c   This is an abbreviation for **−w %c**.

     −s string

          Print data separated by *string*. Normally, newlines separate data.

     −n   Do not print the final newline normally appended to the output.

     −p precision

          Print only as many digits or characters of the data as indicated by the integer *precision*. In the absence of **−p**, the precision is the greater of the precisions of *begin* and *end*. The **−p** option is overridden by whatever appears in a *printf*(3) conversion following **−w**.

     The last four arguments indicate, respectively, the number of data, the lower bound, the upper bound, and the step size or, for random data, the seed. While at least one of them must appear, any of the other three may be omitted, and will be considered as such if given as −. Any three of these arguments determines the fourth. If four are specified and the given and computed values of *reps* conflict, the lower value is used. If fewer than three are specified, defaults are assigned left to right, except for *s*, which assumes its default unless both *begin* and *end* are given.

     Defaults for the four arguments are, respectively, 100, 1, 100, and 1, except that when random data are requested, *s* defaults to a seed depending upon the time of day. *Reps* is expected to be an unsigned integer, and if given as zero is taken to be infinite. *Begin* and *end* may be given as real numbers or as characters representing the corresponding value in ASCII. The last argument must be a real number.

     Random numbers are obtained through *random*(3). The name *jot* derives in part from *iota*, a function in APL.

EXAMPLES

     The command

          jot 21 −1 1.00

     prints 21 evenly spaced numbers increasing from −1 to 1. The ASCII character set is generated with

          jot −c 128 0

     and the strings xaa through xaz with

          jot −w xa%c 26 a

     while 20 random 8-letter strings are produced with

          jot −r −c 160 a z | rs −g 0 8

Infinitely many *yes*'s may be obtained through

> **jot**   **−b**   **yes**   **0**

and thirty *ed*(1) substitution commands applying to lines 2, 7, 12, etc. is the result of

> **jot**   **−w**   **%ds/old/new/**   **30**   **2**   **−**   **5**

The stuttering sequence 9, 9, 8, 8, 7, etc. can be produced by suitable choice of precision and step size, as in

> **jot**   **0**   **9**   **−**   **−.5**

and a file containing exactly 1024 bytes is created with

> **jot**   **−b**   **x**   **512**   **>**   **block**

Finally, to set tabs four spaces apart starting from column 10 and ending in column 132, use

> **expand**   **−`jot**   **−s,**   **−**   **10**   **132**   **4`**

and to print all lines 80 characters or longer,

> **grep**   **`jot**   **−s**   **""**   **−b**   **.**   **80`**

SEE ALSO

> ed(1), expand(1), rs(1), yes(1), printf(3), random(3), expand(1)

1

NAME

kdestroy – destroy Kerberos tickets

SYNOPSIS

kdestroy [–f] [–q]

DESCRIPTION

The *kdestroy* utility destroys the user's active Kerberos authorization tickets by writing zeros to the file that contains them. If the ticket file does not exist, *kdestroy* displays a message to that effect.

After overwriting the file, *kdestroy* removes the file from the system. The utility displays a message indicating the success or failure of the operation. If *kdestroy* is unable to destroy the ticket file, the utility will warn you by making your terminal beep.

In the Athena workstation environment, the *toehold* service automatically destroys your tickets when you end a workstation session. If your site does not provide a similar ticket-destroying mechanism, you can place the *kdestroy* command in your *.logout* file so that your tickets are destroyed automatically when you logout.

The options to *kdestroy* are as follows:

–f   *kdestroy* runs without displaying the status message.

–q   *kdestroy* will not make your terminal beep if it fails to destroy the tickets.

FILES

KRBTKFILE environment variable if set, otherwise
/tmp/tkt[uid]

SEE ALSO

kerberos(1), kinit(1), klist(1)

BUGS

Only the tickets in the user's current ticket file are destroyed. Separate ticket files are used to hold root instance and password changing tickets. These files should probably be destroyed too, or all of a user's tickets kept in a single ticket file.

AUTHORS

Steve Miller, MIT Project Athena/Digital Equipment Corporation
Clifford Neuman, MIT Project Athena
Bill Sommerfeld, MIT Project Athena

1

NAME
kdump – display kernel trace data

SYNOPSIS
kdump [**–dnlRT**] [**–f** *file*] [**–m** *maxdata*] [**–t** [cnis]]

DESCRIPTION
Kdump displays the kernel trace files produced with ktrace(1) in human readable format. By default, the file ktrace.out in the current directory is displayed.

The options are as follows:

–d   Display all numbers in decimal.

–f *file*   Display the specified file instead of ktrace.out.

–l   Loop reading the trace file, once the end-of-file is reached, waiting for more data.

–m *maxdata*
        Display at most *maxdata* bytes when decoding I/O.

–n   Suppress ad hoc translations. Normally **kdump** tries to decode many system calls into a more human readable format. For example, ioctl(2) values are replaced with the macro name and *errno* values are replaced with the strerror(3) string. Suppressing this feature yields a more consistent output format and is easily amenable to further processing.

–R   Display relative timestamps (time since previous entry).

–T   Display absolute timestamps for each entry (seconds since epoch).

–t *cnis*   See the **–t** option of ktrace(1).

SEE ALSO
ktrace(1)

HISTORY
The **kdump** command appears in 4.4BSD.

1

NAME

kerberos – introduction to the Kerberos system

DESCRIPTION

The Kerberos system authenticates individual users in a network environment. After authenticating yourself to Kerberos, you can use network utilities such as *rlogin*, *rcp*, and *rsh* without having to present passwords to remote hosts and without having to bother with *.rhosts* files. Note that these utilities will work without passwords only if the remote machines you deal with support the Kerberos system. All Athena timesharing machines and public workstations support Kerberos.

Before you can use Kerberos, you must register as an Athena user, and you must make sure you have been added to the Kerberos database. You can use the *kinit* command to find out. This command tries to log you into the Kerberos system. *kinit* will prompt you for a username and password. Enter your username and password. If the utility lets you login without giving you a message, you have already been registered.

If you enter your username and *kinit* responds with this message:

Principal unknown (kerberos)

you haven't been registered as a Kerberos user. See your system administrator.

A Kerberos name contains three parts. The first is the *principal name*, which is usually a user's or service's name. The second is the *instance*, which in the case of a user is usually null. Some users may have privileged instances, however, such as "root" or "admin". In the case of a service, the instance is the name of the machine on which it runs; i.e. there can be an *rlogin* service running on the machine ABC, which is different from the rlogin service running on the machine XYZ. The third part of a Kerberos name is the *realm*. The realm corresponds to the Kerberos service providing authentication for the principal. For example, at MIT there is a Kerberos running at the Laboratory for Computer Science and one running at Project Athena.

When writing a Kerberos name, the principal name is separated from the instance (if not null) by a period, and the realm (if not the local realm) follows, preceded by an "@" sign. The following are examples of valid Kerberos names:

> billb
> jis.admin
> srz@lcs.mit.edu
> treese.root@athena.mit.edu

When you authenticate yourself with Kerberos, through either the workstation *toehold* system or the *kinit* command, Kerberos gives you an initial Kerberos *ticket*. (A Kerberos ticket is an encrypted protocol message that provides authentication.) Kerberos uses this ticket for network utilities such as *rlogin* and *rcp*. The ticket transactions are done transparently, so you don't have to worry about their management.

Note, however, that tickets expire. Privileged tickets, such as root instance tickets, expire in a few minutes, while tickets that carry more ordinary privileges may be good for several hours or a day, depending on the installation's policy. If your login session extends beyond the time limit, you will have to re-authenticate yourself to Kerberos to get new tickets. Use the *kinit* command to re-authenticate yourself.

If you use the *kinit* command to get your tickets, make sure you use the *kdestroy* command to destroy your tickets before you end your login session. You should probably put the *kdestroy* command in your *.logout* file so that your tickets will be destroyed automatically when you logout. For more information about the *kinit* and *kdestroy* commands, see the *kinit(1)* and *kdestroy(1)* manual pages.

Currently, Kerberos supports the following network services: *rlogin*, *rsh*, and *rcp*. Other services are being worked on, such as the *pop* mail system and NFS (network file system), but are not yet available.

1

SEE ALSO

kdestroy(1), kinit(1), klist(1), kpasswd(1), des_crypt(3), kerberos(3), kadmin(8)

BUGS

Kerberos will not do authentication forwarding. In other words, if you use *rlogin* to login to a remote host, you cannot use Kerberos services from that host until you authenticate yourself explicitly on that host. Although you may need to authenticate yourself on the remote host, be aware that when you do so, *rlogin* sends your password across the network in clear text.

AUTHORS

Steve Miller, MIT Project Athena/Digital Equipment Corporation
Clifford Neuman, MIT Project Athena

The following people helped out on various aspects of the system:

Jeff Schiller designed and wrote the administration server and its user interface, kadmin. He also wrote the dbm version of the database management system.

Mark Colan developed the Kerberos versions of *rlogin*, *rsh*, and *rcp*, as well as contributing work on the servers.

John Ostlund developed the Kerberos versions of *passwd* and *userreg*.

Stan Zanarotti pioneered Kerberos in a foreign realm (LCS), and made many contributions based on that experience.

Many people contributed code and/or useful ideas, including Jim Aspnes, Bob Baldwin, John Barba, Richard Basch, Jim Bloom, Bill Bryant, Rob French, Dan Geer, David Jedlinsky, John Kohl, John Kubiatowicz, Bob McKie, Brian Murphy, Ken Raeburn, Chris Reed, Jon Rochlis, Mike Shanzer, Bill Sommerfeld, Jennifer Steiner, Ted Ts'o, and Win Treese.

RESTRICTIONS

COPYRIGHT 1985,1986 Massachusetts Institute of Technology

NAME

keylogin – decrypt and store secret key

SYNOPSIS

keylogin

DESCRIPTION

keylogin prompts the user for their login password, and uses it do decrypt the user's secret key stored in the **publickey**(5) database. Once decrypted, the user's key is stored by the local key server process **keyserv**(8C) to be used by any secure network services, such as NFS.

Normally, **login**(1) does this work when the user logs onto the system, but running **keylogin** may be necessary if the user did not type a password to **login**(1).

SEE ALSO

chkey(1), **login**(1), **publickey**(5), **keyserv**(8C), **newkey**(8)

1

NAME
    kill – terminate or signal a process

SYNOPSIS
    kill [–signal_name] pid ...
    kill [–signal_number] pid ...
    kill [–l]

DESCRIPTION
The kill utility sends the TERM signal to the processes specified by the pid operand(s).

Only the super-user may send signals to other users' processes.

The options are as follows:

–l   List the signal names.

–signal_name
        A symbolic signal name specifying the signal to be sent instead of the default TERM. The –l option
        displays the signal names.

–signal_number
        A non-negative decimal integer, specifying the signal to be sent instead of the default TERM.

Some of the more commonly used signals:

-1	-1	(super-user broadcast to all processes, or user broadcast to user's processes)
0	0	(sh(1) only, signals all members of process group)
2	INT	(interrupt)
3	QUIT	(quit)
6	ABRT	(abort)
9	KILL	(non-catchable, non-ignorable kill)
14	ALRM	(alarm clock)
15	TERM	(software termination signal)

Kill is a built-in to csh(1); it allows job specifiers of the form ''%...'' as arguments so process id's are
not as often used as kill arguments. See csh(1) for details.

SEE ALSO
    csh(1), ps(1), kill(2), sigvec(2)

HISTORY
    A kill command appeared in Version 6 AT&T UNIX.

BUGS
    A replacement for the command ''kill 0'' for csh(1) users should be provided.

NAME
      kinit – Kerberos login utility

SYNOPSIS
      kinit [**–irvl**]

DESCRIPTION
      The *kinit* command is used to login to the Kerberos authentication and authorization system. Note that only registered Kerberos users can use the Kerberos system. For information about registering as a Kerberos user, see the *kerberos(1)* manual page.

      If you are logged in to a workstation that is running the *toehold* service, you do not have to use *kinit*. The *toehold* login procedure will log you into Kerberos automatically. You will need to use *kinit* only in those situations in which your original tickets have expired. (Tickets expire in about a day.) Note as well that *toehold* will automatically destroy your tickets when you logout from the workstation.

      When you use *kinit* without options, the utility prompts for your username and Kerberos password, and tries to authenticate your login with the local Kerberos server.

      If Kerberos authenticates the login attempt, *kinit* retrieves your initial ticket and puts it in the ticket file specified by your KRBTKFILE environment variable. If this variable is undefined, your ticket will be stored in the */tmp* directory, in the file *tktuid* , where *uid* specifies your user identification number.

      If you have logged in to Kerberos without the benefit of the workstation *toehold* system, make sure you use the *kdestroy* command to destroy any active tickets before you end your login session. You may want to put the *kdestroy* command in your *.logout* file so that your tickets will be destroyed automatically when you logout.

      The options to *kinit* are as follows:

      –i   *kinit* prompts you for a Kerberos instance.

      –r   *kinit* prompts you for a Kerberos realm. This option lets you authenticate yourself with a remote Kerberos server.

      –v   Verbose mode. *kinit* prints the name of the ticket file used, and a status message indicating the success or failure of your login attempt.

      –l   *kinit* prompts you for a ticket lifetime in minutes. Due to protocol restrictions in Kerberos Version 4, this value must be between 5 and 1275 minutes.

SEE ALSO
      kerberos(1), kdestroy(1), klist(1), toehold(1)

BUGS
      The –r option has not been fully implemented.

AUTHORS
      Steve Miller, MIT Project Athena/Digital Equipment Corporation
      Clifford Neuman, MIT Project Athena

1

NAME

klist – list currently held Kerberos tickets

SYNOPSIS

klist [–s | –t] [–**file** name] [–**srvtab**]

DESCRIPTION

klist prints the name of the tickets file and the identity of the principal the tickets are for (as listed in the tickets file), and lists the principal names of all Kerberos tickets currently held by the user, along with the issue and expire time for each authenticator. Principal names are listed in the form *name.instance@realm*, with the '.' omitted if the instance is null, and the '@' omitted if the realm is null.

If given the –s option, *klist* does not print the issue and expire times, the name of the tickets file, or the identity of the principal.

If given the –t option, **klist** checks for the existence of a non-expired ticket-granting-ticket in the ticket file. If one is present, it exits with status 0, else it exits with status 1. No output is generated when this option is specified.

If given the –**file** option, the following argument is used as the ticket file. Otherwise, if the **KRBTKFILE** environment variable is set, it is used. If this environment variable is not set, the file **/tmp/tkt[uid]** is used, where **uid** is the current user-id of the user.

If given the –**srvtab** option, the file is treated as a service key file, and the names of the keys contained therein are printed. If no file is specified with a –**file** option, the default is */etc/kerberosIV/srvtab*.

FILES

/etc/kerberosIV/krb.conf	to get the name of the local realm
/tmp/tkt[uid]	as the default ticket file ([uid] is the decimal UID of the user).
/etc/kerberosIV/srvtab	as the default service key file

SEE ALSO

kerberos(1), kinit(1), kdestroy(1)

BUGS

When reading a file as a service key file, very little sanity or error checking is performed.

1

NAME

ksrvtgt – fetch and store Kerberos ticket-granting-ticket using a service key

SYNOPSIS

ksrvtgt name instance [[realm] srvtab]

DESCRIPTION

ksrvtgt retrieves a ticket-granting ticket with a lifetime of five (5) minutes for the principal *name.instance@realm* (or *name.instance@localrealm* if *realm* is not supplied on the command line), decrypts the response using the service key found in *srvtab* (or in **/etc/kerberosIV/srvtab** if *srvtab* is not specified on the command line), and stores the ticket in the standard ticket cache.

This command is intended primarily for use in shell scripts and other batch-type facilities.

DIAGNOSTICS

"Generic kerberos failure (kfailure)" can indicate a whole range of problems, the most common of which is the inability to read the service key file.

FILES

/etc/kerberosIV/krb.conf	to get the name of the local realm.
/tmp/tkt[uid]	The default ticket file.
/etc/kerberosIV/srvtab	The default service key file.

SEE ALSO

kerberos(1), kinit(1), kdestroy(1)

NAME

ktrace – enable kernel process tracing

SYNOPSIS

ktrace [–aCcdi] [–f *trfile*] [–g *pgrp*] [–p *pid*] [–t *trstr*]
ktrace [–adi] [–f *trfile*] [–t *trstr*] command

DESCRIPTION

Ktrace enables kernel trace logging for the specified processes. Kernel trace data is logged to the file ktrace.out. The kernel operations that are traced include system calls, namei translations, signal processing, and I/O.

Once tracing is enabled on a process, trace data will be logged until either the process exits or the trace point is cleared. A traced process can generate enormous amounts of log data quickly; It is strongly suggested that users memorize how to disable tracing before attempting to trace a process. The following command is sufficient to disable tracing on all user owned processes, and, if executed by root, all processes:

```
$ trace -C
```

The trace file is not human readable; use kdump(1) to decode it.

The options are as follows:

–a　　　　Append to the trace file instead of truncating it.

–C　　　　Disable tracing on all user owned processes, and, if executed by root, all processes in the system.

–c　　　　Clear the trace points associated with the specified file or processes.

–d　　　　Descendants; perform the operation for all current children of the designated processes.

–f *file*
　　　　　Log trace records to *file* instead of ktrace.out.

–g *pgid*
　　　　　Enable (disable) tracing on all processes in the process group (only one –g flag is permitted).

–i　　　　Inherit; pass the trace flags to all future children of the designated processes.

–p *pid*
　　　　　Enable (disable) tracing on the indicated process id (only one –p flag is permitted).

–t *trstr*
　　　　　The string argument represents the kernel trace points, one per letter. The following table equates the letters with the tracepoints:

　　　　　c　　　trace system calls
　　　　　n　　　trace namei translations
　　　　　i　　　trace I/O
　　　　　s　　　trace signal processing

command
　　　　　Execute *command* with the specified trace flags.

The –p, –g, and *command* options are mutually exclusive.

EXAMPLES

> # trace all kernel operations of process id 34
> ```
> $ ktrace -p 34
> ```
>
> # trace all kernel operations of processes in process group 15 and # pass the trace flags to all current and future children
> ```
> $ ktrace -idg 15
> ```
>
> # disable all tracing of process 65
> ```
> $ ktrace -cp 65
> ```
>
> # disable tracing signals on process 70 and all current children
> ```
> $ ktrace -t s -cdp 70
> ```
>
> # enable tracing of I/O on process 67
> ```
> $ ktrace -ti -p 67
> ```
>
> # run the command "w", tracing only system calls
> ```
> $ ktrace -tc w
> ```
>
> # disable all tracing to the file "tracedata"
> ```
> $ ktrace -c -f tracedata
> ```
>
> # disable tracing of all processes owned by the user
> ```
> $ ktrace -C
> ```

SEE ALSO

> kdump(1)

HISTORY

> The `ktrace` command appears in 4.4BSD.

NAME

    lam – laminate files

SYNOPSIS

    lam [–[fp] min.max] [–s sepstring] [–t c] file ...

DESCRIPTION

    Lam copies the named files side by side onto the standard output. The *n*-th input lines from the input *files* are considered fragments of the single long *n*-th output line into which they are assembled. The name '–' means the standard input, and may be repeated.

    Normally, each option affects only the *file* after it. If the option letter is capitalized it affects all subsequent files until it appears again uncapitalized. The options are described below.

    –f min.max

        Print line fragments according to the format string *min.max*, where *min* is the minimum field width and *max* the maximum field width. If *min* begins with a zero, zeros will be added to make up the field width, and if it begins with a '–', the fragment will be left-adjusted within the field.

    –p min.max

        Like **–f**, but pad this file's field when end-of-file is reached and other files are still active.

    –s sepstring

        Print *sepstring* before printing line fragments from the next file. This option may appear after the last file.

    –t c   The input line terminator is *c* instead of a newline. The newline normally appended to each output line is omitted.

    To print files simultaneously for easy viewing use *pr*(1).

EXAMPLES

    The command

        lam file1 file2 file3 file4

    joins 4 files together along each line. To merge the lines from four different files use

        lam file1 –S "
        " file2 file3 file4

    Every 2 lines of a file may be joined on one line with

        lam – – < file

    and a form letter with substitutions keyed by '@' can be done with

        lam –t @ letter changes

SEE ALSO

    join(1), pr(1), printf(3)

NAME

last – indicate last logins of users and ttys

SYNOPSIS

last [*–n*] [*–f file*] [*–h host*] [*–t tty*] [user ...]

DESCRIPTION

Last will list the sessions of specified *users*, *ttys*, and *hosts*, in reverse time order. Each line of output contains the user name, the tty from which the session was conducted, any hostname, the start and stop times for the session, and the duration of the session. If the session is still continuing or was cut short by a crash or shutdown, **last** will so indicate.

–f *file*   **Last** reads the file *file* instead of the default, /var/log/wtmp.

–n   Limits the report to *n* lines.

–t *tty*   Specify the *tty*. Tty names may be given fully or abbreviated, for example, "last -t 03" is equivalent to "last -t tty03".

–h *host*   *Host* names may be names or internet numbers.

If multiple arguments are given, the information which applies to any of the arguments is printed, e.g., "last root -t console" would list all of "root's" sessions as well as all sessions on the console terminal. If no users, hostnames or terminals are specified, **last** prints a record of all logins and logouts.

The pseudo-user *reboot* logs in at reboots of the system, thus "last reboot" will give an indication of mean time between reboot.

If **last** is interrupted, it indicates to what date the search has progressed. If interrupted with a quit signal **last** indicates how far the search has progressed and then continues.

FILES

/var/log/wtmp login data base

SEE ALSO

lastcomm(1), utmp(5), ac(8)

HISTORY

Last appeared in 3.0BSD.

NAME

`lastcomm` – show last commands executed in reverse order

SYNOPSIS

`lastcomm` [–f *file*] [*command* ...] [*user* ...] [*terminal* ...]

DESCRIPTION

`Lastcomm` gives information on previously executed commands. With no arguments, `lastcomm` prints information about all the commands recorded during the current accounting file's lifetime.

Option:

–f *file*   Read from *file* rather than the default accounting file.

If called with arguments, only accounting entries with a matching *command* name, *user* name, or *terminal* name are printed. So, for example:

```
lastcomm a.out root ttyd0
```

would produce a listing of all the executions of commands named a.out by user *root* on the terminal *ttyd0*.

For each process entry, the following are printed.

- The name of the user who ran the process.
- Flags, as accumulated by the accounting facilities in the system.
- The command name under which the process was called.
- The amount of cpu time used by the process (in seconds).
- The time the process exited.

The flags are encoded as follows: "S" indicates the command was executed by the super-user, "F" indicates the command ran after a fork, but without a following exec, "C" indicates the command was run in PDP-11 compatibility mode (VAX only), "D" indicates the command terminated with the generation of a core file, and "X" indicates the command was terminated with a signal.

FILES

`/var/account/acct` Default accounting file.

SEE ALSO

last(1), sigvec(2), acct(5), core(5)

HISTORY

The `lastcomm` command appeared in 3.0BSD.

1

NAME
ld – link editor

SYNOPSIS
ld [option] ... *file* ...

DESCRIPTION
Ld combines several object programs into one, resolves external references, and searches libraries. In the simplest case several object *files* are given, and ld combines them, producing an object module which can be either executed or become the input for a further ld run. (In the latter case, the −r option must be given to preserve the relocation bits.) The output of ld is left on a.out. This file is made executable only if no errors occurred during the load.

The argument routines are concatenated in the order specified. The entry point of the output is the beginning of the first routine (unless the −e option is specified).

If any argument is a library, it is searched exactly once at the point it is encountered in the argument list. Only those routines defining an unresolved external reference are loaded. If a routine from a library references another routine in the library, and the library has not been processed by ranlib(1), the referenced routine must appear after the referencing routine in the library. Thus the order of programs within libraries may be important. The first member of a library should be a file named '__.SYMDEF', which is understood to be a dictionary for the library as produced by ranlib(1); the dictionary is searched iteratively to satisfy as many references as possible.

The symbols '_etext', '_edata' and '_end' ('etext', 'edata' and 'end' in C) are reserved, and if referred to, are set to the first location above the program, the first location above initialized data, and the first location above all data respectively. It is erroneous to define these symbols.

Ld understands several options. Except for −l, they should appear before the file names.

−A   This option specifies incremental loading, i.e. linking is to be done in a manner so that the resulting object may be read into an already executing program. The next argument is the name of a file whose symbol table will be taken as a basis on which to define additional symbols. Only newly linked material will be entered into the text and data portions of a.out, but the new symbol table will reflect every symbol defined before and after the incremental load. This argument must appear before any other object file in the argument list. The −T option may be used as well, and will be taken to mean that the newly linked segment will commence at the corresponding address (which must be a multiple of 1024). The default value is the old value of _end.

−D   Take the next argument as a hexadecimal number and pad the data segment with zero bytes to the indicated length.

−d   Force definition of common storage even if the −r flag is present.

−e   The following argument is taken to be the name of the entry point of the loaded program; location 0 is the default.

−L*dir*
        Add *dir* to the list of directories in which libraries are searched for. Directories specified with −L are searched before the standard directories.

1

−lx   This option is an abbreviation for the library name 'libx.a,' where x is a string. Ld searches for libraries first in any directories specified with −L options, then in the standard directories /lib, /usr/lib, and /usr/local/lib. A library is searched when its name is encountered, so the placement of a −l is significant.

−M   produce a primitive load map, listing the names of the files which will be loaded.

−N   Do not make the text portion read only or sharable. (Use "magic number" 0407.)

−n   Arrange (by giving the output file a 0410 "magic number") that when the output file is executed, the text portion will be read-only and shared among all users executing the file. This involves moving the data areas up to the first possible 1024 byte boundary following the end of the text.

−o   The *name* argument after −o is used as the name of the ld output file, instead of a.out.

−r   Generate relocation bits in the output file so that it can be the subject of another ld run. This flag also prevents final definitions from being given to common symbols, and suppresses the 'undefined symbol' diagnostics.

−S   'Strip' the output by removing all symbols except locals and globals.

−s   'Strip' the output, that is, remove the symbol table and relocation bits to save space (but impair the usefulness of the debuggers). This information can also be removed by strip(1).

−T   The next argument is a hexadecimal number which sets the text segment origin. The default origin is 0.

−t   ("trace") Print the name of each file as it is processed.

−u   Take the following argument as a symbol and enter it as undefined in the symbol table. This is useful for loading wholly from a library, since initially the symbol table is empty and an unresolved reference is needed to force the loading of the first routine.

−X   Save local symbols except for those whose names begin with 'L'. This option is used by cc(1) to discard internally-generated labels while retaining symbols local to routines.

−x   Do not preserve local (non-.globl) symbols in the output symbol table; only enter external symbols. This option saves some space in the output file.

−ysym

      Indicate each file in which *sym* appears, its type and whether the file defines or references it. Many such options may be given to trace many symbols. (It is usually necessary to begin *sym* with an '_', as external C, FORTRAN and Pascal variables begin with underscores.)

−z   Arrange for the process to be loaded on demand from the resulting executable file (413 format) rather than preloaded. This is the default. Results in a 1024 byte header on the output file followed by a text and data segment each of which have size a multiple of 1024 bytes (being padded out with nulls in the file if necessary). With this format the first few BSS segment symbols may actually appear (from the output of size(1)) to live in the data segment; this to avoid wasting the space resulting from data segment size roundup.

FILES
```
/usr/lib/lib*.a          Libraries.
/usr/local/lib/lib*.a    More libraries.
a.out                    Output file.
```

SEE ALSO
    as(1), ar(1), cc(1), ranlib(1)

HISTORY
    The ld command appeared in Version 6 AT&T UNIX.

BUGS
    There is no way to force data to be page aligned. Ld pads images which are to be demand loaded from the file system to the next page boundary to avoid a bug in the system.

1

NAME

`learn` – computer aided instruction about UNIX

SYNOPSIS

`learn` [`-directory`] [`subject` [`lesson`]]

DESCRIPTION

`Learn` gives Computer Aided Instruction courses and practice in the use of UNIX, the C Shell, and the Berkeley text editors. To get started simply type `learn`. If you had used `learn` before and left your last session without completing a subject, the program will use information in `$HOME/.learnrc` to start you up in the same place you left off. Your first time through, `learn` will ask questions to find out what you want to do. Some questions may be bypassed by naming a `subject`, and more yet by naming a `lesson`. You may enter the `lesson` as a number that `learn` gave you in a previous session. If you do not know the lesson number, you may enter the `lesson` as a word, and `learn` will look for the first lesson containing it. If the `lesson` is ' − ', `learn` prompts for each lesson; this is useful for debugging.

The `subject`s presently handled are

> files
> editor
> vi
> morefiles
> macros
> eqn
> C

There are a few special commands. The command `bye` terminates a `learn` session and `where` tells you of your progress, with `where m` telling you more. The command `again` re-displays the text of the lesson and `again lesson` lets you review `lesson`. There is no way for `learn` to tell you the answers it expects in English, however, the command `hint` prints the last part of the lesson script used to evaluate a response, while `hint m` prints the whole lesson script. This is useful for debugging lessons and might possibly give you an idea about what it expects.

Normally, lesson scripts are found in the directory `/usr/libata/learn`. The **−directory** option allows one to specify a nonstandard place to look for scripts.

FILES

`/usr/lib/learn`	Subtree for all dependent directories and files.
`/usr/tmp/pl*`	Playpen directories.
`$HOME/.learnrc`	Startup information.

SEE ALSO

csh(1), ex(1)

B. W. Kernighan, and M. E. Lesk, *LEARN – Computer-Aided Instruction on UNIX.*

BUGS

The main strength of `learn`, that it asks the student to use the real UNIX, also makes possible baffling mistakes. It is helpful, especially for nonprogrammers, to have a UNIX initiate near at hand during the first sessions. (.Pp Occasionally lessons are incorrect, sometimes because the local version of a command operates in a non-standard way. Occasionally a lesson script does not recognize all the different correct responses, in which case the 'hint' command may be useful. Such lessons may be skipped with the 'skip' command, but it takes some sophistication to recognize the situation.

To find a *lesson* given as a word, **learn** does a simple fgrep(1) through the lessons. It is unclear whether this sort of subject indexing is better than none.

Spawning a new shell is required for each of many user and internal functions.

The vi lessons are provided separately from the others. To use them see your system administrator.

HISTORY
The **learn** command appeared in Version 32V AT&T UNIX.

1

NAME
     leave – remind you when you have to leave

SYNOPSIS
     leave [[+]*hhmm*]

DESCRIPTION
     Leave waits until the specified time, then reminds you that you have to leave. You are reminded 5 minutes
     and 1 minute before the actual time, at the time, and every minute thereafter. When you log off, **leave** ex-
     its just before it would have printed the next message.

     Options:

     hhmm The time of day is in the form *hhmm* where *hh* is a time in hours (on a 12 or 24 hour clock), and *mm*
            are minutes. All times are converted to a 12 hour clock, and assumed to be in the next 12 hours.

     +   If the time is preceded by '+', the alarm will go off in hours and minutes from the current time.

     If no argument is given, **leave** prompts with "When do you have to leave?". A reply of newline causes
     leave to exit, otherwise the reply is assumed to be a time. This form is suitable for inclusion in a .login
     or .profile.

     Leave ignores interrupts, quits, and terminates. To get rid of it you should either log off or use kill −9
     giving its process id.

SEE ALSO
     calendar(1)

HISTORY
     The **leave** command appeared in 3.0BSD.

NAME

    lex – fast lexical analyzer generator

SYNOPSIS

    lex [–bcdfhilnpstvwBFILTV78 –C[aefFmr] –Pprefix –Sskeleton] *[filename ...]*

DESCRIPTION

    lex is a tool for generating *scanners:* programs which recognized lexical patterns in text. *lex* reads the given input files, or its standard input if no file names are given, for a description of a scanner to generate. The description is in the form of pairs of regular expressions and C code, called *rules. lex* generates as output a C source file, **lex.yy.c,** which defines a routine **yylex().** This file is compiled and linked with the **–ll** library to produce an executable. When the executable is run, it analyzes its input for occurrences of the regular expressions. Whenever it finds one, it executes the corresponding C code.

    For full documentation, see **lexdoc(1).** This manual entry is intended for use as a quick reference.

OPTIONS

    lex has the following options:

    –b   generate backing-up information to *lex.backup.* This is a list of scanner states which require backing up and the input characters on which they do so. By adding rules one can remove backing-up states. If all backing-up states are eliminated and **–Cf** or **–CF** is used, the generated scanner will run faster.

    –c   is a do-nothing, deprecated option included for POSIX compliance.

               NOTE: in previous releases of *lex* **–c** specified table-compression options. This functionality is now given by the **–C** flag. To ease the the impact of this change, when *lex* encounters **–c,** it currently issues a warning message and assumes that **–C** was desired instead. In the future this "promotion" of **–c** to **–C** will go away in the name of full POSIX compliance (unless the POSIX meaning is removed first).

    –d   makes the generated scanner run in *debug* mode. Whenever a pattern is recognized and the global **yy_flex_debug** is non-zero (which is the default), the scanner will write to *stderr* a line of the form:

               --accepting rule at line 53 ("the matched text")

               The line number refers to the location of the rule in the file defining the scanner (i.e., the file that was fed to lex). Messages are also generated when the scanner backs up, accepts the default rule, reaches the end of its input buffer (or encounters a NUL; the two look the same as far as the scanner's concerned), or reaches an end-of-file.

    –f   specifies *fast scanner.* No table compression is done and stdio is bypassed. The result is large but fast. This option is equivalent to **–Cfr** (see below).

    –h   generates a "help" summary of *lex's* options to *stderr* and then exits.

    –i   instructs *lex* to generate a *case-insensitive* scanner. The case of letters given in the *lex* input patterns will be ignored, and tokens in the input will be matched regardless of case. The matched text given in *yytext* will have the preserved case (i.e., it will not be folded).

    –l   turns on maximum compatibility with the original AT&T lex implementation, at a considerable performance cost. This option is incompatible with **–f, –F, –Cf,** or **–CF.** See *lexdoc(1)* for details.

    –n   is another do-nothing, deprecated option included only for POSIX compliance.

    –p   generates a performance report to stderr. The report consists of comments regarding features of the *lex* input file which will cause a loss of performance in the resulting scanner. If you give the flag twice, you will also get comments regarding features that lead to minor performance losses.

1

−s   causes the *default rule* (that unmatched scanner input is echoed to *stdout)* to be suppressed. If the scanner encounters input that does not match any of its rules, it aborts with an error.

−t   instructs *lex* to write the scanner it generates to standard output instead of **lex.yy.c.**

−v   specifies that *lex* should write to *stderr* a summary of statistics regarding the scanner it generates.

−w   suppresses warning messages.

−B   instructs *lex* to generate a *batch* scanner instead of an *interactive* scanner (see −I below). See *lex-doc(1)* for details. Scanners using −Cf or −CF compression options automatically specify this option, too.

−F   specifies that the *fast* scanner table representation should be used (and stdio bypassed). This representation is about as fast as the full table representation (**-f),** and for some sets of patterns will be considerably smaller (and for others, larger). See **lexdoc(1)** for more details.

This option is equivalent to **−CFr** (see below).

−I   instructs *lex* to generate an *interactive* scanner, that is, a scanner which stops immediately rather than looking ahead if it knows that the currently scanned text cannot be part of a longer rule's match. This is the opposite of *batch* scanners (see −B above). See **lexdoc(1)** for details.

Note, −I cannot be used in conjunction with *full* or *fast tables,* i.e., the −f, −F, −Cf, or −CF flags. For other table compression options, −I is the default.

−L   instructs *lex* not to generate **#line** directives in **lex.yy.c.** The default is to generate such directives so error messages in the actions will be correctly located with respect to the original *lex* input file, and not to the fairly meaningless line numbers of **lex.yy.c.**

−T   makes *lex* run in *trace* mode. It will generate a lot of messages to *stderr* concerning the form of the input and the resultant non-deterministic and deterministic finite automata. This option is mostly for use in maintaining *lex.*

−V   prints the version number to *stderr* and exits.

−7   instructs *lex* to generate a 7-bit scanner, which can save considerable table space, especially when using −Cf or −CF (and, at most sites, −7 is on by default for these options. To see if this is the case, use the **-v** verbose flag and check the flag summary it reports).

−8   instructs *lex* to generate an 8-bit scanner. This is the default except for the −Cf and −CF compression options, for which the default is site-dependent, and can be checked by inspecting the flag summary generated by the −v option.

−C[aefFmr]
       controls the degree of table compression and scanner optimization.

       −Ca trade off larger tables in the generated scanner for faster performance because the elements of the tables are better aligned for memory access and computation. This option can double the size of the tables used by your scanner.

       −Ce directs *lex* to construct *equivalence classes,* i.e., sets of characters which have identical lexical properties. Equivalence classes usually give dramatic reductions in the final table/object file sizes (typically a factor of 2-5) and are pretty cheap performance-wise (one array look-up per character scanned).

       −Cf specifies that the *full* scanner tables should be generated - *lex* should not compress the tables by taking advantages of similar transition functions for different states.

       −CF specifies that the alternate fast scanner representation (described in **lexdoc(1)**) should be used.

       −Cm directs *lex* to construct *meta-equivalence classes,* which are sets of equivalence classes (or characters, if equivalence classes are not being used) that are commonly used together. Meta-equivalence classes are often a big win when using compressed tables, but they have a moderate performance impact (one or two "if" tests and one array look-up per character scanned).

−Cr causes the generated scanner to *bypass* using stdio for input. In general this option results in a minor performance gain only worthwhile if used in conjunction with **−Cf** or **−CF**. It can cause surprising behavior if you use stdio yourself to read from *yyin* prior to calling the scanner.

A lone **−C** specifies that the scanner tables should be compressed but neither equivalence classes nor meta-equivalence classes should be used.

The options **−Cf** or **−CF** and **−Cm** do not make sense together - there is no opportunity for meta-equivalence classes if the table is not being compressed. Otherwise the options may be freely mixed.

The default setting is **−Cem,** which specifies that *lex* should generate equivalence classes and meta-equivalence classes. This setting provides the highest degree of table compression. You can trade off faster-executing scanners at the cost of larger tables with the following generally being true:

> slowest & smallest
> -Cem
> -Cm
> -Ce
> -C
> -C{f,F}e
> -C{f,F}
> -C{f,F}a
> fastest & largest

> **−C** options are cumulative.

−Pprefix

> changes the default *yy* prefix used by *lex* to be *prefix* instead. See *lexdoc(1)* for a description of all the global variables and file names that this affects.

−Sskeleton_file

> overrides the default skeleton file from which *lex* constructs its scanners. You'll never need this option unless you are doing *lex* maintenance or development.

SUMMARY OF LEX REGULAR EXPRESSIONS

The patterns in the input are written using an extended set of regular expressions. These are:

x	match the character 'x'
.	any character except newline
[xyz]	a "character class"; in this case, the pattern matches either an 'x', a 'y', or a 'z'
[abj-oZ]	a "character class" with a range in it; matches an 'a', a 'b', any letter from 'j' through 'o', or a 'Z'
[^A-Z]	a "negated character class", i.e., any character but those in the class. In this case, any character EXCEPT an uppercase letter.
[^A-Z\n]	any character EXCEPT an uppercase letter or a newline
r*	zero or more r's, where r is any regular expression
r+	one or more r's
r?	zero or one r's (that is, "an optional r")
r{2,5}	anywhere from two to five r's

1

r{2,}	two or more r's
r{4}	exactly 4 r's
{name}	the expansion of the "name" definition (see above)

"[xyz]\"foo"
    the literal string: [xyz]"foo

\X   if X is an 'a', 'b', 'f', 'n', 'r', 't', or 'v', then the ANSI-C interpretation of \x. Otherwise, a literal 'X' (used to escape operators such as '*')

\123   the character with octal value 123

\x2a   the character with hexadecimal value 2a

(r)   match an r; parentheses are used to override precedence (see below)

rs   the regular expression r followed by the regular expression s; called "concatenation"

r|s   either an r or an s

r/s   an r but only if it is followed by an s. The s is not part of the matched text. This type of pattern is called as "trailing context".

^r   an r, but only at the beginning of a line

r$ an r, but only at the end of a line. Equivalent to "r/\n".

<s>r   an r, but only in start condition s (see below for discussion of start conditions)

<s1,s2,s3>r   same, but in any of start conditions s1, s2, or s3

<*>r   an r in any start condition, even an exclusive one.

<<EOF>>   an end-of-file

<s1,s2><<EOF>>   an end-of-file when in start condition s1 or s2

The regular expressions listed above are grouped according to precedence, from highest precedence at the top to lowest at the bottom. Those grouped together have equal precedence.

Some notes on patterns:

-    Negated character classes *match newlines* unless "\n" (or an equivalent escape sequence) is one of the characters explicitly present in the negated character class (e.g., "[^A-Z\n]").

-    A rule can have at most one instance of trailing context (the '/' operator or the '$' operator). The start condition, '^', and "<<EOF>>" patterns can only occur at the beginning of a pattern, and, as well as with '/' and '$', cannot be grouped inside parentheses. The following are all illegal:

1

```
foo/bar$
foo|(bar$)
foo|^bar
<sc1>foo<sc2>bar
```

SUMMARY OF SPECIAL ACTIONS

In addition to arbitrary C code, the following can appear in actions:

- **ECHO** copies yytext to the scanner's output.

- **BEGIN** followed by the name of a start condition places the scanner in the corresponding start condition.

- **REJECT** directs the scanner to proceed on to the "second best" rule which matched the input (or a prefix of the input). **yytext** and **yyleng** are set up appropriately. Note that **REJECT** is a particularly expensive feature in terms scanner performance; if it is used in *any* of the scanner's actions it will slow down *all* of the scanner's matching. Furthermore, **REJECT** cannot be used with the −**f** or −**F** options.

  Note also that unlike the other special actions, **REJECT** is a *branch;* code immediately following it in the action will *not* be executed.

- **yymore()** tells the scanner that the next time it matches a rule, the corresponding token should be *appended* onto the current value of **yytext** rather than replacing it.

- **yyless(n)** returns all but the first *n* characters of the current token back to the input stream, where they will be rescanned when the scanner looks for the next match. **yytext** and **yyleng** are adjusted appropriately (e.g., **yyleng** will now be equal to *n*).

- **unput(c)** puts the character *c* back onto the input stream. It will be the next character scanned.

- **input()** reads the next character from the input stream (this routine is called **yyinput()** if the scanner is compiled using **C++).**

- **yyterminate()** can be used in lieu of a return statement in an action. It terminates the scanner and returns a 0 to the scanner's caller, indicating "all done".

  By default, **yyterminate()** is also called when an end-of-file is encountered. It is a macro and may be redefined.

- **YY_NEW_FILE** is an action available only in <<EOF>> rules. It means "Okay, I've set up a new input file, continue scanning". It is no longer required; you can just assign *yyin* to point to a new file in the <<EOF>> action.

- **yy_create_buffer(file, size)** takes a *FILE* pointer and an integer *size*. It returns a YY_BUFFER_STATE handle to a new input buffer large enough to accommodate *size* characters and associated with the given file. When in doubt, use **YY_BUF_SIZE** for the size.

- **yy_switch_to_buffer(new_buffer)** switches the scanner's processing to scan for tokens from the given buffer, which must be a YY_BUFFER_STATE.

- **yy_delete_buffer(buffer)** deletes the given buffer.

VALUES AVAILABLE TO THE USER

- **char *yytext** holds the text of the current token. It may be modified but not lengthened (you cannot append characters to the end). Modifying the last character may affect the activity of rules anchored using '^' during the next scan; see **lexdoc(1)** for details.

  If the special directive **%array** appears in the first section of the scanner description, then **yytext** is instead declared **char yytext[YYLMAX],** where **YYLMAX** is a macro definition that you can redefine in the first section if you don't like the default value (generally 8KB). Using **%array** results in somewhat slower scanners, but the value of **yytext** becomes immune to calls to *input()* and *unput(),* which potentially destroy its value when **yytext** is a character pointer. The opposite of **%array** is **%pointer,** which is the default.

- **int yyleng** holds the length of the current token.

- **FILE *yyin** is the file which by default *lex* reads from. It may be redefined but doing so only makes sense before scanning begins or after an EOF has been encountered. Changing it in the midst of scanning will have unexpected results since *lex* buffers its input; use **yyrestart()** instead. Once scanning terminates because an end-of-file has been seen, **you can assign** *yyin* at the new input file and then call the scanner again to continue scanning.

- **void yyrestart(FILE *new_file**) may be called to point *yyin* at the new input file. The switch-over to the new file is immediate (any previously buffered-up input is lost). Note that calling **yyrestart()** with *yyin* as an argument thus throws away the current input buffer and continues scanning the same input file.

- **FILE *yyout** is the file to which **ECHO** actions are done. It can be reassigned by the user.

- **YY_CURRENT_BUFFER** returns a **YY_BUFFER_STATE** handle to the current buffer.

- **YY_START** returns an integer value corresponding to the current start condition. You can subsequently use this value with **BEGIN** to return to that start condition.

MACROS AND FUNCTIONS YOU CAN REDEFINE

- **YY_DECL** controls how the scanning routine is declared. By default, it is "int yylex()", or, if prototypes are being used, "int yylex(void)". This definition may be changed by redefining the "YY_DECL" macro. Note that if you give arguments to the scanning routine using a K&R-style/non-prototyped function declaration, you must terminate the definition with a semi-colon (;).

- The nature of how the scanner gets its input can be controlled by redefining the **YY_INPUT** macro. YY_INPUT's calling sequence is "YY_INPUT(buf,result,max_size)". Its action is to place up to *max_size* characters in the character array *buf* and return in the integer variable *result* either the number of characters read or the constant YY_NULL (0 on Unix systems) to indicate EOF. The default YY_INPUT reads from the global file-pointer "yyin". A sample redefinition of YY_INPUT (in the definitions section of the input file):

```
%{
#undef YY_INPUT
#define YY_INPUT(buf,result,max_size) \
    {\
    int c = getchar(); \
    result = (c == EOF) ? YY_NULL : (buf[0] = c, 1); \
    }
%}
```

- When the scanner receives an end-of-file indication from YY_INPUT, it then checks the function **yywrap()** function. If **yywrap()** returns false (zero), then it is assumed that the function has gone ahead and set up *yyin* to point to another input file, and scanning continues. If it returns true (non-zero), then the scanner terminates, returning 0 to its caller.

  The default **yywrap()** always returns 1.

- **YY_USER_ACTION** can be redefined to provide an action which is always executed prior to the matched rule's action.

- The macro **YY_USER_INIT** may be redefined to provide an action which is always executed before the first scan.

- In the generated scanner, the actions are all gathered in one large switch statement and separated using **YY_BREAK,** which may be redefined. By default, it is simply a "break", to separate each rule's action from the following rule's.

FILES

    −ll   library with which scanners may be linked to obtain default versions of *yywrap( )* and *main( ).*

    lex.yy.c generated scanner (called *lexyy.c* on some systems).

    lex.backup
              backing-up information for −**b** flag (called *lex.bck* on some systems).

SEE ALSO

    lexdoc(1), yacc(1), sed(1), awk(1).

    M. E. Lesk and E. Schmidt, *LEX − Lexical Analyzer Generator*

DIAGNOSTICS

    reject_used_but_not_detected undefined or

    yymore_used_but_not_detected undefined - These errors can occur at compile time. They indicate that the scanner uses **REJECT** or **yymore**() but that *lex* failed to notice the fact, meaning that *lex* scanned the first two sections looking for occurrences of these actions and failed to find any, but somehow you snuck some in (via a #include file, for example). Make an explicit reference to the action in your *lex* input file. (Note that previously *lex* supported a **%used/%unused** mechanism for dealing with this problem; this feature is still supported but now deprecated, and will go away soon unless the author hears from people who can argue compellingly that they need it.)

    lex scanner jammed - a scanner compiled with −**s** has encountered an input string which wasn't matched by any of its rules.

    warning, rule cannot be matched indicates that the given rule cannot be matched because it follows other rules that will always match the same text as it. See *lexdoc(1)* for an example.

    warning, −s option given but default rule can be matched means that it is possible (perhaps only in a particular start condition) that the default rule (match any single character) is the only one that will match a particular input. Since

    scanner input buffer overflowed - a scanner rule matched more text than the available dynamic memory.

    token too large, exceeds YYLMAX - your scanner uses **%array** and one of its rules matched a string longer than the **YYLMAX** constant (8K bytes by default). You can increase the value by #define'ing **YYLMAX** in the definitions section of your *lex* input.

    scanner requires −8 flag to use the character 'x' - Your scanner specification includes recognizing the 8-bit character *'x'* and you did not specify the −8 flag, and your scanner defaulted to 7-bit because you used the −**Cf** or −**CF** table compression options.

    lex scanner push-back overflow - you used **unput**() to push back so much text that the scanner's buffer could not hold both the pushed-back text and the current token in **yytext**. Ideally the scanner should dynamically resize the buffer in this case, but at present it does not.

    input buffer overflow, can't enlarge buffer because scanner uses REJECT - the scanner was working on matching an extremely large token and needed to expand the input buffer. This doesn't work with scanners that use **REJECT.**

    fatal lex scanner internal error--end of buffer missed - This can occur in an scanner which is reentered after a long-jump has jumped out (or over) the scanner's activation frame. Before reentering the scanner, use:

        yyrestart(yyin);

AUTHOR

    Vern Paxson, with the help of many ideas and much inspiration from Van Jacobson. Original version by Jef Poskanzer.

See lexdoc(1) for additional credits and the address to send comments to.

DEFICIENCIES / BUGS

Some trailing context patterns cannot be properly matched and generate warning messages ("dangerous trailing context"). These are patterns where the ending of the first part of the rule matches the beginning of the second part, such as "zx*/xy*", where the 'x*' matches the 'x' at the beginning of the trailing context. (Note that the POSIX draft states that the text matched by such patterns is undefined.)

For some trailing context rules, parts which are actually fixed-length are not recognized as such, leading to the abovementioned performance loss. In particular, parts using '|' or {n} (such as "foo{3}") are always considered variable-length.

Combining trailing context with the special '|' action can result in *fixed* trailing context being turned into the more expensive *variable* trailing context. For example, in the following:

```
%%
abc     |
xyz/def
```

Use of **unput()** or **input()** invalidates yytext and yyleng, unless the **%array** directive or the −l option has been used.

Use of unput() to push back more text than was matched can result in the pushed-back text matching a beginning-of-line ('^') rule even though it didn't come at the beginning of the line (though this is rare!).

Pattern-matching of NUL's is substantially slower than matching other characters.

Dynamic resizing of the input buffer is slow, as it entails rescanning all the text matched so far by the current (generally huge) token.

lex does not generate correct #line directives for code internal to the scanner; thus, bugs in its skeleton file yield bogus line numbers.

Due to both buffering of input and read-ahead, you cannot intermix calls to <stdio.h> routines, such as, for example, **getchar()**, with *lex* rules and expect it to work. Call **input()** instead.

The total table entries listed by the −v flag excludes the number of table entries needed to determine what rule has been matched. The number of entries is equal to the number of DFA states if the scanner does not use **REJECT,** and somewhat greater than the number of states if it does.

REJECT cannot be used with the −f or −F options.

The *lex* internal algorithms need documentation.

NAME

     lkbib – search bibliographic databases

SYNOPSIS

     lkbib [−v] [−i*fields*] [−p*filename*] [−t*n*] *key* . . .

DESCRIPTION

     lkbib searches bibliographic databases for references that contain the keys *key* . . . and prints any refer-
ences found on the standard output. **lkbib** will search any databases given by −**p** options, and then a
default database. The default database is taken from the environment variable if it is set, otherwise it is
/usr/share/dict/papers/Ind. For each database *filename* to be searched, if an index *filename*.**i** created by
indxbib(1) exists, then it will be searched instead; each index can cover multiple databases.

OPTIONS

     −**v**   Print the version number.

     −**p***filename*

          Search *filename*. Multiple −**p** options can be used.

     −**i***string*   When searching files for which no index exists, ignore the contents of fields whose names are in
          string.

     −**t***n*   Only require the first *n* characters of keys to be given. Initially *n* is 6.

ENVIRONMENT

     Default database.

FILES

     /usr/share/dict/papers/Ind   Default database to be used if the environment variable is not set. *filename*.**i**
          Index files.

SEE ALSO

     refer(1), **lookbib**(1), **indxbib**(1)

1

NAME
`ln` – make links

SYNOPSIS
`ln` [`-fs`] *source_file* [target_file]
`ln` [`-fs`] *source_file* ... [target_dir]

DESCRIPTION
The `ln` utility creates a new directory entry (linked file) which has the same modes as the original file. It is useful for maintaining multiple copies of a file in many places at once without using up storage for the ''copies''; instead, a link ''points'' to the original copy. There are two types of links; hard links and symbolic links. How a link ''points'' to a file is one of the differences between a hard or symbolic link.

The options are as follows:

`-f`   Unlink any already existing file, permitting the link to occur.

`-s`   Create a symbolic link.

By default `ln` makes *hard* links. A hard link to a file is indistinguishable from the original directory entry; any changes to a file are effective independent of the name used to reference the file. Hard links may not normally refer to directories and may not span file systems.

A symbolic link contains the name of the file to which it is linked. The referenced file is used when an open(2) operation is performed on the link. A stat(2) on a symbolic link will return the linked-to file; an lstat(2) must be done to obtain information about the link. The readlink(2) call may be used to read the contents of a symbolic link. Symbolic links may span file systems and may refer to directories.

Given one or two arguments, `ln` creates a link to an existing file *source_file*. If *target_file* is given, the link has that name; *target_file* may also be a directory in which to place the link; otherwise it is placed in the current directory. If only the directory is specified, the link will be made to the last component of *source_file*.

Given more than two arguments, `ln` makes links in *target_dir* to all the named source files. The links made will have the same name as the files being linked to.

SEE ALSO
link(2), lstat(2), readlink(2), stat(2), symlink(2), symlink(7)

HISTORY
A `ln` command appeared in Version 6 AT&T UNIX.

1

NAME
locate – find files

SYNOPSIS
locate pattern

DESCRIPTION
Locate searches a database for all pathnames which match the specified *pattern*. The database is recomputed periodically, and contains the pathnames of all files which are publicly accessible.

Shell globbing and quoting characters (''*'', ''?'', ''\'', ''['' and '']'') may be used in *pattern*, although they will have to be escaped from the shell. Preceding any character with a backslash (''\'') eliminates any special meaning which it may have. The matching differs in that no characters must be matched explicitly, including slashes (''/'').

As a special case, a pattern containing no globbing characters (''foo'') is matched as though it were ''*foo*''.

FILES
/var/db/locate.database

SEE ALSO
find(1), fnmatch(3)

Woods, James A., "Finding Files Fast", *;login*, 8:1, pp. 8-10, 1983.

HISTORY
The locate command appears in 4.4BSD.

1

NAME
lock – reserve a terminal

SYNOPSIS
lock [–p] [–t *timeout*]

DESCRIPTION
Lock requests a password from the user, reads it again for verification and then will normally not relinquish the terminal until the password is repeated. There are two other conditions under which it will terminate: it will timeout after some interval of time and it may be killed by someone with the appropriate permission.

Options:

–p   A password is not requested, instead the user's current login password is used.

–t *timeout*
The time limit (default 15 minutes) is changed to *timeout* minutes.

HISTORY
The lock command appeared in 3.0BSD.

1

NAME
logger – make entries in the system log

SYNOPSIS
logger [–is] [–f *file*] [–p *pri*] [–t *tag*] [*message* ...]

DESCRIPTION
Logger provides a shell command interface to the syslog(3) system log module.

Options:

–i   Log the process id of the logger process with each line.

–s   Log the message to standard error, as well as the system log.

–f *file*
        Log the specified file.

–p *pri* Enter the message with the specified priority. The priority may be specified numerically or as a "facility.level" pair. For example, "–p local3.info" logs the message(s) as *info*rmational level in the *local3* facility. The default is "user.notice."

–t *tag* Mark every line in the log with the specified *tag*.

message Write the message to log; if not specified, and the –f flag is not provided, standard input is logged.

The **logger** utility exits 0 on success, and >0 if an error occurs.

EXAMPLES

```
logger System rebooted

logger -p local0.notice -t HOSTIDM -f /dev/idmc
```

SEE ALSO
syslog(3), syslogd(8)

STANDARDS
The **logger** command is expected to be IEEE Std1003.2 ("POSIX") compatible.

NAME

login – log into the computer

SYNOPSIS

login [**–fp**] [**–h** *hostname*] [*user*]

DESCRIPTION

The **login** utility logs users (and pseudo-users) into the computer system.

If no user is specified, or if a user is specified and authentication of the user fails, **login** prompts for a user name. Authentication of users is done via passwords.

The options are as follows:

–f   The **–f** option is used when a user name is specified to indicate that proper authentication has already been done and that no password need be requested. This option may only be used by the super-user or when an already logged in user is logging in as themselves.

–h   The **–h** option specifies the host from which the connection was received. It is used by various daemons such as telnetd(8). This option may only be used by the super-user.

–p   By default, **login** discards any previous environment. The **–p** option disables this behavior.

If the file /etc/nologin exists, **login** dislays its contents to the user and exits. This is used by shutdown(8) to prevent users from logging in when the system is about to go down.

Immediately after logging a user in, **login** displays the system copyright notice, the date and time the user last logged in, the message of the day as well as other information. If the file ''.hushlogin'' exists in the user's home directory, all of these messages are suppressed. This is to simplify logins for non-human users, such as uucp(1). **Login** then records an entry in the wtmp(5) and utmp(5) files and executes the user's command interpretor.

Login enters information into the environment (see environ(7)) specifying the user's home directory (HOME), command interpreter (SHELL), search path (PATH), terminal type (TERM) and user name (both LOGNAME and USER).

The standard shells, csh(1) and sh(1), do not fork before executing the **login** utility.

FILES

/etc/motd	message-of-the-day
/etc/nologin	disallows logins
/var/run/utmp	current logins
/var/log/lastlog	last login account records
/var/log/wtmp	login account records
/var/mail/user	system mailboxes
.hushlogin	makes login quieter

SEE ALSO

chpass(1), passwd(1), rlogin(1), getpass(3), utmp(5), environ(7),

HISTORY

A **login** appeared in Version 6 AT&T UNIX.

1

NAME

   `logname` – display user's login name

SYNOPSIS

   `logname`

DESCRIPTION

   The `logname` utility writes the user's login name to standard output followed by a newline.

   The `logname` utility explicitly ignores the LOGNAME and USER environment variables because the environment cannot be trusted.

   The `logname` utility exits 0 on success, and >0 if an error occurs.

SEE ALSO

   who(1), whoami(1), getlogin(3)

STANDARDS

   The `logname` function is expected to conform to IEEE Std1003.2 (''POSIX'').

HISTORY

   The `logname` command appears in 4.4BSD.

1

NAME
look – display lines beginning with a given string

SYNOPSIS
look [–df] [–t *termchar*] *string* [*file*]

DESCRIPTION
The **look** utility displays any lines in *file* which contain *string* as a prefix. As **look** performs a binary search, the lines in *file* must be sorted.

If *file* is not specified, the file /usr/share/dict/words is used, only alphanumeric characters are compared and the case of alphabetic characters is ignored.

Options:

–d   Dictionary character set and order, i.e. only alphanumeric characters are compared.

–f   Ignore the case of alphabetic characters.

–t   Specify a string termination character, i.e. only the characters in *string* up to and including the first occurrence of *termchar* are compared.

The **look** utility exits 0 if one or more lines were found and displayed, 1 if no lines were found, and >1 if an error occurred.

FILES
/usr/share/dict/words the dictionary

SEE ALSO
grep(1), sort(1)

COMPATIBILITY
The original manual page stated that tabs and blank characters participated in comparisons when the –d option was specified. This was incorrect and the current man page matches the historic implementation.

HISTORY
Look appeared in Version 7 AT&T Unix.

NAME

   lookbib – search bibliographic databases

SYNOPSIS

   lookbib [−v] [−i*string*] [−t*n*] *filename* ...

DESCRIPTION

   lookbib prints a prompt on the standard error (unless the standard input is not a terminal), reads from the
   standard input a line containing a set of keywords, searches the bibliographic databases *filename* ... for
   references containing those keywords, prints any references found on the standard output, and repeats this
   process until the end of input. For each database *filename* to be searched, if an index *filename*.i created by
   indxbib(1) exists, then it will be searched instead; each index can cover multiple databases.

OPTIONS

   −v   Print the version number.

   −i*string* When searching files for which no index exists, ignore the contents of fields whose names are in
             string.

   −t*n*   Only require the first *n* characters of keys to be given. Initially *n* is 6.

FILES

   filename.i   Index files.

SEE ALSO

   refer(1), **lkbib**(1), **indxbib**(1)

NAME

lorder – list dependencies for object files

SYNOPSIS

lorder *file* ...

DESCRIPTION

The **lorder** utility uses nm(1) to determine interdependencies in the list of object files specified on the command line. **Lorder** outputs a list of file names where the first file contains a symbol which is defined by the second file.

The output is normally used with tsort(1) when a library is created to determine the optimum ordering of the object modules so that all references may be resolved in a single pass of the loader.

EXAMPLES

```
ar cr library.a 'lorder ${OBJS}  tsort'
```

SEE ALSO

ar(1), ld(1), nm(1), ranlib(1), tsort(1)

HISTORY

An **lorder** utility appeared in Version 7 AT&T UNIX.

NAME

lpq – spool queue examination program

SYNOPSIS

lpq [**-l**] [**-P***printer*] [job # ...] [user ...]

DESCRIPTION

Lpq examines the spooling area used by lpd(8) for printing files on the line printer, and reports the status of the specified jobs or all jobs associated with a user. **Lpq** invoked without any arguments reports on any jobs currently in the queue.

Options:

-P   Specify a particular printer, otherwise the default line printer is used (or the value of the PRINTER variable in the environment). All other arguments supplied are interpreted as user names or job numbers to filter out only those jobs of interest.

-l   Information about each of the files comprising the job entry is printed. Normally, only as much information as will fit on one line is displayed.

For each job submitted (i.e. invocation of lpr(1)) **lpq** reports the user's name, current rank in the queue, the names of files comprising the job, the job identifier (a number which may be supplied to lprm(1) for removing a specific job), and the total size in bytes. Job ordering is dependent on the algorithm used to scan the spooling directory and is supposed to be FIFO (First in First Out). File names comprising a job may be unavailable (when lpr(1) is used as a sink in a pipeline) in which case the file is indicated as ''(standard input)''.

If **lpq** warns that there is no daemon present (i.e. due to some malfunction), the lpc(8) command can be used to restart the printer daemon.

ENVIRONMENT

If the following environment variable exists, it is used by **lpq**:

PRINTER Specifies an alternate default printer.

FILES

/etc/printcap	To determine printer characteristics.
/var/spool/*	The spooling directory, as determined from printcap.
/var/spool/*/cf*	Control files specifying jobs.
/var/spool/*/lock	The lock file to obtain the currently active job.
/usr/share/misc/termcap	For manipulating the screen for repeated display.

SEE ALSO

lpr(1), lprm(1), lpc(8), lpd(8)

HISTORY

Lpq appeared in 3BSD.

BUGS

Due to the dynamic nature of the information in the spooling directory **lpq** may report unreliably. Output formatting is sensitive to the line length of the terminal; this can results in widely spaced columns.

DIAGNOSTICS

Unable to open various files. The lock file being malformed. Garbage files when there is no daemon active, but files in the spooling directory.

NAME

lpr – off line print

SYNOPSIS

lpr [-Pprinter] [-#num] [-C class] [-J job] [-T title] [-U user] [-i [numcols]]
[-1234 font] [-wnum] [-cdfghlnmprstv] [name ...]

DESCRIPTION

Lpr uses a spooling daemon to print the named files when facilities become available. If no names appear, the standard input is assumed.

The following single letter options are used to notify the line printer spooler that the files are not standard text files. The spooling daemon will use the appropriate filters to print the data accordingly.

-c   The files are assumed to contain data produced by cifplot(1)

-d   The files are assumed to contain data from *tex* (DVI format from Stanford).

-f   Use a filter which interprets the first character of each line as a standard FORTRAN carriage control character.

-g   The files are assumed to contain standard plot data as produced by the plot routines (see also plot for the filters used by the printer spooler).

-l   Use a filter which allows control characters to be printed and suppresses page breaks.

-n   The files are assumed to contain data from *ditroff* (device independent troff).

-p   Use pr(1) to format the files (equivalent to print).

-t   The files are assumed to contain data from troff(1) (cat phototypesetter commands).

-v   The files are assumed to contain a raster image for devices like the Benson Varian.

These options apply to the handling of the print job:

-P   Force output to a specific printer. Normally, the default printer is used (site dependent), or the value of the environment variable PRINTER is used.

-h   Suppress the printing of the burst page.

-m   Send mail upon completion.

-r   Remove the file upon completion of spooling or upon completion of printing (with the -s option).

-s   Use symbolic links. Usually files are copied to the spool directory. The -s option will use symlink(2) to link data files rather than trying to copy them so large files can be printed. This means the files should not be modified or removed until they have been printed.

The remaining options apply to copies, the page display, and headers:

-#num   The quantity num is the number of copies desired of each file named. For example,

          lpr -#3 foo.c bar.c more.c
would result in 3 copies of the file foo.c, followed by 3 copies of the file bar.c, etc. On the other hand,

          cat foo.c bar.c more.c | lpr -#3

will give three copies of the concatenation of the files. Often a site will disable this feature to encourage use of a photocopier instead.

−[1234]*font*

Specifies a *font* to be mounted on font position *i*. The daemon will construct a `.railmag` file referencing the font pathname.

−C *class*

Job classification to use on the burst page. For example,

```
lpr −C EECS foo.c
```

causes the system name (the name returned by `hostname(1)`) to be replaced on the burst page by EECS, and the file foo.c to be printed.

−J *job*

Job name to print on the burst page. Normally, the first file's name is used.

−T *title*

Title name for pr(1), instead of the file name.

−U *user*

User name to print on the burst page, also for accounting purposes. This option is only honored if the real user-id is daemon (or that specified in the printcap file instead of daemon), and is intended for those instances where print filters wish to requeue jobs.

−i [numcols]

The output is indented. If the next argument is numeric (*numcols*), it is used as the number of blanks to be printed before each line; otherwise, 8 characters are printed.

−w*num*   Uses *num* as the page width for pr(1).

ENVIRONMENT

If the following environment variable exists, it is used by **lpr**:

PRINTER Specifies an alternate default printer.

FILES

`/etc/passwd`	Personal identification.
`/etc/printcap`	Printer capabilities data base.
`/usr/sbin/lpd*`	Line printer daemons.
`/var/spool/output/*`	Directories used for spooling.
`/var/spool/output/*/cf*`	Daemon control files.
`/var/spool/output/*/df*`	Data files specified in "cf" files.
`/var/spool/output/*/tf*`	Temporary copies of "cf" files.

SEE ALSO

lpq(1), lprm(1), pr(1), symlink(2), printcap(5), lpc(8), lpd(8)

HISTORY

The **lpr** command appeared in 3BSD.

DIAGNOSTICS

If you try to spool too large a file, it will be truncated. **Lpr** will object to printing binary files. If a user other than root prints a file and spooling is disabled, **lpr** will print a message saying so and will not put jobs in the queue. If a connection to lpd(1) on the local machine cannot be made, **lpr** will say that the daemon

cannot be started. Diagnostics may be printed in the daemon's log file regarding missing spool files by
lpd(1).

BUGS

Fonts for troff(1) and tex reside on the host with the printer. It is currently not possible to use local font
libraries.

1

NAME
lprm – remove jobs from the line printer spooling queue

SYNOPSIS
lprm [−Pprinter] [−] [job # ...] [user ...]

DESCRIPTION
Lprm will remove a job, or jobs, from a printer's spool queue. Since the spooling directory is protected from users, using lprm is normally the only method by which a user may remove a job. The owner of a job is determined by the user's login name and host name on the machine where the lpr(1) command was invoked.

Options and arguments:

−Pprinter
> Specify the queue associated with a specific *printer* (otherwise the default printer is used).

−
> If a single '−' is given, lprm will remove all jobs which a user owns. If the super-user employs this flag, the spool queue will be emptied entirely.

user
> Causes lprm to attempt to remove any jobs queued belonging to that user (or users). This form of invoking lprm is useful only to the super-user.

job #
> A user may dequeue an individual job by specifying its job number. This number may be obtained from the lpq(1) program, e.g.

```
% lpq −l

1st:ken                        [job #013ucbarpa]
        (standard input)       100 bytes
% lprm 13
```

If neither arguments or options are given, Lprm will delete the currently active job if it is owned by the user who invoked lprm.

Lprm announces the names of any files it removes and is silent if there are no jobs in the queue which match the request list.

Lprm will kill off an active daemon, if necessary, before removing any spooling files. If a daemon is killed, a new one is automatically restarted upon completion of file removals.

ENVIRONMENT
If the following environment variable exists, it is utilized by lprm.

PRINTER If the environment variable PRINTER exists, and a printer has not been specified with the −P option, the default printer is assumed from PRINTER.

FILES
/etc/printcap	Printer characteristics file.
/var/spool/*	Spooling directories.
/var/spool/*/lock	Lock file used to obtain the pid of the current daemon and the job number of the currently active job.

SEE ALSO

lpr(1), lpq(1), lpd(8)

DIAGNOSTICS

"Permission denied" if the user tries to remove files other than his own.

BUGS

Since there are race conditions possible in the update of the lock file, the currently active job may be incorrectly identified.

HISTORY

The **lprm** command appeared in 3.0BSD.

1

NAME

lptest – generate lineprinter ripple pattern

SYNOPSIS

lptest [*length*] [*count*]

DESCRIPTION

Lptest writes the traditional "ripple test" pattern on standard output. In 96 lines, this pattern will print all 96 printable ASCII characters in each position. While originally created to test printers, it is quite useful for testing terminals, driving terminal ports for debugging purposes, or any other task where a quick supply of random data is needed.

The *length* argument specifies the output line length if the default length of 79 is inappropriate.

The *count* argument specifies the number of output lines to be generated if the default count of 200 is inappropriate. Note that if *count* is to be specified, *length* must be also be specified.

HISTORY

Lptest appeared in 4.3BSD.

1

NAME

ls – list directory contents

SYNOPSIS

ls [−ACFLRTacdfiloqrstul] [*file* ...]

DESCRIPTION

For each operand that names a *file* of a type other than directory, ls displays its name as well as any requested, associated information. For each operand that names a *file* of type directory, ls displays the names of files contained within that directory, as well as any requested, associated information.

If no operands are given, the contents of the current directory are displayed. If more than one operand is given, non-directory operands are displayed first; directory and non-directory operands are sorted separately and in lexicographical order.

The following options are available:

−A   List all entries except for '.' and '..'. Always set for the super-user.

−C   Force multi-column output; this is the default when output is to a terminal.

−F   Display a slash (/) immediately after each pathname that is a directory, an asterisk (∗) after each that is executable, and an at sign (@) after each symbolic link.

−L   If argument is a symbolic link, list the file or directory the link references rather than the link itself.

−R   Recursively list subdirectories encountered.

−T   Display complete time information for the file, including month, day, hour, minute, second, and year.

−a   Include directory entries whose names begin with a dot (.).

−c   Use time when file status was last changed for sorting or printing.

−d   Directories are listed as plain files (not searched recursively) and symbolic links in the argument list are not indirected through.

−f   Output is not sorted.

−i   For each file, print the file's file serial number (inode number).

−l   (The lowercase letter "ell.") List in long format. (See below.) If the output is to a terminal, a total sum for all the file sizes is output on a line before the long listing.

−o   Include the file flags in a long (−l) output

−q   Force printing of non-graphic characters in file names as the character '?'; this is the default when output is to a terminal.

−r   Reverse the order of the sort to get reverse lexicographical order or the oldest entries first.

−s   Display the number of file system blocks actually used by each file, in units of 512 bytes, where partial units are rounded up to the next integer value. If the output is to a terminal, a total sum for all the file sizes is output on a line before the listing.

1

-t   Sort by time modified (most recently modified first) before sorting the operands by lexicographical order.

-u   Use time of last access, instead of last modification of the file for sorting (-t) or printing (-1).

-1   (The numeric digit "one.") Force output to be one entry per line. This is the default when output is not to a terminal.

The -1, -c, and -1 options all override each other; the last one specified determines the format used.

The -c, and -u options override each other; the last one specified determines the file time used.

By default, ls lists one entry per line to standard output; the exceptions are to terminals or when the -c option is specified.

File information is displayed with one or more <blank>s separating the information associated with the -i, -s, and -1 options.

The Long Format

If the -1 option is given, the following information is displayed for each file: file mode, number of links, owner name, group name, number of bytes in the file, abbreviated month, day-of-month file was last modified, hour file last modified, minute file last modified, and the pathname. In addition, for each directory whose contents are displayed, the total number of 512-byte blocks used by the files in the directory is displayed on a line by itself immediately before the information for the files in the directory.

If the owner or group names are not a known user or group name the numeric ID's are displayed.

If the file is a character special or block special file, the major and minor device numbers for the file are displayed in the size field. If the file is a symbolic link the pathname of the linked-to file is preceded by "->".

The file mode printed under the -l option consists of the entry type, owner permissions, and group permissions. The entry type character describes the type of file, as follows:

b   Block special file.
c   Character special file.
d   Directory.
l   Symbolic link.
s   Socket link.
–   Regular file.

The next three fields are three characters each: owner permissions, group permissions, and other permissions. Each field has three character positions:

1.   If **r**, the file is readable; if –, it is not readable.

2.   If **w**, the file is writable; if –, it is not writable.

3.   The first of the following that applies:

       S   If in the owner permissions, the file is not executable and set-user-ID mode is set. If in the group permissions, the file is not executable and set-group-ID mode is set.

       s   If in the owner permissions, the file is executable and set-user-ID mode is set. If in the group permissions, the file is executable and setgroup-ID mode is set.

       x   The file is executable or the directory is searchable.

     −   The file is neither readable, writeable, executable, nor set-user-ID nor set-group-ID mode, nor sticky. (See below.)

These next two apply only to the third character in the last group (other permissions).

     T   The sticky bit is set (mode 1000), but not execute or search permission. (See chmod(1) or sticky(8).)

     t   The sticky bit is set (mode 1000), and is searchable or executable. (See chmod(1) or sticky(8).)

The `ls` utility exits 0 on success, and >0 if an error occurs.

ENVIRONMENTAL VARIABLES

The following environment variables affect the execution of `ls`:

BLOCKSIZE If the environmental variable BLOCKSIZE is set, the block counts (see −s) will be displayed in units of that size block.

COLUMNS If this variable contains a string representing a decimal integer, it is used as the column position width for displaying multiple-text-column output. The `ls` utility calculates how many pathname text columns to display based on the width provided. (See −C.)

TZ The timezone to use when displaying dates. See environ(7) for more information.

COMPATIBILITY

The group field is now automatically included in the long listing for files in order to be compatible with the IEEE Std1003.2 (''POSIX'') specification.

SEE ALSO

chmod(1), symlink(7), sticky(8)

HISTORY

An `ls` command appeared in Version 6 AT&T UNIX.

STANDARDS

The `ls` function is expected to be a superset of the IEEE Std1003.2 (''POSIX'') specification.

1

NAME

m4 – macro language preprocessor for ratfor(1) and pascal(1)

SYNOPSIS

m4 [options]

DESCRIPTION

M4 is a macro language preprocessor for Ratfor, Pascal, and similar languages which do not have a built-in macro processing capability. **M4** reads standard input, and writes the results to the standard output.

The options and their effects are as follows:

−D*name*[=*Val*] Defines *name* to *val* or to null in the absence of *val*.

−U*name*   Undefines *name*.

The **m4** processor provides a kind of C like syntax and some of the macro functions will be familiar:

define   *define(name [, val])* the second argument is installed as the value of the macro whose name is the first argument. If there is no second argument, the value is null. Each occurrence of $*n* in the replacement text, where *n* is a digit, is replaced by the *n*'th argument. Argument 0 is the name of the macro; missing arguments are replaced by the null string.

defn   *defn(name [, name ...])* returns the quoted definition of its argument(s). Useful in renaming macros.

undefine

        undefine(name [, name ...]) removes the definition of the macro(s) named. If there is more than one definition for the named macro, (due to previous use of **pushdef**) all definitions are removed.

pushdef   *pushdef(name [, val])* like **define**, but saves any previous definition by stacking the current definition.

popdef   *popdef(name [, name ...])* removes current definition of its argument(s), exposing the previous one if any.

ifdef   *ifdef(name, if-def [, ifnot-def])* if the first argument is defined, the value is the second argument, otherwise the third. If there is no third argument, the value is null. A word indicating the current operating system is predefined (e.g. or

shift   *shift(arg, arg, arg, ...)* returns all but its first argument. The other arguments are quoted and pushed back with commas in between. The quoting nullifies the effect of the extra scan that will subsequently be performed.

changequote

        changequote(lqchar, rqchar) change quote symbols to the first and second arguments. With no arguments, the quotes are reset back to the default characters (i.e., ` and) .

changecom

        changecom(lcchar, rcchar) change left and right comment markers from the default # and **newline**. With no arguments, the comment mechanism is reset back to the default characters. With one argument, the left marker becomes the argument and the right marker becomes newline. With two arguments, both markers are affected.

divert   *divert(divnum)* **m4** maintains 10 output streams, numbered 0-9. initially stream 0 is the
current stream. The **divert** macro changes the current output stream to its (digit-string) argument. Output diverted to a stream other than 0 through 9 disappears into bitbucket.

undivert
undivert([divnum [, divnum ...]) causes immediate output of text from diversions
named as argument(s), or all diversions if no argument. Text may be undiverted into another
diversion. Undiverting discards the diverted text. At the end of input processing, **M4** forces an
automatic **undivert**, unless **m4wrap** is defined.

divnum   *divnum()* returns the value of the current output stream.

dnl   *dnl()* reads and discards characters up to and including the next newline.

ifelse   *ifelse(arg, arg, if-same [, ifnot-same | arg, arg ...])* has three or
more arguments. If the first argument is the same string as the second, then the value is the third
argument. If not, and if there are more than four arguments, the process is repeated with arguments 4, 5, 6 and 7. Otherwise, the value is either the fourth string, or, if it is not present, null.

incr   *incr(num)* returns the value of its argument incremented by 1. The value of the argument is
calculated by interpreting an initial digit-string as a decimal number.

decr   *decr(num)* returns the value of its argument decremented by 1.

eval   *eval(expression)* evaluates its argument as a constant expression, using integer arithmetic.
The evaluation mechanism is very similar to that of cpp (#if expression). The expression can
involve only integer constants and character constants, possibly connected by the binary operators

$$* \quad / \quad \% \quad + \quad - \quad >> \quad << \quad < \quad >$$
$$<= \quad >= \quad == \quad != \quad \& \quad \char`\^ \quad \&\&$$

or the unary operators ~ ! or by the ternary operator ? :. Parentheses may be used for grouping. Octal numbers may be specified as in C.

len   *len(string)* returns the number of characters in its argument.

index   *index(search-string, string)* returns the position in its first argument where the
second argument begins (zero origin), or −1 if the second argument does not occur.

substr   *substr(string, index [, length])* returns a substring of its first argument. The
second argument is a zero origin number selecting the first character (internally treated as an expression); the third argument indicates the length of the substring. A missing third argument is
taken to be large enough to extend to the end of the first string.

translit
translit(source, from [, to]) transliterates the characters in its first argument from
the set given by the second argument to the set given by the third. If the third argument is shorter
than the second, all extra characters in the second argument are deleted from the first argument.
If the third argument is missing altogether, all characters in the second argument are deleted from
the first argument.

include *include(filename)* returns the contents of the file named in the argument.

1

sinclude
> *sinclude(filename)* is identical to **include**, except that it says nothing if the file is inaccessible.

paste   *paste(filename)* returns the contents of the file named in the argument without any processing, unlike **include**.

spaste   *spaste(filename)* is identical to **paste**, except that it says nothing if the file is inaccessible.

syscmd   *syscmd(command)* executes the UNIX command given in the first argument. No value is returned.

sysval   *sysval()* is the return code from the last call to **syscmd**.

maketemp
> *maketemp(string)* fills in a string of XXXXXX in its argument with the current process ID.

m4exit   *m4exit([exitcode])* causes immediate exit from **m4**. Argument 1, if given, is the exit code; the default is 0.

m4wrap   *m4wrap(m4-macro-or-built-in)* argument 1 will be pushed back at final **EOF**;
> example: m4wrap('dumptable()').

errprint
> *errprint(str [, str, str, ...])* prints its argument(s) on stderr. If there is more than one argument, each argument is separated by a space during the output.

dumpdef   *dumpdef([name, name, ...])* prints current names and definitions, for the named items, or for all if no arguments are given.

AUTHOR
> Ozan S. Yigit (oz)

BUGS
> A sufficiently complex **M4** macro set is about as readable as APL.

> All complex uses of **M4** require the ability to program in deep recursion. Previous lisp experience is recommended.

EXAMPLES
> The following macro program illustrates the type of things that can be done with **M4**.

```
changequote(<,>) define(HASHVAL,99) dnl
define(hash,<expr(str(substr($1,1),0)%HASHVAL)>) dnl
define(str,
        <ifelse($1,",$2,
        <str(substr(<$1>,1),<expr($2+'substr($1,0,1)')>)>)
        >) dnl
define(KEYWORD,<$1,hash($1),>) dnl
define(TSTART,
<struct prehash {
        char *keyword;
        int   hashval;
} keytab[] = {>) dnl
define(TEND,<  "",0
};>)
dnl
```

Thus a keyword table containing the keyword string and its pre-calculated hash value may be generated thus:

```
TSTART
        KEYWORD("foo")
        KEYWORD("bar")
        KEYWORD("baz")
TEND
```

which will expand into:

```
struct prehash {
        char *keyword;
        int   hashval;
} keytab[] = {
        "foo",27,
        "bar",12,
        "baz",20,
        "",0
};
```

Presumably, such a table would speed up the installation of the keywords into a dynamic hash table. (Note that the above macro cannot be used with **m4**, since **eval** does not handle character constants.)

SEE ALSO
cpp(1)

B. W. Kernighan, and D. M. Ritchie., *The M4 Macro Processor*.

HISTORY
An **M4** command appeared in Version 7 AT&T UNIX. The **M4** command this page describes is derived from code contributed by Ozan S. Yigit.

1

NAME
mail – send and receive mail

SYNOPSIS
mail [–iInv] [–s *subject*] [–c *cc-addr*] [–b *bcc-addr*] *to-addr*...
mail [–iInNv] –f [*name*]
mail [–iInNv] [–u *user*]

INTRODUCTION
Mail is an intelligent mail processing system, which has a command syntax reminiscent of ed(1) with lines replaced by messages.

–v   Verbose mode. The details of delivery are displayed on the user's terminal.

–i   Ignore tty interrupt signals. This is particularly useful when using **mail** on noisy phone lines.

–I   Forces mail to run in interactive mode even when input isn't a terminal. In particular, the '~' special character when sending mail is only active in interactive mode.

–n   Inhibits reading /etc/mail.rc upon startup.

–N   Inhibits the initial display of message headers when reading mail or editing a mail folder.

–s   Specify subject on command line (only the first argument after the –s flag is used as a subject; be careful to quote subjects containing spaces.)

–c   Send carbon copies to *list* of users.

–b   Send blind carbon copies to *list*. List should be a comma-separated list of names.

–f   Read in the contents of your *mbox* (or the specified file) for processing; when you *quit*, **mail** writes undeleted messages back to this file.

–u   Is equivalent to:

            mail -f /var/spool/mail/user

Sending mail
To send a message to one or more people, **mail** can be invoked with arguments which are the names of people to whom the mail will be sent. You are then expected to type in your message, followed by an 'control–D' at the beginning of a line. The section below *Replying to or originating mail*, describes some features of **mail** available to help you compose your letter.

Reading mail
In normal usage **mail** is given no arguments and checks your mail out of the post office, then prints out a one line header of each message found. The current message is initially the first message (numbered 1) and can be printed using the **print** command (which can be abbreviated 'p'). You can move among the messages much as you move between lines in ed(1), with the commands '+' and '–' moving backwards and forwards, and simple numbers.

Disposing of mail.
After examining a message you can **delete** 'd') the message or **reply** 'r') to it. Deletion causes the **mail** program to forget about the message. This is not irreversible; the message can be **undeleted** 'u') by giving its number, or the **mail** session can be aborted by giving the **exit** 'x') command. Deleted messages will, however, usually disappear never to be seen again.

1

Specifying messages

Commands such as **print** and **delete** can be given a list of message numbers as arguments to apply to a number of messages at once. Thus "delete 1 2" deletes messages 1 and 2, while "delete 1–5" deletes messages 1 through 5. The special name '*' addresses all messages, and '$' addresses the last message; thus the command **top** which prints the first few lines of a message could be used in "top *" to print the first few lines of all messages.

Replying to or originating mail.

You can use the **reply** command to set up a response to a message, sending it back to the person who it was from. Text you then type in, up to an end-of-file, defines the contents of the message. While you are composing a message, **mail** treats lines beginning with the character '~' specially. For instance, typing '~m' (alone on a line) will place a copy of the current message into the response right shifting it by a tabstop (see *indentprefix* variable, below). Other escapes will set up subject fields, add and delete recipients to the message and allow you to escape to an editor to revise the message or to a shell to run some commands. (These options are given in the summary below.)

Ending a mail processing session.

You can end a **mail** session with the **quit** 'q') command. Messages which have been examined go to your *mbox* file unless they have been deleted in which case they are discarded. Unexamined messages go back to the post office. (See the −**f** option above).

Personal and systemwide distribution lists.

It is also possible to create a personal distribution lists so that, for instance, you can send mail to "cohorts" and have it go to a group of people. Such lists can be defined by placing a line like

        alias cohorts bill ozalp jkf mark kridle@ucbcory

in the file .mailrc in your home directory. The current list of such aliases can be displayed with the **alias** command in **mail**. System wide distribution lists can be created by editing /etc/aliases, see aliases(5) and sendmail(8); these are kept in a different syntax. In mail you send, personal aliases will be expanded in mail sent to others so that they will be able to **reply** to the recipients. System wide **aliases** are not expanded when the mail is sent, but any reply returned to the machine will have the system wide alias expanded as all mail goes through sendmail.

Network mail (ARPA, UUCP, Berknet)

See mailaddr(7) for a description of network addresses.

Mail has a number of options which can be set in the .mailrc file to alter its behavior; thus "set askcc" enables the *askcc* feature. (These options are summarized below.)

SUMMARY

(Adapted from the 'Mail Reference Manual')

Each command is typed on a line by itself, and may take arguments following the command word. The command need not be typed in its entirety – the first command which matches the typed prefix is used. For commands which take message lists as arguments, if no message list is given, then the next message forward which satisfies the command's requirements is used. If there are no messages forward of the current message, the search proceeds backwards, and if there are no good messages at all, **mail** types "applicable messages" and aborts the command.

−   Print out the preceding message. If given a numeric argument *n*, goes to the *n*'th previous message and prints it.

?   Prints a brief summary of commands.

1

!   Executes the shell (see sh(1) and csh(1)) command which follows.

Print   (**P**) Like **print** but also prints out ignored header fields. See also **print**, **ignore** and **retain**.

Reply   (**R**) Reply to originator. Does not reply to other recipients of the original message.

Type   (**T**) Identical to the **Print** command.

alias   (**a**) With no arguments, prints out all currently-defined aliases. With one argument, prints out that alias. With more than one argument, creates a new alias or changes an old one.

alternates
          (**alt**) The **alternates** command is useful if you have accounts on several machines. It can be used to inform **mail** that the listed addresses are really you. When you **reply** to messages, **mail** will not send a copy of the message to any of the addresses listed on the **alternates** list. If the **alternates** command is given with no argument, the current set of alternate names is displayed.

chdir   (**c**) Changes the user's working directory to that specified, if given. If no directory is given, then changes to the user's login directory.

copy   (**co**) The **copy** command does the same thing that **save** does, except that it does not mark the messages it is used on for deletion when you quit.

delete   (**d**) Takes a list of messages as argument and marks them all as deleted. Deleted messages will not be saved in *mbox*, nor will they be available for most other commands.

dp   (also **dt**) Deletes the current message and prints the next message. If there is no next message, **mail** says "at EOF".

edit   (**e**) Takes a list of messages and points the text editor at each one in turn. On return from the editor, the message is read back in.

exit   (**ex** or **x**) Effects an immediate return to the Shell without modifying the user's system mailbox, his *mbox* file, or his edit file in −**f**.

file   (**fi**) The same as **folder**.

folders
          List the names of the folders in your folder directory.

folder (**fo**) The **folder** command switches to a new mail file or folder. With no arguments, it tells you which file you are currently reading. If you give it an argument, it will write out changes (such as deletions) you have made in the current file and read in the new file. Some special conventions are recognized for the name. # means the previous file, % means your system mailbox, %user means user's system mailbox, & means your *mbox* file, and +folder means a file in your folder directory.

from   (**f**) Takes a list of messages and prints their message headers.

headers
          (**h**) Lists the current range of headers, which is an 18−message group. If a '+' argument is given, then the next 18−message group is printed, and if a '−' argument is given, the previous 18−message group is printed.

help   A synonym for **?**

hold   (**ho**, also **preserve**) Takes a message list and marks each message therein to be saved in the user's system mailbox instead of in *mbox*. Does not override the **delete** command.

ignore   Add the list of header fields named to the *ignored list*. Header fields in the ignore list are not printed on your terminal when you print a message. This command is very handy for suppression of certain machine-generated header fields. The **Type** and **Print** commands can be used to print a message in its entirety, including ignored fields. If **ignore** is executed with no arguments, it lists the current set of ignored fields.

mail   (**m**) Takes as argument login names and distribution group names and sends mail to those people.

mbox   Indicate that a list of messages be sent to **mbox** in your home directory when you quit. This is the default action for messages if you do *not* have the **hold** option set.

next   (**n**) like + or CR) Goes to the next message in sequence and types it. With an argument list, types the next matching message.

preserve
              (**pre**) A synonym for **hold**.

print   (**p**) Takes a message list and types out each message on the user's terminal.

quit   (**q**) Terminates the session, saving all undeleted, unsaved messages in the user's *mbox* file in his login directory, preserving all messages marked with **hold** or **preserve** or never referenced in his system mailbox, and removing all other messages from his system mailbox. If new mail has arrived during the session, the message "You have new mail" is given. If given while editing a mailbox file with the −**f** flag, then the edit file is rewritten. A return to the Shell is effected, unless the rewrite of edit file fails, in which case the user can escape with the **exit** command.

reply   (**r**) Takes a message list and sends mail to the sender and all recipients of the specified message. The default message must not be deleted.

respond
              A synonym for **reply**.

retain   Add the list of header fields named to the *retained list* Only the header fields in the retain list are shown on your terminal when you print a message. All other header fields are suppressed. The **Type** and **Print** commands can be used to print a message in its entirety. If **retain** is executed with no arguments, it lists the current set of retained fields.

save   (**s**) Takes a message list and a filename and appends each message in turn to the end of the file. The filename in quotes, followed by the line count and character count is echoed on the user's terminal.

set   (**se**) With no arguments, prints all variable values. Otherwise, sets option. Arguments are of the form *option=value* (no space before or after =) or *option*. Quotation marks may be placed around any part of the assignment statement to quote blanks or tabs, i.e. "set indentprefix= ->"""

saveignore
              Saveignore is to **save** what **ignore** is to **print** and **type**. Header fields thus marked are filtered out when saving a message by **save** or when automatically saving to *mbox*.

saveretain
              Saveretain is to **save** what **retain** is to **print** and **type**. Header fields thus marked are the only ones saved with a message when saving by **save** or when automatically saving to *mbox*. **Saveretain** overrides **saveignore**.

1

shell   (sh) Invokes an interactive version of the shell.

size   Takes a message list and prints out the size in characters of each message.

source The **source** command reads commands from a file.

top   Takes a message list and prints the top few lines of each. The number of lines printed is controlled by the variable **toplines** and defaults to five.

type   (t) A synonym for **print**.

unalias
Takes a list of names defined by **alias** commands and discards the remembered groups of users. The group names no longer have any significance.

undelete
(u) Takes a message list and marks each message as **not** being deleted.

unread (U) Takes a message list and marks each message as **not** having been read.

unset   Takes a list of option names and discards their remembered values; the inverse of **set**.

visual (v) Takes a message list and invokes the display editor on each message.

write   (w) Similar to **save**, except that **only** the message body (*without*) the header) is saved. Extremely useful for such tasks as sending and receiving source program text over the message system.

xit   (x) A synonym for **exit**.

z   **Mail** presents message headers in windowfuls as described under the **headers** command. You can move **mail**'s attention forward to the next window with the **z** command. Also, you can move to the previous window by using **z−**.

Tilde/Escapes

Here is a summary of the tilde escapes, which are used when composing messages to perform special functions. Tilde escapes are only recognized at the beginning of lines. The name ''*tilde escape*'' is somewhat of a misnomer since the actual escape character can be set by the option **escape**.

~! *command*
Execute the indicated shell command, then return to the message.

~b *name* ...
Add the given names to the list of carbon copy recipients but do not make the names visible in the Cc: line ("blind" carbon copy).

~c *name* ...
Add the given names to the list of carbon copy recipients.

~d   Read the file ''dead.letter'' from your home directory into the message.

~e   Invoke the text editor on the message collected so far. After the editing session is finished, you may continue appending text to the message.

~f *messages*
Read the named messages into the message being sent. If no messages are specified, read in the current message. Message headers currently being ignored (by the **ignore** or **retain** command) are not included.

1

~F*messages*
    Identical to ~**f**, except all message headers are included.

~**h**   Edit the message header fields by typing each one in turn and allowing the user to append text to the end or modify the field by using the current terminal erase and kill characters.

~**m***messages*
    Read the named messages into the message being sent, indented by a tab or by the value of *indentprefix*. If no messages are specified, read the current message. Message headers currently being ignored (by the **ignore** or **retain** command) are not included.

~**M***messages*
    Identical to ~**m**, except all message headers are included.

~**p**   Print out the message collected so far, prefaced by the message header fields.

~**q**   Abort the message being sent, copying the message to ''**dead.letter**'' in your home directory if **save** is set.

~**r***filename*
    Read the named file into the message.

~**s***string*
    Cause the named string to become the current subject field.

~**t***name . . .*
    Add the given names to the direct recipient list.

~**v**   Invoke an alternate editor (defined by the VISUAL option) on the message collected so far. Usually, the alternate editor will be a screen editor. After you quit the editor, you may resume appending text to the end of your message.

~**w***filename*
    Write the message onto the named file.

~**|***command*
    Pipe the message through the command as a filter. If the command gives no output or terminates abnormally, retain the original text of the message. The command fmt(1) is often used as **command** to rejustify the message.

~**:***mail-command*
    Execute the given mail command. Not all commands, however, are allowed.

~~*string*
    Insert the string of text in the message prefaced by a single ~. If you have changed the escape character, then you should double that character in order to send it.

Mail Options

Options are controlled via **set** and **unset** commands. Options may be either binary, in which case it is only significant to see whether they are set or not; or string, in which case the actual value is of interest. The binary options include the following:

append   Causes messages saved in *mbox* to be appended to the end rather than prepended. This should always be set (perhaps in /etc/mail.rc).

ask   Causes **mail** to prompt you for the subject of each message you send. If you respond with simply a newline, no subject field will be sent.

1

askcc   Causes you to be prompted for additional carbon copy recipients at the end of each message. Responding with a newline indicates your satisfaction with the current list.

autoprint

Causes the **delete** command to behave like **dp** – thus, after deleting a message, the next one will be typed automatically.

debug   Setting the binary option *debug* is the same as specifying −d on the command line and causes **mail** to output all sorts of information useful for debugging **mail**.

dot   The binary option *dot* causes **mail** to interpret a period alone on a line as the terminator of a message you are sending.

hold   This option is used to hold messages in the system mailbox by default.

ignore   Causes interrupt signals from your terminal to be ignored and echoed as @'s.

ignoreeof

An option related to *dot* is *ignoreeof* which makes **mail** refuse to accept a control-d as the end of a message. *Ignoreeof* also applies to **mail** command mode.

metoo   Usually, when a group is expanded that contains the sender, the sender is removed from the expansion. Setting this option causes the sender to be included in the group.

noheader

Setting the option *noheader* is the same as giving the −N flag on the command line.

nosave   Normally, when you abort a message with two RUBOUT (erase or delete) **mail** copies the partial letter to the file ''dead.letter'' in your home directory. Setting the binary option *nosave* prevents this.

Replyall

Reverses the sense of **reply** and **Reply** commands.

quiet   Suppresses the printing of the version when first invoked.

searchheaders

If this option is set, then a message-list specifier in the form ''/x:y'' will expand to all messages containing the substring ''y'' in the header field ''x''. The string search is case insensitive.

verbose

Setting the option *verbose* is the same as using the −v flag on the command line. When mail runs in verbose mode, the actual delivery of messages is displayed on the user's terminal.

Option String Values

EDITOR   Pathname of the text editor to use in the **edit** command and ~e escape. If not defined, then a default editor is used.

LISTER   Pathname of the directory lister to use in the **folders** command. Default is /bin/ls.

PAGER   Pathname of the program to use in the **more** command or when **crt** variable is set. The default paginator more(1) is used if this option is not defined.

SHELL   Pathname of the shell to use in the ! command and the ~! escape. A default shell is used if this option is not defined.

VISUAL   Pathname of the text editor to use in the **visual** command and ~v escape.

crt   The valued option *crt* is used as a threshold to determine how long a message must be before PAGER is used to read it. If *crt* is set without a value, then the height of the terminal screen stored in the system is used to compute the threshold (see stty(1)).

escape   If defined, the first character of this option gives the character to use in the place of ˜ to denote escapes.

folder   The name of the directory to use for storing folders of messages. If this name begins with a '/', **mail** considers it to be an absolute pathname; otherwise, the folder directory is found relative to your home directory.

MBOX   The name of the *mbox* file. It can be the name of a folder. The default is "mbox" in the user's home directory.

record   If defined, gives the pathname of the file used to record all outgoing mail. If not defined, then outgoing mail is not so saved.

indentprefix
             String used by the "˜m" tilde escape for indenting messages, in place of the normal tab character (ˆI). Be sure to quote the value if it contains spaces or tabs.

toplines   If defined, gives the number of lines of a message to be printed out with the **top** command; normally, the first five lines are printed.

ENVIRONMENT
Mail utilizes the HOME and USER environment variables.

FILES
/var/spool/mail/*	Post office.
˜/mbox	User's old mail.
˜/.mailrc	File giving initial mail commands.
/tmp/R*	Temporary files.
/usr/share/misc/Mail.help*	Help files.
/etc/mail.rc	System initialization file.

SEE ALSO
fmt(1), newaliases(1), vacation(1), aliases(5), mailaddr(7), sendmail(8) and

The Mail Reference Manual..

HISTORY
A **mail** command appeared in Version 6 AT&T UNIX. This man page is derived from *The Mail Reference Manual* originally written by Kurt Shoens.

BUGS
There are some flags that are not documented here. Most are not useful to the general user.

Usually, **mail** is just a link to **Mail**, which can be confusing.

1

NAME
mailq – print the mail queue

SYNOPSIS
mailq [–v]

DESCRIPTION
Mailq prints a summary of the mail messages queued for future delivery.

The first line printed for each message shows the internal identifier used on this host for the message, the size of the message in bytes, the date and time the message was accepted into the queue, and the envelope sender of the message. The second line shows the error message that caused this message to be retained in the queue; it will not be present if the message is being processed for the first time. The following lines show message recipients, one per line.

Mailq is identical to "sendmail -bp".

The options are as follows:

–v   Print verbose information. This adds the priority of the message and a single character indicator ("+" or blank) indicating whether a warning message has been sent on the first line of the message. Additionally, extra lines may be intermixed with the recipients indicating the "controlling user" information; this shows who will own any programs that are executed on behalf of this message and the name of the alias this command expanded from, if any.

The mailq utility exits 0 on success, and >0 if an error occurs.

SEE ALSO
sendmail(8)

HISTORY
The mailq command appeared in 4.0BSD.

NAME

    make – maintain program dependencies

SYNOPSIS

    make [**−eiknqrstv**] [**−D** *variable*] [**−d** *flags*] [**−f** *makefile*] [**−I** *directory*]
        [**−j** *max_jobs*] [*variable=value*] [*target ...*]

DESCRIPTION

    Make is a program designed to simplify the maintenance of other programs. Its input is a list of specifications as to the files upon which programs and other files depend. If the file 'makefile' exists, it is read for this list of specifications. If it does not exist, the file 'Makefile' is read. If the file '.depend' exists, it is read (see mkdep(1)).

    This manual page is intended as a reference document only. For a more thorough description of **make** and makefiles, please refer to *Make – A Tutorial*.

    The options are as follows:

−D *variable*
    Define Ar variable to be 1, in the global context.

−d *flags*
    Turn on debugging, and specify which portions of **make** are to print debugging information. *Flags* is one or more of the following:

        A   Print all possible debugging information; equivalent to specifying all of the debugging flags.

        a   Print debugging information about archive searching and caching.

        c   Print debugging information about conditional evaluation.

        d   Print debugging information about directory searching and caching.

        g1   Print the input graph before making anything.

        g2   Print the input graph after making everything, or before exiting on error.

        j   Print debugging information about running multiple shells.

        m   Print debugging information about making targets, including modification dates.

        s   Print debugging information about suffix-transformation rules.

        t   Print debugging information about target list maintenance.

        v   Print debugging information about variable assignment.

−e   Specify that environmental variables override macro assignments within makefiles.

−f *makefile*
    Specify a makefile to read instead of the default 'makefile' and 'Makefile'. If *makefile* is '−', standard input is read. Multiple makefile's may be specified, and are read in the order specified.

1

−I *directory*
>   Specify a directory in which to search for makefiles and included makefiles. The system makefile directory is automatically included as part of this list.

−i
>   Ignore non-zero exit of shell commands in the makefile. Equivalent to specifying '−' before each command line in the makefile.

−j *max_jobs*
>   Specify the maximum number of jobs that **make** may have running at any one time.

−k
>   Continue processing after errors are encountered, but only on those targets that do not depend on the target whose creation caused the error.

−n
>   Display the commands that would have been executed, but do not actually execute them.

−q
>   Do not execute any commands, but exit 0 if the specified targets are up-to-date and 1, otherwise.

−r
>   Do not use the built-in rules specified in the system makefile.

−s
>   Do not echo any commands as they are executed. Equivalent to specifying '@' before each command line in the makefile.

−t
>   Rather than re-building a target as specified in the makefile, create it or update its modification time to make it appear up-to-date.

variable=value
>   Set the value of the variable *variable* to *value*.

There are seven different types of lines in a makefile: file dependency specifications, shell commands, variable assignments, include statements, conditional directives, for loops, and comments.

In general, lines may be continued from one line to the next by ending them with a backslash ('\'). The trailing newline character and initial whitespace on the following line are compressed into a single space.

FILE DEPENDENCY SPECIFICATIONS

Dependency lines consist of one or more targets, an operator, and zero or more sources. This creates a relationship where the targets "depend" on the sources and are usually created from them. The exact relationship between the target and the source is determined by the operator that separates them. The three operators are as follows:

:
>   A target is considered out-of-date if its modification time is less than those of any of its sources. Sources for a target accumulate over dependency lines when this operator is used. The target is removed if **make** is interrupted.

!
>   Targets are always re-created, but not until all sources have been examined and re-created as necessary. Sources for a target accumulate over dependency lines when this operator is used. The target is removed if **make** is interrupted.

::
>   If no sources are specified, the target is always re-created. Otherwise, a target is considered out-of-date if any of its sources has been modified more recently than the target. Sources for a target do not accumulate over dependency lines when this operator is used. The target will not be removed if **make** is interrupted.

Targets and sources may contain the shell wildcard values '?', '*', '[ ]' and '{ }'. The values '?', '*' and '[ ]' may only be used as part of the final component of the target or source, and must be used to describe existing files. The value '{ }' need not necessarily be used to describe existing files. Expansion is in directory order, not alphabetically as done in the shell.

SHELL COMMANDS

Each target may have associated with it a series of shell commands, normally used to create the target. Each of the commands in this script *must* be preceded by a tab. While any target may appear on a dependency line, only one of these dependencies may be followed by a creation script, unless the ' : : ' operator is used.

If the first or first two characters of the command line are '@' and/or '−', the command is treated specially. A '@' causes the command not to be echoed before it is executed. A '−' causes any non-zero exit status of the command line to be ignored.

VARIABLE ASSIGNMENTS

Variables in make are much like variables in the shell, and, by tradition, consist of all upper-case letters. The five operators that can be used to assign values to variables are as follows:

=　　　　Assign the value to the variable. Any previous value is overridden.

+=　　　Append the value to the current value of the variable.

?=　　　Assign the value to the variable if it is not already defined.

:=　　　Assign with expansion, i.e. expand the value before assigning it to the variable. Normally, expansion is not done until the variable is referenced.

!=　　　Expand the value and pass it to the shell for execution and assign the result to the variable. Any newlines in the result are replaced with spaces.

Any white-space before the assigned *value* is removed; if the value is being appended, a single space is inserted between the previous contents of the variable and the appended value.

Variables are expanded by surrounding the variable name with either curly braces ('{}') or parenthesis ('()') and preceding it with a dollar sign ('$'). If the variable name contains only a single letter, the surrounding braces or parenthesis are not required. This shorter form is not recommended.

Variable substitution occurs at two distinct times, depending on where the variable is being used. Variables in dependency lines are expanded as the line is read. Variables in shell commands are expanded when the shell command is executed.

The four different classes of variables (in order of increasing precedence) are:

Environment variables
　　　　Variables defined as part of make's environment.

Global variables
　　　　Variables defined in the makefile or in included makefiles.

Command line variables
　　　　Variables defined as part of the command line.

Local variables
　　　　Variables that are defined specific to a certain target. The seven local variables are as follows:

　　　　.ALLSRC　　The list of all sources for this target; also known as '>'.

　　　　.ARCHIVE　The name of the archive file.

　　　　.IMPSRC　　The name/path of the source from which the target is to be transformed (the "implied" source); also known as '<'.

　　　　.MEMBER　The name of the archive member.

.OODATE   The list of sources for this target that were deemed out-of-date; also known as '?'.

.PREFIX   The file prefix of the file, containing only the file portion, no suffix or preceding direc-
           tory components; also known as '*'.

.TARGET   The name of the target; also known as '@'.

The shorter forms '@', '?', '>' and '*' are permitted for backward compatibility with historical
makefiles and are not recommended. The six variables '@F', '@D', '<F', '<D', '*F' and '*D' are
permitted for compatibility with AT&T System V UNIX makefiles and are not recommended.

Four of the local variables may be used in sources on dependency lines because they expand to the
proper value for each target on the line. These variables are '.TARGET', '.PREFIX', '.ARCHIVE',
and '.MEMBER'.

In addition, **make** sets or knows about the following variables:

$ A single dollar sign '$', i.e. '$$' expands to a single dollar sign.

.MAKE   The name that **make** was executed with (*argv* [0])

.CURDIR   A path to the directory where **make** was executed.

.OBJDIR   A path to the directory where the targets are built.

MAKEFLAGS The environment variable 'MAKEFLAGS' may contain anything that may be specified
           on **make**'s command line. Anything specified on **make**'s command line is appended
           to the 'MAKEFLAGS' variable which is then entered into the environment for all pro-
           grams which **make** executes.

Variable expansion may be modified to select or modify each word of the variable (where a
''word'' is white-space delimited sequence of characters). The general format of a variable expan-
sion is as follows:

```
{variable[:modifier[:...]]}
```

Each modifier begins with a colon and one of the following special characters. The colon may be
escaped with a backslash ('\').

E   Replaces each word in the variable with its suffix.

H   Replaces each word in the variable with everything but the last component.

M*pattern* Select only those words that match the rest of the modifier. The standard shell wild-
           card characters ('*', '?', and '[]') may be used. The wildcard characters may be es-
           caped with a backslash ('\').

N*pattern* This is identical to 'M', but selects all words which do not match the rest of the
           modifier.

R   Replaces each word in the variable with everything but its suffix.

S/*old_pattern*/*new_pattern*/[g]
           Modify the first occurrence of *old_pattern* in each word to be replaced with
           new_pattern. If a 'g' is appended to the last slash of the pattern, all occurrences in
           each word are replaced. If *old_pattern* begins with a carat ('^'),
           old_pattern is anchored at the beginning of each word. If *old_pattern* ends
           with a dollar sign ('$'), it is anchored at the end of each word. Inside
           new_string, an ampersand ('&') is replaced by *old_pattern*. Any character
           may be used as a delimiter for the parts of the modifier string. The anchoring, amper-
           sand and delimiter characters may be escaped with a backslash ('\').

Variable expansion occurs in the normal fashion inside both *old_string* and *new_string* with the single exception that a backslash is used to prevent the expansion of a dollar sign ('$') not a preceding dollar sign as is usual.

T   Replaces each word in the variable with its last component.

old_string=new_string
        This is the AT&T System V UNIX style variable substitution. It must be the last modifier specified. If *old_string* or *new_string* do not contain the pattern matching character $ then it is assumed that they are anchored at the end of each word, so only suffixes or entire words may be replaced. Otherwise $ is the substring of *old_string* to be replaced in *new_string*

INCLUDE STATEMENTS, CONDITIONALS AND FOR LOOPS

Makefile inclusion, conditional structures and for loops reminiscent of the C programming language are provided in **make**. All such structures are identified by a line beginning with a single dot ('.') character. Files are included with either .include <file> or .include "file". Variables between the angle brackets or double quotes are expanded to form the file name. If angle brackets are used, the included makefile is expected to be in the system makefile directory. If double quotes are used, the including makefile's directory and any directories specified using the −I option are searched before the system makefile directory.

Conditional expressions are also preceded by a single dot as the first character of a line. The possible conditionals are as follows:

.undef *variable*
        Un-define the specified global variable. Only global variables may be un-defined.

.if [!]*expression* [*operator expression* ...]
        Test the value of an expression.

.ifdef [!]*variable* [*operator variable* ...]
        Test the value of a variable.

.ifndef [!]*variable* [*operator variable* ...]
        Test the value of a variable.

.ifmake [!]*target* [*operator target* ...]
        Test the the target being built.

.ifnmake [!]*target* [*operator target* ...]
        Test the target being built.

.else Reverse the sense of the last conditional.

.elif [!]*expression* [*operator expression* ...]
        A combination of '.else' followed by '.if'.

.elifdef [!]*variable* [*operator variable* ...]
        A combination of '.else' followed by '.ifdef'.

.elifndef [!]*variable* [*operator variable* ...]
        A combination of '.else' followed by '.ifndef'.

.elifmake [!]*target* [*operator target* ...]
        A combination of '.else' followed by '.ifmake'.

.elifnmake[!]*target* [*operator target ...*]
>   A combination of '`.else`' followed by '`.ifnmake`'.

.endif
>   End the body of the conditional.

The *operator* may be any one of the following:

|| logical OR

&&   Logical AND; of higher precedence than "".

As in C, **make** will only evaluate a conditional as far as is necessary to determine its value. Parentheses may be used to change the order of evaluation. The boolean operator '`!`' may be used to logically negate an entire conditional. It is of higher precedence than '`&&`'.

The value of *expression* may be any of the following:

defined   Takes a variable name as an argument and evaluates to true if the variable has been defined.

make   Takes a target name as an argument and evaluates to true if the target was specified as part of **make**'s command line or was declared the default target (either implicitly or explicitly, see *.MAIN*) before the line containing the conditional.

empty   Takes a variable, with possible modifiers, and evaluates to true if the expansion of the variable would result in an empty string.

exists   Takes a file name as an argument and evaluates to true if the file exists. The file is searched for on the system search path (see *.PATH*).

target   Takes a target name as an argument and evaluates to true if the target has been defined.

Expression may also be an arithmetic or string comparison. Variable expansion is performed on both sides of the comparison, after which the integral values are compared. A value is interpreted as hexadecimal if it is preceded by 0x, otherwise it is decimal; octal numbers are not supported. The standard C relational operators are all supported. If after variable expansion, either the left or right hand side of a '`==`' or '`!=`' operator is not an integral value, then string comparison is performed between the expanded variables. If no relational operator is given, it is assumed that the expanded variable is being compared against 0.

When **make** is evaluating one of these conditional expression, and it encounters a word it doesn't recognize, either the "make" or "defined" expression is applied to it, depending on the form of the conditional. If the form is '`.ifdef`' or '`.ifndef`', the "defined" expression is applied. Similarly, if the form is '`.ifmake`' or '`.ifnmake`, the "make" ' expression is applied.

If the conditional evaluates to true the parsing of the makefile continues as before. If it evaluates to false, the following lines are skipped. In both cases this continues until a '`.else`' or '`.endif`' is found.

For loops are typically used to apply a set of rules to a list of files. The syntax of a for loop is:

.for *variable* **in** *expression*
>   <make-rules>

.endfor
After the for **expression** is evaluated, it is split into words. The iteration **variable** is successively set to each word, and substituted in the **make-rules** inside the body of the for loop.

COMMENTS

Comments begin with a hash ('#') character, anywhere but in a shell command line, and continue to the end of the line.

SPECIAL SOURCES

.IGNORE   Ignore any errors from the commands associated with this target, exactly as if they all were preceded by a dash ('−').

.MAKE   Execute the commands associated with this target even if the −n or −t options were specified. Normally used to mark recursive **make**'s.

.NOTMAIN   Normally **make** selects the first target it encounters as the default target to be built if no target was specified. This source prevents this target from being selected.

.OPTIONAL

      If a target is marked with this attribute and **make** can't figure out how to create it, it will ignore this fact and assume the file isn't needed or already exists.

.PRECIOUS

      When **make** is interrupted, it removes any partially made targets. This source prevents the target from being removed.

.SILENT   Do not echo any of the commands associated with this target, exactly as if they all were preceded by an at sign ('@').

.USE   Turn the target into **make**'s. version of a macro. When the target is used as a source for another target, the other target acquires the commands, sources, and attributes (except for .USE) of the source. If the target already has commands, the .USE target's commands are appended to them.

SPECIAL TARGETS

Special targets may not be included with other targets, i.e. they must be the only target specified.

.BEGIN   Any command lines attached to this target are executed before anything else is done.

.DEFAULT   This is sort of a .USE rule for any target (that was used only as a source) that **make** can't figure out any other way to create. Only the shell script is used. The .IMPSRC variable of a target that inherits .DEFAULT's commands is set to the target's own name.

.END   Any command lines attached to this target are executed after everything else is done.

.IGNORE   Mark each of the sources with the .IGNORE attribute. If no sources are specified, this is the equivalent of specifying the −i option.

.INTERRUPT

      If **make** is interrupted, the commands for this target will be executed.

.MAIN   If no target is specified when **make** is invoked, this target will be built.

.MAKEFLAGS

      This target provides a way to specify flags for **make** when the makefile is used. The flags are as if typed to the shell, though the −f option will have no effect.

.PATH   The sources are directories which are to be searched for files not found in the current directory. If no sources are specified, any previously specified directories are deleted.

1

.PRECIOUS
> Apply the .PRECIOUS attribute to any specified sources. If no sources are specified, the .PRECIOUS attribute is applied to every target in the file.

.SILENT   Apply the .SILENT attribute to any specified sources. If no sources are specified, the .SILENT attribute is applied to every command in the file.

.SUFFIXES
> Each source specifies a suffix to **make**. If no sources are specified, any previous specified suffices are deleted.

ENVIRONMENT
Make utilizes the following environment variables, if they exist: MAKE, MAKEFLAGS and MAKEOBJDIR.

FILES
.depend	list of dependencies
Makefile	list of dependencies
makefile	list of dependencies
sys.mk	system makefile
/usr/share/mk	system makefile directory

SEE ALSO
mkdep(1)

HISTORY
A **Make** command appeared in Version 7 AT&T UNIX.

1

NAME

man – display the on-line manual pages

SYNOPSIS

man [–achw] [–C *file*] [–M *path*] [–m *path*] [*section*] *name* ...

DESCRIPTION

The **man** utility displays the BSD manual pages entitled *name*.

The options are as follows:

–a Display all of the manual pages for a specified *section* and *name* combination. (Normally, only the first manual page found is displayed.)

–C Use the specified *file* instead of the default configuration file. This permits users to configure their own manual environment. See man.conf(5) for a description of the contents of this file.

–c Copy the manual page to the standard output instead of using more(1) to paginate it. This is done by default if the standard output is not a terminal device.

–h Display only the ''SYNOPSIS'' lines of the requested manual pages.

–M Override the list of standard directories which **man** searches for manual pages. The supplied *path* must be a colon ('':'') separated list of directories. This search path may also be set using the environment variable MANPATH. The subdirectories to be searched, and their search order, is specified by the ''_subdir'' line in the **man** configuration file.

–m Augment the list of standard directories which **man** searches for manual pages. The supplied *path* must be a colon ('':'') separated list of directories. These directories will be searched before the standard directories or the directories specified using the –M option or the MANPATH environment variable. The subdirectories to be searched, and their search order, is specified by the ''_subdir'' line in the **man** configuration file.

–w List the pathnames of the manual pages which **man** would display for the specified *section* and *name* combination.

The optional *section* argument restricts the directories that **man** will search. The **man** configuration file (see man.conf(5)) specifies the possible *section* values that are currently available. If only a single argument is specified or if the first argument is not a valid section, **man** assumes that the argument is the name of a manual page to be displayed.

ENVIRONMENT

MACHINE As some manual pages are intended only for specific architectures, **man** searches any subdirectories, with the same name as the current architecture, in every directory which it searches. Machine specific areas are checked before general areas. The current machine type may be overridden by setting the environment variable MACHINE to the name of a specific architecture.

MANPATH The standard search path used by **man** may be overridden by specifying a path in the MANPATH environment variable. The format of the path is a colon ('':'') separated list of directories. The subdirectories to be searched as well as their search order is specified by the ''_subdir'' line in the **man** configuration file.

PAGER Any value of the environment variable PAGER will be used instead of the standard pagination program, more(1).

FILES
> /etc/man.conf default man configuration file.

SEE ALSO
> apropos(1), whatis(1), whereis(1), man.conf(5)

BUGS
> The on-line manual pages are, by necessity, forgiving toward stupid display devices, causing a few manual
> pages to not as nicely formatted as their typeset counterparts.

HISTORY
> A **man** command appeared in Version 6 AT&T UNIX.

1

NAME

merge – three-way file merge

SYNOPSIS

merge [**−L** *label1* [**−L** *label3*]] [**−p**] [**−q**] *file1 file2 file3*

DESCRIPTION

merge incorporates all changes that lead from *file2* to *file3* into *file1*. The result goes to standard output if **−p** is present, into *file1* otherwise. **merge** is useful for combining separate changes to an original. Suppose *file2* is the original, and both *file1* and *file3* are modifications of *file2*. Then **merge** combines both changes.

An overlap occurs if both *file1* and *file3* have changes in a common segment of lines. On a few older hosts where **diff3** does not support the **−E** option, **merge** does not detect overlaps, and merely supplies the changed lines from *file3*. On most hosts, if overlaps occur, **merge** outputs a message (unless the **−q** option is given), and includes both alternatives in the result. The alternatives are delimited as follows:

> <<<<<<< *file1*
> *lines in file1*
> =======
> *lines in file3*
> >>>>>>> *file3*

If there are overlaps, the user should edit the result and delete one of the alternatives. If the **−L** *label1* and **−L** *label3* options are given, the labels are output in place of the names *file1* and *file3* in overlap reports.

DIAGNOSTICS

Exit status is 0 for no overlaps, 1 for some overlaps, 2 for trouble.

IDENTIFICATION

Author: Walter F. Tichy.
Revision Number: 5.3; Release Date: 1991/02/28.
Copyright © 1982, 1988, 1989 by Walter F. Tichy.
Copyright © 1990, 1991 by Paul Eggert.

SEE ALSO

diff3(1), diff(1), rcsmerge(1), co(1).

NAME

mesg – display (do not display) messages from other users

SYNOPSIS

mesg [**n** | **y**]

DESCRIPTION

The **mesg** utility is invoked by a users to control write access others have to the terminal device associated with the standard error output. Write access is allowed by default, and programs such as talk(1) and write(1) may display messages on the terminal.

Options available:

n   Disallows messages.

y   Permits messages to be displayed.

If no arguments are given, **mesg** displays the present message status to the standard error output.

The **mesg** utility exits with one of the following values:

0	Messages are allowed.
1	Messages are not allowed.
>1	An error has occurred.

FILES

/dev/[pt]ty[pq]?

SEE ALSO

biff(1), talk(1), write(1)

HISTORY

A **mesg** command appeared in Version 6 AT&T UNIX.

NAME

   mh – Message Handler

DESCRIPTION

   Mh is the name of a powerful message handling system. Rather then being a single comprehensive program, mh consists of a collection of fairly simple single-purpose programs to send, receive, save, and retrieve messages. The user should refer to the *UNIX User's Supplementary Documents*, document 8 (USD:8).

   Unlike mail, the standard UNIX mail user interface program, mh is not a closed system which must be explicitly run, then exited when you wish to return to the shell. You may freely intersperse mh commands with other shell commands, allowing you to read and answer your mail while you have (for example) a compilation running, or search for a file or run programs as needed to find the answer to someone's question before answering their mail.

   The rest of this manual entry is a quick tutorial which will teach you the basics of mh. You should read the manual entries for the individual programs for complete documentation.

   To get started using mh, put the directory /usr/contrib/mh-6.8/bin in your $PATH. This is best done in one of the files: .profile, .login, or .cshrc in your home directory. (Check the manual entry for the shell you use, in case you don't know how to do this.) Run the inc command. If you've never used mh before, it will create the necessary default files and directories after asking you if you wish it to do so.

   Inc moves mail from your system maildrop into your mh '+inbox' folder, breaking it up into separate files and converting it to mh format as it goes. It prints one line for each message it processes, containing the from field, the subject field and as much of the first line of the message as will fit. It leaves the first message it processes as your current message. You'll need to run inc each time you wish to incorporate new mail into your mh file.

   scan prints a list of the messages in your current folder.

   The commands: show, next, and prev are used to read specific messages from the current folder. Show displays the current message, or a specific message, which may be specified by its number, which you pass as an argument to show, next, and prev display, respectively, the message numerically after or before the current message. In all cases, the message displayed becomes the current message. If there is no current message, show may be called with an argument, or next may be used to advance to the first message.

   Rmm (remove message) deletes the current message. It may be called with message numbers passed as arguments, to delete specific messages.

   repl is used to respond to the current message (by default). It places you in the editor with a prototype response form. While you're in the editor, you may peruse the item you're responding to by reading the file @. After completing your response, type l to review it, or s to send it.

   Comp allows you to compose a message by putting you in the editor on a prototype message form, and then lets you send it.

   All the mh commands may be run with the single argument: '–help', which causes them to print a list of the arguments they may be invoked with.

   Commands which take a message number as an argument (scan, show, repl, ...) also take one of the words: first, prev, cur, next, or last to indicate (respectively) the first, previous, current, next, or last message in the current folder (assuming they are defined).

Commands which take a range of message numbers (`rmm`, `scan`, `show`, ...) also take any of the abbreviations:

\<num1>–\<num2>	Indicates all messages in the range \<num1> to \<num2>, inclusive. The range must be nonempty.
\<num>:+N	Up to *N* messages beginning with message *num*. *Num* may be any of the pre-defined symbols: `first`, `prev`, `cur`, `next`, or `last`.
\<num>:-N	Up to *N* messages ending with) message *num*. *Num* may be any of the pre-defined symbols: `first`, `prev`, `cur`, `next`, or `last`.
first:N	The first *N* messages, if they exist.
prev:N	The previous *N* messages, if they exist.
next:N	The next *N* messages, if they exist.
last:N	The last *N* messages, if they exist.

There are many other possibilities such as creating multiple folders for different topics, and automatically refiling messages according to subject, source, destination, or content. These are beyond the scope of this manual entry.

Following is a list of all the *MH* commands:

ali(1)	list mail aliases
anno(1)	annotate messages
bbc(1)	check on BBoards
bboards(1)	the UCI BBoards facility
burst(1)	explode digests into messages
comp(1)	compose a message
dist(1)	redistribute a message to additional addresses
folder(1)	set/list current folder/message
folders(1)	list all folders
forw(1)	forward messages
inc(1)	incorporate new mail
mark(1)	mark messages
mhl(1)	produce formatted listings of MH messages
mhmail(1)	send or read mail
mhook(1)	MH receive–mail hooks
mhparam(1)	print MH profile components
mhpath(1)	print full pathnames of MH messages
msgchk(1)	check for messages
msh(1)	MH shell (and BBoard reader)
next(1)	show the next message
packf(1)	compress a folder into a single
pick(1)	select messages by content
prev(1)	show the previous message
prompter(1)	prompting editor front end
rcvstore(1)	incorporate new mail asynchronously
refile(1)	file messages in other folders
repl(1)	reply to a message
rmf(1)	remove folder

rmm(1)	remove messages
scan(1)	produce a one line per message
send(1)	send a message
show(1)	show (list) messages
slocal(1)	special local mail delivery
sortm(1)	sort messages
vmh(1)	visual front–end to MH
whatnow(1)	prompting front–end for send
whom(1)	report to whom a message would
mh–alias(5)	alias file for MH message system
mh–format(5)	format file for MH message system
mh–mail(5)	message format for MH message system
mh–profile(5)	user customization for MH message system
mh–sequence(5)	sequence specification for MH message system
ap(8)	parse addresses 822–style
conflict(8)	search for alias/password conflicts
dp(8)	parse dates 822–style
fmtdump(8)	decode MH format files
install–mh(8)	initialize the MH environment
post(8)	deliver a message

If problems are encountered with an **mh** program, the problems should be reported to the local maintainers of **mh**. When doing this, the name of the program should be reported, along with the version information for the program. To find out what version of an **mh** program is being run, invoke the program with the '–help' switch. In addition to listing the syntax of the command, the program will list information pertaining to its version. This information includes the version of **mh**, the host it was generated on, and the date the program was loaded. A second line of information, found on versions of **mh** after #5.380 include **mh** configuration options. For example,

```
version: MH 6.8.1a #8[UCI] (vangogh.CS.Berkeley.EDU)
        of Sun Jun 13 02:55:52 PDT 1993
options: [BIND] [BPOP] [BSD42] [BSD43] [BSD44] [DBMPWD] [MHE] [MHRC]
        [MIME] [MORE='"/usr/bin/more"'] [NNTP] [NTOHLSWAP] [OVERHEAD]
        [POP] [POP2] [POPSERVICE='"pop3"'] [POSIX] [RPOP] [SENDMTS]
        [SMTP] [SPRINTFTYPE=int] [SYS5DIR] [TYPESIG=void] [UNISTD]
        [VSPRINTF] [WAITINT] [WHATNOW] [ZONEINFO]
```

The '6.8.1a #8[UCI]' indicates that the program is from the UCI **mh** 6.8.1a version of **mh**. The program was generated on the host 'vangogh.CS.Berkeley.EDU' on 'Sun Jun 13 02:55:52 PDT 1993'. It's usually a good idea to send the output of the '–help' switch along with your report.

If there is no local **mk** maintainer, try the address **Bug-MH**. If that fails, use the Internet mailbox **Bug-MH@ICS.UCI.EDU**.

1

NAME
mkdep – construct Makefile dependency list

SYNOPSIS
mkdep [−ap] [−f *file*] [*flags*] *file* ...

DESCRIPTION
Mkdep takes a set of flags for the C compiler and a list of C source files as arguments and constructs a set of include file dependencies which are written into the file ''.depend''. An example of its use in a Makefile might be:

```
CFLAGS= -O -I../include
SRCS= file1.c file2.c

depend:
        mkdep ${CFLAGS} ${SRCS}
```

where the macro SRCS is the list of C source files and the macro CFLAGS is the list of flags for the C compiler.

The options are as follows:

−a   Append to the output file, so that multiple **mkdep**'s may be run from a single Makefile.

−f   Write the include file dependencies to *file*, instead of the default ''.depend''.

−p   Cause **mkdep** to produce dependencies of the form:

         program: program.c

so that subsequent makes will produce *program* directly from its C module rather than using an intermediate .o module. This is useful for programs whose source is contained in a single module.

SEE ALSO
cc(1), cpp(1), make(1)

FILES
.depend   File containing list of dependencies.

HISTORY
The **mkdep** command appeared in 4.3BSD–Tahoe.

1

NAME

mkdir – make directories

SYNOPSIS

mkdir [–p] [–m *mode*] *directory_name ...*

DESCRIPTION

Mkdir creates the directories named as operands, in the order specified, using mode rwxrwxrwx (0777) as modified by the current umask(2).

The options are as follows:

–m   Set the file permission bits of the final created directory to the specified mode. The mode argu-
        ment can be in any of the formats specified to the chmod(1) command. If a symbolic mode is
        specified, the operation characters "+" and "-" are interpreted relative to an initial mode of
        "a=rwx".

–p   Create intermediate directories as required. If this option is not specified, the full path prefix of
        each operand must already exist. Intermediate directories are created with permission bits of
        rwxrwxrwx (0777) as modified by the current umask, plus write and search permission for
        the owner.

The user must have write permission in the parent directory.

Mkdir exits 0 if successful, and >0 if an error occurred.

SEE ALSO

rmdir(1)

STANDARDS

The mkdir utility is expected to be IEEE Std1003.2 ("POSIX") compatible.

1

NAME

    mkfifo – make fifos

SYNOPSIS

    mkfifo *fifo_name* ...

DESCRIPTION

    Mkfifo creates the fifos requested, in the order specified, using mode 0777.

    Mkfifo requires write permission in the parent directory.

    Mkfifo exits 0 if successful, and >0 if an error occurred.

STANDARDS

    The **mkfifo** utility is expected to be IEEE Std1003.2 (''POSIX'') compliant.

SEE ALSO

    mkdir(1), mknod(1), rm(1), mkfifo(2)

HISTORY

    The **mkfifo** command appears in 4.4BSD.

1

NAME

  `mklocale` – make LC_CTYPE locale files

SYNOPSIS

  `mklocale <` *src-file* `>` *language*`/LC_CTYPE`

DESCRIPTION

  The **mklocale** utility reads a LC_CTYPE source file from standard input and produces a LC_CTYPE binary file on standard output suitable for placement in `/usr/share/locale/`*language*`/LC_CTYPE`.

  The format of *src-file* is quite simple. It consists of a series of lines which start with a keyword and have associated data following. C style comments are used to place comments in the file.

  Besides the keywords which will be listed below, the following are valid tokens in *src-file*:

  RUNE   A RUNE may be any of the following:

  `'x'`   The ascii character *x*.

  `'\x'`   The ANSI C character `\x` where `\x` is one of `\a`, `\b`, `\f`, `\n`, `\r`, `\t`, or `\v`.

  `0x[0-9a-z]*`   A hexadecimal number representing a rune code.

  `0[0-7]*`   An octal number representing a rune code.

  `[1-9][0-9]*`   A decimal number representing a rune code.

  STRING   A string enclosed in double quotes (").

  THRU   Either . . . or -. Used to indicate ranges.

  literal The follow characters are taken literally:

  `< ( [`   Used to start a mapping. All are equivalent.

  `> ) ]`   Used to end a mapping. All are equivalent.

  `:`   Used as a delimiter in mappings.

  Key words which should only appear once are:

  ENCODING   Followed by a STRING which indicates the encoding mechanism to be used for this locale. The current encodings are:

  NONE No translation and the default.

  UTF2 Universal character set Transformation Format adopted from **Plan 9 from Bell Labs**. This is the preferred encoding.

  EUC   EUC encoding as used by several vendors of UNIX systems.

  VARIABLE   This keyword must be followed by a single tab or space character, after which encoding specific data is placed. Currently only the EUC encoding requires variable data. See euc(4) for further details.

  INVALID   A single RUNE follows and is used as the invalid rune for this locale.

  The following keywords may appear multiple times and have the following format for data:

`<RUNE1 RUNE2>`	RUNE1 is mapped to RUNE2.
`<RUNE1 THRU RUNEn: RUNE2>`	Runes RUNE1 through RUNEn are mapped to RUNE2 through RUNE2 + n-1.

MAPLOWER   Defines the tolower mappings. RUNE2 is the lower case representation of RUNE1.

MAPUPPER   Defines the toupper mappings. RUNE2 is the upper case representation of RUNE1.

TODIGIT   Defines a map from runes to their digit value. RUNE2 is the integer value represented by RUNE1. For example, the ascii character ' 0 ' would map to the decimal value 0. Only values up to 255 are allowed.

The following keywords may appear multiple times and have the following format for data:

RUNE	This rune has the property defined by the keyword.
RUNE1 THRU RUNEn	All the runes between and including RUNE1 and RUNEn have the property defined by the keyword.

ALPHA   Defines runes which are alphabetic, printable and graphic.

CONTROL   Defines runes which are control characters.

DIGIT   Defines runes which are decimal digits, printable and graphic.

GRAPH   Defines runes which are graphic and printable.

LOWER   Defines runes which are lower case, printable and graphic.

PUNCT   Defines runes which are punctuation, printable and graphic.

SPACE   Defines runes which are spaces.

UPPER   Defines runes which are upper case, printable and graphic.

XDIGIT   Defines runes which are hexadecimal digits, printable and graphic.

BLANK   Defines runes which are blank.

PRINT   Defines runes which are printable.

IDEOGRAM   Defines runes which are ideograms, printable and graphic.

SPECIAL   Defines runes which are special characters, printable and graphic.

PHONOGRAM   Defines runes which are phonograms, printable and graphic.

SEE ALSO
     mbrune(3), rune(3), setlocale(3), euc(4), utf2(4)

BUGS
     The **mklocale** utility is overly simplistic.

HISTORY
     The **mklocale** utility first appeared in 4.4BSD.

1

NAME
mkstr – create an error message file by massaging C source

SYNOPSIS
mkstr [–] *messagefile prefix file* ...

DESCRIPTION
Mkstr creates files containing error messages extracted from C source, and restructures the same C source, to utilize the created error message file. The intent of **mkstr** was to reduce the size of large programs and reduce swapping (see BUGS section below).

Mkstr processes each of the specified *files*, placing a restructured version of the input in a file whose name consists of the specified *prefix* and the original name. A typical usage of **mkstr** is

        mkstr pistrings xx *.c

This command causes all the error messages from the C source files in the current directory to be placed in the file *pistrings* and restructured copies of the sources to be placed in files whose names are prefixed with *xx*.

Options:

–   Error messages are placed at the end of the specified message file for recompiling part of a large **mkstr** ed program.

mkstr finds error messages in the source by searching for the string ′error("′ in the input stream. Each time it occurs, the C string starting at the l" .   if "Sq"Op" .ds A1 " is stored in the message file followed by a null character and a new-line character; The new source is restructured with ′′ pointers into the error message file for retrieval.

```
char efilname = "/usr/lib/pi_strings";
int efil = -1;

error(a1, a2, a3, a4)
{
        char buf[256];

        if (efil < 0) {
                efil = open(efilname, 0);
                if (efil < 0) {
oops:
                        perror(efilname);
                        exit 1 ;
                }
        }
        if (lseek(efil, (long) a1, 0)  read(efil, buf, 256) <= 0)
                goto oops;
        printf(buf, a2, a3, a4);
}
```

SEE ALSO
lseek(2), xstr(1)

HISTORY

   Mkstr appeared in 3.0BSD.

BUGS

   mkstr was intended for the limited architecture of the PDP 11 family. Very few programs actually use it.
   The pascal interpreter, pi(1) and the editor, ex(1) are two programs that are built this way. It is not an
   efficient method, the error messages should be stored in the program text.

NAME

more – file perusal filter for crt viewing

SYNOPSIS

more [−ceinus] [−t *tag*] [−x *tabs*] [−/ *pattern*] [−#] [*file ...*]

DESCRIPTION

More is a filter for paging through text one screenful at a time. It uses termcap(3) so it can run on a variety of terminals. There is even limited support for hardcopy terminals. (On a hardcopy terminal, lines which should be printed at the top of the screen are prefixed with an up-arrow.) *File* may be a single dash ("-"), implying stdin.

OPTIONS

Command line options are described below. Options are also taken from the environment variable MORE (make sure to precede them with a dash ("-")) but command line options will override them.

−c   Normally, **more** will repaint the screen by scrolling from the bottom of the screen. If the −c option is set, when **more** needs to change the entire display, it will paint from the top line down.

−e   Normally, if displaying a single file, **more** exits as soon as it reaches end-of-file. The −e option tells more to exit if it reaches end-of-file twice without an intervening operation. If the file is shorter than a single screen **more** will exit at end-of-file regardless.

−i   The −i option causes searches to ignore case; that is, uppercase and lowercase are considered identical.

−n   The −n flag suppresses line numbers. The default (to use line numbers) may cause **more** to run more slowly in some cases, especially with a very large input file. Suppressing line numbers with the −n flag will avoid this problem. Using line numbers means: the line number will be displayed in the = command, and the **v** command will pass the current line number to the editor.

−s   The −s option causes consecutive blank lines to be squeezed into a single blank line.

−t   The −t option, followed immediately by a tag, will edit the file containing that tag. For more information, see the ctags(1) command.

−u   By default, **more** treats backspaces and CR-LF sequences specially. Backspaces which appear adjacent to an underscore character are displayed as underlined text. Backspaces which appear between two identical characters are displayed as emboldened text. CR-LF sequences are compressed to a single linefeed character. The −u option causes backspaces to always be displayed as control characters, i.e. as the two character sequence "^H", and CR-LF to be left alone.

−x   The −x option sets tab stops every *N* positions. The default for *N* is 8.

−/   The −/ option specifies a string that will be searched for before each file is displayed.

COMMANDS

Interactive commands for **more** are based on vi(1). Some commands may be preceded by a decimal number, called N in the descriptions below. In the following descriptions, ^X means control-X.

h   Help: display a summary of these commands. If you forget all the other commands, remember this one.

1

SPACE or **f** or **^F**
> Scroll forward N lines, default one window. If N is more than the screen size, only the final screenful is displayed.

b or **^B**   Scroll backward N lines, default one window (see option -z below). If N is more than the screen size, only the final screenful is displayed.

j or **RETURN**
> Scroll forward N lines, default 1. The entire N lines are displayed, even if N is more than the screen size.

k   Scroll backward N lines, default 1. The entire N lines are displayed, even if N is more than the screen size.

d or **^D**   Scroll forward N lines, default one half of the screen size. If N is specified, it becomes the new default for subsequent d and u commands.

u or **^U**   Scroll backward N lines, default one half of the screen size. If N is specified, it becomes the new default for subsequent d and u commands.

g   Go to line N in the file, default 1 (beginning of file).

G   Go to line N in the file, default the end of the file.

p or **%**   Go to a position N percent into the file. N should be between 0 and 100. (This works if standard input is being read, but only if **more** has already read to the end of the file. It is always fast, but not always useful.)

r or **^L**   Repaint the screen.

R   Repaint the screen, discarding any buffered input. Useful if the file is changing while it is being viewed.

m   Followed by any lowercase letter, marks the current position with that letter.

'   (Single quote.) Followed by any lowercase letter, returns to the position which was previously marked with that letter. Followed by another single quote, returns to the position at which the last "large" movement command was executed, or the beginning of the file if no such movements have occurred. All marks are lost when a new file is examined.

/pattern Search forward in the file for the N-th line containing the pattern. N defaults to 1. The pattern is a regular expression, as recognized by ed. The search starts at the second line displayed.

?pattern Search backward in the file for the N-th line containing the pattern. The search starts at the line immediately before the top line displayed.

/!pattern
> Like /, but the search is for the N-th line which does NOT contain the pattern.

?!pattern
> Like ?, but the search is for the N-th line which does NOT contain the pattern.

n   Repeat previous search, for N-th line containing the last pattern (or NOT containing the last pattern, if the previous search was /! or ?!).

E[*filename*]
> Examine a new file. If the filename is missing, the "current" file (see the N and P commands below) from the list of files in the command line is re-examined. If the filename is a pound sign (#), the previously examined file is re-examined.

N or :n
> Examine the next file (from the list of files given in the command line). If a number N is specified (not to be confused with the command N), the N-th next file is examined.

P or :p
> Examine the previous file. If a number N is specified, the N-th previous file is examined.

:t
> Go to supplied tag.

v
> Invokes an editor to edit the current file being viewed. The editor is taken from the environment variable EDITOR, or defaults to vi(1).

= or ^G
> These options print out the number of the file currently being displayed relative to the total number of files there are to display, the current line number, the current byte number and the total bytes to display, and what percentage of the file has been displayed. If more is reading from stdin, or the file is shorter than a single screen, some of these items may not be available. Note, all of these items reference the first byte of the last line displayed on the screen.

q or :q or ZZ
> Exits more.

ENVIRONMENT

More utilizes the following environment variables, if they exist:

MORE
> This variable may be set with favored options to more.

EDITOR
> Specify default editor.

SHELL
> Current shell in use (normally set by the shell at login time).

TERM
> Specifies terminal type, used by more to get the terminal characteristics necessary to manipulate the screen.

SEE ALSO
ctags(1), vi(1)

AUTHOR
This software is derived from software contributed to Berkeley by Mark Nudleman.

HISTORY
The more command appeared in 3.0BSD.

1

NAME

mset – retrieve ASCII to IBM 3270 keyboard map

SYNOPSIS

mset [**−picky**] [**−shell**] [*keyboardname*]

DESCRIPTION

Mset retrieves mapping information for the ASCII keyboard to IBM 3270 terminal special functions. Normally, these mappings are found in /usr/share/misc/map3270 (see map3270(5)). This information is used by the tn3270 command (see tn3270(1)).

The default **mset** output can be used to store the mapping information in the process environment in order to avoid scanning **map3270** each time **tn3270** is invoked. To do this, place the following command in your .login file:

        set noglob; setenv MAP3270 "`mset`"; unset noglob

If the *keyboardname* argument is not supplied, **mset** attempts to determine the name of the keyboard the user is using, by checking the KEYBD environment variable. If the KEYBD environment variable is not set, then **mset** uses the user's terminal type from the environment variable TERM as the keyboard name. Normally, **mset** then uses the file map3270(5) to find the keyboard mapping for that terminal. However, if the environment variable MAP3270 exists and contains the entry for the specified keyboard, then that definition is used. If the value of MAP3270 begins with a slash ('/') then it is assumed to be the full pathname of an alternate mapping file and that file is searched first. In any case, if the mapping for the keyboard is not found in the environment, nor in an alternate map file, nor in the standard map file, then the same search is performed for an entry for a keyboard with the name *unknown*. If that search also fails, then a default mapping is used.

The arguments to **mset** are:

−picky   When processing the various map3270 entries (for the user's keyboard, and all those encountered before the one for the user's keyboard), **mset** normally will not complain about entries for unknown functions (like ''PFX1''; the **−picky** argument causes **mset** to issue warning messages about these unknown entries.

−shell   If the map3270 entry is longer than the shell's 1024 environmental variable length limit, the default **mset** output cannot be used to store the mapping information in the process environment to avoid scanning map3270 each time **tn3270** is invoked. The **−shell** argument causes **mset** to generate shell commands to set the environmental variables MAP3270, MAP3270A, and so on, breaking up the entry to fit within the shell environmental variable length limit. To set these variables, place the following command in your .login file:

        mset -shell > tmp ; source tmp ; /bin/rm tmp

keyboardname
               When searching for the map3270 entry that matches the user's keyboard, **mset** will use *keyboardname* instead of determining the keyboard name from the KEYBD or TERM environmental variables.

FILES

/usr/share/misc/map3270 keyboard mapping for known keyboards

SEE ALSO

    tn3270(1), map3270(5)

HISTORY

    The **mset** command appeared in 4.3BSD.

1

NAME

msgs – system messages and junk mail program

SYNOPSIS

msgs [–fhlpq] [*number*] [–*number*]

msgs [–s]

msgs [–c] [–days]

DESCRIPTION

Msgs is used to read system messages. These messages are sent by mailing to the login 'msgs' and should be short pieces of information which are suitable to be read once by most users of the system.

Msgs is normally invoked each time you login, by placing it in the file .login (or .profile if you use sh(1)). It will then prompt you with the source and subject of each new message. If there is no subject line, the first few non-blank lines of the message will be displayed. If there is more to the message, you will be told how long it is and asked whether you wish to see the rest of the message. The possible responses are:

–y   Type the rest of the message.

RETURN   Synonym for y.

–n   Skip this message and go on to the next message.

–   Redisplay the last message.

–q   Drop out of msgs; the next time msgs will pick up where it last left off.

–s   Append the current message to the file ''Messages'' in the current directory; 's–' will save the previously displayed message. A 's' or 's–' may be followed by a space and a file name to receive the message replacing the default ''Messages''.

–m   A copy of the specified message is placed in a temporary mailbox and mail(1) is invoked on that mailbox. Both 'm' and 's' accept a numeric argument in place of the '–'.

Msgs keeps track of the next message you will see by a number in the file .msgsrc in your home directory. In the directory /var/msgs it keeps a set of files whose names are the (sequential) numbers of the messages they represent. The file /var/msgs/bounds shows the low and high number of the messages in the directory so that msgs can quickly determine if there are no messages for you. If the contents of bounds is incorrect it can be fixed by removing it; msgs will make a new bounds file the next time it is run.

The –s option is used for setting up the posting of messages. The line

        msgs: "| /usr/ucb/msgs –s"

should be included in /etc/aliases (see newaliases(1)) to enable posting of messages.

The –c option is used for performing cleanup on /var/msgs. An entry with the –c option should be placed in /etc/crontab to run every night. This will remove all messages over 21 days old. A different expiration may be specified on the command line to override the default.

Options when reading messages include:

–f   Do not to say ''No new messages.''. This is useful in a .login file since this is often the case here.

1

−q   Queries whether there are messages, printing ''There are new messages.'' if there are. The command ''msgs −q'' is often used in login scripts.

−h   Print the first part of messages only.

−l   Option causes only locally originated messages to be reported.

num   A message number can be given on the command line, causing **msgs** to start at the specified message rather than at the next message indicated by your .msgsrc file. Thus

               msgs −h 1

prints the first part of all messages.

−*number*   Start *number* messages back from the one indicated in the .msgsrc file, useful for reviews of recent messages.

−p   Pipe long messages through more(1).

Within **msgs** you can also go to any specific message by typing its number when **msgs** requests input as to what to do.

ENVIRONMENT

Msgs uses the HOME and TERM environment variables for the default home directory and terminal type.

FILES

/usr/msgs/* database
~/.msgsrc   number of next message to be presented

SEE ALSO

aliases(5), mail(1), more(1)

HISTORY

The **msgs** command appeared in 3.0BSD.

1

NAME

mt – magnetic tape manipulating program

SYNOPSIS

mt [−f *tapename*] *command* [*count*]

DESCRIPTION

Mt is used to give commands to a magnetic tape drive. By default mt performs the requested operation once. Operations may be performed multiple times by specifying *count*. Note that *tapename* must reference a raw (not block) tape device.

The available commands are listed below. Only as many characters as are required to uniquely identify a command need be specified.

eof, weof   Write *count* end-of-file marks at the current position on the tape.

fsf   Forward space *count* files.

fsr   Forward space *count* records.

bsf   Back space *count* files.

bsr   Back space *count* records.

rewind   Rewind the tape (Count is ignored).

offline, rewoffl
            Rewind the tape and place the tape unit off-line (Count is ignored).

status   Print status information about the tape unit.

If a tape name is not specified, and the environment variable TAPE does not exist; mt uses the device /dev/rmt12.

Mt returns a 0 exit status when the operation(s) were successful, 1 if the command was unrecognized, and 2 if an operation failed.

ENVIRONMENT

If the following environment variable exists, it is utilized by mt.

TAPE   Mt checks the TAPE environment variable if the argument *tapename* is not given.

FILES

/dev/rmt* Raw magnetic tape interface

SEE ALSO

dd(1), ioctl(2), environ(7)

HISTORY

The mt command appeared in 4.3BSD.

NAME

mv – move files

SYNOPSIS

mv [**−f** | **−i**] *source target*
mv [**−f** | **−i**] *source ... source directory*

DESCRIPTION

In its first form, the **mv** utility renames the file named by the *source* operand to the destination path named by the *target* operand. This form is assumed when the last operand does not name an already existing directory.

In its second form, **mv** moves each file named by a *source* operand to a destination file in the existing directory named by the *directory* operand. The destination path for each operand is the pathname produced by the concatenation of the last operand, a slash, and the final pathname component of the named file.

The following options are available:

−f   Do not prompt for confirmation before overwriting the destination path. (The **−i** option is ignored if the **−f** option is specified.)

−i   Causes **mv** to write a prompt to standard error before moving a file that would overwrite an existing file. If the response from the standard input begins with the character ''y'', the move is attempted.

It is an error for either the *source* operand or the destination path to specify a directory unless both do.

If the destination path does not have a mode which permits writing, **mv** prompts the user for confirmation as specified for the **−i** option.

As the rename(2) call does not work across file systems, **mv** uses cp(1) and rm(1) to accomplish the move. The effect is equivalent to:

```
rm -f destination_path && \
cp -pr source_file destination && \
rm -rf source_file
```

The **mv** utility exits 0 on success, and >0 if an error occurs.

SEE ALSO

cp(1), symlink(7)

STANDARDS

The **mv** utility is expected to be IEEE Std1003.2 (''POSIX'') compatible.

NAME

netstat – show network status

SYNOPSIS

netstat [–Aan] [–f *address_family*] [–M *core*] [–N *system*]
netstat [–dghimnrs] [–f *address_family*] [–M *core*] [–N *system*]
netstat [–dn] [–I *interface*] [–M *core*] [–N *system*] [–w *wait*]
netstat [–p *protocol*] [–M *core*] [–N *system*]

DESCRIPTION

The **netstat** command symbolically displays the contents of various network-related data structures. There are a number of output formats, depending on the options for the information presented. The first form of the command displays a list of active sockets for each protocol. The second form presents the contents of one of the other network data structures according to the option selected. Using the third form, with a *wait* interval specified, **netstat** will continuously display the information regarding packet traffic on the configured network interfaces. The fourth form displays statistics about the named protocol.

The options have the following meaning:

–A   With the default display, show the address of any protocol control blocks associated with sockets; used for debugging.

–a   With the default display, show the state of all sockets; normally sockets used by server processes are not shown.

–d   With either interface display (option –i or an interval, as described below), show the number of dropped packets.

–f *address_family*
     Limit statistics or address control block reports to those of the specified *address family*. The following address families are recognized: *inet*, for AF_INET, *ns*, for AF_NS, *iso*, for AF_ISO, and *unix*, for AF_UNIX.

–g   Show information related to multicast (group address) routing. By default, show the IP Multicast virtual-interface and routing tables. If the –s option is also present, show multicast routing statistics.

–h   Show the state of the IMP host table (obsolete).

–I *interface*
     Show information about the specified interface; used with a *wait* interval as described below.

–i   Show the state of interfaces which have been auto-configured (interfaces statically configured into a system, but not located at boot time are not shown). If the –a options is also present, multicast addresses currently in use are shown for each Ethernet interface and for each IP interface address. Multicast addresses are shown on separate lines following the interface address with which they are associated.

–M   Extract values associated with the name list from the specified core instead of the default /dev/kmem.

–m   Show statistics recorded by the memory management routines (the network manages a private pool of memory buffers).

–N   Extract the name list from the specified system instead of the default /vmunix.

1

    −n   Show network addresses as numbers (normally **netstat** interprets addresses and attempts to display them symbolically). This option may be used with any of the display formats.

−p *protocol*
    Show statistics about *protocol*, which is either a well-known name for a protocol or an alias for it. Some protocol names and aliases are listed in the file /etc/protocols. A null response typically means that there are no interesting numbers to report. The program will complain if *protocol* is unknown or if there is no statistics routine for it.

    −s   Show per-protocol statistics. If this option is repeated, counters with a value of zero are suppressed.

    −r   Show the routing tables. When −s is also present, show routing statistics instead.

−w *wait*
    Show network interface statistics at intervals of *wait* seconds.

The default display, for active sockets, shows the local and remote addresses, send and receive queue sizes (in bytes), protocol, and the internal state of the protocol. Address formats are of the form "host.port" or "network.port" if a socket's address specifies a network but no specific host address. When known the host and network addresses are displayed symbolically according to the data bases /etc/hosts and /etc/networks, respectively. If a symbolic name for an address is unknown, or if the −n option is specified, the address is printed numerically, according to the address family. For more information regarding the Internet "dot format," refer to inet(3)). Unspecified, or "wildcard", addresses and ports appear as "*".

The interface display provides a table of cumulative statistics regarding packets transferred, errors, and collisions. The network addresses of the interface and the maximum transmission unit ("mtu") are also displayed.

The routing table display indicates the available routes and their status. Each route consists of a destination host or network and a gateway to use in forwarding packets. The flags field shows a collection of information about the route stored as binary choices. The individual flags are discussed in more detail in the route(8) and route(4) manual pages. The mapping between letters and flags is:

1	RTF_PROTO2	Protocol specific routing flag #1
2	RTF_PROTO1	Protocol specific routing flag #2
B	RTF_BLACKHOLE	Just discard pkts (during updates)
C	RTF_CLONING	Generate new routes on use
D	RTF_DYNAMIC	Created dynamically (by redirect)
G	RTF_GATEWAY	Destination requires forwarding by intermediary
H	RTF_HOST	Host entry (net otherwise)
L	RTF_LLINFO	Valid protocol to link address translation.
M	RTF_MODIFIED	Modified dynamically (by redirect)
R	RTF_REJECT	Host or net unreachable
S	RTF_STATIC	Manually added
U	RTF_UP	Route usable
X	RTF_XRESOLVE	External daemon translates proto to link address

Direct routes are created for each interface attached to the local host; the gateway field for such entries shows the address of the outgoing interface. The refcnt field gives the current number of active uses of the route. Connection oriented protocols normally hold on to a single route for the duration of a connection while connectionless protocols obtain a route while sending to the same destination. The use field provides a count of the number of packets sent using that route. The interface entry indicates the network interface utilized for the route.

When **netstat** is invoked with the −w option and a *wait* interval argument, it displays a running count of statistics related to network interfaces. An obsolescent version of this option used a numeric parameter with no option, and is currently supported for backward compatibility. This display consists of a column for the primary interface (the first interface found during autoconfiguration) and a column summarizing information for all interfaces. The primary interface may be replaced with another interface with the −I option. The first line of each screen of information contains a summary since the system was last rebooted. Subsequent lines of output show values accumulated over the preceding interval.

SEE ALSO

iostat(1), nfsstat(1), ps(1), vmstat(1), hosts(5), networks(5), protocols(5), services(5), trpt(8), trsp(8)

HISTORY

The **netstat** command appeared in 4.2BSD.

BUGS

The notion of errors is ill-defined.

NAME

    `newaliases` – rebuild the data base for the mail aliases file

SYNOPSIS

    `newaliases`

DESCRIPTION

    `Newaliases` rebuilds the random access data base for the mail aliases file `/etc/aliases`. It must be run each time this file is changed in order for the change to take effect.

    `Newaliases` is identical to ''`sendmail -bi`''.

    The `newaliases` utility exits 0 on success, and >0 if an error occurs.

FILES

    `/etc/aliases` The mail aliases file

SEE ALSO

    aliases(5), sendmail(8)

HISTORY

    The `newaliases` command appeared in 4.0BSD.

NAME

nfsstat – display NFS statistics

SYNOPSIS

nfsstat [−**M** *core*] [−**N** *system*] [−**w** *wait*]

DESCRIPTION

Nfsstat displays statistics kept about NFS client and server activity.

The options are as follows:

−**M**   Extract values associated with the name list from the specified core instead of the default /dev/kmem.

−**N**   Extract the name list from the specified system instead of the default /vmunix.

−**w**   Display a shorter summary of NFS activity for both the client and server at *wait* second intervals.

FILES

/vmunix   default kernel namelist
/dev/kmem default memory file

SEE ALSO

fstat(1), netstat(1), ps(1), systat(1), vmstat(1), iostat(8), pstat(8),

HISTORY

The **nfsstat** command appears in 4.4BSD.

1

NAME

nice – execute a command at a low scheduling priority

SYNOPSIS

nice [*–number*] *command* [*arguments*]

DESCRIPTION

Nice runs *command* at a low priority. (Think of low and slow). If *–number* is specified, and if it is greater than or equal to 10 (the default), **nice** will execute *command* at that priority. The upper bound, or lowest priority that **nice** will run a command is 20. The lower bounds or higher priorities (integers less than 10) can only be requested by the super-user. Negative numbers are expressed as *–– number*.

The returned exit status is the exit value from the command executed by **nice**.

SEE ALSO

csh(1), renice(8)

HISTORY

A **nice** command appeared in Version 6 AT&T UNIX.

BUGS

Nice is particular to sh(1). If you use csh(1), then commands executed with "&" are automatically immune to hangup signals while in the background.

Nice is built into csh(1) with a slightly different syntax than described here. The form nice +10 nices to positive nice, and nice −10 can be used by the super-user to give a process more of the processor.

1

NAME

nm – display name list (symbol table)

SYNOPSIS

nm [–agnopruw] *file* ...

DESCRIPTION

The symbol table (name list) of each object in *file(s)* is displayed. If a library (archive) is given, **nm** displays a list for each object archive member. If *file* is not present, **nm** searches for the file a.out and if present, displays the symbol table for a.out.

–a   Display symbol table entries inserted for use by debuggers.

–g   Restrict display to external (global) symbols.

–n   Present results in numerical order.

–o   Display full path or library name of object on every line.

–p   Do not sort at all.

–r   Reverse order sort.

–u   Display undefined symbols only.

–w   Warn about non-object archive members. Normally, nm will silently ignore all archive members which are not object files.

Each symbol name is preceded by its value (a blank field if the symbol is undefined) and one of the following letters:

–	debugger symbol table entries (see the –a option).
A	absolute
B	bss segment symbol
C	common symbol
D	data segment symbol
f	file name
T	text segment symbol
U	undefined

If the symbol is local (non-external) the type letter is in lower case. The output is sorted alphabetically.

SEE ALSO

ar(1), ar(5), a.out(5), stab(5)

HISTORY

An **nm** command appeared in Version 6 AT&T UNIX.

1

NAME

nohup – invoke a command immune to hangups

SYNOPSIS

nohup *command* [arg ...]

DESCRIPTION

The **nohup** utility invokes *command* with its arguments and at this time sets the signal SIGHUP to be ignored. The signal SIGQUIT may also be set to be ignored. If the standard output is a terminal, the standard output is appended to the file nohup.out in the current directory. If standard error is a terminal, it is directed to the same place as the standard output.

Nohup exits 1 if an error occurs, otherwise the exit status is that of *command*.

ENVIRONMENT

The following variable is utilized by **nohup**.

HOME   If the output file nohup.out cannot be created in the current directory, the **nohup** utility uses the directory named by HOME to create the file.

SEE ALSO

signal(3)

STANDARDS

The **nohup** command is expected to be IEEE Std1003.2 (''POSIX'') compatible.

1

NAME

nroff – emulate nroff command with groff

SYNOPSIS

nroff [**–hi**] [**–m***name*] [**–n***num*] [**–o***list*] [**–r***cn*] [**–T***name*] [*file . . .*]

DESCRIPTION

The **nroff** script emulates the **nroff** command using groff. The **–T** option with an argument other than **ascii** and **latin1** will be ignored. The **–h** option is equivalent to the **grotty –h** option. Other options are as described in **troff**(1). In addition the **–e**, **–q** and **–s** options are silently ignored.

SEE ALSO

groff(1), **troff**(1), **grotty**(1)

1

NAME
od – octal, decimal, hex, ascii dump

SYNOPSIS
od [**−aBbcDdeFfHhIiLlOovXx**] [[+]offset[**.**][**Bb**]] *file*

DESCRIPTION
Od has been deprecated in favor of hexdump(1).

Hexdump, if called as **od**, provides compatibility for the options listed above.

It does not provide compatibility for the **−s** option (see strings(1)) or the **−P**, **−p**, or **−w** options, nor is compatibility provided for the ''label'' component of the offset syntax.

SEE ALSO
hexdump(1), strings(1)

BUGS
Quite a few.

1

NAME
pagesize – print system page size

SYNOPSIS
pagesize

DESCRIPTION
Pagesize prints the size of a page of memory in bytes, as returned by getpagesize(2). This program is useful in constructing portable shell scripts.

SEE ALSO
getpagesize(2)

HISTORY
The pagesize command appeared in 4.2BSD.

NAME

    passwd – modify a user's password

SYNOPSIS

    passwd [**–l**] [*user*]

DESCRIPTION

    Passwd changes the user's Kerberos password. First, the user is prompted for their current password. If the current password is correctly typed, a new password is requested. The new password must be entered twice to avoid typing errors.

    The new password should be at least six characters long and not purely alphabetic. Its total length must be less than _PASSWORD_LEN (currently 128 characters). Numbers, upper case letters and meta characters are encouraged.

    Once the password has been verified, **passwd** communicates the new password information to the Kerberos authenticating host.

    –l   This option causes the password to be updated only in the local password file, and not with the Kerberos database. When changing only the local password, pwd_mkdb(8) is used to update the password databases.

    To change another user's Kerberos password, one must first run kinit(1) followed by passwd(1). The super-user is not required to provide a user's current password if only the local password is modified.

FILES

    /etc/master.passwd The user database
    /etc/passwd   A Version 7 format password file
    /etc/passwd.XXXXXX Temporary copy of the password file

SEE ALSO

    chpass(1), kerberos(1), kinit(1), login(1), passwd(5), kpasswdd(8), pwd_mkdb(8), vipw(8)

    Robert Morris, and Ken Thompson, *UNIX password security.*

HISTORY

    A **passwd** command appeared in Version 6 AT&T UNIX.

1

NAME
   paste – merge corresponding or subsequent lines of files

SYNOPSIS
   paste [–s] [–d *list*] *file* ...

DESCRIPTION
   The **paste** utility concatenates the corresponding lines of the given input files, replacing all but the last file's newline characters with a single tab character, and writes the resulting lines to standard output. If end-of-file is reached on an input file while other input files still contain data, the file is treated as if it were an endless source of empty lines.

   The options are as follows:

   –d *list*   Use one or more of the provided characters to replace the newline characters instead of the default tab. The characters in *list* are used circularly, i.e., when *list* is exhausted the first character from *list* is reused. This continues until a line from the last input file (in default operation) or the last line in each file (using the -s option) is displayed, at which time **paste** begins selecting characters from the beginning of *list* again.

   The following special characters can also be used in list:

   \n   newline character
   \t   tab character
   \\   backslash character
   \0   Empty string (not a null character).

   Any other character preceded by a backslash is equivalent to the character itself.

   –s   Concatenate all of the lines of each separate input file in command line order. The newline character of every line except the last line in each input file is replaced with the tab character, unless otherwise specified by the -d option.

   If ' – ' is specified for one or more of the input files, the standard input is used; standard input is read one line at a time, circularly, for each instance of ' – '.

   The **paste** utility exits 0 on success, and >0 if an error occurs.

SEE ALSO
   cut(1)

STANDARDS
   The **paste** utility is expected to be IEEE Std1003.2 (''POSIX'') compatible.

NAME

patch – a program for applying a diff file to an original

SYNOPSIS

patch [options] orig patchfile [+ [options] orig]

but usually just

patch <patchfile

DESCRIPTION

Patch will take a patch file containing any of the three forms of difference listing produced by the *diff* program and apply those differences to an original file, producing a patched version. By default, the patched version is put in place of the original, with the original file backed up to the same name with the extension ".orig", or as specified by the **-b** switch. You may also specify where you want the output to go with a **-o** switch. If *patchfile* is omitted, or is a hyphen, the patch will be read from standard input.

Upon startup, patch will attempt to determine the type of the diff listing, unless over-ruled by a **-c**, **-e**, or **-n** switch. Context diffs and normal diffs are applied by the *patch* program itself, while ed diffs are simply fed to the *ed* editor via a pipe.

Patch will try to skip any leading garbage, apply the diff, and then skip any trailing garbage. Thus you could feed an article or message containing a diff listing to *patch*, and it should work. If the entire diff is indented by a consistent amount, this will be taken into account.

With context diffs, and to a lesser extent with normal diffs, *patch* can detect when the line numbers mentioned in the patch are incorrect, and will attempt to find the correct place to apply each hunk of the patch. As a first guess, it takes the line number mentioned for the hunk, plus or minus any offset used in applying the previous hunk. If that is not the correct place, *patch* will scan both forwards and backwards for a set of lines matching the context given in the hunk. First *patch* looks for a place where all lines of the context match. If no such place is found, and it's a context diff, and the maximum fuzz factor is set to 1 or more, then another scan takes place ignoring the first and last line of context. If that fails, and the maximum fuzz factor is set to 2 or more, the first two and last two lines of context are ignored, and another scan is made. (The default maximum fuzz factor is 2.) If *patch* cannot find a place to install that hunk of the patch, it will put the hunk out to a reject file, which normally is the name of the output file plus ".rej". (Note that the rejected hunk will come out in context diff form whether the input patch was a context diff or a normal diff. If the input was a normal diff, many of the contexts will simply be null.) The line numbers on the hunks in the reject file may be different than in the patch file: they reflect the approximate location patch thinks the failed hunks belong in the new file rather than the old one.

As each hunk is completed, you will be told whether the hunk succeeded or failed, and which line (in the new file) *patch* thought the hunk should go on. If this is different from the line number specified in the diff you will be told the offset. A single large offset MAY be an indication that a hunk was installed in the wrong place. You will also be told if a fuzz factor was used to make the match, in which case you should also be slightly suspicious.

If no original file is specified on the command line, *patch* will try to figure out from the leading garbage what the name of the file to edit is. In the header of a context diff, the filename is found from lines beginning with "***" or "---", with the shortest name of an existing file winning. Only context diffs have lines like that, but if there is an "Index:" line in the leading garbage, *patch* will try to use the filename from that line. The context diff header takes precedence over an Index line. If no filename can be intuited from the leading garbage, you will be asked for the name of the file to patch.

(If the original file cannot be found, but a suitable SCCS or RCS file is handy, *patch* will attempt to get or check out the file.)

Additionally, if the leading garbage contains a "Prereq: " line, *patch* will take the first word from the prerequisites line (normally a version number) and check the input file to see if that word can be found. If not, *patch* will ask for confirmation before proceeding.

1

The upshot of all this is that you should be able to say, while in a news interface, the following:

    | patch -d /usr/src/local/blurfl

and patch a file in the blurfl directory directly from the article containing the patch.

If the patch file contains more than one patch, *patch* will try to apply each of them as if they came from separate patch files. This means, among other things, that it is assumed that the name of the file to patch must be determined for each diff listing, and that the garbage before each diff listing will be examined for interesting things such as filenames and revision level, as mentioned previously. You can give switches (and another original file name) for the second and subsequent patches by separating the corresponding argument lists by a '+'. (The argument list for a second or subsequent patch may not specify a new patch file, however.)

Patch recognizes the following switches:

−b   causes the next argument to be interpreted as the backup extension, to be used in place of ''.orig''.

−c   forces *patch* to interpret the patch file as a context diff.

−d   causes *patch* to interpret the next argument as a directory, and cd to it before doing anything else.

−D   causes *patch* to use the "#ifdef...#endif" construct to mark changes. The argument following will be used as the differentiating symbol. Note that, unlike the C compiler, there must be a space between the −D and the argument.

−e   forces *patch* to interpret the patch file as an ed script.

−f   forces *patch* to assume that the user knows exactly what he or she is doing, and to not ask any questions. It does not suppress commentary, however. Use **−s** for that.

−F<number>
    sets the maximum fuzz factor. This switch only applied to context diffs, and causes *patch* to ignore up to that many lines in looking for places to install a hunk. Note that a larger fuzz factor increases the odds of a faulty patch. The default fuzz factor is 2, and it may not be set to more than the number of lines of context in the context diff, ordinarily 3.

−l   causes the pattern matching to be done loosely, in case the tabs and spaces have been munged in your input file. Any sequence of whitespace in the pattern line will match any sequence in the input file. Normal characters must still match exactly. Each line of the context must still match a line in the input file.

−n   forces *patch* to interpret the patch file as a normal diff.

−N   causes *patch* to ignore patches that it thinks are reversed or already applied. See also **−R** .

−o   causes the next argument to be interpreted as the output file name.

−p<number>
    sets the pathname strip count, which controls how pathnames found in the patch file are treated, in case the you keep your files in a different directory than the person who sent out the patch. The strip count specifies how many backslashes are to be stripped from the front of the pathname. (Any intervening directory names also go away.) For example, supposing the filename in the patch file was

        /u/howard/src/blurfl/blurfl.c

setting **−p** or **−p0** gives the entire pathname unmodified, **−p1** gives

        u/howard/src/blurfl/blurfl.c

without the leading slash, **−p4** gives

        blurfl/blurfl.c

1

and not specifying −**p** at all just gives you "blurfl.c". Whatever you end up with is looked for either in the current directory, or the directory specified by the −**d** switch.

−**r**   causes the next argument to be interpreted as the reject file name.

−**R**   tells *patch* that this patch was created with the old and new files swapped. (Yes, I'm afraid that does happen occasionally, human nature being what it is.) *Patch* will attempt to swap each hunk around before applying it. Rejects will come out in the swapped format. The −**R** switch will not work with ed diff scripts because there is too little information to reconstruct the reverse operation.

If the first hunk of a patch fails, *patch* will reverse the hunk to see if it can be applied that way. If it can, you will be asked if you want to have the −**R** switch set. If it can't, the patch will continue to be applied normally. (Note: this method cannot detect a reversed patch if it is a normal diff and if the first command is an append (i.e. it should have been a delete) since appends always succeed, due to the fact that a null context will match anywhere. Luckily, most patches add or change lines rather than delete them, so most reversed normal diffs will begin with a delete, which will fail, triggering the heuristic.)

−**s**   makes *patch* do its work silently, unless an error occurs.

−**S**   causes *patch* to ignore this patch from the patch file, but continue on looking for the next patch in the file. Thus

        patch -S + -S + <patchfile

will ignore the first and second of three patches.

−**v**   causes *patch* to print out it's revision header and patch level.

−**x<number>**
        sets internal debugging flags, and is of interest only to *patch* patchers.

ENVIRONMENT
        No environment variables are used by *patch*.

FILES
        /tmp/patch*

SEE ALSO
        diff(1)

NOTES FOR PATCH SENDERS
        There are several things you should bear in mind if you are going to be sending out patches. First, you can save people a lot of grief by keeping a patchlevel.h file which is patched to increment the patch level as the first diff in the patch file you send out. If you put a Prereq: line in with the patch, it won't let them apply patches out of order without some warning. Second, make sure you've specified the filenames right, either in a context diff header, or with an Index: line. If you are patching something in a subdirectory, be sure to tell the patch user to specify a −**p** switch as needed. Third, you can create a file by sending out a diff that compares a null file to the file you want to create. This will only work if the file you want to create doesn't exist already in the target directory. Fourth, take care not to send out reversed patches, since it makes people wonder whether they already applied the patch. Fifth, while you may be able to get away with putting 582 diff listings into one file, it is probably wiser to group related patches into separate files in case something goes haywire.

DIAGNOSTICS
        Too many to list here, but generally indicative that *patch* couldn't parse your patch file.

        The message "Hmm..." indicates that there is unprocessed text in the patch file and that *patch* is attempting to intuit whether there is a patch in that text and, if so, what kind of patch it is.

CAVEATS

Patch cannot tell if the line numbers are off in an ed script, and can only detect bad line numbers in a normal diff when it finds a "change" or a "delete" command. A context diff using fuzz factor 3 may have the same problem. Until a suitable interactive interface is added, you should probably do a context diff in these cases to see if the changes made sense. Of course, compiling without errors is a pretty good indication that the patch worked, but not always.

Patch usually produces the correct results, even when it has to do a lot of guessing. However, the results are guaranteed to be correct only when the patch is applied to exactly the same version of the file that the patch was generated from.

BUGS

Could be smarter about partial matches, excessively deviant offsets and swapped code, but that would take an extra pass.

If code has been duplicated (for instance with #ifdef OLDCODE ... #else ... #endif), *patch* is incapable of patching both versions, and, if it works at all, will likely patch the wrong one, and tell you that it succeeded to boot.

If you apply a patch you've already applied, *patch* will think it is a reversed patch, and offer to un-apply the patch. This could be construed as a feature.

NAME

pax – read and write file archives and copy directory hierarchies

SYNOPSIS

pax [**-cdnv**] [**-f** *archive*] [**-s** *replstr*] ... [**-U** *user*] ... [**-G** *group*] ...
   [**-T** [*from_date*] [*,to_date*]] ... [*pattern* ...]

pax **-r** [**-cdiknuvDYZ**] [**-f** *archive*] [**-o** *options*] ... [**-p** *string*] ... [**-s** *replstr*]
   ... [**-E** *limit*] [**-U** *user*] ... [**-G** *group*] ... [**-T** [*from_date*] [*,to_date*]] ...
   [*pattern* ...]

pax **-w** [**-dituvHLPX**] [**-b** *blocksize*] [[**-a**] [**-f** *archive*]] [**-x** *format*] [**-s** *replstr*]
   ... [**-o** *options*] ... [**-U** *user*] ... [**-G** *group*] ... [**-B** *bytes*]
   [**-T** [*from_date*] [*,to_date*] [*/[c][m]*]] ... [*file* ...]

pax **-r** **-w** [**-diklntuvDHLPXYZ**] [**-p** *string*] ... [**-s** *replstr*] ... [**-U** *user*] ...
   [**-G** *group*] ... [**-T** [*from_date*] [*,to_date*] [*/[c][m]*]] ... [*file* ...]
   directory

DESCRIPTION

Pax will read, write, and list the members of an archive file, and will copy directory hierarchies. **Pax** operation is independent of the specific archive format, and supports a wide variety of different archive formats. A list of supported archive formats can be found under the description of the **-x** option.

The presence of the **-r** and the **-w** options specifies which of the following functional modes **pax** will operate under: *list*, *read*, *write*, and *copy*.

<none>
       List. **Pax** will write to standard output a table of contents of the members of the archive file read from standard input, whose pathnames match the specified *patterns*. The table of contents contains one filename per line and is written using single line buffering.

-r
       Read. **Pax** extracts the members of the archive file read from the standard input, with pathnames matching the specified *patterns*. The archive format and blocking is automatically determined on input. When an extracted file is a directory, the entire file hierarchy rooted at that directory is extracted. All extracted files are created relative to the current file hierarchy. The setting of ownership, access and modification times, and file mode of the extracted files are discussed in more detail under the **-p** option.

-w
       Write. **Pax** writes an archive containing the *file* operands to standard output using the specified archive format. When no *file* operands are specified, a list of files to copy with one per line is read from standard input. When a *file* operand is also a directory, the entire file hierarchy rooted at that directory will be included.

-r **-w**
       Copy. **Pax** copies the *file* operands to the destination *directory*. When no *file* operands are specified, a list of files to copy with one per line is read from the standard input. When a *file* operand is also a directory the entire file hierarchy rooted at that directory will be included. The effect of the *copy* is as if the copied files were written to an archive file and then subsequently extracted, except that there may be hard links between the original and the copied files (see the **-l** option below).

       Warning: The destination *directory* must not be one of the *file* operands or a member of a file hierarchy rooted at one of the *file* operands. The result of a *copy* under these conditions is unpredictable.

While processing a damaged archive during a *read* or *list* operation, **pax** will attempt to recover from media defects and will search through the archive to locate and process the largest number of archive members possible (see the −**E** option for more details on error handling).

OPERANDS

The *directory* operand specifies a destination directory pathname. If the *directory* operand does not exist, or it is not writable by the user, or it is not of type directory, **Pax** will exit with a non-zero exit status.

The *pattern* operand is used to select one or more pathnames of archive members. Archive members are selected using the pattern matching notation described by fnmatch(3). When the *pattern* operand is not supplied, all members of the archive will be selected. When a *pattern* matches a directory, the entire file hierarchy rooted at that directory will be selected. When a *pattern* operand does not select at least one archive member, **pax** will write these *pattern* operands in a diagnostic message to standard error and then exit with a non-zero exit status.

The *file* operand specifies the pathname of a file to be copied or archived. When a *file* operand does not select at least one archive member, **pax** will write these *file* operand pathnames in a diagnostic message to standard error and then exit with a non-zero exit status.

OPTIONS

The following options are supported:

−**r**   Read an archive file from standard input and extract the specified *files*. If any intermediate directories are needed in order to extract an archive member, these directories will be created as if mkdir(2) was called with the bitwise inclusive OR of S_IRWXU, S_IRWXG, and S_IRWXO as the mode argument. When the selected archive format supports the specification of linked files and these files cannot be linked while the archive is being extracted, **pax** will write a diagnostic message to standard error and exit with a non-zero exit status at the completion of operation.

−**w**   Write files to the standard output in the specified archive format. When no *file* operands are specified, standard input is read for a list of pathnames with one per line without any leading or trailing <blanks>.

−**a**   Append *files* to the end of an archive that was previously written. If an archive format is not specified with a −**x** option, the format currently being used in the archive will be selected. Any attempt to append to an archive in a format different from the format already used in the archive will cause **pax** to exit immediately with a non-zero exit status. The blocking size used in the archive volume where writing starts will continue to be used for the remainder of that archive volume.

Warning: Many storage devices are not able to support the operations necessary to perform an append operation. Any attempt to append to an archive stored on such a device may damage the archive or have other unpredictable results. Tape drives in particular are more likely to not support an append operation. An archive stored in a regular file system file or on a disk device will usually support an append operation.

−**b** *blocksize*
When *writing* an archive, block the output at a positive decimal integer number of bytes per write to the archive file. The *blocksize* must be a multiple of 512 bytes with a maximum of 32256 bytes. A *blocksize* can end with k or b to specify multiplication by 1024 (1K) or 512, respectively. A pair of *blocksizes* can be separated by x to indicate a product. A specific archive device may impose additional restrictions on the size of blocking it will support. When blocking is not specified, the default *blocksize* is dependent on the specific archive format being used (see the −**x** option).

-c   Match all file or archive members *except* those specified by the `pattern` and `file` operands.

-d   Cause files of type directory being copied or archived, or archive members of type directory being extracted, to match only the directory file or archive member and not the file hierarchy rooted at the directory.

-f `archive`
      Specify `archive` as the pathname of the input or output archive, overriding the default `standard input` (for *list* and *read*) or `standard output` (for *write*). A single archive may span multiple files and different archive devices. When required, **pax** will prompt for the pathname of the file or device of the next volume in the archive.

-i   Interactively rename files or archive members. For each archive member matching a `pattern` operand or each file matching a `file` operand, **pax** will prompt to /dev/tty giving the name of the file, its file mode and its modification time. **Pax** will then read a line from /dev/tty. If this line is blank, the file or archive member is skipped. If this line consists of a single period, the file or archive member is processed with no modification to its name. Otherwise, its name is replaced with the contents of the line. **Pax** will immediately exit with a non-zero exit status if <EOF> is encountered when reading a response or if /dev/tty cannot be opened for reading and writing.

-k   Do not overwrite existing files.

-l   Link files. (The letter ell). In the *copy* mode (−r −w), hard links are made between the source and destination file hierarchies whenever possible.

-n   Select the first archive member that matches each `pattern` operand. No more than one archive member is matched for each `pattern`. When members of type directory are matched, the file hierarchy rooted at that directory is also matched (unless −d is also specified).

-o `options`
      Information to modify the algorithm for extracting or writing archive files which is specific to the archive format specified by −x. In general, `options` take the form: **name=value**

-p `string`
      Specify one or more file characteristic options (privileges). The `string` option-argument is a string specifying file characteristics to be retained or discarded on extraction. The string consists of the specification characters **a**, **e**, **m**, **o**, and **p**. Multiple characteristics can be concatenated within the same string and multiple −p options can be specified. The meaning of the specification characters are as follows:

      a   Do not preserve file access times. By default, file access times are preserved whenever possible.

      e   'Preserve everything', the user ID, group ID, file mode bits, file access time, and file modification time. This is intended to be used by *root*, someone with all the appropriate privileges, in order to preserve all aspects of the files as they are recorded in the archive. The **e** flag is the sum of the **o** and **p** flags.

      m   Do not preserve file modification times. By default, file modification times are preserved whenever possible.

      o   Preserve the user ID and group ID.

      p   'Preserve' the file mode bits. This intended to be used by a *user* with regular privileges who wants to preserve all aspects of the file other than the ownership. The file times are preserved by default, but two other flags are offered to disable this and use the time of extraction instead.

      In the preceding list, 'preserve' indicates that an attribute stored in the archive is given to the extracted file, subject to the permissions of the invoking process. Otherwise the attribute of the extracted file is determined as part of the normal file creation action. If neither the **e** nor the **o** specification character is specified, or the user ID and group ID are not preserved for any reason, **pax** will not set the S_ISUID (*setuid*) and S_ISGID (*setgid*) bits of the file mode. If the preservation of any of these items fails for any reason, **pax** will write a diagnostic message to standard error. Failure to preserve these items will affect the final exit status, but will not cause the extracted file to be deleted. If the file characteristic letters in any of the string option-arguments are duplicated or conflict with each other, the one(s) given last will take precedence. For example, if

   -p *eme*

is specified, file modification times are still preserved.

-s *replstr*

Modify the file or archive member names specified by the *pattern* or *file* operands according to the substitution expression *replstr*, using the syntax of the ed(1) utility regular expressions. The format of these regular expressions are:

   /*old*/*new*/[**gp**]

As in ed(1), **old** is a basic regular expression and **new** can contain an ampersand (&), \n (where n is a digit) back-references, or subexpression matching. The **old** string may also contain <newline> characters. Any non-null character can be used as a delimiter (/ is shown here). Multiple **-s** expressions can be specified. The expressions are applied in the order they are specified on the command line, terminating with the first successful substitution. The optional trailing **g** continues to apply the substitution expression to the pathname substring which starts with the first character following the end of the last successful substitution. The first unsuccessful substitution stops the operation of the **g** option. The optional trailing **p** will cause the final result of a successful substitution to be written to standard error in the following format:

   <original pathname> >> <new pathname>

File or archive member names that substitute to the empty string are not selected and will be skipped.

-t   Reset the access times of any file or directory read or accessed by **pax** to be the same as they were before being read or accessed by **pax**.

-u   Ignore files that are older (having a less recent file modification time) than a pre-existing file or archive member with the same name. During *read*, an archive member with the same name as a file in the file system will be extracted if the archive member is newer than the file. During *write*, a file system member with the same name as an archive member will be written to the archive if it is newer than the archive member. During *copy*, the file in the destination hierarchy is replaced by the file in the source hierarchy or by a link to the file in the source hierarchy if the file in the source hierarchy is newer.

-v   During a *list* operation, produce a verbose table of contents using the format of the ls(1) utility with the **-l** option. For pathnames representing a hard link to a previous member of the archive, the output has the format:

   <ls -l listing> == <link name>

For pathnames representing a symbolic link, the output has the format:

   <ls -l listing> => <link name>

Where <ls -l listing> is the output format specified by the ls(1) utility when used with the **-l** option. Otherwise for all the other operational modes (*read*, *write*, and *copy*), pathnames are written and flushed to standard error without a trailing <newline> as soon as processing begins on that file or archive member. The trailing <newline>, is not buffered, and is written only after the file has been read or written.

-x *format*

Specify the output archive format, with the default format being *ustar*. **Pax** currently supports the following formats:

1

cpio   The extended cpio interchange format specified in the IEEE Std1003.2 ("POSIX") stan-
          dard. The default blocksize for this format is 5120 bytes. Inode and device information
          about a file (used for detecting file hard links by this format) which may be truncated by
          this format is detected by **pax** and is repaired.

bcpio   The old binary cpio format. The default blocksize for this format is 5120 bytes. This for-
          mat is not very portable and should not be used when other formats are available. Inode
          and device information about a file (used for detecting file hard links by this format) which
          may be truncated by this format is detected by **pax** and is repaired.

sv4cpio   The System V release 4 cpio. The default blocksize for this format is 5120 bytes. Inode
          and device information about a file (used for detecting file hard links by this format) which
          may be truncated by this format is detected by **pax** and is repaired.

sv4crc   The System V release 4 cpio with file crc checksums. The default blocksize for this for-
          mat is 5120 bytes. Inode and device information about a file (used for detecting file hard
          links by this format) which may be truncated by this format is detected by **pax** and is
          repaired.

tar   The old BSD tar format as found in BSD4.3. The default blocksize for this format is
          10240 bytes. Pathnames stored by this format must be 100 characters or less in length.
          Only *regular* files, *hard links*, *soft links*, and *directories* will be archived (other file system
          types are not supported). For backwards compatibility with even older tar formats, a −o
          option can be used when writing an archive to omit the storage of directories. This option
          takes the form:
              −o write_opt=nodir

ustar   The extended tar interchange format specified in the IEEE Std1003.2 ("POSIX") standard.
          The default blocksize for this format is 10240 bytes. Pathnames stored by this format must
          be 250 characters or less in length.

Pax will detect and report any file that it is unable to store or extract as the result of any specific archive format restrictions. The individual archive formats may impose additional restrictions on use.
Typical archive format restrictions include (but are not limited to): file pathname length, file size, link
pathname length and the type of the file.

−B *bytes*
          Limit the number of bytes written to a single archive volume to *bytes*. The *bytes* limit can end
          with m, k, or b to specify multiplication by 1048576 (1M), 1024 (1K) or 512, respectively. A pair of
          bytes limits can be separated by x to indicate a product.

          Warning: Only use this option when writing an archive to a device which supports an end of file read
          condition based on last (or largest) write offset (such as a regular file or a tape drive). The use of this
          option with a floppy or hard disk is not recommended.

−D   This option is the same as the −u option, except that the file inode change time is checked instead of
          the file modification time. The file inode change time can be used to select files whose inode informa-
          tion (e.g. uid, gid, etc.) is newer than a copy of the file in the destination *directory*.

−E *limit*
          Limit the number of consecutive read faults while trying to read a flawed archives to *limit*. With a
          positive *limit*, **pax** will attempt to recover from an archive read error and will continue processing
          starting with the next file stored in the archive. A *limit* of 0 will cause **pax** to stop operation after
          the first read error is detected on an archive volume. A *limit* of NONE will cause **pax** to attempt to
          recover from read errors forever. The default *limit* is a small positive number of retries.

1

Warning: Using this option with NONE should be used with extreme caution as **pax** may get stuck in an infinite loop on a very badly flawed archive.

−G *group*

Select a file based on its *group* name, or when starting with a #, a numeric gid. A '\' can be used to escape the #. Multiple −G options may be supplied and checking stops with the first match.

−H   Follow only command line symbolic links while performing a physical file system traversal.

−L   Follow all symbolic links to perform a logical file system traversal.

−P   Do not follow symbolic links, perform a physical file system traversal. This is the default mode.

−T *[from_date][,to_date][/[c][m]]*

Allow files to be selected based on a file modification or inode change time falling within a specified time range of *from_date* to *to_date* (the dates are inclusive). If only a *from_date* is supplied, all files with a modification or inode change time equal to or younger are selected. If only a *to_date* is supplied, all files with a modification or inode change time equal to or older will be selected. When the *from_date* is equal to the *to_date*, only files with a modification or inode change time of exactly that time will be selected.

When **pax** is in the *write* or *copy* mode, the optional trailing field *[c][m]* can be used to determine which file time (inode change, file modification or both) are used in the comparison. If neither is specified, the default is to use file modification time only. The *m* specifies the comparison of file modification time (the time when the file was last written). The *c* specifies the comparison of inode change time (the time when the file inode was last changed; e.g. a change of owner, group, mode, etc). When *c* and *m* are both specified, then the modification and inode change times are both compared. The inode change time comparison is useful in selecting files whose attributes were recently changed or selecting files which were recently created and had their modification time reset to an older time (as what happens when a file is extracted from an archive and the modification time is preserved). Time comparisons using both file times is useful when **pax** is used to create a time based incremental archive (only files that were changed during a specified time range will be archived).

A time range is made up of six different fields and each field must contain two digits. The format is:

    [yy[mm[dd[hh]]]]mm[.ss]

Where **yy** is the last two digits of the year, the first **mm** is the month (from 01 to 12), **dd** is the day of the month (from 01 to 31), **hh** is the hour of the day (from 00 to 23), the second **mm** is the minute (from 00 to 59), and **ss** is the seconds (from 00 to 59). The minute field **mm** is required, while the other fields are optional and must be added in the following order:

    hh, dd, mm, yy.

The **ss** field may be added independently of the other fields. Time ranges are relative to the current time, so

    −T *1234/cm*

would select all files with a modification or inode change time of 12:34 PM today or later. Multiple −T time range can be supplied and checking stops with the first match.

−U *user*

Select a file based on its *user* name, or when starting with a #, a numeric uid. A '\' can be used to escape the #. Multiple −U options may be supplied and checking stops with the first match.

−X   When traversing the file hierarchy specified by a pathname, do not descend into directories that have a different device ID. See the st_dev field as described in stat(2) for more information about device ID's.

-Y   This option is the same as the −D option, except that the inode change time is checked using the path-
     name created after all the file name modifications have completed.

-Z   This option is the same as the −u option, except that the modification time is checked using the path-
     name created after all the file name modifications have completed.

The options that operate on the names of files or archive members (−c, −i, −n, −s, −u, −v, −D, −C, −T,
−U, −Y, and −Z) interact as follows.

When extracting files during a *read* operation, archive members are 'selected', based only on the user
specified pattern operands as modified by the −c, −n, −u, −D, −G, −T, −U options. Then any −s and −i
options will modify in that order, the names of these selected files. Then the −Y and −Z options will be applied based on the final pathname. Finally the −v option will write the names resulting from these
modifications.

When archiving files during a *write* operation, or copying files during a *copy* operation, archive members are
'selected', based only on the user specified pathnames as modified by the −n, −u, −D, −G, −T, and −U options (the −D option only applies during a copy operation). Then any −s and −i options will modify in that
order, the names of these selected files. Then during a *copy* operation the −Y and the −Z options will be applied based on the final pathname. Finally the −v option will write the names resulting from these
modifications.

When one or both of the −u or −D options are specified along with the −n option, a file is not considered
selected unless it is newer than the file to which it is compared.

EXAMPLES

The command:
```
pax -w -f /dev/rst0 .
```
copies the contents of the current directory to the device /dev/rst0.

The command:
```
pax -r -v -f filename
```
gives the verbose table of contents for an archive stored in filename.

The following commands:
```
mkdir newdir
cd olddir
pax -rw . newdir
```
will copy the entire olddir directory hierarchy to newdir.

The command:
```
pax -r -s ',^//*usr//*,,' -f a.pax
```
reads the archive a.pax, with all files rooted in ''/usr'' into the archive extracted relative to the current
directory.

The command:
```
pax -rw -i . dest_dir
```
can be used to interactively select the files to copy from the current directory to dest_dir.

The command:
```
pax -r -pe -U root -G bin -f a.pax
```
will extract all files from the archive a.pax which are owned by *root* with group *bin* and will preserve all
file permissions.

1

The command:

    pax -r -w -v -Y -Z home /backup

will update (and list) only those files in the destination directory /backup which are older (less recent inode change or file modification times) than files with the same name found in the source file tree home.

STANDARDS

The **pax** utility is a superset of the IEEE Std1003.2 ("POSIX") standard. The options −B, −D, −E, −G, −H, −L, −P, −T, −U, −Y, −Z, the archive formats *bcpio, sv4cpio, sv4crc, tar*, and the flawed archive handling during *list* and *read* operations are extensions to the POSIX standard.

AUTHOR

Keith Muller at the University of California, San Diego

ERRORS

pax will exit with one of the following values:

0   All files were processed successfully.

1   An error occurred.

Whenever **pax** cannot create a file or a link when reading an archive or cannot find a file when writing an archive, or cannot preserve the user ID, group ID, or file mode when the −p option is specified, a diagnostic message is written to standard error and a non-zero exit status will be returned, but processing will continue. In the case where pax cannot create a link to a file, **pax** will not create a second copy of the file.

If the extraction of a file from an archive is prematurely terminated by a signal or error, **pax** may have only partially extracted a file the user wanted. Additionally, the file modes of extracted files and directories may have incorrect file bits, and the modification and access times may be wrong.

If the creation of an archive is prematurely terminated by a signal or error, **pax** may have only partially created the archive which may violate the specific archive format specification.

If while doing a *copy*, **pax** detects a file is about to overwrite itself, the file is not copied, a diagnostic message is written to standard error and when **pax** completes it will exit with a non-zero exit status.

NAME

    perl – practical extraction and report language

SYNOPSIS

    perl [options] filename args

DESCRIPTION

    Perl is an interpreted language optimized for scanning arbitrary text files, extracting information from those text files, and printing reports based on that information. It's also a good language for many system management tasks. The language is intended to be practical (easy to use, efficient, complete) rather than beautiful (tiny, elegant, minimal). It combines (in the author's opinion, anyway) some of the best features of C, *sed*, *awk*, and *sh*, so people familiar with those languages should have little difficulty with it. (Language historians will also note some vestiges of *csh*, Pascal, and even BASIC-PLUS.) Expression syntax corresponds quite closely to C expression syntax. Unlike most Unix utilities, *perl* does not arbitrarily limit the size of your data—if you've got the memory, *perl* can slurp in your whole file as a single string. Recursion is of unlimited depth. And the hash tables used by associative arrays grow as necessary to prevent degraded performance. *Perl* uses sophisticated pattern matching techniques to scan large amounts of data very quickly. Although optimized for scanning text, *perl* can also deal with binary data, and can make dbm files look like associative arrays (where dbm is available). Setuid *perl* scripts are safer than C programs through a dataflow tracing mechanism which prevents many stupid security holes. If you have a problem that would ordinarily use *sed* or *awk* or *sh*, but it exceeds their capabilities or must run a little faster, and you don't want to write the silly thing in C, then *perl* may be for you. There are also translators to turn your *sed* and *awk* scripts into *perl* scripts.

    Upon startup, *perl* looks for your script in one of the following places: Specified line by line via −e switches on the command line. Contained in the file specified by the first filename on the command line. (Note that systems supporting the #! notation invoke interpreters this way.) Passed in implicitly via standard input. This only works if there are no filename arguments—to pass arguments to a *stdin* script you must explicitly specify a − for the script name.

    After locating your script, *perl* compiles it to an internal form. If the script is syntactically correct, it is executed.

    A single-character option may be combined with the following option, if any. This is particularly useful when invoking a script using the #! construct which only allows one argument. Example:

        #!/usr/bin/perl −spi.bak   # same as −s −p −i.bak
        . . .

    Options include:

−0*digits*

        specifies the record separator ($/) as an octal number. If there are no digits, the null character is the separator. Other switches may precede or follow the digits. For example, if you have a version of *find* which can print filenames terminated by the null character, you can say this:

        find . −name '*.bak' −print0 I perl −n0e unlink

        The special value 00 will cause Perl to slurp files in paragraph mode. The value 0777 will cause Perl to slurp files whole since there is no legal character with that value.

−a   turns on autosplit mode when used with a −**n** or −**p**. An implicit split command to the @F array is done as the first thing inside the implicit while loop produced by the −**n** or −**p**.

        perl −ane ´print pop(@F), "\n";´

    is equivalent to

1

```
while (<>) {
        @F = split(' ');
        print pop(@F), "\n";
}
```

−c   causes *perl* to check the syntax of the script and then exit without executing it.

−d   runs the script under the perl debugger. See the section on Debugging.

−D*number*
> sets debugging flags. To watch how it executes your script, use **−D14**. (This only works if debugging is compiled into your *perl*.) Another nice value is −D1024, which lists your compiled syntax tree. And −D512 displays compiled regular expressions.

−e *commandline*
> may be used to enter one line of script. Multiple **−e** commands may be given to build up a multi-line script. If **−e** is given, *perl* will not look for a script filename in the argument list.

−i*extension*
> specifies that files processed by the <> construct are to be edited in-place. It does this by renaming the input file, opening the output file by the same name, and selecting that output file as the default for print statements. The extension, if supplied, is added to the name of the old file to make a backup copy. If no extension is supplied, no backup is made. Saying perl −p −i.bak −e "s/foo/bar/;" ... is the same as using the script:

>> #!/usr/bin/perl −pi.bak
>> s/foo/bar/;

> which is equivalent to

>> #!/usr/bin/perl
>> while (<>) {
>>   if ($ARGV ne $oldargv) {
>>   rename($ARGV, $ARGV . '.bak');
>>   open(ARGVOUT, ">$ARGV");
>>   select(ARGVOUT);
>> $oldargv = $ARGV;
>>   }
>>   s/foo/bar/;
>> }
>> continue {
>>   print; # this prints to original filename
>> }
>> select(STDOUT);

> except that the −i form doesn't need to compare $ARGV to $oldargv to know when the filename has changed. It does, however, use ARGVOUT for the selected filehandle. Note that *STDOUT* is restored as the default output filehandle after the loop. You can use eof to locate the end of each input file, in case you want to append to each file, or reset line numbering (see example under eof).

−I*directory*
> may be used in conjunction with **−P** to tell the C preprocessor where to look for include files. By default /usr/include and /usr/lib/perl are searched.

−l*octnum*
> enables automatic line-ending processing. It has two effects: first, it automatically chops the line terminator when used with **−n** or **−p** , and second, it assigns $\ to have the value of *octnum* so that any

print statements will have that line terminator added back on. If *octnum* is omitted, sets $\backslash$ to the current value of $/. For instance, to trim lines to 80 columns:

```
perl -lpe 'substr($_, 80) = ""'
```

Note that the assignment $\backslash$ = $/ is done when the switch is processed, so the input record separator can be different than the output record separator if the −l switch is followed by a −0 switch:

```
gnufind / -print0 | perl -ln0e 'print "found $_" if -p'
```

This sets $\backslash$ to newline and then sets $/ to the null character.

−n   causes *perl* to assume the following loop around your script, which makes it iterate over filename arguments somewhat like sed −n or *awk*:

```
while (<>) {
        ...                     # your script goes here
}
```

Note that the lines are not printed by default. See −p to have lines printed. Here is an efficient way to delete all files older than a week:

```
find . −mtime +7 −print | perl −nle 'unlink;'
```

This is faster than using the −exec switch of find because you don't have to start a process on every filename found.

−p   causes *perl* to assume the following loop around your script, which makes it iterate over filename arguments somewhat like *sed*:

```
while (<>) {
        ...                     # your script goes here
} continue {
        print;
}
```

Note that the lines are printed automatically. To suppress printing use the −n switch. A −p overrides a −n switch.

−P   causes your script to be run through the C preprocessor before compilation by *perl*. (Since both comments and cpp directives begin with the # character, you should avoid starting comments with any words recognized by the C preprocessor such as if, else or define.)

−s   enables some rudimentary switch parsing for switches on the command line after the script name but before any filename arguments (or before a −−). Any switch found there is removed from @ARGV and sets the corresponding variable in the *perl* script. The following script prints true if and only if the script is invoked with a −xyz switch.

```
#!/usr/bin/perl −s
if ($xyz) { print "true\n"; }
```

−S   makes *perl* use the PATH environment variable to search for the script (unless the name of the script starts with a slash). Typically this is used to emulate #! startup on machines that don't support #!, in the following manner:

```
#!/usr/bin/perl
```

1

```
eval "exec /usr/bin/perl −S $0 $*"
        if $running_under_some_shell;
```

The system ignores the first line and feeds the script to /bin/sh, which proceeds to try to execute the *perl* script as a shell script. The shell executes the second line as a normal shell command, and thus starts up the *perl* interpreter. On some systems $0 doesn't always contain the full pathname, so the −S tells *perl* to search for the script if necessary. After *perl* locates the script, it parses the lines and ignores them because the variable $running_under_some_shell is never true. A better construct than $* would be ${1+"$@"}, which handles embedded spaces and such in the filenames, but doesn't work if the script is being interpreted by csh. In order to start up sh rather than csh, some systems may have to replace the #! line with a line containing just a colon, which will be politely ignored by perl. Other systems can't control that, and need a totally devious construct that will work under any of csh, sh or perl, such as the following:

```
eval '(exit $?0)' && eval 'exec /usr/bin/perl -S $0 ${1+"$@"}'
& eval 'exec /usr/bin/perl -S $0 $argv:q'
        if 0;
```

−u   causes *perl* to dump core after compiling your script. You can then take this core dump and turn it into an executable file by using the undump program (not supplied). This speeds startup at the expense of some disk space (which you can minimize by stripping the executable). (Still, a "hello world" executable comes out to about 200K on my machine.) If you are going to run your executable as a set-id program then you should probably compile it using taintperl rather than normal perl. If you want to execute a portion of your script before dumping, use the dump operator instead. Note: availability of undump is platform specific and may not be available for a specific port of perl.

−U   allows *perl* to do unsafe operations. Currently the only unsafe operations are the unlinking of directories while running as superuser, and running setuid programs with fatal taint checks turned into warnings.

−v   prints the version and patchlevel of your *perl* executable.

−w   prints warnings about identifiers that are mentioned only once, and scalar variables that are used before being set. Also warns about redefined subroutines, and references to undefined filehandles or filehandles opened readonly that you are attempting to write on. Also warns you if you use == on values that don't look like numbers, and if your subroutines recurse more than 100 deep.

−x*directory*

tells *perl* that the script is embedded in a message. Leading garbage will be discarded until the first line that starts with #! and contains the string "perl". Any meaningful switches on that line will be applied (but only one group of switches, as with normal #! processing). If a directory name is specified, Perl will switch to that directory before running the script. The −x switch only controls the the disposal of leading garbage. The script must be terminated with _ _END_ _ if there is trailing garbage to be ignored (the script can process any or all of the trailing garbage via the DATA filehandle if desired).

ENVIRONMENT

Used if chdir has no argument. Used if chdir has no argument and HOME is not set. Used in executing subprocesses, and in finding the script if −S is used. A colon-separated list of directories in which to look for Perl library files before looking in the standard library and the current directory. The command used to get the debugger code. If unset, uses

```
require 'perldb.pl'
```

Apart from these, *perl* uses no other environment variables, except to make them available to the script being executed, and to child processes. However, scripts running setuid would do well to execute the following lines before doing anything else, just to keep people honest:

```
$ENV{'PATH'} = '/bin:/usr/bin';   # or whatever you need
$ENV{'SHELL'} = '/bin/sh' if $ENV{'SHELL'} ne '';
$ENV{'IFS'} = '' if $ENV{'IFS'} ne '';
```

FILES

/tmp/perl–eXXXXXX   temporary file for –e commands.

SEE ALSO

The complete perl documentation can be found in the UNIX System manager's Manual (SMM:19).

a2p   awk to perl translator

s2p   sed to perl translator

DIAGNOSTICS

Compilation errors will tell you the line number of the error, with an indication of the next token or token type that was to be examined. (In the case of a script passed to *perl* via –e switches, each –e is counted as one line.)

Setuid scripts have additional constraints that can produce error messages such as Insecure dependency. See the section on setuid scripts.

TRAPS

Accustomed *awk* users should take special note of the following: Semicolons are required after all simple statements in *perl* (except at the end of a block). Newline is not a statement delimiter. Curly brackets are required on ifs and whiles. Variables begin with $ or @ in *perl*. Arrays index from 0 unless you set $[. Likewise string positions in substr() and index(). You have to decide whether your array has numeric or string indices. Associative array values do not spring into existence upon mere reference. You have to decide whether you want to use string or numeric comparisons. Reading an input line does not split it for you. You get to split it yourself to an array. And the *split* operator has different arguments. The current input line is normally in $_, not $0. It generally does not have the newline stripped. ($0 is the name of the program executed.) $<digit> does not refer to fields—it refers to substrings matched by the last match pattern. The *print* statement does not add field and record separators unless you set $, and $\. You must open your files before you print to them. The range operator is . ., not comma. (The comma operator works as in C.) The match operator is =~, not ~. (~ is the one's complement operator, as in C.) The exponentiation operator is **, not ^. (^ is the XOR operator, as in C.) The concatenation operator is ., not the null string. (Using the null string would render /pat/ /pat/ unparsable, since the third slash would be interpreted as a division operator—the tokener is in fact slightly context sensitive for operators like /, ?, and <. And in fact, . itself can be the beginning of a number.) *Next*, *exit* and *continue* work differently. The following variables work differently

Awk	Perl
ARGC	$#ARGV
ARGV[0]	$0
FILENAME	$ARGV
FNR	$. – something
FS	(whatever you like)
NF	$#Fld, or some such
NR	$.
OFMT	$#
OFS	$,
ORS	$\
RLENGTH	length($&)
RS	$/

1

RSTART	length($`)
SUBSEP	$;

When in doubt, run the *awk* construct through a2p and see what it gives you.

Cerebral C programmers should take note of the following: Curly brackets are required on ifs and whiles. You should use elsif rather than else if *Break* and *continue* become *last* and *next*, respectively. There's no switch statement. Variables begin with $ or @ in *perl*. Printf does not implement *. Comments begin with #, not /*. You can't take the address of anything. ARGV must be capitalized. The system calls link, unlink, rename, etc. return nonzero for success, not 0. Signal handlers deal with signal names, not numbers.

Seasoned *sed* programmers should take note of the following: Backreferences in substitutions use $ rather than \. The pattern matching metacharacters (,), and | do not have backslashes in front. The range operator is . . rather than comma.

Sharp shell programmers should take note of the following: The backtick operator does variable interpretation without regard to the presence of single quotes in the command. The backtick operator does no translation of the return value, unlike csh. Shells (especially csh) do several levels of substitution on each command line. *Perl* does substitution only in certain constructs such as double quotes, backticks, angle brackets and search patterns. Shells interpret scripts a little bit at a time. *Perl* compiles the whole program before executing it. The arguments are available via @ARGV, not $1, $2, etc. The environment is not automatically made available as variables.

BUGS

Perl is at the mercy of your machine's definitions of various operations such as type casting, atof() and sprintf().

If your stdio requires a seek or eof between reads and writes on a particular stream, so does *perl*. (This doesn't apply to sysread() and syswrite().)

While none of the built-in data types have any arbitrary size limits (apart from memory size), there are still a few arbitrary limits: a given identifier may not be longer than 255 characters, and no component of your PATH may be longer than 255 if you use −S. A regular expression may not compile to more than 32767 bytes internally.

Perl actually stands for Pathologically Eclectic Rubbish Lister, but don't tell anyone I said that.

AUTHOR
Larry Wall <lwall@netlabs.com>
MS-DOS port by Diomidis Spinellis <dds@cc.ic.ac.uk>

NAME

    pfbtops – translate a PostScript font in .pfb format to ASCII

SYNOPSIS

    pfbtops [*pfb_file*]

DESCRIPTION

    pfbtops translates a PostScript font in **.pfb** format to ASCII. If *pfb_file* is omitted the pfb file will be read from the standard input. The ASCII format PostScript font will be written on the standard output. PostScript fonts for MS-DOS are normally supplied in **.pfb** format.

    The resulting ASCII format PostScript font can be used with groff. It must first be listed in **/usr/share/groff_font/devps/download**.

SEE ALSO

    grops(1)

1

NAME

pic – compile pictures for troff or TeX

SYNOPSIS

pic [**−nvC**] [*filename ...*]

pic −t [**−cvzC**] [*filename ...*]

DESCRIPTION

This manual page descibes the GNU version of **pic**, which is part of the groff document formatting system.
pic compiles descriptions of pictures embedded within **troff** or TEX input files into commands that are
understood by TEX or **troff**. Each picture starts with a line beginning with **.PS** and ends with a line beginning with **.PE**. Anything outside of **.PS** and **.PE** is passed through without change.

It is the user's responsibility to provide appropriate definitions of the **PS** and **PE** macros. When the macro
package being used does not supply such definitions (for example, old versions of −ms), appropriate
definitions can be obtained with **−mpic**: these will center each picture.

OPTIONS

Options that do not take arguments may be grouped behind a single −. The special option −− can be used
to mark the end of the options. A filename of − refers to the standard input.

−C   Recognize **.PS** and **.PE** even when followed by a character other than space or newline.

−n   Don't use the groff extensions to the troff drawing commands. You should use this if you are
using a postprocessor that doesn't support these extensions. The extensions are described in
groff_out(5). The −n option also causes pic not to use zero-length lines to draw dots in troff
mode.

−t   TEX mode.

−c   Be more compatible with **tpic**. Implies −t. Lines beginning with \ are not passed through transparently. Lines beginning with **.** are passed through with the initial **.** changed to \ A line beginning with **.ps** is given special treatment: it takes an optional integer argument specifying the line
thickness (pen size) in milliinches; a missing argument restores the previous line thickness; the
default line thickness is 8 milliinches. The line thickness thus specified takes effect only when a
non-negative line thickness has not been specified by use of the **thickness** attribute or by setting
the **linethick** variable.

−v   Print the version number.

−z   In TEX mode draw dots using zero-length lines.

The following options supported by other versions of **pic** are ignored:

−D   Draw all lines using the \D escape sequence. **pic** always does this.

−T *dev* Generate output for the **troff** device *dev*. This is unnecessary because the **troff** output generated
by **pic** is device-independent.

USAGE

This section describes only the differences between GNU pic and the original version of pic. Many of
these differences also apply to newer versions of Unix pic.

TEX mode

TEX mode is enabled by the −t option. In TEX mode, pic will define a vbox called **\graph** for each picture.
You must yourself print that vbox using, for example, the command

\centerline{\box\graph}

Actually, since the vbox has a height of zero this will produce slightly more vertical space above the picture than below it;

\centerline{\raise 1em\box\graph}

would avoid this.

You must use a TEX driver that supports the **tpic** specials, version 2.

Lines beginning with \ are passed through transparently; a % is added to the end of the line to avoid unwanted spaces. You can safely use this feature to change fonts or to change the value of **\baselineskip**. Anything else may well produce undesirable results; use at your own risk. Lines beginning with a period are not given any special treatment.

Commands

for *variable* = *expr1* **to** *expr2* [**by** [*]*expr3*] **do** *X body X*

> Set *variable* to *expr1*. While the value of *variable* is less than or equal to *expr2*, do *body* and increment *variable* by *expr3*; if **by** is not given, increment *variable* by 1. If *expr3* is prefixed by * then *variable* will instead be multiplied by *expr3*. *X* can be any character not occurring in *body*.

if *expr* **then** *X if-true X* [**else** *Y if-false Y*]

> Evaluate *expr*; if it is non-zero then do *if-true*, otherwise do *if-false*. *X* can be any character not occurring in *if-true*. *Y* can be any character not occurring in *if-false*.

print *arg*...

> Concatenate the arguments and print as a line on stderr. Each *arg* must be an expression, a position, or text. This is useful for debugging.

command *arg*...

> Concatenate the arguments and pass them through as a line to troff orTEX. Each *arg* must be an expression, a position, or text. This has a similar effect to a line beginning with . or \, but allows the values of variables to be passed through.

sh *X command X*

> Pass *command* to a shell. *X* can be any character not occurring in *command*.

copy *"filename"*

> Include *filename* at this point in the file.

copy [*"filename"*] **thru** *X body X* [**until** *"word"*]
copy [*"filename"*] **thru** *macro* [**until** *"word"*]

> This construct does *body* once for each line of *filename*; the line is split into blank-delimited words, and occurrences of $*i* in *body*, for *i* between 1 and 9, are replaced by the *i*-th word of the line. If *filename* is not given, lines are taken from the current input up to **.PE**. If an **until** clause is specified, lines will be read only until a line the first word of which is *word*; that line will then be discarded. *X* can be any character not occurring in *body*. For example,

> > .PS
> > **copy thru % circle at ($1,$2) % until "END"**
> > **1 2**
> > **3 4**
> > **5 6**
> > **END**
> > **box**
> > **.PE**

> is equivalent to

> > .PS
> > **circle at (1,2)**
> > **circle at (3,4)**
> > **circle at (5,6)**

box
.PE

The commands to be performed for each line can also be taken from a macro defined earlier by giving the name of the macro as the argument to **thru**.

reset
reset *variable1*, *variable2* ...

Reset pre-defined variables *variable1*, *variable2* ... to their default values. If no arguments are given, reset all pre-defined variables to their default values. Note that assigning a value to **scale** also causes all pre-defined variables that control dimensions to be reset to their default values times the new value of scale.

plot *expr* [*"text"*]

This is a text object which is constructed by using *text* as a format string for sprintf with an argument of *expr*. If *text* is omitted a format string of "**%g**" is used. Attributes can be specified in the same way as for a normal text object. Be very careful that you specify an appropriate format string; pic does only very limited checking of the string. This is deprecated in favour of **sprintf**.

variable:=*expr*

This is similar to = except *variable* must already be defined, and the value of *variable* will be changed only in the innermost block in which it is defined. (By contrast, = defines the variable in the current block if it is not already defined there, and then changes the value in the current block.)

Arguments of the form

  X anything *X*

are also allowed to be of the form

  { *anything* }

In this case *anything* can contain balanced occurrences of { and }. Strings may contain *X* or imbalanced occurrences of { and }.

Expressions
The syntax for expressions has been significantly extended:

$x \char94 y$ (exponentiation)
sin(x)
cos(x)
atan2(y, x)
log(x) (base 10)
exp(x) (base 10, ie 10^x)
sqrt(x)
int(x)
rand() (return a random number between 0 and 1)
rand(x) (return a random number between 1 and x; deprecated)
max(*e1*, *e2*)
min(*e1*, *e2*)
!*e*
e1 **&&** *e2*
e1 **||** *e2*
e1 == *e2*
e1 != *e2*
e1 >= *e2*
e1 > *e2*
e1 <= *e2*
e1 < *e2*
"*str1*" == "*str2*"

"*str1*" != "*str2*"

String comparison expressions must be parenthesised in some contexts to avoid ambiguity.

Other Changes

A bare expression, *expr*, is acceptable as an attribute; it is equivalent to *dir expr*, where *dir* is the current direction. For example

> **line 2i**

means draw a line 2 inches long in the current direction.

The maximum width and height of the picture are taken from the variables **maxpswid** and **maxpsht**. Initially these have values 8.5 and 11.

Scientific notation is allowed for numbers. For example

> **x = 5e–2**

Text attributes can be compounded. For example,

> **"foo" above ljust**

is legal.

There is no limit to the depth to which blocks can be examined. For example,

> **[A: [B: [C: box]]] with .A.B.C.sw at 1,2**
> **circle at last [].A.B.C**

is acceptable.

Arcs now have compass points determined by the circle of which the arc is a part.

Circles and arcs can be dotted or dashed. In TEX mode splines can be dotted or dashed.

Boxes can have rounded corners. The **rad** attribute specifies the radius of the quarter-circles at each corner. If no **rad** or **diam** attribute is given, a radius of **boxrad** is used. Initially, **boxrad** has a value of 0. A box with rounded corners can be dotted or dashed.

The **.PS** line can have a second argument specifying a maximum height for the picture. If the width of zero is specified the width will be ignored in computing the scaling factor for the picture. Note that GNU pic will always scale a picture by the same amount vertically as horizontally. This is different from the DWB 2.0 pic which may scale a picture by a different amount vertically than horizontally if a height is specified.

Each text object has an invisible box associated with it. The compass points of a text object are determined by this box. The implicit motion associated with the object is also determined by this box. The dimensions of this box are taken from the width and height attributes; if the width attribute is not supplied then the width will be taken to be **textwid**; if the height attribute is not supplied then the height will be taken to be the number of text strings associated with the object times **textht**. Initially **textwid** and **textht** have a value of 0.

In places where a quoted text string can be used, an expression of the form

> **sprintf("*format*", *arg*,...)**

can also be used; this will produce the arguments formatted according to *format*, which should be a string as described in **printf**(3) appropriate for the number of arguments supplied, using only the **e, f, g** or **%** format characters.

The thickness of the lines used to draw objects is controlled by the **linethick** variable. This gives the thickness of lines in points. A negative value means use the default thickness: in TEX output mode, this means use a thickness of 8 milliinches; in TEX output mode with the **-c** option, this means use the line thickness specified by **.ps** lines; in troff output mode, this means use a thickness proportional to the pointsize. A zero value means draw the thinnest possible line supported by the output device. Initially it has a value of -1. There is also a **thick[ness]** attribute. For example,

1

circle thickness 1.5

would draw a circle using a line with a thickness of 1.5 points. The thickness of lines is not affected by the value of the **scale** variable, nor by the width or height given in the **.PS** line.

Boxes (including boxes with rounded corners), circles and ellipses can be filled by giving then an attribute of **fill[ed]**. This takes an optional argument of an expression with a value between 0 and 1; 0 will fill it with white, 1 with black, values in between with a proportionally gray shade. A value greater than 1 can also be used: this means fill with the shade of gray that is currently being used for text and lines. Normally this will be black, but output devices may provide a mechanism for changing this. Without an argument, then the value of the variable **fillval** will be used. Initially this has a value of 0.5. The invisible attribute does not affect the filling of objects. Any text associated with a filled object will be added after the object has been filled, so that the text will not be obscured by the filling.

Arrow heads will be drawn as solid triangles if the variable **arrowhead** is non-zero and either TEX mode is enabled or the −**x** option has been given. Initially **arrowhead** has a value of 1.

The troff output of pic is device-independent. The −**T** option is therefore redundant. All numbers are taken to be in inches; numbers are never interpreted to be in troff machine units.

Objects can have an **aligned** attribute. This will only work when the postprocessor is **grops**. Any text associated with an object having the **aligned** attribute will be rotated about the center of the object so that it is aligned in the direction from the start point to the end point of the object. Note that this attribute will have no effect for objects whose start and end points are coincident.

In places where n**th** is allowed '*expr*'**th** is also allowed. Note that '**th** is a single token: no space is allowed between the ' and the **th**. For example,

```
for i = 1 to 4 do {
  line from 'i'th box.nw to 'i+1'th box.se
}
```

FILES

    /usr/share/tmac/tmac.pic   Example definitions of the **PS** and **PE** macros.

SEE ALSO

    troff(1), **groff_out**(5), **tex**(1)
    Tpic: Pic for TEX
    AT&T Bell Laboratories, Computing Science Technical Report No. 116, PIC — A Graphics Language for Typesetting. (This can be obtained by sending a mail message to netlib@research.att.com with a body of 'send 116 from research/cstr'.)

BUGS

    Input characters that are illegal for **groff** (ie those with ASCII code 0 or between 013 and 037 octal or between 0200 and 0237 octal) are rejected even in TEX mode.

    The interpretation of **fillval** is incompatible with the pic in 10th edition Unix, which interprets 0 as black and 1 as white.

1

NAME
plot – graphics filters

SYNOPSIS
plot [−T *terminal*] [−r *resolution*] *file* ...

DESCRIPTION
These commands read plotting instructions (see plot(5)) from the standard input or the specified *files*, and in general produce plotting instructions suitable for a particular *terminal* on the standard output. The −r flag may be used to specify the device's output resolution (currently only the Imagen laser printer understands this option).

If no *terminal* type is specified, the environment parameter $TERM (see environ(7)) is used. Known *terminals* are:

4013   Tektronix 4013 storage scope.

4014 or **tek**
Tektronix 4014 or 4015 storage scope with Enhanced Graphics Module. (Use 4013 for Tektronix 4014 or 4015 without the Enhanced Graphics Module).

450   DASI Hyterm 450 terminal (Diablo mechanism).

300   DASI 300 or GSI terminal (Diablo mechanism).

300S   DASI 300S terminal (Diablo mechanism).

aed   AED 512 color graphics terminal.

bitgraph or **bg**
BBN bitgraph graphics terminal.

imagen or **ip**
Imagen laser printer (default 240 dots-per-inch resolution).

crt   Any crt terminal capable of running vi(1).

dumb   Dumb terminals without cursor addressing or line printers.

vt125   DEC vt125 terminal.

hp2648 or **hp** or **hp8**
Hewlett Packard 2648 graphics terminal.

ver   Versatec D1200A printer-plotter.

var   Benson Varian printer-plotter.

These versions of **plot** use the −g option of lpr(1) to send the result directly to the plotter device rather than to the standard output.

ENVIRONMENT
TERM   Used to determine the terminal type if not given as an argument.

FILES
/usr/libexec/plot/t4013

1

```
/usr/libexec/plot/tek
/usr/libexec/plot/t450
/usr/libexec/plot/t300
/usr/libexec/plot/t300s
/usr/libexec/plot/aedplot
/usr/libexec/plot/bgplot
/usr/libexec/plot/crtplot
/usr/libexec/plot/dumbplot
/usr/libexec/plot/gigiplot
/usr/libexec/plot/hpplot
/usr/libexec/plot/implot
/usr/bin/lpr
```

SEE ALSO

plot(3), plot(5), lpr(1)

HISTORY

The `plot` command appeared in Version 6 AT&T UNIX.

NAME
pr – print files

SYNOPSIS
pr [*+page*] [*-column*] [*-adFmrt*] [[**-e**] [*char*] [*gap*]] [**-h** *header*] [[**-i**] [*char*] [*gap*]]
  [**-l** *lines*] [**-o** *offset*] [[**-s**] [*char*]] [[**-n**] [*char*] [*width*]] [**-w** *width*] [-] [*file*
  ...]

DESCRIPTION
The **pr** utility is a printing and pagination filter for text files. When multiple input files are specified, each is read, formatted, and written to standard output. By default, the input is separated into 66-line pages, each with

• A 5-line header with the page number, date, time, and the pathname of the file.

• A 5-line trailer consisting of blank lines.

If standard output is associated with a terminal, diagnostic messages are suppressed until the **pr** utility has completed processing.

When multiple column output is specified, text columns are of equal width. By default text columns are separated by at least one *<blank>*. Input lines that do not fit into a text column are truncated. Lines are not truncated under single column output.

OPTIONS
In the following option descriptions, column, lines, offset, page, and width are positive decimal integers and gap is a nonnegative decimal integer.

+page
> Begin output at page number *page* of the formatted input.

-column
> Produce output that is *columns* wide (default is 1) that is written vertically down each column in the order in which the text is received from the input file. The options −**e** and −**i** are assumed. This option should not be used with −**m**. When used with −**t**, the minimum number of lines is used to display the output.

−**a**
> Modify the effect of the −**column** option so that the columns are filled across the page in a round-robin order (e.g., when column is 2, the first input line heads column 1, the second heads column 2, the third is the second line in column 1, etc.). This option requires the use of the −**column** option.

−**d**
> Produce output that is double spaced. An extra *<newline>* character is output following every *<newline>* found in the input.

−**e** *[char] [gap]*
> Expand each input *<tab>* to the next greater column position specified by the formula $n*gap+1$, where *n* is an integer > 0. If *gap* is zero or is omitted the default is 8. All *<tab>* characters in the input are expanded into the appropriate number of *<space>s*. If any nondigit character, *char*, is specified, it is used as the input tab character.

−**F**
> Use a *<form-feed>* character for new pages, instead of the default behavior that uses a sequence o *<newline>* characters.

1

−h *header*

  header Use the string *header* to replace the *file name* in the header line.

−i *[char][gap]*

  In output, replace multiple <space>s with <tab>s whenever two or more adjacent <space>s reach column positions *gap+1*, *2*gap+1*, etc. If *gap* is zero or omitted, default *<tab>* settings at every eighth column position is used. If any nondigit character, *char*, is specified, it is used as the output *<tab>* character.

−l *lines*

  Override the 66 line default and reset the page length to *lines*. If *lines* is not greater than the sum of both the header and trailer depths (in lines), the **pr** utility suppresses output of both the header and trailer, as if the **−t** option were in effect.

−m　Merge the contents of multiple files. One line from each file specified by a file operand is written side by side into text columns of equal fixed widths, in terms of the number of column positions. The number of text columns depends on the number of file operands successfully opened. The maximum number of files merged depends on page width and the per process open file limit. The options **−e** and **−i** are assumed.

−n *[char][width]*

  Provide *width* digit line numbering. The default for *width*, if not specified, is 5. The number occupies the first *width* column positions of each text column or each line of **−m** output. If *char* (any nondigit character) is given, it is appended to the line number to separate it from whatever follows. The default for *char* is a *<tab>*. Line numbers longer than *width* columns are truncated.

−o *offset*

  Each line of output is preceded by *offset* *<spaces>s*. If the option is not specified, the default is zero. The space taken is in addition to the output line width.

−r　Write no diagnostic reports on failure to open a file.

−s *char*

  Separate text columns by the single character *char* instead of by the appropriate number of *<space>s* (default for *char* is the *<tab>* character).

−t　Print neither the five-line identifying header nor the five-line trailer usually supplied for each page. Quit printing after the last line of each file without spacing to the end of the page.

−w *width*

  Set the width of the line to *width* column positions for multiple text-column output only. If the **−w** option is not specified and the **−s** option is not specified, the default width is 72. If the **−w** option is not specified and the **−s** option is specified, the default width is 512.

file

  A pathname of a file to be printed. If no *file* operands are specified, or if a *file* operand is '−', the standard input is used. The standard input is used only if no *file* operands are specified, or if a *file* operand is '−'.

The **−s** option does not allow the option letter to be separated from its argument, and the options **−e**, **−i**, and **−n** require that both arguments, if present, not be separated from the option letter.

ERRORS

  If **pr** receives an interrupt while printing to a terminal, it flushes all accumulated error messages to the screen before terminating.

The **pr** utility exits 0 on success, and 1 if an error occurs.

Error messages are written to standard error during the printing process (if output is redirected) or after all successful file printing is complete (when printing to a terminal).

SEE ALSO
cat(1), more(1)

STANDARDS
The **pr** utility is IEEE Std1003.2 (''POSIX'') compatible.

1

NAME

printenv, env – print out the environment, set and print environment

SYNOPSIS

printenv [*name*]

env [–] [*name=value* ...] [*command*]

DESCRIPTION

Printenv prints out the names and values of the variables in the environment, with one name/value pair per line. If *name* is specified, only its value is printed.

If a *name* is specified and it is not defined in the environment, **printenv** returns exit status 1, else it returns status 0.

Env executes *command* after modifying the environment as specified on the command line. The option *name=value* specifies an environmental variable, *name*, with a value of *value*. The option ' – ' causes env to completely ignore the environment it inherits.

If no command is specified, **env** prints out the names and values of the variables in the environment, with one name/value pair per line.

SEE ALSO

csh(1), sh(1), execvp(3), environ(7)

HISTORY

The **printenv** command appeared in 3.0BSD.

BUGS

Env doesn't handle commands with equal (''**=**'') signs in their names, for obvious reasons.

NAME

    `printf` – formatted output

SYNOPSIS

    `printf format` [arguments ...]

DESCRIPTION

    `Printf` formats and prints its arguments, after the first, under control of the `format`. The `format` is a character string which contains three types of objects: plain characters, which are simply copied to standard output, character escape sequences which are converted and copied to the standard output, and format specifications, each of which causes printing of the next successive `argument`.

    The `arguments` after the first are treated as strings if the corresponding format is either c or **s**; otherwise it is evaluated as a C constant, with the following extensions:

- A leading plus or minus sign is allowed.
- If the leading character is a single or double quote, or not a digit, plus, or minus sign, the value is the ASCII code of the next character.

    The format string is reused as often as necessary to satisfy the `arguments`. Any extra format specifications are evaluated with zero or the null string.

    Character escape sequences are in backslash notation as defined in the draft proposed ANSI C Standard X3J11. The characters and their meanings are as follows:

`\a`	Write a <bell> character.
`\b`	Write a <backspace> character.
`\f`	Write a <form-feed> character.
`\n`	Write a <new-line> character.
`\r`	Write a <carriage return> character.
`\t`	Write a <tab> character.
`\v`	Write a <vertical tab> character.
`\´`	Write a <single quote> character.
`\\`	Write a backslash character.
`\num`	Write an 8-bit character whose ASCII value is the 1-, 2-, or 3-digit octal number `num`.

    Each format specification is introduced by the percent character ("%"). The remainder of the format specification includes, in the following order:

    Zero or more of the following flags:

#	A '#' character specifying that the value should be printed in an "alternate form". For c, d, and s, formats, this option has no effect. For the o formats the precision of the number is increased to force the first character of the output string to a zero. For the **x** (**X**) format, a non-zero result has the string `0x` (`0X`) prepended to it. For e, **E**, **f**, **g**, and G, formats, the result will always contain a decimal point, even if no digits follow the point (normally, a decimal point only appears in the results of those formats if a digit follows the decimal point). For g and G formats, trailing zeros are not removed from the result as they would otherwise be;

1

–   A minus sign '–' which specifies *left adjustment* of the output in the indicated field;

+   A '+' character specifying that there should always be a sign placed before the number when using signed formats.

' '   A space specifying that a blank should be left before a positive number for a signed format. A '+' overrides a space if both are used;

0   A zero '0' character indicating that zero-padding should be used rather than blank-padding. A '–' overrides a '0' if both are used;

Field Width:
An optional digit string specifying a *field width*; if the output string has fewer characters than the field width it will be blank-padded on the left (or right, if the left-adjustment indicator has been given) to make up the field width (note that a leading zero is a flag, but an embedded zero is part of a field width);

Precision:
An optional period, '.', followed by an optional digit string giving a *precision* which specifies the number of digits to appear after the decimal point, for e and f formats, or the maximum number of characters to be printed from a string; if the digit string is missing, the precision is treated as zero;

Format:
A character which indicates the type of format to use (one of **diouxXfwEgGcs**).

A field width or precision may be '*' instead of a digit string. In this case an *argument* supplies the field width or precision.

The format characters and their meanings are:

diouXx   The *argument* is printed as a signed decimal (d or i), unsigned decimal, unsigned octal, or unsigned hexadecimal (X or x), respectively.

f   The *argument* is printed in the style '[–]ddd.ddd' where the number of d's after the decimal point is equal to the precision specification for the argument. If the precision is missing, 6 digits are given; if the precision is explicitly 0, no digits and no decimal point are printed.

eE   The *argument* is printed in the style e where there is one digit before the decimal point and the number after is equal to the precision specification for the argument; when the precision is missing, 6 digits are produced. An upper-case E is used for an 'E' format.

gG   The *argument* is printed in style **f** or in style **e** (**E**) whichever gives full precision in minimum space.

c   The first character of *argument* is printed.

s   Characters from the string *argument* are printed until the end is reached or until the number of characters indicated by the precision specification is reached; however if the precision is 0 or missing, all characters in the string are printed.

%   Print a '%'; no argument is used.

In no case does a non-existent or small field width cause truncation of a field; padding takes place only if the specified field width exceeds the actual width.

RETURN VALUES
Printf exits 0 on success, 1 on failure.

1

SEE ALSO
    printf(3)

HISTORY
The `printf` command appeared in 4.3BSD–Reno. It is modeled after the standard library function, printf(3).

BUGS
Since the floating point numbers are translated from ASCII to floating-point and then back again, floating-point precision may be lost.

ANSI hexadecimal character constants were deliberately not provided.

1

NAME
ps – process status

SYNOPSIS
ps [−aCehjlmrSTuvwx] [−M *core*] [−N *system*] [−O *fmt*] [−o *fmt*] [−p *pid*] [−t *tty*]
[−W *swap*]
ps [−L]

DESCRIPTION
Ps displays a header line followed by lines containing information about your processes that have controlling terminals. This information is sorted by process ID.

The information displayed is selected based on a set of keywords (see the −L −O and −o options). The default output format includes, for each process, the process' ID, controlling terminal, cpu time (including both
user and system time), state, and associated command.

The options are as follows:

−a   Display information about other users' processes as well as your own.

−C   Change the way the cpu percentage is calculated by using a ''raw'' cpu calculation that ignores
''resident'' time (this normally has no effect).

−e   Display the environment as well.

−h   Repeat the information header as often as necessary to guarantee one header per page of information.

−j   Print information associated with the following keywords: user, pid, ppid, pgid, sess, jobc, state, tt,
time and command.

−L   List the set of available keywords.

−l   Display information associated with the following keywords: uid, pid, ppid, cpu, pri, nice, vsz, rss,
wchan, state, tt, time and command.

−M   Extract values associated with the name list from the specified core instead of the default
''/dev/kmem''.

−m   Sort by memory usage, instead of by process ID.

−N   Extract the name list from the specified system instead of the default ''/vmunix''.

−O   Add the information associated with the space or comma separated list of keywords specified,
after the process ID, in the default information display. Keywords may be appended with an
equals (''='') sign and a string. This causes the printed header to use the specified string instead
of the standard header.

−o   Display information associated with the space or comma separated list of keywords specified.
Keywords may be appended with an equals (''='') sign and a string. This causes the printed
header to use the specified string instead of the standard header.

−p   Display information associated with the specified process ID.

−r   Sort by current cpu usage, instead of by process ID.

1

-s   Change the way the process time is calculated by summing all exited children to their parent process.

-T   Display information about processes attached to the device associated with the standard input.

-t   Display information about processes attached to the specified terminal device.

-u   Display information associated with the following keywords: user, pid, %cpu, %mem, vsz, rss, tt, state, start, time and command. The -u option implies the -r option.

-v   Display information associated with the following keywords: pid, state, time, sl, re, pagein, vsz, rss, lim, tsiz, %cpu, %mem and command. The -v option implies the -m option.

-W   Extract swap information from the specified file instead of the default "/dev/swap".

-w   Use 132 columns to display information, instead of the default which is your window size. If the -w option is specified more than once, ps will use as many columns as necessary without regard for your window size.

-x   Display information about processes without controlling terminals.

A complete list of the available keywords are listed below. Some of these keywords are further specified as follows:

%cpu   The cpu utilization of the process; this is a decaying average over up to a minute of previous (real) time. Since the time base over which this is computed varies (since processes may be very young) it is possible for the sum of all %CPU fields to exceed 100%.

%mem   The percentage of real memory used by this process.

flags   The flags (in hexadecimal) associated with the process as in the include file <sys/proc.h>:

SLOAD	0x0000001	in core
SSYS	0x0000002	swapper or pager process
SLOCK	0x0000004	process being swapped out
SSWAP	0x0000008	save area flag
STRC	0x0000010	process is being traced
SWTED	0x0000020	another tracing flag
SSINTR	0x0000040	sleep is interruptible
SKEEP	0x0000100	another flag to prevent swap out
SOMASK	0x0000200	restore old mask after taking signal
SWEXIT	0x0000400	working on exiting
SPHYSIO	0x0000800	doing physical I/O
SVFORK	0x0001000	process resulted from vfork(2)
SVFDONE	0x0002000	another vfork flag
SNOVM	0x0004000	no vm, parent in a vfork
SPAGV	0x0008000	init data space on demand, from vnode
SSEQL	0x0010000	user warned of sequential vm behavior
SUANOM	0x0020000	user warned of random vm behavior
STIMO	0x0040000	timing out during sleep
SNOCLDSTOP	0x0080000	no SIGCHLD when children stop
SCTTY	0x0100000	has a controlling terminal
SOWEUPC	0x0200000	owe process an addupc() call at next ast
SSEL	0x0400000	selecting; wakeup/waiting danger
SEXEC	0x0800000	process called exec(2)

SHPUX	0x1000000	HP-UX process (HPUXCOMPAT)
SULOCK	0x2000000	locked in core after swap error
SPTECHG	0x4000000	pte's for process have changed

lim   The soft limit on memory used, specified via a call to setrlimit(2).

lstart   The exact time the command started, using the "%C" format described in strftime(3).

nice   The process scheduling increment (see setpriority(2)).

rss   the real memory (resident set) size of the process (in 1024 byte units).

start   The time the command started. If the command started less than 24 hours ago, the start time is displayed using the "%l:ps.1p" format described in strftime(3). If the command started less than 7 days ago, the start time is displayed using the "%a6.15p" format. Otherwise, the start time is displayed using the "%e%b%y" format.

state   The state is given by a sequence of letters, for example, "RWNA". The first letter indicates the run state of the process:

D   Marks a process in disk (or other short term, uninterruptible) wait.
I   Marks a process that is idle (sleeping for longer than about 20 seconds).
R   Marks a runnable process.
S   Marks a process that is sleeping for less than about 20 seconds.
T   Marks a stopped process.
Z   Marks a dead process (a "zombie").

Additional characters after these, if any, indicate additional state information:

+   The process is in the foreground process group of its control terminal.
<   The process has raised CPU scheduling priority.
>   The process has specified a soft limit on memory requirements and is currently exceeding that limit; such a process is (necessarily) not swapped.
A   the process has asked for random page replacement (VA_ANOM, from vadvise(2), for example, lisp(1) in a garbage collect).
E   The process is trying to exit.
L   The process has pages locked in core (for example, for raw I/O).
N   The process has reduced CPU scheduling priority (see setpriority(2)).
S   The process has asked for FIFO page replacement (VA_SEQL, from vadvise(2), for example, a large image processing program using virtual memory to sequentially address voluminous data).
s   The process is a session leader.
V   The process is suspended during a vfork.
W   The process is swapped out.
X   The process is being traced or debugged.

tt   An abbreviation for the pathname of the controlling terminal, if any. The abbreviation consists of the two letters following "/dev/tty", or, for the console, "co". This is followed by a "-" if the process can no longer reach that controlling terminal (i.e., it has been revoked).

wchan The event (an address in the system) on which a process waits. When printed numerically, the initial part of the address is trimmed off and the result is printed in hex, for example, 0x80324000 prints as 324000.

When printing using the command keyword, a process that has exited and has a parent that has not yet waited for the process (in other words, a zombie) is listed as "<defunct>", and a process which is blocked while trying to exit is listed as "<exiting>". Ps makes an educated guess as to the file name and arguments given when the process was created by examining memory or the swap area. The method is inherently somewhat unreliable and in any event a process is entitled to destroy this information, so the names cannot be depended on too much. The ucomm (accounting) keyword can, however, be depended on.

KEYWORDS

The following is a complete list of the available keywords and their meanings. Several of them have aliases (keywords which are synonyms).

%cpu	percentage cpu usage (alias pcpu)
%mem	percentage memory usage (alias pmem)
acflag	accounting flag (alias acflg)
command	command and arguments
cpu	short-term cpu usage factor (for scheduling)
flags	the process flags, in hexadecimal (alias f)
inblk	total blocks read (alias inblock)
jobc	job control count
ktrace	tracing flags
ktracep	tracing vnode
lim	memoryuse limit
logname	login name of user who started the process
lstart	time started
majflt	total page faults
minflt	total page reclaims
msgrcv	total messages received (reads from pipes/sockets)
msgsnd	total messages sent (writes on pipes/sockets)
nice	nice value (alias ni)
nivcsw	total involuntary context switches
nsigs	total signals taken (alias nsignals)
nswap	total swaps in/out
nvcsw	total voluntary context switches
nwchan	wait channel (as an address)
oublk	total blocks written (alias oublock)
p_ru	resource usage (valid only for zombie)
paddr	swap address
pagein	pageins (same as majflt)
pgid	process group number
pid	process ID
poip	pageouts in progress
ppid	parent process ID
pri	scheduling priority
re	core residency time (in seconds; 127 = infinity)
rgid	real group ID
rlink	reverse link on run queue, or 0
rss	resident set size
rsz	resident set size + (text size / text use count) (alias rssize)
ruid	real user ID
ruser	user name (from ruid)
sess	session pointer
sig	pending signals (alias pending)
sigcatch	caught signals (alias caught)
sigignore	ignored signals (alias ignored)

1

sigmask	blocked signals (alias blocked)
sl	sleep time (in seconds; 127 = infinity)
start	time started
state	symbolic process state (alias stat)
svgid	saved gid from a setgid executable
svuid	saved uid from a setuid executable
tdev	control terminal device number
time	accumulated cpu time, user + system (alias cputime)
tpgid	control terminal process group ID
tsess	control terminal session pointer
tsiz	text size (in Kbytes)
tt	control terminal name (two letter abbreviation)
tty	full name of control terminal
uprocp	process pointer
ucomm	name to be used for accounting
uid	effective user ID
upr	scheduling priority on return from system call (alias usrpri)
user	user name (from uid)
vsz	virtual size in Kbytes (alias vsize)
wchan	wait channel (as a symbolic name)
xstat	exit or stop status (valid only for stopped or zombie process)

FILES

/dev	special files and device names
/dev/drum	default swap device
/dev/kmem	default kernel memory
/var/run/dev.db	/dev name database
/var/run/kvm_vmunix.db	system namelist database
/vmunix	default system namelist

SEE ALSO

kill(1), w(1), kvm(3), strftime(3), pstat(8)

BUGS

Since `ps` cannot run faster than the system and is run as any other scheduled process, the information it displays can never be exact.

1

NAME

psbb – extract bounding box from PostScript document

SYNOPSIS

psbb *file*

DESCRIPTION

psbb reads *file* which should be a PostScript document conforming to the Document Structuring conventions and looks for a **%%BoundingBox** comment. If it finds one, it prints a line

llx lly urx ury

on the standard output and exits with zero status. If it doesn't find such a line or if the line is invalid it prints a message and exits with non-zero status.

SEE ALSO

grops(1)

1

NAME
ptx – permuted index

SYNOPSIS
ptx [option] . . . [input [output]]

DESCRIPTION
Ptx generates a permuted index to file *input* on file *output* (standard input and output default). It has three phases: the first does the permutation, generating one line for each keyword in an input line. The keyword is rotated to the front. The permuted file is then sorted. Finally, the sorted lines are rotated so the keyword comes at the middle of the page. Ptx produces output in the form:

```
.xx tail before keyword keyword and after head
```

where `.xx` may be an nroff(1) or troff(1) macro for user-defined formatting. The *before keyword* and *keyword and after* fields incorporate as much of the line as will fit around the keyword when it is printed at the middle of the page. *Tail* and *head*, at least one of which is an empty string "", are wrapped-around pieces small enough to fit in the unused space at the opposite end of the line. When original text must be discarded, '/' marks the spot.

The following options can be applied:

−f   Fold upper and lower case letters for sorting.

−t   Prepare the output for the phototypesetter; the default line length is 100 characters.

−w *n*
             Use the next argument, *n*, as the width of the output line. The default line length is 72 characters.

−g *n*
             Use the next argument, *n*, as the number of characters to allow for each gap among the four parts of the line as finally printed. The default gap is 3 characters.

−o *only*
             Use as keywords only the words given in the *only* file.

−i *ignore*
             Do not use as keywords any words given in the ignore file. If the −i and −o options are missing, use /usr/share/dict/eign as the ignore file.

−b *break*
             Use the characters in the break file to separate words. In any case, tab, newline, and space characters are always used as break characters.

−r   Take any leading nonblank characters of each input line to be a reference identifier (as to a page or chapter) separate from the text of the line. Attach that identifier as a 5th field on each output line.

The index for this manual was generated using ptx.

FILES
/usr/bin/sort
/usr/share/dict/eign

HISTORY
The ptx command appeared in Version 7 AT&T UNIX.

BUGS
　　Line length counts do not account for overstriking or proportional spacing.

1

NAME
pwd – return working directory name

SYNOPSIS
pwd

DESCRIPTION
Pwd writes the absolute pathname of the current working directory to the standard output.

The pwd utility exits 0 on success, and >0 if an error occurs.

STANDARDS
The **pwd** command is expected to be IEEE Std1003.2 (''POSIX'') compatible .

SEE ALSO
cd(1), csh(1), getwd(3)

BUGS
In csh(1) the command **dirs** is always faster (although it can give a different answer in the rare case that the current directory or a containing directory was moved after the shell descended into it).

1

NAME

quota – display disk usage and limits

SYNOPSIS

quota [–g] [–u] [–v | –q]
quota [–u] [–v | –q] *user*
quota [–g] [–v | –q] *group*

DESCRIPTION

Quota displays users' disk usage and limits. By default only the user quotas are printed.

Options:

–g   Print group quotas for the group of which the user is a member. The optional –u flag is equivalent to the default.

–v   quota will display quotas on filesystems where no storage is allocated.

–q   Print a more terse message, containing only information on filesystems where usage is over quota.

Specifying both –g and –u displays both the user quotas and the group quotas (for the user).

Only the super-user may use the –u flag and the optional *user* argument to view the limits of other users. Non-super-users can use the the –g flag and optional *group* argument to view only the limits of groups of which they are members.

The –q flag takes precedence over the –v flag.

Quota reports the quotas of all the filesystems listed in /etc/fstab. If quota exits with a non-zero status, one or more filesystems are over quota.

FILES

quota.user   located at the filesystem root with user quotas
quota.group   located at the filesystem root with group quotas
/etc/fstab   to find filesystem names and locations

HISTORY

The quota command appeared in 4.2BSD.

SEE ALSO

quotactl(2), fstab(5), edquota(8), quotacheck(8), quotaon(8), repquota(8)

1

NAME
ranlib – table-of-contents for archive libraries

SYNOPSIS
ranlib [−t] *file ...*

DESCRIPTION
Ranlib creates a table of external references for archive libraries, normally used by the loader, ld(1). This table is is named "__.SYMDEF" and is prepended to the archive. Files in the archive which are not executable and symbols which are uninteresting to the loader are ignored.

The options are as follows:

−t   Set the modification time of the __.SYMDEF file. This time is compared by the loader with the modification time of the archive to verify that the table is up-to-date with respect to the archive. If the modification time has been changed without any change to the archive (for example, by a cp(1)), the −t option can be used to "touch" the modification time so that it appears that the table is up-to-date. This is also useful after using the −t option of make(1).

FILES
/tmp/ranlib.XXXXXX Temporary file names.

SEE ALSO
ar(1), ld(1), lorder(1), nm(1), ranlib(5)

HISTORY
A ranlib command appeared in Version 7 AT&T UNIX.

1

NAME
rcp – remote file copy

SYNOPSIS
rcp [**–Kpx**] [**–k** *realm*] *file1 file2*
rcp [**–Kprx**] [**–k** *realm*] *file ... directory*

DESCRIPTION
Rcp copies files between machines. Each *file* or *directory* argument is either a remote file name of the form ''rname@rhost:path'', or a local file name (containing no ':' characters, or a '/' before any ':'s).

–K   The **–K** option turns off all Kerberos authentication.

–k   The **–k** option requests **rcp** to obtain tickets for the remote host in realm *realm* instead of the remote host's realm as determined by **krb_realmofhost**(3).

–p   The **–p** option causes **rcp** to attempt to preserve (duplicate) in its copies the modification times and modes of the source files, ignoring the *umask*. By default, the mode and owner of *file2* are preserved if it already existed; otherwise the mode of the source file modified by the **umask**(2) on the destination host is used.

–r   If any of the source files are directories, **rcp** copies each subtree rooted at that name; in this case the destination must be a directory.

–x   The **–x** option turns on DES encryption for all data passed by **rcp**. This may impact response time and CPU utilization, but provides increased security.

If *path* is not a full path name, it is interpreted relative to the login directory of the specified user *ruser* on *rhost*, or your current user name if no other remote user name is specified. A *path* on a remote host may be quoted (using \ ", or ´) so that the metacharacters are interpreted remotely.

Rcp does not prompt for passwords; it performs remote execution via **rsh**(1), and requires the same authorization.

Rcp handles third party copies, where neither source nor target files are on the current machine.

SEE ALSO
cp(1), ftp(1), rsh(1), rlogin(1)

HISTORY
The **rcp** command appeared in 4.2BSD. The version of **rcp** described here has been reimplemented with Kerberos in 4.3BSD–Reno.

BUGS
Doesn't detect all cases where the target of a copy might be a file in cases where only a directory should be legal.

Is confused by any output generated by commands in a .login, .profile, or .cshrc file on the remote host.

The destination user and hostname may have to be specified as ''rhost.rname'' when the destination machine is running the 4.2BSD version of **rcp**.

1

NAME

rcs – change RCS file attributes

SYNOPSIS

rcs [*options*] *file* ...

DESCRIPTION

rcs creates new RCS files or changes attributes of existing ones. An RCS file contains multiple revisions of text, an access list, a change log, descriptive text, and some control attributes. For **rcs** to work, the caller's login name must be on the access list, except if the access list is empty, the caller is the owner of the file or the superuser, or the –i option is present.

Pathnames matching an RCS suffix denote RCS files; all others denote working files. Names are paired as explained in **ci**(1). Revision numbers use the syntax described in **ci**(1).

OPTIONS

–i Create and initialize a new RCS file, but do not deposit any revision. If the RCS file has no path prefix, try to place it first into the subdirectory *./RCS*, and then into the current directory. If the RCS file already exists, print an error message.

–a*logins*
Append the login names appearing in the comma-separated list *logins* to the access list of the RCS file.

–A*oldfile*
Append the access list of *oldfile* to the access list of the RCS file.

–e[*logins*]
Erase the login names appearing in the comma-separated list *logins* from the access list of the RCS file. If *logins* is omitted, erase the entire access list.

–b[*rev*] Set the default branch to *rev*. If *rev* is omitted, the default branch is reset to the (dynamically) highest branch on the trunk.

–c*string*
sets the comment leader to *string*. The comment leader is printed before every log message line generated by the keyword **Log** during checkout (see **co**(1)). This is useful for programming languages without multi-line comments. An initial **ci** , or an **rcs** –i without –c, guesses the comment leader from the suffix of the working file.

–k*subst* Set the default keyword substitution to *subst*. The effect of keyword substitution is described in **co**(1). Giving an explicit –k option to **co**, **rcsdiff**, and **rcsmerge** overrides this default. Beware **rcs** –kv, because –kv is incompatible with **co** –l. Use **rcs** –kkv to restore the normal default keyword substitution.

–l[*rev*] Lock the revision with number *rev*. If a branch is given, lock the latest revision on that branch. If *rev* is omitted, lock the latest revision on the default branch. Locking prevents overlapping changes. A lock is removed with **ci** or **rcs** –u (see below).

–u[*rev*] Unlock the revision with number *rev*. If a branch is given, unlock the latest revision on that branch. If *rev* is omitted, remove the latest lock held by the caller. Normally, only the locker of a revision may unlock it. Somebody else unlocking a revision breaks the lock. This causes a mail message to be sent to the original locker. The message contains a commentary solicited from the breaker. The commentary is terminated by end-of-file or by a line containing . by itself.

–L Set locking to *strict*. Strict locking means that the owner of an RCS file is not exempt from locking for checkin. This option should be used for files that are shared.

–U Set locking to non-strict. Non-strict locking means that the owner of a file need not lock a revision for checkin. This option should *not* be used for files that are shared. Whether default locking is strict is determined by your system administrator, but it is normally strict.

1

−m*rev*:*msg*

> Replace revision *rev*'s log message with *msg*.

−n*name*[:[*rev*]]

> Associate the symbolic name *name* with the branch or revision *rev*. Delete the symbolic name if both : and *rev* are omitted; otherwise, print an error message if *name* is already associated with another number. If *rev* is symbolic, it is expanded before association. A *rev* consisting of a branch number followed by a . stands for the current latest revision in the branch. A : with an empty *rev* stands for the current latest revision on the default branch, normally the trunk. For example, **rcs −n***name*: **RCS/∗** associates *name* with the current latest revision of all the named RCS files; this contrasts with **rcs −n***name*:**$ RCS/∗** which associates *name* with the revision numbers extracted from keyword strings in the corresponding working files.

−N*name*[:[*rev*]]

> Act like −**n**, except override any previous assignment of *name*.

−o*range*

> deletes ("outdates") the revisions given by *range*. A range consisting of a single revision number means that revision. A range consisting of a branch number means the latest revision on that branch. A range of the form *rev1*:*rev2* means revisions *rev1* to *rev2* on the same branch, :*rev* means from the beginning of the branch containing *rev* up to and including *rev*, and *rev*: means from revision *rev* to the end of the branch containing *rev*. None of the outdated revisions may have branches or locks.

−**q**　　　Run quietly; do not print diagnostics.

−**I**　　　Run interactively, even if the standard input is not a terminal.

−s*state*[:*rev*]

> Set the state attribute of the revision *rev* to *state*. If *rev* is a branch number, assume the latest revision on that branch. If *rev* is omitted, assume the latest revision on the default branch. Any identifier is acceptable for *state*. A useful set of states is **Exp** (for experimental), **Stab** (for stable), and **Rel** (for released). By default, **ci**(1) sets the state of a revision to **Exp**.

−**t**[*file*]　Write descriptive text from the contents of the named *file* into the RCS file, deleting the existing text. The *file* pathname may not begin with −. If *file* is omitted, obtain the text from standard input, terminated by end-of-file or by a line containing . by itself. Prompt for the text if interaction is possible; see −**I**. With −**i**, descriptive text is obtained even if −**t** is not given.

−**t**−*string*

> Write descriptive text from the *string* into the RCS file, deleting the existing text.

−**V***n*　　Emulate RCS version *n*. See **co**(1) for details.

−**x***suffixes*

> Use *suffixes* to characterize RCS files. See **ci**(1) for details.

COMPATIBILITY

> The −**b***rev* option generates an RCS file that cannot be parsed by RCS version 3 or earlier.
>
> The −**k***subst* options (except −**kkv**) generate an RCS file that cannot be parsed by RCS version 4 or earlier.
>
> Use **rcs −V***n* to make an RCS file acceptable to RCS version *n* by discarding information that would confuse version *n*.
>
> RCS version 5.5 and earlier does not support the −**x** option, and requires a **,v** suffix on an RCS pathname.

FILES

> **rcs** accesses files much as **ci**(1) does, except that it uses the effective user for all accesses, it does not write the working file or its directory, and it does not even read the working file unless a revision number of **$** is specified.

1

ENVIRONMENT

RCSINIT

options prepended to the argument list, separated by spaces. See **ci**(1) for details.

DIAGNOSTICS

The RCS pathname and the revisions outdated are written to the diagnostic output. The exit status is zero if and only if all operations were successful.

IDENTIFICATION

Author: Walter F. Tichy.
Revision Number: 5.6; Release Date: 1991/09/26.
Copyright © 1982, 1988, 1989 by Walter F. Tichy.
Copyright © 1990, 1991 by Paul Eggert.

SEE ALSO

co(1), ci(1), ident(1), rcsdiff(1), rcsintro(1), rcsmerge(1), rlog(1), rcsfile(5)
Walter F. Tichy, RCS—A System for Version Control, *Software—Practice & Experience* **15**, 7 (July 1985), 637-654.

BUGS

The separator for revision ranges in the −**o** option used to be − instead of **:**, but this leads to confusion when symbolic names contain −. For backwards compatibility **rcs −o** still supports the old − separator, but it warns about this obsolete use.

Symbolic names need not refer to existing revisions or branches. For example, the −**o** option does not remove symbolic names for the outdated revisions; you must use −**n** to remove the names.

1

NAME

rcsclean – clean up working files

SYNOPSIS

rcsclean [*options*] [*file* ...]

DESCRIPTION

rcsclean removes working files that were checked out and never modified. For each *file* given, **rcsclean** compares the working file and a revision in the corresponding RCS file. If it finds a difference, it does nothing. Otherwise, it first unlocks the revision if the −**u** option is given, and then removes the working file unless the working file is writable and the revision is locked. It logs its actions by outputting the corresponding **rcs** −**u** and **rm** −**f** commands on the standard output.

If no *file* is given, all working files in the current directory are cleaned. Pathnames matching an RCS suffix denote RCS files; all others denote working files. Names are paired as explained in **ci**(1).

The number of the revision to which the working file is compared may be attached to any of the options −**n**, −**q**, −**r**, or −**u**. If no revision number is specified, then if the −**u** option is given and the caller has one revision locked, **rcsclean** uses that revision; otherwise **rcsclean** uses the latest revision on the default branch, normally the root.

rcsclean is useful for **clean** targets in Makefiles. See also **rcsdiff**(1), which prints out the differences, and **ci**(1), which normally asks whether to check in a file if it was not changed.

OPTIONS

−**k***subst*   Use *subst* style keyword substitution when retrieving the revision for comparison. See **co**(1) for details.

−**n**[*rev*]   Do not actually remove any files or unlock any revisions. Using this option will tell you what **rcsclean** would do without actually doing it.

−**q**[*rev*]   Do not log the actions taken on standard output.

−**r**[*rev*]   This option has no effect other than specifying the revision for comparison.

−**u**[*rev*]   Unlock the revision if it is locked and no difference is found.

−**V***n*   Emulate RCS version *n*. See **co**(1) for details.

−**x***suffixes*

Use *suffixes* to characterize RCS files. See **ci**(1) for details.

EXAMPLES

rcsclean *.c *.h

removes all working files ending in **.c** or **.h** that were not changed since their checkout.

rcsclean

removes all working files in the current directory that were not changed since their checkout.

FILES

rcsclean accesses files much as **ci**(1) does.

ENVIRONMENT

RCSINIT

options prepended to the argument list, separated by spaces. A backslash escapes spaces within an option. The **RCSINIT** options are prepended to the argument lists of most RCS commands. Useful **RCSINIT** options include −**q**, −**V**, and −**x**.

DIAGNOSTICS

The exit status is zero if and only if all operations were successful. Missing working files and RCS files are silently ignored.

1

IDENTIFICATION

Author: Walter F. Tichy.
Revision Number: 1.8; Release Date: 1991/11/03.
Copyright © 1982, 1988, 1989 by Walter F. Tichy.
Copyright © 1990, 1991 by Paul Eggert.

SEE ALSO

ci(1), co(1), ident(1), rcs(1), rcsdiff(1), rcsintro(1), rcsmerge(1), rlog(1), rcsfile(5)

Walter F. Tichy, RCS—A System for Version Control, *Software—Practice & Experience* **15**, 7 (July 1985), 637-654.

BUGS

At least one *file* must be given in older Unix versions that do not provide the needed directory scanning operations.

1

NAME
rcsdiff – compare RCS revisions

SYNOPSIS
rcsdiff [−k*subst*] [−q] [−r*rev1* [−r*rev2*]] [−V*n*] [−x*suffixes*] [*diff options*] *file* ...

DESCRIPTION
rcsdiff runs **diff**(1) to compare two revisions of each RCS file given.

Pathnames matching an RCS suffix denote RCS files; all others denote working files. Names are paired as explained in **ci**(1).

The option −q suppresses diagnostic output. Zero, one, or two revisions may be specified with −r. The option −k*subst* affects keyword substitution when extracting revisions, as described in **co**(1); for example, −**kk** −r**1.1** −r**1.2** ignores differences in keyword values when comparing revisions **1.1** and **1.2**. To avoid excess output from locker name substitution, −**kkvl** is assumed if (1) at most one revision option is given, (2) no −k option is given, (3) −**kkv** is the default keyword substitution, and (4) the working file's mode would be produced by **co** −**l**. See **co**(1) for details about −V and −x. Otherwise, all options of **diff**(1) that apply to regular files are accepted, with the same meaning as for **diff**.

If both *rev1* and *rev2* are omitted, **rcsdiff** compares the latest revision on the default branch (by default the trunk) with the contents of the corresponding working file. This is useful for determining what you changed since the last checkin.

If *rev1* is given, but *rev2* is omitted, **rcsdiff** compares revision *rev1* of the RCS file with the contents of the corresponding working file.

If both *rev1* and *rev2* are given, **rcsdiff** compares revisions *rev1* and *rev2* of the RCS file.

Both *rev1* and *rev2* may be given numerically or symbolically.

EXAMPLE
The command

> **rcsdiff f.c**

compares the latest revision on the default branch of the RCS file to the contents of the working file **f.c**.

ENVIRONMENT
RCSINIT
> options prepended to the argument list, separated by spaces. See **ci**(1) for details.

DIAGNOSTICS
Exit status is 0 for no differences during any comparison, 1 for some differences, 2 for trouble.

IDENTIFICATION
Author: Walter F. Tichy.
Revision Number: 5.3; Release Date: 1991/04/21.
Copyright © 1982, 1988, 1989 by Walter F. Tichy.
Copyright © 1990, 1991 by Paul Eggert.

SEE ALSO
ci(1), co(1), diff(1), ident(1), rcs(1), rcsintro(1), rcsmerge(1), rlog(1)
Walter F. Tichy, RCS—A System for Version Control, *Software—Practice & Experience* **15**, 7 (July 1985), 637-654.

1

NAME

rcsfreeze – freeze a configuration of sources checked in under RCS

SYNOPSIS

rcsfreeze [*name*]

DESCRIPTION

rcsfreeze assigns a symbolic revision number to a set of RCS files that form a valid configuration.

The idea is to run **rcsfreeze** each time a new version is checked in. A unique symbolic name (**C**_*number*, where *number* is increased each time **rcsfreeze** is run) is then assigned to the most recent revision of each RCS file of the main trunk.

An optional *name* argument to **rcsfreeze** gives a symbolic name to the configuration. The unique identifier is still generated and is listed in the log file but it will not appear as part of the symbolic revision name in the actual RCS files.

A log message is requested from the user for future reference.

The shell script works only on all RCS files at one time. All changed files must be checked in already. Run *rcsclean*(1) first and see whether any sources remain in the current directory.

FILES

RCS/.rcsfreeze.ver
> version number

RCS/.rcsfreeze.log
> log messages, most recent first

AUTHOR

Stephan v. Bechtolsheim

SEE ALSO

co(1), rcs(1), rcsclean(1), rlog(1)

BUGS

rcsfreeze does not check whether any sources are checked out and modified.

Although both source file names and RCS file names are accepted, they are not paired as usual with RCS commands.

Error checking is rudimentary.

rcsfreeze is just an optional example shell script, and should not be taken too seriously. See CVS for a more complete solution.

1

NAME

rcsintro – introduction to RCS commands

DESCRIPTION

The Revision Control System (RCS) manages multiple revisions of files. RCS automates the storing, retrieval, logging, identification, and merging of revisions. RCS is useful for text that is revised frequently, for example programs, documentation, graphics, papers, and form letters.

The basic user interface is extremely simple. The novice only needs to learn two commands: **ci**(1) and **co**(1). **ci**, short for "check in", deposits the contents of a file into an archival file called an RCS file. An RCS file contains all revisions of a particular file. **co**, short for "check out", retrieves revisions from an RCS file.

Functions of RCS

- Store and retrieve multiple revisions of text. RCS saves all old revisions in a space efficient way. Changes no longer destroy the original, because the previous revisions remain accessible. Revisions can be retrieved according to ranges of revision numbers, symbolic names, dates, authors, and states.

- Maintain a complete history of changes. RCS logs all changes automatically. Besides the text of each revision, RCS stores the author, the date and time of check-in, and a log message summarizing the change. The logging makes it easy to find out what happened to a module, without having to compare source listings or having to track down colleagues.

- Resolve access conflicts. When two or more programmers wish to modify the same revision, RCS alerts the programmers and prevents one modification from corrupting the other.

- Maintain a tree of revisions. RCS can maintain separate lines of development for each module. It stores a tree structure that represents the ancestral relationships among revisions.

- Merge revisions and resolve conflicts. Two separate lines of development of a module can be coalesced by merging. If the revisions to be merged affect the same sections of code, RCS alerts the user about the overlapping changes.

- Control releases and configurations. Revisions can be assigned symbolic names and marked as released, stable, experimental, etc. With these facilities, configurations of modules can be described simply and directly.

- Automatically identify each revision with name, revision number, creation time, author, etc. The identification is like a stamp that can be embedded at an appropriate place in the text of a revision. The identification makes it simple to determine which revisions of which modules make up a given configuration.

- Minimize secondary storage. RCS needs little extra space for the revisions (only the differences). If intermediate revisions are deleted, the corresponding deltas are compressed accordingly.

Getting Started with RCS

Suppose you have a file **f.c** that you wish to put under control of RCS. If you have not already done so, make an RCS directory with the command

mkdir RCS

Then invoke the check-in command

ci f.c

This command creates an RCS file in the **RCS** directory, stores **f.c** into it as revision 1.1, and deletes **f.c**. It also asks you for a description. The description should be a synopsis of the contents of the file. All later check-in commands will ask you for a log entry, which should summarize the changes that you made.

1

Files in the RCS directory are called RCS files; the others are called working files. To get back the working file **f.c** in the previous example, use the check-out command

> **co f.c**

This command extracts the latest revision from the RCS file and writes it into **f.c**. If you want to edit **f.c**, you must lock it as you check it out with the command

> **co −l f.c**

You can now edit **f.c**.

Suppose after some editing you want to know what changes that you have made. The command

> **rcsdiff f.c**

tells you the difference between the most recently checked-in version and the working file. You can check the file back in by invoking

> **ci f.c**

This increments the revision number properly.

If **ci** complains with the message

> **ci error: no lock set by** *your name*

then you have tried to check in a file even though you did not lock it when you checked it out. Of course, it is too late now to do the check-out with locking, because another check-out would overwrite your modifications. Instead, invoke

> **rcs −l f.c**

This command will lock the latest revision for you, unless somebody else got ahead of you already. In this case, you'll have to negotiate with that person.

Locking assures that you, and only you, can check in the next update, and avoids nasty problems if several people work on the same file. Even if a revision is locked, it can still be checked out for reading, compiling, etc. All that locking prevents is a *check-in* by anybody but the locker.

If your RCS file is private, i.e., if you are the only person who is going to deposit revisions into it, strict locking is not needed and you can turn it off. If strict locking is turned off, the owner of the RCS file need not have a lock for check-in; all others still do. Turning strict locking off and on is done with the commands

> **rcs −U f.c**   and   **rcs −L f.c**

If you don't want to clutter your working directory with RCS files, create a subdirectory called **RCS** in your working directory, and move all your RCS files there. RCS commands will look first into that directory to find needed files. All the commands discussed above will still work, without any modification. (Actually, pairs of RCS and working files can be specified in three ways: (a) both are given, (b) only the working file is given, (c) only the RCS file is given. Both RCS and working files may have arbitrary path prefixes; RCS commands pair them up intelligently.)

To avoid the deletion of the working file during check-in (in case you want to continue editing or compiling), invoke

> **ci −l f.c**   or   **ci −u f.c**

These commands check in **f.c** as usual, but perform an implicit check-out. The first form also locks the checked in revision, the second one doesn't. Thus, these options save you one check-out operation. The first form is useful if you want to continue editing, the second one if you just want to read the file. Both update the identification markers in your working file (see below).

You can give **ci** the number you want assigned to a checked in revision. Assume all your revisions were numbered 1.1, 1.2, 1.3, etc., and you would like to start release 2. The command

    ci −r2 f.c   or   ci −r2.1 f.c

assigns the number 2.1 to the new revision. From then on, **ci** will number the subsequent revisions with 2.2, 2.3, etc. The corresponding **co** commands

    co −r2 f.c   and   co −r2.1 f.c

retrieve the latest revision numbered 2.*x* and the revision 2.1, respectively. **co** without a revision number selects the latest revision on the *trunk*, i.e. the highest revision with a number consisting of two fields. Numbers with more than two fields are needed for branches. For example, to start a branch at revision 1.3, invoke

    ci −r1.3.1 f.c

This command starts a branch numbered 1 at revision 1.3, and assigns the number 1.3.1.1 to the new revision. For more information about branches, see **rcsfile**(5).

Automatic Identification

RCS can put special strings for identification into your source and object code. To obtain such identification, place the marker

    Id

into your text, for instance inside a comment. RCS will replace this marker with a string of the form

    $Id: *filename revision date time author state* **$**

With such a marker on the first page of each module, you can always see with which revision you are working. RCS keeps the markers up to date automatically. To propagate the markers into your object code, simply put them into literal character strings. In C, this is done as follows:

    static char rcsid[] = "Id";

The command **ident** extracts such markers from any file, even object code and dumps. Thus, **ident** lets you find out which revisions of which modules were used in a given program.

You may also find it useful to put the marker **Log** into your text, inside a comment. This marker accumulates the log messages that are requested during check-in. Thus, you can maintain the complete history of your file directly inside it. There are several additional identification markers; see **co**(1) for details.

IDENTIFICATION

Author: Walter F. Tichy.
Revision Number: 5.1; Release Date: 1991/04/21.
Copyright © 1982, 1988, 1989 by Walter F. Tichy.
Copyright © 1990, 1991 by Paul Eggert.

SEE ALSO

ci(1), co(1), ident(1), rcs(1), rcsdiff(1), rcsintro(1), rcsmerge(1), rlog(1)
Walter F. Tichy, RCS—A System for Version Control, *Software—Practice & Experience* **15**, 7 (July 1985), 637-654.

1

NAME
rcsmerge – merge RCS revisions

SYNOPSIS
rcsmerge [*options*] *file*

DESCRIPTION
rcsmerge incorporates the changes between two revisions of an RCS file into the corresponding working file.

Pathnames matching an RCS suffix denote RCS files; all others denote working files. Names are paired as explained in **ci**(1).

At least one revision must be specified with one of the options described below, usually −**r**. At most two revisions may be specified. If only one revision is specified, the latest revision on the default branch (normally the highest branch on the trunk) is assumed for the second revision. Revisions may be specified numerically or symbolically.

rcsmerge prints a warning if there are overlaps, and delimits the overlapping regions as explained in **merge**(1). The command is useful for incorporating changes into a checked-out revision.

OPTIONS
−**k***subst*　Use *subst* style keyword substitution. See **co**(1) for details. For example, −**kk** −**r1.1** −**r1.2** ignores differences in keyword values when merging the changes from **1.1** to **1.2**.

−**p**[*rev*]　Send the result to standard output instead of overwriting the working file.

−**q**[*rev*]　Run quietly; do not print diagnostics.

−**r**[*rev*]　Merge with respect to revision *rev*. Here an empty *rev* stands for the latest revision on the default branch, normally the head.

−**V***n*　　Emulate RCS version *n*. See **co**(1) for details.

−**x***suffixes*
　　　　Use *suffixes* to characterize RCS files. See **ci**(1) for details.

EXAMPLES
Suppose you have released revision 2.8 of **f.c**. Assume furthermore that after you complete an unreleased revision 3.4, you receive updates to release 2.8 from someone else. To combine the updates to 2.8 and your changes between 2.8 and 3.4, put the updates to 2.8 into file f.c and execute

　　rcsmerge −p −r2.8 −r3.4 f.c >f.merged.c

Then examine **f.merged.c**. Alternatively, if you want to save the updates to 2.8 in the RCS file, check them in as revision 2.8.1.1 and execute **co −j**:

　　ci −r2.8.1.1 f.c
　　co −r3.4 −j2.8:2.8.1.1 f.c

As another example, the following command undoes the changes between revision 2.4 and 2.8 in your currently checked out revision in **f.c**.

　　rcsmerge −r2.8 −r2.4 f.c

Note the order of the arguments, and that **f.c** will be overwritten.

ENVIRONMENT
RCSINIT
　　　　options prepended to the argument list, separated by spaces. See **ci**(1) for details.

DIAGNOSTICS
Exit status is 0 for no overlaps, 1 for some overlaps, 2 for trouble.

IDENTIFICATION

    Author: Walter F. Tichy.

    Revision Number: 5.3; Release Date: 1991/08/19.

    Copyright © 1982, 1988, 1989 by Walter F. Tichy.

    Copyright © 1990, 1991 by Paul Eggert.

SEE ALSO

    ci(1), co(1), ident(1), merge(1), rcs(1), rcsdiff(1), rcsintro(1), rlog(1), rcsfile(5)

    Walter F. Tichy, RCS—A System for Version Control, *Software—Practice & Experience* **15**, 7 (July 1985), 637-654.

1

. NAME

rdist – remote file distribution program

SYNOPSIS

rdist [–nqbRhivwy] [–f *distfile*] [–d *var=value*] [–m *host*] [*name* ...]
rdist [–nqbRhivwy] –c *name* ... [login@]*host*[:dest]

DESCRIPTION

Rdist is a program to maintain identical copies of files over multiple hosts. It preserves the owner, group, mode, and mtime of files if possible and can update programs that are executing. **Rdist** reads commands from *distfile* to direct the updating of files and/or directories.

Options specific to the first SYNOPSIS form:

–   If *distfile* is '–', the standard input is used.

–**f** *distfile*
          Use the specified *distfile*.

If either the –**f** or '–' option is not specified, the program looks first for "distfile", then "Distfile" to use as the input. If no names are specified on the command line, **rdist** will update all of the files and directories listed in *distfile*. Otherwise, the argument is taken to be the name of a file to be updated or the label of a command to execute. If label and file names conflict, it is assumed to be a label. These may be used together to update specific files using specific commands.

Options specific to the second SYNOPSIS form:

–**c**   Forces **rdist** to interpret the remaining arguments as a small *distfile*.

          The equivalent distfile is as follows.

                    (*name* ...) -> [*login@*] *host*
                         install [*dest*];

Options common to both forms:

–**b**   Binary comparison. Perform a binary comparison and update files if they differ rather than comparing dates and sizes.

–**d** *var=value*
          Define *var* to have *value*. The –**d** option is used to define or override variable definitions in the *distfile*. *Value* can be the empty string, one name, or a list of names surrounded by parentheses and separated by tabs and/or spaces.

–**h**   Follow symbolic links. Copy the file that the link points to rather than the link itself.

–**i**   Ignore unresolved links. **Rdist** will normally try to maintain the link structure of files being transferred and warn the user if all the links cannot be found.

–**m** *host*   Limit which machines are to be updated. Multiple –**m** arguments can be given to limit updates to a subset of the hosts listed in the *distfile*.

–**n**   Print the commands without executing them. This option is useful for debugging *distfile*.

–**q**   Quiet mode. Files that are being modified are normally printed on standard output. The –**q** option suppresses this.

−R   Remove extraneous files. If a directory is being updated, any files that exist on the remote host
            that do not exist in the master directory are removed. This is useful for maintaining truly ident-
            ical copies of directories.

−v   Verify that the files arc up to date on all the hosts. Any files that are out of date will be
            displayed but no files will be changed nor any mail sent.

−w   Whole mode. The whole file name is appended to the destination directory name. Normally,
            only the last component of a name is used when renaming files. This will preserve the directo-
            ry structure of the files being copied instead of flattening the directory structure. For example,
            renaming a list of files such as (dir1/f1 dir2/f2) to dir3 would create files dir3/dir1/f1 and
            dir3/dir2/f2 instead of dir3/f1 and dir3/f2.

−y   Younger mode. Files are normally updated if their *mtime* and *size* (see stat(2)) disagree.
            The −y option causes **rdist** not to update files that are younger than the master copy. This
            can be used to prevent newer copies on other hosts from being replaced. A warning message is
            printed for files which are newer than the master copy.

Distfile contains a sequence of entries that specify the files to be copied, the destination hosts, and what
operations to perform to do the updating. Each entry has one of the following formats.

```
<variable name> '=' <name list>
[label:]<source list> '->' <destination list> <command list>
[label:]<source list> '::' <time_stamp file> <command list>
```

The first format is used for defining variables. The second format is used for distributing files to other hosts.
The third format is used for making lists of files that have been changed since some given date. The
source list specifies a list of files and/or directories on the local host which are to be used as the master
copy for distribution. The *destination list* is the list of hosts to which these files are to be copied.
Each file in the source list is added to a list of changes if the file is out of date on the host which is being updated (second format) or the file is newer than the time stamp file (third format).

Labels are optional. They are used to identify a command for partial updates.

Newlines, tabs, and blanks are only used as separators and are otherwise ignored. Comments begin with '#'
and end with a newline.

Variables to be expanded begin with '$' followed by one character or a name enclosed in curly braces (see
the examples at the end).

The source and destination lists have the following format:

```
<name>
```
or
```
'(' <zero or more names separated by white-space> ')'
```

The shell meta-characters '[', ']', '{', '}', '*', and '?' are recognized and expanded (on the local host only)
in the same way as csh(1). They can be escaped with a backslash. The '~' character is also expanded in the
same way as csh(1) but is expanded separately on the local and destination hosts. When the −w option is
used with a file name that begins with '~', everything except the home directory is appended to the destination name. File names which do not begin with '/' or '~' use the destination user's home directory as the root
directory for the rest of the file name.

The command list consists of zero or more commands of the following format.

```
'install'      <options>      opt_dest_name ';'
'notify'       <name list>    ';'
'except'       <name list>    ';'
'except_pat'   <pattern list> ';'
'special'      <name list>    string ';'
```

The **install** command is used to copy out of date files and/or directories. Each source file is copied to each host in the destination list. Directories are recursively copied in the same way. *Opt_dest_name* is an optional parameter to rename files. If no **install** command appears in the command list or the destination name is not specified, the source file name is used. Directories in the path name will be created if they do not exist on the remote host. To help prevent disasters, a non-empty directory on a target host will never be replaced with a regular file or a symbolic link. However, under the '–R' option a non-empty directory will be removed if the corresponding filename is completely absent on the master host. The *options* are '–R', '–h', '–i', '–v', '–w', '–y', and '–b' and have the same semantics as options on the command line except they only apply to the files in the source list. The login name used on the destination host is the same as the local host unless the destination name is of the format ''login@host''.

The **notify** command is used to mail the list of files updated (and any errors that may have occurred) to the listed names. If no '@' appears in the name, the destination host is appended to the name (e.g., name1@host, name2@host, ...).

The **except** command is used to update all of the files in the source list **except** for the files listed in *name list*. This is usually used to copy everything in a directory except certain files.

The **except_pat** command is like the **except** command except that *pattern list* is a list of regular expressions (see ed(1) for details). If one of the patterns matches some string within a file name, that file will be ignored. Note that since '\' is a quote character, it must be doubled to become part of the regular expression. Variables are expanded in *pattern list* but not shell file pattern matching characters. To include a '$', it must be escaped with '\'.

The **special** command is used to specify sh(1) commands that are to be executed on the remote host after the file in *name list* is updated or installed. If the *name list* is omitted then the shell commands will be executed for every file updated or installed. The shell variable 'FILE' is set to the current filename before executing the commands in *string*. *String* starts and ends with '"' and can cross multiple lines in *distfile*. Multiple commands to the shell should be separated by ';'. Commands are executed in the user's home directory on the host being updated. The *special* command can be used to rebuild private databases, etc. after a program has been updated.

The following is a small example:

```
HOSTS = ( matisse root@arpa )

FILES = ( /bin /lib /usr/bin /usr/games
/usr/include/{*.h,{stand,sys,vax*,pascal,machine}/*.h}
/usr/lib /usr/man/man? /usr/ucb /usr/local/rdist )

EXLIB = ( Mail.rc aliases aliases.dir aliases.pag crontab dshrc
sendmail.cf sendmail.fc sendmail.hf sendmail.st uucp vfont )

${FILES} -> ${HOSTS}
install -R ;
except /usr/lib/${EXLIB} ;
except /usr/games/lib ;
special /usr/lib/sendmail "/usr/lib/sendmail -bz" ;
```

```
srcs:
/usr/src/bin -> arpa
except_pat ( \\.o\$ /SCCS\$ ) ;

IMAGEN = (ips dviimp catdvi)

imagen:
/usr/local/${IMAGEN} -> arpa
install /usr/local/lib ;
notify ralph ;

${FILES} :: stamp.cory
notify root@cory ;
```

FILES

distfile   input command file
/tmp/rdist* temporary file for update lists

SEE ALSO

sh(1), csh(1), stat(2)

HISTORY

The rdist command appeared in 4.3BSD.

DIAGNOSTICS

A complaint about mismatch of rdist version numbers may really stem from some problem with starting your shell, e.g., you are in too many groups.

BUGS

Source files must reside on the local host where rdist is executed.

There is no easy way to have a special command executed after all files in a directory have been updated.

Variable expansion only works for name lists; there should be a general macro facility.

Rdist aborts on files which have a negative mtime (before Jan 1, 1970).

There should be a 'force' option to allow replacement of non-empty directories by regular files or symlinks. A means of updating file modes and owners of otherwise identical files is also needed.

1

NAME

    refer – preprocess bibliographic references for groff

SYNOPSIS

    refer [−benvCPRS] [−a*n*] [−c*fields*] [−f*n*] [−i*fields*] [−k*field*] [−l*m,n*] [−p*filename*] [−s*fields*]
    [−t*n*] [−B*field.macro*] [*filename* ...]

DESCRIPTION

    This file documents the GNU version of **refer**, which is part of the groff document formatting system.
refer copies the contents of *filename* ... to the standard output, except that lines between **.[** and **.]** are interpreted as citations, and lines between **.R1** and **.R2** are interpreted as commands about how citations are to be processed.

    Each citation specifies a reference. The citation can specify a reference that is contained in a bibliographic database by giving a set of keywords that only that reference contains. Alternatively it can specify a reference by supplying a database record in the citation. A combination of these alternatives is also possible.

    For each citation, **refer** can produce a mark in the text. This mark consists of some label which can be separated from the text and from other labels in various ways. For each reference it also outputs **groff** commands that can be used by a macro package to produce a formatted reference for each citation. The output of **refer** must therefore be processed using a suitable macro package. The −**ms** and −**me** macros are both suitable. The commands to format a citation's reference can be output immediately after the citation, or the references may be accumulated, and the commands output at some later point. If the references are accumulated, then multiple citations of the same reference will produce a single formatted reference.

    The interpretation of lines between **.R1** and **.R2** as commands is a new feature of GNU refer. Documents making use of this feature can still be processed by Unix refer just by adding the lines

        .de R1
        .ig R2
        ..

to the beginning of the document. This will cause **troff** to ignore everything between **.R1** and **.R2**. The effect of some commands can also be achieved by options. These options are supported mainly for compatibility with Unix refer. It is usually more convenient to use commands.

    refer generates **.lf** lines so that filenames and line numbers in messages produced by commands that read **refer** output will be correct; it also interprets lines beginning with **.lf** so that filenames and line numbers in the messages and **.lf** lines that it produces will be accurate even if the input has been preprocessed by a command such as **soelim**(1).

OPTIONS

    Most options are equivalent to commands (for a description of these commands see the **Commands** subsection):

    −**b**   **no-label-in-text; no-label-in-reference**

    −**e**   **accumulate**

    −**n**   **no-default-database**

    −**C**   **compatible**

    −**P**   **move-puntuation**

    −**S**   **label "(A.n|Q) ', ' (D.y|D)"; bracket-label " (") "; "**

    −**a***n*   **reverse A***n*

    −**c***fields* **capitalize** *fields*

    −**f***n*   **label %***n*

    −**i***fields* **search-ignore** *fields*

1

-k   **label L%a**

-k*field*   **label** *field* **%a**

-l   **label A.nD.y%a**

-l*m*   **label A.n+*m*D.y%a**

-l,*n*   **label A.nD.y-*n*%a**

-l*m*,*n*   **label A.n+*m*D.y-*n*%a**

-p*filename*
        database *filename*

-s*spec*   **sort** *spec*

-t*n*   **search-truncate** *n*

These options are equivalent to the following commands with the addition that the filenames specified on the command line are processed as if they were arguments to the **bibliography** command instead of in the normal way:

-B   **annotate X AP; no-label-in-reference**

-B*field.macro*
        annotate *field macro*; **no-label-in-reference**

The following options have no equivalent commands:

-v   Print the version number.

-R   Don't recognize lines beginning with **.R1/.R2**.

USAGE

Bibliographic databases

The bibliographic database is a text file consisting of records separated by one or more blank lines. Within each record fields start with a % at the beginning of a line. Each field has a one character name that immediately follows the %. It is best to use only upper and lower case letters for the names of fields. The name of the field should be followed by exactly one space, and then by the contents of the field. Empty fields are ignored. The conventional meaning of each field is as follows:

A   The name of an author. If the name contains a title such as **Jr.** at the end, it should be separated from the last name by a comma. There can be multiple occurences of the A field. The order is siginificant. It is a good idea always to supply an A field or a **Q** field.

B   For an article that is part of a book, the title of the book

C   The place (city) of publication.

D   The date of publication. The year should be specified in full. If the month is specified, the name rather than the number of the month should be used, but only the first three letters are required. It is a good idea always to supply a **D** field; if the date is unknown, a value such as **in press** or **unknown** can be used.

E   For an article that is part of a book, the name of an editor of the book. Where the work has editors and no authors, the names of the editors should be given as A fields and **, (ed)** or **, (eds)** should be appended to the last author.

G   US Government ordering number.

I   The publisher (issuer).

J   For an article in a journal, the name of the journal.

K   Keywords to be used for searching.

L   Label.

N   Journal issue number.

O   Other information. This is usually printed at the end of the reference.

P   Page number. A range of pages can be specified as $m-n$.

Q   The name of the author, if the author is not a person. This will only be used if there are no **A** fields. There can only be one **Q** field.

R   Technical report number.

S   Series name.

T   Title. For an article in a book or journal, this should be the title of the article.

V   Volume number of the journal or book.

X   Annotation.

For all fields except **A** and **E**, if there is more than one occurence of a particular field in a record, only the last such field will be used.

If accent strings are used, they should follow the charater to be accented. This means that the **AM** macro must be used with the −**ms** macros. Accent strings should not be quoted: use one \ rather than two.

Citations

The format of a citation is

     .[*opening-text*
     flags keywords
     fields
     .]*closing-text*

The *opening-text*, *closing-text* and *flags* components are optional. Only one of the *keywords* and *fields* components need be specified.

The *keywords* component says to search the bibliographic databases for a reference that contains all the words in *keywords*. It is an error if more than one reference if found.

The *fields* components specifies additional fields to replace or supplement those specified in the reference. When references are being accumulated and the *keywords* component is non-empty, then additional fields should be specified only on the first occasion that a particular reference is cited, and will apply to all citations of that reference.

The *opening-text* and *closing-text* component specifies strings to be used to bracket the label instead of the strings specified in the **bracket-label** command. If either of these components is non-empty, the strings specified in the **bracket-label** command will not be used; this behaviour can be altered using the [and] flags. Note that leading and trailing spaces are significant for these components.

The *flags* component is a list of non-alphanumeric characters each of which modifies the treatment of this particular citation. Unix refer will treat these flags as part of the keywords and so will ignore them since they are non-alphanumeric. The following flags are currently recognized:

\#   This says to use the label specified by the **short-label** command, instead of that specified by the **label** command. If no short label has been specified, the normal label will be used. Typically the short label is used with author-date labels and consists of only the date and possibly a disambiguating letter; the # is supposed to be suggestive of a numeric type of label.

[Precede *opening-text* with the first string specified in the **bracket-label** command.

]   Follow *closing-text* with the second string specified in the **bracket-label** command.

One advantages of using the [and] flags rather than including the brackets in *opening-text* and *closing-text* is that you can change the style of bracket used in the document just by changing the **bracket-label** command. Another advantage is that sorting and merging of citations will not necessarily be inhibited if the flags are used.

If a label is to be inserted into the text, it will be attached to the line preceding the **.[** line. If there is no such line, then an extra line will be inserted before the **.[** line and a warning will be given.

There is no special notation for making a citation to multiple references. Just use a sequence of citations, one for each reference. Don't put anything between the citations. The labels for all the citations will be attached to the line preceding the first citation. The labels may also be sorted or merged. See the description of the <> label expression, and of the **sort-adjacent-labels** and **abbreviate-label-ranges** command. A label will not be merged if its citation has a non-empty *opening-text* or *closing-text*. However, the labels for a citation using the] flag and without any *closing-text* immediately followed by a citation using the [flag and without any *opening-text* may be sorted and merged even though the first citation's *opening-text* or the second citation's *closing-text* is non-empty. (If you wish to prevent this just make the first citation's *closing-text* **\&**.)

Commands

Commands are contained between lines starting with **.R1** and **.R2**. Recognition of these lines can be prevented by the **−R** option. When a **.R1** line is recognized any accumulated references are flushed out. Neither **.R1** nor **.R2** lines, nor anything between them is output.

Commands are separated by newlines or **;**s. **#** introduces a comment that extends to the end of the line (but does not conceal the newline). Each command is broken up into words. Words are separated by spaces or tabs. A word that begins with **"** extends to the next **"** that is not followed by another **"**. If there is no such **"** the word extends to the end of the line. Pairs of **"** in a word beginning with **"** collapse to a single **"**. Neither **#** nor **;** are recognized inside **"**s. A line can be continued by ending it with ****; this works everywhere except after a **#**.

Each command *name* that is marked with ∗ has an associated negative command **no-***name* that undoes the effect of *name*. For example, the **no-sort** command specifies that references should not be sorted. The negative commands take no arguments.

In the following description each argument must be a single word; *field* is used for a single upper or lower case letter naming a field; *fields* is used for a sequence of such letters; *m* and *n* are used for a non-negative numbers; *string* is used for an arbitrary string; *filename* is used for the name of a file.

abbreviate∗ *fields string1 string2 string3 string4*

> Abbreviate the first names of *fields*. An initial letter will be separated from another initial letter by *string1*, from the last name by *string2*, and from anything else (such as a **von** or **de**) by *string3*. These default to a period followed by a space. In a hyphenated first name, the initial of the first part of the name will be separated from the hyphen by *string4*; this defaults to a period. No attempt is made to handle any ambiguities that might result from abbreviation. Names are abbreviated before sorting and before label construction.

abbreviate-label-ranges∗ *string*

> Three or more adjacent labels that refer to consecutive references will be abbreviated to a label consisting of the first label, followed by *string* followed by the last label. This is mainly useful with numeric labels. If *string* is omitted it defaults to −.

accumulate∗

> Accumulate references instead of writing out each reference as it is encountered. Accumulated references will be written out whenever a reference of the form
>
> > .[
> > $LIST$
> > .]
>
> is encountered, after all input files hve been processed, and whenever **.R1** line is recognized.

annotate∗ *field string*   *field* is an annotation; print it at the end of the reference as a paragraph preceded by the line

.*string*

If *macro* is omitted it will default to **AP**; if *field* is also omitted it will default to **X**. Only one field can be an annotation.

articles *string* ...   *string* ... are definite or indefinite articles, and should be ignored at the beginning of **T** fields when sorting. Initially, **the**, **a** and **an** are recognized as articles.

bibliography *filename* ... Write out all the references contained in the bibliographic databases *filename* ...

bracket-label *string1 string2 string3*

In the text, bracket each label with *string1* and *string2*. An occurrence of *string2* immediately followed by *string1* will be turned into *string3*. The default behaviour is

bracket-label \∗([. \∗(.] ", "

capitalize *fields*   Convert *fields* to caps and small caps.

compatible∗   Recognize **.R1** and **.R2** even when followed by a character other than space or newline.

database *filename* ...   Search the bibliographic databases *filename* ... For each *filename* if an index *filename*.**i** created by **indxbib**(1) exists, then it will be searched instead; each index can cover multiple databases.

date-as-label∗ *string*   *string* is a label expression that specifies a string with which to replace the **D** field after constructing the label. See the **Label expressions** subsection for a description of label expressions. This command is useful if you do not want explicit labels in the reference list, but instead want to handle any necessary disambiguation by qualifying the date in some way. The label used in the text would typically be some combination of the author and date. In most cases you should also use the **no-label-in-reference** command. For example,

date-as-label D.+yD.y%a∗D.-y

would attach a disambiguating letter to the year part of the **D** field in the reference.

default-database∗   The default database should be searched. This is the default behaviour, so the negative version of this command is more useful. refer determines whether the default database should be searched on the first occasion that it needs to do a search. Thus a **no-default-database** command must be given before then, in order to be effective.

discard∗ *fields*   When the reference is read, *fields* should be discarded; no string definitions for *fields* will be output. Initially, *fields* are **XYZ**.

et-al∗ *string m n*   Control use of **et al** in the evaluation of **@** expressions in label expressions. If the number of authors needed to make the author sequence unambiguous is u and the total number of authors is t then the last $t - u$ authors will be replaced by *string* provided that $t - u$ is not less than m and t is not less than n. The default behaviour is

et-al " et al" 2 3

include *filename*   Include *filename* and interpret the contents as commands.

join-authors *string1 string2 string3*

This says how authors should be joined together. When there are exactly two authors, they will be joined with *string1*. When there are more than two authors, all but the last two will be joined with *string2*, and the last two authors will be joined with *string3*. If *string3* is omitted, it will default to *string1*; if *string2* is also omitted it will also default to *string1*. For example,

> **join-authors " and " ", " ", and "**

will restore the default method for joining authors.

label-in-reference*   When outputting the reference, define the string **[F** to be the reference's label. This is the default behaviour; so the negative version of this command is more useful.

label-in-text*   For each reference output a label in the text. The label will be separated from the surrounding text as described in the **bracket-label** command. This is the default behaviour; so the negative version of this command is more useful.

label *string*   *string* is a label expression describing how to label each reference.

separate-label-second-parts *string*
    When merging two-part labels, separate the second part of the second label from the first label with *string*. See the description of the <> label expression.

move-punctuation*   In the text, move any punctuation at the end of line past the label. It is usually a good idea to give this command unless you are using superscripted numbers as labels.

reverse* *string*   Reverse the fields whose names are in *string*. Each field name can be followed by a number which says how many such fields should be reversed. If no number is given for a field, all such fields will be reversed.

search-ignore* *fields*   While searching for keys in databases for which no index exists, ignore the contents of *fields*. Initially, fields **XYZ** are ignored.

search-truncate* *n*   Only require the first *n* characters of keys to be given. In effect when searching for a given key, words in the database keys are truncated to the maximum of *n* and the length of the key. Initially *n* is 6.

short-label* *string*   *string* is a label expression that specifies an alternative (usually shorter) style of label. This is used when the # flag is given in the citation. When using author-date style labels, the identity of the author or authors is sometimes clear from the context, and so it may be desirable to omit the author or authors from the label. The **short-label** command will typically be used to specify a label containing just a date and possibly a disambiguating letter.

sort* *string*   Sort references according to **string**. References will automatically be accumulated. *string* should be a list of field names, each followed by a number, indicating how many fields with the name should be used for sorting. + can be used to indicate that all the fields with the name should be used. Also . can be used to indicate the references should be sorted using the (tentative) label. (The **Label expressions** subsection describes the concept of a tentative label.)

sort-adjacent-labels*   Sort labels that are adjacent in the text according to their position in the reference list. This command should usually be given if the **abbreviate-label-ranges** command has been given, or if the label expression contains a <> expression. This will have no effect unless references are being accumulated.

Label expressions

Label expressions can be evaluated both normally and tentatively. The result of normal evaluation is used for output. The result of tentative evaluation, called the *tentative label*, is used to gather the information that normal evaluation needs to disambiguate the label. Label expressions specified by the **date-as-label** and **short-label** commands are not evaluated tentatively. Normal and tentative evaluation are the same for all types of expression other than **@**, *****, and **%** expressions. The description below applies to normal evaluation, except where otherwise specified.

field
field n   The *n*-th part of *field*. If *n* is omitted, it defaults to 1.

'string'   The characters in *string* literally.

@   All the authors joined as specified by the **join-authors** command. The whole of each author's name will be used. However, if the references are sorted by author (that is the sort specification starts with A+), then authors' last names will be used instead, provided that this does not introduce ambiguity, and also an initial subsequence of the authors may be used instead of all the authors, again provided that this does not introduce ambiguity. The use of only the last name for the *i*-th author of some reference is considered to be ambiguous if there is some other reference, such that the first *i* - 1 authors of the references are the same, the *i*-th authors are not the same, but the *i*-th authors' last names are the same. A proper initial subsequence of the sequence of authors for some reference is considered to be ambiguous if there is a reference with some other sequence of authors which also has that subsequence as a proper initial subsequence. When an initial subsequence of authors is used, the remaining authors are replaced by the string specified by the **et-al** command; this command may also specify additional requirements that must be met before an initial subsequence can be used. **@** tentatively evaluates to a canonical representation of the authors, such that authors that compare equally for sorting purpose will have the same representation.

%*n*
%a
%A
%i
%I   The serial number of the reference formatted according to the character following the **%**. The serial number of a reference is 1 plus the number of earlier references with same tentative label as this reference. These expressions tentatively evaluate to an empty string.

expr *****   If there is another reference with the same tentative label as this reference, then *expr*, otherwise an empty string. It tentatively evaluates to an empty string.

*expr***+***n*
*expr***−***n*   The first (+) or last (−) *n* upper or lower case letters or digits of *expr*. Troff special characters (such as \\('a) count as a single letter. Accent strings are retained but do not count towards the total.

*expr***.l**   *expr* converted to lowercase.

*expr***.u**   *expr* converted to uppercase.

*expr***.c**   *expr* converted to caps and small caps.

*expr***.r**   *expr* reversed so that the last name is first.

*expr***.a**   *expr* with first names abbreviated. Note that fields specified in the **abbreviate** command are abbreviated before any labels are evaluated. Thus **.a** is useful only when you want a field to be abbreviated in a label but not in a reference.

*expr***.y**   The year part of *expr*.

*expr***.+y**   The part of *expr* before the year, or the whole of *expr* if it does not contain a year.

*expr***.−y**   The part of *expr* after the year, or an empty string if *expr* does not contain a year.

*expr***.n**   The last name part of *expr*.

expr1   *expr1* except that if the last character of *expr1* is − then it will be replaced by *expr2*.

expr1 expr2
         The concatenation of *expr1* and *expr2*.

expr1 | *expr2*

>   If *expr1* is non-empty then *expr1* otherwise *expr2*.

expr1 & *expr2*

>   If *expr1* is non-empty then *expr2* otherwise an empty string.

expr1 ? *expr2* : *expr3*

>   If *expr1* is non-empty then *expr2* otherwise *expr3*.

<expr>   The label is in two parts, which are separated by *expr*. Two adjacent two-part labels which have the same first part will be merged by appending the second part of the second label onto the first label separated by the string specified in the **separate-label-second-parts** command (initially, a comma followed by a space); the resulting label will also be a two-part label with the same first part as before merging, and so additional labels can be merged into it. Note that it is permissible for the first part to be empty; this maybe desirable for expressions used in the **short-label** command.

(expr)   The same as *expr*. Used for grouping.

The above expressions are listed in order of precedence (highest first); **&** and | have the same precedence.

Macro interface

Each reference starts with a call to the macro]-. The string [F will be defined to be the label for this reference, unless the **no-label-in-reference** command has been given. There then follows a series of string definitions, one for each field: string [X corresponds to field *X*. The number register [P is set to 1 if the **P** field contains a range of pages. The [T, [A and [O number registers are set to 1 according as the **T**, **A** and **O** fields end with one of the characters .?!. The [E number register will be set to 1 if the [E string contains more than one name. The reference is followed by a call to the][macro. The first argument to this macro gives a number representing the type of the reference. If a reference contains a **J** field, it will be classified as type 1, otherwise if it contains a **B** field, it will type 3, otherwise if it contains a **G** or **R** field it will be type 4, otherwise if contains a **I** field it will be type 2, otherwise it will be type 0. The second argument is a symbolic name for the type: **other, journal-article, book, article-in-book** or **tech-report**. Groups of references that have been accumulated or are produced by the **bibliography** command are preceded by a call to the]< macro and followed by a call to the]> macro.

FILES

>   **/usr/share/dict/papers/Ind**   Default database.
>
>   *file*.**i**   Index files.

SEE ALSO

>   **indxbib**(1), **lookbib**(1), **lkbib**(1)

BUGS

>   In label expressions, <> expressions are ignored inside *.char* expressions.

1

NAME
    register – register with Kerberos

SYNOPSIS
    register

DESCRIPTION
    The *register* command is used to register a new user with Kerberos. The Kerberos server keeps record of certain trusted hosts from which it will accept new registrations. If the host on which *register* is run is trusted by Kerberos, the user is asked for his current password, and then a new password to be used with Kerberos. A user may only register with Kerberos one time.

FILES
    /.update.keyxx.xx.xx.xx   shared DES key with server

SEE ALSO
    registerd(8), kerberos(1)

DIAGNOSTICS
    ''Principal not unique'' if the user already exists in the Kerberos database.
    ''Permission Denied,'' if the host on which register is being run is untrusted.

NAME
     rev – reverse lines of a file

SYNOPSIS
     rev [*file*]

DESCRIPTION
     The **rev** utility copies the specified files to the standard output, reversing the order of characters in every
     line. If no files are specified, the standard input is read.

1

NAME

rlog – print log messages and other information about RCS files

SYNOPSIS

rlog [*options*] *file* ...

DESCRIPTION

rlog prints information about RCS files.

Pathnames matching an RCS suffix denote RCS files; all others denote working files. Names are paired as explained in **ci**(1).

rlog prints the following information for each RCS file: RCS pathname, working pathname, head (i.e., the number of the latest revision on the trunk), default branch, access list, locks, symbolic names, suffix, total number of revisions, number of revisions selected for printing, and descriptive text. This is followed by entries for the selected revisions in reverse chronological order for each branch. For each revision, **rlog** prints revision number, author, date/time, state, number of lines added/deleted (with respect to the previous revision), locker of the revision (if any), and log message. All times are displayed in Coordinated Universal Time (UTC). Without options, **rlog** prints complete information. The options below restrict this output.

−L   Ignore RCS files that have no locks set. This is convenient in combination with **−h**, **−l**, and **−R**.

−R   Print only the name of the RCS file. This is convenient for translating a working pathname into an RCS pathname.

−h   Print only the RCS pathname, working pathname, head, default branch, access list, locks, symbolic names, and suffix.

−t   Print the same as **−h**, plus the descriptive text.

−b   Print information about the revisions on the default branch, normally the highest branch on the trunk.

−d*dates*

Print information about revisions with a checkin date/time in the ranges given by the semicolon-separated list of *dates*. A range of the form *d1<d2* or *d2>d1* selects the revisions that were deposited between *d1* and *d2* inclusive. A range of the form *<d* or *d>* selects all revisions dated *d* or earlier. A range of the form *d<* or *>d* selects all revisions dated *d* or later. A range of the form *d* selects the single, latest revision dated *d* or earlier. The date/time strings *d*, *d1*, and *d2* are in the free format explained in **co**(1). Quoting is normally necessary, especially for < and >. Note that the separator is a semicolon.

−l[*lockers*]

Print information about locked revisions only. In addition, if the comma-separated list *lockers* of login names is given, ignore all locks other than those held by the *lockers*. For example, **rlog −L −R −lwft RCS/∗** prints the name of RCS files locked by the user **wft**.

−r[*revisions*]

prints information about revisions given in the comma-separated list *revisions* of revisions and ranges. A range *rev1* :*rev2* means revisions *rev1* to *rev2* on the same branch, :*rev* means revisions from the beginning of the branch up to and including *rev*, and *rev*: means revisions starting with *rev* to the end of the branch containing *rev*. An argument that is a branch means all revisions on that branch. A range of branches means all revisions on the branches in that range. A branch followed by a . means the latest revision in that branch. A bare **−r** with no *revisions* means the latest revision on the default branch, normally the trunk.

−s*states*

prints information about revisions whose state attributes match one of the states given in the comma-separated list *states*.

−w[*logins*]

prints information about revisions checked in by users with login names appearing in the comma-separated list *logins*. If *logins* is omitted, the user's login is assumed.

−V*n*   Emulate RCS version *n* when generating logs. See **co**(1) for more.

−x*suffixes*

> Use *suffixes* to characterize RCS files. See **ci**(1) for details.

rlog prints the intersection of the revisions selected with the options **−d**, **−l**, **−s**, and **−w**, intersected with the union of the revisions selected by **−b** and **−r**.

EXAMPLES

> **rlog −L −R RCS/∗**
> **rlog −L −h RCS/∗**
> **rlog −L −l RCS/∗**
> **rlog RCS/∗**

The first command prints the names of all RCS files in the subdirectory **RCS** that have locks. The second command prints the headers of those files, and the third prints the headers plus the log messages of the locked revisions. The last command prints complete information.

ENVIRONMENT

> RCSINIT
>
> > options prepended to the argument list, separated by spaces. See **ci**(1) for details.

DIAGNOSTICS

> The exit status is zero if and only if all operations were successful.

IDENTIFICATION

> Author: Walter F. Tichy.
> Revision Number: 5.3; Release Date: 1991/08/22.
> Copyright © 1982, 1988, 1989 by Walter F. Tichy.
> Copyright © 1990, 1991 by Paul Eggert.

SEE ALSO

> ci(1), co(1), ident(1), rcs(1), rcsdiff(1), rcsintro(1), rcsmerge(1), rcsfile(5)
> Walter F. Tichy, RCS—A System for Version Control, *Software—Practice & Experience* **15**, 7 (July 1985), 637-654.

BUGS

> The separator for revision ranges in the **−r** option used to be − instead of **:**, but this leads to confusion when symbolic names contain −. For backwards compatibility **rlog −r** still supports the old − separator, but it warns about this obsolete use.

NAME

      rlogin – remote login

SYNOPSIS

      rlogin [**–8EKLdx**] [**–e** *char*] [**–k** *realm*] [**–l** *username*] *host*

DESCRIPTION

      Rlogin starts a terminal session on a remote host *host*.

      Rlogin first attempts to use the Kerberos authorization mechanism, described below. If the remote host does not supporting Kerberos the standard Berkeley `rhosts` authorization mechanism is used. The options are as follows:

    –8   The **–8** option allows an eight-bit input data path at all times; otherwise parity bits are stripped except when the remote side's stop and start characters are other than ^S/^Q .

    –E   The **–E** option stops any character from being recognized as an escape character. When used with the **–8** option, this provides a completely transparent connection.

    –K   The **–K** option turns off all Kerberos authentication.

    –L   The **–L** option allows the rlogin session to be run in ''litout'' (see `tty(4)`) mode.

    –d   The **–d** option turns on socket debugging (see `setsockopt(2)`) on the TCP sockets used for communication with the remote host.

    –e   The **–e** option allows user specification of the escape character, which is ''~'' by default. This specification may be as a literal character, or as an octal value in the form \nnn.

    –k   The option requests rlogin to obtain tickets for the remote host in realm *realm* instead of the remote host's realm as determined by `krb_realmofhost(3)`.

    –x   The **–x** option turns on DES encryption for all data passed via the rlogin session. This may impact response time and CPU utilization, but provides increased security.

      A line of the form ''<escape char>.'' disconnects from the remote host. Similarly, the line ''<escape char>^Z'' will suspend the **rlogin** session, and ''<escape char><delayed-suspend char>'' suspends the send portion of the rlogin, but allows output from the remote system. By default, the tilde (''~'') character is the escape character, and normally control-Y (''^Y'') is the delayed-suspend character.

      All echoing takes place at the remote site, so that (except for delays) the **rlogin** is transparent. Flow control via ^S/^Q and flushing of input and output on interrupts are handled properly.

KERBEROS AUTHENTICATION

      Each user may have a private authorization list in the file `.klogin` in their home directory. Each line in this file should contain a Kerberos principal name of the form *principal.instance@realm*. If the originating user is authenticated to one of the principals named in `.klogin`, access is granted to the account. The principal *accountname.@localrealm* is granted access if there is no `.klogin` file. Otherwise a login and password will be prompted for on the remote machine as in `login(1)`. To avoid certain security problems, the `.klogin` file must be owned by the remote user.

      If Kerberos authentication fails, a warning message is printed and the standard Berkeley **rlogin** is used instead.

1

ENVIRONMENT

The following environment variable is utilized by **rlogin**:

TERM Determines the user's terminal type.

SEE ALSO

rsh(1), kerberos(3), krb_sendauth(3), krb_realmofhost(3)

HISTORY

The **rlogin** command appeared in 4.2BSD.

BUGS

Rlogin will be replaced by telnet(1) in the near future.

More of the environment should be propagated.

1

NAME

rm – remove directory entries

SYNOPSIS

rm [**-f** | **-i**] [**-dPRr**] *file* ...

DESCRIPTION

The **rm** utility attempts to remove the non-directory type files specified on the command line. If the permissions of the file do not permit writing, and the standard input device is a terminal, the user is prompted (on the standard error output) for confirmation.

The options are as follows:

-d   Attempt to remove directories as well as other types of files.

-f   Attempt to remove the files without prompting for confirmation, regardless of the file's permissions. If the file does not exist, do not display a diagnostic message or modify the exit status to reflect an error. The -f option overrides any previous -i options.

-i   Request confirmation before attempting to remove each file, regardless of the file's permissions, or whether or not the standard input device is a terminal. The -i option overrides any previous -f options.

-P   Overwrite regular files before deleting them. Files are overwritten three times, first with the byte pattern 0xff, then 0x00, and then 0xff again, before they are deleted.

-R   Attempt to remove the file hierarchy rooted in each file argument. The -R option implies the -d option. If the -i option is specified, the user is prompted for confirmation before each directory's contents are processed (as well as before the attempt is made to remove the directory). If the user does not respond affirmatively, the file hierarchy rooted in that directory is skipped.

-r   Equivalent to -R.

The **rm** utility removes symbolic links, not the files referenced by the links.

It is an error to attempt to remove the files "." and "..".

The **rm** utility exits 0 if all of the named files or file hierarchies were removed, or if the -f option was specified and all of the existing files or file hierarchies were removed. If an error occurs, **rm** exits with a value >0.

SEE ALSO

rmdir(1), unlink(2), fts(3), symlink(7)

BUGS

The -P option assumes that the underlying file system is a fixed-block file system. UFS is a fixed-block file system, LFS is not. In addition, only regular files are overwritten, other types of files are not.

COMPATIBILITY

The **rm** utility differs from historical implementations in that the -f option only masks attempts to remove non-existent files instead of masking a large variety of errors.

Also, historical BSD implementations prompted on the standard output, not the standard error output.

STANDARDS

The **rm** command is expected to be IEEE Std1003.2 ("POSIX") compatible.

1

NAME

    `rmdir` – remove directories

SYNOPSIS

    `rmdir` *directory* ...

DESCRIPTION

The rmdir utility removes the directory entry specified by each *directory* argument, provided it is empty.

Arguments are processed in the order given. In order to remove both a parent directory and a subdirectory of that parent, the subdirectory must be specified first so the parent directory is empty when `rmdir` tries to remove it.

The `rmdir` utility exits with one of the following values:

0   Each directory entry specified by a dir operand referred to an empty directory and was removed successfully.

> 0   An error occurred.

SEE ALSO

    rm(1)

STANDARDS

The `rmdir` command is expected to be IEEE Std1003.2 (''POSIX'') compatible.

1

NAME

   rpcgen – an RPC protocol compiler

SYNOPSIS

   rpcgen *infile*
   rpcgen –c | –h | –l | –m [–o *outfile*] [*infile*]
   rpcgen –s *transport* [–o *outfile*] [*infile*]

DESCRIPTION

   rpcgen is a tool that generates C code to implement an RPC protocol. The input to rpcgen is a language similar to C known as RPC Language (Remote Procedure Call Language). Information about the syntax of RPC Language is available in the *Rpcgen Programming Guide*.

   Available options:

   –c   Compile into XDR routines.

   –h   Compile into C data-definitions (a header file)

   –l   Compile into client-side stubs.

   –m   Compile into server-side stubs, but do not generate a *main* routine. This option is useful for doing callback-routines and for people who need to write their own *main* routine to do initialization.

   –o *outfile*
             Specify the name of the output file. If none is specified, standard output is used (–c, –h, –l and –s modes only).

   –s *transport*
             Compile into server-side stubs, using the given transport. The supported transports are UDP and TCP. This option may be invoked more than once so as to compile a server that serves multiple transports.

   rpcgen is normally used as in the first synopsis where it takes an input file and generates four output files. If the *infile* is named proto.x, then rpcgen will generate a header file in proto.h, XDR routines in proto_xdr.c, server-side stubs in proto_svc.c, and client-side stubs in proto_clnt.c.

   The other synopses shown above are used when one does not want to generate all the output files, but only a particular one. Their usage is described in the USAGE section below.

   The C-preprocessor, cpp(1), is run on all input files before they are actually interpreted by rpcgen, so all the cpp directives are legal within an rpcgen input file. For each type of output file, rpcgen defines a special cpp symbol for use by the rpcgen programmer:

   RPC_HDR   defined when compiling into header files

   RPC_XDR   defined when compiling into XDR routines

   RPC_SVC   defined when compiling into server-side stubs

   RPC_CLNT   defined when compiling into client-side stubs

   In addition, rpcgen does a little preprocessing of its own. Any line beginning with '%' is passed directly into the output file, uninterpreted by rpcgen.

   You can customize some of your XDR routines by leaving those data types undefined. For every data type that is undefined, rpcgen will assume that there exists a routine with the name *xdr_* prepended to the name of the undefined type.

SEE ALSO

cpp(1)

Rpcgen Programming Guide, Sun Microsystems.

BUGS

Nesting is not supported. As a work-around, structures can be declared at top-level, and their name used inside other structures in order to achieve the same effect.

Name clashes can occur when using program definitions, since the apparent scoping does not really apply. Most of these can be avoided by giving unique names for programs, versions, procedures and types.

NAME

    rs – reshape a data array

SYNOPSIS

    rs [–[csCS][x][kKgGw][N]tTeEnyjhHm] [rows [cols]]

DESCRIPTION

Rs reads the standard input, interpreting each line as a row of blank-separated entries in an array, transforms the array according to the options, and writes it on the standard output. With no arguments it transforms stream input into a columnar format convenient for terminal viewing.

The shape of the input array is deduced from the number of lines and the number of columns on the first line. If that shape is inconvenient, a more useful one might be obtained by skipping some of the input with the **–k** option. Other options control interpretation of the input columns.

The shape of the output array is influenced by the *rows* and *cols* specifications, which should be positive integers. If only one of them is a positive integer, *rs* computes a value for the other which will accommodate all of the data. When necessary, missing data are supplied in a manner specified by the options and surplus data are deleted. There are options to control presentation of the output columns, including transposition of the rows and columns.

The options are described below.

–cx	Input columns are delimited by the single character *x*. A missing *x* is taken to be '^I'.
–sx	Like **–c**, but maximal strings of *x* are delimiters.
–Cx	Output columns are delimited by the single character *x*. A missing *x* is taken to be '^I'.
–Sx	Like **–C**, but padded strings of *x* are delimiters.
–t	Fill in the rows of the output array using the columns of the input array, that is, transpose the input while honoring any *rows* and *cols* specifications.
–T	Print the pure transpose of the input, ignoring any *rows* or *cols* specification.
–kN	Ignore the first *N* lines of input.
–KN	Like **–k**, but print the ignored lines.
–gN	The gutter width (inter-column space), normally 2, is taken to be *N*.
–GN	The gutter width has *N* percent of the maximum column width added to it.
–e	Consider each line of input as an array entry.
–n	On lines having fewer entries than the first line, use null entries to pad out the line. Normally, missing entries are taken from the next line of input.
–y	If there are too few entries to make up the output dimensions, pad the output by recycling the input from the beginning. Normally, the output is padded with blanks.
–h	Print the shape of the input array and do nothing else. The shape is just the number of lines and the number of entries on the first line.
–H	Like **–h**, but also print the length of each line.
–j	Right adjust entries within columns.
–wN	The width of the display, normally 80, is taken to be the positive integer *N*.
–m	Do not trim excess delimiters from the ends of the output array.

With no arguments, *rs* transposes its input, and assumes one array entry per input line unless the first non-ignored line is longer than the display width. Option letters which take numerical arguments interpret a missing number as zero unless otherwise indicated.

1

EXAMPLES

Rs can be used as a filter to convert the stream output of certain programs (e.g., *spell*, *du*, *file*, *look*, *nm*, *who*, and *wc*(1)) into a convenient "window" format, as in

    who | rs

This function has been incorporated into the *ls*(1) program, though for most programs with similar output *rs* suffices.

To convert stream input into vector output and back again, use

    rs 1 0 | rs 0 1

A 10 by 10 array of random numbers from 1 to 100 and its transpose can be generated with

    jot −r 100 | rs 10 10 | tee array | rs −T > tarray

In the editor *vi*(1), a file consisting of a multi-line vector with 9 elements per line can undergo insertions and deletions, and then be neatly reshaped into 9 columns with

    :1,$!rs 0 9

Finally, to sort a database by the first line of each 4-line field, try

    rs −eC 0 4 | sort | rs −c 0 1

SEE ALSO

jot(1), vi(1), sort(1), pr(1)

BUGS

Handles only two dimensional arrays.

The algorithm currently reads the whole file into memory, so files that do not fit in memory will not be reshaped.

Fields cannot be defined yet on character positions.

Re-ordering of columns is not yet possible.

There are too many options.

1

NAME

  rsh – remote shell

SYNOPSIS

  rsh [**–Kdnx**] [**–k** *realm*] [**–l** *username*] *host* [command]

DESCRIPTION

  Rsh executes *command* on *host*.

  Rsh copies its standard input to the remote command, the standard output of the remote command to its standard output, and the standard error of the remote command to its standard error. Interrupt, quit and terminate signals are propagated to the remote command; **rsh** normally terminates when the remote command does. The options are as follows:

  –K The **–K** option turns off all Kerberos authentication.

  –d The **–d** option turns on socket debugging (using `setsockopt(2)`) on the TCP sockets used for communication with the remote host.

  –k The **–k** option causes **rsh** to obtain tickets for the remote host in *realm* instead of the remote host's realm as determined by `krb_realmofhost(3)`.

  –l By default, the remote username is the same as the local username. The **–l** option allows the remote name to be specified. Kerberos authentication is used, and authorization is determined as in `rlogin(1)`.

  –n The **–n** option redirects input from the special device `/dev/null` (see the BUGS section of this manual page).

  –x The **–x** option turns on DES encryption for all data exchange. This may introduce a significant delay in response time.

  If no *command* is specified, you will be logged in on the remote host using `rlogin(1)`.

  Shell metacharacters which are not quoted are interpreted on local machine, while quoted metacharacters are interpreted on the remote machine. For example, the command

    `rsh otherhost cat remotefile >> localfile`

  appends the remote file *remotefile* to the local file *localfile*, while

    `rsh otherhost cat remotefile ">>" other_remotefile`

  appends *remotefile* to *other_remotefile*.

FILES

  `/etc/hosts`

SEE ALSO

  `rlogin(1)`, `kerberos(3)`, `krb_sendauth(3)`, `krb_realmofhost(3)`

HISTORY

  The **rsh** command appeared in 4.2BSD.

BUGS

  If you are using `csh(1)` and put a **rsh** in the background without redirecting its input away from the terminal, it will block even if no reads are posted by the remote command. If no input is desired you should redirect the input of **rsh** to `/dev/null` using the **−n** option.

You cannot run an interactive command (like `rogue`(6) or `vi`(1)) using **rsh**; use `rlogin`(1) instead.

Stop signals stop the local **rsh** process only; this is arguably wrong, but currently hard to fix for reasons too complicated to explain here.

1

NAME

rstat – remote status display

SYNOPSIS

rstat host

DESCRIPTION

rstat displays a summary of the current system status of a particular **host**. The output shows the current time of day, how long the system has been up, and the load averages. The load average numbers give the number of jobs in the run queue averaged over 1, 5 and 15 minutes.

The **rstat_svc(8c)** daemon must be running on the remote host for this command to work. **rstat** uses an RPC protocol defined in /usr/include/rpcsvc/rstat.x.

EXAMPLE

example% rstat otherhost
7:36am up 6 days, 16:45, load average: 0.20, 0.23, 0.18
example%

DIAGNOSTICS

rstat: RPC: Program not registered

The **rstat_svc** daemon has not been started on the remote host.

rstat: RPC: Timed out

A communication error occurred. Either the network is excessively congested, or the **rstat_svc** daemon has terminated on the remote host.

rstat: RPC: Port mapper failure - RPC: Timed out

The remote host is not running the portmapper (see **portmap(8c)**), and cannot accommodate any RPC-based services. The host may be down.

SEE ALSO

portmap(8c), **rstat_svc**(8c)

1

NAME

`ruptime` – show host status of local machines

SYNOPSIS

`ruptime [ -alrtu ]`

DESCRIPTION

`Ruptime` gives a status line like *uptime* for each machine on the local network; these are formed from packets broadcast by each host on the network once a minute.

Machines for which no status report has been received for 11 minutes are shown as being down.

The options are as follows:

−a   Users idle an hour or more are not counted unless the −a flag is given.

−l   Sort by load average.

−r   Reverses the sort order.

−t   Sort by uptime.

−u   Sort by number of users.

The default listing is sorted by host name.

FILES

`/var/rwho/whod.*` data files

SEE ALSO

rwho(1) uptime(1)

HISTORY

`Ruptime` appeared in 4.2BSD.

1

NAME

rwho – who is logged in on local machines

SYNOPSIS

rwho [−a]

DESCRIPTION

The **rwho** command produces output similar to who, but for all machines on the local network. If no report has been received from a machine for 5 minutes then **rwho** assumes the machine is down, and does not report users last known to be logged into that machine.

If a users hasn't typed to the system for a minute or more, then **rwho** reports this idle time. If a user hasn't typed to the system for an hour or more, then the user will be omitted from the output of **rwho** unless the −a flag is given.

FILES

/var/rwho/whod.*   information about other machines

SEE ALSO

ruptime(1), rwhod(8)

HISTORY

The **rwho** command appeared in 4.3BSD.

BUGS

This is unwieldy when the number of machines on the local net is large.

NAME

    sccs – front end for the SCCS subsystem

SYNOPSIS

    sccs [–**r**] [–**d** *path*] [–**p** *path*] *command* [flags] [*file* . . .]

DESCRIPTION

    Sccs is a front end to the SCCS programs that helps them mesh more cleanly with the rest of UNIX. It also includes the capability to run "set user id" to another user to provide additional protection.

    Basically, **sccs** runs the command with the specified *flags* and *args*. Each argument is normally modified to be prepended with "SCCS/s.".

    Flags to be interpreted by the **sccs** program must be before the *command* argument. Flags to be passed to the actual SCCS program must come after the *command* argument. These flags are specific to the command and are discussed in the documentation for that command.

    Besides the usual SCCS commands, several "pseudo-commands" can be issued. These are:

    edit   Equivalent to "get –e".

    delget   Perform a delta on the named files and then get new versions. The new versions will have id keywords expanded, and will not be editable. The –m, –p, –r, –s, and –y flags will be passed to **delta**, and the –b, –c, –e, –i, –k, –l, –s, and –x flags will be passed to get.

    deledit Equivalent to **delget** except that the **get** phase includes the –e flag. This option is useful for making a *checkpoint* of your current editing phase. The same flags will be passed to delta as described above, and all the flags listed for above except –e and –k are passed to **edit**.

    create   Creates an SCCS file , taking the initial contents from the file of the same name. Any flags to **admin** are accepted. If the creation is successful, the files are renamed with a comma on the front. These should be removed when you are convinced that the SCCS files have been created successfully.

    fix   Must be followed by a –r flag. This command essentially removes the named delta, but leaves you with a copy of the delta with the changes that were in it. It is useful for fixing small compiler bugs, etc. Since it doesn't leave audit trails, it should be used carefully.

    clean   This routine removes everything from the current directory that can be recreated from SCCS files. It will not remove any files being edited. If the –b flag is given, branches are ignored in the determination of whether they are being edited; this is dangerous if you are keeping the branches in the same directory.

    unedit This is the opposite of an **edit** or a "get –e". It should be used with extreme caution, since any changes you made since the get will be irretrievably lost.

    info   Gives a listing of all files being edited. If the –b flag is given, branches (i.e., SID's with two or fewer components) are ignored. If the –u flag is given (with an optional argument) then only files being edited by you (or the named user) are listed.

    check   Like **info** except that nothing is printed if nothing is being edited, and a non-zero exit status is returned if anything is being edited. The intent is to have this included in an *install* entry in a makefile to insure that everything is included into the SCCS file before a version is installed.

tell   Gives a newline-separated list of the files being edited on the standard output. Takes the −b and −u flags like **info** and **check**.

diffs   Gives a **diff** listing between the current version of the program(s) you have out for editing and the versions in SCCS format. The −r, −c, −i, −x, and −t flags are passed to **get**; the −l, −s, −e, −f, −h, and −b options are passed to **diff**. The −C flag is passed to **diff** as −c.

print   This command prints out verbose information about the named files.

−r   Runs **sccs** as the real user rather than as whatever effective user **sccs** is "set user id" to.

−d   Specifies a root directory for the SCCS files. The default is the current directory. If environment variable PROJECT is set, it will be used to determine the −d flag.

−p   Defines the pathname of the directory in which the SCCS files will be found; "SCCS" is the default. The −p flag differs from the −d flag in that the −d argument is prepended to the entire pathname and the −p argument is inserted before the final component of the pathname. For example, "sccs −d/x −py get a/b" will convert to "get /x/a/y/s.b". The intent here is to create aliases such as "alias syssccs sccs -d/usr/src" which will be used as "syssccs get cmd/who.c".

        Certain commands (such as **admin**) cannot be run "set user id" by all users, since this would allow anyone to change the authorizations. These commands are always run as the real user.

EXAMPLES

To get a file for editing, edit it, and produce a new delta:

```
sccs get −e file.c
ex file.c
sccs delta file.c
```

To get a file from another directory:

```
sccs −p/usr/src/sccs/s. get cc.c
```

or

```
sccs get /usr/src/sccs/s.cc.c
```

To make a delta of a large number of files in the current directory:

```
sccs delta *.c
```

To get a list of files being edited that are not on branches:

```
sccs info −b
```

To delta everything being edited by you:

```
sccs delta `sccs tell −u`
```

In a makefile, to get source files from an SCCS file if it does not already exist:

```
SRCS = <list of source files>
$(SRCS):
        sccs get $(REL) $@
```

1

ENVIRONMENT

PROJECT   The PROJECT environment variable is checked by the −d flag. If it begins with a slash, it
            is taken directly; otherwise, the home directory of a user of that name is examined for a sub-
            directory "src" or "source". If such a directory is found, it is used.

SEE ALSO

what(1) admin(SCCS), chghist(SCCS), comb(SCCS), delta(SCCS), get(SCCS), help(SCCS),
prt(SCCS), rmdel(SCCS), sccsdiff(SCCS),

Eric Allman, *An Introduction to the Source Code Control System.*

HISTORY

The sccs command appeared in 4.3BSD.

BUGS

It should be able to take directory arguments on pseudo-commands like the SCCS commands do.

1

NAME
script – make typescript of terminal session

SYNOPSIS
script [–a] [*file*]

DESCRIPTION
Script makes a typescript of everything printed on your terminal. It is useful for students who need a hardcopy record of an interactive session as proof of an assignment, as the typescript file can be printed out later with lpr(1).

If the argument *file* is given, script saves all dialogue in *file*. If no file name is given, the typescript is saved in the file typescript.

Option:

–a   Append the output to *file* or typescript, retaining the prior contents.

The script ends when the forked shell exits (a *control-D* to exit the Bourne shell (sh(1)), and *exit*, *logout* or *control-d* (if *ignoreeof* is not set) for the C-shell, csh(1)).

Certain interactive commands, such as vi(1), create garbage in the typescript file. Script works best with commands that do not manipulate the screen, the results are meant to emulate a hardcopy terminal.

ENVIRONMENT
The following environment variable is utilized by script:

SHELL If the variable SHELL exists, the shell forked by script will be that shell. If SHELL is not set, the Bourne shell is assumed. (Most shells set this variable automatically).

SEE ALSO
csh(1) (for the *history* mechanism).

HISTORY
The script command appeared in 3.0BSD.

BUGS
Script places **everything** in the log file, including linefeeds and backspaces. This is not what the naive user expects.

1

NAME
sed – stream editor

SYNOPSIS
sed [−an] command [file ...]
sed [−an] [−e command] [−f command_file] [file ...]

DESCRIPTION
The **sed** utility reads the specified files, or the standard input if no files are specified, modifying the input as specified by a list of commands. The input is then written to the standard output.

A single command may be specified as the first argument to **sed**. Multiple commands may be specified by using the −e or −f options. All commands are applied to the input in the order they are specified regardless of their origin.

The following options are available:

−a   The files listed as parameters for the ''w'' functions are created (or truncated) before any process-
        ing begins, by default. The −a option causes **sed** to delay opening each file until a command
        containing the related ''w'' function is applied to a line of input.

−e command
        Append the editing commands specified by the command argument to the list of commands.

−f command_file
        Append the editing commands found in the file command_file to the list of commands. The
        editing commands should each be listed on a separate line.

−n   By default, each line of input is echoed to the standard output after all of the commands have been
        applied to it. The −n option suppresses this behavior.

The form of a **sed** command is as follows:

        [address [,address]] function [arguments]

Whitespace may be inserted before the first address and the function portions of the command.

Normally, **sed** cyclically copies a line of input, not including its terminating newline character, into a *pattern space*, (unless there is something left after a ''D'' function), applies all of the commands with addresses that select that pattern space, copies the pattern space to the standard output, appending a newline, and deletes the pattern space.

Some of the functions use a *hold space* to save all or part of the pattern space for subsequent retrieval.

Sed Addresses
An address is not required, but if specified must be a number (that counts input lines cumulatively across input files), a dollar (''$'') character that addresses the last line of input, or a context address (which consists of a regular expression preceded and followed by a delimiter).

A command line with no addresses selects every pattern space.

A command line with one address selects all of the pattern spaces that match the address.

A command line with two addresses selects the inclusive range from the first pattern space that matches the first address through the next pattern space that matches the second. (If the second address is a number less than or equal to the line number first selected, only that line is selected.) Starting at the first line following the selected range, **sed** starts looking again for the first address.

Editing commands can be applied to non-selected pattern spaces by use of the exclamation character (''!'') function.

Sed Regular Expressions

The **sed** regular expressions are basic regular expressions (BRE's, see regex(3) for more information). In addition, **sed** has the following two additions to BRE's:

1. In a context address, any character other than a backslash (''\'') or newline character may be used to delimit the regular expression. Also, putting a backslash character before the delimiting character causes the character to be treated literally. For example, in the context address \xabc\xdefx, the RE delimiter is an ''x'' and the second ''x'' stands for itself, so that the regular expression is ''abcxdef''.

2. The escape sequence \n matches a newline character embedded in the pattern space. You can't, however, use a literal newline character in an address or in the substitute command.

One special feature of **sed** regular expressions is that they can default to the last regular expression used. If a regular expression is empty, i.e. just the delimiter characters are specified, the last regular expression encountered is used instead. The last regular expression is defined as the last regular expression used as part of an address or substitute command, and at run-time, not compile-time. For example, the command ''/abc/s//XXX/'' will substitute ''XXX'' for the pattern ''abc''.

Sed Functions

In the following list of commands, the maximum number of permissible addresses for each command is indicated by [0addr], [1addr], or [2addr], representing zero, one, or two addresses.

The argument *text* consists of one or more lines. To embed a newline in the text, precede it with a backslash. Other backslashes in text are deleted and the following character taken literally.

The ''r'' and ''w'' functions take an optional file parameter, which should be separated from the function letter by white space. Each file given as an argument to **sed** is created (or its contents truncated) before any input processing begins.

The ''b'', ''r'', ''s'', ''t'', ''w'', ''y'', ''!'', and '':''' functions all accept additional arguments. The following synopses indicate which arguments have to be separated from the function letters by white space characters.

Two of the functions take a function-list. This is a list of **sed** functions separated by newlines, as follows:

```
{ function
  function
  ...
  function
}
```

The ''{'' can be preceded by white space and can be followed by white space. The function can be preceded by white space. The terminating ''}'' must be preceded by a newline or optional white space.

[2addr] function-list

    Execute function-list only when the pattern space is selected.

[1addr]a\
text

    Write *text* to standard output immediately before each attempt to read a line of input, whether by executing the ''N'' function or by beginning a new cycle.

1

[2addr]b[lable]
> Branch to the ":" function with the specified label. If the label is not specified, branch to the end of the script.

[2addr]c\
text
> Delete the pattern space. With 0 or 1 address or at the end of a 2-address range, *text* is written to the standard output.

[2addr]d   Delete the pattern space and start the next cycle.

[2addr]D
> Delete the initial segment of the pattern space through the first newline character and start the next cycle.

[2addr]g   Replace the contents of the pattern space with the contents of the hold space.

[2addr]G
> Append a newline character followed by the contents of the hold space to the pattern space.

[2addr]h   Replace the contents of the hold space with the contents of the pattern space.

[2addr]H
> Append a newline character followed by the contents of the pattern space to the hold space.

[1addr]i\
text
> Write *text* to the standard output.

[2addr]l   (The letter ell.) Write the pattern space to the standard output in a visually unambiguous form. This form is as follows:

backslash	\
alert	\a
form-feed	\f
newline	\n
carriage-return	\r
tab	\t
vertical tab	\v

> Nonprintable characters are written as three-digit octal numbers (with a preceding backslash) for each byte in the character (most significant byte first). Long lines are folded, with the point of folding indicated by displaying a backslash followed by a newline. The end of each line is marked with a "$".

[2addr]n   Write the pattern space to the standard output if the default output has not been suppressed, and replace the pattern space with the next line of input.

[2addr]N
> Append the next line of input to the pattern space, using an embedded newline character to separate the appended material from the original contents. Note that the current line number changes.

1

[2addr]p   Write the pattern space to standard output.

[2addr]P   Write the pattern space, up to the first newline character to the standard output.

[1addr]q   Branch to the end of the script and quit without starting a new cycle.

[1addr]r file
           Copy the contents of *file* to the standard output immediately before the next attempt to read a line
           of input. If *file* cannot be read for any reason, it is silently ignored and no error condition is set.

[2addr]s/regular expression/replacement/flags
           Substitute the replacement string for the first instance of the regular expression in the pattern
           space. Any character other than backslash or newline can be used instead of a slash to delimit the
           RE and the replacement. Within the RE and the replacement, the RE delimiter itself can be used
           as a literal character if it is preceded by a backslash.

           An ampersand (''&'') appearing in the replacement is replaced by the string matching the RE.
           The special meaning of ''&'' in this context can be suppressed by preceding it by a backslash.
           The string ''\#'', where ''#'' is a digit, is replaced by the text matched by the corresponding
           backreference expression (see re_format(7)).

           A line can be split by substituting a newline character into it. To specify a newline character in the
           replacement string, precede it with a backslash.

           The value of *flags* in the substitute function is zero or more of the following:

                      0 ... 9   Make the substitution only for the N'th occurrence of the regular expression in
                                the pattern space.

                      g   Make the substitution for all non-overlapping matches of the regular expression,
                                not just the first one.

                      p   Write the pattern space to standard output if a replacement was made. If the re-
                                placement string is identical to that which it replaces, it is still considered to have
                                been a replacement.

                      w *file* Append the pattern space to *file* if a replacement was made. If the replacement
                                string is identical to that which it replaces, it is still considered to have been a re-
                                placement.

[2addr]t [label]
           Branch to the ''''': function bearing the label if any substitutions have been made since the most
           recent reading of an input line or execution of a ''t'' function. If no label is specified, branch to
           the end of the script.

[2addr]w *file*
           Append the pattern space to the *file*.

[2addr]x   Swap the contents of the pattern and hold spaces.

[2addr]y/string1/string2/
           Replace all occurrences of characters in *string1* in the pattern space with the corresponding char-
           acters from *string2*. Any character other than a backslash or newline can be used instead of a slash
           to delimit the strings. Within *string1* and *string2*, a backslash followed by any character other
           than a newline is that literal character, and a backslash followed by an ''n'' is replaced by a new-
           line character.

1

[2addr]!function
[2addr]!function-list
      Apply the function or function-list only to the lines that are *not* selected by the address(es).

[0addr]:label
      This function does nothing; it bears a label to which the ''b'' and ''t'' commands may branch.

[1addr]= Write the line number to the standard output followed by a newline character.

[0addr]   Empty lines are ignored.

[0addr]# The ''#'' and the remainder of the line are ignored (treated as a comment), with the single exception that if the first two characters in the file are ''#n'', the default output is suppressed. This is the same as specifying the −n option on the command line.

The **sed** utility exits 0 on success and >0 if an error occurs.

SEE ALSO
awk(1), ed(1), grep(1), regex(3), re_format(7)

HISTORY
A **sed** command appeared in Version 7 AT&T UNIX.

STANDARDS
The **sed** function is expected to be a superset of the IEEE Std1003.2 (''POSIX'') specification.

1

NAME
sendbug – mail a system bug report to 4bsd-bugs

SYNOPSIS
sendbug [*address*]

DESCRIPTION
Bug reports sent to '4bsd-bugs@Berkeley.EDU' are intercepted by a program which expects bug reports to conform to a standard format. **Sendbug** is a shell script to help the user compose and mail bug reports in the correct format. **Sendbug** works by invoking the editor specified by the environment variable EDITOR on a temporary copy of the bug report format outline. The user must fill in the appropriate fields and exit the editor. **Sendbug** then mails the completed report to '4bsd-bugs@Berkeley.EDU' or the *address* specified on the command line.

ENVIRONMENT
Sendbug will utilize the following environment variable if it exists:

EDITOR Specifies the preferred editor. If EDITOR is not set, **sendbug** defaults to vi(1).

FILES
/usr/share/misc/bugformat Contains the bug report outline.

SEE ALSO
vi(1), environ(7), bugfiler(8), sendmail(8)

HISTORY
The **sendbug** command appeared in 4.2BSD.

NAME

   sh – command interpreter (shell)

SYNOPSIS

   sh [-/+aCefnuvxIimsVEb] [-/+o longname] [arg ...]

DESCRIPTION

   Sh is the standard command interpreter for the system. The current version of sh is in the process of being changed to conform with the POSIX 1003.2 and 1003.2a specifications for the shell. This version has many features which make it appear similar in some respects to the Korn shell, but it is not a Korn shell clone (run GNU's bash if you want that). Only features designated by POSIX, plus a few Berkeley extensions, are being incorporated into this shell. We expect POSIX conformance by the time 4.4 BSD is released. This man page is not intended to be a tutorial or a complete specification of the shell.

   Overview

   The shell is a command that reads lines from either a file or the terminal, interprets them, and generally executes other commands. It is the program that is running when a user logs into the system (although a user can select a different shell with the chsh(1) command). The shell implements a language that has flow control constructs, a macro facility that provides a variety of features in addition to data storage, along with built in history and line editing capabilities. It incorporates many features to aid interactive use and has the advantage that the interpretative language is common to both interactive and non-interactive use (shell scripts). That is, commands can be typed directly to the running shell or can be put into a file and the file can be executed directly by the shell.

   Invocation

   If no args are present and if the standard input of the shell is connected to a terminal (or if the -i flag is set), the shell is considered an interactive shell. An interactive shell generally prompts before each command and handles programming and command errors differently (as described below). When first starting, the shell inspects argument 0, and if it begins with a dash '-', the shell is also considered a login shell. This is normally done automatically by the system when the user first logs in. A login shell first reads commands from the files /etc/profile and .profile if they exist. If the environment variable ENV is set on entry to a shell, or is set in the .profile of a login shell, the shell next reads commands from the file named in ENV. Therefore, a user should place commands that are to be executed only at login time in the .profile file, and commands that are executed for every shell inside the ENV file. To set the ENV variable to some file, place the following line in your .profile of your home directory

                 ENV=$HOME/.shinit; export ENV

   substituting for ".shinit" any filename you wish. Since the ENV file is read for every invocation of the shell, including shell scripts and non-interactive shells, the following paradigm is useful for restricting commands in the ENV file to interactive invocations. Place commands within the "case" and "esac" below (these commands are described later):

           case $- in *i*)
                       # commands for interactive use only
                       ...
           esac

   If command line arguments besides the options have been specified, then the shell treats the first argument as the name of a file from which to read commands (a shell script), and the remaining arguments are set as

1

the positional parameters of the shell ($1, $2, etc). Otherwise, the shell reads commands from its standard input.

Argument List Processing

All of the single letter options have a corresponding name that can be used as an argument to the '-o' option. The set -o name is provided next to the single letter option in the description below. Specifying a dash "-" turns the option on, while using a plus "+" disables the option. The following options can be set from the command line or with the set(1) builtin (described later).

-a   allexport
      Export all variables assigned to. (UNIMPLEMENTED for 4.4alpha)

-C   noclobber
      Don't overwrite existing files with ">". (UNIMPLEMENTED for 4.4alpha)

-e   errexit
      If not interactive, exit immediately if any untested command fails. The exit status of a command is considered to be explicitly tested if the command is used to control an if, elif, while, or until; or if the command is the left hand operand of an "&&" or "||" operator.

-f   noglob
      Disable pathname expansion.

-n   noexec
      If not interactive, read commands but do not execute them. This is useful for checking the syntax of shell scripts.

-u   nounset
      Write a message to standard error when attempting to expand a variable that is not set, and if the shell is not interactive, exit immediately. (UNIMPLEMENTED for 4.4alpha)

-v   verbose
      The shell writes its input to standard error as it is read. Useful for debugging.

-x   xtrace
      Write each command to standard error (preceded by a '+ ') before it is executed. Useful for debugging.

-I   ignoreeof
      Ignore EOF's from input when interactive.

-i   interactive
      Force the shell to behave interactively.

-m   monitor
      Turn on job control (set automatically when interactive).

-s   stdin
      Read commands from standard input (set automatically if no file arguments are present). This option has no effect when set after the shell has already started running (i.e. with set(1)).

-V   vi   Enable the builtin vi(1) command line editor (disables -E if it has been set).

-E   emacs
      Enable the builtin emacs(1) command line editor (disables -V if it has been set).

-b   notify
      Enable asynchronous notification of background job completion. (UNIMPLEMENTED for 4.4alpha)

Lexical Structure

The shell reads input in terms of lines from a file and breaks it up into words at whitespace (blanks and tabs), and at certain sequences of characters that are special to the shell called "operators". There are two types of operators: control operators and redirection operators (their meaning is discussed later). Following is a list of operators:

Control operators: & && ( ) ; ;; | || <newline>

Redirection operator: < > >| << >> <& >& <<- <>

Quoting

Quoting is used to remove the special meaning of certain characters or words to the shell, such as operators, whitespace, or keywords. There are three types of quoting: matched single quotes, matched double quotes, and backslash.

Backslash

A backslash preserves the literal meaning of the following character, with the exception of <newline>. A backslash preceding a <newline> is treated as a line continuation.

Single Quotes

Enclosing characters in single quotes preserves the literal meaning of all the characters.

Double Quotes

Enclosing characters within double quotes preserves the literal meaning of all characters except dollarsign ($), backquote ('), and backslash (\). The backslash inside double quotes is historically weird, and serves to quote only the following characters: $ ' " \ <newline>. Otherwise it remains literal.

Reserved Words

Reserved words are words that have special meaning to the shell and are recognized at the beginning of a line and after a control operator. The following are reserved words:

!	elif	fi	while	case
else	for	then	{	}
do	done	until	if	esac

Their meaning is discussed later.

Aliases

An alias is a name and corresponding value set using the alias(1) builtin command. Whenever a reserved word may occur (see above), and after checking for reserved words, the shell checks the word to see if it matches an alias. If it does, it replaces it in the input stream with its value. For example, if there is an alias called ''lf'' with the value ''ls -F'', then the input

lf foobar <return>

would become

ls -F foobar <return>

Aliases provide a convenient way for naive users to create shorthands for commands without having to learn how to create functions with arguments. They can also be used to create lexically obscure code. This use is discouraged.

Commands

The shell interprets the words it reads according to a language, the specification of which is outside the scope of this man page (refer to the BNF in the POSIX 1003.2 document). Essentially though, a line is read and if the first word of the line (or after a control operator) is not a reserved word, then the shell has recognized a simple command. Otherwise, a complex command or some other special construct may have been recognized.

Simple Commands

If a simple command has been recognized, the shell performs the following actions:

1) Leading words of the form ''name=value'' are stripped off and assigned to the environment of the simple command. Redirection operators and their arguments (as described below) are stripped off and saved for processing.

2) The remaining words are expanded as described in the section called ''Expansions'', and the first remaining word is considered the command name and the command is located. The remaining words are considered the arguments of the command. If no command name resulted, then the ''name=value'' variable assignments recognized in 1) affect the current shell.

3) Redirections are performed as described in the next section.

Redirections

Redirections are used to change where a command reads its input or sends its output. In general, redirections open, close, or duplicate an existing reference to a file. The overall format used for redirection is:

[n] redir-op file

where redir-op is one of the redirection operators mentioned previously. Following is a list of the possible redirections. The [n] is an optional number, as in '3' (not '[3]'), that refers to a file descriptor.

1

[n]> file
> Redirect standard output (or n) to file.

[n]>l file
> Same, but override the -C option.

[n]>> file
> Append standard output (or n) to file.

[n]< file
> Redirect standard input (or n) from file.

[n1]<&n2
> Duplicate standard input (or n1) from file descriptor n2.

[n]<&-
> Close standard input (or n).

[n1]>&n2
> Duplicate standard output (or n) from n2.

[n]>&-
> Close standard output (or n).

[n]<> file
> Open file for reading and writing on standard input (or n).

The following redirection is often called a "here-document".

    [n]<< delimiter
       here-doc-text...
    delimiter

All the text on successive lines up to the delimiter is saved away and made available to the command on standard input, or file descriptor n if it is specified. If the delimiter as specified on the initial line is quoted, then the here-doc-text is treated literally, otherwise the text is subjected to parameter expansion, command substitution, and arithmetic expansion (as described in the section on "Expansions"). If the operator is "<<-" instead of "<<", then leading tabs in the here-doc-text are stripped.

Search and Execution

There are three types of commands: shell functions, builtin commands, and normal programs -- and the command is searched for (by name) in that order. They each are executed in a different way.

When a shell function is executed, all of the shell positional parameters (except $0, which remains unchanged) are set to the arguments of the shell function. The variables which are explicitly placed in the environment of the command (by placing assignments to them before the function name) are made local to the function and are set to the values given. Then the command given in the function definition is executed. The positional parameters are restored to their original values when the command completes.

Shell builtins are executed internally to the shell, without spawning a new process.

Otherwise, if the command name doesn't match a function or builtin, the command is searched for as a normal program in the filesystem (as described in the next section). When a normal program is executed, the shell runs the program, passing the arguments and the environment to the program. If the program is a shell procedure, the shell will interpret the program in a subshell. The shell will reinitialize itself in this case, so that the effect will be as if a new shell had been invoked to handle the shell procedure, except that the location of commands located in the parent shell will be remembered by the child.

Path Search

When locating a command, the shell first looks to see if it has a shell function by that name. Then it looks for a builtin command by that name. Finally, it searches each entry in PATH in turn for the command.

The value of the PATH variable should be a series of entries separated by colons. Each entry consists of a directory name. The current directory may be indicated by an empty directory name.

Command names containing a slash are simply executed without performing any of the above searches.

Command Exit Status

Each command has an exit status that can influence the behavior of other shell commands. The paradigm is that a command exits with zero for normal or success, and non-zero for failure, error, or a false indication. The man page for each command should indicate the various exit codes and what they mean. Additionally, the builtin commands return exit codes, as does an executed function.

Complex Commands

Complex commands are combinations of simple commands with control operators or reserved words, together creating a larger complex command. More generally, a command is one of the following:

- simple command

- pipeline

- list or compound-list

- compound command

- function definition

Unless otherwise stated, the exit status of a command is that of the last simple command executed by the command.

Pipeline

A pipeline is a sequence of one or more commands separated by the control operator |. The standard output of all but the last command is connected to the standard input of the next command.

The format for a pipeline is:

[!] command1 [| command2 ...]

The standard output of command1 is connected to the standard input of command2. The standard input, standard output, or both of a command is considered to be assigned by the pipeline before any redirection specified by redirection operators that are part of the command.

If the pipeline is not in the background (discussed later), the shell waits for all commands to complete.

If the reserved word ! does not precede the pipeline, the exit status is the exit status of the last command specified in the pipeline. Otherwise, the exit status is the logical NOT of the exit status of the last command. That is, if the last command returns zero, the exit status is 1; if the last command returns greater than zero, the exit status is zero.

Because pipeline assignment of standard input or standard output or both takes place before redirection, it can be modified by redirection. For example:

$ command1 2>&1 | command2

sends both the standard output and standard error of command1 to the standard input of command2.

A ; or <newline> terminator causes the preceding AND-OR-list (described next) to be executed sequentially; a & causes asynchronous execution of the preceding AND-OR-list.

Background Commands -- &

If a command is terminated by the control operator ampersand (&), the shell executes the command asynchronously -- that is, the shell does not wait for the command to finish before executing the next command.

The format for running a command in background is:

command1 & [command2 & ...]

If the shell is not interactive, the standard input of an asynchronous command is set to /dev/null.

Lists -- Generally Speaking

A list is a sequence of zero or more commands separated by newlines, semicolons, or ampersands, and optionally terminated by one of these three characters. The commands in a list are executed in the order they are written. If command is followed by an ampersand, the shell starts the command and immediately proceed onto the next command; otherwise it waits for the command to terminate before proceeding to the next one.

"&&" and "||" are AND-OR list operators. "&&" executes the first command, and then executes the second command iff the exit status of the first command is zero. "||" is similar, but executes the second command iff the exit status of the first command is nonzero. "&&" and "||" both have the same priority.

The syntax of the if command is

```
if list
then list
[ elif list
then   list ] ...
[ else list ]
fi
```

The syntax of the while command is

```
while list
do   list
done
```

The two lists are executed repeatedly while the exit status of the first list is zero. The until command is similar, but has the word until in place of while repeat until the exit status of the first list is zero.

The syntax of the for command is

   for variable in word...
   do list
   done

The words are expanded, and then the list is executed repeatedly with the variable set to each word in turn. do and done may be replaced with ''{'' and ''}''.

The syntax of the break and continue command is

   break [num]
   continue [num]

Break terminates the num innermost for or while loops. Continue continues with the next iteration of the innermost loop. These are implemented as builtin commands.

The syntax of the case command is

   case word in
   pattern) list ;;
   ...
   esac

The pattern can actually be one or more patterns (see Shell Patterns described later), separated by ''|'' characters.

Commands may be grouped by writing either

   (list)

or

   { list; }

The first of these executes the commands in a subshell.

Functions

The syntax of a function definition is

   name ( ) command

A function definition is an executable statement; when executed it installs a function named name and returns an exit status of zero. The command is normally a list enclosed between ''{'' and ''}''.

Variables may be declared to be local to a function by using a local command. This should appear as the first statement of a function, and the syntax is

   local [variable | -] ...

1

Local is implemented as a builtin command.

When a variable is made local, it inherits the initial value and exported and readonly flags from the variable with the same name in the surrounding scope, if there is one. Otherwise, the variable is initially unset. The shell uses dynamic scoping, so that if you make the variable x local to function f, which then calls function g, references to the variable x made inside g will refer to the variable x declared inside f, not to the global variable named x.

The only special parameter than can be made local is "-". Making "-" local any shell options that are changed via the set command inside the function to be restored to their original values when the function returns.

The syntax of the return command is

   return [exitstatus]

It terminates the currently executing function. Return is implemented as a builtin command.

Variables and Parameters

The shell maintains a set of parameters. A parameter denoted by a name is called a variable. When starting up, the shell turns all the environment variables into shell variables. New variables can be set using the form

   name=value

Variables set by the user must have a name consisting solely of alphabetics, numerics, and underscores - the first of which must not be numeric. A parameter can also be denoted by a number or a special character as explained below.

Positional Parameters

A positional parameter is a parameter denoted by a number (n > 0). The shell sets these initially to the values of its command line arguments that follow the name of the shell script. The set(1) builtin can also be used to set or reset them.

Special Parameters

A special parameter is a parameter denoted by one of the following special characters. The value of the parameter is listed next to its character.

* Expands to the positional parameters, starting from one. When the expansion occurs within a double-quoted string it expands to a single field with the value of each parameter separated by the first character of the IFS variable, or by a <space> if IFS is unset.

@ Expands to the positional parameters, starting from one. When the expansion occurs within double-quotes, each positional parameter expands as a separate argument. If there are no positional parameters, the expansion of @ generates zero arguments, even when @ is double-quoted. What this basically means, for example, is if $1 is "abc" and $2 is "def ghi", then "$@" expands to the two arguments:

   "abc"   "def ghi"

1

Expands to the number of positional parameters.

?   Expands to the exit status of the most recent pipeline.

- (Hyphen)
> Expands to the current option flags (the single-letter option names concatenated into a string) as specified on invocation, by the set builtin command, or implicitly by the shell.

$ Expands to the process ID of the invoked shell. A subshell retains the same value of $ as its parent.

!   Expands to the process ID of the most recent background command executed from the current shell. For a pipeline, the process ID is that of the last command in the pipeline.

0 (Zero.)
> Expands to the name of the shell or shell script.

Word Expansions

This clause describes the various expansions that are performed on words. Not all expansions are performed on every word, as explained later.

Tilde expansions, parameter expansions, command substitutions, arithmetic expansions, and quote removals that occur within a single word expand to a single field. It is only field splitting or pathname expansion that can create multiple fields from a single word. The single exception to this rule is the expansion of the special parameter @ within double-quotes, as was described above.

The order of word expansion is:

(1) Tilde Expansion, Parameter Expansion, Command Substitution, Arithmetic Expansion (these all occur at the same time).

(2) Field Splitting is performed on fields generated by step (1) unless the IFS variable is null.

(3) Pathname Expansion (unless set -f is in effect).

(4) Quote Removal.

The $ character is used to introduce parameter expansion, command substitution, or arithmetic evaluation.

Tilde Expansion (substituting a user's home

A word beginning with an unquoted tilde character (˜) is subjected to tilde expansion. All the characters up to a slash (/) or the end of the word are treated as a username and are replaced with the user's home directory. If the username is missing (as in ˜/foobar), the tilde is replaced with the value of the HOME variable (the current user's home directory).

Parameter Expansion

The format for parameter expansion is as follows:

  ${expression}

where expression consists of all characters until the matching }. Any } escaped by a backslash or within a quoted string, and characters in embedded arithmetic expansions, command substitutions, and variable expansions, are not examined in determining the matching }.

The simplest form for parameter expansion is:

${parameter}

The value, if any, of parameter is substituted.

The parameter name or symbol can be enclosed in braces, which are optional except for positional parameters with more than one digit or when parameter is followed by a character that could be interpreted as part of the name. If a parameter expansion occurs inside double-quotes:

1) Pathname expansion is not performed on the results of the expansion.

2) Field splitting is not performed on the results of the expansion, with the exception of @.

In addition, a parameter expansion can be modified by using one of the following formats.

${parameter:-word}
>   Use Default Values. If parameter is unset or null, the expansion of word is substituted; otherwise, the value of parameter is substituted.

${parameter:=word}
>   Assign Default Values. If parameter is unset or null, the expansion of word is assigned to parameter. In all cases, the final value of parameter is substituted. Only variables, not positional parameters or special parameters, can be assigned in this way.

${parameter:?[word]}
>   Indicate Error if Null or Unset. If parameter is unset or null, the expansion of word (or a message indicating it is unset if word is omitted) is written to standard error and the shell exits with a nonzero exit status. Otherwise, the value of parameter is substituted. An interactive shell need not exit.

${parameter:+word}
>   Use Alternate Value. If parameter is unset or null, null is substituted; otherwise, the expansion of word is substituted.

In the parameter expansions shown previously, use of the colon in the format results in a test for a parameter that is unset or null; omission of the colon results in a test for a parameter that is only unset.

${#parameter}
>   String Length. The length in characters of the value of parameter.

The following four varieties of parameter expansion provide for substring processing. In each case, pattern matching notation (see Shell Patterns), rather than regular expression notation, is used to evaluate the patterns. If parameter is * or @, the result of the expansion is unspecified. Enclosing the full parameter expansion string in double-quotes does not cause the following four varieties of pattern characters to be quoted, whereas quoting characters within the braces has this effect. (UNIMPLEMENTED IN 4.4alpha)

${parameter%word}
>   Remove Smallest Suffix Pattern. The word is expanded to produce a pattern. The parameter expansion then results in parameter, with the smallest portion of the suffix matched by the pattern deleted.

${parameter%%word}
>   Remove Largest Suffix Pattern. The word is expanded to produce a pattern. The parameter expansion then results in parameter, with the largest portion of the suffix matched by the pattern deleted.

1

${parameter#word}
>   Remove Smallest Prefix Pattern. The word is expanded to produce a pattern. The parameter expansion then results in parameter, with the smallest portion of the prefix matched by the pattern deleted.

${parameter##word}
>   Remove Largest Prefix Pattern. The word is expanded to produce a pattern. The parameter expansion then results in parameter, with the largest portion of the prefix matched by the pattern deleted.

Command Substitution

Command substitution allows the output of a command to be substituted in place of the command name itself. Command substitution occurs when the command is enclosed as follows:

    $(command)

or ("backquoted" version):

    `command`

The shell expands the command substitution by executing command in a subshell environment and replacing the command substitution with the standard output of the command, removing sequences of one or more <newline>s at the end of the substitution. (Embedded <newline>s before the end of the output are not removed; however, during field splitting, they may be translated into <space>s, depending on the value of IFS and quoting that is in effect.)

Arithmetic Expansion

Arithmetic expansion provides a mechanism for evaluating an arithmetic expression and substituting its value. The format for arithmetic expansion is as follows:

    $((expression))

The expression is treated as if it were in double-quotes, except that a double-quote inside the expression is not treated specially. The shell expands all tokens in the expression for parameter expansion, command substitution, and quote removal.

Next, the shell treats this as an arithmetic expression and substitutes the value of the expression.

White Space Splitting (Field Splitting)

After parameter expansion, command substitution, and arithmetic expansion the shell scans the results of expansions and substitutions that did not occur in double-quotes for field splitting and multiple fields can result.

The shell treats each character of the IFS as a delimiter and use the delimiters to split the results of parameter expansion and command substitution into fields.

Pathname Expansion (File Name Generation)

Unless the -f flag is set, file name generation is performed after word splitting is complete. Each word is viewed as a series of patterns, separated by slashes. The process of expansion replaces the word with the names of all existing files whose names can be formed by replacing each pattern with a string that matches the specified pattern. There are two restrictions on this: first, a pattern cannot match a string containing a slash, and second, a pattern cannot match a string starting with a period unless the first character of the pattern is a period. The next section describes the patterns used for both Pathname Expansion and the case(1) command.

Shell Patterns

A pattern consists of normal characters, which match themselves, and meta-characters. The meta-characters are "!", "*", "?", and "[". These characters lose there special meanings if they are quoted. When command or variable substitution is performed and the dollar sign or back quotes are not double quoted, the value of the variable or the output of the command is scanned for these characters and they are turned into meta-characters.

An asterisk ("*") matches any string of characters. A question mark matches any single character. A left bracket ("[") introduces a character class. The end of the character class is indicated by a "]"; if the "]" is missing then the "[" matches a "[" rather than introducing a character class. A character class matches any of the characters between the square brackets. A range of characters may be specified using a minus sign. The character class may be complemented by making an exclamation point the first character of the character class.

To include a "]" in a character class, make it the first character listed (after the "!", if any). To include a minus sign, make it the first or last character listed

Builtins

This section lists the builtin commands which are builtin because they need to perform some operation that can't be performed by a separate process. In addition to these, there are several other commands that may be builtin for efficiency (e.g. printf(1), echo(1), test(1), etc).

alias [name[=string] ...]
> If name=string is specified, the shell defines the alias "name" with value "string". If just "name" is specified, the value of the alias "name" is printed. With no arguments, the alias builtin prints the names and values of all defined aliases (see unalias).

bg [job] ...
> Continue the specified jobs (or the current job if no jobs are given) in the background.

command command arg...
> Execute the specified builtin command. (This is useful when you have a shell function with the same name as a builtin command.)

cd [directory]
> Switch to the specified directory (default $HOME). If the an entry for CDPATH appears in the environment of the cd command or the shell variable CDPATH is set and the directory name does not begin with a slash, then the directories listed in CDPATH will be searched for the specified directory. The format of CDPATH is the same as that of PATH. In an interactive shell, the cd command will print out the name of the directory that it actually switched to if this is different

from the name that the user gave. These may be different either because the CDPATH mechanism was used or because a symbolic link was crossed.

. file   The commands in the specified file are read and executed by the shell.

eval string...

Concatenate all the arguments with spaces. Then re-parse and execute the command.

exec [command arg...]

Unless command is omitted, the shell process is replaced with the specified program (which must be a real program, not a shell builtin or function). Any redirections on the exec command are marked as permanent, so that they are not undone when the exec command finishes.

exit [exitstatus]

Terminate the shell process. If exitstatus is given it is used as the exit status of the shell; otherwise the exit status of the preceding command is used.

export name...

The specified names are exported so that they will appear in the environment of subsequent commands. The only way to un-export a variable is to unset it. The shell allows the value of a variable to be set at the same time it is exported by writing

    export name=value

With no arguments the export command lists the names of all exported variables.

fc [-e editor] [first [last]]

fc -l [-nr] [first [last]]

fc -s [old=new] [first]

The fc builtin lists, or edits and re-executes, commands previously entered to an interactive shell.

-e editor

Use the editor named by editor to edit the commands. The editor string is a command name, subject to search via the PATH variable. The value in the FCEDIT variable is used as a default when -e is not specified. If FCEDIT is null or unset, the value of the EDITOR variable is used. If EDITOR is null or unset, ed(1) is used as the editor.

-l (ell)

List the commands rather than invoking an editor on them. The commands are written in the sequence indicated by the first and last operands, as affected by -r, with each command preceded by the command number.

-n

Suppress command numbers when listing with -l.

-r Reverse the order of the commands listed (with -l) or edited (with neither -l nor -s).

-s

Re-execute the command without invoking an editor.

first

last

Select the commands to list or edit. The number of previous commands that can be accessed are determined by the value of the HISTSIZE variable. The value of first or last or both are one of the following:

[+]number

A positive number representing a command number; command numbers can be displayed with the -l option.

1

-number
> A negative decimal number representing the command that was executed number of commands previously. For example, -1 is the immediately previous command.

string
> A string indicating the most recently entered command that begins with that string. If the old=new operand is not also specified with -s, the string form of the first operand cannot contain an embedded equal sign.

The following environment variables affect the execution of fc:

FCEDIT
> Name of the editor to use.

HISTSIZE
> The number of previous commands that are accessible.

fg [job]
> Move the specified job or the current job to the foreground.

getopts optstring var
> The POSIX getopts command.

hash -rv command...
> The shell maintains a hash table which remembers the locations of commands. With no arguments whatsoever, the hash command prints out the contents of this table. Entries which have not been looked at since the last cd command are marked with an asterisk; it is possible for these entries to be invalid.
>
> With arguments, the hash command removes the specified commands from the hash table (unless they are functions) and then locates them. With the -v option, hash prints the locations of the commands as it finds them. The -r option causes the hash command to delete all the entries in the hash table except for functions.

jobid [job]
> Print the process id's of the processes in the job. If the job argument is omitted, use the current job.

jobs
> This command lists out all the background processes which are children of the current shell process.

pwd
> Print the current directory. The builtin command may differ from the program of the same name because the builtin command remembers what the current directory is rather than recomputing it each time. This makes it faster. However, if the current directory is renamed, the builtin version of pwd will continue to print the old name for the directory.

read [-p prompt] [-e] variable...
> The prompt is printed if the -p option is specified and the standard input is a terminal. Then a line is read from the standard input. The trailing newline is deleted from the line and the line is split as described in the section on word splitting above, and the pieces are assigned to the variables in order. If there are more pieces than variables, the remaining pieces (along with the characters in IFS that separated them) are assigned to the last variable. If there are more variables than pieces, the remaining variables are assigned the null string.
>
> The -e option causes any backslashes in the input to be treated specially. If a backslash is followed by a newline, the backslash and the newline will be deleted. If a backslash is followed by any other character, the backslash will be deleted and the following character will be treated as though it were not in IFS, even if it is.

readonly name...
> The specified names are marked as read only, so that they cannot be subsequently modified or

1

unset. The shell allows the value of a variable to be set at the same time it is marked read only by writing

readonly name=value

> With no arguments the readonly command lists the names of all read only variables.

set [{ -options | +options | -- }] arg...

> The set command performs three different functions.

> With no arguments, it lists the values of all shell variables.

> If options are given, it sets the specified option flags, or clears them as described in the section called "Argument List Processing".

> The third use of the set command is to set the values of the shell's positional parameters to the specified args. To change the positional parameters without changing any options, use "--" as the first argument to set. If no args are present, the set command will clear all the positional parameters (equivalent to executing "shift $#".

setvar variable value

> Assigns value to variable. (In general it is better to write variable=value rather than using setvar. Setvar is intended to be used in functions that assign values to variables whose names are passed as parameters.)

shift [n]

> Shift the positional parameters n times. A shift sets the value of $1 to the value of $2, the value of $2 to the value of $3, and so on, decreasing the value of $# by one. If there are zero positional parameters, shifting doesn't do anything.

trap [action] signal...

> Cause the shell to parse and execute action when any of the specified signals are received. The signals are specified by signal number. Action may be null or omitted; the former causes the specified signal to be ignored and the latter causes the default action to be taken. When the shell forks off a subshell, it resets trapped (but not ignored) signals to the default action. The trap command has no effect on signals that were ignored on entry to the shell.

umask [mask]

> Set the value of umask (see umask(2)) to the specified octal value. If the argument is omitted, the umask value is printed.

unalias [-a] [name]

> If "name" is specified, the shell removes that alias. If "-a" is specified, all aliases are removed.

unset name...

> The specified variables and functions are unset and unexported. If a given name corresponds to both a variable and a function, both the variable and the function are unset.

wait [job]

> Wait for the specified job to complete and return the exit status of the last process in the job. If the argument is omitted, wait for all jobs to complete and the return an exit status of zero.

Command Line Editing

When sh is being used interactively from a terminal, the current command and the command history (see fc in Builtins) can be edited using vi-mode command-line editing. This mode uses commands, described below, similar to a subset of those described in the vi man page. The command set -o vi enables vi-mode editing and place sh into vi insert mode. With vi-mode enabled, sh can be switched between insert mode and command mode. The editor is not described in full here, but will be in a later document. It's similar to vi: typing <ESC> will throw you into command VI command mode. Hitting <return> while in command mode will pass the line to the shell.

1

NAME
     shar – create a shell archive of files

SYNOPSIS
     shar *file ...*

DESCRIPTION
     Shar writes an sh(1) shell script to the standard output which will recreate the file hierarchy specified by
     the command line operands. Directories will be recreated and must be specified before the files they contain
     (the find(1) utility does this correctly).

     Shar is normally used for distributing files by ftp(1) or mail(1).

SEE ALSO
     compress(1), mail(1), uuencode(1), tar(1)

BUGS
     Shar makes no provisions for special types of files or files containing magic characters.

     It is easy to insert trojan horses into **shar** files. It is strongly recommended that all shell archive files be ex-
     amined before running them through sh(1). Archives produced using this implementation of **shar** may be
     easily examined with the command:

          egrep -v '^[X#]' shar.file

EXAMPLES
     To create a shell archive of the program ls(1) and mail it to Rick:

          cd ls
          shar 'find . -print' | mail -s "ls source" rick

     To recreate the program directory:

          mkdir ls
          cd ls
          <delete header lines and examine mailed archive>
          sh archive

HISTORY
     The **shar** command appears in 4.4BSD.

NAME

    `size` – display object file segment sizes (text, data and bss)

SYNOPSIS

    `size` [`object_file ...`]

DESCRIPTION

    `Size` displays the text, data and bss segment sizes of the specified `object_file` in bytes (in decimal), and the sum of the three segments (in decimal and hexadecimal). If no `object_file` is specified `size` attempts to report on the file `a.out`.

SEE ALSO

    `a.out`(5)

HISTORY

    A `size` command appeared in Version 6 AT&T Unix.

1

NAME
`sleep` – suspend execution for an interval of time

SYNOPSIS
`sleep` *seconds*

DESCRIPTION
The `sleep` command suspends execution for a minimum of *seconds*. `Sleep` is used to schedule the execution of other commands (see EXAMPLES below).

The `Sleep` utility exits with one of the following values:

0   On successful completion, or if the signal `SIGALRM` was received.

>0   An error occurred.

EXAMPLES
To schedule the execution of a command for *x* number seconds later:

```
(sleep 1800; sh command_file >& errors)&
```

This incantation would wait a half hour before running the script command_file. (See the `at`(1) utility.)

To reiteratively run a command (with the `csh`(1)):

```
while (1)
        if (! -r zzz.rawdata) then
                sleep 300
        else
                foreach i ('ls *.rawdata')
                        sleep 70
                        awk -f collapse_data $i >> results
                end
                break
        endif
end
```

The scenario for a script such as this might be: a program currently running is taking longer than expected to process a series of files, and it would be nice to have another program start processing the files created by the first program as soon as it is finished (when zzz.rawdata is created). The script checks every five minutes for the file zzz.rawdata, when the file is found, then another portion processing is done courteously by sleeping for 70 seconds in between each awk job.

SEE ALSO
setitimer(2), alarm(3), sleep(3), at(1)

STANDARDS
The `sleep` command is expected to be IEEE Std1003.2 ("POSIX") compatible.

1

NAME

soelim – eliminate .so's from nroff input

SYNOPSIS

soelim [*file ...*]

DESCRIPTION

Soelim reads the specified files or the standard input and performs the textual inclusion implied by the `nroff(1)` directives of the form:

```
.so somefile
```

The directives need to appear at the beginning of input lines. This is useful since programs such as `tbl(1)` do not normally do this; it allows the placement of individual tables in separate files to be run as a part of a large document.

An argument consisting of a single minus ' – ' is taken to be a file name corresponding to the standard input.

Note that inclusion can be suppressed by using '\'' instead of '\.', i.e.

```
´so /usr/lib/tmac.s
```

A sample usage of **soelim** would be

```
soelim exum?.n | tbl | nroff −ms | col | lpr
```

SEE ALSO

colcrt(1), more(1)

BUGS

The format of the source commands must involve no strangeness – exactly one blank must precede and no blanks follow the file name.

HISTORY

The **soelim** command appeared in 3.0BSD.

NAME

sort – sort or merge text files

SYNOPSIS

sort [–mubdfinrtx][+pos1 [–pos2]] . . . [–o output] [–T directory][file] . . .

DESCRIPTION

The sort utility sorts text files by lines. Comparisons are based on one or more sort keys (or fields) extract-ed from each line of input, and are performed lexicographically. By default, if keys are not given, sort re-gards each input line as a single field.

The following options are available:

–c   Check that the single input file is sorted lexicographically. If the file is not sorted, sort sorts it and writes the sorted output to the standard output or the filename specified by the –o option.

–m   Merge only; the input files are assumed to be pre-sorted.

–o output

The argument given is the name of an output file to be used instead of the standard output. This file can be the same as one of the input files.

–T directory

The argument directory is used for creating temporary files.

–u   Unique: suppress all but one in each set of lines having equal keys. If used with the –c option, check that there are no lines with duplicate keys.

The following options override the default ordering rules. When ordering options appear independent of key field specifications, the requested field ordering rules are applied globally to all sort keys.

–d   Only blank space and alphanumeric characters are used in making comparisons.

–f   Considers all lowercase characters that have uppercase equivalents to be the same for purposes of comparison.

–i   Ignore all non-printable characters.

–n   An initial numeric string, consisting of optional blank space, optional minus sign, and zero or more digits (including decimal point) is sorted by arithmetic value. The –n option implies the –b op-tion. (See below.) Note that the –b option is only effective when key fields have been specified and that –0 is considered equal to zero. Reverse the sense of comparisons.

The treatment of field separators can be altered using the options:

–b   Leading blank spaces are ignored when determining the starting ending positions of a restricted sort key. If the –b option is specified before the first +pos1 argument, it shall be applied to all +pos1 arguments. Otherwise, the –b option can be attached independently to each +pos1 or –pos2 argument (see below).

–t char

Char is used as the field separator character; char is not considered to be part of a field (although it can be included in a sort key). Each occurrence of char is significant (for example, "charchar" delimits an empty field). If –t is not specified, blank space characters are used as default field separators.

+*pos1*   Designates the start position of a key field.

−*pos1*   Designates the end position of a key field.

The following operands are available: *file* The pathname of a file to be sorted, merged, or checked. If no file operands are specified, or if a file operand is −, the standard input is used.

A field is defined as a minimal sequence of characters followed by a field separator or a newline character. By default, the first blank space of a sequence of blank spaces acts as the field separator. All blank spaces in a sequence of blank spaces are considered to be part of the next field; for example, all blank spaces at the beginning of a line are considered to be part of the first field.

Fields are specified by the +*pos1* and −*pos2* arguments. A missing +*pos1* argument defaults to the beginning of a line. A missing −*pos2* argument defaults to the end of a line.

The arguments +*pos1* and −*pos2* have the form *m.n* followed by one or more of the options −b, −d, −f, −i, −n, −r. A +*pos1* position specified by *m.n* is interpreted to mean the *n*th character in the *m*+1th field. A missing *.n* means '.0', indicating the first character of the *m*+1th field. If the −b option is in effect, *n* is counted from the first non-blank character in the *m*+1th field; *m*.0b refers to the first non-blank character in the *m*+1th field.

A −*pos2* position specified by *m.n* is interpreted to mean the *n*th character (including separators) after the last character of the *m*th field. A missing *.n* means '.0', indicating the last character of the *m*th field. If the −b option is in effect, *n* is counted from the last leading blank character in the *m*+1th field; *m*.1b refers to the first non-blank character in the *m*+1th field.

FILES
    /var/tmp/stm*, /tmp/*   Default temporary directories (in order of search).

SEE ALSO
    comm(1), uniq(1), join(1)

DIAGNOSTICS
BUGS
    Lines which are longer than 4096 are discarded and processing continues.

HISTORY
    A **sort** command appeared in Version 6 AT&T UNIX.

1

NAME

spell, spellin, spellout – find spelling errors

SYNOPSIS

spell [−v] [−b] [−x] [−d *hlist*] [−s *hstop*] [−h *spellhist*] [*file*] ...
spellin [*list*]
spellout [−d] Ar list

DESCRIPTION

Spell collects words from the named documents, and looks them up in a spelling list. Words that neither occur among nor are derivable (by applying certain inflections, prefixes or suffixes) from words in the spelling list are printed on the standard output. If no files are named, words are collected from the standard input.

Spell ignores most troff(1), tbl(1) and eqn(1) constructions.

Under the −v option, all words not literally in the spelling list are printed, and plausible derivations from spelling list words are indicated.

Under the −b option, British spelling is checked. Besides preferring *centre*, *colour*, *speciality*, *travelled*, etc., this option insists upon −**ise** in words like *standardise*, Fowler and the OED to the contrary notwithstanding.

Under the −x option, every plausible stem is printed with '=' for each word.

The spelling list is based on many sources. While it is more haphazard than an ordinary dictionary, it is also more effective with proper names and popular technical words. Coverage of the specialized vocabularies of biology, medicine and chemistry is light.

The auxiliary files used for the spelling list, stop list, and history file may be specified by arguments following the −d, −s, and −h options. The default files are indicated below. Copies of all output may be accumulated in the history file. The stop list filters out misspellings (e.g. thier=thy−y+ier) that would otherwise pass.

Two routines help maintain the hash lists used by spell. Both expect a set of words, one per line, from the standard input. Spellin combines the words from the standard input and the preexisting *list* file and places a new list on the standard output. If no *list* file is specified, the new list is created from scratch. Spellout looks up each word from the standard input and prints on the standard output those that are missing from (or present on, with option −d) the hashed *list* file. For example, to verify that *hookey* is not on the default spelling list, add it to your own private list, and then use it with spell,

```
echo  hookey  |  spellout  /usr/share/dict/hlista
echo  hookey  |  spellin  /usr/share/dict/hlista  >  myhlist
spell  −d  myhlist  huckfinn
```

FILES

/usr/dict/hlist[ab]	Hashed spelling lists, American & British, default for −d.
/usr/dict/hstop	Hashed stop list, default for −s.
/dev/null	History file, default for −h.
/tmp/spell.$$*	Temporary files.
/usr/libexec/spell	Binary executed by the shell script /usr/bin/spell.

SEE ALSO

    deroff(1), sort(1), tee(1), sed(1)

BUGS

The spelling list's coverage is uneven; new installations will probably wish to monitor the output for several months to gather local additions.

British spelling was done by an American.

HISTORY

The **spell** command appeared in Version 6 AT&T UNIX.

NAME

    spline – interpolate smooth curve

SYNOPSIS

    spline [option] ...

DESCRIPTION

    Spline takes pairs of numbers from the standard input as abcissas and ordinates of a function. It produces a similar set, which is approximately equally spaced and includes the input set, on the standard output. The cubic spline output (R. W. Hamming, *Numerical Methods for Scientists and Engineers,* 2nd ed., 349ff) has two continuous derivatives, and sufficiently many points to look smooth when plotted, for example by *graph*(1G).

    The following options are recognized, each as a separate argument.

    –a   Supply abscissas automatically (they are missing from the input); spacing is given by the next argument, or is assumed to be 1 if next argument is not a number.

    –k   The constant k used in the boundary value computation

$$y_0'' = ky_1'', \quad y_n'' = ky_{n-1}''$$

    is set by the next argument. By default $k = 0$.

    –n   Space output points so that approximately n intervals occur between the lower and upper x limits. (Default $n = 100$.)

    –p   Make output periodic, i.e. match derivatives at ends. First and last input values should normally agree.

    –x   Next 1 (or 2) arguments are lower (and upper) x limits. Normally these limits are calculated from the data. Automatic abcissas start at lower limit (default 0).

SEE ALSO

    graph(1), plot(1)

DIAGNOSTICS

    When data is not strictly monotone in x, *spline* reproduces the input without interpolating extra points.

BUGS

    A limit of 1000 input points is enforced silently.

NAME

split – split a file into pieces

SYNOPSIS

split [–b *byte_count[k/m]*] [–l *line_count*] [*file* [*name*]]

DESCRIPTION

The **split** utility reads the given *file* (or standard input if no file is specified) and breaks it up into files of 1000 lines each.

The options are as follows:

–b   Create smaller files *byte_count* bytes in length. If "k" is appended to the number, the file is split into *byte_count* kilobyte pieces. If "m" is appended to the number, the file is split into *byte_count* megabyte pieces.

–l   Create smaller files *n* lines in length.

If additional arguments are specified, the first is used as the name of the input file which is to be split. If a second additional argument is specified, it is used as a prefix for the names of the files into which the file is split. In this case, each file into which the file is split is named by the prefix followed by a lexically ordered suffix in the range of "aa-zz".

If the *name* argument is not specified, the file is split into lexically ordered files named in the range of "xaa-zzz".

BUGS

For historical reasons, if you specify *name*, **split** can only create 676 separate files. The default naming convention allows 2028 separate files.

HISTORY

A **split** command appeared in Version 6 AT&T UNIX.

1

NAME
  startslip – dial up and login to a slip server

SYNOPSIS
  startslip [–d] [–s *string*] [–A *annexname*] [–F *flowcontrol*] *device user passwd*

DESCRIPTION
  Startslip opens the specified *device*.

  Once carrier is asserted startslip attempts to login as the specified *user* with the given *password*. If successful, it puts the device into the slip line discipline. If carrier drops and a SIGHUP is sent to startslip, it closes the device and attempts to repeat the dialup and login sequence.

  Available options:

  –d   Startslip prints out debugging information about what it is trying to do.

  –s *string* The optional *string* is written to *device*. For a dialup modem, the string is used to specify a dial sequence.

  –A *annexname*
            Startslip assumes it is connecting to a Xylogics Annex box and engages in an appropriate dialog using the *user* and *passwd* arguments. The *annexname* argument is a string that is used to match against the Annex prompt to determine when a connection has been established.

  –F *flowcontrol*
            Determines the type of flow control used on *device*. Choices for *flowcontrol* are "none" for no flow control (the default), "hw" for hardware RTS/CTS flow control and "sw" for software XON/XOFF flow control.

SEE ALSO
  sliplogin(8)

HISTORY
  The startslip appeared in 4.4BSD.

1

NAME
strings – find printable strings in a file

SYNOPSIS
strings [–afo] [–n *number*] [*file* ...]

DESCRIPTION
Strings displays the sequences of printable characters in each of the specified files, or in the standard input, by default. By default, a sequence must be at least four characters in length before being displayed.

The options are as follows:

–a   By default, strings only searches the text and data segments of object files. The –a option causes strings to search the entire object file.

–f   Each string is preceded by the name of the file in which it was found.

–n   Specifies the minimum number of characters in a sequence to be *number*, instead of four.

–o   Each string is preceded by its decimal offset in the file.

Strings is useful for identifying random binaries, among other things.

SEE ALSO
hexdump(1)

BUGS
The algorithm for identifying strings is extremely primitive. In particular, machine code instructions on certain architectures can resemble sequences of ASCII bytes, which will fool the algorithm.

COMPATIBILITY
Historic implementations of strings only search the initialized data portion of the object file. This was reasonable as strings were normally stored there. Given new compiler technology which installs strings in the text portion of the object file, the default behavior was changed.

HISTORY
The strings command appeared in 3.0BSD.

NAME

    `strip` – remove unnecessary information from executable files

SYNOPSIS

    `strip` [–d] *file* ...

DESCRIPTION

    The `strip` utility deletes the relocation information and symbol table used by assemblers, loaders and de-
buggers. This significantly decreases the size of the installed binaries and saves disk space.

    The options are as follows:

    –d   Delete only debugging and empty symbols.

    `Strip` exits 0 on success and 1 if an error occurred.

SEE ALSO

    cc(1), ld(1), stab(5)

HISTORY

    A `strip` command appeared in Version 6 AT&T UNIX.

NAME

　　struct – structure Fortran programs

SYNOPSIS

　　struct [option] ... file

DESCRIPTION

　　Struct translates the Fortran program specified by *file* (standard input default) into a Ratfor program. Wherever possible, Ratfor control constructs replace the original Fortran. Statement numbers appear only where still necessary. Cosmetic changes are made, including changing Hollerith strings into quoted strings and relational operators into symbols (.e.g. ".GT." into ">"). The output is appropriately indented.

　　The following options may occur in any order.

　　−s　　Input is accepted in standard format, i.e. comments are specified by a c, C, or * in column 1, and continuation lines are specified by a nonzero, nonblank character in column 6. Normally input is in the form accepted by *f77*(1)

　　−i　　Do not turn computed goto statements into switches. (Ratfor does not turn switches back into computed goto statements.)

　　−a　　Turn sequences of else ifs into a non-Ratfor switch of the form

　　　　　switch
　　　　　　　　{　　case pred1: code
　　　　　　　　　　case pred2: code
　　　　　　　　　　case pred3: code
　　　　　　　　　　default: code
　　　　　　　　}

　　　　　The case predicates are tested in order; the code appropriate to only one case is executed. This generalized form of switch statement does not occur in Ratfor.

　　−b　　Generate goto's instead of multilevel break statements.

　　−n　　Generate goto's instead of multilevel next statements.

　　−t*n*　　Make the nonzero integer *n* the lowest valued label in the output program (default 10).

　　−c*n*　　Increment successive labels in the output program by the nonzero integer *n* (default 1).

　　−e*n*　　If *n* is 0 (default), place code within a loop only if it can lead to an iteration of the loop. If *n* is nonzero, admit a small code segments to a loop if otherwise the loop would have exits to several places including the segment, and the segment can be reached only from the loop. 'Small' is close to, but not equal to, the number of statements in the code segment. Values of n under 10 are suggested.

FILES

　　/tmp/struct*

SEE ALSO

　　f77(1)

BUGS

　　Struct knows Fortran 66 syntax, but not full Fortran 77.

　　If an input Fortran program contains identifiers which are reserved words in Ratfor, the structured version of the program will not be a valid Ratfor program.

　　The labels generated cannot go above 32767.

　　If you get a goto without a target, try −e .

NAME
stty – set the options for a terminal device interface

SYNOPSIS
stty [−a ❘ −e ❘ −g] [−f *file*] [operands]

DESCRIPTION
The stty utility sets or reports on terminal characteristics for the device that is its standard input. If no options or operands are specified, it reports the settings of a subset of characteristics as well as additional ones if they differ from their default values. Otherwise it modifies the terminal state according to the specified arguments. Some combinations of arguments are mutually exclusive on some terminal types.

The following options are available:

−a   Display all the current settings for the terminal to standard output as per IEEE Std1003.2 (''POSIX'').

−e   Display all the current settings for the terminal to standard output in the traditional BSD ''all'' and ''everything'' formats.

−f   Open and use the terminal named by *file* rather than using standard input. The file is opened using the O_NONBLOCK flag of **open**(), making it possible to set or display settings on a terminal that might otherwise block on the open.

−g   Display all the current settings for the terminal to standard output in a form that may be used as an argument to a subsequent invocation of stty to restore the current terminal state as per IEEE Std1003.2 (''POSIX'').

The following arguments are available to set the terminal characteristics:

Control Modes:
Control mode flags affect hardware characteristics associated with the terminal. This corresponds to the c_cflag in the termios structure.

parenb (−parenb)
> Enable (disable) parity generation and detection.

parodd (−parodd)
> Select odd (even) parity.

cs5 cs6 cs7 cs8
> Select character size, if possible.

number
> Set terminal baud rate to the number given, if possible. If the baud rate is set to zero, modem control is no longer asserted.

ispeed *number*
> Set terminal input baud rate to the number given, if possible. If the input baud rate is set to zero, the input baud rate is set to the value of the output baud rate.

ospeed *number*
> Set terminal output baud rate to the number given, if possible. If the output baud rate is set to zero, modem control is no longer asserted.

speed *number*
> This sets both **ispeed** and **ospeed** to *number*.

hupcl (**–hupcl**)
> Stop asserting modem control (do not stop asserting modem control) on last close.

hup (**–hup**)
> Same as hupcl (**–hupcl**).

cstopb (**–cstopb**)
> Use two (one) stop bits per character.

cread (**–cread**)
> Enable (disable) the receiver.

clocal (**–clocal**)
> Assume a line without (with) modem control.

crtscts (**–crtscts**)
> Enable RTS/CTS flow control.

Input Modes:
> This corresponds to the c_iflag in the termios structure.

ignbrk (**–ignbrk**)
> Ignore (do not ignore) break on input.

brkint (**–brkint**)
> Signal (do not signal) INTR on break.

ignpar (**–ignpar**)
> Ignore (do not ignore) parity errors.

parmrk (**–parmrk**)
> Mark (do not mark) parity errors.

inpck (**–inpck**)
> Enable (disable) input parity checking.

istrip (**–istrip**)
> Strip (do not strip) input characters to seven bits.

inlcr (**–inlcr**)
> Map (do not map) NL to CR on input.

igncr (**–igncr**)
> Ignore (do not ignore) CR on input.

icrnl (**–icrnl**)
> Map (do not map) CR to NL on input.

ixon (**–ixon**)
> Enable (disable) START/STOP output control. Output from the system is stopped when the system receives STOP and started when the system receives START, or if **ixany** is set, any character restarts output.

1

ixoff (**–ixoff**)
> Request that the system send (not send) START/STOP characters when the input queue is nearly empty/full.

ixany (**–ixany**)
> Allow any character (allow only START) to restart output.

imaxbel (**–imaxbel**)
> The system imposes a limit of MAX_INPUT (currently 255) characters in the input queue. If **imaxbel** is set and the input queue limit has been reached, subsequent input causes the system to send an ASCII BEL character to the output queue (the terminal beeps at you). Otherwise, if **imaxbel** is unset and the input queue is full, the next input character causes the entire input and output queues to be discarded.

Output Modes:

This corresponds to the c_oflag of the termios structure.

opost (**–opost**)
> Post-process output (do not post-process output; ignore all other output modes).

onlcr (**–onlcr**)
> Map (do not map) NL to on output.

oxtabs (**–oxtabs**)
> Expand (do not expand) tabs to spaces on output.

Local Modes:

Local mode flags (lflags) affect various and sundry characteristics of terminal processing. Historically the term "local" pertained to new job control features implemented by Jim Kulp on a Pdp 11/70 at IIASA. Later the driver ran on the first VAX at Evans Hall, UC Berkeley, where the job control details were greatly modified but the structure definitions and names remained essentially unchanged. The second interpretation of the 'l' in lflag is ''line discipline flag'' which corresponds to the *c_lflag* of the *termios* structure.

isig (**–isig**)
> Enable (disable) the checking of characters against the special control characters INTR, QUIT, and SUSP.

icanon (**–icanon**)
> Enable (disable) canonical input (ERASE and KILL processing).

iexten (**–iexten**)
> Enable (disable) any implementation defined special control characters not currently controlled by icanon, isig, or ixon.

echo (**–echo**)
> Echo back (do not echo back) every character typed.

echoe (**–echoe**)
> The ERASE character shall (shall not) visually erase the last character in the current line from the display, if possible.

echok (**–echok**)
> Echo (do not echo) NL after KILL character.

echoke (**−echoke**)
> The KILL character shall (shall not) visually erase the the current line from the display, if possible.

echonl (**−echonl**)
> Echo (do not echo) NL, even if echo is disabled.

echoctl (**−echoctl**)
> If **echoctl** is set, echo control characters as ^X. Otherwise control characters echo as themselves.

echoprt (**−echoprt**)
> For printing terminals. If set, echo erased characters backwards within '' \ '' and '' / ''. Otherwise, disable this feature.

noflsh (**−noflsh**)
> Disable (enable) flush after INTR, QUIT, SUSP.

tostop (**−tostop**)
> Send (do not send) SIGTTOU for background output. This causes background jobs to stop if they attempt terminal output.

altwerase (**−altwerase**)
> Use (do not use) an alternate word erase algorithm when processing WERASE characters. This alternate algorithm considers sequences of alphanumeric/underscores as words. It also skips the first preceding character in its classification (as a convenience since the one preceding character could have been erased with simply an ERASE character.)

mdmbuf (**−mdmbuf**)
> If set, flow control output based on condition of Carrier Detect. Otherwise writes return an error if Carrier Detect is low (and Carrier is not being ignored with the CLOCAL flag.)

flusho (**−flusho**)
> Indicates output is (is not) being discarded.

pendin (**−pendin**)
> Indicates input is (is not) pending after a switch from non-canonical to canonical mode and will be re-input when a read becomes pending or more input arrives.

Control Characters:

control-character string
> Set *control-character* to *string*. If string is a single character, the control character is set to that character. If string is the two character sequence "^-" or the string "undef" the control character is disabled (i.e. set to {_POSIX_VDISABLE}.)

> Recognized control-characters:

control-character	Subscript	Description
eof	VEOF	EOF character
eol	VEOL	EOL character
eol2	VEOL2	EOL2 character

1

erase	VERASE	ERASE character
werase	VWERASE	WERASE character
intr	VINTR	INTR character
kill	VKILL	KILL character
quit	VQUIT	QUIT character
susp	VSUSP	SUSP character
start	VSTART	START character
stop	VSTOP	STOP character
dsusp	VDSUSP	DSUSP character
lnext	VLNEXT	LNEXT character
reprint	VREPRINT	REPRINT character
status	VSTATUS	STATUS character

min *number*

time *number*
> Set the value of min or time to number. MIN and TIME are used in Non-Canonical mode input processing (-icanon).

Combination Modes:

saved settings
> Set the current terminal characteristics to the saved settings produced by the −g option.

evenp or **parity**
> Enable parenb and cs7; disable parodd.

oddp   Enable parenb, cs7, and parodd.

−parity, −evenp, −oddp
> Disable parenb, and set cs8.

nl (−nl)
> Enable (disable) icrnl. In addition -nl unsets inlcr and igncr.

ek   Reset ERASE and KILL characters back to system defaults.

sane   Resets all modes to reasonable values for interactive terminal use.

tty   Set the line discipline to the standard terminal line discipline TTYDISC.

crt (−crt)
> Set (disable) all modes suitable for a CRT display device.

kerninfo (−kerninfo)
> Enable (disable) the system generated status line associated with processing a STATUS character (usually set to ^T). The status line consists of the system load average, the current command name, its process ID, the event the process is waiting on (or the status of the process), the user and system times, percent cpu, and current memory usage.

columns *number*
> The terminal size is recorded as having *number* columns.

cols *number*
> is an alias for **columns** .

1

rows *number*

The terminal size is recorded as having *number* rows.

dec   Set modes suitable for users of Digital Equipment Corporation systems (ERASE, KILL, and INTR characters are set to ^?, ^U, and ^C; ixany is disabled, and crt is enabled.)

extproc (**−extproc**)

If set, this flag indicates that some amount of terminal processing is being performed by either the terminal hardware or by the remote side connected to a pty.

raw (**−raw**)

If set, change the modes of the terminal so that no input or output processing is performed. If unset, change the modes of the terminal to some reasonable state that performs input and output processing. Note that since the terminal driver no longer has a single RAW bit, it is not possible to intuit what flags were set prior to setting **raw**. This means that unsetting **raw** may not put back all the setting that were previously in effect. To set the terminal into a raw state and then accurately restore it, the following shell code is recommended:

```
save_state=$(stty -g)
stty raw
...
stty "$save_state"
```

size   The size of the terminal is printed as two numbers on a single line, first rows, then columns.

Compatibility Modes:

These modes remain for compatibility with the previous version of the stty command.

all   Reports all the terminal modes as with **stty** **−a** except that the control characters are printed in a columnar format.

everything

Same as **all**.

cooked   Same as **sane**.

cbreak   If set, enables **brkint**, **ixon**, **imaxbel**, **opost**, **isig**, **iexten**, and **−icanon**. If unset, same as **sane**.

new   Same as **tty**.

old   Same as **tty**.

newcrt (**−newcrt**)

Same as **crt**.

pass8   The converse of **parity**.

tandem (**−tandem**)

Same as **ixoff**.

decctlq (**−decctlq**)

The converse of **ixany**.

1

crterase (**–crterase**)
>   Same as **echoe**.

crtbs (**–crtbs**)
>   Same as **echoe**.

crtkill (**–crtkill**)
>   Same as **echoke**.

ctlecho (**–ctlecho**)
>   Same as **echoctl**.

prterase (**–prterase**)
>   Same as **echoprt**.

litout (**–litout**)
>   The converse of **opost**.

tabs (**–tabs**)
>   The converse of **tabs**.

brk *value*
>   Same as the control character **eol**.

flush *value*
>   Same as the control character **discard**.

rprnt *value*
>   Same as the control character **reprint**.

The **stty** utility exits with a value of 0 if successful, and >0 if an error occurs.

SEE ALSO
termios(4)

STANDARDS
The **stty** function is expected to be IEEE Std1003.2 ("POSIX") compatible. The flags **–e** and **–f** are extensions to the standard.

1

NAME
`style` – analyze surface characteristics of a document

SYNOPSIS
`style` [−ml] [−mm] [−a] [−e] [−lnum] [−rnum] [−p] [−P] *file* ...

DESCRIPTION
Style analyzes the surface characteristics of the writing style of a document. It reports on readability, sentence length and structure, word length and usage, verb type, and sentence openers. Because **style** runs `deroff` before looking at the text, formatting header files should be included as part of the input.

Options available:

−a   print all sentences with their length and readability index.

−e   print all sentences that begin with an expletive.

−p   print all sentences that contain a passive verb.

−l *num*   print all sentences longer than *num*.

−ml   The flag −ml, which causes `deroff` to skip lists, should be used if the document contains many lists of non-sentences.

−mm   The default macro package −**ms** may be overridden with the flag −**mm**.

−r *num*   print all sentences whose readability index is greater than *num*.

−P   print parts of speech of the words in the document.

SEE ALSO
`deroff`(1), `diction`(1)

BUGS
Use of non-standard formatting macros may cause incorrect sentence breaks.

HISTORY
The **style** command appeared in 4BSD.

1

NAME

su – substitute user identity

SYNOPSIS

su [−**Kflm**] [*login*]

DESCRIPTION

Su requests the Kerberos password for *login* (or for ''*login*.root'', if no login is provided), and switches to that user and group ID after obtaining a Kerberos ticket granting ticket. A shell is then executed. **Su** will resort to the local password file to find the password for *login* if there is a Kerberos error. If **su** is executed by root, no password is requested and a shell with the appropriate user ID is executed; no additional Kerberos tickets are obtained.

By default, the environment is unmodified with the exception of USER, HOME, and SHELL. HOME and SHELL are set to the target login's default values. USER is set to the target login, unless the target login has a user ID of 0, in which case it is unmodified. The invoked shell is the target login's. This is the traditional behavior of **su**.

The options are as follows:

−**K**   Do not attempt to use Kerberos to authenticate the user.

−**f**   If the invoked shell is csh(1), this option prevents it from reading the ''.cshrc'' file.

−**l**   Simulate a full login. The environment is discarded except for HOME, SHELL, PATH, TERM, and USER. HOME and SHELL are modified as above. USER is set to the target login. PATH is set to ''/bin:/usr/bin''. TERM is imported from your current environment. The invoked shell is the target login's, and **su** will change directory to the target login's home directory.

−**m**   Leave the environment unmodified. The invoked shell is your login shell, and no directory changes are made. As a security precaution, if the target user's shell is a non-standard shell (as defined by getusershell(3)) and the caller's real uid is non-zero, **su** will fail.

The −**l** and −**m** options are mutually exclusive; the last one specified overrides any previous ones.

Only users in group 0 (normally ''wheel'') can **su** to ''root''.

By default (unless the prompt is reset by a startup file) the super-user prompt is set to ''#'' to remind one of its awesome power.

SEE ALSO

csh(1), login(1), sh(1), kinit(1), kerberos(1), passwd(5), group(5), environ(7)

ENVIRONMENT

Environment variables used by **su**:

HOME Default home directory of real user ID unless modified as specified above.

PATH Default search path of real user ID unless modified as specified above.

TERM Provides terminal type which may be retained for the substituted user ID.

USER The user ID is always the effective ID (the target user ID) after an **su** unless the user ID is 0 (root).

HISTORY

A **su** command appeared in Version 7 AT&T UNIX.

NAME
sum – calculate file checksums and block counts

SYNOPSIS
sum *file*

DESCRIPTION
The **sum** utility calculates and writes to standard output a checksum (16 bit CRC) for each input file, and also writes to the standard output the number of blocks in each file.

The following operand is available:

file The pathname of the *file* to checksum. If no file operands are specified, the standard input is used.

SEE ALSO
wc(1)

DIAGNOSTICS
The **sum** utility exits zero on success, and >0 if an error occurs.

End-of-file may return a read-error.

HISTORY
A **sum** command appeared in Version 7 AT&T UNIX.

1

NAME
symorder – rearrange name list

SYNOPSIS
symorder –t *symlist file*

DESCRIPTION
The file *symlist* contains a list of symbols to be found in *file,* one symbol per line.

The symbol table of *file* is updated in place; symbols read from *symlist* are relocated to the beginning of the table and in the order given.

–t　　Restrict the symbol table to the symbols listed in *symlist.*

This program was specifically designed to cut down on the overhead of getting symbols from /vmunix .

DIAGNOSTICS
The symorder utility exits 0 on success, 1 if a symbol listed in the *symlist* file was not found in the symbol table, and >1 if an error occurs.

SEE ALSO
nm(3), nlist(3), strip(3)

HISTORY
The symorder command appeared in 3.0BSD.

NAME

　　　　systat – display system statistics on a crt

SYNOPSIS

　　　　systat [–display] [refresh-interval]

DESCRIPTION

　　　　Systat displays various system statistics in a screen oriented fashion using the curses screen display library, curses(3).

　　　　While systat is running the screen is usually divided into two windows (an exception is the vmstat display which uses the entire screen). The upper window depicts the current system load average. The information displayed in the lower window may vary, depending on user commands. The last line on the screen is reserved for user input and error messages.

　　　　By default systat displays the processes getting the largest percentage of the processor in the lower window. Other displays show swap space usage, disk I/O statistics (a la iostat(1)), virtual memory statistics (a la vmstat(1)), network "mbuf" utilization, and network connections (a la netstat(1)).

　　　　Input is interpreted at two different levels. A "global" command interpreter processes all keyboard input. If this command interpreter fails to recognize a command, the input line is passed to a per-display command interpreter. This allows each display to have certain display-specific commands.

　　　　Command line options:

　　　　–display　　　　The – flag expects display to be one of: **pigs**, **iostat**, **swap**, **mbufs**, **vmstat** or **netstat**. These displays can also be requested interactively (without the " – ") and are described in full detail below.

　　　　refresh-interval The refresh-value specifies the screen refresh time interval in seconds.

　　　　Certain characters cause immediate action by **systat**. These are

　　　　^L　　　　　　Refresh the screen.

　　　　^G　　　　　　Print the name of the current "display" being shown in the lower window and the refresh interval.

　　　　^Z　　　　　　Stop **systat**.

　　　　:　　　　　　　Move the cursor to the command line and interpret the input line typed as a command. While entering a command the current character erase, word erase, and line kill characters may be used.

　　　　The following commands are interpreted by the "global" command interpreter.

　　　　help　　　　　Print the names of the available displays on the command line.

　　　　load　　　　　Print the load average over the past 1, 5, and 15 minutes on the command line.

　　　　stop　　　　　Stop refreshing the screen.

　　　　[start] [number]

　　　　　　　　　　　Start (continue) refreshing the screen. If a second, numeric, argument is provided it is interpreted as a refresh interval (in seconds). Supplying only a number will set the refresh interval to this value.

　　　　quit　　　　　Exit **systat**. (This may be abbreviated to q.)

The available displays are:

pigs   Display, in the lower window, those processes resident in main memory and getting the largest portion of the processor (the default display). When less than 100% of the processor is scheduled to user processes, the remaining time is accounted to the "idle" process.

iostat   Display, in the lower window, statistics about processor use and disk throughput. Statistics on processor use appear as bar graphs of the amount of time executing in user mode ("user"), in user mode running low priority processes ("nice"), in system mode ("system"), and idle ("idle"). Statistics on disk throughput show, for each drive, kilobytes of data transferred, number of disk transactions performed, and average seek time (in milliseconds). This information may be displayed as bar graphs or as rows of numbers which scroll downward. Bar graphs are shown by default;

The following commands are specific to the **iostat** display; the minimum unambiguous prefix may be supplied.

    numbers Show the disk I/O statistics in numeric form. Values are displayed in numeric columns which scroll downward.

    bars   Show the disk I/O statistics in bar graph form (default).

    msps   Toggle the display of average seek time (the default is to not display seek times).

swap   Show information about swap space usage on all the swap areas compiled into the kernel. The first column is the device name of the partition. The next column is the total space available in the partition. The *Used* column indicates the total blocks used so far; the graph shows the percentage of space in use on each partition. If there are more than one swap partition in use, a total line is also shown. Areas known to the kernel, but not in use are shown as not available.

mbufs   Display, in the lower window, the number of mbufs allocated for particular uses, i.e. data, socket structures, etc.

vmstat   Take over the entire display and show a (rather crowded) compendium of statistics related to virtual memory usage, process scheduling, device interrupts, system name translation cacheing, disk I/O etc.

The upper left quadrant of the screen shows the number of users logged in and the load average over the last one, five, and fifteen minute intervals. Below this line are statistics on memory utilization. The first row of the table reports memory usage only among active processes, that is processes that have run in the previous twenty seconds. The second row reports on memory usage of all processes. The first column reports on the number of physical pages claimed by processes. The second column reports the number of physical pages that are devoted to read only text pages. The third and fourth columns report the same two figures for virtual pages, that is the number of pages that would be needed if all processes had all of their pages. Finally the last column shows the number of physical pages on the free list.

Below the memory display is the disk usage display. It reports the number of seeks, transfers, and number of kilobyte blocks transferred per second averaged over the refresh period of the display (by default, five seconds). For some disks it also reports the average milliseconds per seek. Note that the system only keeps statistics on at most four disks.

Below the disk display is a list of the average number of processes (over the last refresh interval) that are runnable ('r'), in page wait ('p'), in disk wait other than paging ('d'), sleeping ('s'), and swapped out but desiring to run ('w'). Below the queue length listing is a numerical listing and a bar graph showing the amount of system (shown as '='), user (shown as '>'), nice (shown as '-'), and idle time (shown as ' ').

1

At the bottom left are statistics on name translations. It lists the number of names translated in the previous interval, the number and percentage of the translations that were handled by the system wide name translation cache, and the number and percentage of the translations that were handled by the per process name translation cache.

Under the date in the upper right hand quadrant are statistics on paging and swapping activity. The first two columns report the average number of pages brought in and out per second over the last refresh interval due to page faults and the paging daemon. The third and fourth columns report the average number of pages brought in and out per second over the last refresh interval due to swap requests initiated by the scheduler. The first row of the display shows the average number of disk transfers per second over the last refresh interval; the second row of the display shows the average number of pages transferred per second over the last refresh interval.

Below the paging statistics is a line listing the average number of total reclaims ('Rec'), intransit blocking page faults ('It'), swap text pages found in free list ('F/S'), file system text pages found in free list ('F/F'), reclaims from free list pages freed by the clock daemon ('Fre'), and sequential process pages freed ('SFr') per second over the refresh interval.

Below this line are statistics on the average number of zero filled pages ('zf') and demand filled text pages ('xf') per second over the refresh period. The first row indicates the number of requests that were resolved, the second row shows the number that were set up, and the last row shows the percentage of setup requests that were actually used. Note that this percentage is usually less than 100%, however it may exceed 100% if a large number of requests are actually used long after they were set up during a period when no new pages are being set up. Thus this figure is most interesting when observed over a long time period, such as from boot time (see below on getting such a display).

Below the page fill statistics is a column that lists the average number of context switches ('Csw'), traps ('Trp'; includes page faults), system calls ('Sys'), interrupts ('Int'), characters output to DZ ports using pseudo-DMA ('Pdm'), network software interrupts ('Sof'), page faults ('Flt'), pages scanned by the page daemon ('Scn'), and revolutions of the page daemon's hand ('Rev') per second over the refresh interval.

Running down the right hand side of the display is a breakdown of the interrupts being handled by the system. At the top of the list is the total interrupts per second over the time interval. The rest of the column breaks down the total on a device by device basis. Only devices that have interrupted at least once since boot time are shown.

The following commands are specific to the **vmstat** display; the minimum unambiguous prefix may be supplied.

boot	Display cumulative statistics since the system was booted.
run	Display statistics as a running total from the point this command is given.
time	Display statistics averaged over the refresh interval (the default).
zero	Reset running statistics to zero.

netstat   Display, in the lower window, network connections. By default, network servers awaiting requests are not displayed. Each address is displayed in the format ''host.port'', with each shown symbolically, when possible. It is possible to have addresses displayed numerically, limit the display to a set of ports, hosts, and/or protocols (the minimum unambiguous prefix may be supplied):

1

> **all**   Toggle the displaying of server processes awaiting requests (this is the equivalent of the −a flag to *netstat 1*).
>
> **numbers**   Display network addresses numerically.
>
> **names**   Display network addresses symbolically.
>
> *protocol*   Display only network connections using the indicated protocol (currently either "tcp" or "udp").
>
> **ignore** [*items*]
> > Do not display information about connections associated with the specified hosts or ports. Hosts and ports may be specified by name ("vangogh", "ftp"), or numerically. Host addresses use the Internet dot notation ("128.32.0.9"). Multiple items may be specified with a single command by separating them with spaces.
>
> **display** [*items*]
> > Display information about the connections associated with the specified hosts or ports. As for *ignore*, [*items*] may be names or numbers.
>
> **show** [*ports|hosts*]
> > Show, on the command line, the currently selected protocols, hosts, and ports. Hosts and ports which are being ignored are prefixed with a '!'. If *ports* or *hosts* is supplied as an argument to **show**, then only the requested information will be displayed.
>
> **reset**   Reset the port, host, and protocol matching mechanisms to the default (any protocol, port, or host).

Commands to switch between displays may be abbreviated to the minimum unambiguous prefix; for example, "io" for "iostat". Certain information may be discarded when the screen size is insufficient for display. For example, on a machine with 10 drives the **iostat** bar graph displays only 3 drives on a 24 line terminal. When a bar graph would overflow the allotted screen space it is truncated and the actual value is printed "over top" of the bar.

The following commands are common to each display which shows information about disk drives. These commands are used to select a set of drives to report on, should your system have more drives configured than can normally be displayed on the screen.

> **ignore** [*drives*]   Do not display information about the drives indicated. Multiple drives may be specified, separated by spaces.
>
> **display** [*drives*]   Display information about the drives indicated. Multiple drives may be specified, separated by spaces.

FILES

> /vmunix   For the namelist.
> /dev/kmem   For information in main memory.
> /dev/drum   For information about swapped out processes.
> /etc/hosts   For host names.
> /etc/networks For network names.
> /etc/services For port names.

HISTORY

> The **systat** program appeared in 4.3BSD.

BUGS

> Takes 2-10 percent of the cpu. Certain displays presume a minimum of 80 characters per line. The **vmstat** display looks out of place because it is (it was added in as a separate display rather than created as a new program).

1

NAME

tail – display the last part of a file

SYNOPSIS

tail [−f | −r][−b *number* | −c *number* | −n *number*] [*file* ...]

DESCRIPTION

The tail utility displays the contents of *file* or, by default, its standard input, to the standard output.

The display begins at a byte, line or 512-byte block location in the input. Numbers having a leading plus (''+'') sign are relative to the beginning of the input, for example, ''-c +2'' starts the display at the second byte of the input. Numbers having a leading minus (''-'') sign or no explicit sign are relative to the end of the input, for example, ''-n 2'' displays the last two lines of the input. The default starting location is ''-n 10'', or the last 10 lines of the input.

The options are as follows:

−b *number*
> The location is *number* 512-byte blocks.

−c *number*
> The location is *number* bytes.

−f
> The −f option causes tail to not stop when end of file is reached, but rather to wait for additional data to be appended to the input. The −f option is ignored if the standard input is a pipe, but not if it is a FIFO.

−n *number*
> The location is *number* lines.

−r
> The −r option causes the input to be displayed in reverse order, by line. Additionally, this option changes the meaning of the −b, −c and −n options. When the −r option is specified, these options specify the number of bytes, lines or 512-byte blocks to display, instead of the bytes, lines or blocks from the beginning or end of the input from which to begin the display. The default for the −r option is to display all of the input.

If more than a single file is specified, each file is preceded by a header consisting of the string ''==> XXX <=='' where ''XXX'' is the name of the file.

The tail utility exits 0 on success, and >0 if an error occurs.

SEE ALSO

cat(1), head(1), sed(1)

STANDARDS

The tail utility is expected to be a superset of the POSIX 1003.2 specification. In particular, the −b and −r options are extensions to that standard.

The historic command line syntax of tail is supported by this implementation. The only difference between this implementation and historic versions of tail, once the command line syntax translation has been done, is that the −b, −c and −n options modify the −r option, i.e. ''-r -c 4'' displays the last 4 characters of the last line of the input, while the historic tail (using the historic syntax ''-4cr'') would ignore the −c option and display the last 4 lines of the input.

HISTORY

A **tail** command appeared in Version 7 AT&T UNIX.

NAME

`talk` – talk to another user

SYNOPSIS

`talk` *person* [*ttyname*]

DESCRIPTION

Talk is a visual communication program which copies lines from your terminal to that of another user.

Options available:

person   If you wish to talk to someone on your own machine, then *person* is just the person's login name. If you wish to talk to a user on another host, then *person* is of the form user@host.

ttyname   If you wish to talk to a user who is logged in more than once, the *ttyname* argument may be used to indicate the appropriate terminal name, where *ttyname* is of the form ttyXX.

When first called, `talk` sends the message

```
Message from TalkDaemon@his_machine...
talk: connection requested by your_name@your_machine.
talk: respond with: talk your_name@your_machine
```

to the user you wish to talk to. At this point, the recipient of the message should reply by typing

```
talk  your_name@your_machine
```

It doesn't matter from which machine the recipient replies, as long as his login-name is the same. Once communication is established, the two parties may type simultaneously, with their output appearing in separate windows. Typing control-L '^L' will cause the screen to be reprinted, while your erase, kill, and word kill characters will behave normally. To exit, just type your interrupt character; `talk` then moves the cursor to the bottom of the screen and restores the terminal to its previous state.

Permission to talk may be denied or granted by use of the mesg(1) command. At the outset talking is allowed. Certain commands, in particular nroff(1) and pr(1), disallow messages in order to prevent messy output.

FILES

```
/etc/hosts       to find the recipient's machine
/var/run/utmp  to find the recipient's tty
```

SEE ALSO

mail(1), mesg(1), who(1), write(1)

BUGS

The version of talk(1) released with 4.3BSD uses a protocol that is incompatible with the protocol used in the version released with 4.2BSD.

HISTORY

The `talk` command appeared in 4.2BSD.

NAME

tar – tape archiver

SYNOPSIS

tar [key] [name ...]

DESCRIPTION

Tar saves and restores multiple files on a single file (usually a magnetic tape, but it can be any file). Tar's actions are controlled by the key argument. The key is a string of characters containing at most one function letter and possibly one or more function modifiers. Other arguments to tar are file or directory names specifying which files to dump or restore. In all cases, appearance of a directory name refers to the files and (recursively) subdirectories of that directory.

The function portion of the key is specified by one of the following letters:

r   The named files are written on the end of the tape. The c function implies this.

x   The named files are extracted from the tape. If the named file matches a directory whose contents had been written onto the tape, this directory is (recursively) extracted. The owner, modification time, and mode are restored (if possible). If no file argument is given, the entire content of the tape is extracted. Note that if multiple entries specifying the same file are on the tape, the last one overwrites all earlier.

t   The names of the specified files are listed each time they occur on the tape. If no file argument is given, all of the names on the tape are listed.

u   The named files are added to the tape if either they are not already there or have been modified since last put on the tape.

c   Create a new tape; writing begins on the beginning of the tape instead of after the last file. This command implies r.

The following characters may be used in addition to the letter which selects the function desired.

o   On output, tar normally places information specifying owner and modes of directories in the archive. Former versions of tar, when encountering this information will give error message of the form

         <name>/: cannot create.

This modifier will suppress the directory information.

p   This modifier says to restore files to their original modes, ignoring the present umask(2). Setuid and sticky information will also be restored to the super-user.

0, ..., 9
This modifier selects an alternate drive on which the tape is mounted. The default is drive 0 at 1600 bpi, which is normally /dev/rmt8.

v   Normally tar does its work silently. The v (verbose) option makes tar print the name of each file it treats preceded by the function letter. With the t function, the verbose option gives more information about the tape entries than just their names.

w   Tar prints the action to be taken followed by file name, then wait for user confirmation. If a word beginning with 'y' is given, the action is done. Any other input means don't do it.

f   *Tar* uses the next argument as the name of the archive instead of /dev/rmt?. If the name of the file is '−', tar writes to standard output or reads from standard input, whichever is appropriate. Thus, **tar** can be used as the head or tail of a filter chain. **Tar** can also be used to move hierarchies with the command

```
cd fromdir; tar cf - .  |  (cd todir; tar xf -)
```

b   *Tar* uses the next argument as the blocking factor for tape records. The default is 20 (the maximum). This option should only be used with raw magnetic tape archives (See **f** above). The block size is determined automatically when reading tapes (key letters **x** and **t**).

s   tells **tar** to strip off any leading slashes from pathnames.

l   tells **tar** to complain if it cannot resolve all of the links to the files dumped. If this is not specified, no error messages are printed.

m   tells **tar** not to restore the modification times. The modification time will be the time of extraction.

h   Force **tar** to follow symbolic links as if they were normal files or directories. Normally, **tar** does not follow symbolic links.

H   Force **tar** to follow symbolic links on the command line only as if they were normal files or directories. Normally, **tar** does not follow symbolic links. Note that −**h** supercedes −**H**.

B   Forces input and output blocking to 20 blocks per record. This option was added so that **tar** can work across a communications channel where the blocking may not be maintained.

C   If a file name is preceded by −**C**, then **tar** will perform a chdir(2) to that file name. This allows multiple directories not related by a close common parent to be archived using short relative path names. For example, to archive files from /usr/include and from /etc, one might use

```
tar c -C /usr include -C / etc
```

Previous restrictions dealing with **tar**'s inability to properly handle blocked archives have been lifted.

FILES
```
/dev/rmt?
/tmp/tar*
```

SEE ALSO
tar(5), format(5), symlink(7)

DIAGNOSTICS
Complaints about bad key characters and tape read/write errors.

Complaints if enough memory is not available to hold the link tables.

BUGS
There is no way to ask for the *n*-th occurrence of a file.

Tape errors are handled ungracefully.

The **u** option can be slow.

The current limit on file name length is 100 characters.

There is no way selectively to follow symbolic links.

When extracting tapes created with the **r** or **u** options, directory modification times may not be set correctly.

HISTORY

The **tar** command appeared in Version 7 AT&T UNIX.

NAME

    tbl – format tables for troff

SYNOPSIS

    tbl [**−Cv**] [*files . . .*]

DESCRIPTION

    This manual page describes the GNU version of **tbl**, which is part of the groff document formatting system. **tbl** compiles descriptions of tables embedded within **troff** input files into commands that are understood by **troff**. Normally, it should be invoked using the −**t** option of **groff**. It is highly compatible with Unix **tbl**. The output generated by GNU **tbl** cannot be processed with Unix **troff**; it must be processed with GNU **troff**. If no files are given on the command line, the standard input will be read. A filename of − will cause the standard input to be read.

OPTIONS

    −**C**   Recognize **.TS** and **.TE** even when followed by a character other than space or newline.

    −**v**   Print the version number.

USAGE

    Only the differences between GNU **tbl** and Unix **tbl** are described here.

    Normally **tbl** attempts to prevent undesirable breaks in the table by using diversions. This can sometimes interact badly with macro packages' own use of diversions, when footnotes, for example, are used. The **nokeep** option tells **tbl** not to try and prevent breaks in this way.

    The **decimalpoint** option specifies the character to be recognized as the decimal point character in place of the default period. It takes an argument in parentheses, which must be a single character, as for the **tab** option.

    The **f** format modifier can be followed by an arbitrary length font name in parentheses.

    There is a **d** format modifier which means that a vertically spanning entry should be aligned at the bottom of its range.

    There is no limit on the number of columns in a table, nor any limit on the number of text blocks. All the lines of a table are considered in deciding column widths, not just the first 200. Table continuation (**.T&**) lines are not restricted to the first 200 lines.

    Numeric and alphabetic items may appear in the same column.

    Numeric and alphabetic items may span horizontally.

    tbl uses register, string, macro and diversion names beginning with **3**. When using **tbl** you should avoid using any names beginning with a **3**.

BUGS

    You should use **.TS H/.TH** in conjunction with a supporting macro package for *all* multi-page boxed tables. If there is no header that you wish to appear at the top of each page of the table, place the **.TH** line immediately after the format section. Do not enclose a multi-page table within keep/release macros, or divert it in any other way.

    A text block within a table must be able to fit on one page.

    The **bp** request cannot be used to force a page-break in a multi-page table. Instead, define **BP** as follows

```
.de BP
.ie '\\n(.z'' .bp \\$1
.el \!.BP \\$1
..
```

    and use **BP** instead of **bp**.

SEE ALSO

groff(1), troff(1)

1

NAME

tcopy – copy and/or verify mag tapes

SYNOPSIS

tcopy [–cvx] [–s *maxblk*] [*src* [*dest*]]

DESCRIPTION

Tcopy is designed to copy magnetic tapes. The only assumption made about the tape is that there are two tape marks at the end. Tcopy with only a source tape (*rmt0* by default) specified will print information about the sizes of records and tape files. If a destination is specified a copy will be made of the source tape. The blocking on the destination tape will be identical to that used on the source tape. Copying a tape will yield the same output as if just printing the sizes.

Options:

–c   Copy *src* to *dest* and then verify that the two tapes are identical.

–s *maxblk*
        Specify a maximum block size, *maxblk*.

–v   Given the two tapes, and *dest* verify that they are identical.

–x   Output all informational messages to the standard error. This option is useful when *dest* is /dev/stdout.

SEE ALSO

mtio(4)

HISTORY

The tcopy command appeared in 4.3BSD.

1

NAME
　　tee – pipe fitting

SYNOPSIS
　　tee [**−ai**] [*file* ...]

DESCRIPTION
　　The **tee** utility copies standard input to standard output, making a copy in zero or more files.　The output is unbuffered.

　　The following options are available:

　　−a　　Append the output to the files rather than overwriting them.

　　−i　　Ignore the SIGINT signal.

　　The following operands are available:

　　file　　A pathname of an output *file*.

　　The **tee** utility takes the default action for all signals, except in the event of the **−i** option.

　　The **tee** utility exits 0 on success, and >0 if an error occurs.

STANDARDS
　　The **tee** function is expected to be POSIX IEEE Std1003.2 (''POSIX'') compatible.

NAME

telnet – user interface to the TELNET protocol

SYNOPSIS

telnet [**–8EFKLacdfrx**] [**–S** *tos*] [**–X** *authtype*] [**–e** *escapechar*] [**–k** *realm*] [**–l** *user*] [**–n** *tracefile*] [*host* [port]]

DESCRIPTION

The **telnet** command is used to communicate with another host using the TELNET protocol. If **telnet** is invoked without the *host* argument, it enters command mode, indicated by its prompt (**telnet>**). In this mode, it accepts and executes the commands listed below. If it is invoked with arguments, it performs an **open** command with those arguments.

Options:

–8   Specifies an 8-bit data path. This causes an attempt to negotiate the TELNET BINARY option on both input and output.

–E   Stops any character from being recognized as an escape character.

–F   If Kerberos V5 authentication is being used, the **–F** option allows the local credentials to be forwarded to the remote system, including any credentials that have already been forwarded into the local environment.

–K   Specifies no automatic login to the remote system.

–L   Specifies an 8-bit data path on output. This causes the BINARY option to be negotiated on output.

–S *tos*

Sets the IP type-of-service (TOS) option for the telnet connection to the value *tos,* which can be a numeric TOS value or, on systems that support it, a symbolic TOS name found in the /etc/iptos file.

–X *atype*

Disables the *atype* type of authentication.

–a   Attempt automatic login. Currently, this sends the user name via the USER variable of the ENVIRON option if supported by the remote system. The name used is that of the current user as returned by getlogin(2) if it agrees with the current user ID, otherwise it is the name associated with the user ID.

–c   Disables the reading of the user's .telnetrc file. (See the **toggle skiprc** command on this man page.)

–d   Sets the initial value of the **debug** toggle to TRUE

–e *escape char*

Sets the initial **telnet telnet** escape character to *escape char.* If *escape char* is omitted, then there will be no escape character.

–f   If Kerberos V5 authentication is being used, the **–f** option allows the local credentials to be forwarded to the remote system.

1

−k *realm*

    If Kerberos authentication is being used, the **−k** option requests that telnet obtain tickets for the remote host in realm realm instead of the remote host's realm, as determined by krb_realmofhost(3).

−l *user*

    When connecting to the remote system, if the remote system understands the ENVIRON option, then *user* will be sent to the remote system as the value for the variable USER. This option implies the **−a** option. This option may also be used with the **open** command.

−n *tracefile*

    Opens *tracefile* for recording trace information. See the **set tracefile** command below.

−r   Specifies a user interface similar to rlogin(1). In this mode, the escape character is set to the tilde (˜) character, unless modified by the -e option.

−x   Turns on encryption of the data stream if possible. This option is not available outside of the United States and Canada.

host   Indicates the official name, an alias, or the Internet address of a remote host.

port   Indicates a port number (address of an application). If a number is not specified, the default **telnet** port is used.

When in rlogin mode, a line of the form ˜. disconnects from the remote host; ˜ is the telnet escape character. Similarly, the line ˜^Z suspends the telnet session. The line ˜] escapes to the normal telnet escape prompt.

Once a connection has been opened, **telnet** will attempt to enable the TELNET LINEMODE option. If this fails, then **telnet** will revert to one of two input modes: either ''character at a time'' or ''old line by line'' depending on what the remote system supports.

When LINEMODE is enabled, character processing is done on the local system, under the control of the remote system. When input editing or character echoing is to be disabled, the remote system will relay that information. The remote system will also relay changes to any special characters that happen on the remote system, so that they can take effect on the local system.

In ''character at a time'' mode, most text typed is immediately sent to the remote host for processing.

In ''old line by line'' mode, all text is echoed locally, and (normally) only completed lines are sent to the remote host. The ''local echo character'' (initially ''^E'') may be used to turn off and on the local echo (this would mostly be used to enter passwords without the password being echoed).

If the LINEMODE option is enabled, or if the **localchars** toggle is TRUE (the default for ''old line by line''; see below), the user's quit, **intr**, and **flush** characters are trapped locally, and sent as TELNET protocol sequences to the remote side. If LINEMODE has ever been enabled, then the user's **susp** and **eof** are also sent as TELNET protocol sequences, and **quit** is sent as a TELNET ABORT instead of BREAK There are options (see **toggle autoflush** and **toggle autosynch** below) which cause this action to flush subsequent output to the terminal (until the remote host acknowledges the TELNET sequence) and flush previous terminal input (in the case of **quit** and **intr**).

While connected to a remote host, **telnet** command mode may be entered by typing the **telnet** ''escape character'' (initially ''^]''). When in command mode, the normal terminal editing conventions are available.

The following **telnet** commands are available. Only enough of each command to uniquely identify it need be typed (this is also true for arguments to the **mode**, **set**, **toggle**, **unset**, **slc**, **environ**, and **display** commands).

auth *argument* ...

> The auth command manipulates the information sent through the `TELNET AUTHENTICATE` option. Valid arguments for the auth command are as follows:

> **disable** *type* — Disables the specified type of authentication. To obtain a list of available types, use the `auth disable ?` command.

> **enable** *type* — Enables the specified type of authentication. To obtain a list of available types, use the `auth enable ?` command.

> **status** — Lists the current status of the various types of authentication.

close — Close a TELNET session and return to command mode.

display *argument* ...

> Displays all, or some, of the **set** and **toggle** values (see below).

encrypt *argument* ...

> The encrypt command manipulates the information sent through the `TELNET ENCRYPT` option.

> Note: Because of export controls, the `TELNET ENCRYPT` option is not supported outside of the United States and Canada.

> Valid arguments for the encrypt command are as follows:

> **disable** *type* **[input|output]**
> > Disables the specified type of encryption. If you omit the input and output, both input and output are disabled. To obtain a list of available types, use the `encrypt disable ?` command.

> **enable** *type* **[input|output]**
> > Enables the specified type of encryption. If you omit input and output, both input and output are enabled. To obtain a list of available types, use the `encrypt enable ?` command.

> **input** — This is the same as the `encrypt start input` command.

> **-input** — This is the same as the `encrypt stop input` command.

> **output** — This is the same as the `encrypt start output` command.

> **-output** — This is the same as the `encrypt stop output` command.

> **start [input|output]**
> > Attempts to start encryption. If you omit **input** and **output,** both input and output are enabled. To obtain a list of available types, use the `encrypt enable ?` command.

> **status** — Lists the current status of encryption.

> **stop [input|output]**
> > Stops encryption. If you omit input and output, encryption is on both input and output.

> **type** *type* — Sets the default type of encryption to be used with later `encrypt start` or `encrypt stop` commands.

environ *arguments...*

> The **environ** command is used to manipulate the the variables that my be sent through the `TELNET ENVIRON` option. The initial set of variables is taken from the users environment,

1

with only the DISPLAY and PRINTER variables being exported by default. The USER variable is also exported if the −a or −l options are used.

Valid arguments for the **environ** command are:

define *variable value*
>   Define the variable *variable* to have a value of *value*. Any variables defined by this command are automatically exported. The *value* may be enclosed in single or double quotes so that tabs and spaces may be included.

undefine *variable*
>   Remove *variable* from the list of environment variables.

export *variable*
>   Mark the variable *variable* to be exported to the remote side.

unexport *variable*
>   Mark the variable *variable* to not be exported unless explicitly asked for by the remote side.

list   List the current set of environment variables. Those marked with a * will be sent automatically, other variables will only be sent if explicitly requested.

?   Prints out help information for the **environ** command.

logout   Sends the TELNET LOGOUT option to the remote side. This command is similar to a **close** command; however, if the remote side does not support the LOGOUT option, nothing happens. If, however, the remote side does support the LOGOUT option, this command should cause the remote side to close the TELNET connection. If the remote side also supports the concept of suspending a user's session for later reattachment, the logout argument indicates that you should terminate the session immediately.

mode *type* *Type* is one of several options, depending on the state of the TELNET session. The remote host is asked for permission to go into the requested mode. If the remote host is capable of entering that mode, the requested mode will be entered.

character   Disable the TELNET LINEMODE option, or, if the remote side does not understand the LINEMODE option, then enter "character at a time" mode.

line   Enable the TELNET LINEMODE option, or, if the remote side does not understand the LINEMODE option, then attempt to enter "old-line-by-line" mode.

isig (−isig)
>   Attempt to enable (disable) the TRAPSIG mode of the LINEMODE option. This requires that the LINEMODE option be enabled.

edit (−edit)
>   Attempt to enable (disable) the EDIT mode of the LINEMODE option. This requires that the LINEMODE option be enabled.

softtabs (−softtabs)
>   Attempt to enable (disable) the SOFT_TAB mode of the LINEMODE option. This requires that the LINEMODE option be enabled.

litecho (–litecho)
> Attempt to enable (disable) the LIT_ECHO mode of the LINEMODE option. This requires that the LINEMODE option be enabled.

? Prints out help information for the **mode** command.

open *host* [[–1] *user*][–*port*]
> Open a connection to the named host. If no port number is specified, **telnet** will attempt to contact a TELNET server at the default port. The host specification may be either a host name (see hosts(5)) or an Internet address specified in the "dot notation" (see inet(3)). The [–1] option may be used to specify the user name to be passed to the remote system via the ENVIRON option. When connecting to a non-standard port, **telnet** omits any automatic initiation of TELNET options. When the port number is preceded by a minus sign, the initial option negotiation is done. After establishing a connection, the file .telnetrc in the users home directory is opened. Lines beginning with a # are comment lines. Blank lines are ignored. Lines that begin without white space are the start of a machine entry. The first thing on the line is the name of the machine that is being connected to. The rest of the line, and successive lines that begin with white space are assumed to be **telnet** commands and are processed as if they had been typed in manually to the **telnet** command prompt.

quit Close any open TELNET session and exit **telnet**. An end of file (in command mode) will also close a session and exit.

send *arguments*
> Sends one or more special character sequences to the remote host. The following are the arguments which may be specified (more than one argument may be specified at a time):

abort Sends the TELNET ABORT (Abort processes) sequence.

ao Sends the TELNET AO (Abort Output) sequence, which should cause the remote system to flush all output *from* the remote system *to* the user's terminal.

ayt Sends the TELNET AYT (Are You There) sequence, to which the remote system may or may not choose to respond.

brk Sends the TELNET BRK (Break) sequence, which may have significance to the remote system.

ec Sends the TELNET EC (Erase Character) sequence, which should cause the remote system to erase the last character entered.

el Sends the TELNET EL (Erase Line) sequence, which should cause the remote system to erase the line currently being entered.

eof Sends the TELNET EOF (End Of File) sequence.

eor Sends the TELNET EOR (End of Record) sequence.

escape Sends the current **telnet** escape character (initially "^").

ga Sends the TELNET GA (Go Ahead) sequence, which likely has no significance to the remote system.

getstatus
> If the remote side supports the TELNET STATUS command, **getstatus** will send the subnegotiation to request that the server send its current option status.

ip   Sends the TELNET IP (Interrupt Process) sequence, which should cause the re-
          mote system to abort the currently running process.

nop   Sends the TELNET NOP (No OPeration) sequence.

susp   Sends the TELNET SUSP (SUSPend process) sequence.

synch   Sends the TELNET SYNCH sequence. This sequence causes the remote system to
          discard all previously typed (but not yet read) input. This sequence is sent as TCP
          urgent data (and may not work if the remote system is a 4.2BSD system -- if it
          doesn't work, a lower case ''r'' may be echoed on the terminal).

do *cmd*

dont *cmd*

will *cmd*

wont *cmd*
          Sends the TELNET DO *cmd* sequence. *Cmd* can be either a decimal number
          between 0 and 255, or a symbolic name for a specific TELNET command. *Cmd* can
          also be either **help** or **?** to print out help information, including a list of known
          symbolic names.

?   Prints out help information for the **send** command.

set *argument value*

unset *argument value*
          The **set** command will set any one of a number of **telnet** variables to a specific value or to
          TRUE. The special value **off** turns off the function associated with the variable, this is
          equivalent to using the **unset** command. The **unset** command will disable or set to
          FALSE any of the specified functions. The values of variables may be interrogated with the
          display command. The variables which may be set or unset, but not toggled, are listed
          here. In addition, any of the variables for the **toggle** command may be explicitly set or un-
          set using the **set** and **unset** commands.

ayt   If TELNET is in localchars mode, or LINEMODE is enabled, and the status character
          is typed, a TELNET AYT sequence (see **send ayt** preceding) is sent to the re-
          mote host. The initial value for the "Are You There" character is the terminal's
          status character.

echo   This is the value (initially '''^E''') which, when in ''line by line'' mode, toggles
          between doing local echoing of entered characters (for normal processing), and
          suppressing echoing of entered characters (for entering, say, a password).

eof   If **telnet** is operating in LINEMODE or ''old line by line'' mode, entering this
          character as the first character on a line will cause this character to be sent to the re-
          mote system. The initial value of the eof character is taken to be the terminal's **eof**
          character.

erase   If **telnet** is in **localchars** mode (see **toggle localchars** below), **and** if
          telnet is operating in ''character at a time'' mode, then when this character is
          typed, a TELNET EC sequence (see **send ec** above) is sent to the remote system.
          The initial value for the erase character is taken to be the terminal's **erase** charac-
          ter.

escape This is the **telnet** escape character (initially "`^[`") which causes entry into **telnet** command mode (when connected to a remote system).

flushoutput

If **telnet** is in **localchars** mode (see **toggle localchars** below) and the **flushoutput** character is typed, a TELNET AO sequence (see **send ao** above) is sent to the remote host. The initial value for the flush character is taken to be the terminal's **flush** character.

forw1

forw2 If TELNET is operating in LINEMODE, these are the characters that, when typed, cause partial lines to be forwarded to the remote system. The initial value for the forwarding characters are taken from the terminal's eol and eol2 characters.

interrupt

If **telnet** is in **localchars** mode (see **toggle localchars** below) and the **interrupt** character is typed, a TELNET IP sequence (see **send ip** above) is sent to the remote host. The initial value for the interrupt character is taken to be the terminal's **intr** character.

kill If **telnet** is in **localchars** mode (see **toggle localchars** below), **and if telnet** is operating in "character at a time" mode, then when this character is typed, a TELNET EL sequence (see **send el** above) is sent to the remote system. The initial value for the kill character is taken to be the terminal's **kill** character.

lnext If **telnet** is operating in LINEMODE or "old line by line" mode, then this character is taken to be the terminal's **lnext** character. The initial value for the lnext character is taken to be the terminal's **lnext** character.

quit If **telnet** is in **localchars** mode (see **toggle localchars** below) and the **quit** character is typed, a TELNET BRK sequence (see **send brk** above) is sent to the remote host. The initial value for the quit character is taken to be the terminal's **quit** character.

reprint

If **telnet** is operating in LINEMODE or "old line by line" mode, then this character is taken to be the terminal's **reprint** character. The initial value for the reprint character is taken to be the terminal's **reprint** character.

rlogin This is the rlogin escape character. If set, the normal TELNET escape character is ignored unless it is preceded by this character at the beginning of a line. This character, at the beginning of a line followed by a "." closes the connection; when followed by a ^Z it suspends the telnet command. The initial state is to disable the rlogin escape character.

start If the TELNET TOGGLE-FLOW-CONTROL option has been enabled, then this character is taken to be the terminal's **start** character. The initial value for the kill character is taken to be the terminal's **start** character.

stop If the TELNET TOGGLE-FLOW-CONTROL option has been enabled, then this character is taken to be the terminal's **stop** character. The initial value for the kill character is taken to be the terminal's **stop** character.

susp If **telnet** is in **localchars** mode, or LINEMODE is enabled, and the **suspend** character is typed, a TELNET SUSP sequence (see **send susp** above) is sent to the remote host. The initial value for the suspend character is taken to be the terminal's **suspend** character.

tracefile
> This is the file to which the output, caused by **netdata** or **option** tracing being TRUE, will be written. If it is set to '' − '', then tracing information will be written to standard output (the default).

worderase
> If **telnet** is operating in LINEMODE or ''old line by line'' mode, then this character is taken to be the terminal's **worderase** character. The initial value for the worderase character is taken to be the terminal's **worderase** character.

? Displays the legal **set** (**unset**) commands.

slc *state* The **slc** command (Set Local Characters) is used to set or change the state of the the special characters when the TELNET LINEMODE option has been enabled. Special characters are characters that get mapped to TELNET commands sequences (like **ip** or **quit**) or line editing characters (like **erase** and **kill**). By default, the local special characters are exported.

> **check** Verify the current settings for the current special characters. The remote side is requested to send all the current special character settings, and if there are any discrepancies with the local side, the local side will switch to the remote value.

> **export** Switch to the local defaults for the special characters. The local default characters are those of the local terminal at the time when **telnet** was started.

> **import** Switch to the remote defaults for the special characters. The remote default characters are those of the remote system at the time when the TELNET connection was established.

> **?** Prints out help information for the **slc** command.

status Show the current status of **telnet**. This includes the peer one is connected to, as well as the current mode.

toggle *arguments ...*
> Toggle (between TRUE and FALSE) various flags that control how **telnet** responds to events. These flags may be set explicitly to TRUE or FALSE using the **set** and **unset** commands listed above. More than one argument may be specified. The state of these flags may be interrogated with the **display** command. Valid arguments are:

> **authdebug** Turns on debugging information for the authentication code.

> **autoflush** If **autoflush** and **localchars** are both TRUE, then when the **ao**, or **quit** characters are recognized (and transformed into TELNET sequences; see **set** above for details), **telnet** refuses to display any data on the user's terminal until the remote system acknowledges (via a TELNET TIMING MARK option) that it has processed those TELNET sequences. The initial value for this toggle is TRUE if the terminal user had not done an "stty noflsh", otherwise FALSE (see stty(1)).

autodecrypt
> When the TELNET ENCRYPT option is negotiated, by default the actual encryption (decryption) of the data stream does not start automatically. The autoencrypt (autodecrypt) command states that encryption of the output (input) stream should be enabled as soon as possible.

Note: Because of export controls, the TELNET ENCRYPT option is not supported outside the United States and Canada.

autologin   If the remote side supports the TELNET AUTHENTICATION option TELNET attempts to use it to perform automatic authentication. If the AUTHENTICATION option is not supported, the user's login name are propagated through the TELNET ENVIRON option. This command is the same as specifying a option on the **open** command.

autosynch   If **autosynch** and **localchars** are both TRUE, then when either the **intr** or **quit** characters is typed (see **set** above for descriptions of the **intr** and **quit** characters), the resulting TELNET sequence sent is followed by the TELNET SYNCH sequence. This procedure **should** cause the remote system to begin throwing away all previously typed input until both of the TELNET sequences have been read and acted upon. The initial value of this toggle is FALSE.

binary   Enable or disable the TELNET BINARY option on both input and output.

inbinary   Enable or disable the TELNET BINARY option on input.

outbinary   Enable or disable the TELNET BINARY option on output.

crlf   If this is TRUE, then carriage returns will be sent as <CR><LF>. If this is FALSE, then carriage returns will be send as <CR><NUL>. The initial value for this toggle is FALSE.

crmod   Toggle carriage return mode. When this mode is enabled, most carriage return characters received from the remote host will be mapped into a carriage return followed by a line feed. This mode does not affect those characters typed by the user, only those received from the remote host. This mode is not very useful unless the remote host only sends carriage return, but never line feed. The initial value for this toggle is FALSE.

debug   Toggles socket level debugging (useful only to the **super user**). The initial value for this toggle is FALSE.

encdebug   Turns on debugging information for the encryption code.

localchars   If this is TRUE, then the **flush**, **interrupt**, **quit**, **erase**, and **kill** characters (see **set** above) are recognized locally, and transformed into (hopefully) appropriate TELNET control sequences (respectively **ao**, **ip**, **brk**, **ec**, and **el**; see **send** above). The initial value for this toggle is TRUE in "old line by line" mode, and FALSE in "character at a time" mode. When the LINEMODE option is enabled, the value of **localchars** is ignored, and assumed to always be TRUE. If LINEMODE has ever been enabled, then **quit** is sent as **abort**, and **eof and** are sent as **eof and susp**, see **send** above).

netdata   Toggles the display of all network data (in hexadecimal format). The initial value for this toggle is FALSE.

options   Toggles the display of some internal **telnet** protocol processing (having to do with TELNET options). The initial value for this toggle is FALSE.

1

<table>
<tr><td>prettydump</td><td>When the netdata toggle is enabled, if prettydump is enabled the output from the netdata command will be formatted in a more user readable format. Spaces are put between each character in the output, and the beginning of any TELNET escape sequence is preceded by a '*' to aid in locating them.</td></tr>
</table>

skiprc   When the skiprc toggle is TRUE, TELNET skips the reading of the
              .telnetrc file in the users home directory when connections are opened.
              The initial value for this toggle is FALSE.

termdata   Toggles the display of all terminal data (in hexadecimal format). The initial
              value for this toggle is FALSE.

verbose_encrypt
              When the verbose_encrypt toggle is TRUE, TELNET prints out a message each time encryption is enabled or disabled. The initial value for this toggle is FALSE. Note: Because of export controls, data encryption is not supported outside of the United States and Canada.

?   Displays the legal **toggle** commands.

z   Suspend **telnet**. This command only works when the user is using the csh(1).

! [*command*]
              Execute a single command in a subshell on the local system. If **command** is omitted, then an interactive subshell is invoked.

? [*command*]
              Get help. With no arguments, **telnet** prints a help summary. If a command is specified, **telnet** will print the help information for just that command.

ENVIRONMENT
Telnet uses at least the HOME, SHELL, DISPLAY, and TERM environment variables. Other environment variables may be propagated to the other side via the TELNET ENVIRON option.

FILES
~/.telnetrc user customized telnet startup values

HISTORY
The **Telnet** command appeared in 4.2BSD.

NOTES
On some remote systems, echo has to be turned off manually when in "old line by line" mode.

In "old line by line" mode or LINEMODE the terminal's **eof** character is only recognized (and sent to the remote system) when it is the first character on a line.

NAME

test – condition evaluation utility

SYNOPSIS

test *expression*

DESCRIPTION

The **test** utility evaluates the expression and, if it evaluates to true, returns a zero (true) exit status; otherwise it returns 1 (false). If there is no expression, test also returns 1 (false).

All operators and flags are separate arguments to the **test** utility.

The following primaries are used to construct expression:

-b *file*	True if *file* exists and is a block special file.
-c *file*	True if *file* exists and is a character special file.
-d *file*	True if *file* exists and is a directory.
-e *file*	True if *file* exists (regardless of type).
-f *file*	True if *file* exists and is a regular file.
-g *file*	True if *file* exists and its set group ID flag is set.
-h *file*	True if *file* exists and is a symbolic link.
-n *string*	True if the length of *string* is nonzero.
-p *file*	True if *file* is a named pipe (FIFO).
-r *file*	True if *file exists and is readable.*
-s *file*	True if *file* exists and has a size greater than zero.
-t *[file_descriptor]*	True if the file whose file descriptor number is *file_descriptor* (default 1) is open and is associated with a terminal.
-u *file*	True if *file* exists and its set user ID flag is set.
-w *file*	True if *file* exists and is writable. True indicates only that the write flag is on. The file is not writable on a read-only file system even if this test indicates true.
-x *file*	True if *file* exists and is executable. True indicates only that the execute flag is on. If *file* is a directory, true indicates that *file* can be searched.
-z *string*	True if the length of *string* is zero.
string	True if *string* is not the null string.
s1 = *s2*	True if the strings *s1* and *s2* are identical.
s1 != *s2*	True if the strings *s1* and *s2* are not identical.
n1 **-eq** *n2*	True if the integers *n1* and *n2* are algebraically equal.
n1 **-ne** *n2*	True if the integers *n1* and *n2* are not algebraically equal.

1

n1 **−gt** *n2*   True if the integer *n1* is algebraically greater than the integer *n2*.

n1 **−ge** *n2*   True if the integer *n1* is algebraically greater than or equal to the integer *n2*.

n1 **−lt** *n2*   True if the integer *n1* is algebraically less than the integer *n2*.

n1 **−le** *n2*   True if the integer *n1* is algebraically less than or equal to the integer *n2*.

These primaries can be combined with the following operators:

! *expression*
>   True if *expression* is false.

expression1 **−a** *expression2*
>   True if both *expression1* and *expression2* are true.

expression1 **−o** *expression2*
>   True if either *expression1* or *expression2* are true.

(*expression* **)**
>   True if expression is true.

The **−a** operator has higher precedence than the **−o** operator.

GRAMMAR AMBIGUITY

The **test** grammar is inherently ambiguous. In order to assure a degree of consistency, the cases described in the IEEE Std1003.2 (''POSIX''), section D11.2/4.62.4, standard are evaluated consistently according to the rules specified in the standards document. All other cases are subject to the ambiguity in the command semantics.

RETURN VALUES

The **test** utility exits with one of the following values:

0   expression evaluated to true.

1   expression evaluated to false or expression was missing.

>1   An error occurred.

STANDARDS

The **test** function is expected to be IEEE Std1003.2 (''POSIX'') compatible.

NAME

      tfmtodit − create font files for use with groff −Tdvi

SYNOPSIS

      tfmtodit [−sv] [−g*gf_file*] [−k*skewchar*] *tfm_file map_file font*

DESCRIPTION

      tfmtodit creates a font file for use with **groff** −Tdvi. *tfm_file* is the name of the TEX font metric file for the font. *map_file* is a file giving the groff names for characters in the font; this file should consist of a sequence of lines of the form:

           n c1 c2 ...

      where *n* is a decimal integer giving the position of the character in the font, and *c1* , *c2* ,... are the groff names of the character. If a character has no groff names but exists in the tfm file, then it will be put in the groff font file as an unnamed character. *font* is the name of the groff font file. The groff font file is written to *font*.

      The −s option should be given if the font is special (a font is *special* if **troff** should search it whenever a character is not found in the current font.) If the font is special, it should be listed in the **fonts** command in the DESC file; if it is not special, there is no need to list it, since **troff** can automatically mount it when it's first used.

      To do a good job of math typesetting, groff requires font metric information not present in the tfm file. The reason for this is that TEX has separate math italic fonts whereas groff uses normal italic fonts for math. The additional information required by groff is given by the two arguments to the **math_fit** macro in the Metafont programs for the Computer Modern fonts. In a text font (a font for which **math_fitting** is false), Metafont normally ignores these two arguments. Metafont can be made to put this information in the gf file by loading the following definition after **cmbase** when creating **cm.base**:

           def ignore_math_fit(expr left_adjustment,right_adjustment) =
              special "adjustment";
              numspecial left_adjustment∗16/designsize;
              numspecial right_adjustment∗16/designsize;
              enddef;

      The gf file created using this modified **cm.base** should be specified with the −**g** option. The −**g** option should not be given for a font for which **math_fitting** is true.

OPTIONS

      −**v**   Print the version number.

      −**s**   The font is special. The effect of this option is to add the **special** command to the font file.

      −**k***n*   The skewchar of this font is at position *n*. *n* should be an integer; it may be given in decimal, or with a leading **0** in octal, or with a leading **0x** in hexadecimal. The effect of this option is to ignore any kerns whose second component is the specified character.

      −**g***gf_file*

           gf_file is a gf file produced by Metafont containing special and numspecial commands giving additional font metric information.

FILES

      /usr/share/groff_font/devdvi/DESC   Device desciption file.

      /usr/share/groff_font/devdvi/*F*   Font description file for font *F*.

SEE ALSO

      groff(1), **grodvi**(1), **groff_font**(5)

1

NAME
   tftp – trivial file transfer program

SYNOPSIS
   tftp [*host*]

DESCRIPTION
   Tftp is the user interface to the Internet TFTP (Trivial File Transfer Protocol), which allows users to transfer files to and from a remote machine. The remote *host* may be specified on the command line, in which case **tftp** uses *host* as the default host for future transfers (see the **connect** command below).

COMMANDS
   Once **tftp** is running, it issues the prompt and recognizes the following commands:

? *command-name* ...
   Print help information.

ascii   Shorthand for "mode ascii"

binary   Shorthand for "mode binary"

connect *host-name* [*port*]
   Set the *host* (and optionally *port*) for transfers. Note that the TFTP protocol, unlike the FTP protocol, does not maintain connections between transfers; thus, the **connect** command does not actually create a connection, but merely remembers what host is to be used for transfers. You do not have to use the **connect** command; the remote host can be specified as part of the **get** or **put** commands.

get *filename*
get *remotename localname*
get *file1 file2* ... *fileN*
   Get a file or set of files from the specified *sources*. *Source* can be in one of two forms: a filename on the remote host, if the host has already been specified, or a string of the form *hosts:filename* to specify both a host and filename at the same time. If the latter form is used, the last hostname specified becomes the default for future transfers.

mode *transfer-mode*
   Set the mode for transfers; *transfer-mode* may be one of *ascii* or *binary*. The default is *ascii*.

put *file*
put *localfile remotefile*
put *file1 file2* ... *fileN remote-directory*
   Put a file or set of files to the specified remote file or directory. The destination can be in one of two forms: a filename on the remote host, if the host has already been specified, or a string of the form *hosts:filename* to specify both a host and filename at the same time. If the latter form is used, the hostname specified becomes the default for future transfers. If the remote-directory form is used, the remote host is assumed to be a UNIX machine.

quit   Exit **tftp**. An end of file also exits.

rexmt *retransmission-timeout*
   Set the per-packet retransmission timeout, in seconds.

status   Show current status.

timeout *total-transmission-timeout*
           Set the total transmission timeout, in seconds.

trace   Toggle packet tracing.

verbose Toggle verbose mode.

BUGS

Because there is no user-login or validation within the TFTP protocol, the remote site will probably have some sort of file-access restrictions in place. The exact methods are specific to each site and therefore difficult to document here.

HISTORY

The **tftp** command appeared in 4.3BSD.

NAME

time – time command execution

SYNOPSIS

time [**–l**] *command*

DESCRIPTION

The **time** utility executes and times *command* by initiating a timer and passing the *command* to the shell. After the *command* finishes, **time** writes to the standard error stream, (in seconds): the total time elapsed, time consumed by system overhead, and the time used to execute the *command* process.

Available options:

–l   The contents of the *rusage* structure are printed as well.

The csh(1) has its own and syntactically different builtin version of **time.** The command described here is available as /usr/bin/time to csh users.

BUGS

The granularity of seconds on micro processors is crude and can result in times being reported for CPU usage which are too large by a second.

SEE ALSO

csh(1)

FILES

/usr/include/sys/h/resource.h

HISTORY

A **time** command appeared in Version 6 AT&T UNIX.

NAME

tip, cu – connect to a remote system

SYNOPSIS

tip [–v] *–speed system–name*
tip [–v] *–speed phone–number*
cu *phone–number* [–t] [–s *speed*] [–a *acu*] [–l *line*] [–#]

DESCRIPTION

Tip and *cu* establish a full-duplex connection to another machine, giving the appearance of being logged in directly on the remote cpu. It goes without saying that you must have a login on the machine (or equivalent) to which you wish to connect. The preferred interface is tip. The *cu* interface is included for those people attached to the "call UNIX" command of version 7. This manual page describes only tip.

Available Option:

–v   Set verbose mode.

Typed characters are normally transmitted directly to the remote machine (which does the echoing as well). A tilde ('~') appearing as the first character of a line is an escape signal; the following are recognized:

~^D or ~.
          Drop the connection and exit (you may still be logged in on the remote machine).

~c [*name*]
          Change directory to *name* (no argument implies change to your home directory).

~!   Escape to a shell (exiting the shell will return you to tip).

~>   Copy file from local to remote. Tip prompts for the name of a local file to transmit.

~<   Copy file from remote to local. Tip prompts first for the name of the file to be sent, then for a command to be executed on the remote machine.

~p *from* [*to*]
          Send a file to a remote UNIX host. The put command causes the remote UNIX system to run the command string "cat > 'to'", while tip sends it the "from" file. If the "to" file isn't specified the "from" file name is used. This command is actually a UNIX specific version of the "~>" command.

~t *from* [*to*]
          Take a file from a remote UNIX host. As in the put command the "to" file defaults to the "from" file name if it isn't specified. The remote host executes the command string "cat 'from';echo ^A" to send the file to tip.

~| Pipe the output from a remote command to a local UNIX process. The command string sent to the local UNIX system is processed by the shell.

~$ Pipe the output from a local UNIX process to the remote host. The command string sent to the local UNIX system is processed by the shell.

~C   Fork a child process on the local system to perform special protocols such as XMODEM. The child program will be run with the following somewhat unusual arrangement of file descriptors:

                              0 <-> local tty in
                              1 <-> local tty out
                              2 <-> local tty out
                              3 <-> remote tty in
                              4 <-> remote tty out

1

~#   Send a BREAK to the remote system. For systems which don't support the necessary *ioctl* call the break is simulated by a sequence of line speed changes and DEL characters.

~s   Set a variable (see the discussion below).

~^z   Stop **tip** (only available with job control).

~^Y   Stop only the ''local side'' of **tip** (only available with job control); the ''remote side'' of **tip**, the side that displays output from the remote host, is left running.

~?   Get a summary of the tilde escapes

Tip uses the file /etc/remote to find how to reach a particular system and to find out how it should operate while talking to the system; refer to remote(5) for a full description. Each system has a default baud rate with which to establish a connection. If this value is not suitable, the baud rate to be used may be specified on the command line, e.g. tip -300 mds.

When **tip** establishes a connection it sends out a connection message to the remote system; the default value, if any, is defined in /etc/remote (see remote(5)).

When **tip** prompts for an argument (e.g. during setup of a file transfer) the line typed may be edited with the standard erase and kill characters. A null line in response to a prompt, or an interrupt, will abort the dialogue and return you to the remote machine.

Tip guards against multiple users connecting to a remote system by opening modems and terminal lines with exclusive access, and by honoring the locking protocol used by uucico(8).

During file transfers **tip** provides a running count of the number of lines transferred. When using the ~> and ~< commands, the ''eofread'' and ''eofwrite'' variables are used to recognize end-of-file when reading, and specify end-of-file when writing (see below). File transfers normally depend on tandem mode for flow control. If the remote system does not support tandem mode, ''echocheck'' may be set to indicate **tip** should synchronize with the remote system on the echo of each transmitted character.

When **tip** must dial a phone number to connect to a system it will print various messages indicating its actions. **Tip** supports the DEC DN Ns-11 and Racal-Vadic 831 auto-call-units; the and Ventel 212+, Racal-Vadic 3451, and Bizcomp 1031 and 1032 integral call unit/modems.

VARIABLES

DEC DF**tip** maintains a set of *variables* which control its operation. Some of these variables are read-only to normal users (root is allowed to change anything of interest). Variables may be displayed and set through the ''s'' escape. The syntax for variables is patterned after vi(1) and Mail(1). Supplying ''all'' as an argument to the set command displays all variables readable by the user. Alternatively, the user may request display of a particular variable by attaching a '?' to the end. For example ''escape?'' displays the current escape character.

Variables are numeric, string, character, or boolean values. Boolean variables are set merely by specifying their name; they may be reset by prepending a '!' to the name. Other variable types are set by concatenating an '=' and the value. The entire assignment must not have any blanks in it. A single set command may be used to interrogate as well as set a number of variables. Variables may be initialized at run time by placing set commands (without the ''~s'' prefix in a file .tiprc in one's home directory). The −v option causes **tip** to display the sets as they are made. Certain common variables have abbreviations. The following is a list of common variables, their abbreviations, and their default values.

beautify   (bool) Discard unprintable characters when a session is being scripted; abbreviated *be*.

1

baudrate   (num) The baud rate at which the connection was established; abbreviated *ba*.

dialtimeout
              (num) When dialing a phone number, the time (in seconds) to wait for a connection to be established; abbreviated *dial*.

echocheck   (bool) Synchronize with the remote host during file transfer by waiting for the echo of the last character transmitted; default is *off*.

eofread   (str) The set of characters which signify an end-of-transmission during a ˜< file transfer command; abbreviated *eofr*.

eofwrite   (str) The string sent to indicate end-of-transmission during a ˜> file transfer command; abbreviated *eofw*.

eol   (str) The set of characters which indicate an end-of-line. **Tip** will recognize escape characters only after an end-of-line.

escape   (char) The command prefix (escape) character; abbreviated *es*; default value is '˜'.

exceptions (str) The set of characters which should not be discarded due to the beautification switch; abbreviated *ex*; default value is ''\t\n\f\b''.

force   (char) The character used to force literal data transmission; abbreviated *fo*; default value is '^P'.

framesize   (num) The amount of data (in bytes) to buffer between file system writes when receiving files; abbreviated *fr*.

host   (str) The name of the host to which you are connected; abbreviated *ho*.

prompt   (char) The character which indicates an end-of-line on the remote host; abbreviated *pr*; default value is '\n'. This value is used to synchronize during data transfers. The count of lines transferred during a file transfer command is based on receipt of this character.

raise   (bool) Upper case mapping mode; abbreviated *ra*; default value is *off*. When this mode is enabled, all lower case letters will be mapped to upper case by **tip** for transmission to the remote machine.

raisechar   (char) The input character used to toggle upper case mapping mode; abbreviated *rc*; default value is '^A'.

record   (str) The name of the file in which a session script is recorded; abbreviated *rec*; default value is ''tip.record''.

script   (bool) Session scripting mode; abbreviated *sc*; default is *off*. When *script* is true, **tip** will record everything transmitted by the remote machine in the script record file specified in *record*. If the *beautify* switch is on, only printable ASCII characters will be included in the script file (those characters betwee 040 and 0177). The variable *exceptions* is used to indicate characters which are an exception to the normal beautification rules.

tabexpand   (bool) Expand tabs to spaces during file transfers; abbreviated *tab*; default value is *false*. Each tab is expanded to 8 spaces.

verbose   (bool) Verbose mode; abbreviated *verb*; default is *true*. When verbose mode is enabled, **tip** prints messages while dialing, shows the current number of lines transferred during a file transfer operations, and more.

1

ENVIRONMENT

Tip uses the following environment variables:

SHELL   (str) The name of the shell to use for the ~! command; default value is "/bin/sh", or taken from the environment.

HOME   (str) The home directory to use for the ~c command; default value is taken from the environment.

HOST   Check for a default host if none specified.

The variables ${REMOTE} and ${PHONES} are also exported.

FILES

/etc/remote	Global system descriptions.
/etc/phones	Global phone number data base.
${REMOTE}	Private system descriptions.
${PHONES}	Private phone numbers.
~/.tiprc	Initialization file.
tip.record	Record file.
/var/log/aculog	Line access log.
/var/spool/uucp/LCK..*	Lock file to avoid conflicts with uucp.

DIAGNOSTICS

Diagnostics are, hopefully, self explanatory.

SEE ALSO

remote(5), phones(5)

HISTORY

The **tip** appeared command in 4.2BSD.

BUGS

The full set of variables is undocumented and should, probably, be pared down.

NAME

tn3270 – full-screen remote login to IBM VM/CMS

SYNOPSIS

tn3270 [–d] [–n *filename*] [–t *commandname*] [*sysname* [port]]

DESCRIPTION

Tn3270 permits a full-screen, full-duplex connection from a UNIX machine to an IBM (or compatible) machine. Tn3270 gives the appearance of being logged in to the remote machine from an IBM 3270 terminal. Of course, you must have an account on the machine to which you connect in order to log in. Tn3270 looks to the user in many respects like the Yale ASCII Terminal Communication System II. Tn3270 is actually a modification of the Arpanet TELNET user interface (see telnet(1)) which will, in certain circumstances, interpret and generate raw 3270 control streams.

The flags to tn3270 are as follows:

–d   Turn on socket-level tracing (for super-user only) –n*filename* Specify a file to receive network trace data output (from commands "toggle netdata" and "toggle options", see telnet(1));   the default is for output to be directed to the standard error file. –t*commandname* Specify a UNIX command to process IBM 4994 style transparent mode data received from the remote IBM machine.

sysname   The name of the remote system. If the remote name is NOT specified, the user will be prompted for a command (see below).

port   The port to connect to on the remote system. Normally, tn3270 attempts to connect to the standard TELNET port (port 23) on the remote machine.

When tn3270 first connects to the remote system, it will negotiate to go into 3270 mode. Part of this negotiation involves telling the remote system what model 3270 it is emulating. In all cases, tn3270 emulates a 3278 terminal. To decide which specific model, tn3270 looks at the number of lines and columns on the actual terminal (as defined in the TERM environment variable; see termcap(5)). The terminal (or window in which tn3270 is running, on multiple window systems) must have at least 80 columns and 24 lines, or tn3270 will not go into emulation mode. If the terminal does have at least 80 columns and at least 24 lines, the following table describes the emulation:

minimum_size (rows*columns)	emulated terminal
27*132	3278 model 5
43*80	3278 model 4
32*80	3278 model 3
24*80	3278 model 2.

Emulation of the 3270 terminal is done in the UNIX process. This emulation involves mapping 3270-style commands from the host into appropriate sequences to control the user's terminal screen. Tn3270 uses curses(3) and the /usr/share/misc/termcap file to do this. The emulation also involves simulating the special 3270 keyboard keys (program function keys, etc.) by mapping sequences of keystrokes from the ASCII keyboard into appropriate 3270 control strings. This mapping is terminal dependent and is specified in a description file, /usr/share/misc/map3270, (see map3270(5)) or in an environment variable MAP3270 (and, if necessary, MAP3270A, MAP3270B, and so on - see mset(1)). Any special function keys on the ASCII keyboard are used whenever possible. If an entry for the user's terminal is not found, tn3270 looks for an entry for the terminal type *unknown*. If this is not found, tn3270 uses a default keyboard mapping (see map3270(5)).

1

The first character of each special keyboard mapping sequence is either an ASCII escape (ESC), a control character, or an ASCII delete (DEL). If the user types an unrecognized function key sequence, **tn3270** sends an ASCII bell (BEL), or a visual bell if defined in the user's termcap entry, to the user's terminal and nothing is sent to the IBM host.

If **tn3270** is invoked without specifying a remote host system name, it enters local command mode, indicated by the prompt "tn3270> ". In this mode, **tn3270** accepts and executes all the commands of telnet(1), plus one additional command:

transcom   Specify UNIX command for IBM 4994 style transparent mode processing.

Tn3270 command mode may also be entered, after connecting to a host, by typing a special escape sequence. If **tn3270** has succeeded in negotiating 3270 mode with the remote host, the escape sequence will be as defined by the map3270 (see map3270(5)) entry for the user's terminal type (typically control-C); otherwise the escape sequence will initially be set to the single character '^]' (control right square bracket).

While in command mode, any host login session is still alive but temporarily suspended. The host login session may be resumed by entering an empty line (press the RETURN key) in response to the command prompt. A session may be terminated by logging off the foreign host, or by typing "quit" or "close" while in local command mode.

FILES
```
/usr/share/misc/termcap
/usr/share/misc/map3270
```

NOTES
The IBM 4994 style transparent mode command is invoked when **tn3270** receives IBM 4994 style transparent output from the remote host. Output and input pipes are created for communication between the two processes. The pipes are closed when a 3270 clear command is received from the remote hosts, signaling the end of transparent mode output. Transparent mode is necessary for sending ASCII control characters over the 3270 terminal connection; ASCII graphics terminal support is accomplished this way. Developers of **transcom** commands should note that the **transcom** stdin pipe end will be in CBREAK mode, with ECHO and CRMOD turned off.

ENVIRONMENT
Tn3270 checks the following environment variables: TERM, MAP3270, MAP3270[A...]. Information on these can be found in mset(1). **Tn3270** also checks SHELL, KEYBD and API3270.

SEE ALSO
mset(1), telnet(1), curses(3), termcap(3), termcap(5), map3270(5),

"Yale ASCII Terminal Communication", *System II Program Description/Operator's Manual*, IBM SB30-1911.

HISTORY
The **tn3270** command appeared in 4.3BSD.

BUGS
Tn3270 is slow and uses system resources prodigiously.

Not all 3270 functions are supported, nor all Yale enhancements.

Error conditions (attempting to enter data in a protected field, for example) should cause a message to be sent to the user's terminal instead of just ringing a bell.

1

NAME

touch – change file access and modification times

SYNOPSIS

touch [-acfm] [-r *file*] [-t -[[CC]YY]MMDDhhmm[.SS]] *file* ...

DESCRIPTION

The touch utility sets the modification and access times of files to the current time of day. If the file doesn't exist, it is created with default permissions.

The following options are available:

-a   Change the access time of the file. The modification time of the file is not changed unless the -m flag is also specified.

-c   Do not create the file if it does not exist. The touch utility does not treat this as an error. No error messages are displayed and the exit value is not affected.

-f   Attempt to force the update, even if the file permissions do not currently permit it.

-m   Change the modification time of the file. The access time of the file is not changed unless the -a flag is also specified.

-r   Use the access and modifications times from the specified file instead of the current time of day.

-t   Change the access and modification times to the specified time. The argument should be in the form ''[[CC]YY]MMDDhhmm[.SS]'' where each pair of letters represents the following:

> CC   The first two digits of the year (the century).
> YY   The second two digits of the year. If ''YY'' is specified, but ''CC'' is not, a value for ''YY'' between 69 and 99 results in a ''YY'' value of 19. Otherwise, a ''YY'' value of 20 is used.
> MM   The month of the year, from 1 to 12.
> DD   the day of the month, from 1 to 31.
> hh   The hour of the day, from 0 to 23.
> mm   The minute of the hour, from 0 to 59.
> SS   The second of the minute, from 0 to 61.

If the ''CC'' and ''YY'' letter pairs are not specified, the values default to the current year. If the ''SS'' letter pair is not specified, the value defaults to 0.

The touch utility exits 0 on success, and >0 if an error occurs.

SEE ALSO

utimes(2)

COMPATIBILITY

The obsolescent form of touch, where a time format is specified as the first argument, is supported. When no -r or -t option is specified, there are at least two arguments, and the first argument is a string of digits either eight or ten characters in length, the first argument is interpreted as a time specification of the form ''MMDDhhmm[YY]''.

The ''MM'', ''DD'', ''hh'' and ''mm'' letter pairs are treated as their counterparts specified to the -t option. If the ''YY'' letter pair is in the range 69 to 99, the year is set to 1969 to 1999, otherwise, the year is set in the 21st century.

1

HISTORY
A `touch` command appeared in Version 7 AT&T UNIX.

STANDARDS
The `touch` function is expected to be a superset of the IEEE Std1003.2 (''POSIX'') specification.

NAME

tput – terminal capability interface

SYNOPSIS

tput [–T *term*] *attribute*

DESCRIPTION

Tput makes terminal-dependent information available to users or shell applications. The options are as follows:

–T   The terminal name as specified in the termcap database, for example, ''vt100'' or ''xterm''. If not specified, **tput** retrieves the ''TERM'' variable from the environment.

Tput outputs a string if the *attribute* is of type string; a number if it is of type integer. Otherwise, **tput** exits 0 if the terminal has the capability and 1 if it does not, without further action.

If the *attribute* is of type string, and takes arguments (e.g. cursor movement, the termcap ''cm'' sequence) the arguments are taken from the command line immediately following the attribute.

The following special attributes are available:

clear   Clear the screen (the termcap ''cl'' sequence).

init   Initialize the terminal (the termcap ''is'' sequence).

longname   Print the descriptive name of the user's terminal type.

reset   Reset the terminal (the termcap ''rs'' sequence).

DIAGNOSTICS

The exit value of **tput** is based on the last attribute specified. If the attribute is of type string or of type integer, **tput** exits 0 if the attribute is defined for this terminal type and 1 if it is not. If the attribute is of type boolean, **tput** exits 0 if the terminal has this attribute, and 1 if it does not. **Tput** exits 2 if any error occurred.

SEE ALSO

termcap(3), termcap(5)

BUGS

Tput can't really distinguish between different types of attributes.

HISTORY

The **tput** command appears in 4.4BSD.

1

NAME
tr – translate characters

SYNOPSIS
tr [**–cs**] *string1* *string2*
tr [**–c**] **–d** *string1*
tr [**–c**] **–s** *string1*
tr [**–c**] **–ds** *string1* *string2*

DESCRIPTION
The **tr** utility copies the standard input to the standard output with substitution or deletion of selected characters.

The following options are available:

–c   Complements the set of characters in *string1*, that is "-c ab" includes every character except for "a" and "b".

–d   The –d option causes characters to be deleted from the input.

–s   The –s option squeezes multiple occurrences of the characters listed in the last operand (either *string1* or *string2*) in the input into a single instance of the character. This occurs after all deletion and translation is completed.

In the first synopsis form, the characters in *string1* are translated into the characters in *string2* where the first character in *string1* is translated into the first character in *string2* and so on. If *string1* is longer than *string2*, the last character found in *string2* is duplicated until *string1* is exhausted.

In the second synopsis form, the characters in *string1* are deleted from the input.

In the third synopsis form, the characters in *string1* are compressed as described for the –s option.

In the fourth synopsis form, the characters in *string1* are deleted from the input, and the characters in *string2* are compressed as described for the –s option.

The following conventions can be used in *string1* and *string2* to specify sets of characters:

character   Any character not described by one of the following conventions represents itself.

\octal   A backslash followed by 1, 2 or 3 octal digits represents a character with that encoded value. To follow an octal sequence with a digit as a character, left zero-pad the octal sequence to the full 3 octal digits.

\character   A backslash followed by certain special characters maps to special values.

        \a   <alert character>
        \b   <backspace>
        \f   <form-feed>
        \n   <newline>
        \r   <carriage return>
        \t   <tab>
        \v   <vertical tab>

A backslash followed by any other character maps to that character.

c-c   Represents the range of characters between the range endpoints, inclusively.

[:class:]   Represents all characters belonging to the defined character class. Class names are:

    alnum   <alphanumeric characters>
    alpha   <alphabetic characters>
    cntrl   <control characters>
    digit   <numeric characters>
    graph   <graphic characters>
    lower   <lower-case alphabetic characters>
    print   <printable characters>
    punct   <punctuation characters>
    space   <space characters>
    upper   <upper-case characters>
    xdigit   <hexadecimal characters>

With the exception of the "upper" and "lower" classes, characters in the classes are in unspecified order. In the "upper" and "lower" classes, characters are entered in ascending order.

For specific information as to which ASCII characters are included in these classes, see ctype(3) and related manual pages.

[=equiv=]   Represents all characters or collating (sorting) elements belonging to the same equivalence class as *equiv*. If there is a secondary ordering within the equivalence class, the characters are ordered in ascending sequence. Otherwise, they are ordered after their encoded values. An example of an equivalence class might be "c" and "ch" in Spanish; English has no equivalence classes.

[#*n]   Represents *n* repeated occurrences of the character represented by #. This expression is only valid when it occurs in *string2*. If *n* is omitted or is zero, it is be interpreted as large enough to extend *string2* sequence to the length of *string1*. If *n* has a leading zero, it is interpreted as an octal value, otherwise, it's interpreted as a decimal value.

The **tr** utility exits 0 on success, and >0 if an error occurs.

EXAMPLES

The following examples are shown as given to the shell:

Create a list of the words in file1, one per line, where a word is taken to be a maximal string of letters.

```
tr -cs  [:alpha:]" "\n" < file1"
```

Translate the contents of file1 to upper-case.

```
tr  [:lower:]" "[:upper:]" < file1"
```

Strip out non-printable characters from file1.

```
tr -cd  [:print:]" < file1"
```

COMPATIBILITY

System V has historically implemented character ranges using the syntax "[c-c]" instead of the "c-c" used by historic BSD implementations and standardized by POSIX. System V shell scripts should work under this implementation as long as the range is intended to map in another range, i.e. the command "tr [a-z] [A-

1

Z]'' will work as it will map the "[" character in *string1* to the "[" character in *string2*. However, if the shell script is deleting or squeezing characters as in the command "tr -d [a-z]'', the characters "[" and "]" will be included in the deletion or compression list which would not have happened under an historic System V implementation. Additionally, any scripts that depended on the sequence "a-z" to represent the three characters "a", "-" and "z" will have to be rewritten as "a\-z''.

The **tr** utility has historically not permitted the manipulation of NUL bytes in its input and, additionally, stripped NUL's from its input stream. This implementation has removed this behavior as a bug.

The **tr** utility has historically been extremely forgiving of syntax errors, for example, the −c and −s options were ignored unless two strings were specified. This implementation will not permit illegal syntax.

STANDARDS

The **tr** utility is expected to be IEEE Std1003.2 ("POSIX") compatible. It should be noted that the feature wherein the last character of *string2* is duplicated if *string2* has less characters than *string1* is permitted by POSIX but is not required. Shell scripts attempting to be portable to other POSIX systems should use the "[#*]" convention instead of relying on this behavior.

NAME

troff – format documents

SYNOPSIS

troff [−**abivzCER**] [−**w**_name_] [−**W**_name_] [−**d**_cs_] [−**f**_fam_] [−**m**_name_] [−**n**_num_] [−**o**_list_] [−**r**_cn_]
[−**T**_name_] [−**F**_dir_] [−**M**_dir_] [_files_ . . .]

DESCRIPTION

This manual page describes the GNU version of **troff**, which is part of the groff document formatting system. It is highly compatible with Unix troff. Usually it should be invoked using the groff command, which will also run preprocessors and postprocessors in the appropriate order and with the appropriate options.

OPTIONS

−**a**   Generate an ASCII approximation of the typeset output.

−**b**   Print a backtrace with each warning or error message. This backtrace should help track down the cause of the error. The line numbers given in the backtrace may not always be correct: troff's idea of line numbers gets confused by **as** or **am** requests.

−**i**   Read the standard input after all the named input files have been processed.

−**v**   Print the version number.

−**w**_name_   Enable warning _name_. Available warnings are described in the Warnings subsection below. Multiple −**w** options are allowed.

−**W**_name_   Inhibit warning _name_. Multiple −**W** options are allowed.

−**E**   Inhibit all error messages.

−**z**   Suppress formatted output.

−**C**   Enable compatibility mode.

−**d**_cs_
−**d**_name_=_s_ Define _c_ or _name_ to be a string _s_; _c_ must be a one letter name.

−**f**_fam_   Use _fam_ as the default font family.

−**m**_name_   Read in the file **tmac.**_name_. Normally this will be searched for in /usr/share/tmac.

−**R**   Don't load **troffrc**.

−**n**_num_   Number the first page _num_.

−**o**_list_   Output only pages in _list_, which is a comma-separated list of page ranges; _n_ means print page _n_, _m_−_n_ means print every page between _m_ and _n_, −_n_ means print every page up to _n_, _n_− means print every page from _n_.

−**r**_cn_
−**r**_name_=_n_ Set number register _c_ or _name_ to _n_; _c_ must be a one character name; _n_ can be any troff numeric expression.

−**T**_name_   Prepare output for device _name_, rather than the default **/usr/share/groff_font**.

−**F**_dir_   Search _dir_ for subdirectories **dev**_name_ (_name_ is the name of the device) for the **DESC** file and font files before the normal **/usr/share/groff_font**.

−**M**_dir_   Search directory _dir_ for macro files before the normal **/usr/share/tmac**.

USAGE

Only the features not in Unix troff are described here.

Long names

The names of number registers, fonts, strings/macros/diversions, special characters can be of any length. In escape sequences, where you can use (_xx_ for a two character name, you can use [_xxx_] for a name of arbitrary length:

1

\[*xxx*]   Print the special character called *xxx*.

\f[*xxx*]   Set font *xxx*.

*[*xxx*]   Interpolate string *xxx*.

\n[*xxx*]   Interpolate number register *xxx*.

Fractional pointsizes

A *scaled point* is equal to 1/sizescale points, where sizescale is specified in the **DESC** file (1 by default.) There is a new scale indicator **z** which has the effect of multiplying by sizescale. Requests and escape sequences in troff interpret arguments that represent a pointsize as being in units of scaled points, but they evaluate each such argument using a default scale indicator of **z**. Arguments treated in this way are the argument to the **ps** request, the third argument to the **cs** request, the second and fourth arguments to the **tkf** request, the argument to the \H escape sequence, and those variants of the \s escape sequence that take a numeric expression as their argument.

For example, suppose sizescale is 1000; then a scaled point will be equivalent to a millipoint; the request **.ps 10.25** is equivalent to **.ps 10.25z** and so sets the pointsize to 10250 scaled points, which is equal to 10.25 points.

The number register \n(.s returns the pointsize in points as a decimal fraction. There is also a new number register \n[.ps] that returns the pointsize in scaled points.

It would make no sense to use the **z** scale indicator in a numeric expression whose default scale indicator was neither **u** nor **z**, and so **troff** disallows this. Similarily it would make no sense to use a scaling indicator other than **z** or **u** in a numeric expression whose default scale indicator was **z**, and so **troff** disallows this as well.

There is also a new scale indicator **s** which multiplies by the number of units in a scaled point. So, for example, \n[.ps]s is equal to **1m**. Be sure not to confuse the **s** and **z** scale indicators.

Numeric expressions

Spaces are permitted in a number expression within parentheses.

M indicates a scale of 100ths of an em.

e1>?*e2*   The maximum of *e1* and *e2*.

e1<?*e2*   The minimum of *e1* and *e2*.

(*c*;*e*)   Evaluate *e* using *c* as the default scaling indicator. If *c* is missing, ignore scaling indicators in the evaluation of *e*.

New escape sequences

\A'*anything*'
          This expands to **1** or **0** according as *anything* is or is not acceptable as the name of a string, macro, diversion, number register, environment or font. It will return **0** if *anything* is empty. This is useful if you want to lookup user input in some sort of associative table.

\C'*xxx*'   Typeset character named *xxx*. Normally it is more convenient to use \[*xxx*]. But \C has the advantage that it is compatible with recent versions of UNIX and is available in compatibility mode.

\E   This is equivalent to an escape character, but it's not interpreted in copy-mode. For example, strings to start and end superscripting could be defined like this:

```
.ds { \v'-.3m'\s'\En[.s]*6u/10u'
.ds } \s0\v'.3m'
```

          The use of \E ensures that these definitions will work even if *{ gets interpreted in copy-mode (for example, by being used in a macro argument.)

\N'*n*'   Typeset the character with code *n* in the current font. *n* can be any integer. Most devices only have characters with codes between 0 and 255. If the current font does not contain a character with that code, special fonts will *not* be searched. The \N escape sequence can be conveniently used on conjunction with the **char** request:

> .char \[phone] \f(ZD\N'37'

The code of each character is given in the fourth column in the font description file after the **charset** command. It is possible to include unnamed characters in the font description file by using a name of ——; the \N escape sequence is the only way to use these.

\R'*name* ±*n*'
> This has the same effect as
>
> > .nr *name* ±*n*

\s(*nn*
\s±(*nn*   Set the point size to *nn* points; *nn* must be exactly two digits.

\s[±*n*]
\s±[*n*]
\s'±*n*'
\s±'*n*'   Set the point size to *n* scaled points; *n* is a numeric expression with a default scale indicator of **z**.

\V*x*
\V(*xx*
\V[*xxx*]   Interpolate the contents of the environment variable *xxx* , as returned by **getenv**(3). \V is interpreted in copy-mode.

\Y*x*
\Y(*xx*
\Y[*xxx*]   This is approximately equivalent to \X'*[*xxx*]'. However the contents of the string or macro *xxx* are not interpreted; also it is permitted for *xxx* to have been defined as a macro and thus contain newlines (it is not permitted for the argument to \X to contain newlines). The inclusion of newlines requires an extension to the Unix troff output format, and will confuse drivers that do not know about this extension.

\Z'*anything*'
> Print anything and then restore the horizontal and vertical position; *anything* may not contain tabs or leaders.

\$0   The name by which the current macro was invoked. The **als** request can make a macro have more than one name.

\$*   In a macro, the concatenation of all the arguments separated by spaces.

\$@   In a macro, the concatenation of all the arguments with each surrounded by double quotes, and separated by spaces.

\$(*nn*
\$[*nnn*]   In a macro, this gives the *nn*-th or *nnn*-th argument. Macros can have a unlimited number of arguments.

\?*anything*\?
> When used in a diversion, this will transparently embed *anything* in the diversion. *anything* is read in copy mode. When the diversion is reread, *anything* will be interpreted. *anything* may not contain newlines; use \! if you want to embed newlines in a diversion. The escape sequence \? is also recognised in copy mode and turned into a single internal code; it is this code that terminates *anything*. Thus

1

```
.nr x 1
.nf
.di d
\?\\?\\\\?\\\\\\\nx\\\\?\\?\?
.di
.nr x 2
.di e
.d
.di
.nr x 3
.di f
.e
.di
.nr x 4
.f
```

will print **4**.

\V   This increases the width of the preceding character so that the spacing between that character and the following character will be correct if the following character is a roman character. For example, if an italic f is immediately followed by a roman right parenthesis, then in many fonts the top right portion of the f will overlap the top left of the right parenthesis producing *f*), which is ugly. Inserting \V produces *f*) and avoids this problem. It is a good idea to use this escape sequence whenever an italic character is immediately followed by a roman character without any intervening space.

\,   This modifies the spacing of the following character so that the spacing between that character and the preceding character will correct if the preceding character is a roman character. For example, inserting \, between the parenthesis and the f changes (*f* to (*f*. It is a good idea to use this escape sequence whenever a roman character is immediately followed by an italic character without any intervening space.

\)   Like \& except that it behaves like a character declared with the **cflags** request to be transparent for the purposes of end of sentence recognition.

\~   This produces an unbreakable space that stretches like a normal inter-word space when a line is adjusted.

\#   Everything up to and including the next newline is ignored. This is interpreted in copy mode. This is like \% except that \% does not ignore the terminating newline.

New requests

.aln *xx yy*

      Create an alias *xx* for number register object named *yy*. The new name and the old name will be exactly equivalent. If *yy* is undefined, a warning of type **reg** will be generated, and the request will be ignored.

.als *xx yy*

      Create an alias *xx* for request, string, macro, or diversion object named *yy*. The new name and the old name will be exactly equivalent (it is similar to a hard rather than a soft link). If *yy* is undefined, a warning of type **mac** will be generated, and the request will be ignored. The **de, am, di, da, ds**, and **as** requests only create a new object if the name of the macro, diversion or string diversion is currently undefined or if it is defined to be a request; normally they modify the value of an existing object.

.asciify *xx*

      This request only exists in order to make it possible to make certain gross hacks work with GNU troff. It 'unformats' the diversion *xx* in such a way that ASCII characters that were formatted and diverted into *xx* will be treated like ordinary input characters when *xx* is reread. For example, this

```
            .tr @.
            .di x
            @nr\ n\ 1
            .br
            .di
            .tr @@
            .asciify x
            .x
```

will set register **n** to 1.

.backtrace
> Print a backtrace of the input stack on stderr.

.break Break out of a while loop. See also the **while** and **continue** requests. Be sure not to confuse this
> with the **br** request.

.cflags *n c1 c2*...
> Characters *c1*, *c2*,... have properties determined by *n*, which is ORed from the following:

> 1   the character ends sentences (initially characters **.?!** have this property);

> 2   lines can be broken before the character (initially no characters have this property);

> 4   lines can be broken after the character (initially characters −\(hy\(em have this property);

> 8   the character overlaps horizontally (initially characters \(ul\(rn\(ru have this property);

> 16   the character overlaps vertically (initially character \(br has this property);

> 32   an end of sentence character followed by any number of characters with this property
> will be treated as the end of a sentence if followed by a newline or two spaces; in other
> words the character is transparent for the purposes of end of sentence recognition; this is
> the same as having a zero space factor in TEX (initially characters "')]*\(dg\(rq have this
> property).

.char *c string*
> Define character *c* to be *string*. Every time character *c* needs to be printed, *string* will be pro-
> cessed in a temporary environment and the result will be wrapped up into a single object. Compa-
> tibility mode will be turned off and the escape character will be set to \ while *string* is being pro-
> cessed. Any emboldening, constant spacing or track kerning will be applied to this object rather
> than to individual characters in *string*. A character defined by this request can be used just like a
> normal character provided by the output device. In particular other characters can be translated to
> it with the **tr** request; it can be made the leader character by the **lc** request; repeated patterns can
> be drawn with the character using the \l and \L escape sequences; words containing the character
> can be hyphenated correctly, if the **hcode** request is used to give the character a hyphenation code.
> There is a special anti-recursion feature: use of character within the character's definition will be
> handled like normal characters not defined with **char**. A character definition can be removed with
> the **rchar** request.

.chop *xx*
> Chop the last character off macro, string, or diversion *xx*. This is useful for removing the newline
> from the end of diversions that are to be interpolated as strings.

.close *stream*
> Close the stream named *stream*; *stream* will no longer be an acceptable argument to the **write**
> request. See the **open** request.

.continue
> Finish the current iteration of a while loop. See also the **while** and **break** requests.

1

.cp *n*   If *n* is non-zero or missing, enable compatibility mode, otherwise disable it. In compatibility mode, long names are not recognised, and the incompatibilities caused by long names do not arise.

.do *xxx* Interpret .*xxx* with compatibility mode disabled. For example,

> **.do fam T**

would have the same effect as

> **.fam T**

except that it would work even if compatibility mode had been enabled. Note that the previous compatibility mode is restored before any files sourced by *xxx* are interpreted.

.fam *xx* Set the current font family to *xx*. The current font family is part of the current environment. See the description of the **sty** request for more information on font families.

.fspecial *f s1 s2 ...*

> When the current font is *f*, fonts *s1*, *s2*,... will be special, that is, they will searched for characters not in the current font. Any fonts specified in the **special** request will be searched before fonts specified in the **fspecial** request.

.ftr *f g* Translate font *f* to *g*. Whenever a font named *f* is referred to in \f escape sequence, or in the **ft**, **ul**, **bd**, **cs**, **tkf**, **special**, **fspecial**, **fp**, or **sty** requests, font *g* will be used. If *g* is missing, or equal to *f* then font *f* will not be translated.

.hcode *c1 code1 c2 code2 ...*

> Set the hyphenation code of character *c1* to *code1* and that of *c2* to *code2*. A hyphenation code must be a single input character (not a special character) other than a digit or a space. Initially each lower-case letter has a hyphenation code, which is itself, and each upper-case letter has a hyphenation code which is the lower case version of itself. See also the **hpf** request.

.hla *lang*

> Set the current hyphenation language to *lang*. Hyphenation exceptions specified with the **hw** request and hyphenation patterns specified with the **hpf** request are both associated with the current hyphenation language. The **hla** request is usually invoked by the **troffrc** file.

.hlm *n* Set the maximum number of consecutive hyphenated lines to *n*. If *n* is negative, there is no maximum. The default value is −1. This value is associated with the current environment. Only lines output from an environment count towards the maximum associated with that environment. Hyphens resulting from \% are counted; explicit hyphens are not.

.hpf *file* Read hyphenation patterns from *file*; this will be searched for in the same way that **tmac.**name is searched for when the −m*name* option is specified. It should have the same format as the argument to the \patterns primitive in TEX; the letters appearing in this file are interpreted as hyphenation codes. A % character in the patterns file introduces a comment that continues to the end of the line. The set of hyphenation patterns is associated with the current language set by the **hla** request. The **hpf** request is usually invoked by the **troffrc** file.

.hym *n* Set the *hyphenation margin* to *n*: when the current adjustment mode is not **b**, the line will not be hyphenated if the line is no more than *n* short. The default hyphenation margin is 0. The default scaling indicator for this request is *m*. The hyphenation margin is associated with the current environment. The current hyphenation margin is available in the \n[.hym] register.

.hys *n* Set the *hyphenation space* to *n*: when the current adjustment mode is **b** don't hyphenate the line if the line can be justified by adding no more than *n* extra space to each word space. The default hyphenation space is 0. The default scaling indicator for this request is **m**. The hyphenation space is associated with the current environment. The current hyphenation space is available in the \n[.hys] register.

.kern *n* If *n* is non-zero or missing, enable pairwise kerning, otherwise disable it.

.mso *file*

The same as the **so** request except that *file* is searched for in the same way that **tmac.***name* is searched for when the **−m***name* option is specified.

.nroff　　Make the **n** built-in condition true and the **t** built-in condition false. This can be reversed using the **troff** request.

.open *stream filename*

Open *filename* for writing and associate the stream named *stream* with it. See also the **close** and **write** requests.

.opena *stream filename*

Like **open**, but if *filename* exists, append to it instead of truncating it.

.pnr　　Print the names and contents of all currently defined number registers on stderr.

.ptr　　Print the names and positions of all traps (not including input line traps and diversion traps) on stderr. Empty slots in the page trap list are printed as well, because they can affect the priority of subsequently planted traps.

.rchar *c1 c2 ...*

Remove the definitions of characters *c1*, *c2*, ... This undoes the effect of a **char** request.

.rj

.rj *n*　　Right justify the next *n* input lines. Without an argument right justify the next input line. The number of lines to be right justifed is available in the **\n[.rj]** register. This implicitly does **.ce 0**. The **ce** request implicitly does **.rj 0**.

.rnn *xx yy*

Rename number register *xx* to *yy*.

.shc *c*　　Set the soft hyphen character to *c*. If *c* is omitted, the soft hyphen character will be set to the default **\(hy**. The soft hyphen character is the character which will be inserted when a word is hyphenated at a line break. If the soft hyphen character does not exist in the font of the character immediately preceding a potential break point, then the line will not be broken at that point. Neither definitions (specified with the **char** request) nor translations (specified with the **tr** request) are considered when finding the soft hyphen character.

.shift *n*　　In a macro, shift the arguments by *n* positions: argument *i* becomes argument *i−n*; arguments 1 to *n* will no longer be available. If *n* is missing, arguments will be shifted by 1. Shifting by negative amounts is currently undefined.

.special *s1 s2 ...*

Fonts *s1*, *s2*, are special and will be searched for characters not in the current font.

.sty *n f*　　Associate style *f* with font position *n*. A font position can be associated either with a font or with a style. The current font is the index of a font position and so is also either a font or a style. When it is a style, the font that is actually used is the font the name of which is the concatenation of the name of the current family and the name of the current style. For example, if the current font is 1 and font position 1 is associated with style **R** and the current font family is **T**, then font **TR** will be used. If the current font is not a style, then the current family is ignored. When the requests **cs**, **bd**, **tkf**, **uf**, or **fspecial** are applied to a style, then they will instead be applied to the member of the current family corresponding to that style. The default family can be set with the **−f** option. The **styles** command in the DESC file controls which font positions (if any) are initially associated with styles rather than fonts.

.tkf *f s1 n1 s2 n2*

Enable track kerning for font *f*. When the current font is *f* the width of every character will be increased by an amount between *n1* and *n2*; when the current point size is less than or equal to *s1* the width will be increased by *n1*; when it is greater than or equal to *s2* the width will be increased by *n2*; when the point size is greater than or equal to *s1* and less than or equal to *s2* the increase in

1

width is a linear function of the point size.

.trf *filename*

Transparently output the contents of file *filename*. Each line is output as it would be were it preceded by \!; however, the lines are not subject to copy-mode interpretation. If the file does not end with a newline, then a newline will be added. For example, you can define a macro *x* containing the contents of file *f*, using

    .di *x*
    .trf *f*
    .di

Unlike with the **cf** request, the file cannot contain characters such as NUL that are not legal troff input characters.

.trnt abcd

This is the same as the **tr** request except that the translations do not apply to text that is transparently throughput into a diversion with \!. For example,

    .tr ab
    .di x
    \!.tm a
    .di
    .x

will print **b**; if **trnt** is used instead of **tr** it will print **a**.

.troff   Make the **n** built-in condition false, and the **t** built-in condition true. This undoes the effect of the **nroff** request.

.vpt *n*   Enable vertical position traps if *n* is non-zero, disable them otherwise. Vertical position traps are traps set by the **wh** or **dt** requests. Traps set by the **it** request are not vertical position traps. The parameter that controls whether vertical position traps are enabled is global. Initially vertical position traps are enabled.

.warn *n* Control warnings. *n* is the sum of the numbers associated with each warning that is to be enabled; all other warnings will be disabled. The number associated with each warning is listed in the 'Warnings' section. For example, **.warn 0** will disable all warnings, and **.warn 1** will disable all warnings except that about missing characters. If *n* is not given, all warnings will be enabled.

.while *c anything*

While condition *c* is true, accept *anything* as input; *c* can be any condition acceptable to an **if** request; *anything* can comprise multiple lines if the first line starts with \{ and the last line ends with \}. See also the **break** and **continue** requests.

.write *stream anything*

Write *anything* to the stream named *stream*. *stream* must previously have been the subject of an **open** request. *anything* is read in copy mode; a leading " will be stripped.

Extended requests

.cf *filename*

When used in a diversion, this will embed in the diversion an object which, when reread, will cause the contents of *filename* to be transparently copied through to the output. In Unix troff, the contents of *filename* is immediately copied through to the output regardless of whether there is a current diversion; this behavior is so anomalous that it must be considered a bug.

.ev *xx*   If *xx* is not a number, this will switch to a named environment called *xx*. The environment should be popped with a matching **ev** request without any arguments, just as for numbered environments. There is no limit on the number of named environments; they will be created the first time that they are referenced.

.fp *n f1 f2*

> The **fp** request has an optional third argument. This argument gives the external name of the font, which is used for finding the font description file. The second argument gives the internal name of the font which is used to refer to the font in troff after it has been mounted. If there is no third argument then the internal name will be used as the external name. This feature allows you to use fonts with long names in compatibility mode.

.ss *m n* When two arguments are given to the **ss** request, the second argument gives the *sentence space size*. If the second argument is not given, the sentence space size will be the same as the word space size. Like the word space size, the sentence space is in units of one twelfth of the spacewidth parameter for the current font. Initially both the word space size and the sentence space size are 12. The sentence space size is used in two circumstances: if the end of a sentence occurs at the end of a line in fill mode, then both an inter-word space and a sentence space will be added; if two spaces follow the end of a sentence in the middle of a line, then the second space will be a sentence space. Note that the behaviour of Unix troff will be exactly that exhibited by GNU troff if a second argument is never given to the **ss** request. In GNU troff, as in Unix troff, you should always follow a sentence with either a newline or two spaces.

.ta *n1 n2...nn* **T** *r1 r2...rn*

> Set tabs at positions *n1* , *n2*,..., *nn* and then set tabs at *nn+r1* , *nn+r2*,...., *nn+rn* and then at *nn+rn+r1* , *nn+rn+r2*,..., *nn+rn+rn*, and so on. For example,

> > **.ta T .5i**

> will set tabs every half an inch.

New number registers

The following read-only registers are available:

\n[.C]   1 if compatibility mode is in effect, 0 otherwise.

\n[.cdp]

> The depth of the last character added to the current environment. It is positive if the character extends below the baseline.

\n[.ce]   The number of lines remaining to be centered, as set by the **ce** request.

\n[.cht] The height of the last character added to the current environment. It is positive if the character extends above the baseline.

\n[.csk] The skew of the last character added to the current environment. The *skew* of a character is how far to the right of the center of a character the center of an accent over that character should be placed.

\n[.ev]   The name or number of the current environment. This is a string-valued register.

\n[.fam]

> The current font family. This is a string-valued register.

\n[.fp]   The number of the next free font position.

\n[.g]   Always 1. Macros should use this to determine whether they are running under GNU troff.

\n[.hla] The current hyphenation language as set by the **hla** request.

\n[.hlc] The number of immediately preceding consecutive hyphenated lines.

\n[.hlm]

> The maximum allowed number of consecutive hyphenated lines, as set by the **hlm** request.

\n[.hy]   The current hyphenation flags (as set by the **hy** request.)

\n[.hym]

> The current hyphenation margin (as set by the **hym** request.)

\n[.hys] The current hyphenation space (as set by the **hys** request.)

\n[.in]   The indent that applies to the current output line.

\n[.kern]
> **1** if pairwise kerning is enabled, **0** otherwise.

\n[.lg]   The current ligature mode (as set by the **lg** request.)

\n[.ll]   The line length that applies to the current output line.

\n[.lt]   The title length as set by the **lt** request.

\n[.ne]   The amount of space that was needed in the last **ne** request that caused a trap to be sprung. Useful in conjunction with the **\n[.trunc]** register.

\n[.pn]   The number of the next page: either the value set by a **pn** request, or the number of the current page plus 1.

\n[.ps]   The current pointsize in scaled points.

\n[.psr] The last-requested pointsize in scaled points.

\n[.rj]   The number of lines to be right-justified as set by the **rj** request.

\n[.sr]   The last requested pointsize in points as a decimal fraction. This is a string-valued register.

\n[.tabs]
> A string representation of the current tab settings suitable for use as an argument to the **ta** request.

\n[.trunc]
> The amount of vertical space truncated by the most recently sprung vertical position trap, or, if the trap was sprung by a **ne** request, minus the amount of vertical motion produced by the **ne** request. In other words, at the point a trap is sprung, it represents the difference of what the vertical position would have been but for the trap, and what the vertical position actually is. Useful in conjunction with the **\n[.ne]** register.

\n[.ss]

\n[.sss] These give the values of the parameters set by the first and second arguments of the ss request.

\n[.vpt] 1 if vertical position traps are enabled, 0 otherwise.

\n[.warn]
> The sum of the numbers associated with each of the currently enabled warnings. The number associated with each warning is listed in the 'Warnings' subsection.

\n(.x   The major version number. For example, if the version number is **1.03** then **\n(.x** will contain **1**.

\n(.y   The minor version number. For example, if the version number is **1.03** then **\n(.y** will contain **03**.

The following registers are set by the **\w** escape sequence:

\n[rst]

\n[rsb] Like the **st** and **sb** registers, but takes account of the heights and depths of characters.

\n[ssc] The amount of horizontal space (possibly negative) that should be added to the last character before a subscript.

\n[skw] How far to right of the center of the last character in the **\w** argument, the center of an accent from a roman font should be placed over that character.

The following read/write number registers are available:

\n[systat]
> The return value of the system() function executed by the last **sy** request.

\n[slimit]
> If greater than 0, the maximum number of objects on the input stack. If less than or equal to 0, there is no limit on the number of objects on the input stack. With no limit, recursion can continue

until virtual memory is exhausted.

Miscellaneous

Fonts not listed in the DESC file are automatically mounted on the next available font position when they are referenced. If a font is to be mounted explicitly with the **fp** request on an unused font position, it should be mounted on the first unused font position, which can be found in the **\n[.fp]** register; although **troff** does not enforce this strictly, it will not allow a font to be mounted at a position whose number is much greater than that of any currently used position.

Interpolating a string does not hide existing macro arguments. Thus in a macro, a more efficient way of doing

.xx \\$@

is

*[xx]\\

If the font description file contains pairwise kerning information, characters from that font will be kerned. Kerning between two characters can be inhibited by placing a \& between them.

In a string comparison in a condition, characters that appear at different input levels to the first delimiter character will not be recognized as the second or third delimiters. This applies also to the **tl** request. In a \w escape sequence, a character that appears at a different input level to the starting delimiter character will not be recognised as the closing delimiter character. When decoding a macro argument that is delimited by double quotes, a character that appears at a different input level to the starting delimiter character will not be recognised as the closing delimiter character. The implementation of \$@ ensures that the double quotes surrounding an argument will appear at the same input level, which will be different to the input level of the argument itself. In a long escape name] will not be recognized as a closing delimiter except when it occurs at the same input level as the opening]. In compatibility mode, no attention is paid to the input-level.

There are some new types of condition:

.if rxxx True if there is a number register named xxx.

.if dxxx True if there is a string, macro, diversion, or request named xxx.

.if cch True if there is a character ch available; ch is either an ASCII character or a special character \(xx or \[xxx]; the condition will also be true if ch has been defined by the **char** request.

Warnings

The warnings that can be given by **troff** are divided into the following categories. The name associated with each warning is used by the −w and −W options; the number is used by the **warn** request, and by the **.warn** register.

char	1	Non-existent characters. This is enabled by default.
number	2	Invalid numeric expressions. This is enabled by default.
break	4	In fill mode, lines which could not be broken so that their length was less than the line length. This is enabled by default.
delim	8	Missing or mismatched closing delimiters.
el	16	Use of the **el** request with no matching **ie** request.
scale	32	Meaningless scaling indicators.
range	64	Out of range arguments.
syntax	128	Dubious syntax in numeric expressions.
di	256	Use of **di** or **da** without an argument when there is no current diversion.

mac	512	Use of undefined strings, macros and diversions. When an undefined string, macro or diversion is used, that string is automatically defined as empty. So, in most cases, at most one warning will be given for each name.
reg	1024	Use of undefined number registers. When an undefined number register is used, that register is automatically defined to have a value of 0. a definition is automatically made with a value of 0. So, in most cases, at most one warning will be given for use of a particular name.
tab	2048	Use of a tab character where a number was expected.
right-brace	4096	Use of \} where a number was expected.
missing	8192	Requests that are missing non-optional arguments.
input	16384	Illegal input characters.
escape	32768	Unrecognized escape sequences. When an unrecognized escape sequence is encountered, the escape character is ignored.
space	65536	Missing space between a request or macro and its argument. This warning will be given when an undefined name longer than two characters is encountered, and the first two characters of the name make a defined name. The request or macro will not be invoked. When this warning is given, no macro is automatically defined. This is enabled by default. This warning will never occur in compatibility mode.
font	131072	Non-existent fonts. This is enabled by default.

There are also names that can be used to refer to groups of warnings:

all   All warnings except **di**, **mac** and **reg**. It is intended that this covers all warnings that are useful with traditional macro packages.

w   All warnings.

Incompatibilities

Long names cause some incompatibilities. Unix troff will interpret

> **.dsabcd**

as defining a string **ab** with contents **cd**. Normally, GNU troff will interpret this as a call of a macro named **dsabcd**. Also Unix troff will interpret *[or \n[as references to a string or number register called [. In GNU troff, however, this will normally be interpreted as the start of a long name. In *compatibility mode* GNU troff will interpret these things in the traditional way. In compatibility mode, however, long names are not recognised. Compatibility mode can be turned on with the −C command line option, and turned on or off with the **cp** request. The number register \n(.C is 1 if compatibility mode is on, 0 otherwise.

GNU troff does not allow the use of the escape sequences \\\\\&\\}\\{\(space)\'\`\-_\!\%\c in names of strings, macros, diversions, number registers, fonts or environments; Unix troff does. The \A escape sequence may be helpful in avoiding use of these escape sequences in names.

Fractional pointsizes cause one noteworthy incompatibility. In Unix troff the **ps** request ignores scale indicators and so

> **.ps 10u**

will set the pointsize to 10 points, whereas in GNU troff it will set the pointsize to 10 scaled points.

In GNU troff there is a fundamental difference between unformatted, input characters, and formatted, output characters. Everything that affects how an output character will be output is stored with the character; once an output character has been constructed it is unaffected by any subsequent requests that are executed, including **bd**, **cs**, **tkf**, **tr**, or **fp** requests. Normally output characters are constructed from input characters at the moment immediately before the character is added to the current output line. Macros, diversions and strings are all, in fact, the same type of object; they contain lists of input characters and output characters in any combination. An output character does not behave like an input character for the purposes of macro processing; it does not inherit any of the special properties that the input character from which it was constructed might have had. For example,

> **.di x**
> ****
> **.br**
> **.di**
> **.x**

will print \\ in GNU troff; each pair of input \s is turned into one output \ and the resulting output \s are not interpreted as escape characters when they are reread. Unix troff would interpret them as escape characters when they were reread and would end up printing one \. The correct way to obtain a printable \ is to use the \e escape sequence: this will always print a single instance of the current escape character, regardless of whether or not it is used in a diversion; it will also work in both GNU troff and Unix troff. If you wish for some reason to store in a diversion an escape sequence that will be interpreted when the diversion is reread, you can either use the traditional \! transparent output facility, or, if this is unsuitable, the new \? escape sequence.

ENVIRONMENT

GROFF_TMAC_PATH
A colon separated list of directories in which to search for macro files.

GROFF_TYPESETTER
Default device.

GROFF_FONT_PATH
A colon separated list of directories in which to search for the **dev**name directory. **troff** will search in directories given in the **−F** option before these, and in standard directories (**/usr/share/groff_font**) after these.

FILES

/usr/share/tmac/troffrc	Initialization file
/usr/share/tmac/tmac.name	Macro files
/usr/share/groff_font/devname**/DESC**	Device description file for device name.
/usr/share/groff_font/devname**/**F	Font file for font F of device name.

SEE ALSO
groff(1) **tbl**(1), **pic**(1), **eqn**(1), **grops**(1), **grodvi**(1), **grotty**(1), **groff_font**(5), **groff_out**(5), **groff_char**(7)

1

NAME
true – return true value

SYNOPSIS
true

DESCRIPTION
True is normally used in a Bourne shell script. **True** tests for the appropriate status "false" before running (or failing to run) a list of commands.

SEE ALSO
csh(1), sh(1), false(1)

DIAGNOSTICS
The **true** utility always returns with exit code zero.

STANDARDS
The **true** function is expected to be POSIX 1003.2 compatible.

NAME
   tset – terminal initialization

SYNOPSIS
   tset [**-IQrSs**] [**-**] [**-e** *ch*] [**-i** *ch*] [**-k** *ch*] [**-m** *mapping*] [*terminal*]
   reset [**-IQrSs**] [**-**] [**-e** *ch*] [**-i** *ch*] [**-k** *ch*] [**-m** *mapping*] [*terminal*]

DESCRIPTION
   Tset initializes terminals. **Tset** first determines the type of terminal that you are using. This determination is done as follows, using the first terminal type found.

   - The *terminal* argument specified on the command line.
   - The value of the TERM environmental variable.
   - The terminal type associated with the standard error output device in the /etc/ttys file.
   - The default terminal type, "unknown".

   If the terminal type was not specified on the command-line, the **-m** option mappings are then applied (see below for more information). Then, if the terminal type begins with a question mark ("?"), the user is prompted for confirmation of the terminal type. An empty response confirms the type, or, another type can be entered to specify a new type. Once the terminal type has been determined, the termcap entry for the terminal is retrieved. If no termcap entry is found for the type, the user is prompted for another terminal type.

   Once the termcap entry is retrieved, the window size, backspace, interrupt and line kill characters (among many other things) are set and the terminal and tab initialization strings are sent to the standard error output. Finally, if the erase, interrupt and line kill characters have changed, or are not set to their default values, their values are displayed to the standard error output.

   When invoked as **reset**, **tset** sets cooked and echo modes, turns off cbreak and raw modes, turns on newline translation and resets any unset special characters to their default values before doing the terminal initialization described above. This is useful after a program dies leaving a terminal in an abnormal state. Note, you may have to type "<LF>reset<LF>" (the line-feed character is normally control-J) to get the terminal to work, as carriage-return may no longer work in the abnormal state. Also, the terminal will often not echo the command.

   The options are as follows:

   -   The terminal type is displayed to the standard output, and the terminal is not initialized in any way.

   -e   Set the erase character to *ch*.

   -I   Do not send the terminal or tab initialization strings to the terminal.

   -i   Set the interrupt character to *ch*.

   -k   Set the line kill character to *ch*.

   -m   Specify a mapping from a port type to a terminal. See below for more information.

   -Q   Don't display any values for the erase, interrupt and line kill characters.

   -r   Print the terminal type to the standard error output.

   -S   Print the terminal type and the termcap entry to the standard output. See the section below on setting the environment for details.

   -s   Print the sequence of shell commands to initialize the environment variables TERM and TERMCAP to the standard output. See the section below on setting the environment for details.

The arguments for the −e, −i and −k options may either be entered as actual characters or by using the "hat" notation, i.e. control-h may be specified as "^H" or "^h".

SETTING THE ENVIRONMENT

It is often desirable to enter the terminal type and information about the terminal's capabilities into the shell's environment. This is done using the −S and −s options.

When the −S option is specified, the terminal type and the termcap entry are written to the standard output, separated by a space and without a terminating newline. This can be assigned to an array by **csh** and **ksh** users and then used like any other shell array.

When the −s option is specified, the commands to enter the information into the shell's environment are written to the standard output. If the SHELL environmental variable ends in "csh", the commands are for the **csh**, otherwise, they are for sh. Note, the **csh** commands set and unset the shell variable "noglob", leaving it unset. The following line in the .login or .profile files will initialize the environment correctly:

```
eval `tset -s options ...
```

To demonstrate a simple use of the −S option, the following lines in the .login file have an equivalent effect:

```
set noglob
set term=('tset -S options ...')
setenv TERM $term[1]
setenv TERMCAP "$term[2]"
unset term
unset noglob
```

TERMINAL TYPE MAPPING

When the terminal is not hardwired into the system (or the current system information is incorrect) the terminal type derived from the /etc/ttys file or the TERM environmental variable is often something generic like "network", "dialup", or "unknown". When **tset** is used in a startup script (.profile for sh(1) users or .login for csh(1) users) it is often desirable to provide information about the type of terminal used on such ports. The purpose of the −m option is to "map" from some set of conditions to a terminal type, that is, to tell **tset** "If I'm on this port at a particular speed, guess that I'm on that kind of terminal".

The argument to the −m option consists of an optional port type, an optional operator, an optional baud rate specification, an optional colon (":") character and a terminal type. The port type is a string (delimited by either the operator or the colon character). The operator may be any combination of: ">", "<", "@", and "!"; ">" means greater than, "<" means less than, "@" means equal to and "!" inverts the sense of the test. The baud rate is specified as a number and is compared with the speed of the standard error output (which should be the control terminal). The terminal type is a string.

If the terminal type is not specified on the command line, the −m mappings are applied to the terminal type. If the port type and baud rate match the mapping, the terminal type specified in the mapping replaces the current type. If more than one mapping is specified, the first applicable mapping is used.

For example, consider the following mapping: "dialup>9600:vt100". The port type is "dialup", the operator is ">", the baud rate specification is "9600", and the terminal type is "vt100". The result of this mapping is to specify that if the terminal type is "dialup", and the baud rate is greater than 9600 baud, a terminal type of "vt100" will be used.

If no port type is specified, the terminal type will match any port type, for example, "-m dialup:vt100 -m :?xterm" will cause any dialup port, regardless of baud rate, to match the terminal type "vt100", and any non-dialup port type to match the terminal type "?xterm". Note, because of the leading question mark, the user will be queried on a default port as to whether they are actually using an *xterm* terminal.

No whitespace characters are permitted in the −m option argument. Also, to avoid problems with metacharacters, it is suggested that the entire −m option argument be placed within single quote characters, and that **csh** users insert a backslash character (''\'') before any exclamation marks (''!'').

ENVIRONMENT

The **tset** command utilizes the SHELL and TERM environment variables.

FILES

/etc/ttys   system port name to terminal type mapping database
/usr/share/misc/termcap terminal capability database

SEE ALSO

csh(1), sh(1), stty(1), tty(4), termcap(5), ttys(5), environ(7)

HISTORY

The **tset** command appeared in 3.0BSD.

COMPATIBILITY

The −A, −E, −h, −u and −v options have been deleted from the **tset** utility. None of them were documented in 4.3BSD and all are of limited utility at best. The −a, −d and −p options are similarly not documented or useful, but were retained as they appear to be in widespread use. It is strongly recommended that any usage of these three options be changed to use the −m option instead. The −n option remains, but has no effect. It is still permissible to specify the −e, −i and −k options without arguments, although it is strongly recommended that such usage be fixed to explicitly specify the character.

Executing **tset** as **reset** no longer implies the −Q option. Also, the interaction between the − option and the *terminal* argument in some historic implementations of **tset** has been removed.

Finally, the **tset** implementation has been completely redone (as part of the addition to the system of a IEEE Std1003.1-1988 (''POSIX'') compliant terminal interface) and will no longer compile on systems with older terminal interfaces.

1

NAME

tsort – topological sort of a directed graph

SYNOPSIS

tsort [−l] [*file*]

DESCRIPTION

Tsort takes a list of pairs of node names representing directed arcs in a graph and prints the nodes in topological order on standard output. Input is taken from the named *file*, or from standard input if no file is given.

Node names in the input are separated by white space and there must be an even number of node pairs.

Presence of a node in a graph can be represented by an arc from the node to itself. This is useful when a node is not connected to any other nodes.

If the graph contains a cycle (and therefore cannot be properly sorted), one of the arcs in the cycle is ignored and the sort continues. Cycles are reported on standard error.

The options are as follows:

−l   Search for and display the longest cycle. Can take a very long time.

SEE ALSO

ar(1)

HISTORY

A **tsort** command appeared in Version 7 AT&T UNIX. This **tsort** command and manual page are derived from sources contributed to Berkeley by Michael Rendell of Memorial University of Newfoundland.

NAME

   tty – return user's terminal name

SYNOPSIS

   tty [−s]

DESCRIPTION

   The tty utility writes the name of the terminal attached to standard input to standard output. The name that
   is written is the string returned by ttyname(3). If the standard input is not a terminal, the message "not a
   tty" is written. The options are as follows:

   −s   Don't write the terminal name; only the exit status is affected when this option is specified. The −s
          option is deprecated in favor of the "test -t 0" command.

   Tty exits 0 if the standard input is a terminal, 1 if the standard input is not a terminal, and >1 if an error occurs.

SEE ALSO

   test(1), ttyname(3)

STANDARDS

   The tty function is expected to be IEEE Std1003.2 ("POSIX") compatible.

1

NAME

ul – do underlining

SYNOPSIS

ul [−i] [−t *terminal*] [*name* ...]

DESCRIPTION

Ul reads the named files (or standard input if none are given) and translates occurrences of underscores to the sequence which indicates underlining for the terminal in use, as specified by the environment variable TERM. The file /etc/termcap is read to determine the appropriate sequences for underlining. If the terminal is incapable of underlining, but is capable of a standout mode then that is used instead. If the terminal can overstrike, or handles underlining automatically, ul degenerates to cat(1). If the terminal cannot underline, underlining is ignored.

The following options are available:

−i   Underlining is indicated by a separate line containing appropriate dashes '−'; this is useful when you want to look at the underlining which is present in an nroff output stream on a crt-terminal.

−t *terminal*
        Overrides the terminal type specified in the environment with *terminal*.

ENVIRONMENT

The following environment variable is used:

TERM The TERM variable is used to relate a tty device with its device capability description (see termcap(5)). TERM is set at login time, either by the default terminal type specified in /etc/ttys or as set during the login process by the user in their login file (see setenv(1)).

SEE ALSO

man(1), nroff(1), colcrt(1)

BUGS

Nroff usually outputs a series of backspaces and underlines intermixed with the text to indicate underlining. No attempt is made to optimize the backward motion.

HISTORY

The ul command appeared in 3.0BSD.

NAME

uname – display information about the system

SYNOPSIS

uname [−amnrsv]

DESCRIPTION

The **uname** command writes the name of the operating system implementation to standard output. When options are specified, strings representing one or more system characteristics are written to standard output.

The options are as follows:

−a   Behave as though the options −m, −n, −r, −s, and −v were specified.

−m   Write the type of the current hardware platform to standard output.

−n   Write the name of the system to standard output.

−r   Write the current release level of the operating system to standard output.

−s   Write the name of the operating system implementation to standard output.

−v   Write the version level of this release of the operating system to standard output.

If the −a flag is specified, or multiple flags are specified, all output is written on a single line, separated by spaces.

The **uname** utility exits 0 on success, and >0 if an error occurs.

SEE ALSO

sysctl(8), sysctl(3), uname(3)

HISTORY

The **uname** command appeared in 4.4BSD.

STANDARDS

The **uname** command is expected to conform to the IEEE Std1003.2 (''POSIX'') specification.

NAME

unifdef – remove ifdef'ed lines

SYNOPSIS

unifdef [**–clt**] [**–D***sym* **–U***sym* **–iD***sym* **–iD***sym*] ... [*file*]

DESCRIPTION

Unifdef is useful for removing ifdef'ed lines from a file while otherwise leaving the file alone. **Unifdef** acts on #ifdef, #ifndef, #else, and #endif lines, and it knows only enough about C to know when one of these is inactive because it is inside a comment, or a single or double quote. Parsing for quotes is very simplistic: when it finds an open quote, it ignores everything (except escaped quotes) until it finds a close quote, and it will not complain if it gets to the end of a line and finds no backslash for continuation.

Available options:

–D*sym*
–U*sym*

> Specify which symbols to define or undefine. and the lines inside those ifdefs will be copied to the output or removed as appropriate. The ifdef, ifndef, else, and endif lines associated with *sym* will also be removed. Ifdefs involving symbols you don't specify and "#if" control lines are untouched and copied out along with their associated ifdef, else, and endif lines. If an ifdef X occurs nested inside another ifdef X, then the inside ifdef is treated as if it were an unrecognized symbol. If the same symbol appears in more than one argument, the last occurrence dominates.

–c   If the **–c** flag is specified, then the operation of **unifdef** is complemented, i.e. the lines that would have been removed or blanked are retained and vice versa.

–l   Replace removed lines with blank lines instead of deleting them.

–t   Disables parsing for C comments and quotes, which is useful for plain text.

–iD*sym*
–iU*sym*

> Ignore ifdefs. If your C code uses ifdefs to delimit non-C lines, such as comments or code which is under construction, then you must tell **unifdef** which symbols are used for that purpose so that it won't try to parse for quotes and comments inside those ifdefs. One specifies ignored ifdefs with **–iD***sym* and **–iU***sym* similar to **–D***sym* and **–U***sym* above.

Unifdef copies its output to *stdout* and will take its input from *stdin* if no *file* argument is given.

Unifdef works nicely with the **–D***sym* option added to diff(1) as of the 4.1 Berkeley Software Distribution.

SEE ALSO

diff(1)

DIAGNOSTICS

Inappropriate else or endif.
Premature EOF with line numbers of the unterminated #ifdefs.

Exit status is 0 if output is exact copy of input, 1 if not, 2 if trouble.

1

BUGS

Should try to deal with ''#if'' lines.

Doesn't work correctly if input contains null characters.

HISTORY

The `unifdef` command appeared in 4.3BSD.

1

NAME
     uniq – report or filter out repeated lines in a file

SYNOPSIS
     uniq [–c | –d | –u] [–f *fields*] [–s *chars*] [*input_file* [*output_file*]]

DESCRIPTION
     The uniq utility reads the standard input comparing adjacent lines, and writes a copy of each unique input
     line to the standard output. The second and succeeding copies of identical adjacent input lines are not writ-
     ten. Repeated lines in the input will not be detected if they are not adjacent, so it may be necessary to sort
     the files first.

     The following options are available:

     –c   Precede each output line with the count of the number of times the line occurred in the input, fol-
             lowed by a single space.

     –d   Don't output lines that are not repeated in the input.

     –f *fields*
             Ignore the first *fields* in each input line when doing comparisons. A field is a string of non-blank
             characters separated from adjacent fields by blanks. Field numbers are one based, i.e. the first field
             is field one.

     –s *chars*
             Ignore the first *chars* characters in each input line when doing comparisons. If specified in con-
             junction with the –f option, the first *chars* characters after the first *fields* fields will be ig-
             nored. Character numbers are one based, i.e. the first character is character one.

     –u   Don't output lines that are repeated in the input.

     If additional arguments are specified on the command line, the first such argument is used as the name of an
     input file, the second is used as the name of an output file.

     The uniq utility exits 0 on success, and >0 if an error occurs.

COMPATIBILITY
     The historic +*number* and –*number* options have been deprecated but are still supported in this imple-
     mentation.

SEE ALSO
     sort(1)

STANDARDS
     The uniq utility is expected to be IEEE Std1003.2 (''POSIX'') compatible.

NAME

 units – conversion program

SYNOPSIS

 units

DESCRIPTION

 Units converts quantities expressed in various standard scales to their equivalents in other scales. It works interactively in this fashion:

> *You have:* inch
> *You want:* cm
>   * 2.54000e+00
>   / 3.93701e−01

 A quantity is specified as a multiplicative combination of units optionally preceded by a numeric multiplier. Powers are indicated by suffixed positive integers, division by the usual sign:

> *You have:* 15 pounds force/in2
> *You want:* atm
>   * 1.02069e+00
>   / 9.79730e−01

 Units only does multiplicative scale changes. Thus it can convert Kelvin to Rankine, but not Centigrade to Fahrenheit. Most familiar units, abbreviations, and metric prefixes are recognized, together with a generous leavening of exotica and a few constants of nature including:

pi	ratio of circumference to diameter
c	speed of light
e	charge on an electron
g	acceleration of gravity
force	same as g
mole	Avogadro's number
water	pressure head per unit height of water
au	astronomical unit

 'Pound' is a unit of mass. Compound names are run together, e.g. 'lightyear'. British units that differ from their US counterparts are prefixed thus: 'brgallon'. Currency is denoted 'belgiumfranc', 'britainpound', ...

 For a complete list of units, 'cat /usr/share/misc/units'.

FILES

 /usr/lib/units

BUGS

 Don't base your financial plans on the currency conversions.

1

NAME

    unvis – revert a visual representation of data back to original form

SYNOPSIS

    unvis [*file ...*]

DESCRIPTION

    Unvis is the inverse function of vis(1). It reverts a visual representation of data back to its original form
    on standard output.

SEE ALSO

    vis(1), unvis(3), vis(3)

HISTORY

    The **unvis** command appears in 4.4BSD.

NAME

    `uptime` – show how long system has been running

SYNOPSIS

    `uptime`

DESCRIPTION

    The `uptime` utility displays the current time, the length of time the system has been up, the number of users, and the load average of the system over the last 1, 5, and 15 minutes.

FILES

    `/vmunix` system name list

SEE ALSO

    w(1)

HISTORY

    The `uptime` command appeared in 3.0BSD.

1

NAME
users – list current users

SYNOPSIS
users

DESCRIPTION
Users lists the login names of the users currently on the system, in sorted order, space separated, on a single line.

FILES
/etc/utmp

SEE ALSO
finger(1), last(1), who(1), utmp(5)

HISTORY
The **users** command appeared in 3.0BSD.

NAME

    uucp – unix to unix copy

SYNOPSIS

    uucp [**–acCdfmr**] [**–n**_user_] [**–g**_grade_] [**–s**_spool_] [**–x**_debug_] source-file.... destination-file

DESCRIPTION

    Uucp copies files named by the source-file arguments to the destination-file argument. A file name may be a pathname on your machine, or may have the form

        system-name!pathname

    where 'system-name' is taken from a list of system names that _uucp_ knows about. Shell metacharacters ?*[] appearing in the pathname part will be expanded on the appropriate system.

    Pathnames may be one of:

    (1)   a full pathname;

    (2)   a pathname preceded by ~_user;_ where _user_ is a userid on the specified system and is replaced by that user's login directory;

    (3)   a pathname prefixed by ~, where ~ is expanded into the system's public directory (usually /var/spool/uucppublic);

    (4)   a partial pathname, which is prefixed by the current directory.

    If the result is an erroneous pathname for the remote system, the copy will fail. If the destination-file is a directory, the last part of the source-file name is used.

    Uucp preserves execute permissions across the transmission and gives 0666 read and write permissions (see _chmod_(2)).

    The following options are interpreted by _uucp_.

    –a   Avoid doing a _getwd_ to find the current directory. (This is sometimes used for efficiency.)

    –c   Use the source file when copying out rather than copying the file to the spool directory. (This is the default.)

    –C   Copy the source file to the spool directory and transmit the copy.

    –d   Make all necessary directories for the file copy. (This is the default.)

    –f   Do not make intermediate directories for the file copy.

    –g_grade_

        Grade is a single letter/number; lower ASCII sequence characters will cause a job to be transmitted earlier during a particular conversation. Default is 'n'. By way of comparison, _uux_(1) defaults to 'A'; mail is usually sent at 'C'.

    –m   Send mail to the requester when the copy is complete.

    –n_user_ Notify _user_ on remote system (i.e., send _user_ mail) that a file was sent.

    –r   Do not start the transfer, just queue the job.

    –s_spool_ Use _spool_ as the spool directory instead of the default.

    –x_debug_

        Turn on the debugging at level _debug_.

FILES

    /var/spool/uucp - spool directory

    /usr/lib/uucp/* - other data and program files

SEE ALSO

    uux(1), mail(1)

1

D. A. Nowitz and M. E. Lesk, *A Dial-Up Network of UNIX Systems*.

D. A. Nowitz, *Uucp Implementation Description*.

WARNING

The domain of remotely accessible files can (and for obvious security reasons, usually should) be severely restricted. You will very likely not be able to fetch files by pathname; ask a responsible person on the remote system to send them to you. For the same reasons you will probably not be able to send files to arbitrary pathnames.

BUGS

All files received by *uucp* will be owned by the uucp administrator (usually UID 5).

The −m option will only work sending files or receiving a single file. (Receiving multiple files specified by special shell characters ?*[] will not activate the −m option.)

At present *uucp* cannot copy to a system several "hops" away, that is, a command of the form

      uucp myfile system1!system2!system3!yourfile

is not permitted. Use *uusend*(1) instead.

When invoking *uucp* from *csh*(1), the '!' character must be prefixed by the '\' escape to inhibit *csh*'s history mechanism. (Quotes are not sufficient.)

Uucp refuses to copy a file that does not give read access to ''other''; that is, the file must have at least 0444 modes.

1

NAME
uuencode, uudecode – encode/decode a binary file

SYNOPSIS
uuencode [*file*] *name*
uudecode [*file* ...]

DESCRIPTION
Uuencode and uudecode are used to transmit binary files over transmission mediums that do not support other than simple ASCII data.

Uuencode reads *file* (or by default the standard input) and writes an encoded version to the standard output. The encoding uses only printing ASCII characters and includes the mode of the file and the operand *name* for use by uudecode.

Uudecode transforms *uuencoded* files (or by default, the standard input) into the original form. The resulting file is named *name* and will have the mode of the original file except that setuid and execute bits are not retained. Uudecode ignores any leading and trailing lines.

EXAMPLES
The following example packages up a source tree, compresses it, uuencodes it and mails it to a user on another system. When uudecode is run on the target system, the file "src_tree.tar.Z" will be created which may then be uncompressed and extracted into the original tree.

```
tar cf – src_tree | compress |
uuencode src_tree.tar.Z | mail sys1!sys2!user
```

SEE ALSO
compress(1), mail(1), uucp(1), uuencode(5), format(5)

BUGS
The encoded form of the file is expanded by 35% (3 bytes become 4 plus control information).

HISTORY
The uuencode command appeared in 4.0BSD.

NAME
uulog – display UUCP log entries

SYNOPSIS
uulog [–s *sys*] [–u *user*]

DESCRIPTION
The **uulog** program displays uucp(1) and uux(1) log entries from the file `/var/spool/uucp/LOGFILE`.

Options supported by **uulog**:

–s *sys*   Display all entries logged which include the system named *sys*.

–u *user*   Display only entries which include the user name *user*.

FILES
`/usr/spool/uucp/LOGFILE`   Logfile of all uucp events.

SEE ALSO
uucp(1), uux(1).

NOTES
Very early releases of UUCP used separate log files for each of the UUCP utilities; **uulog** was used to merge the individual logs into a master file. This capability has not been necessary for some time and is no longer supported.

BUGS
UUCP's recording of which user issued a request is unreliable.

The **uulog** program is little more than an overspecialized version of grep(1).

HISTORY
A **uulog** command appeared in Version 32V AT&T UNIX.

1

NAME
uuname – list names of UUCP hosts

SYNOPSIS
uuname [–l]

DESCRIPTION
Uuname lists the UUCP names of known systems.

Available option:

–l　　Return the local system name; this may differ from the hostname(1) for the system if the hostname is very long.

SEE ALSO
uucp(1), uux(1).

HISTORY
The uuname command appeared in 4.0BSD.

1

NAME

uuq – examine or manipulate the uucp queue

SYNOPSIS

uuq [–l] [–h] [–s*system*] [–u*user*] [–d*jobno*] [–r*sdir*] [–b*baud*]

DESCRIPTION

Uuq is used to examine (and possibly delete) entries in the uucp queue.

When listing jobs, uuq uses a format reminiscent of ls. For the long format, information for each job listed includes job number, number of files to transfer, user who spooled the job, number of bytes to send, type of command requested (S for sending files, R for receiving files, X for remote uucp), and file or command desired.

Several options are available:

–h   Print only the summary lines for each system. Summary lines give system name, number of jobs for the system, and total number of bytes to send.

–l   Specifies a long format listing. The default is to list only the job numbers sorted across the page.

–s*system*   Limit output to jobs for systems whose system names begin with *system*.

–u*user*   Limit output to jobs for users whose login names begin with *user*.

–d*jobno*   Delete job number *jobno* (as obtained from a previous uuq command) from the uucp queue. Only the UUCP Administrator is permitted to delete jobs.

–r*sdir*   Look for files in the spooling directory *sdir* instead of the default directory.

–b*baud*   Use *baud* to compute the transfer time instead of the default 1200 baud.

FILES

/usr/spool/uucp/	Default spool directory
/usr/spool/uucp/C./C.*	Control files
/usr/spool/uucp/D*hostname* ./D.*	Outgoing data files
/usr/spool/uucp/X./X.*	Outgoing execution files

SEE ALSO

uucp(1), uux(1), uulog(1), uusnap(8)

BUGS

No information is available on work requested by the remote machine.

The user who requests a remote uucp command is unknown.

"uq –l" can be horrendously slow.

HISTORY

The uuq command appeared in 4.3BSD.

1

NAME
uusend – send a file to a remote host

SYNOPSIS
uusend [–m *mode*] *sourcefile sys1!sys2!..!remotefile*

DESCRIPTION
Uusend sends a file to a given location on a remote system. The system need not be directly connected to the local system, but a chain of uucp(1) links must to connect the two systems.

Available option:

–m *mode*   The mode of the file on the remote end is taken from the octal number given. Otherwise, the mode of the input file will be used.

The sourcefile can be ' – ', meaning to use the standard input. Both of these options are primarily intended for internal use of uusend.

The remotefile can include the ˜userid syntax.

DIAGNOSTICS
If anything goes wrong any further away than the first system down the line, you will never hear about it.

SEE ALSO
uux(1), uucp(1), uuencode(1)

BUGS
This command should not exist, since uucp should handle it.

All systems along the line must have the uusend command available and allow remote execution of it.

Some uucp systems have a bug where binary files cannot be the input to a uux(1) command. If this bug exists in any system along the line, the file will show up severely munged.

HISTORY
The uusend command appeared in 4.0BSD.

1

NAME

uux – unix to unix command execution

SYNOPSIS

uux [**-**] [**-cClLnprz**] [**-a**_name_] [**-g**_grade_] [**-x**_debug_] command-string

DESCRIPTION

Uux will gather zero or more files from various systems, execute a command on a specified system and then send standard output to a file on a specified system.

The _command-string_ is made up of one or more arguments that look like a Shell command line, except that the command and file names may be prefixed by _system-name_!. A null _system-name_ is interpreted as the local system.

File names may be one of

> (1) a full path name;

> (2) a path name preceded by ˜_user_ where _user_ is a login name on the specified system and is replaced by that user's login directory;

> (3) a path name prefixed by ˜; where ˜ is expanded to the system's public directory (usually /var/spool/uucppublic);

> (4) a partial pathname, which is prefixed by the current directory.

As an example, the command

> uux "!diff usg!/usr/dan/file1 pwba!/a4/dan/file2 > !˜/dan/file.diff"

will get the **file1** and **file2** files from the "usg" and "pwba" machines, execute a _diff_(1) command and put the results in **file.diff** in the local /var/spool/uucppublic/dan/ directory.

Any special shell characters, such as <>;|, should be quoted either by quoting the entire _command-string_, or quoting the special characters as individual arguments.

Uux will attempt to get all files to the execution system. For files that are output files, the file name must be escaped using parentheses. For example, the command

> uux a!wc b!/usr/file1 \(c!/usr/file2 \)

gets **/usr/file1** from system "b" and sends it to system "a", performs a _wc_ command on that file and sends the result of the _wc_ command to system "c".

Uux will notify you by mail if the requested command on the remote system was disallowed. This notification can be turned off by the −**n** option.

The following _options_ are interpreted by _uux_:

− The standard input to _uux_ is made the standard input to the _command-string_.

−a_name_ Use _name_ as the user identification replacing the initiator user-id.

−c Do not copy local file to the spool directory for transfer to the remote machine (this is the default).

−C Force the copy of local files to the spool directory for transfer.

−g_grade_
> _Grade_ is a single letter/number, from **0** to **9**, **A** to **Z**, or **a** to **z**; **0** is the highest, and **z** is the lowest grade. The default is **A**; by comparison _uucp_(1) defaults to **n** and mail is usually sent at grade **C**. Lower grades should be specified for high-volume jobs, such as news.

−l Try and make a link from the original file to the spool directory. If the link cannot be made, copy the file.

−n Do not notify the user when the command completes.

−p Same as −: The standard input to _uux_ is made the standard input to the _command-string_.

−r   Do not start the file transfer, just queue the job.

−x*debug*

Produce debugging output on stdout. The debug is a number between 0 and 9; higher numbers give more detailed information. Debugging is permitted only for privileged users (specifically, those with read access to *L.sys*(5).

−z   Notify the user only if the command fails.

−L   Start up *uucico* with the **-L** flag. This will force calls to be made to local sites only (see *uucico*(8)).

FILES

/var/spool/uucp   spool directories
/usr/lib/uucp/*   UUCP configuration data and daemons

SEE ALSO

uucp(1), uucico(8), uuxqt(8).

WARNING

For security reasons, many installations will limit the list of commands executable on behalf of an incoming request from *uux*. Many sites will permit little more than the receipt of mail (see *mail*(1)) via *uux*.

BUGS

Only the first command of a shell pipeline may have a *system-name*!. All other commands are executed on the system of the first command.

The use of the shell metacharacter * will probably not do what you want it to do.

The shell tokens << and >> are not implemented.

When invoking *uux* from *csh*(1), the '!' character must be prefixed by the '\' escape to inhibit *csh*'s history mechanism. (Quotes are not sufficient.)

1

NAME

vacation – return ''I am not here'' indication

SYNOPSIS

vacation –i [–r *interval*]
vacation [–a *alias*] *login*

DESCRIPTION

Vacation returns a message to the sender of a message telling them that you are currently not reading your mail. The intended use is in a .forward file. For example, your .forward file might have:

        \eric, "|/usr/bin/vacation -a allman eric"

which would send messages to you (assuming your login name was eric) and reply to any messages for ''eric'' or ''allman''.

Available options:

–a *alias*

        Handle messages for *alias* in the same manner as those received for the user's login name.

–i   Initialize the vacation database files. It should be used before you modify your .forward file.

–r   Set the reply interval to *interval* days. The default is one week. An interval of ''0'' means that a reply is sent to each message, and an interval of ''infinite'' (actually, any non-numeric character) will never send more than one reply. It should be noted that intervals of ''0'' are quite dangerous, as it allows mailers to get into ''I am on vacation'' loops.

No message will be sent unless *login* (or an *alias* supplied using the –a option) is part of either the ''To:'' or ''Cc:'' headers of the mail. No messages from ''???-REQUEST'', ''Postmaster'', ''UUCP'', ''MAILER'', or ''MAILER-DAEMON'' will be replied to (where these strings are case insensitive) nor is a notification sent if a ''Precedence: bulk'' or ''Precedence: junk'' line is included in the mail headers. The people who have sent you messages are maintained as an ndbm(3) database in the file .vacation.db in your home directory.

Vacation expects a file .vacation.msg, in your home directory, containing a message to be sent back to each sender. It should be an entire message (including headers). For example, it might contain:

        From: eric@CS.Berkeley.EDU (Eric Allman)
        Subject: I am on vacation
        Delivered-By-The-Graces-Of: The Vacation program
        Precedence: bulk

        I am on vacation until July 22. If you have something urgent,
        please contact Keith Bostic <bostic@CS.Berkeley.EDU>.
        --eric

Vacation reads the first line from the standard input for a UNIX ''From'' line to determine the sender. Sendmail(8) includes this ''From'' line automatically.

Fatal errors, such as calling **vacation** with incorrect arguments, or with non-existent *logins*, are logged in the system log file, using syslog(8).

FILES

    `~/.vacation.db`   database file

    `~/.vacation.msg` message to send

SEE ALSO

    `sendmail`(8), `syslog`(8)

HISTORY

    The **vacation** command appeared in 4.3BSD.

1

NAME

vgrind – grind nice listings of programs

SYNOPSIS

vgrind [−] [−W] [−d *file*] [−f] [−h *header*] [−l *language*] [−n] [−sn] [−t] [−x] *name*
. . .

DESCRIPTION

Vgrind formats the program sources which are arguments in a nice style using troff(1) Comments are placed in italics, keywords in bold face, and the name of the current function is listed down the margin of each page as it is encountered.

Vgrind runs in two basic modes, filter mode (see the −f option) or regular mode. In filter mode **vgrind** acts as a filter in a manner similar to tbl(1). The standard input is passed directly to the standard output except for lines bracketed by the *troff-like* macros:

.vS   starts processing

.vE   ends processing

These lines are formatted as described above. The output from this filter can be passed to troff for output. There need be no particular ordering with eqn(1) or tbl(1).

In regular mode **vgrind** accepts input files, processes them, and passes them to troff(1) for output.

In both modes **vgrind** passes any lines beginning with a decimal point without conversion.

The options are:

−	forces input to be taken from standard input (default if −f is specified)
−W	forces output to the (wide) Versatec printer rather than the (narrow) Varian
−d *file*	specifies an alternate language definitions file (default is /usr/share/misc/vgrindefs)
−f	forces filter mode
−h *header*	specifies a particular header to put on every output page (default is the file name)
−l	specifies the language to use. Currently known are PASCAL (−l*p*), MODEL (−l*m*), C (−l*c* or the default), CSH (−l*csh*), SHELL (−l*sh*), RATFOR (−l*r*), MODULA2 (−l*mod2*), YACC (−l*yacc*), LISP (−l*isp*), and ICON (−l*I*).
−n	forces no keyword bolding
−s	specifies a point size to use on output (exactly the same as the argument of a .ps)
−t	similar to the same option in troff causing formatted text to go to the standard output
−x	outputs the index file in a "pretty" format. The index file itself is produced whenever **vgrind** is run with a file called index in the current directory. The index of function definitions can then be run off by giving **vgrind** the −x option and the file index as argument.

FILES

index   file where source for index is created

```
/usr/share/tmac/tmac.vgrind   macro package
/usr/libexec/vfontedpr        preprocessor
/usr/share/misc/vgrindefs     language descriptions
```

SEE ALSO

getcap(3), vgrindefs(5)

BUGS

Vfontedpr assumes that a certain programming style is followed:

For C – function names can be preceded on a line only by spaces, tabs, or an asterisk. The parenthesized arguments must also be on the same line.

For PASCAL – function names need to appear on the same line as the keywords *function* or *procedure*.

For MODEL – function names need to appear on the same line as the keywords *is beginproc*.

If these conventions are not followed, the indexing and marginal function name comment mechanisms will fail.

More generally, arbitrary formatting styles for programs mostly look bad. The use of spaces to align source code fails miserably; if you plan to **vgrind** your program you should use tabs. This is somewhat inevitable since the font used by **vgrind** is variable width.

The mechanism of ctags(1) in recognizing functions should be used here.

Filter mode does not work in documents using the −me or −ms macros. (So what use is it anyway?)

HISTORY

The **vgrind** command appeared in 3.0BSD.

1

NAME

    ex, vi, view – text editors

SYNOPSIS

    ex [–eFRrsv] [–c cmd] [–t tag] [–w size] [file ...]
    vi [–eFRrv] [–c cmd] [–t tag] [–w size] [file ...]
    view [–eFRrv] [–c cmd] [–t tag] [–w size] [file ...]

DESCRIPTION

Vi is a screen oriented text editor. Ex is a line-oriented text editor. Ex and vi are different interfaces to the same program, and it is possible to switch back and forth during an edit session. View is the equivalent of using the –R (read-only) option of vi.

This manual page is the one provided with the **nex/nvi** versions of the **ex/vi** text editors. **Nex/nvi** are intended as bug-for-bug compatible replacements for the original Fourth Berkeley Software Distribution (4BSD) **ex** and **vi** programs. For the rest of this manual page, **nex/nvi** is used only when it's necessary to distinguish it from the historic implementations of **ex/vi**.

This manual page is intended for users already familiar with **ex/vi**. Anyone else should almost certainly read a good tutorial on the editor before this manual page. If you're in an unfamiliar environment, and you absolutely have to get work done immediately, read the section after the options description, entitled ''Fast Startup''. It's probably enough to get you going.

The following options are available:

–c   Execute *cmd* immediately after starting the edit session. Particularly useful for initial positioning in the file, however *cmd* is not limited to positioning commands. This is the POSIX 1003.2 interface for the historic ''+cmd'' syntax. **Nex/nvi** supports both the old and new syntax.

–e   Start editing in ex mode, as if the command name were **ex**.

–F   Don't copy the entire file when first starting to edit. (The default is to make a copy in case someone else modifies the file during your edit session.)

–R   Start editing in read-only mode, as if the command name was **view**, or the readonly option was set.

–r   Recover the specified file, or, if no files are specified, list the files that could be recovered.

–s   Enter batch mode; applicable only to **ex** edit sessions. Batch mode is useful when running **ex** scripts. Prompts, informative messages and other user oriented message are turned off, and no start-up files or environmental variables are read. This is the POSIX 1003.2 interface for the historic ''–'' argument. **Nex/nvi** supports both the old and new syntax.

–t   Start editing at the specified tag. (See ctags(1)).

–w   Set the initial window size to the specified number of lines.

–v   Start editing in vi mode, as if the command name was **vi** or **view**.

–X   Reserved for X11 interfaces. *No X11 support is currently implemented.*

Command input for **ex/vi** is read from the standard input. In the **vi** interface, it is an error if standard input is not a terminal. In the **ex** interface, if standard input is not a terminal, **ex** will read commands from it regardless, however, the session will a batch mode session, exactly as if the **−s** option had been specified.

Ex/vi exits 0 on success, and greater than 0 if an error occurs.

FAST STARTUP

This section will tell you the minimum amount that you need to do simple editing tasks using **vi**. If you've never used any screen editor before, you're likely to have problems even with this simple introduction. In that case you should find someone that already knows **vi** and have them walk you through this section.

Vi is a screen editor. This means that it takes up almost the entire screen, displaying part of the file on each screen line, except for the last line of the screen. The last line of the screen is used for you to give commands to **vi**, and for **vi** to give information to you.

The other fact that you need to understand is that **vi** is a modeful editor, i.e. you are either entering text or you are executing commands, and you have to be in the right mode to do one or the other. You will be in command mode when you first start editing a file. There are commands that switch you into input mode. There is only one key that takes you out of input mode, and that is the <escape> key. (Key names are written using less-than and greater-than signs, e.g. <escape> means the "escape" key, usually labeled "esc" on your terminal's keyboard.) If you're ever confused as to which mode you're in, keep entering the <escape> key until **vi** beeps at you. (Generally, **vi** will beep at you if you try and do something that's not allowed. It will also display error messages.)

To start editing a file, enter the command "vi file_name<carriage-return>". The command you should enter as soon as you start editing is ": set verbose showmode<carriage-return>". This will make the editor give you verbose error messages and display the current mode at the bottom of the screen.

The commands to move around the file are:
h   Move the cursor left one character.
j   Move the cursor down one line.
k   Move the cursor up one line.
l   Move the cursor right one character.
<cursor-arrows>
    The cursor arrow keys should work, too.
/text<carriage-return>
    Search for the string "text" in the file, and move the cursor to its first character.

The commands to enter new text are:
a   Append new text, *after* the cursor.
i   Insert new text, *before* the cursor.
o   Open a new line below the line the cursor is on, and start entering text.
O   Open a new line above the line the cursor is on, and start entering text.
<escape>
    Once you've entered input mode using the one of the **a, i, O,** or **o** commands, use **<escape>** to quit entering text and return to command mode.

The commands to copy text are:
yy   Copy the line the cursor is on.
p   Append the copied line after the line the cursor is on.

The commands to delete text are:

dd   Delete the line the cursor is on.

x   Delete the character the cursor is on.

The commands to write the file are:

:w<carriage-return>

> Write the file back to the file with the name that you originally used as an argument on the **vi** command line.

:w file_name<carriage-return>

> Write the file back to the file with the name "file_name".

The commands to quit editing and exit the editor are:

:q<carriage-return>

> Quit editing and leave vi (if you've modified the file, but not saved your changes, **vi** will refuse to quit).

:q!<carriage-return>

> Quit, discarding any modifications that you may have made.

One final caution. Unusual characters can take up more than one column on the screen, and long lines can take up more than a single screen line. The above commands work on "physical" characters and lines, i.e. they affect the entire line no matter how many screen lines it takes up and the entire character no matter how many screen columns it takes up.

VI COMMANDS

The following section describes the commands available in the command mode of the **vi** editor. In each entry below, the tag line is a usage synopsis for the command character.

[count] <control-A>

> Search forward count times for the occurrence of the word upon which the cursor is positioned.

[count] <control-B>

> Page backwards count screens.

[count] <control-D>

> Scroll forwards count lines.

[count] <control-E>

> Scroll forward count lines, leaving the current line and column as is, if possible.

[count] <control-F>

> Page forward count screens.

<control-G>

> Display the file information.

<control-H>
[count] h

> Move the cursor back count characters in the current line.

[count] <control-J>
[count] <control-N>
[count] j

> Move the cursor down count lines without changing the current column.

<control-L>
<control-R>

> Repaint the screen.

[count] <control-M>
[count] +
> Move the cursor down count lines to the first nonblank character of that line.

[count] <control-P>
[count] k
> Move the cursor up count lines, without changing the current column.

<control-T>
> Return to the most recent tag context.

<control-U>
> Scroll backwards count lines.

<control-W>
> Switch to the next lower window in the screen.

<control-Y>
> Scroll backwards count lines, leaving the current line and column as is, if possible.

<control-Z>
> Suspend the current editor session.

<escape>
> Execute **ex** commands or cancel partial commands.

<control-]>
> Push a tag reference onto the tag stack.

<control-^>
> Switch to the most recently edited file.

[count] <space>
[count] l
> Move the cursor forwards count characters without changing the current line.

[count] ! motion shell-command(s) <newline>
> Replace text with results from shell command.

[count] #
> Increment the cursor word.

[count] $
> Move the cursor to the end of a line.

% Move to the matching character.

& Repeat the previous substitution command on the current line.

'<character>
'<character>
> Return to a context marked by the character <character>.

[count] (
> Back up count sentences.

[count])
> Move forward count sentences.

[count] ,
> Reverse find character count times.

[count] -
> Move to first nonblank of previous line, count times.

[count] .
> Repeat the last command that modified text.

1

/RE<carriage-return>
/RE/ [offset]<carriage-return>
?RE<carriage-return>
?RE? [offset]<carriage-return>
N
n   Search forward or backward for a regular expression.
0   Move to the first character in the current line.
:   Execute an ex command.
[count] ;
     Repeat the last character find count times.
[count] < motion
[count] > motion
     Shift lines left or right.
@ buffer
     Execute a named buffer.
[count] A
     Enter input mode, appending the text after the end of the line.
[count] B
     Move backwards count bigwords.
[buffer] [count] C
     Change text from the current position to the end-of-line.
[buffer] D
     Delete text from the current position to the end-of-line.
[count] E
     Move forward count end-of-bigwords.
[count] F <character>
     Search count times backward through the current line for <character>.
[count] G
     Move to line count, or the last line of the file if count not specified.
[count] H
     Move to the line count - 1 lines below the top of the screen.
[count] I
     Enter input mode, inserting the text at the beginning of the line.
[count] J
     Join lines.
[count] L
     Move to the line count - 1 lines above the bottom of the screen.
M   Move to the line in the middle of the screen.
[count] O
     Enter input mode, appending text in a new line above the current line.
[buffer] P
     Insert text from a buffer.
Q   Exit vi (or visual) mode and switch to ex mode.
[count] R
     Enter input mode, replacing the characters in the current line.
[buffer] [count] S
     Substitute count lines.

[count] T <character>
>   Search backwards, count times, through the current line for the character *after* the specified <character>.

U   Restore the current line to its state before the cursor last moved to it.

[count] W
>   Move forward count bigwords.

[buffer] [count] X
>   Delete count characters before the cursor.

[buffer] [count] Y
>   Copy (or ''yank'') count lines into the specified buffer.

ZZ   Write the file and exit **vi**.

[count] [[
>   Back up count section boundaries.

[count]]]
>   Move forward count section boundaries.

^   Move to first nonblank character on the current line.

[count] _
>   Move down count - 1 lines, to the first nonblank character.

[count] a
>   Enter input mode, appending the text after the cursor.

[count] b
>   Move backwards count words.

[buffer] [count] c motion
>   Change a region of text.

[buffer] [count] d motion
>   Delete a region of text.

[count] e
>   Move forward count end-of-words.

[count] f<character>
>   Search forward, count times, through the rest of the current line for <character>.

[count] i
>   Enter input mode, inserting the text before the cursor.

m <character>
>   Save the current context (line and column) as <character>.

[count] o
>   Enter input mode, appending text in a new line under the current line.

[buffer] p
>   Append text from a buffer.

[count] r <character>
>   Replace characters.

[buffer] [count] s
>   Substitute count characters in the current line starting with the current character.

[count] t <character>
>   Search forward, count times, through the current line for the character immediately *before* <character>.

u   Undo the last change made to the file.

[count] w
>   Move forward count words.

[buffer] [count] x

    Delete count characters.

[buffer] [count] y motion

    Copy (or "yank") a text region specified by the count and motion into a buffer.

[count1] z [count2] [-|.|+|^]<carriage-return>

    Redraw, optionally repositioning, the screen.

[count] {

    Move backward count paragraphs.

[count] |

    Move to a specific *column* position on the current line.

[count] }

    Move forwards count paragraphs.

[count] ˜

    Reverse the case of the count character(s).

<interrupt>

    Interrupt the current operation.

VI TEXT INPUT COMMANDS

    The following section describes the commands available in the text input mode of the **vi** editor.

<control-D>

    Erase the previous autoindent character.

^<control-D>

    Erase all of the autoindent characters, and reset the autoindent level.

0<control-D>

    Erase all of the autoindent characters.

<control-T>

    Insert sufficient <tab> and <space> characters to move the cursor forward to a column immediately after a column which is an even multiple of the **shiftwidth** option.

<erase>

<control-H>

    Erase the last character.

<literal next>

    Quote the next character.

<escape>

    Resolve all text input into the file, and return to command mode.

<line erase>

    Erase the current line.

<control-W>

<word erase>

    Erase the last word. The definition of word in this case is dependent on the **altwerase** and **ttywerase** options.

<control-X>[0-9A-Fa-f]*

    Insert a character with the hexadecimal value specified into the text.

<interrupt>

    Interrupt text input mode, returning to command mode.

EX COMMANDS

    The following section describes the commands available in the **ex** editor. In each entry below, the tag line is a usage synopsis for the command.

<end-of-file>
> Scroll the screen.

! command
[range]! command
> Execute a shell command, or filter lines through a shell command.

"   A comment.

[range] nu[mber] [count] [flags]
[range] # [count] [flags]
> Display the selected lines, each preceded with its line number.

@ buffer
* buffer
> Execute a buffer.

[range] d[elete] [buffer] [count] [flags]
> Delete the lines from the file.

di[splay] b[uffers] | s[creens] | t[ags]
> Display buffers, screens or tags.

e[dit][!] [+cmd] [file]
ex[!] [+cmd] [file]
> Edit a different file.

exu[sage] [command]
> Display usage for an ex command.

f[ile] [file]
> Display and optionally change the file name.

fg [name]
> Visual mode only. Foreground the specified screen.

[range] g[lobal] /pattern/ [commands]
[range] v /pattern/ [commands]
> Apply commands to lines matching (or not matching) a pattern.

he[lp]
> Display a help message.

[line] i[nsert][!]
> The input text is inserted before the specified line.

[range] j[oin][!] [count] [flags]
> Join lines of text together.

[range] l[ist] [count] [flags]
> Display the lines unambiguously.

map[!] [lhs rhs]
> Define or display maps (for vi only).

[line] ma[rk] <character>
[line] k <character>
> Mark the line with the mark <character>.

[range] m[ove] line
> Move the specified lines after the target line.

mk[exrc][!] file
> Write the abbreviations, editor options and maps to the specified file.

n[ext][!] [file ...]
> Edit the next file from the argument list.

[line] o[pen] /pattern/ [flags]
> Enter open mode.

pre[serve]
> Save the file in a form that can later be recovered by using **ex −l** and **−r** options.

prev[ious][!]
> Edit the previous file from the argument list.

[range] p[rint] [count] [flags]
> Display the specified lines.

[line] pu[t] [buffer]
> Append buffer contents to the current line.

q[uit][!]
> End the editing session.

[line] r[ead][!] [file]
> Read a file.

rec[over] file
> Recover `file` if it was previously saved.

res[ize] [+|-]size
> Visual mode only. Grow or shrink the current screen.

rew[ind][!]
> Rewind the argument list.

se[t] [option[=[value]] ...] [nooption ...] [option? ...] [all]
> Display or set editor options.

sh[ell]
> Run a shell program.

so[urce] file
> Read and execute **ex** commands from a file.

sp[lit] [file ...]
> Visual mode only. Split the screen.

[range] s[ubstitute] [/pattern/replace/] [options] [count] [flags]
[range] & [options] [count] [flags]
[range] ˜ [options] [count] [flags]
> Make substitutions.

su[spend][!]
st[op][!]
<suspend>
> Suspend the edit session.

ta[g][!] tagstring
> Edit the file containing the specified tag.

tagp[op][!] [file | number]
> Pop to the specified tag in the tags stack.

unm[ap][!] lhs
> Unmap a mapped string.

ve[rsion]
> Display the version of the **ex/vi** editor.

[line] vi[sual] [type] [count] [flags]
> Ex mode only. Enter **vi**.

vi[sual][!] [+cmd] [file]
> Visual mode only. Edit a new file.

viu[sage] [command]
> Display usage for a **vi** command.

[range] w[rite][!] [>>] [file]
[range] w[rite] [!] [file]
[range] wn[!] [>>] [file]
[range] wq[!] [>>] [file]
> Write the file.

[range] x[it][!] [file]
> Write the file if it has been modified.

[range] ya[nk] [buffer] [count]
> Copy the specified lines to a buffer.

[line] z [type] [count] [flags]
> Adjust the window.

SET OPTIONS

There are a large number of options that may be set (or unset) to change the editor's behavior. This section describes the options, their abbreviations and their default values.

In each entry below, the first part of the tag line is the full name of the option, followed by any equivalent abbreviations. The part in square brackets is the default value of the option. Most of the options are boolean, i.e. they are either on or off, and do not have an associated value.

Options apply to both **ex** and **vi** modes, unless otherwise specified.

altwerase [off]
> Vi only. Select an alternate word erase algorithm.

autoindent, ai [off]
> Automatically indent new lines.

autoprint, ap [off]
> Ex only. Display the current line automatically.

autowrite, aw [off]
> Write modified files automatically when changing files.

beautify, bf [off]
> Discard control characters.

cdpath [environment variable CDPATH, or current directory]
> The directory paths used as path prefixes for the **cd** command.

columns, co [80]
> Set the number of columns in the screen.

comment [off]
> Vi only. Skip leading comments in files.

directory, dir [environment variable TMPDIR, or /tmp]
> The directory where temporary files are created.

edcompatible, ed [off]
> Remember the values of the ''c'' and ''g'' suffices to the **substitute** commands, instead of initializing them as unset for each new command.

errorbells, eb [off]
> Ex only. Announce error messages with a bell.

exrc, ex [off]
> Never read startup files in the local directory.

extended [off]
> Regular expressions are extended (i.e. egrep(1) style) expressions.

flash [on]
>   Flash the screen instead of beeping the keyboard on error.

hardtabs, ht [8]
>   Set the spacing between hardware tab settings.

ignorecase, ic [off]
>   Ignore case differences in regular expressions.

keytime [6]
>   The 10th's of a second **ex/vi** waits for a subsequent key to complete a key mapping.

leftright [off]
>   Vi only. Do left-right scrolling.

lines, li [24]
>   Vi only. Set the number of lines in the screen.

lisp [off]
>   Vi only. Modify various search commands and options to work with Lisp.

>   *This option is not yet implemented.*

list [off]
>   Display lines in an unambiguous fashion.

magic [on]
>   Treat certain characters specially in regular expressions.

matchtime [7]
>   Vi only. The 10th's of a second **ex/vi** pauses on the matching character when the **showmatch** option is set.

mesg [on]
>   Permit messages from other users.

modelines, modeline [off]
>   Read the first and last few lines of each file for **ex** commands.

>   *This option will never be implemented.*

number, nu [off]
>   Precede each line displayed with its current line number.

octal [off]
>   Display unknown characters as octal numbers, instead of the default hexadecimal.

open [on]
>   Ex only. If this option is not set, the **open** and **visual** commands are disallowed.

optimize, opt [on]
>   Vi only. Optimize text throughput to dumb terminals.

>   *This option is not yet implemented.*

paragraphs, para [IPLPPPQPP LIpplpipbp]
>   Vi only. Define additional paragraph boundaries for the { and } commands.

prompt [on]
>   Ex only. Display a command prompt.

readonly, ro [off]
>   Mark the file as read-only.

recdir [/var/tmp/vi.recover]
>   The directory where recovery files are stored.

redraw, re [off]
>   Vi only. Simulate an intelligent terminal on a dumb one.

>   *This option is not yet implemented.*

remap [on]

    Remap keys until resolved.

report [5]

    Set the number of lines about which the editor reports changes.

ruler [off]

    Vi only. Display a row/column ruler on the colon command line.

scroll, scr [window / 2]

    Set the number of lines scrolled.

sections, sect [NHSHH HUnhsh]

    Vi only. Define additional section boundaries for the [[and]] commands.

shell, sh [environment variable SHELL, or /bin/sh]

    Select the shell used by the editor.

shiftwidth, sw [8]

    Set the autoindent and shift command indentation width.

showdirty [off]

    Vi only. Display an asterisk on the colon command line if the file has been modified.

showmatch, sm [off]

    Vi only. Note matching ''{'' and ''('' for ''}'' and '')'' characters.

showmode [off]

    Vi only. Display the current editor mode (command or input).

sidescroll [16]

    Vi only. Set the amount a left-right scroll will shift.

slowopen, slow [off]

    Delay display updating during text input.

    This option is not yet implemented.

sourceany [off]

    Read startup files not owned by the current user.

    This option will never be implemented.

tabstop, ts [8]

    This option sets tab widths for the editor display.

taglength, tl [0]

    Set the number of significant characters in tag names.

tags, tag [tags /var/db/libc.tags /sys/kern/tags]

    Set the list of tags files.

term, ttytype, tty [environment variable TERM]

    Set the terminal type.

terse [off]

    This option has historically made editor messages less verbose. It has no effect in this implementation.

timeout, to [on]

    Time out on keys which may be mapped.

ttywerase [off]

    Vi only. Select an alternate erase algorithm.

verbose [off]

    only. Display an error message for every error.

w300 [no default]

    Vi only. Set the window size if the baud rate is less than 1200 baud.

1

w1200 [no default]
> Vi only. Set the window size if the baud rate is equal to 1200 baud.

w9600 [no default]
> Vi only. Set the window size if the baud rate is greater than 1200 baud.

warn [on]
> Ex only. This option causes a warning message to the terminal if the file has been modified, since it was last written, before a **!** command.

window, w, wi [environment variable LINES]
> Set the window size for the screen.

wrapmargin, wm [0]
> Vi only. Break lines automatically when they reach the right-hand margin.

wrapscan, ws [on]
> Set searches to wrap around the end or beginning of the file.

writeany, wa [off]
> Turn off file-overwriting checks.

ENVIRONMENTAL VARIABLES

COLUMNS The number of columns on the screen. This value overrides any system or terminal specific values. If the COLUMNS environmental variable is not set when **ex/vi** runs, or the **columns** option is explicitly reset by the user, **ex/vi** enters the value into the environment.

EXINIT A list of **ex** startup commands, read if the variable NEXINIT is not set.

HOME The user's home directory, used as the initial directory path for the startup $HOME/.nexrc and $HOME/.exrc files. This value is also used as the default directory for the **vi cd** command.

LINES The number of rows on the screen. This value overrides any system or terminal specific values. If the LINES environmental variable is not set when **ex/vi** runs, or the **lines** option is explicitly reset by the user, **ex/vi** enters the value into the environment.

NEXINIT A list of **ex** startup commands.

SHELL The user's shell of choice (see also the **shell** option).

TERM The user's terminal type. The default is the type "unknown". If the TERM environmental variable is not set when **ex/vi** runs, or the **term** option is explicitly reset by the user, **ex/vi** enters the value into the environment.

TMPDIR The location used to stored temporary files (see also the **directory** option).

ASYNCHRONOUS EVENTS

Vi/ex handles six signals specially.

SIGALRM Vi/ex uses this signal for periodic backups of file modifications and to display "busy" messages when operations are likely to take a long time.

SIGCONT If the editor is running in visual mode, the screen is repainted.
SIGHUP

SIGTERM If the current buffer has changed since it was last written in its entirety, the editor attempts to save the modified file so it can be later recovered. See the **vi/ex** Reference manual section entitled "Recovery" for more information.

SIGINT When an interrupt occurs, the current operation is halted, and the editor returns to the command level. If interrupted during text input, the text already input is resolved into the file as if the text input had been normally terminated.

SIGQUIT Vi/ex ignores this signal.

SIGWINCH The screen is resized. See the **vi/ex** Reference manual section entitled "Sizing the Screen" for more information.

BUGS

    See the file `nvi/docs/bugs.current` for a list of the known bugs in this version.

FILES

`/bin/sh`	The default user shell.
`/etc/vi.exrc`	System-wide vi startup file.
`/tmp`	Temporary file directory.
`/var/tmp/vi.recover`	Recovery file directory.
`$HOME/.nexrc`	1st choice for user's home directory startup file.
`$HOME/.exrc`	2nd choice for user's home directory startup file.
`.nexrc`	1st choice for local directory startup file.
`.exrc`	2nd choice for local directory startup file.

SEE ALSO

    `ctags(1)`, `more(1)`, `curses(3)`, `dbopen(3)`

    The "Vi Quick Reference" card.

    "An Introduction to Display Editing with Vi", found in the "UNIX User's Manual Supplementary Documents" section of both the 4.3BSD and 4.4BSD manual sets. This document is the closest thing available to an introduction to the **vi** screen editor.

    "Ex Reference Manual (Version 3.7)", found in the "UNIX User's Manual Supplementary Documents" section of both the 4.3BSD and 4.4BSD manual sets. This document is the final reference for the **ex** editor, as distributed in most historic 4BSD and System V systems.

    "Edit: A tutorial", found in the "UNIX User's Manual Supplementary Documents" section of the 4.3BSD manual set. This document is an introduction to a simple version of the **ex** screen editor.

    "Ex/Vi Reference Manual", found in the "UNIX User's Manual Supplementary Documents" section of the 4.4BSD manual set. This document is the final reference for the **nex/nvi** text editors, as distributed in 4.4BSD and 4.4BSD-Lite.

    Roff source for all of these documents is distributed with **nex/nvi** in the `nvi/USD.doc` directory of the **nex/nvi** source code.

    The files "autowrite", "input", "quoting", and "structures", found in the `nvi/docs/internals` directory of the **nex/nvi** source code.

HISTORY

    The **nex/nvi** replacements for the **ex/vi** editor first appeared in 4.4BSD.

STANDARDS

    Nex/nvi is close to IEEE Std1003.2 ("POSIX"). That document differs from historical **ex/vi** practice in several places; there are changes to be made on both sides.

1

NAME

vis – display non-printable characters in a visual format

SYNOPSIS

vis [–cbflnostw] [–F *foldwidth*] [*file* ...]

DESCRIPTION

Vis is a filter for converting non-printable characters into a visual representation. It differs from cat -v in that the form is unique and invertible. By default, all non-graphic characters except space, tab, and new-line are encoded. A detailed description of the various visual formats is given in vis(3).

The options are as follows:

–b   Turns off prepending of backslash before up-arrow control sequences and meta characters, and disables the doubling of backslashes. This produces output which is neither invertible or precise, but does represent a minimum of change to the input. It is similar to "cat -v".

–c   Request a format which displays a small subset of the non-printable characters using C-style backslash sequences.

–F   Causes vis to fold output lines to foldwidth columns (default 80), like fold(1), except that a hidden newline sequence is used, (which is removed when inverting the file back to its original form with unvis(1)). If the last character in the encoded file does not end in a newline, a hidden newline sequence is appended to the output. This makes the output usable with various editors and other utilities which typically don't work with partial lines.

–f   Same as –F.

–l   Mark newlines with the visible sequence '\$', followed by the newline.

–n   Turns off any encoding, except for the fact that backslashes are still doubled and hidden newline sequences inserted if –f or –F is selected. When combined with the –f flag, vis becomes like an invertible version of the fold(1) utility. That is, the output can be unfolded by running the output through

–o   Request a format which displays non-printable characters as an octal number, \ddd.

–s   Only characters considered unsafe to send to a terminal are encoded. This flag allows backspace, bell, and carriage return in addition to the default space, tab and newline. unvis(1).

–t   Tabs are also encoded.

–w   White space (space-tab-newline) is also encoded.

SEE ALSO

unvis(1), vis(3)

HISTORY

The vis command appears in 4.4BSD.

1

NAME

w – who present users are and what they are doing

SYNOPSIS

w [**–hin**] [**–M** *core*] [**–N** *system*] [*user*]

DESCRIPTION

The **w** utility prints a summary of the current activity on the system, including what each user is doing. The first line displays the current time of day, how long the system has been running, the number of users logged into the system, and the load averages. The load average numbers give the number of jobs in the run queue averaged over 1, 5 and 15 minutes.

The fields output are the user's login name, the name of the terminal the user is on, the host from which the user is logged in, the time the user logged on, the time since the user last typed anything, and the name and arguments of the current process.

The options are as follows:

–h   Suppress the heading.

–i   Output is sorted by idle time.

–M   Extract values associated with the name list from the specified core instead of the default "/dev/kmem".

–N   Extract the name list from the specified system instead of the default "/vmunix".

–n   Show network addresses as numbers (normally **w** interprets addresses and attempts to display them symbolically).

If a *user* name is specified, the output is restricted to that user.

FILES

/var/run/utmp list of users on the system

SEE ALSO

who(1), finger(1), ps(1), uptime(1),

BUGS

The notion of the "current process" is muddy. The current algorithm is "the highest numbered process on the terminal that is not ignoring interrupts, or, if there is none, the highest numbered process on the terminal". This fails, for example, in critical sections of programs like the shell and editor, or when faulty programs running in the background fork and fail to ignore interrupts. (In cases where no process can be found, **w** prints "–".)

The CPU time is only an estimate, in particular, if someone leaves a background process running after logging out, the person currently on that terminal is "charged" with the time.

Background processes are not shown, even though they account for much of the load on the system.

Sometimes processes, typically those in the background, are printed with null or garbaged arguments. In these cases, the name of the command is printed in parentheses.

The **w** utility does not know about the new conventions for detection of background jobs. It will sometimes find a background job instead of the right one.

1

COMPATIBILITY
The −f, −1, −s, and −w flags are no longer supported.

HISTORY
The w command appeared in UNIX3.0.

1

NAME

wait – await process completion

SYNOPSIS

wait [*pid*]

DESCRIPTION

If invoked with no arguments, the **wait** utility waits until all existing child processes in the background have terminated.

Available operands:

pid   If a *pid* operand is specified, and it is the process ID of a background child process that still exists, the **wait** utility waits until that process has completed and consumes its status information, without consuming the status information of any other process.

        If a pid operand is specified that is not the process ID of a child background process that still exists, **wait** exits without waiting for any processes to complete.

The **wait** utility exits with one of the following values:

0   The **wait** utility was invoked with no operands and all of the existing background child processes have terminated, or the process specified by the pid operand exited normally with 0 as its exit status.

>0   The specified process did not exist and its exit status information was not available, or the specified process existed or its exit status information was available, and it terminated with a non-zero exit status.

If the specified process terminated abnormally due to the receipt of a signal, the exit status information of **wait** contains that termination status as well.

STANDARDS

The **wait** command is expected to be IEEE Std1003.2 (''POSIX'') compatible.

1

NAME
wall – write a message to users

SYNOPSIS
wall [*file*]

DESCRIPTION
Wall displays the contents of *file* or, by default, its standard input, on the terminals of all currently logged in users.

Only the super-user can write on the terminals of users who have chosen to deny messages or are using a program which automatically denies messages.

SEE ALSO
mesg(1), talk(1), write(1), shutdown(8)

HISTORY
A wall command appeared in Version 7 AT&T UNIX.

1

NAME

wc – word, line, and byte count

SYNOPSIS

wc [–clw] [*file* ...]

DESCRIPTION

The wc utility displays the number of lines, words, and bytes contained in each input *file* (or standard input, by default) to the standard output. A line is defined as a string of characters delimited by a <newline> character, and a word is defined as a string of characters delimited by white space characters. White space characters are the set of characters for which the isspace(3) function returns true. If more than one input file is specified, a line of cumulative counts for all the files is displayed on a separate line after the output for the last file.

The following options are available:

–c   The number of bytes in each input file is written to the standard output.

–l   The number of lines in each input file is written to the standard output.

–w   The number of words in each input file is written to the standard output.

When an option is specified, wc only reports the information requested by that option. The default action is equivalent to specifying all of the flags.

If no files are specified, the standard input is used and no file name is displayed.

The wc utility exits 0 on success, and >0 if an error occurs.

SEE ALSO

isspace(3)

COMPATIBILITY

Historically, the wc utility was documented to define a word as a "maximal string of characters delimited by <space>, <tab> or <newline> characters". The implementation, however, didn't handle non-printing characters correctly so that " ^D^E " counted as 6 spaces, while "foo^D^Ebar" counted as 8 characters. 4BSD systems after 4.3BSD modified the implementation to be consistent with the documentation. This implementation defines a "word" in terms of the isspace(3) function, as required by IEEE Std1003.2 ("POSIX").

STANDARDS

The wc function conforms to IEEE Std1003.2 ("POSIX").

1

NAME
what – show what versions of object modules were used to construct a file

SYNOPSIS
what *name* ...

DESCRIPTION
What reads each file *name* and searches for sequences of the form ''@(#)'' as inserted by the source code control system. It prints the remainder of the string following this marker, up to a null character, newline, double quote, or ''> character.''

BUGS
As BSD is not licensed to distribute SCCS this is a rewrite of the **what** command which is part of SCCS, and may not behave exactly the same as that command does.

HISTORY
The **what** command appeared in 4.0BSD.

NAME
  whatis – describe what a command is

SYNOPSIS
  whatis [**−M** *path*] [**−m** *path*] *command* ...

DESCRIPTION
  Whatis looks up a given command and gives the header line from the manual page. You can then use the
  man(1) command to get more information.

  The options are as follows:

  −M *path* Override the list of standard directories **whatis** searches for its database named
      "whatis.db". The supplied *path* must be a colon ":" separated list of directories. This
      search path may also be set using the environment variable MANPATH.

  −m *path* Augment the list of standard directories **whatis** searches for its database named
      "whatis.db". The supplied *path* must be a colon ":" separated list of directories. These
      directories will be searched before the standard directories or the directories supplied with the
      −M option or the MANPATH environment variable are searched.

ENVIRONMENT
  MANPATH The standard search path used by man(1) may be overridden by specifying a path in the
      MANPATH environment variable.

FILES
  whatis.db name of the whatis database

SEE ALSO
  apropos(1), man(1), whereis(1)

HISTORY
  The **whatis** command appeared in 3.0BSD.

1

NAME
> **whereis** – locate programs

SYNOPSIS
> **whereis** [*program ...*]

DESCRIPTION
> The **whereis** utility checks the standard binary directories for the specified programs, printing out the paths of any it finds.
>
> The path searched is the string returned by the **sysctl**(8) utility for the ''user.cs_path'' string.

SEE ALSO
> **sysctl**(8),

COMPATIBILITY
> The historic flags and arguments for the **whereis** utility are no longer available in this version.

HISTORY
> The **whereis** command appeared in 3.0BSD.

1

NAME

which – locate a program file including aliases and paths

SYNOPSIS

which [*name*] ...

DESCRIPTION

Which takes a list of names and looks for the files which would be executed had these names been given as commands. Each argument is expanded if it is aliased, and searched for along the user's path. Both aliases and path are taken from the user's .cshrc file.

FILES

~/.cshrc source of aliases and path values

DIAGNOSTICS

A diagnostic is given for names which are aliased to more than a single word, or if an executable file with the argument name was not found in the path.

BUGS

Must be executed by a csh(1), or some other shell which knows about aliases.

HISTORY

The which command appeared in 3.0BSD.

1

NAME
who – display who is logged in

SYNOPSIS
who [*am I*] [*file*]

DESCRIPTION
The utility **who** displays a list of all users currently logged on, showing for each user the login name, tty name, the date and time of login, and hostname if not local.

Available options:

am I Returns the invoker's real user name.

file By default, **who** gathers information from the file /var/run/utmp. An alternate *file* may be specified which is usually /var/run/wtmp (or /var/run/wtmp.[0-6] depending on site policy as wtmp can grow quite large and daily versions may or may not be kept around after compression by ac(8)). The wtmp file contains a record of every login, logout, crash, shutdown and date change since wtmp was last truncated or created.

If /var/log/wtmp is being used as the file, the user name may be empty or one of the special characters 'l', '}' and '~'. Logouts produce an output line without any user name. For more information on the special characters, see utmp(5).

FILES
/var/run/utmp
/var/log/wtmp
/var/log/wtmp.[0-6]

SEE ALSO
last(1), users(1), getuid(2), utmp(5)

HISTORY
A **who** command appeared in Version 6 AT&T UNIX.

NAME

    whoami – display effective user id

SYNOPSIS

    whoami

DESCRIPTION

    The **whoami** utility has been obsoleted by the id(1) utility, and is equivalent to ''**id** **−un**''. The command ''**id** **−p**'' is suggested for normal interactive use.

    The **whoami** utility displays your effective user ID as a name.

    The **whoami** utility exits 0 on success, and >0 if an error occurs.

SEE ALSO

    id(1)

1

NAME

whois – Internet user name directory service

SYNOPSIS

whois [–h *hostname*] *name* ...

DESCRIPTION

Whois looks up records in the Network Information Center (NIC) database.

The options are as follows:

–h   Use the specified host instead of the default NIC (nic.ddn.mil).

The operands specified to whois are concatenated together (separated by white-space) and presented to the whois server.

The default action, unless directed otherwise with a special *name*, is to do a very broad search, looking for matches to *name* in all types of records and most fields (name, nicknames, hostname, net address, etc.) in the database. For more information as to what *name* operands have special meaning, and how to guide the search, use the special name ''*help*''.

SEE ALSO

RFC 812: Nicname/Whois

HISTORY

The whois command appeared in 4.3BSD.

NAME

window – window environment

SYNOPSIS

window [−t] [−f] [−d] [−e *escape-char*] [−c *command*]

DESCRIPTION

Window implements a window environment on ASCII terminals.

A window is a rectangular portion of the physical terminal screen associated with a set of processes. Its size and position can be changed by the user at any time. Processes communicate with their window in the same way they normally interact with a terminal–through their standard input, output, and diagnostic file descriptors. The window program handles the details of redirecting input and output to and from the windows. At any one time, only one window can receive input from the keyboard, but all windows can simultaneously send output to the display.

When **window** starts up, the commands (see long commands below) contained in the file .windowrc in the user's home directory are executed. If it does not exist, two equal sized windows spanning the terminal screen are created by default.

The command line options are

−t   Turn on terse mode (see **terse** command below).

−f   Fast. Don't perform any startup action.

−d   Ignore .windowrc and create the two default windows instead.

−e *escape-char*
> Set the escape character to *escape-char*. *Escape-char* can be a single character, or in the form ^X where X is any character, meaning control–X.

−c *command*
> Execute the string *command* as a long command (see below) before doing anything else.

Windows can overlap and are framed as necessary. Each window is named by one of the digits "1" to "9". This one-character identifier, as well as a user definable label string, are displayed with the window on the top edge of its frame. A window can be designated to be in the *foreground*, in which case it will always be on top of all normal, non-foreground windows, and can be covered only by other foreground windows. A window need not be completely within the edges of the terminal screen. Thus a large window (possibly larger than the screen) may be positioned to show only a portion of its full size.

Each window has a cursor and a set of control functions. Most intelligent terminal operations such as line and character deletion and insertion are supported. Display modes such as underlining and reverse video are available if they are supported by the terminal. In addition, similar to terminals with multiple pages of memory, each window has a text buffer which can have more lines than the window itself.

Process Environment

With each newly created window, a shell program is spawned with its process environment tailored to that window. Its standard input, output, and diagnostic file descriptors are bound to one end of either a pseudo-terminal (pty(4)) or a UNIX domain socket (socketpair(4)). If a pseudo-terminal is used, then its special characters and modes (see stty(1)) are copied from the physical terminal. A termcap(5) entry tailored to this window is created and passed as environment (environ(5)) variable TERMCAP. The termcap entry contains the window's size and characteristics as well as information from the physical terminal, such as the existence of underline, reverse video, and other display modes, and the codes produced by the terminal's function keys, if any. In addition, the window size attributes of the pseudo-terminal are set to reflect the size of this window, and updated whenever it is changed by the user. In particular, the editor vi(1) uses this information to redraw its display.

Operation

During normal execution, **window** can be in one of two states: conversation mode and command mode. In conversation mode, the terminal's real cursor is placed at the cursor position of a particular window--called the current window--and input from the keyboard is sent to the process in that window. The current window is always on top of all other windows, except those in foreground. In addition, it is set apart by highlighting its identifier and label in reverse video.

Typing **window**'s escape character (normally ^P) in conversation mode switches it into command mode. In command mode, the top line of the terminal screen becomes the command prompt window, and **window** interprets input from the keyboard as commands to manipulate windows.

There are two types of commands: short commands are usually one or two key strokes; long commands are strings either typed by the user in the command window (see the "**:**" command below), or read from a file (see **source** below).

Short Commands

Below, # represents one of the digits "1" to "9" corresponding to the windows 1 to 9. ^X means control–*X*, where *X* is any character. In particular, ^^ is control–^. *Escape* is the escape key, or ^[.

Select window # as the current window and return to conversation mode.

%#   Select window # but stay in command mode.

^^   Select the previous window and return to conversation mode. This is useful for toggling between two windows.

escape
             Return to conversation mode.

^P   Return to conversation mode and write ^P to the current window. Thus, typing two ^P's in conversation mode sends one to the current window. If the **window** escape is changed to some other character, that character takes the place of ^P here.

?   List a short summary of commands.

^L   Refresh the screen.

q   Exit **window**. Confirmation is requested.

^Z   Suspend **window**.

w   Create a new window. The user is prompted for the positions of the upper left and lower right corners of the window. The cursor is placed on the screen and the keys "h", "j", "k", and "l" move the cursor left, down, up, and right, respectively. The keys "H", "J", "K", and "L" move the cursor to the respective limits of the screen. Typing a number before the movement keys repeats the movement that number of times. Return enters the cursor position as the upper left corner of the window. The lower right corner is entered in the same manner. During this process, the placement of the new window is indicated by a rectangular box drawn on the screen, corresponding to where the new window will be framed. Typing escape at any point cancels this command.

This window becomes the current window, and is given the first available ID. The default buffer size is used (see *default_nline* command below).

Only fully visible windows can be created this way.

c #   Close window #. The process in the window is sent the hangup signal (see kill(1)). Csh(1) should handle this signal correctly and cause no problems.

m #   Move window # to another location. A box in the shape of the window is drawn on the screen to indicate the new position of the window, and the same keys as those for the **w** command are used to position the box. The window can be moved partially off-screen.

M #   Move window # to its previous position.

s #   Change the size of window #. The user is prompted to enter the new lower right corner of the window. A box is drawn to indicate the new window size. The same keys used in **w** and **m** are used to enter the position.

S #   Change window # to its previous size.

^Y   Scroll the current window up by one line.

^E   Scroll the current window down by one line.

^U   Scroll the current window up by half the window size.

^D   Scroll the current window down by half the window size.

^B   Scroll the current window up by the full window size.

^F   Scroll the current window down by the full window size.

h   Move the cursor of the current window left by one column.

j   Move the cursor of the current window down by one line.

k   Move the cursor of the current window up by one line.

l   Move the cursor of the current window right by one column.

y   Yank. The user is prompted to enter two points within the current window. Then the content of the current window between those two points is saved in the yank buffer.

p   Put. The content of the yank buffer is written to the current window as input.

^S   Stop output in the current window.

^Q   Start output in the current window.

:   Enter a line to be executed as long commands. Normal line editing characters (erase character, erase word, erase line) are supported.

Long Commands

Long commands are a sequence of statements parsed much like a programming language, with a syntax similar to that of C. Numeric and string expressions and variables are supported, as well as conditional statements.

There are two data types: string and number. A string is a sequence of letters or digits beginning with a letter. ''_'' and ''.'' are considered letters. Alternately, non-alphanumeric characters can be included in strings by quoting them in ''"'' or escaping them with ''\''. In addition, the ''\'' sequences of C are supported, both inside and outside quotes (e.g., ''\n'' is a new line, ''\r'' a carriage return). For example, these are legal strings: abcde01234, "&#$^*&#", ab"'$#"cd, ab\$\#cd, "/usr/ucb/window".

A number is an integer value in one of three forms: a decimal number, an octal number preceded by "0", or a hexadecimal number preceded by "0x" or "0X". The natural machine integer size is used (i.e., the signed integer type of the C compiler). As in C, a non-zero number represents a boolean true.

The character "#" begins a comment which terminates at the end of the line.

A statement is either a conditional or an expression. Expression statements are terminated with a new line or ";". To continue an expression on the next line, terminate the first line with "\".

Conditional Statement

Window has a single control structure: the fully bracketed if statement in the form

```
if <expr> then
<statement>
...
elsif <expr> then
<statement>
...
else
<statement>
...
endif
```

The else and elsif parts are optional, and the latter can be repeated any number of times. <Expr> must be numeric.

Expressions

Expressions in window are similar to those in the C language, with most C operators supported on numeric operands. In addition, some are overloaded to operate on strings.

When an expression is used as a statement, its value is discarded after evaluation. Therefore, only expressions with side effects (assignments and function calls) are useful as statements.

Single valued (no arrays) variables are supported, of both numeric and string values. Some variables are predefined. They are listed below.

The operators in order of increasing precedence:

<expr1> = *<expr2>*

Assignment. The variable of name *<expr1>*, which must be string valued, is assigned the result of *<expr2>*. Returns the value of *<expr2>*.

<expr1> ? *<expr2>* : *<expr3>*

Returns the value of *<expr2>* if *<expr1>* evaluates true (non-zero numeric value); returns the value of *<expr3>* otherwise. Only one of *<expr2>* and *<expr3>* is evaluated. *<Expr1>* must be numeric.

<expr1> || *<expr2>*

Logical or. Numeric values only. Short circuit evaluation is supported (i.e., if *<expr1>* evaluates true, then *<expr2>* is not evaluated).

<expr1> && *<expr2>*

Logical and with short circuit evaluation. Numeric values only.

1

<expr1> | *<expr2>*
>   Bitwise or. Numeric values only.

<expr1> ^ *<expr2>*
>   Bitwise exclusive or. Numeric values only.

<expr1> & *<expr2>*
>   Bitwise and. Numeric values only.

<expr1> == *<expr2>*, *<expr1>* != <expr2>
>   Comparison (equal and not equal, respectively). The boolean result (either 1 or 0) of the comparison is returned. The operands can be numeric or string valued. One string operand forces the other to be converted to a string in necessary.

<expr1> < *<expr2>*, *<expr1>* > *<expr2>*, *<expr1>* <= *<expr2>*,
>   Less than, greater than, less than or equal to, greater than or equal to. Both numeric and string values, with automatic conversion as above.

<expr1> << *<expr2>*, *<expr1>* >> *<expr2>*
>   If both operands are numbers, *<expr1>* is bit shifted left (or right) by *<expr2>* bits. If *<expr1>* is a string, then its first (or last) *<expr2>* characters are returns (if *<expr2>* is also a string, then its length is used in place of its value).

<expr1> + *<expr2>*, *<expr1>* - *<expr2>*
>   Addition and subtraction on numbers. For "+", if one argument is a string, then the other is converted to a string, and the result is the concatenation of the two strings.

<expr1> * *<expr2>*, *<expr1>* / *<expr2>*, *<expr1>* % *<expr2>*
>   Multiplication, division, modulo. Numbers only.

−*<expr>*, ~*<expr>*, !*<expr>*, \$*<expr>*, \$?*<expr>*
>   The first three are unary minus, bitwise complement and logical complement on numbers only. The operator, "\$", takes *<expr>* and returns the value of the variable of that name. If *<expr>* is numeric with value n and it appears within an alias macro (see below), then it refers to the nth argument of the alias invocation. "\$?" tests for the existence of the variable *<expr>*, and returns 1 if it exists or 0 otherwise.

<expr>(`<arglist>`)
>   Function call. *<Expr>* must be a string that is the unique prefix of the name of a builtin **window** function or the full name of a user defined alias macro. In the case of a builtin function, `<arglist>` can be in one of two forms:
>
>   <expr1>, <expr2>, ...
>   argname1 = <expr1>, argname2 = <expr2>, ...
>
>   The two forms can in fact be intermixed, but the result is unpredictable. Most arguments can be omitted; default values will be supplied for them. The *argnames* can be unique prefixes of the argument names. The commas separating arguments are used only to disambiguate, and can usually be omitted.
>
>   Only the first argument form is valid for user defined aliases. Aliases are defined using the **alias** builtin function (see below). Arguments are accessed via a variant of the variable mechanism (see "\$" operator above).
>
>   Most functions return value, but some are used for side effect only and so must be used as statements. When a function or an alias is used as a statement, the parentheses surrounding the argument list may be omitted. Aliases return no value.

1

Builtin Functions

The arguments are listed by name in their natural order. Optional arguments are in square brackets '[ ]'. Arguments that have no names are in angle brackets '<>'. An argument meant to be a boolean flag (often named *flag*) can be one of *on*, *off*, *yes*, *no*, *true*, or *false*, with obvious meanings, or it can be a numeric expression, in which case a non-zero value is true.

alias([*<string>*], [*<string-list)>*])

>If no argument is given, all currently defined alias macros are listed. Otherwise, *<string>* is defined as an alias, with expansion *<string-list >>*. The previous definition of *<string>*, if any, is returned. Default for *<string-list>* is no change.

close(*<window-list>*)

>Close the windows specified in *<window-list>*. If *<window-list>* is the word *all*, than all windows are closed. No value is returned.

cursormodes([*modes*])

>Set the window cursor to *modes*. *Modes* is the bitwise or of the mode bits defined as the variables *m_ul* (underline), *m_rev* (reverse video), *m_blk* (blinking), and *m_grp* (graphics, terminal dependent). Return value is the previous modes. Default is no change. For example, cursor(m_revm_blk) sets the window cursors to blinking reverse video.

default_nline([*nline*])

>Set the default buffer size to *nline*. Initially, it is 48 lines. Returns the old default buffer size. Default is no change. Using a very large buffer can slow the program down considerably.

default_shell([*<string-list>*])

>Set the default window shell program to *<string-list>*. Returns the first string in the old shell setting. Default is no change. Initially, the default shell is taken from the environment variable SHELL.

default_smooth([*flag*])

>Set the default value of the *smooth* argument to the command **window** (see below). The argument is a boolean flag (one of *on*, *off*, *yes*, *no*, *true*, *false*, or a number, as described above). Default is no change. The old value (as a number) is returned. The initial value is 1 (true).

echo([*window*], [*<string-list>*])

>Write the list of strings, *<string-list>*, to **window**, separated by spaces and terminated with a new line. The strings are only displayed in the window, the processes in the window are not involved (see **write** below). No value is returned. Default is the current window.

escape([*escapec*])

>Set the escape character to *escape-char*. Returns the old escape character as a one-character string. Default is no change. *Escapec* can be a string of a single character, or in the form −^X, meaning control−*X*.

foreground([*window*], [*flag*])

>Move **window** in or out of foreground. *Flag* is a boolean value. The old foreground flag is returned. Default for **window** is the current window, default for *flag* is no change.

label([*window*], [*label*])

>Set the label of **window** to *label*. Returns the old label as a string. Default for **window** is the current window, default for *label* is no change. To turn off a label, set it to an empty string ("").

list( ) No arguments. List the identifiers and labels of all windows. No value is returned.

select([*window*]**)**

Make **window** the current window. The previous current window is returned. Default is no change.

source(*filename* **)**

Read and execute the long commands in *filename*. Returns −1 if the file cannot be read, 0 otherwise.

terse([flag]**)**

Set terse mode to *flag*. In terse mode, the command window stays hidden even in command mode, and errors are reported by sounding the terminal's bell. *Flag* can take on the same values as in *foreground* above. Returns the old terse flag. Default is no change.

unalias(*alias* **)**

Undefine *alias*. Returns -1 if *alias* does not exist, 0 otherwise.

unset(*variable* **)**

Undefine *variable*. Returns -1 if *variable* does not exist, 0 otherwise.

variables( )

No arguments. List all variables. No value is returned.

window([*row*], [*column*], [*nrow*], [*ncol*], [*nline*], [*label*], [*pty*], [*frame*], [*mapnl*], [*keepopen*], [*smooth*], [*shell*]**).**

Open a window with upper left corner at *row*, *column* and size *nrow*, *ncol*. If *nline* is specified, then that many lines are allocated for the text buffer. Otherwise, the default buffer size is used. Default values for *row*, *column*, *nrow*, and *ncol* are, respectively, the upper, left-most, lower, or right-most extremes of the screen. *Label* is the label string. *Frame*, *pty*, and *mapnl* are flag values interpreted in the same way as the argument to *foreground* (see above); they mean, respectively, put a frame around this window (default true), allocate pseudo-terminal for this window rather than socketpair (default true), and map new line characters in this window to carriage return and line feed (default true if socketpair is used, false otherwise). Normally, a window is automatically closed when its process exits. Setting *keepopen* to true (default false) prevents this action. When *smooth* is true, the screen is updated more frequently (for this window) to produce a more terminal-like behavior. The default value of *smooth* is set by the *default_smooth* command (see above). *Shell* is a list of strings that will be used as the shell program to place in the window (default is the program specified by *default_shell*, see above). The created window's identifier is returned as a number.

write([*window*], [*<string–list>*]**)**

Send the list of strings, *<string-list>*, to **window**, separated by spaces but not terminated with a new line. The strings are actually given to the window as input. No value is returned. Default is the current window.

Predefined Variables

These variables are for information only. Redefining them does not affect the internal operation of **window**.

baud The baud rate as a number between 50 and 38400.

modes   The display modes (reverse video, underline, blinking, graphics) supported by the physical terminal. The value of *modes* is the bitwise or of some of the one bit values, *m_blk*, *m_grp*, *m_rev*, and *m_ul* (see below). These values are useful in setting the window cursors' modes (see *cursormodes* above).

m_blk   The blinking mode bit.

m_grp   The graphics mode bit (not very useful).

m_rev   The reverse video mode bit.

m_ul   The underline mode bit.

ncol   The number of columns on the physical screen.

nrow   The number of rows on the physical screen.

term   The terminal type. The standard name, found in the second name field of the terminal's TERMCAP entry, is used.

ENVIRONMENT

Window utilizes these environment variables: HOME, SHELL, TERM, TERMCAP, WINDOW_ID.

FILES

~/.windowrc   startup command file.
/dev/[pt]ty[pq]? pseudo-terminal devices.

HISTORY

The window command appeared in 4.3BSD.

DIAGNOSTICS

Should be self explanatory.

1

NAME

write – send a message to another user

SYNOPSIS

write *user* [*ttyname*]

DESCRIPTION

Write allows you to communicate with other users, by copying lines from your terminal to theirs.

When you run the **write** command, the user you are writing to gets a message of the form:

```
Message from yourname@yourhost on yourtty at hh:mm ...
```

Any further lines you enter will be copied to the specified user's terminal. If the other user wants to reply, they must run **write** as well.

When you are done, type an end-of-file or interrupt character. The other user will see the message EOF indicating that the conversation is over.

You can prevent people (other than the super-user) from writing to you with the mesg(1) command. Some commands, for example nroff(1) and pr(1), disallow writing automatically, so that your output isn't overwritten.

If the user you want to write to is logged in on more than one terminal, you can specify which terminal to write to by specifying the terminal name as the second operand to the **write** command. Alternatively, you can let **write** select one of the terminals – it will pick the one with the shortest idle time. This is so that if the user is logged in at work and also dialed up from home, the message will go to the right place.

The traditional protocol for writing to someone is that the string '−o', either at the end of a line or on a line by itself, means that it's the other person's turn to talk. The string 'oo' means that the person believes the conversation to be over.

SEE ALSO

mesg(1), talk(1), who(1)

HISTORY

A **write** command appeared in Version 6 AT&T UNIX.

1

NAME

xargs – construct argument list(s) and execute utility

SYNOPSIS

xargs [–t] [[–x] –n *number*] [–s *size*] [*utility* [*arguments* ...]]

DESCRIPTION

The **xargs** utility reads space, tab, newline and end-of-file delimited arguments from the standard input and executes the specified *utility* with them as arguments.

The utility and any arguments specified on the command line are given to the *utility* upon each invocation, followed by some number of the arguments read from standard input. The *utility* is repeatedly executed until standard input is exhausted.

Spaces, tabs and newlines may be embedded in arguments using single (" ' ") or double (" " ") quotes or backslashes ("\"). Single quotes escape all non-single quote characters, excluding newlines, up to the matching single quote. Double quotes escape all non-double quote characters, excluding newlines, up to the matching double quote. Any single character, including newlines, may be escaped by a backslash.

The options are as follows:

–n *number*
> Set the maximum number of arguments taken from standard input for each invocation of the utility. An invocation of *utility* will use less than *number* standard input arguments if the number of bytes accumulated (see the –s option) exceeds the specified *size* or there are fewer than *number* arguments remaining for the last invocation of *utility*. The current default value for *number* is 5000.

–s *size*
> Set the maximum number of bytes for the command line length provided to *utility*. The sum of the length of the utility name and the arguments passed to *utility* (including NULL terminators) will be less than or equal to this number. The current default value for *size* is ARG_MAX - 2048.

–t
> Echo the command to be executed to standard error immediately before it is executed.

–x
> Force **xargs** to terminate immediately if a command line containing *number* arguments will not fit in the specified (or default) command line length.

If no *utility* is specified, echo(1) is used.

Undefined behavior may occur if *utility* reads from the standard input.

The **xargs** utility exits immediately (without processing any further input) if a command line cannot be assembled, *utility* cannot be invoked, an invocation of the utility is terminated by a signal or an invocation of the utility exits with a value of 255.

The **xargs** utility exits with a value of 0 if no error occurs. If *utility* cannot be invoked, **xargs** exits with a value of 127. If any other error occurs, **xargs** exits with a value of 1.

SEE ALSO

echo(1), find(1)

STANDARDS

The **xargs** utility is expected to be IEEE Std1003.2 ("POSIX") compliant.

1

NAME
xchess – X chess display

SYNOPSIS
xchess [option ...] [white-display] [black-display]

DESCRIPTION
xchess is a chess display program which allows players to play a game on either one or two displays, or play a chess-playing program. It uses the **X** window system. If one or no display names are given, it will open up one window and both black and white at the same board. If two displays are given, **xchess** will accept moves from each player in his turn. Black's board will be drawn with his pieces at the bottom.

xchess will not allow a player to make an illegal move. It accepts all legal moves, including castling and pawn capture *en passant*.

OPTIONS
-d   Turn on debugging.

-f record-file
Use **record-file** for saving the game when the **Save** button is selected, or if the **-s** flag is given. The default is "xchess.game".

-r saved-game
Start with the position at the end of the saved game in the named file. This file may be the result of the **Save** command, and may be in either English or International format. When reading moves, one move it made per second.

-q   Don't pause for a second every time a move is made when a game is being restored.

-v   Whenever a piece is moved, outline the path with a "lightning bolt". This option and the **-n** option are useful if you don't want to miss an opponent's move when he makes it.

-i   Use International format for recording moves (squares numbered 1-8, a-h) as opposed to English (e.g, *p/k4xp/q5*).

-t moves/timeunit
Allows **timeunit** seconds for every **moves** moves. If either player exceeds this allowance both recieve a message saying informing them of this fact.

-c   Play the computer. **xchess** will start up a chess-playing program (currently the only one it knows how to talk to is **GNU Chess**).

-p program
The name of the program to use if the **-c** option is given. The default is "/usr/public/gnuchess". Note that **gnuchess** must be compiled with the *compat* flag (in the file "main.c") set to 1.

-b   If the **-c** flag was given, have the computer play white.

-bnw   If the display has more than one display plane (i.e, is color), pretend it's black and white.

-s   Save the moves in the record file as they are made. This is useful if you don't want your game to be lost when **xchess** core dumps.

-n   Be noisy – beep after every move is made.

-h host Run GNU Chess on the specified **host**.

-R   Randomly chose who plays white and who plays black, if two displays are given.

CONTROLS
The window is divided up into several sub-windows. The pieces are moved by pushing down any mouse button on top of the piece, moving to the destination square, and releasing it. Castling is done by moving the king to the right square. If you push down on a piece and then let the button up without moving it, you must move that piece. ("Touch it, move it.")

The progress of the game is listed in the "Game Record" window. Error messages and such things are printed in the "Message" window. Both these windows have scroll bars that you can use to move around. There are also windows for clocks and for a record of the pieces captured.

If you type any keys in the window, the text will go into the message window of both players. This provides a simple communication facility.

There are 9 buttons in the control window. They are as follows:

Draw   Both players must push this button to agree on a draw (just one is ok if only one display is being used).

Resign   The player whose turn it is to move resigns.

Reset   Start over from the beginning.

Back   Retract a move. If two displays are being used the other player will be asked to confirm this.

Fwd   This will re-play the most recently retracted move. This button in conjunction with **Back** is useful for "scrolling around" in a saved game.

Save   Save the game in the record file.

Flip   Rotate the board so that Black will have his pieces at the bottom.

Switch   Change the mapping of boards to players.

Pause   This button has two functions. When a game is being restored, pieces will be moved once a second. Hitting **Pause** will stop this process, and hitting it again will restart it. During the time that it is stopped no other action can be made except restarting it. While a game is being played, **Pause** will stop the clock and restart it.

DEFAULTS

xchess uses the following *.Xdefaults*:

Noisy   The -n flag.

SaveMoves
        The -s flag.

Algebraic
        The -i flag.

BlackAndWhite
        The -bnw flag.

QuickRestore
        The -q flag.

Flash   The -v flag.

NumFlashes
        How many times to flash the move. The default is 5.

FlashWidth
        How big to make the lightning bolt. The default is 10 pixels.

ProgName
        The -p option. This may also be changed in the Makefile (-DDEF_PROG_NAME).

ProgHost
        The -h option.

RecordFile
        The -f option.

BlackPiece
        The color of the black pieces.

WhitePiece
>   The color of the white pieces.

BorderColor
>   The color of the borders.

BlackSquare
>   The color of the black squares.

WhiteSquare
>   The color of the white squares.

TextColor
>   The color of routine messages and the move record text.

ErrorText
>   The color of error messages.

PlayerText
>   The color of player-entered text.

TextBack
>   The background color for the two text windows.

CursorColor
>   The color of the mouse and the text cursors.

SEE ALSO
>   X(8), gnuchess(1), chess(5)

AUTHOR
>   Wayne A. Christopher (faustus@ic.berkeley.edu)

BUGS

Checkmate and stalemate are not detected, so the appropriate player must resign or agree to a draw respectively.

Switch doesn't work.

If you are playing **gnuchess**, and you select Undo a few times so that it is **gnuchess**'s turn to move, it won't do anything.

NAME

xsend, xget, enroll – private encrypted mail

SYNOPSIS

xsend *person*
xget
enroll

DESCRIPTION

The **xsend**, **xget**, and **enroll** utilities initiate and conduct encrypted mail on top of the regular mail(1) system. To get started, one enrolls with the utility **enroll** which requests a password which is then required before the enrollee can read mail sent via **xsend**.

Xsend is used just like mail, but will not 'cc' messages. The regular mail(1) facilities deliver mail stating when encrypted mail has arrived.

The **xget** command is used to read the encrypted mail; it requests the enrolled password before allowing the receipt of mail sent with **xsend**.

FILES

/var/spool/secretmail/*.key: keys
/var/spool/secretmail/*.[0-9]: messages

SEE ALSO

mail(1)

HISTORY

The **xsend** command appeared in Version 7 AT&T UNIX.

1

NAME

　　　`xstr` – extract strings from C programs to implement shared strings

SYNOPSIS

　　　`xstr` [−c] [−] [*file*]

DESCRIPTION

　　　`Xstr` maintains a file `strings` into which strings in component parts of a large program are hashed. These strings are replaced with references to this common area. This serves to implement shared constant strings, most useful if they are also read-only.

　　　Available options:

　　　−　　　　`Xstr` reads from the standard input.

　　　−c　　　`Xstr` will extract the strings from the C source *file* or the standard input (−), replacing string references by expressions of the form (&xstr[number]) for some number. An appropriate declaration of `xstr` is prepended to the file. The resulting C text is placed in the file x . c, to then be compiled. The strings from this file are placed in the `strings` data base if they are not there already. Repeated strings and strings which are suffixes of existing strings do not cause changes to the data base.

　　　After all components of a large program have been compiled a file xs . c declaring the common `xstr` space can be created by a command of the form

```
xstr
```

　　　The file xs . c should then be compiled and loaded with the rest of the program. If possible, the array can be made read-only (shared) saving space and swap overhead.

　　　`Xstr` can also be used on a single file. A command

```
xstr name
```

　　　creates files x . c and xs . c as before, without using or affecting any `strings` file in the same directory.

　　　It may be useful to run `xstr` after the C preprocessor if any macro definitions yield strings or if there is conditional code which contains strings which may not, in fact, be needed. An appropriate command sequence for running `xstr` after the C preprocessor is:

```
cc −E name.c | xstr −c −
cc −c x.c
mv x.o name.o
```

　　　`Xstr` does not touch the file `strings` unless new items are added, thus make(1) can avoid remaking xs . o unless truly necessary.

FILES

`strings`	Data base of strings
`x.c`	Massaged C source
`xs.c`	C source for definition of array 'xstr'
`/tmp/xs*`	Temp file when 'xstr name' doesn't touch `strings`

1

SEE ALSO
    mkstr(1)

BUGS
    If a string is a suffix of another string in the data base, but the shorter string is seen first by **xstr** both strings will be placed in the data base, when just placing the longer one there will do.

HISTORY
    The **xstr** command appeared in 3.0BSD.

1

NAME

> yacc – an LALR(1) parser generator

SYNOPSIS

> **yacc** [**-dlrtv**] [**-b** *file_prefix*] [**-p** *symbol_prefix*] *filename*

DESCRIPTION

> *Yacc* reads the grammar specification in the file *filename* and generates an LR(1) parser for it. The parsers consist of a set of LALR(1) parsing tables and a driver routine written in the C programming language. *Yacc* normally writes the parse tables and the driver routine to the file *y.tab.c.*

> The following options are available:

> > **-b** *file_prefix*
> >
> > > The **-b** option changes the prefix prepended to the output file names to the string denoted by *file_prefix*. The default prefix is the character *y*.
> >
> > **-d**   The **-d** option causes the header file *y.tab.h* to be written.
> >
> > **-l**   If the **-l** option is not specified, *yacc* will insert #line directives in the generated code. The #line directives let the C compiler relate errors in the generated code to the user's original code. If the **-l** option is specified, *yacc* will not insert the #line directives. Any #line directives specified by the user will be retained.
> >
> > **-p** *symbol_prefix*
> >
> > > The **-p** option changes the prefix prepended to yacc-generated symbols to the string denoted by *symbol_prefix*. The default prefix is the string *yy*.
> >
> > **-r**   The **-r** option causes *yacc* to produce separate files for code and tables. The code file is named *y.code.c,* and the tables file is named *y.tab.c.*
> >
> > **-t**   The **-t** option changes the preprocessor directives generated by *yacc* so that debugging statements will be incorporated in the compiled code.
> >
> > **-v**   The **-v** option causes a human-readable description of the generated parser to be written to the file *y.output*.

> If the environment variable TMPDIR is set, the string denoted by TMPDIR will be used as the name of the directory where the temporary files are created.

FILES

> *y.code.c*
> *y.tab.c*
> *y.tab.h*
> *y.output*
> */tmp/yacc.aXXXXXX*
> */tmp/yacc.tXXXXXX*
> */tmp/yacc.uXXXXXX*

DIAGNOSTICS

> If there are rules that are never reduced, the number of such rules is reported on standard error. If there are any LALR(1) conflicts, the number of conflicts is reported on standard error.

1

NAME
yes – be repetitively affirmative

SYNOPSIS
yes [*expletive*]

DESCRIPTION
Yes outputs *expletive*, or, by default, ''y'', forever.

HISTORY
The yes command appeared in 4.0BSD.

1

NAME

yyfix – extract tables from y.tab.c

SYNOPSIS

yyfix *file* [*tables*]

DESCRIPTION

Programs have historically used a script (often named ":yyfix") to extract tables from the yacc(1) generated file y.tab.c. As the names of the tables generated by the current version of yacc are different from those of historical versions of yacc, the shell script **yyfix** is provided to simplify the transition.

The first (and required) argument to **yyfix** is the name of the file where the extracted tables should be stored.

If further command line arguments are specified, they are taken as the list of tables to be extracted. Otherwise, **yyfix** attempts to determine if the y.tab.c file is from an old or new yacc, and extracts the appropriate tables.

The tables "yyexca", "yyact", "yypact", "yypgo", "yyr1", "yyr2", "yychk", and "yydef" are extracted from historical versions of yacc.

The tables "yylhs", "yylen", "yydefred", "yydgoto", "yysindex", "yyrindex", "yygindex", "yytable", "yyname", "yyrule", and "yycheck", are extracted from the current version of yacc.

FILES

y.tab.c File from which tables are extracted.

SEE ALSO

yacc(1)

HISTORY

The **yyfix** command appears in 4.4BSD.

NAME

    zcmp, zdiff – compare compressed files

SYNOPSIS

    zcmp [cmp_options] file1 [file2]

    zdiff [diff_options] file1 [file2]

DESCRIPTION

    Zcmp and *zdiff* are used to invoke the *cmp* or the *diff* program on compressed files. All options specified are passed directly to *cmp* or *diff*. If only 1 file is specified, then the files compared are *file1* and an uncompressed *file1*.gz. If two files are specified, then they are uncompressed if necessary and fed to *cmp* or *diff*. The exit status from *cmp* or *diff* is preserved.

SEE ALSO

    cmp(1), diff(1), zmore(1), zgrep(1), znew(1), zforce(1), gzip(1), gzexe(1)

BUGS

    Messages from the *cmp* or *diff* programs refer to temporary filenames instead of those specified.

NAME

    zforce – force a '.gz' extension on all gzip files

SYNOPSIS

    zforce [name ...]

DESCRIPTION

    zforce forces a .gz extension on all *gzip* files so that *gzip* will not compress them twice. This can be useful for files with names truncated after a file transfer. On systems with a 14 char limitation on file names, the original name is truncated to make room for the .gz suffix. For example, 12345678901234 is renamed to 12345678901.gz. A file name such as foo.tgz is left intact.

SEE ALSO

    gzip(1), znew(1), zmore(1), zgrep(1), zdiff(1), gzexe(1)

1

NAME

zgrep – search possibly compressed files for a regular expression

SYNOPSIS

zgrep [grep_options] [**-e**] *pattern filename* . . .

DESCRIPTION

Zgrep is used to invoke the *grep* on compress'ed or gzip'ed files. All options specified are passed directly to *grep*. If no file is specified, then the standard input is decompressed if necessary and fed to grep. Otherwise the given files are uncompressed if necessary and fed to *grep*.

If *zgrep* is invoked as *zegrep* or *zfgrep* then *egrep* or *fgrep* is used instead of *grep*. If the GREP environment variable is set, *zgrep* uses it as the *grep* program to be invoked. For example:

    for sh: GREP=fgrep zgrep string files
    for csh: (setenv GREP fgrep; zgrep string files)

AUTHOR

Charles Levert (charles@comm.polymtl.ca)

SEE ALSO

grep(1), egrep(1), fgrep(1), zdiff(1), zmore(1), znew(1), zforce(1), gzip(1), gzexe(1)

1

NAME

zmore – file perusal filter for crt viewing of compressed text

SYNOPSIS

zmore [name ...]

DESCRIPTION

Zmore is a filter which allows examination of compressed or plain text files one screenful at a time on a soft-copy terminal. *zmore* works on files compressed with *compress, pack* or *gzip,* and also on uncompressed files. If a file does not exist, *zmore* looks for a file of the same name with the addition of a .gz, .z or .Z suffix.

Zmore normally pauses after each screenful, printing --More-- at the bottom of the screen. If the user then types a carriage return, one more line is displayed. If the user hits a space, another screenful is displayed. Other possibilities are enumerated later.

Zmore looks in the file */etc/termcap* to determine terminal characteristics, and to determine the default window size. On a terminal capable of displaying 24 lines, the default window size is 22 lines. To use a pager other than the default *more,* set environment variable PAGER to the name of the desired program, such as *less.*

Other sequences which may be typed when *zmore* pauses, and their effects, are as follows (*i* is an optional integer argument, defaulting to 1) :

i <space>
  display *i* more lines, (or another screenful if no argument is given)

^D
  display 11 more lines (a "scroll"). If *i* is given, then the scroll size is set to *i*.

d
  same as ^D (control-D)

i z
  same as typing a space except that *i*, if present, becomes the new window size. Note that the window size reverts back to the default at the end of the current file.

i s
  skip *i* lines and print a screenful of lines

i f
  skip *i* screenfuls and print a screenful of lines

q or Q
  quit reading the current file; go on to the next (if any)

e or q
  When the prompt --More--(Next file: *file*) is printed, this command causes zmore to exit.

s
  When the prompt --More--(Next file: *file*) is printed, this command causes zmore to skip the next file and continue.

=
  Display the current line number.

i /expr
  search for the *i*-th occurrence of the regular expression *expr*. If the pattern is not found, *zmore* goes on to the next file (if any). Otherwise, a screenful is displayed, starting two lines before the place where the expression was found. The user's erase and kill characters may be used to edit the regular expression. Erasing back past the first column cancels the search command.

i n
  search for the *i*-th occurrence of the last regular expression entered.

!command
  invoke a shell with *command*. The character '!' in "command" are replaced with the previous shell command. The sequence "\!" is replaced by "!".

:q or :Q quit reading the current file; go on to the next (if any) (same as q or Q).

.
  (dot) repeat the previous command.

The commands take effect immediately, i.e., it is not necessary to type a carriage return. Up to the time when the command character itself is given, the user may hit the line kill character to cancel the numerical argument being formed. In addition, the user may hit the erase character to redisplay the --More-- message.

At any time when output is being sent to the terminal, the user can hit the quit key (normally control–\). *Zmore* will stop sending output, and will display the usual --More-- prompt. The user may then enter one of the above commands in the normal manner. Unfortunately, some output is lost when this is done, due to the fact that any characters waiting in the terminal's output queue are flushed when the quit signal occurs.

The terminal is set to *noecho* mode by this program so that the output can be continuous. What you type will thus not show on your terminal, except for the / and ! commands.

If the standard output is not a teletype, then *zmore* acts just like *zcat*, except that a header is printed before each file.

FILES

/etc/termcap   Terminal data base

SEE ALSO

more(1), gzip(1), zdiff(1), zgrep(1), znew(1), zforce(1), gzexe(1)

NAME

      znew – recompress .Z files to .gz files

SYNOPSIS

      znew [-ftv9PK] [name.Z ...]

DESCRIPTION

      Znew recompresses files from .Z (compress) format to .gz (gzip) format. If you want to recompress a file already in gzip format, rename the file to force a .Z extension then apply znew.

OPTIONS

      –f   Force recompression from .Z to .gz format even if a .gz file already exists.

      –t   Tests the new files before deleting originals.

      –v   Verbose. Display the name and percentage reduction for each file compressed.

      –9   Use the slowest compression method (optimal compression).

      –P   Use pipes for the conversion to reduce disk space usage.

      –K   Keep a .Z file when it is smaller than the .gz file

SEE ALSO

      gzip(1), zmore(1), zdiff(1), zgrep(1), zforce(1), gzexe(1), compress(1)

BUGS

      Znew does not maintain the time stamp with the -P option if *cpmod(1)* is not available and *touch(1)* does not support the -r option.

Section 6
Games

NAME

 adventure – an exploration game

SYNOPSIS

 adventure [saved-file]

DESCRIPTION

 The object of the game is to locate and explore Colossal Cave, find the treasures hidden there, and bring them back to the building with you. The program is self-descriptive to a point, but part of the game is to discover its rules.

 To terminate a game, enter ''quit''; to save a game for later resumption, enter ''suspend''.

NAME

arithmetic – quiz on simple arithmetic

SYNOPSIS

arithmetic [–o +–x/] [–r range]

DESCRIPTION

Arithmetic asks you to solve problems in simple arithmetic. Each question must be answered correctly before going on to the next. After every 20 problems, it prints the score so far and the time taken. You can quit at any time by typing the interrupt or end-of-file character.

The options are as follows:

–o   By default, *arithmetic* asks questions on addition of numbers from 0 to 10, and corresponding subtraction. By supplying one or more of the characters **+–x/**, you can ask for problems in addition, subtraction, multiplication, and division, respectively. If you give one of these characters more than once, that kind of problem will be asked correspondingly more often.

–r   If a *range* is supplied, *arithmetic* selects the numbers in its problems in the following way. For addition and multiplication, the numbers to be added or multiplied are between 0 and *range*, inclusive. For subtraction and division, both the required result and the number to divide by or subtract will be between 0 and *range*. (Of course, *arithmetic* will not ask you to divide by 0.) The default *range* is 10.

When you get a problem wrong, *arithmetic* will remember the numbers involved, and will tend to select those numbers more often than others, in problems of the same sort. Eventually it will forgive and forget.

Arithmetic cannot be persuaded to tell you the right answer. You must work it out for yourself.

DIAGNOSTICS

"What?" if you get a question wrong. "Right!" if you get it right. "Please type a number." if arithmetic doesn't understand what you typed.

SEE ALSO

bc(1), dc(1)

NAME

 atc – air traffic controller game

SYNOPSIS

 atc -[u?lstp] [-[gf] game_name] [-r random seed]

DESCRIPTION

 Atc lets you try your hand at the nerve wracking duties of the air traffic controller without endangering the lives of millions of travelers each year. Your responsibilities require you to direct the flight of jets and prop planes into and out of the flight arena and airports. The speed (update time) and frequency of the planes depend on the difficulty of the chosen arena.

OPTIONS

 –u Print the usage line and exit.

 –? Same as –**u.**

 –l Print a list of available games and exit. The first game name printed is the default game.

 –s Print the score list (formerly the Top Ten list).

 –t Same as –**s.**

 –p Print the path to the special directory where *atc* expects to find its private files. This is used during the installation of the program.

 –g game Play the named game. If the game listed is not one of the ones printed from the –l option, the default game is played.

 –f game Same as –**g.**

 –r seed Set the random seed. The purpose of this flag is questionable.

GOALS

 Your goal in *atc* is to keep the game going as long as possible. There is no winning state, except to beat the times of other players. You will need to: launch planes at airports (by instructing them to increase their altitude); land planes at airports (by instructing them to go to altitude zero when exactly over the airport); and maneuver planes out of exit points.

 Several things will cause the end of the game. Each plane has a destination (see information area), and sending a plane to the wrong destination is an error. Planes can run out of fuel, or can collide. Collision is defined as adjacency in any of the three dimensions. A plane leaving the arena in any other way than through its destination exit is an error as well.

 Scores are sorted in order of the number of planes safe. The other statistics are provided merely for fun. There is no penalty for taking longer than another player (except in the case of ties).

 Suspending a game is not permitted. If you get a talk message, tough. When was the last time an Air Traffic Controller got called away to the phone?

THE DISPLAY

 Depending on the terminal you run *atc* on, the screen will be divided into 4 areas. It should be stressed that the terminal driver portion of the game was designed to be reconfigurable, so the display format can vary depending the version you are playing. The descriptions here are based on the ascii version of the game. The game rules and input format, however, should remain consistent. Control-L redraws the screen, should it become muddled.

 RADAR

  The first screen area is the radar display, showing the relative locations of the planes, airports, standard entry/exit points, radar beacons, and "lines" which simply serve to aid you in guiding the planes.

  Planes are shown as a single letter with an altitude. If the numerical altitude is a single digit, then it represents thousands of feet. Some distinction is made between the prop planes and the jets. On ascii terminals, prop planes are represented by a upper case letter, jets by a lower case letter.

Airports are shown as a number and some indication of the direction planes must be going to land at the airport. On ascii terminals, this is one of '^', '>', '<', and 'v', to indicate north (0 degrees), east (90), west (270) and south (180), respectively. The planes will also take off in this direction.

Beacons are represented as circles or asterisks and a number. Their purpose is to offer a place of easy reference to the plane pilots. See 'the delay command' under the input section of this manual.

Entry/exit points are displayed as numbers along the border of the radar screen. Planes will enter the arena from these points without warning. These points have a direction associated with them, and planes will always enter the arena from this direction. On the ascii version of *atc*, this direction is not displayed. It will become apparent what this direction is as the game progresses.

Incoming planes will always enter at the same altitude: 7000 feet. For a plane to successfully depart through an entry/exit point, it must be flying at 9000 feet. It is not necessary for the planes to be flying in any particular direction when they leave the arena (yet).

INFORMATION AREA

The second area of the display is the information area, which lists the time (number of updates since start), and the number of planes you have directed safely out of the arena. Below this is a list of planes currently in the air, followed by a blank line, and then a list of planes on the ground (at airports). Each line lists the plane name and its current altitude, an optional asterisk indicating low fuel, the plane's destination, and the plane's current command. Changing altitude is not considered to be a command and is therefore not displayed. The following are some possible information lines:

        B4*A0: Circle @ b1
        g7 E4: 225

The first example shows a prop plane named 'B' that is flying at 4000 feet. It is low on fuel (note the '*'). It's destination is Airport #0. The next command it expects to do is circle when it reaches Beacon #1. The second example shows a jet named 'g' at 7000 feet, destined for Exit #4. It is just now executing a turn to 225 degrees (South-West).

INPUT AREA

The third area of the display is the input area. It is here that your input is reflected. See the INPUT heading of this manual for more details.

AUTHOR AREA

This area is used simply to give credit where credit is due. :-)

INPUT

A command completion interface is built into the game. At any time, typing '?' will list possible input characters. Typing a backspace (your erase character) backs up, erasing the last part of the command. When a command is complete, a return enters it, and any semantic checking is done at that time. If no errors are detected, the command is sent to the appropriate plane. If an error is discovered during the check, the offending statement will be underscored and a (hopefully) descriptive message will be printed under it.

The command syntax is broken into two parts: *Immediate Only* and *Delayable* commands. *Immediate Only* commands happen on the next update. *Delayable* commands also happen on the next update unless they are followed by an optional predicate called the *Delay* command.

In the following tables, the syntax **[0–9]** means any single digit, and **<dir>** refers to the keys around the 's' key, namely ''wedcxzaq''. In absolute references, 'q' refers to North-West or 315 degrees, and 'w' refers to North, or 0 degrees. In relative references, 'q' refers to -45 degrees or 45 degrees left, and 'w' refers to 0 degrees, or no change in direction.

All commands start with a plane letter. This indicates the recipient of the command. Case is ignored.

IMMEDIATE ONLY COMMANDS

> **– a Altitude:**
>> Affect a plane's altitude (and take off).
>> **– [0–9] Number:**
>>> Go to the given altitude (thousands of feet).
>> **– c/+ Climb:**
>>> Relative altitude change.
>>> **– [0–9] Number:**
>>>> Difference in thousands of feet.
>> **– d/– Descend:**
>>> Relative altitude change.
>>> **– [0–9] Number:**
>>>> Difference in thousands of feet.

> **– m Mark:**
>> Display in highlighted mode. Command is displayed normally.

> **– i Ignore:**
>> Do not display highlighted. Command is displayed as a line of dashes if there is no command.

> **– u Unmark:**
>> Same as ignore, but if a delayed command is processed, the plane will become marked. This is useful if you want to forget about a plane during part, but not all, of its journey.

DELAYABLE COMMANDS

> **– c Circle:**
>> Have the plane circle (clockwise by default).
>> **– l Left:**
>>> Circle counterclockwise.
>> **– r Right:**
>>> Circle clockwise.

> **– t Turn:**
>> Change direction.
>> **– l Left:**
>>> Turn counterclockwise (45 degrees by default).
>>> **– <dir> Direction:**
>>>> Turn ccw the given number of degrees. Zero degrees is no turn. A ccw turn of -45 degrees is 45 cw.
>> **– r Right:**
>>> Turn clockwise (45 degrees by default).
>>> **– <dir> Direction:**
>>>> Same as turn left <dir>.
>> **– L Left 90:**
>>> Turn counterclockwise 90 degrees.
>> **– R Right 90:**
>>> Turn clockwise 90 degrees.
>> **– <dir> Direction:**
>>> Turn to the absolute compass heading given. The shortest turn will be taken.
>> **– t Towards:**
>>> Turn towards a beacon, airport or exit. The turn is just an estimate.
>>> **– b/* Beacon:**
>>>> Turn towards the beacon.
>>>> **– [0-9] Number:**
>>>>> The beacon number.
>> **– e Exit:**

Turn towards the exit.
- **[0-9] Number:**
The exit number.
- **a Airport:**
Turn towards the airport.
- **[0-9] Number:**
The airport number.

THE DELAY COMMAND

The **Delay** (a/@) command may be appended to any **Delayable** command. It allows the controller to instruct a plane to do an action when the plane reaches a particular beacon (or other objects in future versions).

- **a/@ At:**
Do the given delayable command when the plane reaches the given beacon.
- **b/* Beacon:**
This is redundant to allow for expansion.
- **[0-9] Number:**
The beacon number.

MARKING, UNMARKING AND IGNORING

Planes are **marked** when they enter the arena. This means they are displayed in highlighted mode on the radar display. A plane may also be either **unmarked** or **ignored**. An **unmarked** plane is drawn in unhighlighted mode, and a line of dashes is displayed in the command field of the information area. The plane will remain this way until a mark command has been issued. Any other command will be issued, but the command line will return to a line of dashes when the command is completed.

An **ignored** plane is treated the same as an unmarked plane, except that it will automatically switch to **marked** status when a delayed command has been processed. This is useful if you want to forget about a plane for a while, but its flight path has not been completely set.

As with all of the commands, marking, unmarking and ignoring will take effect at the beginning of the next update. Do not be surprised if the plane does not immediately switch to unhighlighted mode.

EXAMPLES

atlab1	a: turn left at beacon #1
cc	C: circle
gtte4ab2	g: turn towards exit #4 at beacon #2
ma+2	m: altitude: climb 2000 feet
stq	S: turn to 315
xi	x: ignore

OTHER INFORMATION

Jets move every update; prop planes move every other update.

All planes turn a most 90 degrees per movement.

Planes enter at 7000 feet and leave at 9000 feet.

Planes flying at an altitude of 0 crash if they are not over an airport.

Planes waiting at airports can only be told to take off (climb in altitude).

NEW GAMES

The **Game_List** file lists the currently available play fields. New field description file names must be placed in this file to be 'playable'. If a player specifies a game not in this file, his score will not be logged.

The game field description files are broken into two parts. The first part is the definition section. Here, the four tunable game parameters must be set. These variables are set with the syntax:

    variable = number;

Variable may be one of: **update,** indicating the number of seconds between forced updates; **newplane,** indicating (about) the number of updates between new plane entries; **width,** indicating the width of the play field; and **height,** indicating the height of the play field.

The second part of the field description files describes the locations of the exits, the beacons, the airports and the lines. The syntax is as follows:

    beacon: (x y) ... ;
    airport: (x y direction) ... ;
    exit: (x y direction) ... ;
    line: [(x1 y1) (x2 y2)] ... ;

For beacons, a simple x, y coordinate pair is used (enclosed in parenthesis). Airports and exits require a third value, a direction, which is one of **wedcxzaq.** For airports, this is the direction that planes must be going to take off and land, and for exits, this is the direction that planes will going when they **enter** the arena. This may not seem intuitive, but as there is no restriction on direction of exit, this is appropriate. Lines are slightly different, since they need two coordinate pairs to specify the line endpoints. These endpoints must be enclosed in square brackets.

All statements are semi-colon (;) terminated. Multiple item statements accumulate. Each definition must occur exactly once, before any item statements. Comments begin with a hash (#) symbol and terminate with a newline. The coordinates are between zero and width-1 and height-1 inclusive. All of the exit coordinates must lie on the borders, and all of the beacons and airports must lie inside of the borders. Line endpoints may be anywhere within the field, so long as the lines are horizontal, vertical or **exactly diagonal.**

FIELD FILE EXAMPLE

```
# This is the default game.

update = 5;
newplane = 5;
width = 30;
height = 21;

exit:           ( 12  0 x ) ( 29  0 z ) ( 29  7 a ) ( 29 17 a )
                ( 9 20 e ) ( 0 13 d ) ( 0  7 d ) ( 0  0 c ) ;

beacon:         ( 12  7 ) ( 12 17 ) ;

airport:        ( 20 15 w ) ( 20 18 d ) ;

line:           [ ( 1  1 ) ( 6  6 ) ]
                [ ( 12  1 ) ( 12  6 ) ]
                [ ( 13  7 ) ( 28  7 ) ]
                [ ( 28  1 ) ( 13 16 ) ]
                [ ( 1 13 ) ( 11 13 ) ]
                [ ( 12  8 ) ( 12 16 ) ]
                [ ( 11 18 ) ( 10 19 ) ]
                [ ( 13 17 ) ( 28 17 ) ]
                [ ( 1  7 ) ( 11  7 ) ] ;
```

FILES

Files are kept in a special directory. See the OPTIONS for a way to print this path out.

ATC_score   Where the scores are kept.

Game_List   The list of playable games.

AUTHOR

Ed James, UC Berkeley: edjames@ucbvax.berkeley.edu, ucbvax!edjames

This game is based on someone's description of the overall flavor of a game written for some unknown PC many years ago, maybe.

BUGS

The screen sometimes refreshes after you have quit.

Yet Another Curses Bug was discovered during the development of this game. If your curses library clrtobot.o is version 5.1 or earlier, you will have erase problems with the backspace operator in the input window.

6

NAME

　　backgammon – the game of backgammon

SYNOPSIS

　　backgammon [-] [n r w b pr pw pb t*term* s*file*]

DESCRIPTION

　　This program lets you play backgammon against the computer or against a "friend". All commands only are one letter, so you don't need to type a carriage return, except at the end of a move. The program is mostly self documenting, so that a question mark (?) will usually get some help. If you answer 'y' when the program asks if you want the rules, you will get text explaining the rules of the game, some hints on strategy, instruction on how to use the program, and a tutorial consisting of a practice game against the computer. A description of how to use the program can be obtained by answering 'y' when it asks if you want instructions.

　　The possible arguments for backgammon (most are unnecessary but some are very convenient) consist of:

n	don't ask for rules or instructions
r	player is red (implies n)
w	player is white (implies n)
b	two players, red and white (implies n)
pr	print the board before red's turn
pw	print the board before white's turn
pb	print the board before both player's turn
t*term*	terminal is type *term*, uses /etc/termcap
s*file*	recover previously saved game from *file*. (This can also be done by executing the saved file, i.e., typing its name in as a command)

　　Arguments may be optionally preceded by a '-'. Several arguments may be concatenated together, but not after 's' or 't' arguments, since they can be followed by an arbitrary string. Any unrecognized arguments are ignored. An argument of a lone '-' gets a description of possible arguments.

　　If *term* has capabilities for direct cursor movement (see *termcap*(5)) *backgammon* "fixes" the board after each move, so the board does not need to be reprinted, unless the screen suffers some horrendous malady. Also, any 'p' option will be ignored. (The 't' option is not necessary unless the terminal type does not match the entry in the /etc/termcap data base.)

QUICK REFERENCE

　　When the program prompts by typing only your color, type a space or carriage return to roll, or

d	to double
p	to print the board
q	to quit
s	to save the game for later

　　When the program prompts with 'Move:', type

p	to print the board
q	to quit
s	to save the game

or a *move*, which is a sequence of

s-f   move from **s** to **f**

s/r   move one man on **s** the roll **r**

separated by commas or spaces and ending with a newline. Available abbreviations are

s-f1-f2   means **s-f1,f1-f2**

s/r1r2   means **s/r1,s/r2**

Use 'b' for bar and 'h' for home, or 0 or 25 as appropriate.

AUTHOR
Alan Char

FILES

/usr/games/teachgammon	– rules and tutorial
/etc/termcap	– terminal capabilities

BUGS
The program's strategy needs much work.

NAME

  banner – print large banner on printer

SYNOPSIS

  /usr/games/banner [–w*n*] message ...

DESCRIPTION

  Banner prints a large, high quality banner on the standard output. If the message is omitted, it prompts for and reads one line of its standard input. If –**w** is given, the output is scrunched down from a width of 132 to *n* , suitable for a narrow terminal. If *n* is omitted, it defaults to 80.

  The output should be printed on a hard-copy device, up to 132 columns wide, with no breaks between the pages. The volume is great enough that you may want a printer or a fast hardcopy terminal, but if you are patient, a decwriter or other 300 baud terminal will do.

BUGS

  Several ASCII characters are not defined, notably <, >, [,], \ ^, _, {, }, |, and ˜. Also, the characters ", ', and & are funny looking (but in a useful way.)

  The –**w** option is implemented by skipping some rows and columns. The smaller it gets, the grainier the output. Sometimes it runs letters together.

AUTHOR

  Mark Horton

NAME

    battlestar – a tropical adventure game

SYNOPSIS

    battlestar [-r (recover a saved game)]

DESCRIPTION

    Battlestar is an adventure game in the classic style. However, It's slightly less of a puzzle and more a game of exploration. There are a few magical words in the game, but on the whole, simple English should suffice to make one's desires understandable to the parser.

THE SETTING

    In the days before the darkness came, when battlestars ruled the heavens...

> Three He made and gave them to His daughters,
> Beautiful nymphs, the goddesses of the waters.
> One to bring good luck and simple feats of wonder,
> Two to wash the lands and churn the waves asunder,
> Three to rule the world and purge the skies with thunder.

    In those times great wizards were known and their powers were beyond belief. They could take any object from thin air, and, uttering the word 'su' could disappear.

    In those times men were known for their lust of gold and desire to wear fine weapons. Swords and coats of mail were fashioned that could withstand a laser blast.

    But when the darkness fell, the rightful reigns were toppled. Swords and helms and heads of state went rolling across the grass. The entire fleet of battlestars was reduced to a single ship.

SAMPLE COMMANDS

take	---	take an object
drop	---	drop an object
wear	---	wear an object you are holding
draw	---	carry an object you are wearing
puton	---	take an object and wear it
take off	--	draw an object and drop it

    throw \<object> \<direction>

    !   \<shell esc>

IMPLIED OBJECTS

    >-: take watermelon
    watermelon:
    Taken.
    >-: eat
    watermelon:
    Eaten.
    >-: take knife and sword and apple, drop all
    knife:
    Taken.
    broadsword:
    Taken.
    apple:

Taken.
knife:
Dropped.
broadsword:
Dropped.
apple:
Dropped.
>-: get
knife:
Taken.

6

Notice that the "shadow" of the next word stays around if you want to take advantage of it. That is, saying "take knife" and then "drop" will drop the knife you just took.

SCORE & INVEN

The two commands "score" and "inven" will print out your current status in the game.

SAVING A GAME

The command "save" will save your game in a file called "Bstar." You can recover a saved game by using the "-r" option when you start up the game.

DIRECTIONS

The compass directions N, S, E, and W can be used if you have a compass. If you don't have a compass, you'll have to say R, L, A, or B, which stand for Right, Left, Ahead, and Back. Directions printed in room descriptions are always printed in R, L, A, & B relative directions.

HISTORY

I wrote Battlestar in 1979 in order to experiment with the niceties of the C Language. Most interesting things that happen in the game are hardwired into the code, so don't send me any hate mail about it! Instead, enjoy art for art's sake!

AUTHOR

David Riggle

INSPIRATION & ASSISTANCE

Chris Guthrie
Peter Da Silva
Kevin Brown
Edward Wang
Ken Arnold & Company

BUGS

Countless.

FAN MAIL

Send to edward%ucbarpa@Berkeley.arpa, chris%ucbcory@berkeley.arpa, riggle.pa@xerox.arpa.

NAME
bcd, **ppt**, `morse` – reformat input as punch cards, paper tape or morse code

SYNOPSIS
bcd [*string ...*]
ppt [*string ...*]
`morse` [–s *string ...*]

DESCRIPTION
The commands bcd, **ppt** and `morse` reads the given input and reformats it in the form of punched cards, paper tape or morse code respectively. Acceptable input are command line arguments or the standard input.

Available option:

–s   The –s option for morse produces dots and dashes rather than words.

FILES

NAME

boggle – word search game

SYNOPSIS

boggle [-bd] [-s seed] [-t time] [-w length] [+[+]] [boardspec]

DESCRIPTION

The object of *boggle* is to find as many words as possible on the Boggle board within the three minute time limit. A Boggle board is a four by four arrangement of Boggle cubes, each side of each cube displaying a letter of the alphabet or 'qu'. Words are formed by finding a sequence of cubes (letters) that are in the game's dictionary. The (N+1)th cube in the word must be horizontally, vertically, or diagonally adjacent to the Nth cube. Cubes cannot be reused. Words consist solely of lower case letters and must be at least 3 letters long.

Command line flags can be given to change the rules of the game. The + flag allows a cube to be used multiple times, but not in succession. The ++ flag allows the same cubes to be considered adjacent to itself. **A seed other than the time of day is specified by -s#,** where # is the seed. The time limit can be changed from the default 3 minutes by using the flag **-t#,** where # is the duration (in seconds) of each game. The minimum word length can be changed from 3 letters by specifying **-w#,** where # is the minimum number of letters to use.

A starting board position can be specified on the command line by listing the board left to right and top to bottom.

The **-b** flag puts *boggle* in batch mode. A **boardspec** must also be given. The dictionary is read from stdin and a list of words appearing in **boardspec** is printed to stdout.

Help is available during play by typing '?'. More detailed information on the game is given there.

BUGS

If there are a great many words in the cube the final display of the words may scroll off of the screen. (On a 25 line screen about 130 words can be displayed.)

No word can contain a 'q' that is not immediately followed by a 'u'.

When using the '+' or '++' options the display of words found in the board doesn't indicate reused cubes.

AUTHOR

Boggle is a trademark of Parker Brothers.
Barry Brachman
Dept. of Computer Science
University of British Columbia

NAME
caesar – decrypt caesar cyphers

SYNOPSIS
caesar [*rotation*]

DESCRIPTION
The **caesar** utility attempts to decrypt caesar cyphers using English letter frequency statistics. **Caesar** reads from the standard input and writes to the standard output.

The optional numerical argument Ar rotation may be used to specify a specific rotation value.

The frequency (from most common to least) of English letters is as follows:

ETAONRISHDLFCMUGPYWBVKXJQZ

Their frequencies as a percentage are as follows:

E(13), T(10.5), A(8.1), O(7.9), N(7.1), R(6.8), I(6.3), S(6.1), H(5.2), D(3.8), L(3.4), F(2.9), C(2.7), M(2.5), U(2.4), G(2), P(1.9), Y(1.9), W(1.5), B(1.4), V(.9), K(.4), X(.15), J(.13), Q(.11), Z(.07).

Rotated postings to USENET and some of the databases used by the fortune(6) program are rotated by 13 characters.

6

NAME

canfield, cfscores – the solitaire card game canfield

SYNOPSIS

canfield
cfscores

DESCRIPTION

If you have never played solitaire before, it is recommended that you consult a solitaire instruction book. In Canfield, tableau cards may be built on each other downward in alternate colors. An entire pile must be moved as a unit in building. Top cards of the piles are available to be played on foundations, but never into empty spaces.

Spaces must be filled from the stock. The top card of the stock also is available to be played on foundations or built on tableau piles. After the stock is exhausted, tableau spaces may be filled from the talon and the player may keep them open until he wishes to use them.

Cards are dealt from the hand to the talon by threes and this repeats until there are no more cards in the hand or the player quits. To have cards dealt onto the talon the player types 'ht' for his move. Foundation base cards are also automatically moved to the foundation when they become available.

The command 'c' causes *canfield* to maintain card counting statistics on the bottom of the screen. When properly used this can greatly increase one's chances of winning.

The rules for betting are somewhat less strict than those used in the official version of the game. The initial deal costs $13. You may quit at this point or inspect the game. Inspection costs $13 and allows you to make as many moves as possible without moving any cards from your hand to the talon. (The initial deal places three cards on the talon; if all these cards are used, three more are made available.) Finally, if the game seems interesting, you must pay the final installment of $26. At this point you are credited at the rate of $5 for each card on the foundation; as the game progresses you are credited with $5 for each card that is moved to the foundation. Each run through the hand after the first costs $5. The card counting feature costs $1 for each unknown card that is identified. If the information is toggled on, you are only charged for cards that became visible since it was last turned on. Thus the maximum cost of information is $34. Playing time is charged at a rate of $1 per minute.

With no arguments, the program *cfscores* prints out the current status of your canfield account. If a user name is specified, it prints out the status of their canfield account. If the −a flag is specified, it prints out the canfield accounts for all users that have played the game since the database was set up.

FILES

/usr/games/canfield	the game itself
/usr/games/cfscores	the database printer
/usr/games/lib/cfscores	the database of scores

BUGS

It is impossible to cheat.

AUTHORS

Originally written: Steve Levine
Further random hacking by: Steve Feldman, Kirk McKusick, Mikey Olson, and Eric Allman.

NAME

chess – GNU chess

SYNOPSIS

chess [arg1 arg2]

DESCRIPTION

Chess plays a game of chess against the user or it plays against itself.

Chess has a simple alpha-numeric board display or it can be compiled for use with the CHESSTOOL program on a SUN workstation. The program gets its opening moves from the file gnuchess.book which should be located in the same directory as gnuchess. To invoke the program, type 'gnuchess' or type 'chesstool gnuchess' on a SUN workstation where 'CHESSTOOL' is installed. The 'gnuchess' command can be followed by up to 2 command line arguments. If one argument is given it determines the programs search time in seconds. If two arguments are given, they will be used to set tournament time controls with the first argument being the number of moves and the second being the total clock time in minutes. Thus, entering 'chess 60 5' will set the clocks for 5 minutes (300 seconds) for the first 60 moves. If no argument is given the program will prompt the user for level of play. For use with CHESSTOOL, see the documentation on that program.

Once *Chess* is invoked, the program will display the board and prompt the user for a move. To enter a move, use the notation 'e2e4' where the first letter-number pair indicates the origination square and the second letter-number pair indicates the destination square. An alternative is to use the notation 'nf3' where the first letter indicates the piece type (p,n,b,r,q,k). To castle, type the origin and destination squares of the king just as you would do for a regular move, or type "o-o" for kingside castling and "o-o-o" for queenside.

COMMANDS

In addition to legal moves, the following commands are available as responses.

beep -- causes the program to beep after each move.

bd -- updates the current board position on the display.

book -- turns off use of the opening library.

both -- causes the computer to play both sides of a chess game.

black -- causes the computer to take the black pieces with the move and begin searching.

level -- allows the user to set time controls such as 60 moves in 5 minutes etc. In tournament mode, the program will vary the time it takes for each move depending on the situation. If easy mode is disabled (using the 'easy' command), the program will often respond with its move immediately, saving time on its clock for use later on.

depth -- allows the user to change the search depth of the program. The maximum depth is 29 ply. Normally the depth is set to 29 and the computer terminates its search based on elapsed time rather than depth. Using the depth command allows setting depth to say 4 ply and setting response time to a large number such as 9999 seconds. The program will then search until all moves have been examined to a depth of 4 ply (with extensions up to 11 additional ply for sequences of checks and captures).

easy -- toggles easy mode (thinking on opponents time) on and off. The default is easy mode ON. If easy mode is disabled, the user must enter a 'break' or '^C' to get the programs attention before entering each move.

edit -- allows the user to set up a board position. In this mode, the '#' command will clear the board, the 'c' command will toggle piece color, and the '.' command will exit setup mode. Pieces are entered by typing a letter (p,n,b,r,q,k) for the piece followed by the coordinate. For example "pb3" would place a pawn on square b3.

force -- allows the user to enter moves for both sides. To get the program to play after a sequence of moves has been entered use the 'white' or 'black' commands.

6

get -- retrieves a game from disk. The program will prompt the user for a file name.

help -- displays a short description of the commands.

hint -- causes the program to supply the user with its predicted move.

list -- writes the game moves and some statistics on search depth, nodes, and time to the file 'chess.lst'.

new -- starts a new game.

post -- causes the program to display the principle variation and the score during the search. A score of 100 is equivalent to a 1 pawn advantage for the computer.

random -- causes the program to randomize its move selection slightly.

reverse -- causes the board display to be reversed. That is, the white pieces will now appear at the top of the board.

quit -- exits the game.

save -- saves a game to disk. The program will prompt the user for a file name.

switch -- causes the program to switch places with the opponent and begin searching.

undo -- undoes the last move whether it was the computer's or the human's. You may also type "remove". This is equivalent to two "undo's" (e.g. retract one move for each side).

white -- causes the computer to take the white pieces with the move and begin searching.

BUGS

Pawn promotion to pieces other than a queen is not allowed. En-Passant does not work properly with CHESSTOOOL. The transposition table may not work properly in some positions so the default is to turn this off.

NAME

ching – the book of changes and other cookies

SYNOPSIS

ching [hexagram]

DESCRIPTION

The *I Ching* or *Book of Changes* is an ancient Chinese oracle that has been in use for centuries as a source of wisdom and advice.

The text of the *oracle* (as it is sometimes known) consists of sixty-four *hexagrams,* each symbolized by a particular arrangement of six straight (——) and broken (– –) lines. These lines have values ranging from six through nine, with the even values indicating the broken lines.

Each hexagram consists of two major sections. The **Judgement** relates specifically to the matter at hand (E.g., "It furthers one to have somewhere to go.") while the **Image** describes the general attributes of the hexagram and how they apply to one's own life ("Thus the superior man makes himself strong and untiring.").

When any of the lines have the values six or nine, they are moving lines; for each there is an appended judgement which becomes significant. Furthermore, the moving lines are inherently unstable and change into their opposites; a second hexagram (and thus an additional judgement) is formed.

Normally, one consults the oracle by fixing the desired question firmly in mind and then casting a set of changes (lines) using yarrow–stalks or tossed coins. The resulting hexagram will be the answer to the question.

Using an algorithm suggested by S. C. Johnson, the UNIX *oracle* simply reads a question from the standard input (up to an EOF) and hashes the individual characters in combination with the time of day, process id and any other magic numbers which happen to be lying around the system. The resulting value is used as the seed of a random number generator which drives a simulated coin–toss divination. The answer is then piped through **nroff** for formatting and will appear on the standard output.

For those who wish to remain steadfast in the old traditions, the oracle will also accept the results of a personal divination using, for example, coins. To do this, cast the change and then type the resulting line values as an argument.

The impatient modern may prefer to settle for Chinese cookies; try *fortune*(6).

SEE ALSO

It furthers one to see the great man.

DIAGNOSTICS

The great prince issues commands,
Founds states, vests families with fiefs.
Inferior people should not be employed.

BUGS

Waiting in the mud
Brings about the arrival of the enemy.

If one is not extremely careful,
Somebody may come up from behind and strike him.
Misfortune.

NAME

cribbage – the card game cribbage

SYNOPSIS

/usr/games/cribbage [−req] *name ...*

DESCRIPTION

Cribbage plays the card game cribbage, with the program playing one hand and the user the other. The program will initially ask the user if the rules of the game are needed − if so, it will print out the appropriate section from *According to Hoyle* with *more (I)*.

Cribbage options include:

−e   When the player makes a mistake scoring his hand or crib, provide an explanation of the correct score. (This is especially useful for beginning players.)

−q   Print a shorter form of all messages − this is only recommended for users who have played the game without specifying this option.

−r   Instead of asking the player to cut the deck, the program will randomly cut the deck.

Cribbage first asks the player whether he wishes to play a short game ("once around", to 61) or a long game ("twice around", to 121). A response of 's' will result in a short game, any other response will play a long game.

At the start of the first game, the program asks the player to cut the deck to determine who gets the first crib. The user should respond with a number between 0 and 51, indicating how many cards down the deck is to be cut. The player who cuts the lower ranked card gets the first crib. If more than one game is played, the loser of the previous game gets the first crib in the current game.

For each hand, the program first prints the player's hand, whose crib it is, and then asks the player to discard two cards into the crib. The cards are prompted for one per line, and are typed as explained below.

After discarding, the program cuts the deck (if it is the player's crib) or asks the player to cut the deck (if it's its crib); in the latter case, the appropriate response is a number from 0 to 39 indicating how far down the remaining 40 cards are to be cut.

After cutting the deck, play starts with the non-dealer (the person who doesn't have the crib) leading the first card. Play continues, as per cribbage, until all cards are exhausted. The program keeps track of the scoring of all points and the total of the cards on the table.

After play, the hands are scored. The program requests the player to score his hand (and the crib, if it is his) by printing out the appropriate cards (and the cut card enclosed in brackets). Play continues until one player reaches the game limit (61 or 121).

A carriage return when a numeric input is expected is equivalent to typing the lowest legal value; when cutting the deck this is equivalent to choosing the top card.

Cards are specified as rank followed by suit. The ranks may be specified as one of: 'a', '2', '3', '4', '5', '6', '7', '8', '9', 't', 'j', 'q', and 'k', or alternatively, one of: "ace", "two", "three", "four", "five", "six", "seven", "eight", "nine", "ten", "jack", "queen", and "king". Suits may be specified as: 's', 'h', 'd', and 'c', or alternatively as: "spades", "hearts", "diamonds", and "clubs". A card may be specified as: <rank> " " <suit>, or: <rank> " of " <suit>. If the single letter rank and suit designations are used, the space separating the suit and rank may be left out. Also, if only one card of the desired rank is playable, typing the rank is sufficient. For example, if your hand was "2H, 4D, 5C, 6H, JC, KD" and it was desired to discard the king of diamonds, any of the following could be typed: "k", "king", "kd", "k d", "k of d", "king d", "king of d", "k diamonds", "k of diamonds", "king diamonds", or "king of diamonds".

FILES

/usr/games/cribbage

AUTHORS
Earl T. Cohen wrote the logic. Ken Arnold added the screen oriented interface.

6

NAME

  dungeon – Adventures in the Dungeons of Doom

SYNOPSIS

  dungeon

  dungeon [-r [savefile]]   -- pdp-11 version only

DESCRIPTION

  Dungeon is a game of adventure, danger, and low cunning. In it you will explore some of the most amazing territory ever seen by mortal man. Hardened adventurers have run screaming from the terrors contained within.

  In Dungeon, the intrepid explorer delves into the forgotten secrets of a lost labyrinth deep in the bowels of the earth, searching for vast treasures long hidden from prying eyes, treasures guarded by fearsome monsters and diabolical traps!

  Dungeon was created at the Programming Technology Division of the MIT Laboratory for Computer Science by Tim Anderson, Marc Blank, Bruce Daniels, and Dave Lebling. It was inspired by the Adventure game of Crowther and Woods, and the Dungeons and Dragons game of Gygax and Arneson. The original version was written in MDL (alias MUDDLE). The current version was translated from MDL into FORTRAN IV by a somewhat paranoid DEC engineer who prefers to remain anonymous.

  On-line information may be obtained with the commands HELP and INFO.

OPTIONS

  In the pdp-11 version, the **-r** flag allows restarting a saved game. The default savefile is *dungeon.sav* which may be overriden on the command line. In the Vax version, the game is restored by using the **restore** command.

DETAILS

  Following, is the summary produced by the **info** command:

  Welcome to Dungeon!

  You are near a large dungeon, which is reputed to contain vast quantities of treasure. Naturally, you wish to acquire some of it. In order to do so, you must of course remove it from the dungeon. To receive full credit for it, you must deposit it safely in the trophy case in the living room of the house.

  In addition to valuables, the dungeon contains various objects which may or may not be useful in your attempt to get rich. You may need sources of light, since dungeons are often dark, and weapons, since dungeons often have unfriendly things wandering about. Reading material is scattered around the dungeon as well; some of it is rumored to be useful.

  To determine how successful you have been, a score is kept. When you find a valuable object and pick it up, you receive a certain number of points, which depends on the difficulty of finding the object. You receive extra points for transporting the treasure safely to the living room and placing it in the trophy case. In addition, some particularly interesting rooms have a value associated with visiting them. The only penalty is for getting yourself killed, which you may do only twice.

  Of special note is a thief (always carrying a large bag) who likes to wander around in the dungeon (he has never been seen by the light of day). He likes to take things. Since he steals for pleasure rather than profit and is somewhat sadistic, he only takes things which you have seen. Although he prefers valuables, sometimes in his haste he may take something which is worthless. From time to time, he examines his take and discards objects which he doesn't like. He may occasionally stop in a room you are visiting, but more often he just wanders through and rips you off (he is a skilled pickpocket).

COMMANDS

brief	suppresses printing of long room descriptions for rooms which have been visited.
superbrief	suppresses printing of long room descriptions for all rooms.
verbose	restores long descriptions.
info	prints information which might give some idea of what the game is about.
quit	prints your score and asks whether you wish to continue playing.
save	saves the state of the game for later continuation.
restore	restores a saved game.
inventory	lists the objects in your possession.
look	prints a description of your surroundings.
score	prints your current score and ranking.
time	tells you how long you have been playing.
diagnose	reports on your injuries, if any.

The **inventory** command may be abbreviated **i**; the **look** command may be abbreviated **l**; the **quit** command may be abbreviated **q**.

A command that begins with '!' as the first character is taken to be a shell command and is passed unchanged to the shell via *system(3)*.

CONTAINMENT

Some objects can contain other objects. Many such containers can be opened and closed. The rest are always open. They may or may not be transparent. For you to access (e.g., take) an object which is in a container, the container must be open. For you to see such an object, the container must be either open or transparent. Containers have a capacity, and objects have sizes; the number of objects which will fit therefore depends on their sizes. You may put any object you have access to (it need not be in your hands) into any other object. At some point, the program will attempt to pick it up if you don't already have it, which process may fail if you're carrying too much. Although containers can contain other containers, the program doesn't access more than one level down.

FIGHTING

Occupants of the dungeon will, as a rule, fight back when attacked. In some cases, they may attack even if unprovoked. Useful verbs here are *attack* <villain> *with* <weapon>, *kill*, etc. Knife-throwing may or may not be useful. You have a fighting strength which varies with time. Being in a fight, getting killed, and being injured all lower this strength. Strength is regained with time. Thus, it is not a good idea to fight someone immediately after being killed. Other details should become apparent after a few melees or deaths.

COMMAND PARSER

A command is one line of text terminated by a carriage return. For reasons of simplicity, all words are distinguished by their first six letters. All others are ignored. For example, typing *disassemble the encyclopedia* is not only meaningless, it also creates excess effort for your fingers. Note that this truncation may produce ambiguities in the interpretation of longer words. [Also note that upper and lower case are equivalent.]

You are dealing with a fairly stupid parser, which understands the following types of things:

Actions:
Among the more obvious of these, such as *take, put, drop*, etc. Fairly general forms of these may be used, such as *pick up, put down*, etc.

Directions:
north, south, up, down, etc. and their various abbreviations. Other more obscure directions (*land, cross*) are appropriate in only certain situations.

6

Objects:
Most objects have names and can be referenced by them.

Adjectives:
Some adjectives are understood and required when there are two objects which can be referenced with the same 'name' (e.g., *doors, buttons*).

Prepositions:
It may be necessary in some cases to include prepositions, but the parser attempts to handle cases which aren't ambiguous without. Thus *give car to demon* will work, as will *give demon car*. *give car demon* probably won't do anything interesting. When a preposition is used, it should be appropriate; *give car with demon* won't parse.

Sentences:
The parser understands a reasonable number of syntactic construc- tions. In particular, multiple commands (separated by commas) can be placed on the same line.

Ambiguity:
The parser tries to be clever about what to do in the case of actions which require objects that are not explicitly specified. If there is only one possible object, the parser will assume that it should be used. Otherwise, the parser will ask. Most questions asked by the parser can be answered.

FILES

dindx.dat	- game initialization info
dtext.dat	- encoded messages
rindx.dat	- index into message file for pdp version
dungeon.sav	- default save file for pdp version
dsave.dat	- default save file for non-pdp versions
listen, speak	- co-process routines for pdp version

BUGS

For those familiar with the MDL version of the game on the ARPAnet, the following is a list of the major incompatabilties:

    -The first six letters of a word are considered significant, instead of the first five.

    -The syntax for *tell, answer,* and *incant* is different.

    -Compound objects are not recognized.

    -Compound commands can be delimited with comma as well as period.

Also, the palantir, brochure, and dead man problems are not implemented.

The pdp version is slightly stripped down to fit within the memory contraints. An overlayed pdp version might be made that would allow the complete game to be compiled and loaded, but I don't have the inclination (or machine) to do it.

AUTHORS

Many people have had a hand in this version. See the "History" and "README" files for credits. Send bug reports to billr@tekred.TEK.COM (or ...!tektronix!tekred!billr).

NAME

factor, primes – factor a number, generate primes

SYNOPSIS

factor [number] ...

primes [start [stop]]

DESCRIPTION

The *factor* utility will factor integers between -2147483648 and 2147483647 inclusive. When a number is factored, it is printed, followed by a ":", and the list of factors on a single line. Factors are listed in ascending order, and are preceded by a space. If a factor divides a value more than once, it will be printed more than once.

When *factor* is invoked with one or more arguments, each argument will be factored.

When *factor* is invoked with no arguments, *factor* reads numbers, one per line, from standard input, until end of file or error. Leading white-space and empty lines are ignored. Numbers may be preceded by a single - or +. Numbers are terminated by a non-digit character (such as a newline). After a number is read, it is factored. Input lines must not be longer than 255 characters.

The *primes* utility prints primes in ascending order, one per line, starting at or above **start** and continuing until, but not including **stop.** The **start** value must be at least 0 and not greater than **stop.** The **stop** value must not be greater than 4294967295. The default value of **stop** is 4294967295.

When the *primes* utility is invoked with no arguments, **start** is read from standard input. **Stop** is taken to be 4294967295. The **start** value may be preceded by a single +. The **start** value is terminated by a non-digit character (such as a newline). The input line must not be longer than 255 characters.

DIAGNOSTICS

Out of range or invalid input results in 'ouch' being written to standard error.

BUGS

Factor cannot handle the "10 most wanted" factor list, *primes* won't get you a world record.

NAME

　　　fish – play "Go Fish"

SYNOPSIS

　　　fish [–p]

DESCRIPTION

　　　Fish is the game *Go Fish*, a traditional children's card game.

　　　The computer deals the player and itself seven cards, and places the rest of the deck face-down (figuratively). The object of the game is to collect "books", or all of the members of a single rank. For example, collecting four 2's would give the player a "book of 2's".

　　　The options are as follows:

　　　–p　　　Professional mode.

　　　The computer makes a random decision as to who gets to start the game, and then the computer and player take turns asking each other for cards of a specified rank. If the asked player has any cards of the requested rank, they give them up to the asking player. A player must have at least one of the cards of the rank they request in their hand. When a player asks for a rank of which the other player has no cards, the asker is told to "Go Fish!". Then, the asker draws a card from the non-dealt cards. If they draw the card they asked for, they continue their turn, asking for more ranks from the other player. Otherwise, the other player gets a turn.

　　　When a player completes a book, either by getting cards from the other player or drawing from the deck, they set those cards aside and the rank is no longer in play.

　　　The game ends when either player no longer has any cards in their hand. The player with the most books wins.

　　　Fish provides instructions as to what input it accepts.

BUGS

　　　The computer cheats only rarely.

NAME

fortune – print a random, hopefully interesting, adage

SYNOPSIS

fortune [–aefilosw] [–m *pattern*] [[*N%*] *file/dir/all*]

DESCRIPTION

When fortune is run with no arguments it prints out a random epigram. Epigrams are divided into several categories, where each category is subdivided into those which are potentially offensive and those which are not. The options are as follows:

–a Choose from all lists of maxims, both offensive and not. (See the –o option for more information on offensive fortunes.)

–e Consider all fortune files to be of equal size (see discussion below on multiple files).

–f Print out the list of files which would be searched, but don't print a fortune.

–l Long dictums only.

–m Print out all fortunes which match the regular expression *pattern*. See regex(3) for a description of patterns.

–o Choose only from potentially offensive aphorisms. **Please, please, please request a potentially offensive fortune if and only if you believe, deep down in your heart, that you are willing to be offended. (And that if you are, you'll just quit using –o rather than give us grief about it, okay?)**

> ... let us keep in mind the basic governing philosophy of The Brotherhood, as handsomely summarized in these words: we believe in healthy, hearty laughter -- at the expense of the whole human race, if needs be. Needs be.
> --H. Allen Smith, "Rude Jokes"

–s Short apothegms only.

–i Ignore case for –m patterns.

–w Wait before termination for an amount of time calculated from the number of characters in the message. This is useful if it is executed as part of the logout procedure to guarantee that the message can be read before the screen is cleared.

The user may specify alternate sayings. You can specify a specific file, a directory which contains one or more files, or the special word *all* which says to use all the standard databases. Any of these may be preceded by a percentage, which is a number N between 0 and 100 inclusive, followed by a %. If it is, there will be a N percent probability that an adage will be picked from that file or directory. If the percentages do not sum to 100, and there are specifications without percentages, the remaining percent will apply to those files and/or directories, in which case the probability of selecting from one of them will be based on their relative sizes.

As an example, given two databases *funny* and *not-funny*, with *funny* twice as big, saying

```
fortune funny not-funny
```

will get you fortunes out of *funny* two-thirds of the time. The command

```
fortune 90% funny 10% not-funny
```

will pick out 90% of its fortunes from *funny* (the ''10% not-funny'' is unnecessary, since 10% is all that's left). The −e option says to consider all files equal; thus

```
fortune -e
```

is equivalent to

```
fortune 50% funny 50% not
```
-funny

FILES
```
/usr/share/games/fortune
```

SEE ALSO
```
regex(3),  regcmp(3),
```

NAME

    hack – exploring The Dungeons of Doom

SYNOPSIS

    /usr/games/hack [**–d** *directory*] [**–n**] [**–u** *playername*]

    /usr/games/hack [**–d** *directory*] **–s** [**–X**] [*playernames*]

DESCRIPTION

    Hack is a display oriented dungeons & dragons - like game. Both display and command structure resemble rogue. (For a game with the same structure but entirely different display - a real cave instead of dull rectangles - try Quest.)

    To get started you really only need to know two commands. The command **?** will give you a list of the available commands and the command **/** will identify the things you see on the screen.

    To win the game (as opposed to merely playing to beat other people high scores) you must locate the Amulet of Yendor which is somewhere below the 20th level of the dungeon and get it out. Nobody has achieved this yet and if somebody does, he will probably go down in history as a hero among heroes.

    When the game ends, either by your death, when you quit, or if you escape from the caves, *hack* will give you (a fragment of) the list of top scorers. The scoring is based on many aspects of your behavior but a rough estimate is obtained by taking the amount of gold you've found in the cave plus four times your (real) experience. Precious stones may be worth a lot of gold when brought to the exit. There is a 10% penalty for getting yourself killed.

    The administration of the game is kept in the directory specified with the **–d** option, or, if no such option is given, in the directory specified by the environment variable HACKDIR, or, if no such variable exists, in the current directory. This same directory contains several auxiliary files such as lockfiles and the list of top scorers and a subdirectory *save* where games are saved. The game administrator may however choose to install hack with a fixed playing ground, usually /usr/games/lib/hackdir.

    The **–n** option suppresses printing of the news.

    The **–u** *playername* option supplies the answer to the question "Who are you?". When *playername* has as suffix one of **–T –S –K –F –C –W** then this supplies the answer to the question "What kind of character ... ?".

    The **–s** option will print out the list of your scores. It may be followed by arguments **–X** where X is one of the letters C, F, K, S, T, W to print the scores of Cavemen, Fighters, Knights, Speleologists, Tourists or Wizards. It may also be followed by one or more player names to print the scores of the players mentioned.

AUTHORS

    Jay Fenlason (+ Kenny Woodland, Mike Thome and Jon Payne) wrote the original hack, very much like rogue (but full of bugs).

    Andries Brouwer continuously deformed their sources into the current version - in fact an entirely different game.

FILES

hack	The hack program.
data, rumors	Data files used by hack.
help, hh	Help data files.
record	The list of top scorers.
save	A subdirectory containing the saved games.
bones_dd	Descriptions of the ghost and belongings of a deceased adventurer.
xlock.dd	Description of a dungeon level.
safelock	Lock file for xlock.
record_lock	Lock file for record.

ENVIRONMENT

USER or LOGNAME	Your login name.
HOME	Your home directory.
SHELL	Your shell.
TERM	The type of your terminal.
HACKPAGER, PAGER	Pager used instead of default pager.
MAIL	Mailbox file.
MAILREADER	Reader used instead of default
	(probably /bin/mail or /usr/ucb/mail).
HACKDIR	Playground.
HACKOPTIONS	String predefining several hack options
	(see help file).

Several other environment variables are used in debugging (wizard) mode, like GENOCIDED, INVENT, MAGIC and SHOPTYPE.

BUGS

Probably infinite. Mail complaints to mcvax!aeb .

NAME

hangman – the game of hangman

SYNOPSIS

/usr/games/hangman

DESCRIPTION

In *hangman*, the computer picks a word from the on-line word list and you must try to guess it. The computer keeps track of which letters have been guessed and how many wrong guesses you have made on the screen in a graphic fashion.

FILES

/usr/dict/words   On-line word list

AUTHOR

Ken Arnold

NAME

hunt – a multi-player multi-terminal game

SYNOPSIS

/usr/games/hunt [–qmcsfbS] [–n name] [–t team] [–p port] [–w message] [host]

DESCRIPTION

The object of the game *hunt* is to kill off the other players. There are no rooms, no treasures, and no monsters. Instead, you wander around a maze, find grenades, trip mines, and shoot down walls and players. The more players you kill before you die, the better your score is. If the –m flag is given, you enter the game as a monitor (you can see the action but you cannot play).

Hunt normally looks for an active game on the local network; if none is found, it starts one up on the local host. The location of the game may be specified by giving the *host* argument. This presupposes that a hunt game is already running on that host, see *huntd*(6) for details on how to setup a game on a specific host. If more than one game if found, you may pick which game to play in.

If the –q flag is given, *hunt* queries the local network (or specific host) and reports on all active games found. This is useful for shell startup scripts, *e.g.* csh's .login.

The player name may be specified on the command line by using the –n option.

The –c, –s, and –f options are for entering the game cloaked, scanning, or flying respectively.

The –b option turns off beeping when you reach the typeahead limit.

The –t option aids team playing by making everyone else on one's team appear as the team name. A team name is a single digit to avoid conflicting with other characters used in the game.

The –p *port* option allows the rendezvous port number to be set. This is a useful way for people playing on dialup lines to avoid playing with people on 9600 baud terminals.

The –w *message* option is the only way to send a message to everyone else's screen when you start up. It is most often used to say "eat slime death - NickD's coming in".

When you die and are asked if you wish to re-enter the game, there are other answers than just yes or no. You can also reply with a **w** for write a message before continuing or **o** to change how you enter the game (cloaked, scanning, or flying).

To be notified automatically when a *hunt* starts up, add your login to the *hunt-players* mailing list (see *huntd*(6)).

PLAYING HINTS

Hunt only works on crt (vdt) terminals with at least 24 lines, 80 columns, and cursor addressing. The screen is divided in to 3 areas. On the right hand side is the status area. It shows damage sustained, charges remaining, who's in the game, who's scanning (the "*" in front of the name), who's cloaked (the "+" in front of the name), and other players' scores. The rest of the screen is taken up by your map of the maze. The 24th line is used for longer messages that don't fit in the status area.

Hunt uses the same keys to move as *vi*(1) does, *i.e.*, **h, j, k,** and **l** for left, down, up, right respectively. To change which direction you're facing in the maze, use the upper case version of the movement key (*i.e.*, **HJKL**). You can only fire or throw things in the direction you're facing.

Other commands are:

```
f or 1   – Fire a bullet (Takes 1 charge)
g or 2   – Throw grenade (Takes 9 charges)
F or 3   – Throw satchel charge (Takes 25 charges)
G or 4   – Throw bomb (Takes 49 charges)
5        – Throw big bomb (Takes 81 charges)
6        – Throw even bigger bomb (Takes 121 charges)
7        – Throw even more big bomb (Takes 169 charges)
8        – Throw even more bigger bomb (Takes 225 charges)
```

9	– Throw very big bomb (Takes 289 charges)
0	– Throw very, very big bomb (Takes 361 charges)
@	– Throw biggest bomb (Takes 441 charges)
o	– Throw small slime (Takes 15 charges)
O	– Throw big slime (Takes 30 charges)
p	– Throw bigger slime (Takes 45 charges)
P	– Throw biggest slime (Takes 60 charges)
s	– Scan (show where other players are) (Takes 1 charge)
c	– Cloak (hide from scanners) (Takes 1 charge)
^L	– Redraw screen
q	– Quit

The symbols on the screen are:

−|+	– walls
/\	– diagonal (deflecting) walls
#	– doors (dispersion walls)
;	– small mine
g	– large mine
:	– bullet
o	– grenade
O	– satchel charge
@	– bomb
s	– small slime
$	– big slime
><^v	– you facing right, left, up, or down
}{i!	– other players facing right, left, up, or down
*	– explosion
\	/ −*− /	\	– grenade and large mine explosion

Other helpful hints:

- You can only fire in the direction you are facing.
- You can only fire three shots in a row, then the gun must cool off.
- Shots move 5 times faster than you do.
- To stab someone, you face that player and move at them.
- Stabbing does 2 points worth of damage and shooting does 5 points.
- Slime does 5 points of damage each time it hits.
- You start with 15 charges and get 5 more every time a player enters or re-enters.
- Grenade explosions cover a 3 by 3 area, each larger bomb cover a correspondingly larger area (ranging from 5 by 5 to 21 by 21). All explosions are centered around the square the shot hits and do the most damage in the center.
- Slime affects all squares it oozes over. The number of squares is equal to the number of charges used.
- One small mine and one large mine is placed in the maze for every new player. A mine has a 2% probability of tripping when you walk forward on to it; 50% when going sideways; 95% when backing up. Tripping a mine costs you 5 points or 10 points respectively. Defusing a mine is worth 1 charge or 9 charges respectively.
- You cannot see behind you.
- Cloaking consumes 1 ammo charge per 20 of your moves.
- Scanning consumes 1 ammo charge per (20 × the number of players) of other player moves.
- Turning on cloaking turns off scanning — turning on scanning turns off cloaking.
- When you kill someone, you get 2 more damage capacity points and 2 damage points get taken away.

6

- Maximum typeahead is 5 characters.
- A shot destroys normal (*i.e.,* non-diagonal, non-door) walls.
- Diagonal walls deflect shots and change orientation.
- Doors disperse shots in random directions (up, down, left, right).
- Diagonal walls and doors cannot be destroyed by direct shots but may be destroyed by an adjacent grenade explosion.
- Slime goes around walls, not through them.
- Walls regenerate, reappearing in the order they were destroyed. One percent of the regenerated walls will be diagonal walls or doors. When a wall is generated directly beneath a player, he is thrown in a random direction for a random period of time. When he lands, he sustains damage (up to 20 percent of the amount of damage already sustained); *i.e.*, the less damage he had, the more nimble he is and therefore less likely to hurt himself on landing.
- Every 30 deaths or so, a "?" will appear. It is a wandering bomb which will explode when it hits someone, or when it is slimed.
- If no one moves, everything stands still.
- The environment variable **HUNT** is checked to get the player name. If you don't have this variable set, *hunt* will ask you what name you want to play under. If you wish to set other options than just your name, you can enumerate the options as follows:

         setenv HUNT "name=Sneaky,team=1,cloak,mapkey=zoFfGg1f2g3F4G"

sets the player name to Sneaky, sets the team to one, sets the enter game attribute to cloaked, and the maps **z** to **o**, **F** to **f**, **G** to **g**, **1** to **f**, **2** to **g**, **3** to **F**, and **4** to **G**. The *mapkey* option must be last. Other options are: scan, fly, nobeep, port=string, host=string, and message=string — which correspond to the command line options. String options cannot contain commas since commas are used to separate options.
- It's a boring game if you're the only one playing.

Your score is the decayed average of the ratio of number of kills to number of times you entered the game and is only kept for the duration of a single session of *hunt*.

Hunt normally drives up the load average to be approximately (number_of_players + 0.5) greater than it would be without a *hunt* game executing.

STATISTICS
The –S option fetches the current game statistics. The meaning of the column headings are as follows: *score* — the player's last score; *ducked* — how many shots a player ducked; *absorb* — how many shots a player absorbed; *faced* — how many shots were fired at player's face; *shot* — how many shots were fired at player; *robbed* — how many of player's shots were absorbed; *missed* — how many of player's shots were ducked; *slimeK* — how many slime kills player had; *enemy* — how many enemies were killed; *friend* — how many friends were killed (self and same team); *deaths* — how many times player died; *still* — how many times player died without typing in any commands; *saved* — how many times a shot/bomb would have killed player if he hadn't ducked or absorbed it.

FILES
/usr/games/lib/huntd   game coordinator

SEE ALSO
huntd(6)

AUTHORS
Conrad Huang, Ken Arnold, and Greg Couch;
University of California, San Francisco, Computer Graphics Lab

ACKNOWLEDGEMENTS
We thank Don Kneller, John Thomason, Eric Pettersen, Mark Day, and Scott Weiner for providing endless hours of play-testing to improve the character of the game. We hope their significant others will forgive them; we certainly don't.

BUGS

    To keep up the pace, not everything is as realistic as possible.

6

NAME

huntd – hunt daemon, back-end for hunt game

SYNOPSIS

/usr/games/lib/huntd [−s] [−p port]

DESCRIPTION

huntd controls the multi-player *hunt*(6) game. When it starts up, it tries to notify all members of the *hunt-players* mailing list (see *sendmail*(8)) by faking a *talk*(1) request from user "Hunt Game".

The **−s** option is for running *huntd* forever (server mode). This is similar to running it under the control of *inetd* (see below), but it consumes a process table entry when no one is playing.

The **−p** option changes the udp port number used to rendezvous with the player process and thus allows for private games of hunt. This option turns off the notification of players on the *hunt-players* mailing list.

INETD

To run *huntd* from *inetd*, you'll need to put the *hunt* service in **/etc/services**:

        hunt 26740/udp   # multi-player/multi-host mazewars

and add a line in **/etc/inetd.conf**:

        hunt dgram udp wait nobody /usr/games/lib/huntd HUNT

except for Suns which use **/etc/servers**:

        hunt udp /usr/games/lib/huntd

Do not use any of the command line options — if you want *inetd* to start up *huntd* on a private port, change the port listed in **/etc/services**.

NETWORK RENDEZVOUS

When *hunt*(6) starts up, it broadcasts on the local area net (using the broadcast address for each interface) to find a *hunt* game in progress. If a *huntd* hears the request, it sends back the port number for the *hunt* process to connect to. Otherwise, the *hunt* process starts up a *huntd* on the local machine and trys to rendezvous with it.

SEE ALSO

hunt(6), talk(1), sendmail(8)

AUTHORS

Conrad Huang, Ken Arnold, and Greg Couch;
University of California, San Francisco, Computer Graphics Lab

NAME

`larn` – exploring the caverns of Larn

SYNOPSIS

`larn` [`−r`] [`−H` *number*] [`−n`] [`−h`] [`−o` *optsfile*]

DESCRIPTION

Larn is a fantasy games in which your child has contracted a strange disease, and none of your home remedies seem to have any effect. You set out to find a remedy in a limited amount of time, and to collect gold along the way of course!

The options are:

−r The −r option restores a checkpointed game after it has died.

−H The −H option sets the hardness of the game.

−n The −n option suppresses the welcome message at start up, putting you directly into the game.

−h The −h option prints the command line options.

−o The −o option specifies a different options file than `~/.larnopts`.

COMMANDS

These are the movement commands:

h move to the left	H run left	. stay here
j move down	J run down	Z teleport yourself
k move up	K run up	c cast a spell
l move to the right	L run right	r read a scroll
y move northwest	Y run northwest	q quaff a potion
u move northeast	U run northeast	W wear armor
b move southwest	B run southwest	T take off armor
n move southeast	N run southeast	w wield a weapon
^ identify a trap	g give present pack weight	P give tax status
d drop an item	i inventory your pockets	Q quit the game
v print program version	S save the game	D list all items found
? this help screen	A create diagnostic file (wizards only)	e eat something

OPTIONS FILE

The file `~/.larnopts` may be used to set a few options for **Larn**. A sequence of words terminated by whitespace is used to specify options.

Word	Meaning
bold-objects	Select bold display of objects.
inverse-objects	Select inverse video display of objects.
no-introduction	Do not display intro message.
enable-checkpointing	Turn on periodic checkpointing.
no-beep	Disable beeping of the terminal.
male	Choose your sex to be a man.
female	Choose your sex to be a woman.

name: "your name"	Choose your playing name.
monster: "monst name"	Choose a name for a monster.
savefile: "save-file-name"	Define what the savegame filename will be.

Your name and monster names must be enclosed in double quotation marks and may be up to 34 characters long. Longer names are truncated. Anything enclosed in quotation marks is considered one word, and must be separated from other words by whitespace.

SPECIAL NOTES

When **dropping gold**, if you type '*' as your amount, all your gold gets dropped. In general, typing in '*' means all of what you are interested in. This is true when visiting the bank, or when contributing at altars.

You can get out of the store, trading post, school, or home by hitting **<esc>**.

When casting a spell, if you need a list of spells you can cast, type **D** as the first letter of your spell. The available list of spells will be shown, after which you may enter the spell code. This only works on the 1st letter of the spell you are casting.

AUTHOR
Noah Morgan

FILES
| /var/games/larn.scores | Score file. |
| ~/.larnopts | Options file. |

NAME

mille – play Mille Bornes

SYNOPSIS

/usr/games/mille [file]

DESCRIPTION

Mille plays a two-handed game reminiscent of the Parker Brother's game of Mille Bornes with you. The rules are described below. If a file name is given on the command line, the game saved in that file is started.

When a game is started up, the bottom of the score window will contain a list of commands. They are:

P   Pick a card from the deck. This card is placed in the 'P' slot in your hand.

D   Discard a card from your hand. To indicate which card, type the number of the card in the hand (or ''P'' for the just-picked card) followed by a <RETURN> or <SPACE>. The <RETURN or <SPACE> is required to allow recovery from typos which can be very expensive, like discarding safeties.

U   Use a card. The card is again indicated by its number, followed by a <RETURN> or <SPACE>.

O   Toggle ordering the hand. By default off, if turned on it will sort the cards in your hand appropriately. This is not recommended for the impatient on slow terminals.

Q   Quit the game. This will ask for confirmation, just to be sure. Hitting <DELETE> (or <RUBOUT>) is equivalent.

S   Save the game in a file. If the game was started from a file, you will be given an opportunity to save it on the same file. If you don't wish to, or you did not start from a file, you will be asked for the file name. If you type a <RETURN> without a name, the save will be terminated and the game resumed.

R   Redraw the screen from scratch. The command ^L (control 'L') will also work.

W   Toggle window type. This switches the score window between the startup window (with all the command names) and the end-of-game window. Using the end-of-game window saves time by eliminating the switch at the end of the game to show the final score. Recommended for hackers and other miscreants.

If you make a mistake, an error message will be printed on the last line of the score window, and a bell will beep.

At the end of each hand or game, you will be asked if you wish to play another. If not, it will ask you if you want to save the game. If you do, and the save is unsuccessful, play will be resumed as if you had said you wanted to play another hand/game. This allows you to use the ''S'' command to reattempt the save.

AUTHOR

Ken Arnold

(The game itself is a product of Parker Brothers, Inc.)

SEE ALSO

curses(3X), *Screen Updating and Cursor Movement Optimization: A Library Package*, Ken Arnold

CARDS

Here is some useful information. The number in parentheses after the card name is the number of that card in the deck:

Hazard	Repair	Safety
Out of Gas (2)	Gasoline (6)	Extra Tank (1)
Flat Tire (2)	Spare Tire (6)	Puncture Proof (1)
Accident (2)	Repairs (6)	Driving Ace (1)
Stop (4)	Go (14)	Right of Way (1)
Speed Limit (3)	End of Limit (6)	

$$25 - (10), 50 - (10), 75 - (10), 100 - (12), 200 - (4)$$

6

RULES

Object: The point of this game is to get a total of 5000 points in several hands. Each hand is a race to put down exactly 700 miles before your opponent does. Beyond the points gained by putting down milestones, there are several other ways of making points.

Overview: The game is played with a deck of 101 cards. *Distance* cards represent a number of miles traveled. They come in denominations of 25, 50, 75, 100, and 200. When one is played, it adds that many miles to the player's trip so far this hand. *Hazard* cards are used to prevent your opponent from putting down Distance cards. They can only be played if your opponent has a *Go* card on top of the Battle pile. The cards are *Out of Gas*, *Accident*, *Flat Tire*, *Speed Limit*, and *Stop*. *Remedy* cards fix problems caused by Hazard cards played on you by your opponent. The cards are *Gasoline*, *Repairs*, *Spare Tire*, *End of Limit*, and *Go*. *Safety* cards prevent your opponent from putting specific Hazard cards on you in the first place. They are *Extra Tank*, *Driving Ace*, *Puncture Proof*, and *Right of Way*, and there are only one of each in the deck.

Board Layout: The board is split into several areas. From top to bottom, they are: **SAFETY AREA** (unlabeled): This is where the safeties will be placed as they are played. **HAND**: These are the cards in your hand. **BATTLE**: This is the Battle pile. All the Hazard and Remedy Cards are played here, except the *Speed Limit* and *End of Limit* cards. Only the top card is displayed, as it is the only effective one. **SPEED**: The Speed pile. The *Speed Limit* and *End of Limit* cards are played here to control the speed at which the player is allowed to put down miles. **MILEAGE**: Miles are placed here. The total of the numbers shown here is the distance traveled so far.

Play: The first pick alternates between the two players. Each turn usually starts with a pick from the deck. The player then plays a card, or if this is not possible or desirable, discards one. Normally, a play or discard of a single card constitutes a turn. If the card played is a safety, however, the same player takes another turn immediately.

This repeats until one of the players reaches 700 points or the deck runs out. If someone reaches 700, they have the option of going for an *Extension*, which means that the play continues until someone reaches 1000 miles.

Hazard and Remedy Cards: Hazard Cards are played on your opponent's Battle and Speed piles. Remedy Cards are used for undoing the effects of your opponent's nastiness.

Go (Green Light) must be the top card on your Battle pile for you to play any mileage, unless you have played the *Right of Way* card (see below).

Stop is played on your opponent's *Go* card to prevent them from playing mileage until they play a *Go* card.

Speed Limit is played on your opponent's Speed pile. Until they play an *End of Limit* they can only play 25 or 50 mile cards, presuming their *Go* card allows them to do even that.

End of Limit is played on your Speed pile to nullify a *Speed Limit* played by your opponent.

Out of Gas is played on your opponent's *Go* card. They must then play a *Gasoline* card, and then a *Go* card before they can play any more mileage.

Flat Tire is played on your opponent's *Go* card. They must then play a *Spare Tire* card, and then a *Go* card before they can play any more mileage.

Accident is played on your opponent's *Go* card. They must then play a *Repairs* card, and then a *Go* card before they can play any more mileage.

Safety Cards: Safety cards prevent your opponent from playing the corresponding Hazard cards on you for the rest of the hand. It cancels an attack in progress, and *always entitles the player to an extra turn*.

Right of Way prevents your opponent from playing both *Stop* and *Speed Limit* cards on you. It also acts as a permanent *Go* card for the rest of the hand, so you can play mileage as long as there is not a Hazard card on top of your Battle pile. In this case only, your opponent can play Hazard cards directly on a Remedy card other than a Go card.

Extra Tank When played, your opponent cannot play an *Out of Gas* on your Battle Pile.

Puncture Proof When played, your opponent cannot play a *Flat Tire* on your Battle Pile.

Driving Ace When played, your opponent cannot play an *Accident* on your Battle Pile.

Distance Cards: Distance cards are played when you have a *Go* card on your Battle pile, or a Right of Way in your Safety area and are not stopped by a Hazard Card. They can be played in any combination that totals exactly 700 miles, except that *you cannot play more than two 200 mile cards in one hand*. A hand ends whenever one player gets exactly 700 miles or the deck runs out. In that case, play continues until neither someone reaches 700, or neither player can use any cards in their hand. If the trip is completed after the deck runs out, this is called *Delayed Action*.

Coup Fourré: This is a French fencing term for a counter-thrust move as part of a parry to an opponent's attack. In current French colloquial language it means a sneaky, underhanded blow. In Mille Bornes, it is used as follows: If an opponent plays a Hazard card, and you have the corresponding Safety in your hand, you play it immediately, even *before* you draw. This immediately removes the Hazard card from your Battle pile, and protects you from that card for the rest of the game. This gives you more points (see "Scoring" below).

Scoring: Scores are totaled at the end of each hand, whether or not anyone completed the trip. The terms used in the Score window have the following meanings:

Milestones Played: Each player scores as many miles as they played before the trip ended.

Each Safety: 100 points for each safety in the Safety area.

All 4 Safeties: 300 points if all four safeties are played.

Each Coup Fourré: 300 points for each Coup Fourré accomplished.

The following bonus scores can apply only to the winning player.

Trip Completed: 400 points bonus for completing the trip to 700 or 1000.

Safe Trip: 300 points bonus for completing the trip without using any 200 mile cards.

Delayed Action: 300 points bonus for finishing after the deck was exhausted.

Extension: 200 points bonus for completing a 1000 mile trip.

Shut-Out: 500 points bonus for completing the trip before your opponent played any mileage cards.

Running totals are also kept for the current score for each player for the hand (**Hand Total**), the game (**Overall Total**), and number of games won (**Games**).

6

NAME

monop – Monopoly game

SYNOPSIS

/usr/games/monop [file]

DESCRIPTION

Monop is reminiscent of the Parker Brother's game Monopoly, and monitors a game between 1 to 9 users. It is assumed that the rules of Monopoly are known. The game follows the standard rules, with the exception that, if a property goes up for auction and there are only two solvent players, no auction is held and the property remains unowned.

The game, in effect, lends the player money, so it is possible to buy something which you cannot afford. However, as soon as a person goes into debt, he must "fix the problem", *i.e.*, make himself solvent, before play can continue. If this is not possible, the player's property reverts to his debtee, either a player or the bank. A player can resign at any time to any person or the bank, which puts the property back on the board, unowned.

Any time that the response to a question is a *string*, e.g., a name, place or person, you can type '?' to get a list of valid answers. It is not possible to input a negative number, nor is it ever necessary.

A Summary of Commands:

quit: quit game: This allows you to quit the game. It asks you if you're sure.

print: print board: This prints out the current board. The columns have the following meanings (column headings are the same for the **where**, **own holdings**, and **holdings** commands):

Name   The first ten characters of the name of the square

Own   The *number* of the owner of the property.

Price   The cost of the property (if any)

Mg   This field has a '∗' in it if the property is mortgaged

\#   If the property is a Utility or Railroad, this is the number of such owned by the owner. If the property is land, this is the number of houses on it.

Rent   Current rent on the property. If it is not owned, there is no rent.

where: where players are: Tells you where all the players are. A '∗' indicates the current player.

own holdings:

List your own holdings, *i.e.*, money, get-out-of-jail-free cards, and property.

holdings: holdings list: Look at anyone's holdings. It will ask you whose holdings you wish to look at. When you are finished, type "done".

mortgage: mortgage property: Sets up a list of mortgageable property, and asks which you wish to mortgage.

unmortgage:

unmortgage property: Unmortgage mortgaged property.

buy: buy houses: Sets up a list of monopolies on which you can buy houses. If there is more than one, it asks you which you want to buy for. It then asks you how many for each piece of property, giving the current amount in parentheses after the property name. If you build in an unbalanced manner (a disparity of more than one house within the same monopoly), it asks you to re-input things.

sell: sell houses: Sets up a list of monopolies from which you can sell houses. It operates in an analogous manner to *buy*.

card:　　card for jail: Use a get-out-of-jail-free card to get out of jail. If you're not in jail, or you don't have one, it tells you so.

pay:　　pay for jail: Pay $50 to get out of jail, from whence you are put on Just Visiting. Difficult to do if you're not there.

trade:　　This allows you to trade with another player. It asks you whom you wish to trade with, and then asks you what each wishes to give up. You can get a summary at the end, and, in all cases, it asks for confirmation of the trade before doing it.

resign:　　Resign to another player or the bank. If you resign to the bank, all property reverts to its virgin state, and get-out-of-jail free cards revert to the deck.

save:　　save game: Save the current game in a file for later play. You can continue play after saving, either by adding the file in which you saved the game after the *monop* command, or by using the *restore* command (see below). It will ask you which file you wish to save it in, and, if the file exists, confirm that you wish to overwrite it.

restore:　　restore game: Read in a previously saved game from a file. It leaves the file intact.

roll:　　Roll the dice and move forward to your new location. If you simply hit the <RETURN> key instead of a command, it is the same as typing *roll*.

AUTHOR

Ken Arnold

FILES

/usr/games/lib/cards.pck　　Chance and Community Chest cards

BUGS

No command can be given an argument instead of a response to a query.

NAME

　　number – convert Arabic numerals to English

SYNOPSIS

　　`number` [–l] [# . . .]

DESCRIPTION

　　The `number` utility prints the English equivalent of the number to the standard output, with each 10^3 magnitude displayed on a separate line. If no argument is specified, `number` reads lines from the standard input.

　　The options are as follows:

　　–l　　　Display the number on a single line.

BUGS

　　Although `number` understand fractions, it doesn't understand exponents.

NAME

   phantasia – an interterminal fantasy game

SYNOPSIS

   phantasia [–HSabmpsx]

DESCRIPTION

   Phantasia is a role playing game which allows players to roll up characters of various types to fight monsters and other players. Progression of characters is based upon gaining experience from fighting monsters (and other players).

   Most of the game is menu driven and self-explanatory (more or less). The screen is cursor updated, so be sure to set up the **TERM** variable in your environment.

   The options provide for a variety of functions to support the game. They are:

   –s   Invokes *phantasia* without header information.

   –m   Get a monster listing.

   –a   Get a listing of all character names on file.

   –x   Examine/change a particular character on file.

   –H   Print header only.

   –p   Purge old characters.

   –b   Show scoreboard of top characters per login.

   –S   Turn on wizard options, if allowed, if running as "root".

   The characters are saved on a common file, in order to make the game interactive between players. The characters are given a password in order to retrieve them later. Only characters above **level** zero are saved. Characters unused for awhile will be purged. Characters are only placed on the scoreboard when they die.

AUTHOR

   Edward Estes, AT&T Information Systems, Skokie, IL

PARTICULARS

   Normal Play

   A number of the player's more important statistics are almost always displayed on the screen, with maximums (where applicable) in parentheses.

   The character is placed randomly near the center of a cartesian system. Most commands are selected with a single letter or digit. For example, one may move by hitting 'W', 'S', 'N', or 'E', (lower case may also be used, at no time is the game case dependent). One may also use 'H', 'J', 'K', 'L', for movement, similar to *vi*(1). To move to a specific (x, y) coordinate, use the **move** ('1') command. The distance a character can move is calculated by 1 plus 1.5 per **level.** Moving in a compass direction will move the player the maximum allowed distance in that direction.

   A player may see who else is playing by using the **players** ('2') option. One may see the coordinates of those who are the same distance or closer to the origin as he/she. **Kings,** and **council of the wise** can see and can be seen by everyone. A **palantir** removes these restrictions.

   One can talk to other players with the **talk** ('3') option. In general, this is a line or so of text. To remove a current message, just type <return> when prompted for a message.

   The **stats** ('4') option shows additional characteristics of a player.

   One may leave the game either with the **quit** ('5') option.

   One may rest by default. Resting lets one regain maximum **energy level,** and also lets one find **mana** (more is found for larger levels and further distances from the origin).

One may call a monster by hitting '9' or 'C'.

Use 'X' to examine other players.

One may quit or execute a sub-shell by hitting interrupt. Quitting during battle results in death for obvious reasons.

Several other options become available as the player progresses in **level** and **magic,** or to other stations in the game (**valar, council of the wise, king**). These are described elsewhere. In general, a control-L will force the redrawing of the screen.

Other things which may happen are more or less self-explanatory.

Fighting Monsters

A player has several options while fighting monsters. They are as follows:

melee	Inflicts damage on the monster, based upon **strength.** Also decreases the monster's **strength** some.
skirmish	Inflicts a little less damage than **melee,** but decreases the monster's **quickness** instead.
evade	Attempt to run away. Success is based upon both the player's and the monster's **brains** and **quickness.**
spell	Several options for throwing spells (described elsewhere).
nick	Hits the monster one plus the player's **sword,** and gives the player 10% of the monster's **experience.** Decreases the monster's **experience** an amount proportional to the amount granted. This also increases the monster's quickness. Paralyzed monsters wake up very fast when nicked.
luckout	This is essentially a battle of wits with the monster. Success is based upon the player's and the monster's **brains.** The player gets credit for slaying the monster if he/she succeeds. Otherwise, nothing happens, and the chance to **luckout** is lost.

Character Statistics

strength	determines how much damage a character can inflict.
quickness	determines how many chances a character gets to make decisions while fighting.
energy level	specifies how much damage a character may endure before dying.
magic level	determines which spells a character may throw, and how effective those spells will be.
brains	basically, the character's intelligence; used for various fighting options and spells.
mana	used as a power source for throwing spells.
experience	gained by fighting monsters and other characters.
level	indicative of how much experience a character has accumulated; progresses geometrically as **experience** increases.
poison	sickness which degrades a character's performance (affects **energy level** and **strength**).
sin	accumulated as a character does certain nasty things; used only rarely in normal play of the game.
age	of player; roughly equivalent to number of turns. As **age** increases, many personal statistics degenerate.

Character Types

Character statistics are rolled randomly from the above list, according to character type. The types are as follows:

magic user strong in **magic level** and **brains** , weak in other areas.   Must rely on wits and magic to survive.

fighter good in **strength** and **energy level** , fairly good in other areas. This adds up to a well-equipped fighter.

elf very high **quickness** and above average **magic level** are **elves** selling points.

dwarf very high **strength** and **energy level** , but with a tendency to be rather slow and not too bright.

halfling rather quick and smart, with high **energy level** , but poor in **magic** and **strength**. Born with some **experience.**

experimento very mediocre in all areas. However, the **experimento** may be placed almost anywhere within the playing grid.

The possible ranges for starting statistics are summarized in the following table.

Type	Strength	Quick	Mana	Energy	Brains	Magic
Mag. User	10-15	30-35	50-100	30-45	60-85	5-9
Fighter	40-55	30-35	30-50	45-70	25-45	3-6
Elf	35-45	32-38	45-90	30-50	40-65	4-7
Dwarf	50-70	25-30	25-45	60-100	20-40	2-5
Halfling	20-25	34	25-45	55-90	40-75	1-4
Experimento	25	27	100	35	25	2

Not only are the starting characteristics different for the different character types, the characteristics progress at different rates for the different types as the character goes up in **level**. **Experimentoes'** characteristics progress randomly as one of the other types. The progression as characters increase in **level** is summarized in the following table.

Type	Strength	Mana	Energy	Brains	Magic
Mag. User	2.0	75	20	6	2.75
Fighter	3.0	40	30	3.0	1.5
Elf	2.5	65	25	4.0	2.0
Dwarf	5	30	35	2.5	1
Halfling	2.0	30	30	4.5	1

The character type also determines how much gold a player may carry, how long until **rings** can overcome the player, and how much **poison** the player can withstand.

Spells

During the course of the game, the player may exercise his/her magic powers. These cases are described below.

cloak *magic level necessary:* 20 (plus level 7)
mana used: 35 plus 3 per rest period
Used during normal play. Prevents monsters from finding the character, as well as hiding the player from other players. His/her coordinates show up as '?' in the **players** option. Players cannot collect **mana,** find trading posts, or discover the **grail** while cloaked.   Calling a monster uncloaks, as well as choosing this option while cloaked.

teleport *magic level necessary:* 40 (plus level 12)
mana used: 30 per 75 moved
Used during normal play. Allows the player too move with much more freedom

than with the **move** option, at the price of expending mana. The maximum distance possible to move is based upon **level** and **magic level.**

power blast

magic level necessary: none
mana used: 5 times **level**
Used during inter-terminal battle. Damage is based upon **magic level** and **strength.** Hits much harder than a normal hit.

all or nothing

magic level necessary: none
mana used: 1
Used while combating monsters. Has a 25% chance of working. If it works it hits the monster just enough to kill it. If it fails, it doesn't hit the monster, and doubles the monster's **quickness** and **strength.** Paralyzed monsters wake up much quicker as a result of this spell.

magic bolt

magic level necessary: 5
mana used: variable
Used while combating monsters. Hits the monster based upon the amount of **mana** expended and **magic level.** Guaranteed to hit at least 10 per **mana.**

force field

magic level necessary: 15
mana used: 30
Used during monster combat. Throws up a shield to protect from damage. The shield is added to actual energy level, and is a fixed number, based upon maximum energy. Normally, damage occurs first to the shield, and then to the players actual **energy level.**

transform

magic level necessary: 25
mana used: 50
Used during monster combat. Transforms the monster randomly into one of the 100 monsters from the monster file.

increase might

magic level necessary: 35
mana used: 75
Used during combat with monsters. Increases strength up to a maximum.

invisibility

magic level necessary: 45
mana used: 90
Used while fighting monsters. Makes it harder for the monster to hit, by temporarily increasing the player's **quickness.** This spell may be thrown several times, but a maximum level will be reached.

transport

magic level necessary: 60
mana used: 125
Used during monster combat. Transports the monster away from the player. Success is base upon player's **magic** and **brains,** and the monster's **experience.** If it fails the player is transported instead.   60% of the time, the monster will drop any treasure it was carrying.

paralyze

magic level necessary: 75
mana used: 150
Used during monster combat. "Freezes" the monster by putting its **quickness** slightly negative. The monster will slowly wake up. Success is based upon player's **magic** and the monster's **experience.** If it fails, nothing happens.

specify

magic level necessary: none
mana used: 1000
Used during monster combat only by **valar** or **council of the wise.** Allows the player to pick which monster to fight.

Monsters

Monsters get bigger as one moves farther from the origin (0,0). Rings of distance 125 from the origin determine the size. A monster's **experience, energy level,** and **brains** are multiplied by the size. **Strength** is increase 50% per size over one, and **quickness** remains the same, regardless of size.

Also, nastier monsters are found as one progress farther out from the origin. Monsters also may flock. The percent chance of that happening is designated as **flock %** in the monster listing. Monsters outside the first ring may carry treasure, as determined by their treasure type. Flocking monsters, and bigger monsters increase the chances of treasure.

Certain monsters have special abilities; they are as follows:

Unicorn	can only be subdued if the player is in possession of a **virgin.**
Modnar	has random characteristics, including treasure type.
Mimic	will pick another name from the list of monsters in order to confuse.
Dark Lord	very nasty person. Does not like to be hit (especially nicked), and many spells do not work well (or at all) against him. One can always **evade** from the **Dark Lord.**
Leanan-Sidhe	also a very nasty person. She will permanently sap **strength** from someone.
Saruman	wanders around with **Wormtongue** , who can steal a **palantir.** Also, **Saruman** may turn a player's gems into gold pieces, or scramble her/his stats.
Thaumaturgist	can transport a player.
Balrog	inflicts damage by taking away **experience** , not **energy.**
Vortex	may take some **mana.**
Nazgul	may try to steal a **ring** or neutralize part of one's **brains.**
Tiamat	may take half a player's **gold** and **gems** and escape.
Kobold	may get nasty and steal one gold piece and run away.
Shelob	may bite, inflicting the equivalent of one **poison.**
Assorted Faeries	These are killed if attacking someone carrying **holy water.** These are **Cluricaun, Fir Darrig, Fachan, Ghille Dhu, Bogle, Killmoulis,** and **Bwca.**
Lamprey	may bite, inflicting 1/2 of a **poison.**
Shrieker	will call one of its (much bigger) buddies if picked upon.
Bonnacon	will become bored with battle, fart, and run off.
Smeagol	will try to steal a **ring** from a player, if given the chance.
Succubus	may inflict damage through a **force field.** This subtracts from **energy level** instead of any shield the player may have thrown up. This is a very easy way to die.
Cerberus	loves metal and will steal all the metal treasures from a player if able.
Ungoliant	can bite and poison. This inflicts five **poisons** , and also takes one from the player's **quickness.**
Jabberwock	may tire of battle, and leave after calling one of his friends (**Jubjub Bird** or **Bandersnatch**).
Morgoth	actually **Modnar** , but reserved for **council of the wise, valar,** and **ex-valar.** Fights with **Morgoth** end when either he or the player dies. His characteristics are calculated based upon the player's. The player is given the chance to ally with him. No magic, except **force field** works when battling **Morgoth.**

6

Troll	may regenerate its **energy** and **strength** while in battle.
Wraith	may make a player blind.

Treasures

The various treasure types are as follows:

Type zero	*none*
Type one	*power booster* – adds mana.
	druid – adds experience.
	holy orb – subtracts 0.25 sin.
Type two	*amulet* – protects from cursed treasure.
	holy water – kills **assorted faeries.**
	hermit – reduces sin by 25% and adds some mana.
Type three	*shield* – adds to maximum **energy level**
	virgin – used to subdue a **unicorn** , or to give much **experience** (and some **sin**).
	athelas – subtracts one **poison.**
Type four (scrolls)	*shield* – throws a bigger than normal **force field.**
	invisible – temporarily puts the finder's **quickness** to one million.
	ten fold strength – multiplies finder's strength by ten.
	pick monster – allows finder to pick next monster to battle.
	general knowledge – adds to finder's **brains** and **magic level.**

All the scrolls except **general knowledge** automatically call a monster. These preserve any spells that were already in effect, but are only in effect while in battle.

Type five	*dagger* – adds to **strength.**
	armour – same as a **shield,** but bigger.
	tablet – adds brains.
Type six	*priest* – rests to maximum; adds **mana, brains;** and halves **sin.**
	Robin Hood – increases **shield** and adds permanently to **strength.**
	axe – like **dagger,** but bigger.
Type seven	*charm* – protects from cursed treasure (used before **amulet**); used in conjunction with **blessing** to battle **Dark Lord.**
	Merlyn – adds **brains, magic,** and **mana.**
	war hammer – like an **axe,** but bigger.
Type eight	*healing potion* – sets **poison** to -2, or subtracts two from **poison,** whichever is better.
	transporter – allows finder to move anywhere.
	sword – like a **war hammer** , but bigger.
Type nine	*golden crown* – allows the player to become **king,** by going to (0,0).
	blessing – cuts **sin** to 1/3, adds **mana,** rests to max., kills **Dark Lord** with a **charm,** and gives bearer first hit on all monsters.
	quicksilver – adds to **quickness.**
Type ten	*elven boots* – adds permanently to **quickness.**
Type eleven	*palantir* – allows one to see all the other players; used by **council of the wise** to seek the **grail.**
Type twelve/thirteen	*ring* – allows one to hit much harder in battle, etc.

Any treasure type 10-13 monsters may instead carry a type nine treasure.

A monster may also be carrying **gold** or **gems.** These are used at **trading posts** to buy things.   A **gem** is worth 1000 gold pieces. Too much **gold** will slow a player down. One may carry 1000 plus 200 per **level** of **gold.** A **gem** weighs one half a gold piece. Monsters of treasure type 7 or higher may carry **gems.**

The chance of a cursed treasure is based upon treasure type. The more valuable treasures have a greater chance of being cursed. A cursed treasure knocks **energy level** very low, and adds 0.25 **poison.**

Rings

Rings are only carried by **nazguls** and **Dark Lord.** They come in four different flavors. All **rings** rest the player to maximum and cause him/her to hit much harder in battle with monsters (assuming one has chosen to use the **ring** for battle.)

Two types of **rings** are cursed and come either from **nazguls** or **Dark Lord.** After a few times of using these types, the player falls under the control of the **ring,** and strange, random things will occur. Eventually, the player dies, and gives his/her name to a monster on the file. Dying before the **ring** is used up also renames the monster.

The two remaining types of **rings** are much more benign. The one from a **nazgul** is good for a limited number of battle rounds, and will save the player from death if it was being used when he/she died. The one from **Dark Lord** is the same, except that it never is used up. **rings** disappear after saving someone from death. In general, cursed **rings** occur much more often than normal ones. It is usually not a good idea to pick one up. The only way to get rid of a **ring** is to have a monster steal it.

King

A player may become **king by finding a** *crown* and going to (0,0). Players must have a **level** in the range of 10 to 1000 to be able to find a *crown*. When a player with one or more *crowns* reaches **level** 1000, the *crowns* are converted to *gold.*

Once a player is king, he/she may do certain things while in the Lord's Chamber (0,0). These are exercised with the **decree** ('0') option.

transport	This is done to another player. It randomly moves the affected player about. A **charm** protects from transports.
curse	This is done to another player. It is analogous to cursed treasure, but worse. It inflicts two **poison,** knocks **energy level** very low, and degrades the maximum energy. It also removes a **cloak.** A **blessing** protects from king's curses.
energy void	The king may put a number of these scattered about his/her kingdom as he/she pleases. If a player hits one, he/she loses **mana, energy,** and **gold.** The energy void disappears after being hit.
bestow	This is also done to another player. The king may wish to reward one or more loyal subjects by sharing his/her riches (**gold**). Or it is a convenient way to dispose of some unwanted deadweight.
collect taxes	Everyone pays 7% tax on all **gold** and **gems** acquired, regardless of the existence of a **king.** The king collects the accrued taxes with this option.

The **king** may also **teleport** anywhere for free by using the origin as a starting place.

Council of the Wise, Valar

A player automatically becomes a member of the **council of the wise** upon reaching level 3000. Members of the council cannot have **rings.** Members of the council have a few extra options which they can exercise. These are exercised **intervene** ('8') option. All **intervene** options cost 1000 mana. One **intervene** option is to *heal* another player. This is just a quick way for that player to be rested to maximum and lose a little **poison.** The main purpose in life for members of the council is to seek the **Holy Grail.** This is done with a **palantir** under the *seek grail* option. The distance cited by the seek is accurate within 10%, in order not to make it too easy to find the grail. A player must have infinitesimally small **sin,** or else it's all over upon finding the grail. In order to help members of the council on their quest, they may *teleport* with greater ease.

6

Upon finding the grail, the player advances to position of **valar.** He/she may then exercise more and niftier options under *intervention*. These include all of the council members' options plus the ability to move other players about, bless them, and throw monsters at them. A **valar**'s blessing has the same effect as the treasure *blessing,* except that the affected player does not get his/her *blessing* flag set. All *intervention* options which affect other players age the player who uses them. **Valars** are essentially immortal, but are actually given five lives. If these are used up, the player is left to die, and becomes an **ex-valar.** A **valar** cannot *move, teleport,* or call monsters. (An exception to this is if the *valar* finds a *transporter*. This is to allow him/her to dispose of excess *gold.* Any monsters which a **valar** encounters are based upon his/her size. Only one valar may exist at a time. The current valar is replaced when another player finds the grail. The valar is then bumped back to the council of the wise.

Wizard

The *wizard* is usually the owner of the game, and the one who maintains the associated files. The *wizard* is granted special powers within the game, if it is invoked with the '−S' option. Otherwise, the *wizard* plays no different from other players. The *wizard* abilities are outlined below.

change players
> When examining a player, (game invoked with '-x', or use 'X' from within game), the *wizard* may also change the player.

intervention
> The *wizard* may do all the *intervention* options. One extra option, *vaporize,* is added to kill any offensive players.

super character type
> An extra character type is added. This character starts with the maximum possible in all statistics, selected from the other character types. A **super** character's statistics also progress at the maximum possible rate, selected from the other character types.

Special Places

Certain regions of the playing grid have different names. In general, this is only to give the player some idea of his/her present location. Some special places do exist.

Trading Posts
> These are located at |x| == |y| == n*n*100 for n = 1, 2...1000. Trading posts farther out have more things for sale. Be careful about cheating the merchants there, as they have short tempers. Merchants are dishonest about 5% of the time.

Lord's Chamber
> This is located at (0,0). Only players with **crowns** may enter.

Point of No Return
> This is located beyond 1.2e+6 in any direction. The only way to return from here is a **transporter** or to have a **valar** relocate the player.

Dead Marshes
> This is a band located fairly distant from the origin. The first fourteen monsters (water monsters) can normally only be found here.

Valhala
> This place is where the **valar** resides. It is associated with no particular coordinate on the playing grid.

Miscellaneous

Once a player reaches **level** 5, the game will start to time out waiting for input. This is to try to keep the game a bit faster paced.

A *guru* will never be disgusted with your **sins** if they are less than one.

A *medic* wants half of a player's **gold** to be happy. Offering more than one has, or a negative amount will anger the *medic,* who will make the player worse (add one **poison**).

The **Holy Grail** does little for those who are not ready to behold it. Whenever anyone finds it, it moves. It is always located within 1e+6 in any compass direction of the origin.

There is a maximum amount of **mana** and **charms** a player may posses, based upon **level.** *Quicksilver* is always limited to to a maximum of 99.

Books bought at a **trading post** increase **brains,** based upon the number bought. It is unwise, however to buy more than 1/10 of one's **level** in books at a time.

Players over level 10000 are automatically retired.

A *blindness* goes away in random time.

Players with *crowns* are identified with a '*' before their character type.

Inter-terminal Battle

When two player's coordinates correspond, they may engage in battle. In general, the player with the highest **quickness** gets the first hit. If the two players are severely mis-matched, the stronger player is drastically handicapped for the battle. In order to protect from being stuck in an infinite loop, the player waiting for response may time out. Options for battle are:

fight	Inflicts damage upon other person.
run away	Escape from battle. Has a 75% chance of working.
power blast	Battle spell.
luckout	One-time chance to try to win against the foe. Has a 10% chance of working.

Sometimes waits for the other player may be excessive, because he/she may be battling a monster. Upon slaying a player in battle the winner gets the other's **experience** and treasures. **Rings** do not work for inter-terminal battle.

BUGS

All screen formats assume at least 24 lines by at least 80 columns. No provisions are made for when any of the data items get too big for the allotted space on the screen.

NAME

    `pig` – eformatray inputway asway Igpay Atinlay

SYNOPSIS

    `pig`

DESCRIPTION

    Ethay `igpay` utilityway eadsray ethay andardstay inputway andway iteswray itway outway otay andardstay outputway inway Igpay Atinlay.

    Usefulway orfay eneratinggay onthlymay eportsray.

NAME

pom – display the phase of the moon

SYNOPSIS

pom

DESCRIPTION

The *pom* utility displays the current phase of the moon. Useful for selecting software completion target dates and predicting managerial behavior.

6

NAME

quiz – random knowledge tests

SYNOPSIS

quiz [–t] [–i *file*] [*question answer*]

DESCRIPTION

The quiz utility tests your knowledge of random facts. It has a database of subjects from which you can choose. With no arguments, quiz displays the list of available subjects.

The options are as follows:

–t   Use tutorial mode, in which questions are repeated later if you didn't get them right the first time, and new questions are presented less frequently to help you learn the older ones.

–i   Specify an alternate index file.

Subjects are divided into categories. You can pick any two categories from the same subject. Quiz will ask questions from the first category and it expects answers from the second category. For example, the command "quiz victim killer" asks questions which are the names of victims, and expects you to answer with the cause of their untimely demise, whereas the command "quiz killer victim" works the other way around.

If you get the answer wrong, quiz lets you try again. To see the right answer, enter a blank line.

Index and Data File Syntax

The index and data files have a similar syntax. Lines in them consist of several categories separated by colons. The categories are regular expressions formed using the following meta-characters:

pat|pat	alternate patterns
{pat}	optional pattern
[pat]	delimiters, as in pat[pat|pat]pat

In an index file, each line represents a subject. The first category in each subject is the pathname of the data file for the subject. The remaining categories are regular expressions for the titles of each category in the subject.

In data files, each line represents a question/answer set. Each category is the information for the question/answer for that category.

The backslash character ("\") is used to quote syntactically significant characters, or at the end of a line to signify that a continuation line follows.

If either a question or its answer is empty, quiz will refrain from asking it.

FILES

/usr/share/games/quiz.db   The default index and data files.

BUGS

Quiz is pretty cynical about certain subjects.

NAME

rain – animated raindrops display

SYNOPSIS

rain

DESCRIPTION

Rain's display is modeled after the VAX/VMS program of the same name. The terminal has to be set for 9600 baud to obtain the proper effect.

As with all programs that use *termcap*, the TERM environment variable must be set (and exported) to the type of the terminal being used.

FILES

/etc/termcap

AUTHOR

Eric P. Scott

6

NAME

random – random lines from a file or random numbers

SYNOPSIS

random [**−er**] [*denominator*]

DESCRIPTION

Random reads lines from the standard input and copies them to the standard output with a probability of 1/denominator. The default value for *denominator* is 2.

The options are as follows:

−e   If the **−e** option is specified, **random** does not read or write anything, and simply exits with a random exit value of 0 to *denominator* - 1, inclusive.

−r   The **−r** option guarantees that the output is unbuffered.

SEE ALSO

fortune(6)

6

NAME

robots – fight off villainous robots

SYNOPSIS

robots [**–sjta**] [**scorefile**]

DESCRIPTION

Robots pits you against evil robots, who are trying to kill you (which is why they are evil). Fortunately for you, even though they are evil, they are not very bright and have a habit of bumping into each other, thus destroying themselves. In order to survive, you must get them to kill each other off, since you have no offensive weaponry.

Since you are stuck without offensive weaponry, you are endowed with one piece of defensive weaponry: a teleportation device. When two robots run into each other or a junk pile, they die. If a robot runs into you, you die. When a robot dies, you get 10 points, and when all the robots die, you start on the next field. This keeps up until they finally get you.

Robots are represented on the screen by a '+', the junk heaps from their collisions by a '*', and you (the good guy) by a '**@**'.

The commands are:

h	move one square left
l	move one square right
k	move one square up
j	move one square down
y	move one square up and left
u	move one square up and right
b	move one square down and left
n	move one square down and right
.	(also space) do nothing for one turn
HJKLBNYU	run as far as possible in the given direction
>	do nothing for as long as possible
t	teleport to a random location
w	wait until you die or they all do
q	quit
^L	redraw the screen

All commands can be preceded by a count.

If you use the '**w**' command and survive to the next level, you will get a bonus of 10% for each robot which died after you decided to wait. If you die, however, you get nothing. For all other commands, the program will save you from typos by stopping short of being eaten. However, with '**w**' you take the risk of dying by miscalculation.

Only five scores are allowed per user on the score file. If you make it into the score file, you will be shown the list at the end of the game. If an alternate score file is specified, that will be used instead of the standard file for scores.

The options are

–s	Don't play, just show the score file.
–j	Jump, *i.e.*, when you run, don't show any intermediate positions; only show things at the end. This is useful on slow terminals.
–t	Teleport automatically when you have no other option. This is a little disconcerting until you get used to it, and then it is very nice.
–a	Advance into the higher levels directly, skipping the lower, easier levels.

AUTHOR

    Ken Arnold

FILES

    /usr/games/lib/robots_roll   the score file

BUGS

    Bugs? You *crazy*, man?!?

NAME

　　rogue – exploring The Dungeons of Doom

SYNOPSIS

　　/usr/games/rogue [**−r**] [*save_file*] [**−s**] [**−d**]

DESCRIPTION

　　Rogue is a computer fantasy game with a new twist. It is crt oriented and the object of the game is to survive the attacks of various monsters and get a lot of gold, rather than the puzzle solving orientation of most
computer fantasy games.

　　To get started you really only need to know two commands. The command **?** will give you a list of the
available commands and the command **/** will identify the things you see on the screen.

　　To win the game (as opposed to merely playing to beat other people's high scores) you must locate the
Amulet of Yendor which is somewhere below the 20th level of the dungeon and get it out. Nobody has
achieved this yet and if somebody does, they will probably go down in history as a hero among heroes.

　　When the game ends, either by your death, when you quit, or if you (by some miracle) manage to win,
rogue will give you a list of the top-ten scorers. The scoring is based entirely upon how much gold you
get. There is a 10% penalty for getting yourself killed.

　　If *save_file* is specified, rogue will be restored from the specified saved game file.

　　The **−s** option will print out the list of scores.

　　For more detailed directions, read the document *A Guide to the Dungeons of Doom*.

AUTHORS

　　Timothy Stoehr, Michael C. Toy, Kenneth C. R. C. Arnold, Glenn Wichman

FILES

　　/usr/games/lib/rogue_roll　Score file
　　~/rogue.save　　　　　　　Default save file

SEE ALSO

　　Michael C. Toy and Kenneth C. R. C. Arnold, *A guide to the Dungeons of Doom*

BUGS

　　Probably infinite, although none are known. However, that Ice Monsters sometimes transfix you permanently is *not* a bug. It's a feature.

NAME

sail – multi-user wooden ships and iron men

SYNOPSIS

sail [−s [−l]] [−x] [−b] [num]

DESCRIPTION

Sail is a computer version of Avalon Hill's game of fighting sail originally developed by S. Craig Taylor.

Players of *Sail* take command of an old fashioned Man of War and fight other players or the computer. They may re-enact one of the many historical sea battles recorded in the game, or they can choose a fictional battle.

As a sea captain in the *Sail* Navy, the player has complete control over the workings of his ship. He must order every maneuver, change the set of his sails, and judge the right moment to let loose the terrible destruction of his broadsides. In addition to fighting the enemy, he must harness the powers of the wind and sea to make them work for him. The outcome of many battles during the age of sail was decided by the ability of one captain to hold the 'weather gage.'

The flags are:

−s   Print the names and ships of the top ten sailors.

−l   Show the login name. Only effective with **-s**.

−x   Play the first available ship instead of prompting for a choice.

−b   No bells.

IMPLEMENTATION

Sail is really two programs in one. Each player starts up a process which runs his own ship. In addition, a *driver* process is forked (by the first player) to run the computer ships and take care of global bookkeeping.

Because the *driver* must calculate moves for each ship it controls, the more ships the computer is playing, the slower the game will appear.

If a player joins a game in progress, he will synchronize with the other players (a rather slow process for everyone), and then he may play along with the rest.

To implement a multi-user game in Version 7 UNIX, which was the operating system *Sail* was first written under, the communicating processes must use a common temporary file as a place to read and write messages. In addition, a locking mechanism must be provided to ensure exclusive access to the shared file. For example, *Sail* uses a temporary file named /tmp/#sailsink.21 for scenario 21, and corresponding file names for the other scenarios. To provide exclusive access to the temporary file, *Sail* uses a technique stolen from an old game called "pubcaves" by Jeff Cohen. Processes do a busy wait in the loop

for (n = 0; link(sync_file, sync_lock) < 0 && n < 30; n++)
            sleep(2);

until they are able to create a link to a file named "/tmp/#saillock.??". The "??" correspond to the scenario number of the game. Since UNIX guarantees that a link will point to only one file, the process that succeeds in linking will have exclusive access to the temporary file.

Whether or not this really works is open to speculation. When ucbmiro was rebooted after a crash, the file system check program found 3 links between the *Sail* temporary file and its link file.

CONSEQUENCES OF SEPARATE PLAYER AND DRIVER

When players do something of global interest, such as moving or firing, the driver must coordinate the action with the other ships in the game. For example, if a player wants to move in a certain direction, he writes a message into the temporary file requesting the driver to move his ship. Each "turn," the driver reads all the messages sent from the players and decides what happened. It then writes back into the temporary file new values of variables, etc.

The most noticeable effect this communication has on the game is the delay in moving. Suppose a player types a move for his ship and hits return. What happens then? The player process saves up messages to be written to the temporary file in a buffer. Every 7 seconds or so, the player process gets exclusive access to the temporary file and writes out its buffer to the file. The driver, running asynchronously, must read in the movement command, process it, and write out the results. This takes two exclusive accesses to the temporary file. Finally, when the player process gets around to doing another 7 second update, the results of the move are displayed on the screen. Hence, every movement requires four exclusive accesses to the temporary file (anywhere from 7 to 21 seconds depending upon asynchrony) before the player sees the results of his moves.

In practice, the delays are not as annoying as they would appear. There is room for "pipelining" in the movement. After the player writes out a first movement message, a second movement command can then be issued. The first message will be in the temporary file waiting for the driver, and the second will be in the file buffer waiting to be written to the file. Thus, by always typing moves a turn ahead of the time, the player can sail around quite quickly.

If the player types several movement commands between two 7 second updates, only the last movement command typed will be seen by the driver. Movement commands within the same update "overwrite" each other, in a sense.

THE HISTORY OF SAIL

I wrote the first version of *Sail* on a PDP 11/70 in the fall of 1980. Needless to say, the code was horrendous, not portable in any sense of the word, and didn't work. The program was not very modular and had fseeks() and fwrites() every few lines. After a tremendous rewrite from the top down, I got the first working version up by 1981. There were several annoying bugs concerning firing broadsides and finding angles. *Sail* uses no floating point, by the way, so the direction routines are rather tricky. Ed Wang rewrote my angle() routine in 1981 to be more correct (although it still doesn't work perfectly), and he added code to let a player select which ship he wanted at the start of the game (instead of the first one available).

Captain Happy (Craig Leres) is responsible for making *Sail* portable for the first time. This was no easy task, by the way. Constants like 2 and 10 were very frequent in the code. I also became famous for using "Riggle Memorial Structures" in *Sail*. Many of my structure references are so long that they run off the line printer page. Here is an example, if you promise not to laugh.

specs[scene[flog.fgamenum].ship[flog.fshipnum].shipnum].pts

Sail received its fourth and most thorough rewrite in the summer and fall of 1983. Ed Wang rewrote and modularized the code (a monumental feat) almost from scratch. Although he introduced many new bugs, the final result was very much cleaner and (?) faster. He added window movement commands and find ship commands.

HISTORICAL INFO

Old Square Riggers were very maneuverable ships capable of intricate sailing. Their only disadvantage was an inability to sail very close to the wind. The design of a wooden ship allowed only for the guns to bear to the left and right sides. A few guns of small aspect (usually 6 or 9 pounders) could point forward, but their effect was small compared to a 68 gun broadside of 24 or 32 pounders. The guns bear approximately like so:

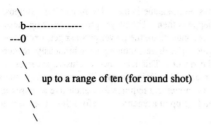

6

An interesting phenomenon occurred when a broadside was fired down the length of an enemy ship. The shot tended to bounce along the deck and did several times more damage. This phenomenon was called a rake. Because the bows of a ship are very strong and present a smaller target than the stern, a stern rake (firing from the stern to the bow) causes more damage than a bow rake.

```
        b
        00   ---- Stern rake!
        a
```

Most ships were equipped with carronades, which were very large, close range cannons. American ships from the revolution until the War of 1812 were almost entirely armed with carronades.

The period of history covered in *Sail* is approximately from the 1770's until the end of Napoleonic France in 1815. There are many excellent books about the age of sail. My favorite author is Captain Frederick Marryat. More contemporary authors include C.S. Forester and Alexander Kent.

Fighting ships came in several sizes classed by armament. The mainstays of any fleet were its "Ships of the Line", or "Line of Battle Ships". They were so named because these ships fought together in great lines. They were close enough for mutual support, yet every ship could fire both its broadsides. We get the modern words "ocean liner," or "liner," and "battleship" from "ship of the line." The most common size was the the 74 gun two decked ship of the line. The two gun decks usually mounted 18 and 24 pounder guns.

The pride of the fleet were the first rates. These were huge three decked ships of the line mounting 80 to 136 guns. The guns in the three tiers were usually 18, 24, and 32 pounders in that order from top to bottom.

Various other ships came next. They were almost all "razees," or ships of the line with one deck sawed off. They mounted 40-64 guns and were a poor cross between a frigate and a line of battle ship. They neither had the speed of the former nor the firepower of the latter.

Next came the "eyes of the fleet." Frigates came in many sizes mounting anywhere from 32 to 44 guns. They were very handy vessels. They could outsail anything bigger and outshoot anything smaller. Frigates didn't fight in lines of battle as the much bigger 74's did. Instead, they harassed the enemy's rear or captured crippled ships. They were much more useful in missions away from the fleet, such as cutting out expeditions or boat actions. They could hit hard and get away fast.

Lastly, there were the corvettes, sloops, and brigs. These were smaller ships mounting typically fewer than 20 guns. A corvette was only slightly smaller than a frigate, so one might have up to 30 guns. Sloops were used for carrying dispatches or passengers. Brigs were something you built for land-locked lakes.

SAIL PARTICULARS

Ships in *Sail* are represented by two characters. One character represents the bow of the ship, and the other represents the stern. Ships have nationalities and numbers. The first ship of a nationality is number 0, the second number 1, etc. Therefore, the first British ship in a game would be printed as "b0". The second Brit would be "b1", and the fifth Don would be "s4".

Ships can set normal sails, called Battle Sails, or bend on extra canvas called Full Sails. A ship under full sail is a beautiful sight indeed, and it can move much faster than a ship under Battle Sails. The only trouble is, with full sails set, there is so much tension on sail and rigging that a well aimed round shot can burst a sail into ribbons where it would only cause a little hole in a loose sail. For this reason, rigging damage is doubled on a ship with full sails set. Don't let that discourage you from using full sails. I like to keep them up right into the heat of battle. A ship with full sails set has a capital letter for its nationality. E.g., a Frog, "f0", with full sails set would be printed as "F0".

When a ship is battered into a listing hulk, the last man aboard "strikes the colors." This ceremony is the ship's formal surrender. The nationality character of a surrendered ship is printed as "!". E.g., the Frog of our last example would soon be "!0".

A ship has a random chance of catching fire or sinking when it reaches the stage of listing hulk. A sinking ship has a "⌐" printed for its nationality, and a ship on fire and about to explode has a "#" printed.

Captured ships become the nationality of the prize crew. Therefore, if an American ship captures a British ship, the British ship will have an "a" printed for its nationality. In addition, the ship number is changed to "&","'", "(", ")", "*", or "+" depending upon the original number, be it 0,1,2,3,4, or 5. E.g., the "b0" captured by an American becomes the "a&". The "s4" captured by a Frog becomes the "f*".

The ultimate example is, of course, an exploding Brit captured by an American: "#&".

MOVEMENT

Movement is the most confusing part of *Sail* to many. Ships can head in 8 directions:

```
          0   0   0
  b   b   b0   b   b   b   0b   b
  0   0                    0
```

The stern of a ship moves when it turns. The bow remains stationary. Ships can always turn, regardless of the wind (unless they are becalmed). All ships drift when they lose headway. If a ship doesn't move forward at all for two turns, it will begin to drift. If a ship has begun to drift, then it must move forward before it turns, if it plans to do more than make a right or left turn, which is always possible.

Movement commands to *Sail* are a string of forward moves and turns. An example is "l3". It will turn a ship left and then move it ahead 3 spaces. In the drawing above, the "b0" made 7 successive left turns. When *Sail* prompts you for a move, it prints three characters of import. E.g.,
move (7, 4):
The first number is the maximum number of moves you can make, including turns. The second number is the maximum number of turns you can make. Between the numbers is sometimes printed a quote "'". If the quote is present, it means that your ship has been drifting, and you must move ahead to regain headway before you turn (see note above). Some of the possible moves for the example above are as follows:

```
move (7, 4): 7
move (7, 4): 1
move (7, 4): d          /* drift, or do nothing */
move (7, 4): 6r
move (7, 4): 5rl
move (7, 4): 4rlr
move (7, 4): llrlr2
move (7, 4): lrlrlrl
```

Because square riggers performed so poorly sailing into the wind, if at any point in a movement command you turn into the wind, the movement stops there. E.g.,

```
move (7, 4): 1114
Movement Error;
Helm: 111
```

Moreover, whenever you make a turn, your movement allowance drops to min(what's left, what you would have at the new attitude). In short, if you turn closer to the wind, you most likely won't be able to sail the full allowance printed in the "move" prompt.

Old sailing captains had to keep an eye constantly on the wind. Captains in *Sail* are no different. A ship's ability to move depends on its attitude to the wind. The best angle possible is to have the wind off your quarter, that is, just off the stern. The direction rose on the side of the screen gives the possible movements for your ship at all positions to the wind. Battle sail speeds are given first, and full sail speeds are given in parenthesis.

```
      0 1(2)
       \|/
      -^-3(6)
       /|\
      | 4(7)
      3(6)
```

Pretend the bow of your ship (the '^') is pointing upward and the wind is blowing from the bottom to the top of the page. The numbers at the bottom "3(6)" will be your speed under battle or full sails in such a situation. If the wind is off your quarter, then you can move "4(7)". If the wind is off your beam, "3(6)". If the wind is off your bow, then you can only move "1(2)". Facing into the wind, you can't move at all. Ships facing into the wind were said to be "in irons".

WINDSPEED AND DIRECTION

The windspeed and direction is displayed as a little weather vane on the side of the screen. The number in the middle of the vane indicates the wind speed, and the + to - indicates the wind direction. The wind blows from the + sign (high pressure) to the - sign (low pressure). E.g.,

```
      |
      3
      +
```

The wind speeds are 0 = becalmed, 1 = light breeze, 2 = moderate breeze, 3 = fresh breeze, 4 = strong breeze, 5 = gale, 6 = full gale, 7 = hurricane. If a hurricane shows up, all ships are destroyed.

GRAPPLING AND FOULING

If two ships collide, they run the risk of becoming tangled together. This is called "fouling." Fouled ships are stuck together, and neither can move. They can unfoul each other if they want to. Boarding parties can only be sent across to ships when the antagonists are either fouled or grappled.

Ships can grapple each other by throwing grapnels into the rigging of the other.

The number of fouls and grapples you have are displayed on the upper right of the screen.

BOARDING

Boarding was a very costly venture in terms of human life. Boarding parties may be formed in *Sail* to either board an enemy ship or to defend your own ship against attack. Men organized as Defensive Boarding Parties fight twice as hard to save their ship as men left unorganized.

The boarding strength of a crew depends upon its quality and upon the number of men sent.

CREW QUALITY

The British seaman was world renowned for his sailing abilities. American sailors, however, were actually the best seamen in the world. Because the American Navy offered twice the wages of the Royal Navy, British seamen who liked the sea defected to America by the thousands.

In *Sail,* crew quality is quantized into 5 energy levels. "Elite" crews can outshoot and outfight all other sailors. "Crack" crews are next. "Mundane" crews are average, and "Green" and "Mutinous" crews are below average. A good rule of thumb is that "Crack" or "Elite" crews get one extra hit per broadside compared to "Mundane" crews. Don't expect too much from "Green" crews.

BROADSIDES

Your two broadsides may be loaded with four kinds of shot: grape, chain, round, and double. You have guns and carronades in both the port and starboard batteries. Carronades only have a range of two, so you have to get in close to be able to fire them. You have the choice of firing at the hull or rigging of another ship. If the range of the ship is greater than 6, then you may only shoot at the rigging.

The types of shot and their advantages are:

ROUND

Range of 10. Good for hull or rigging hits.

DOUBLE

Range of 1. Extra good for hull or rigging hits. Double takes two turns to load.

CHAIN

Range of 3. Excellent for tearing down rigging. Cannot damage hull or guns, though.

GRAPE

Range of 1. Sometimes devastating against enemy crews.

On the side of the screen is displayed some vital information about your ship:

```
Load  D! R!
Hull  9
Crew  4 4 2
Guns  4 4
Carr  2 2
Rigg  5 5 5 5
```

"Load" shows what your port (left) and starboard (right) broadsides are loaded with. A "!" after the type of shot indicates that it is an initial broadside. Initial broadside were loaded with care before battle and before the decks ran red with blood. As a consequence, initial broadsides are a little more effective than broadsides loaded later. A "*" after the type of shot indicates that the gun crews are still loading it, and you cannot fire yet. "Hull" shows how much hull you have left. "Crew" shows your three sections of crew. As your crew dies off, your ability to fire decreases. "Guns" and "Carr" show your port and starboard guns. As you lose guns, your ability to fire decreases. "Rigg" shows how much rigging you have on your 3 or 4 masts. As rigging is shot away, you lose mobility.

EFFECTIVENESS OF FIRE

It is very dramatic when a ship fires its thunderous broadsides, but the mere opportunity to fire them does not guarantee any hits. Many factors influence the destructive force of a broadside. First of all, and the chief factor, is distance. It is harder to hit a ship at range ten than it is to hit one sloshing alongside. Next is raking. Raking fire, as mentioned before, can sometimes dismast a ship at range ten. Next, crew size and quality affects the damage done by a broadside. The number of guns firing also bears on the point, so to speak. Lastly, weather affects the accuracy of a broadside. If the seas are high (5 or 6), then the lower gunports of ships of the line can't even be opened to run out the guns. This gives frigates and other flush decked vessels an advantage in a storm. The scenario *Pellew vs. The Droits de L'Homme* takes advantage of this peculiar circumstance.

REPAIRS

Repairs may be made to your Hull, Guns, and Rigging at the slow rate of two points per three turns. The message "Repairs Completed" will be printed if no more repairs can be made.

PECULIARITIES OF COMPUTER SHIPS

Computer ships in *Sail* follow all the rules above with a few exceptions. Computer ships never repair damage. If they did, the players could never beat them. They play well enough as it is. As a consolation, the computer ships can fire double shot every turn. That fluke is a good reason to keep your distance. The *Driver* figures out the moves of the computer ships. It computes them with a typical A.I. distance function and a depth first search to find the maximum "score." It seems to work fairly well, although I'll be the first to admit it isn't perfect.

HOW TO PLAY

Commands are given to *Sail* by typing a single character. You will then be prompted for further input. A brief summary of the commands follows.

COMMAND SUMMARY

'f' Fire broadsides if they bear
'l' Reload
'L' Unload broadsides (to change ammo)
'm' Move
'i' Print the closest ship
'I' Print all ships
'F' Find a particular ship or ships (e.g. "a?" for all Americans)
's' Send a message around the fleet
'b' Attempt to board an enemy ship
'B' Recall boarding parties
'c' Change set of sail
'r' Repair
'u' Attempt to unfoul
'g' Grapple/ungrapple
'v' Print version number of game
'^L' Redraw screen
'Q' Quit

'C'   Center your ship in the window
'U'   Move window up
'D','N' Move window down
'H'   Move window left
'J'   Move window right
'S'   Toggle window to follow your ship or stay where it is

SCENARIOS

Here is a summary of the scenarios in *Sail:*

Ranger vs. Drake:

Wind from the N, blowing a fresh breeze.

    (a) Ranger   19 gun Sloop (crack crew) (7 pts)
    (b) Drake   17 gun Sloop (crack crew) (6 pts)

The Battle of Flamborough Head:

Wind from the S, blowing a fresh breeze.

This is John Paul Jones' first famous battle. Aboard the Bonhomme Richard, he was able to overcome the Serapis's greater firepower by quickly boarding her.

    (a) Bonhomme Rich   42 gun Corvette (crack crew) (11 pts)

(b) Serapis   44 gun Frigate (crack crew) (12 pts)

Arbuthnot and Des Touches:
Wind from the N, blowing a gale.

(b) America   64 gun Ship of the Line (crack crew) (20 pts)
(b) Befford   74 gun Ship of the Line (crack crew) (26 pts)
(b) Adamant   50 gun Ship of the Line (crack crew) (17 pts)
(b) London   98 gun 3 Decker SOL (crack crew) (28 pts)
(b) Royal Oak   74 gun Ship of the Line (crack crew) (26 pts)
(f) Neptune   74 gun Ship of the Line (average crew) (24 pts)
(f) Duc de Bourgogne 80 gun 3 Decker SOL (average crew) (27 pts)
(f) Conquerant   74 gun Ship of the Line (average crew) (24 pts)
(f) Provence   64 gun Ship of the Line (average crew) (18 pts)
(f) Romulus   44 gun Ship of the Line (average crew) (10 pts)

Suffren and Hughes:
Wind from the S, blowing a fresh breeze.

(b) Monmouth   74 gun Ship of the Line (average crew) (24 pts)
(b) Hero   74 gun Ship of the Line (crack crew) (26 pts)
(b) Isis   50 gun Ship of the Line (crack crew) (17 pts)
(b) Superb   74 gun Ship of the Line (crack crew) (27 pts)
(b) Burford   74 gun Ship of the Line (average crew) (24 pts)
(f) Flamband   50 gun Ship of the Line (average crew) (14 pts)
(f) Annibal   74 gun Ship of the Line (average crew) (24 pts)
(f) Severe   64 gun Ship of the Line (average crew) (18 pts)
(f) Brilliant   80 gun Ship of the Line (crack crew) (31 pts)
(f) Sphinx   80 gun Ship of the Line (average crew) (27 pts)

Nymphe vs. Cleopatre:
Wind from the S, blowing a fresh breeze.

(b) Nymphe   36 gun Frigate (crack crew) (11 pts)
(f) Cleopatre   36 gun Frigate (average crew) (10 pts)

Mars vs. Hercule:
Wind from the S, blowing a fresh breeze.
(b) Mars   74 gun Ship of the Line (crack crew) (26 pts)
(f) Hercule   74 gun Ship of the Line (average crew) (23 pts)

Ambuscade vs. Baionnaise:
Wind from the N, blowing a fresh breeze.

(b) Ambuscade   32 gun Frigate (average crew) (9 pts)
(f) Baionnaise   24 gun Corvette (average crew) (9 pts)

Constellation vs. Insurgent:
Wind from the S, blowing a gale.

(a) Constellation   38 gun Corvette (elite crew) (17 pts)
(f) Insurgent   36 gun Corvette (average crew) (11 pts)

Constellation vs. Vengeance:
Wind from the S, blowing a fresh breeze.

(a) Constellation   38 gun Corvette (elite crew) (17 pts)

6

      (f) Vengeance   40 gun Frigate (average crew) (15 pts)

The Battle of Lissa:
    Wind from the S, blowing a fresh breeze.

      (b) Amphion   32 gun Frigate (elite crew) (13 pts)
      (b) Active   38 gun Frigate (elite crew) (18 pts)
      (b) Volage   22 gun Frigate (elite crew) (11 pts)
      (b) Cerberus   32 gun Frigate (elite crew) (13 pts)
      (f) Favorite   40 gun Frigate (average crew) (15 pts)
      (f) Flore   40 gun Frigate (average crew) (15 pts)
      (f) Danae   40 gun Frigate (crack crew) (17 pts)
      (f) Bellona   32 gun Frigate (green crew) (9 pts)
      (f) Corona   40 gun Frigate (green crew) (12 pts)
      (f) Carolina   32 gun Frigate (green crew) (7 pts)

Constitution vs. Guerriere:
    Wind from the SW, blowing a gale.

      (a) Constitution   44 gun Corvette (elite crew) (24 pts)
      (b) Guerriere   38 gun Frigate (crack crew) (15 pts)

United States vs. Macedonian:
    Wind from the S, blowing a fresh breeze.

      (a) United States   44 gun Frigate (elite crew) (24 pts)
      (b) Macedonian   38 gun Frigate (crack crew) (16 pts)

Constitution vs. Java:
    Wind from the S, blowing a fresh breeze.

      (a) Constitution   44 gun Corvette (elite crew) (24 pts)
      (b) Java   38 gun Corvette (crack crew) (19 pts)

Chesapeake vs. Shannon:
    Wind from the S, blowing a fresh breeze.

      (a) Chesapeake   38 gun Frigate (average crew) (14 pts)
      (b) Shannon   38 gun Frigate (elite crew) (17 pts)

The Battle of Lake Erie:
    Wind from the S, blowing a light breeze.

      (a) Lawrence   20 gun Sloop (crack crew) (9 pts)
      (a) Niagara   20 gun Sloop (elite crew) (12 pts)
      (b) Lady Prevost   13 gun Brig (crack crew) (5 pts)
      (b) Detroit   19 gun Sloop (crack crew) (7 pts)
      (b) Q. Charlotte   17 gun Sloop (crack crew) (6 pts)

Wasp vs. Reindeer:
    Wind from the S, blowing a light breeze.

      (a) Wasp   20 gun Sloop (elite crew) (12 pts)
      (b) Reindeer   18 gun Sloop (elite crew) (9 pts)

Constitution vs. Cyane and Levant:
> Wind from the S, blowing a moderate breeze.

> (a) Constitution   44 gun Corvette (elite crew) (24 pts) (b) Cyane   24 gun Sloop (crack crew) (11
> pts) (b) Levant   20 gun Sloop (crack crew) (10 pts)

Pellew vs. Droits de L'Homme:
> Wind from the N, blowing a gale.

> (b) Indefatigable   44 gun Frigate (elite crew) (14 pts)
> (b) Amazon   36 gun Frigate (crack crew) (14 pts)
> (f) Droits L'Hom   74 gun Ship of the Line (average crew) (24 pts)

Algeciras:
> Wind from the SW, blowing a moderate breeze.

> (b) Caesar   80 gun Ship of the Line (crack crew) (31 pts)
> (b) Pompee   74 gun Ship of the Line (crack crew) (27 pts)
> (b) Spencer   74 gun Ship of the Line (crack crew) (26 pts)
> (b) Hannibal   98 gun 3 Decker SOL (crack crew) (28 pts)
> (s) Real-Carlos   112 gun 3 Decker SOL (green crew) (27 pts)
> (s) San Fernando   96 gun 3 Decker SOL (green crew) (24 pts)
> (s) Argonauta   80 gun Ship of the Line (green crew) (23 pts)
> (s) San Augustine   74 gun Ship of the Line (green crew) (20 pts)
> (f) Indomptable   80 gun Ship of the Line (average crew) (27 pts)
> (f) Desaix   74 gun Ship of the Line (average crew) (24 pts)

Lake Champlain:
> Wind from the N, blowing a fresh breeze.

> (a) Saratoga   26 gun Sloop (crack crew) (12 pts)
> (a) Eagle   20 gun Sloop (crack crew) (11 pts)
> (a) Ticonderoga   17 gun Sloop (crack crew) (9 pts)
> (a) Preble   7 gun Brig (crack crew) (4 pts)
> (b) Confiance   37 gun Frigate (crack crew) (14 pts)
> (b) Linnet   16 gun Sloop (elite crew) (10 pts)
> (b) Chubb   11 gun Brig (crack crew) (5 pts)

Last Voyage of the USS President:
> Wind from the N, blowing a fresh breeze.

> (a) President   44 gun Frigate (elite crew) (24 pts)
> (b) Endymion   40 gun Frigate (crack crew) (17 pts)
> (b) Pomone   44 gun Frigate (crack crew) (20 pts)
> (b) Tenedos   38 gun Frigate (crack crew) (15 pts)

Hornblower and the Natividad:
> Wind from the E, blowing a gale.

> A scenario for you Horny fans. Remember, he sank the Natividad against heavy odds and winds. Hint:
> don't try to board the Natividad, her crew is much bigger, albeit green.

> (b) Lydia   36 gun Frigate (elite crew) (13 pts)
> (s) Natividad   50 gun Ship of the Line (green crew) (14 pts)

Curse of the Flying Dutchman:
Wind from the S, blowing a fresh breeze.

Just for fun, take the Piece of cake.

(s) Piece of Cake   24 gun Corvette (average crew) (9 pts)
(f) Flying Dutchy   120 gun 3 Decker SOL (elite crew) (43 pts)

The South Pacific:
Wind from the S, blowing a strong breeze.

(a) USS Scurvy   136 gun 3 Decker SOL (mutinous crew) (27 pts)
(b) HMS Tahiti   120 gun 3 Decker SOL (elite crew) (43 pts)
(s) Australian   32 gun Frigate (average crew) (9 pts)
(f) Bikini Atoll   7 gun Brig (crack crew) (4 pts)

Hornblower and the battle of Rosas
Wind from the E, blowing a fresh breeze.

The only battle Hornblower ever lost. He was able to dismast one
ship and stern rake the others though. See if you can do as well.

(b) Sutherland   74 gun Ship of the Line (crack crew) (26 pts)
(f) Turenne   80 gun 3 Decker SOL (average crew) (27 pts)
(f) Nightmare   74 gun Ship of the Line (average crew) (24 pts)
(f) Paris   112 gun 3 Decker SOL (green crew) (27 pts)
(f) Napoleon   74 gun Ship of the Line (green crew) (20 pts)

Cape Horn:
Wind from the NE, blowing a strong breeze.

(a) Concord   80 gun Ship of the Line (average crew) (27 pts)
(a) Berkeley   98 gun 3 Decker SOL (crack crew) (28 pts)
(b) Thames   120 gun 3 Decker SOL (elite crew) (43 pts)
(s) Madrid   112 gun 3 Decker SOL (green crew) (27 pts)
(f) Musket   80 gun 3 Decker SOL (average crew) (27 pts)

New Orleans:
Wind from the SE, blowing a fresh breeze.

Watch that little Cypress go!

(a) Alligator   120 gun 3 Decker SOL (elite crew) (43 pts)
(b) Firefly   74 gun Ship of the Line (crack crew) (27 pts)
(b) Cypress   44 gun Frigate (elite crew) (14 pts)

Botany Bay:
Wind from the N, blowing a fresh breeze.

(b) Shark   64 gun Ship of the Line (average crew) (18 pts)
(f) Coral Snake   44 gun Corvette (elite crew) (24 pts)
(f) Sea Lion   44 gun Frigate (elite crew) (24 pts)

Voyage to the Bottom of the
Wind from the NW, blowing a fresh breeze.

This one is dedicated to Richard Basehart and David Hedison.

    (a) Seaview   120 gun 3 Decker SOL (elite crew) (43 pts)
    (a) Flying Sub   40 gun Frigate (crack crew) (17 pts)
    (b) Mermaid   136 gun 3 Decker SOL (mutinous crew) (27 pts)
    (s) Giant Squid   112 gun 3 Decker SOL (green crew) (27 pts)

Frigate Action:
Wind from the E, blowing a fresh breeze.

    (a) Killdeer   40 gun Frigate (average crew) (15 pts)
    (b) Sandpiper   40 gun Frigate (average crew) (15 pts)
    (s) Curlew   38 gun Frigate (crack crew) (16 pts)

The Battle of Midway:
Wind from the E, blowing a moderate breeze.

    (a) Enterprise   80 gun Ship of the Line (crack crew) (31 pts)
    (a) Yorktown   80 gun Ship of the Line (average crew) (27 pts)
    (a) Hornet   74 gun Ship of the Line (average crew) (24 pts)
    (j) Akagi   112 gun 3 Decker SOL (green crew) (27 pts)
    (j) Kaga   96 gun 3 Decker SOL (green crew) (24 pts)
    (j) Soryu   80 gun Ship of the Line (green crew) (23 pts)

Star Trek:
Wind from the S, blowing a fresh breeze.

    (a) Enterprise   450 gun Ship of the Line (elite crew) (75 pts)
    (a) Yorktown   450 gun Ship of the Line (elite crew) (75 pts)
    (a) Reliant   450 gun Ship of the Line (elite crew) (75 pts)
    (a) Galileo   450 gun Ship of the Line (elite crew) (75 pts)
    (k) Kobayashi Maru   450 gun Ship of the Line (elite crew) (75 pts)
    (k) Klingon II   450 gun Ship of the Line (elite crew) (75 pts)
    (o) Red Orion   450 gun Ship of the Line (elite crew) (75 pts)
    (o) Blue Orion   450 gun Ship of the Line (elite crew) (75 pts)

CONCLUSION
Sail has been a group effort.

AUTHOR
    Dave Riggle

CO-AUTHOR
    Ed Wang

REFITTING
    Craig Leres

CONSULTANTS
    Chris Guthrie
    Captain Happy
    Horatio Nelson
        and many valiant others...

REFERENCES

Wooden Ships & Iron Men, by Avalon Hill

Captain Horatio Hornblower Novels, (13 of them) by C.S. Forester

Captain Richard Bolitho Novels, (12 of them) by Alexander Kent

The Complete Works of Captain Frederick Marryat, (about 20) especially

        Mr. Midshipman Easy

        Peter Simple

        Jacob Faithful

        Japhet in Search of a Father

        Snarleyyow, or The Dog Fiend

        Frank Mildmay, or The Naval Officer

BUGS

Probably a few, and please report them to "riggle@ernie.berkeley.edu" and "edward@ucbarpa.berkeley.edu"

NAME

snake, snscore – display chase game

SYNOPSIS

snake [**-w width**] [**-l length**]
snscore

DESCRIPTION

Snake is a display-based game which must be played on a CRT terminal. The object of the game is to make as much money as possible without getting eaten by the snake. The –l and –w options allow you to specify the length and width of the field. By default the entire screen (except for the last column) is used.

You are represented on the screen by an I. The snake is 6 squares long and is represented by S's. The money is $, and an exit is #. Your score is posted in the upper left hand corner.

You can move around using the same conventions as vi(1), the h, j, k, and l keys work, as do the arrow keys. Other possibilities include:

sefc   These keys are like hjkl but form a directed pad around the d key.

HJKL   These keys move you all the way in the indicated direction to the same row or column as the money. This does *not* let you jump away from the snake, but rather saves you from having to type a key repeatedly. The snake still gets all his turns.

SEFC   Likewise for the upper case versions on the left.

ATPB   These keys move you to the four edges of the screen. Their position on the keyboard is the mnemonic, e.g. P is at the far right of the keyboard.

x   This lets you quit the game at any time.

p   Points in a direction you might want to go.

w   Space warp to get out of tight squeezes, at a price.

To earn money, move to the same square the money is on. A new $ will appear when you earn the current one. As you get richer, the snake gets hungrier. To leave the game, move to the exit (#).

A record is kept of the personal best score of each player. Scores are only counted if you leave at the exit, getting eaten by the snake is worth nothing.

As in pinball, matching the last digit of your score to the number which appears after the game is worth a bonus.

To see who wastes time playing snake, run *snscore* .

FILES

/usr/games/lib/snakerawscores database of personal bests
/usr/games/lib/snake.log   log of games played

BUGS

When playing on a small screen, it's hard to tell when you hit the edge of the screen.

The scoring function takes into account the size of the screen. A perfect function to do this equitably has not been devised.

NAME

tetris – the game of tetris

SYNOPSIS

tetris [–s] [–k *keys*] [–l *level*]

DESCRIPTION

The **tetris** command runs display-based game which must be played on a CRT terminal. The object is to fit the shapes together forming complete rows, which then vanish. When the shapes fill up to the top, the game ends. You can optionally select a level of play, or custom-select control keys.

The default level of play is 2.

The default control keys are as follows:

j	move left
k	rotate 1/4 turn counterclockwise
l	move right
<space>	drop
p	pause
q	quit

The options are as follows:

–k   The default control keys can be changed using the **–k –option**. The *keys* argument must have the six keys in order, and, remember to quote any space or tab characters from the shell. For example:

```
tetris -l 2 -k 'jkl pq'
```

will play the default games, i.e. level 2 and with the default control keys. The current key settings are displayed at the bottom of the screen during play.

–l   Select a level of play.

–s   Display the top scores.

PLAY

At the start of the game, a shape will appear at the top of the screen, falling one square at a time. The speed at which it falls is determined directly by the level: if you select level 2, the blocks will fall twice per second; at level 9, they fall 9 times per second. (As the game goes on, things speed up, no matter what your initial selection.) When this shape "touches down" on the bottom of the field, another will appear at the top.

You can move shapes to the left or right, rotate them counterclockwise, or drop them to the bottom by pressing the appropriate keys. As you fit them together, completed horizontal rows vanish, and any blocks above fall down to fill in. When the blocks stack up to the top of the screen, the game is over.

SCORING

You get one point for every block you fit into the stack, and one point for every space a block falls when you hit the drop key. (Dropping the blocks is therefore a good way to increase your score.) Your total score is the product of the level of play and your accumulated points—200 points on level 3 gives you a score of 600. Each player gets at most one entry on any level, for a total of nine scores in the high scores file. Players who no longer have accounts are limited to one score. Also, scores over 5 years old are expired. The exception to these conditions is that the highest score on a given level is *always* kept, so that following generations can pay homage to those who have wasted serious amounts of time.

The score list is produced at the end of the game. The printout includes each player's overall ranking, name, score, and how many points were scored on what level. Scores which are the highest on a given level are marked with asterisks "*".

FILES

/var/games/tetris.scores   high score file

BUGS

The higher levels are unplayable without a fast terminal connection.

AUTHORS

Adapted from a 1989 International Obfuscated C Code Contest winner by Chris Torek and Darren F. Provine.

Manual adapted from the original entry written by Nancy L. Tinkham and Darren F. Provine.

6

6

NAME

trek – trekkie game

SYNOPSIS

/usr/games/trek [[**−a**] file]

DESCRIPTION

Trek is a game of space glory and war. Below is a summary of commands. For complete documentation, see *Trek* by Eric Allman.

If a filename is given, a log of the game is written onto that file. If the **−a** flag is given before the filename, that file is appended to, not truncated.

The game will ask you what length game you would like. Valid responses are ''short'', ''medium'', and ''long''. You may also type ''restart'', which restarts a previously saved game. You will then be prompted for the skill, to which you must respond ''novice'', ''fair'', ''good'', ''expert'', ''commodore'', or ''impossible''. You should normally start out with a novice and work up.

In general, throughout the game, if you forget what is appropriate the game will tell you what it expects if you just type in a question mark.

AUTHOR

Eric Allman

SEE ALSO

/usr/doc/trek

COMMAND SUMMARY

abandon	capture
cloak up/down	
computer request; ...	**da**mages
destruct	**dock**
help	impulse course distance
lrscan	move course distance
phasers automatic amount	
phasers manual amt1 course1 spread1 ...	
torpedo course [yes] angle/**no**	
ram course distance	rest time
shell	shields **up/down**
srscan [yes/**no**]	
status	**terminate** yes/no
undock	visual course
warp warp_factor	

NAME

worm – play the growing worm game

SYNOPSIS

worm [*size*]

DESCRIPTION

In *worm,* you are a little worm, your body is the "o'"s on the screen and your head is the "@". You move with the hjkl keys (as in the game snake). If you don't press any keys, you continue in the direction you last moved. The upper case HJKL keys move you as if you had pressed several (9 for HL and 5 for JK) of the corresponding lower case key (unless you run into a digit, then it stops).

On the screen you will see a digit, if your worm eats the digit is will grow longer, the actual amount longer depends on which digit it was that you ate. The object of the game is to see how long you can make the worm grow.

The game ends when the worm runs into either the sides of the screen, or itself. The current score (how much the worm has grown) is kept in the upper left corner of the screen.

The optional argument, if present, is the initial length of the worm.

BUGS

If the initial length of the worm is set to less than one or more than 75, various strange things happen.

NAME

worms – animate worms on a display terminal

SYNOPSIS

worms [–ft] [–l *length*] [–n *number*]

DESCRIPTION

A UNIX version of the DEC-2136 program "worms".

The options are as follows:

    –f   Makes a "field" for the worm(s) to eat.

    –t   Makes each worm leave a trail behind it.

    –l   Specifies a length for each worm; the default is 16.

    –n   Specifies the number of worms; the default is 3.

BUGS

The lower-right-hand character position will not be updated properly on a terminal that wraps at the right margin.

NAME
    wump – hunt the wumpus in an underground cave

SYNOPSIS
    wump [-h] [-a arrows] [-b bats] [-p pits] [-r rooms] [-t tunnels]

DESCRIPTION
The game *wump* is based on a fantasy game first presented in the pages of *People's Computer Company* in 1973. In Hunt the Wumpus you are placed in a cave built of many different rooms, all interconnected by tunnels. Your quest is to find and shoot the evil Wumpus that resides elsewhere in the cave without running into any pits or using up your limited supply of arrows.

The options are as follows:

-a   Specifies the number of magic arrows the adventurer gets. The default is five.

-b   Specifies the number of rooms in the cave which contain bats. The default is three.

-h   Play the hard version -- more pits, more bats, and a generally more dangerous cave.

-n   Specifies the number of rooms in the cave which contain bottomless pits. The default is three.

-r   Specifies the number of rooms in the cave. The default cave size is twenty-five rooms.

-t   Specifies the number of tunnels connecting each room in the cave to another room. Beware, too many tunnels in a small cave can easily cause it to collapse! The default cave room has three tunnels to other rooms.

While wandering through the cave you'll notice that, while there are tunnels everywhere, there are some mysterious quirks to the cave topology, including some tunnels that go from one room to another, but not necessarily back! Also, most pesky of all are the rooms that are home to large numbers of bats, which, upon being disturbed, will en masse grab you and move you to another portion of the cave (including those housing bottomless pits, sure death for unwary explorers).

Fortunately, you're not going into the cave without any weapons or tools, and in fact your biggest aids are your senses; you can often smell the rather odiferous Wumpus up to *two* rooms away, and you can always feel the drafts created by the occasional bottomless pit and hear the rustle of the bats in caves they might be sleeping within.

To kill the wumpus, you'll need to shoot it with one of your magic arrows. Fortunately, you don't have to be in the same room as the creature, and can instead shoot the arrow from as far as three or four rooms away!

When you shoot an arrow, you do so by typing in a list of rooms that you'd like it to travel to. If at any point in its travels it cannot find a tunnel to the room you specify from the room it's in, it will instead randomly fly down one of the tunnels, possibly, if you're real unlucky, even flying back into the room you're in and hitting you!

6

NAME
    xneko – cat-and-mouse chase in an X window

SYNOPSIS
    xneko [**-display** *display*] [**-geometry** *geometry*] [**-title** *title*] [**-name** *name*] [**-iconic**] [**-speed** *speed*]
    [**-time** *time*] [**-help**]

DESCRIPTION
    Xneko displays a window in which a cat chases your "mouse" cursor.

    All options except the last three above behave in the standard manner for X applications (see *X*(1)). The -
speed option controls the speed of the cat (the default is 16). The **-time** option controls the interval (in
microseconds) between updates of the *xneko* window (the default is 125000). The **-help** option provides a
usage message and exits.

    The word "neko" means "cat" in Japanese.

SEE ALSO
    X(1)

AUTHOR
    Masayuki Koba, 1990

NAME

    xroach – cockroaches hide under your windows

SYNOPSIS

    xroach [-option .,..]

DESCRIPTION

    Xroach displays disgusting cockroaches on your root window. These creepy crawlies scamper around until they find a window to hide under. Whenever you move or iconify a window, the exposed beetles again scamper for cover.

OPTIONS

    –display *display_name*

        Drop the roaches on the given display. Make sure the display is nearby, so you can hear the screams.

    –rc *roach_color*

        Use the given string as the color for the bugs instead of the default "black".

    –speed *roach_speed*

        Use the given speed for the insects instead of the default 20.0. For example, in winter the speed should be set to 5.0. In summer, 30.0 might be about right.

    –roaches *num_roaches*

        This is the number of the little critters. Default is 10.

BUGS

    As given by the -roaches option. Default is 10.

COPYRIGHT

    Copyright 1991 by J.T. Anderson

AUTHORS

    J.T. Anderson (jta@locus.com)

DEDICATION

    Greg McFarlane (gregm@otc.otca.oz.au)

SEE ALSO

    xroachmotel(1), xddt(1)

Section 7
Miscellaneous

NAME

intro – miscellaneous information pages

DESCRIPTION

This section contains miscellaneous documentation, mostly in the area of text processing macro packages for troff(1).

HISTORY

intro appeared in 4.2 BSD.

NAME

ascii – octal, hexadecimal and decimal ASCII character sets

DESCRIPTION

The **octal** set:

```
000 nul  001 soh  002 stx  003 etx  004 eot  005 enq  006 ack  007 bel
010 bs   011 ht   012 nl   013 vt   014 np   015 cr   016 so   017 si
020 dle  021 dc1  022 dc2  023 dc3  024 dc4  025 nak  026 syn  027 etb
030 can  031 em   032 sub  033 esc  034 fs   035 gs   036 rs   037 us
040 sp   041 !    042 "    043 #    044 $    045 %    046 &    047 '
050 (    051 )    052 *    053 +    054 ,    055 -    056 .    057 /
060 0    061 1    062 2    063 3    064 4    065 5    066 6    067 7
070 8    071 9    072 :    073 ;    074 <    075 =    076 >    077 ?
100 @    101 A    102 B    103 C    104 D    105 E    106 F    107 G
110 H    111 I    112 J    113 K    114 L    115 M    116 N    117 O
120 P    121 Q    122 R    123 S    124 T    125 U    126 V    127 W
130 X    131 Y    132 Z    133 [    134 \    135 ]    136 ^    137 _
140 `    141 a    142 b    143 c    144 d    145 e    146 f    147 g
150 h    151 i    152 j    153 k    154 l    155 m    156 n    157 o
160 p    161 q    162 r    163 s    164 t    165 u    166 v    167 w
170 x    171 y    172 z    173 {    174 |    175 }    176 ~    177 del
```

The **hexadecimal** set:

```
00 nul  01 soh  02 stx  03 etx  04 eot  05 enq  06 ack  07 bel
08 bs   09 ht   0a nl   0b vt   0c np   0d cr   0e so   0f si
10 dle  11 dc1  12 dc2  13 dc3  14 dc4  15 nak  16 syn  17 etb
18 can  19 em   1a sub  1b esc  1c fs   1d gs   1e rs   1f us
20 sp   21 !    22 "    23 #    24 $    25 %    26 &    27 '
28 (    29 )    2a *    2b +    2c ,    2d -    2e .    2f /
30 0    31 1    32 2    33 3    34 4    35 5    36 6    37 7
38 8    39 9    3a :    3b ;    3c <    3d =    3e >    3f ?
40 @    41 A    42 B    43 C    44 D    45 E    46 F    47 G
48 H    49 I    4a J    4b K    4c L    4d M    4e N    4f O
50 P    51 Q    52 R    53 S    54 T    55 U    56 V    57 W
58 X    59 Y    5a Z    5b [    5c \    5d ]    5e ^    5f _
60 `    61 a    62 b    63 c    64 d    65 e    66 f    67 g
68 h    69 i    6a j    6b k    6c l    6d m    6e n    6f o
70 p    71 q    72 r    73 s    74 t    75 u    76 v    77 w
78 x    79 y    7a z    7b {    7c |    7d }    7e ~    7f del
```

The **decimal** set:

```
 0 nul   1 soh   2 stx   3 etx   4 eot   5 enq   6 ack   7 bel
 8 bs    9 ht   10 nl   11 vt   12 np   13 cr   14 so   15 si
16 dle  17 dc1  18 dc2  19 dc3  20 dc4  21 nak  22 syn  23 etb
24 can  25 em   26 sub  27 esc  28 fs   29 gs   30 rs   31 us
32 sp   33 !    34 "    35 #    36 $    37 %    38 &    39 '
40 (    41 )    42 *    43 +    44 ,    45 -    46 .    47 /
48 0    49 1    50 2    51 3    52 4    53 5    54 6    55 7
56 8    57 9    58 :    59 ;    60 <    61 =    62 >    63 ?
64 @    65 A    66 B    67 C    68 D    69 E    70 F    71 G
```

72	H	73	I	74	J	75	K	76	L	77	M	78	N	79	O
80	P	81	Q	82	R	83	S	84	T	85	U	86	V	87	W
88	X	89	Y	90	Z	91	[	92	\	93	]	94	^	95	_
96	'	97	a	98	b	99	c	100	d	101	e	102	f	103	g
104	h	105	i	106	j	107	k	108	l	109	m	110	n	111	o
112	p	113	q	114	r	115	s	116	t	117	u	118	v	119	w
120	x	121	y	122	z	123	{	124			125	}	126	~	127	del

FILES

/usr/share/misc/ascii

HISTORY

An `ascii` manual page appeared in Version 7 AT&T UNIX.

7

NAME

    `environ` – user environment

SYNOPSIS

    extern char **environ;

DESCRIPTION

An array of strings called the *environment* is made available by `execve`(2) when a process begins. By convention these strings have the form "*name=value*". The following names are used by various commands:

`BLOCKSIZE` The size of the block units used by several commands, most notably `df`(1), `du`(1) and `ls`(1). BLOCKSIZE may be specified in units of a byte by specifying a number, in units of a kilobyte by specifying a number followed by "K" or "k", in units of a megabyte by specifying a number followed by "M" or "m" and in units of a gigabyte by specifying a number followed by "G" or "g". Sizes less than 512 bytes or greater than a gigabyte are ignored.

`EXINIT` A startup list of commands read by `ex`(1), `edit`(1), and `vi`(1).

`HOME` A user's login directory, set by `login`(1) from the password file `passwd`(5).

`PATH` The sequence of directories, separated by colons, searched by `csh`(1), `sh`(1), `system`(3), `execvp`(3), etc, when looking for an executable file. PATH is set to ":/usr/ucb:/bin:/usr/bin" initially by `login`(1).

`PRINTER` The name of the default printer to be used by `lpr`(1), `lpq`(1), and `lprm`(1).

`SHELL` The full pathname of the user's login shell.

`TERM` The kind of terminal for which output is to be prepared. This information is used by commands, such as `nroff`(1) or `plot`(1) which may exploit special terminal capabilities. See `/usr/share/misc/termcap` (`termcap`(5)) for a list of terminal types.

`TERMCAP` The string describing the terminal in TERM, or, if it begins with a '/', the name of the termcap file. See `TERMPATH` below, `termcap`(5), and `termcap`.

`TERMPATH` A sequence of pathnames of termcap files, separated by colons or spaces, which are searched for terminal descriptions in the order listed. Having no `TERMPATH` is equivalent to a `TERMPATH` of "`$HOME/.termcap:/etc/termcap`". `TERMPATH` is ignored if `TERMCAP` contains a full pathname.

`TMPDIR` The directory in which to store temporary files. Most applications use either "/tmp" or "/var/tmp". Setting this variable will make them use another directory.

`TZ` The timezone to use when displaying dates. The normal format is a pathname relative to "/usr/share/zoneinfo". For example, the command "env TZ=US/Pacific date" displays the current time in California. See `tzset`(3) for more information.

`USER` The login name of the user.

Further names may be placed in the environment by the `export` command and *name=value* arguments in `sh`(1), or by the `setenv` command if you use `csh`(1). It is unwise to change certain `sh`(1) variables that are frequently exported by `.profile` files, such as `MAIL`, `PS1`, `PS2`, and `IFS`, unless you know what you are doing.

SEE ALSO
    csh(1), ex(1), login(1), sh(1), execve(2), execle(3), system(3), termcap(3), termcap(5)

HISTORY
    The **environ** manual page appeared in 4.2BSD.

NAME

eqnchar – special character definitions for eqn

SYNOPSIS

eqn /usr/share/misc/eqnchar [files]| **troff** [options]

neqn /usr/pub/eqnchar [files]| **nroff** [options]

DESCRIPTION

Eqnchar contains *troff* and *nroff* character definitions for constructing characters that are not available on the Graphic Systems typesetter. These definitions are primarily intended for use with *eqn* and *neqn*. It contains definitions for the following characters

ciplus	⊕	||	||	*square*	□
citimes	⊗	*langle*	⟨	*circle*	○
wig	~	*rangle*	⟩	*blot*	⬛
-wig	≈	*hbar*	ℏ	*bullet*	●
>wig	≳	*ppd*	⊥	*prop*	∝
<wig	≲	*<->*	↔	*empty*	∅
=wig	≅	*<=>*	⇔	*member*	∈
star	✱	*|<*	≮	*nomem*	∉
bigstar	✻	*|>*	≯	*cup*	∪
=dot	≐	*ang*	∟	*cap*	∩
orsign	∨	*rang*	⊢	*incl*	⊥
andsign	∧	*3dot*	⋮	*subset*	⊂
=del	≜	*thf*	∴	*supset*	⊃
oppA	⩑	*quarter*	¼	*!subset*	⊆
oppE	∃	*3quarter*	¾	*!supset*	⊇
angstrom	Å	*degree*	°		

FILES

/usr/pub/eqnchar

SEE ALSO

troff(1), eqn(1)

NAME

groff_char – groff character names

DESCRIPTION

This manual page lists the standard **groff** input characters. Only the characters that are available for the device that is being used to print this manual page will be displayed. The *Input code* column applies to characters which can be input with a single character, and gives the ISO Latin-1 code of that input character. The *PostScript name* column gives the usual PostScript name of the output character.

The ISO Latin-1 no-break space (code 0240 octal) is equivalent to \(space). All other ISO Latin-1 characters print as themselves with the following exceptions: ` prints as ', ´ prints as '; the corresponding ISO Latin-1 characters can be obtained with \' and \(aq. The ISO Latin-1 'Hyphen, Minus Sign' (code 45) prints as a hyphen; a minus sign can be obtained with \-. The ISO Latin-1 'Tilde' (code 126) prints as ~; the larger glyph can be obtained with \(ti. The ISO Latin-1 'Circumflex Accent' (code 94) prints as ^; a larger glyph can be obtained with \(ha.

Output	Input name	Input code	PostScript name	Notes
Æ	\(AE		AE	
æ	\(ae		ae	
Œ	\(OE		OE	
œ	\(oe		oe	
ß	\(ss		germandbls	
´	\(aa		acute	acute accent
`	\(ga		grave	grave accent
¢	\(ct		cent	
	\(ff		ff	ff ligature
fi	\(fi		fi	fi ligature
fl	\(fl		fl	fl ligature
	\(Fi		ffi	ffi ligature
	\(Fl		ffl	ffl ligature
←	\(<-		arrowleft	
→	\(->		arrowright	
↔	\(<>		arrowboth	horizontal double-headed arrow
↓	\(da		arrowdown	
↑	\(ua		arrowup	
|	\(br		br	box rule with traditional troff metrics
_	\(ru		ru	baseline rule
	\(ul		ul	underline with traditional troff metrics
⎮	\(bv		bv	bold vertical
♥	\(bs		bell	
O	\(ci		circle	
•	\(bu		bullet	
©	\(co		copyright	
®	\(rg		registered	
™	\(tm		trademark	
‡	\(dd		daggerdbl	double dagger sign
†	\(dg		dagger	
£	\(ps		paragraph	
§	\(sc		section	
°	\(de		degree	
—	\(em		emdash	em dash
–	\(en		endash	en dash
½	\(12		onehalf	

Output	Input name	Input code	PostScript name	Notes
¼	\(14		onequarter	
¾	\(34		threequarters	
′	\(fm		minute	footmark, prime
″	\(sd		second	
-	\(hy		hyphen	
∧	\(la		angleleft	left angle bracket
⇐	\(lh		handleft	
⇒	\(rh		handright	
"	\(lq		quotedblleft	
"	\(rq		quotedblright	
│	\(or		bar	
−	\-		minus	minus sign from current font
/	\(sl		slash	
□	\(sq		square	
∴	\(tf		therefore	
A	\(*A		Alpha	
B	\(*B		Beta	
Ξ	\(*C		Xi	
Δ	\(*D		Delta	
E	\(*E		Epsilon	
Φ	\(*F		Phi	
Γ	\(*G		Gamma	
Θ	\(*H		Theta	
I	\(*I		Iota	
K	\(*K		Kappa	
Λ	\(*L		Lambda	
M	\(*M		Mu	
N	\(*N		Nu	
O	\(*O		Omicron	
Π	\(*P		Pi	
Ψ	\(*Q		Psi	
P	\(*R		Rho	
Σ	\(*S		Sigma	
T	\(*T		Tau	
Υ	\(*U		Upsilon	
Ω	\(*W		Omega	
X	\(*X		Chi	
H	\(*Y		Eta	
Z	\(*Z		Zeta	
α	\(*a		alpha	
β	\(*b		beta	
ξ	\(*c		xi	
δ	\(*d		delta	
ε	\(*e		epsilon	
φ	\(*f		phi	
γ	\(*g		gamma	
θ	\(*h		theta	
ι	\(*i		iota	
κ	\(*k		kappa	
λ	\(*l		lambda	
μ	\(*m		mu	

Output	Input name	Input code	PostScript name	Notes
ν	\(*n		nu	
o	\(*o		omicron	
π	\(*p		pi	
ψ	\(*q		psi	
ρ	\(*r		rho	
σ	\(*s		sigma	
τ	\(*t		tau	
υ	\(*u		upsilon	
ω	\(*w		omega	
χ	\(*x		chi	
η	\(*y		eta	
ζ	\(*z		zeta	
ς	\(ts		sigma1	terminal sigma
	\(~		approxequal	
≈	\(~=		approxequal	
≠	\(!=		notequal	
*	\(**		asteriskmath	
±	\(+-		plusminus	
≤	\(<=		lessequal	
≡	\(==		equivalence	
≥	\(>=		greaterequal	
¬	\(no		logicalnot	
∃	\(te		existential	there exists, existential quantifier
∀	\(fa		universal	for all, universal quantifier
∞	\(if		infinity	
∈	\(mo		element	
×	\(mu		multiply	
+	\(pl		plusmath	plus sign in special font
=	\(eq		equalmath	equals sign in special font
∝	\(pt		proportional	
¶	\(pp		perpendicular	
⊂	\(sb		propersubset	
⊃	\(sp		propersuperset	
⊆	\(ib		reflexsubset	
⊇	\(ip		reflexsuperset	
~	\(ap		similar	
∂	\(pd		partialdiff	partial differentiation sign
∩	\(ca		intersection	intersection, cap
∪	\(cu		union	union, cup
÷	\(di		divide	division sign
∇	\(gr		gradient	
∅	\(es		emptyset	
∧	\(an		arrowhorizex	horizontal arrow extension

SEE ALSO

groff(1)

An extension to the troff character set for Europe, E.G. Keizer, K.J. Simonsen, J. Akkerhuis, EUUG Newsletter, Volume 9, No. 2, Summer 1989

NAME
hier – layout of filesystems

DESCRIPTION
An outline of the filesystem hierarchy.

/   root directory of the system

/COPYRIGHT
system copyright notice

/[a-z]   user filesystems

/altroot/   alternate root filesystem, in case of disaster

/amd/   home directories mount point; see amd(8)

/bin/   utilities used in both single and multi-user environments

/dev/   block, character and other special device files

MAKEDEV
script for creating device files; see makedev(8)

console	the computer's console device
fd/	file descriptor files; see fd(4)
drum	system swap space; see drum(4)
klog	kernel logging device; see syslog(3)
kmem	kernel virtual memory device; see mem(4)
log	UNIX domain datagram log socket; see syslogd(8)
mem	kernel physical memory device; see mem(4)
stderr	
stdin	
stdout	file descriptor files; see fd(4)
null	the null device; see null(4)
tty	process' controlling terminal device; see tty(4)

/dump/   online dump(8) repository

/etc/   system configuration files and scripts

aliases∗	name alias files for sendmail(8)
amd∗	configuration files for amd(8)
changelist	files backed up by the security script
crontab	schedule used by the cron(8) daemon
csh.cshrc	
csh.login	
csh.logout	system-wide scripts for csh(1)
daily	script run each day by cron(8)
disklabels/	backup disklabels; see disklabel(8)
disktab	disk description file, see disktab(5)
dm.conf	dungeon master configuration; see dm.conf(5)
dumpdates	dump history; see dump(8)
exports	filesystem export information; see mountd(8)
fstab	filesystem information; see fstab(5) and mount(8)

ftpusers	users denied ftp(1) access; see ftpd(8)
ftpwelcome	ftp(1) initial message; see ftpd(8)
gettytab	terminal configuration database; see gettytab(8)
group	group permissions file; see group(5)
hosts	host name database backup for named(8); see hosts(5)
hosts.equiv	trusted machines with equivalent user ID's
hosts.lpd	trusted machines with printing privileges
inetd.conf	Internet server configuration file; see inetd(8)
kerberosIV/	configuration files for the kerberos version IV; see kerberos(1)
localtime	local timezone information; see ctime(3)
mail.rc	system-wide initialization script for mail(1)
man.conf	configuration file for man(1); see man.conf(5)
master.passwd	
passwd	
pwd.db	
spwd.db	password files and their databases; see pwd_mkdb(8)
monthly	script run each month by cron(8)
motd	system message of the day
mtree/	mtree configuration files; see mtree(1)
named.*	
namedb/	named configuration files and databases; see named(8)
netgroup	network groups; see netgroup(5)
netstart	network startup script
networks	network name data base; see networks(5)
phones	remote host phone number data base; see phones(5)
printcap	system printer configuration; see printcap(5)
protocols	protocol name database; see protocols(5)
rc	
rc.local	system startup files; see rc(8)
remote	remote host description file; see remote(5)
security	daily (in)security script run by cron(8)
sendmail.*	sendmail(8) configuration information
services	service name data base; see services(5)
shells	list of permitted shells; see shells(5)
sliphome	slip login/logout scripts; see slattach(8)
syslog.conf	syslogd(8) configuration file; see syslog.conf(5)
termcap	terminal type database; see termcap(3)
ttys	terminal initialization information; see ttys(5)
weekly	script run each week by cron(8)

/home/	mount point for the automounter; see amd(8)
/mnt/	empty directory commonly used by system administrators as a temporary mount point
/root/	home directory for the super-user

.rhosts	super-user id mapping between machines
.cshrc	super-user start-up file
.login	super-user start-up file
.profile	super-user start-up file

/sbin/	system programs and administration utilities used in both single-user and multi-user environments	
/stand/	programs used in a standalone environment	
/sys	symbolic link to the operating system source	
/tmp/	temporary files, usually a `mfs`(8) memory-based filesystem (the contents of /tmp are usually NOT preserved across a system reboot)	
/usr/	contains the majority of the system utilities and files	

    X11   X11 files

bin/	X11 binaries
include/	X11 include files
lib/	X11 libraries

    bin/   common utilities, programming tools, and applications
    contrib/   packages maintained by groups other than Berkeley

bin/	contributed binaries
include/	contributed include files
libexec/	contributed daemons
libdata/	contributed data files

    games/   the important stuff
    include/   standard C include files

X11/	include files for X11 window system
arpa/	include files for Internet service protocols
g++/	include files for the C++ compiler
kerberosIV/	include files for kerberos authentication package; see `kerberos`(1)
machine/	machine specific include files
net/	miscellaneous network include files
netccitt/	CCITT networking include files
netinet/	include files for Internet standard protocols; see `inet`(4)
netiso/	include files for ISO standard protocols; see `iso`(4)
netns/	include files for XNS standard protocols; see `ns`(4)
nfs/	include files for NFS (Network File System)
pascal/	include files for `pc`(1)
protocols/	include files for Berkeley service protocols
rpc/	include files for Sun Microsystem's RPC package
sys/	kernel include files
ufs/	include files for UFS
xnscourier/	include files for XNS package

    lib/   system C library archives; see `ar`(1)

uucp/	UUCP binaries and scripts (historically placed; to be moved)

    libdata/   miscellaneous utility data files

libexec/		system daemons and system utilities (executed by other programs)
local/		local executables, libraries, etc.
	bin/	local binaries
	include/	local include files
	libexec/	local daemons
	libdata/	local data files
obj/		architecture-specific target tree produced by building the `/usr/src` tree; normally a symbolic link or mounted filesystem
old/		programs from past lives of 4BSD which may disappear in future releases
	bin/	old binaries
	include/	old include files
	libexec/	old daemons
	libdata/	old data files
sbin/		system daemons and system utilities (normally executed by the super-user)
share/		architecture-independent text files
	calendar/	a variety of calendar files; see `calendar`(1)
	dict/	word lists; see `look`(1) and `spell`(1)

	words	common words
	web2	words of Webster's 2nd International
	papers/	reference databases; see `refer`(1)
	special/	custom word lists; see `spell`(1)

	doc/	miscellaneous documentation; source for most of the printed 4BSD manuals (available from the USENIX association)
	games/	text files used by various games
	man/	formatted manual pages
	me/	macros for use with the me(7) macro package
	misc/	miscellaneous system-wide text files

	termcap	terminal characteristics database; see `termcap`(5)

	mk/	include files for `make`(1)
	ms/	macros for use with the ms(7) macro package
	skel/	sample initialization files for new user accounts
	tabset/	tab description files for a variety of terminals, used in the termcap file; see `termcap`(5)
	tmac/	text processing macros; see `nroff`(1) and `troff`(1)
	zoneinfo/	timezone configuration information; see `tzfile`(5)
usr.bin/		source for utilities/files in `/usr/bin`
usr.sbin/		source for utilities/files in `/usr/sbin`

/usr/src/		4BSD and local source files
	bin/	source for utilities/files in `/bin`
	contrib/	source for utilities/files in `/usr/contrib`
	etc/	source (usually example files) for files in `/etc`
	games/	source for utilities/files in `/usr/games`
	include/	source for files in `/usr/include`
	kerberosIV/	source for Kerberos version IV utilities and libraries
	lib/	source for libraries in `/usr/lib`

libexec/	source for utilities/files in `/usr/libexec`
local/	source for utilities/files in `/usr/local`
old/	source for utilities/files in `/usr/old`
sbin/	source for utilities/files in `/sbin`
share/	source for files in `/usr/share`

doc/

papers/	source for various Berkeley technical papers
psd/	source for Programmer's Supplementary Documents
smm/	source for System Manager's Manual
usd/	source for User's Supplementary Documents

sys/   kernel source files

compile/	kernel compilation directory
conf/	architecture independent configuration directory
deprecated/	deprecated kernel functionality
dev/	architecture independent device support
hp/	general support for Hewlett-Packard architectures
hp300/	support for the Hewlett-Packard 9000/300 68000-based workstations
i386/	support for the Intel 386/486 workstations
isofs/	support for ISO filesystems

cd9660/   support for the ISO-9660 filesystem

kern/	support for the high kernel (system calls)
libkern/	C library routines used in the kernel
luna68k/	Omron Luna 68000-based workstations
mips/	general support for MIPS architectures
miscfs/	miscellaneous file systems
net/	miscellaneous networking support
netccitt/	CCITT networking support
netinet/	TCP/IP networking support
netiso/	ISO networking support
netns/	XNS networking support
news3400/	Sony News MIPS-based workstations
nfs/	NFS support
pmax/	DECstation 3100 and 5000 MIPS-based workstations
scripts/	kernel debugging scripts
sparc/	Sparcstation I & II SPARC-based workstations
stand/	kernel standalone support
sys/	kernel (and system) include files
tahoe/	Computer Consoles Inc. Tahoe architecture (obsolete)
tests/	kernel testing
ufs/	local filesystem support

ffs/	the Berkeley Fast File System
lfs/	the log-structured file system
mfs/	the in-memory file system
ufs/	shared UNIX file system support

vax/	Digital Equipment Corp. VAX architecture (obsolete)
vm/	virtual memory support

/var/   multi-purpose log, temporary, transient, and spool files

    account/   system accounting files

        acct   execution accounting file; see `acct`(5)

    at/   timed command scheduling files; see `at`(1)
    backups/   miscellaneous backup files, largely of files found in `/etc`
    crash/   system crash dumps; see `savecore`(8)
    db/   miscellaneous automatically generated system-specific database files
    games/   miscellaneous game status and log files
    log/   miscellaneous system log files

amd.*	`amd`(8) logs
daily.out	output of the last run of the `/etc/daily` script
ftp.*	`ftp`(1) logs
kerberos.*	`kerberos`(1) logs
lastlog	system last time logged in log; see `utmp`(5)
lpd-errs.*	printer daemon error logs; see `lpd`(8)
maillog.*	`sendmail`(8) log files
messages.*	general system information log
monthly.out	output of the last run of the `/etc/monthly` script
secure	sensitive security information log
sendmail.st	`sendmail`(8) statistics
timed.*	`timed`(8) logs
weekly.out	output of the last run of the `/etc/weekly` script
wtmp	login/logout log; see `utmp`(5)

    mail/   user system mailboxes
    msgs/   system messages; see `msgs`(1)
    preserve/   temporary home of files preserved after an accidental death of `ex`(1) or `vi`(1)
    quotas/   filesystem quota information
    run/   system information files, rebuilt after each reboot

        utmp   database of current users; see `utmp`(5)

    rwho/   rwho data files; see `rwhod`(8), `rwho`(1), and `ruptime`(1)
    spool/   miscellaneous printer and mail system spooling directories

ftp/	commonly ``~ftp'', the anonymous ftp root directory; see `ftpd`(8)
mqueue/	undelivered mail queue; see `sendmail`(8)
news/	Network news archival and spooling directories
output/	printer spooling directories
secretmail/	secretmail spool directory; see `xget`(1)
uucp/	uucp spool directory
uucppublic/	commonly ``~uucp'', the uucp public temporary directory; see `uucp`(1)

    tmp/   temporary files that are not discarded between system reboots

        vi.recover/   recovery directory for `nvi`(1)

/vmunix   the executable for the operating system

SEE ALSO
  apropos(1), ls(1), whatis(1), whereis(1), which(1),

HISTORY
  A **hier** manual page appeared in Version 7 AT&T UNIX.

NAME

hostname – host name resolution description

DESCRIPTION

Hostnames are domains, where a domain is a hierarchical, dot-separated list of subdomains; for example, the machine monet, in the Berkeley subdomain of the EDU subdomain of the Internet would be represented as

        monet.Berkeley.EDU

(with no trailing dot).

Hostnames are often used with network client and server programs, which must generally translate the name to an address for use. (This function is generally performed by the library routine gethostbyname(3).) Hostnames are resolved by the Internet name resolver in the following fashion.

If the name consists of a single component, i.e. contains no dot, and if the environment variable "HOSTALIASES" is set to the name of a file, that file is searched for any string matching the input hostname. The file should consist of lines made up of two white-space separated strings, the first of which is the hostname alias, and the second of which is the complete hostname to be substituted for that alias. If a case-insensitive match is found between the hostname to be resolved and the first field of a line in the file, the substituted name is looked up with no further processing.

If the input name ends with a trailing dot, the trailing dot is removed, and the remaining name is looked up with no further processing.

If the input name does not end with a trailing dot, it is looked up by searching through a list of domains until a match is found. The default search list includes first the local domain, then its parent domains with at least 2 name components (longest first). For example, in the domain CS.Berkeley.EDU, the name lithium.CChem will be checked first as lithium.CChem.CS.Berkeley.EDU and then as lithium.CChem.Berkeley.EDU. Lithium.CChem.EDU will not be tried, as the there is only one component remaining from the local domain. The search path can be changed from the default by a system-wide configuration file (see resolver(5)).

SEE ALSO

gethostbyname(3), resolver(5), mailaddr(7), named(8)

HISTORY

Hostname appeared in 4.2 BSD.

NAME

`mailaddr` – mail addressing description

DESCRIPTION

Mail addresses are based on the Internet protocol listed at the end of this manual page. These addresses are in the general format

        user@domain

where a domain is a hierarchical dot separated list of subdomains. For example, a valid address is:

        eric@CS.Berkeley.EDU

Unlike some other forms of addressing, domains do not imply any routing. Thus, although this address is specified as an Internet address, it might travel by an alternate route if that were more convenient or efficient. For example, at Berkeley, the associated message would probably go directly to CS over the Ethernet rather than going via the Berkeley Internet gateway.

Abbreviation.

Under certain circumstances it may not be necessary to type the entire domain name. In general, anything following the first dot may be omitted if it is the same as the domain from which you are sending the message. For example, a user on "calder.berkeley.edu" could send to "eric@CS" without adding the "berkeley.edu" since it is the same on both sending and receiving hosts.

Compatibility.

Certain old address formats are converted to the new format to provide compatibility with the previous mail system. In particular,

        user@host

and

        user@host.domain

are allowed;

        host.domain!user

is converted to

        user@host.domain

and

        host!user

is converted to

        user@host.UUCP

This is normally converted back to the "host!user" form before being sent on for compatibility with older UUCP hosts.

Case Distinctions.

Domain names (i.e., anything after the "@" sign) may be given in any mixture of upper and lower case with the exception of UUCP hostnames. Most hosts accept any combination of case in user names, with the notable exception of MULTICS sites.

Route-addrs.

Under some circumstances it may be necessary to route a message through several hosts to get it to the final destination. Normally this routing is done automatically, but sometimes it is desirable to route the message manually. Addresses which show these relays are termed "route-addrs." These use the syntax:

        <@hosta,@hostb:user@hostc>

This specifies that the message should be sent to hosta, from there to hostb, and finally to hostc. This path is forced even if there is a more efficient path to hostc.

Route-addrs occur frequently on return addresses, since these are generally augmented by the software at each host. It is generally possible to ignore all but the "user@hostc" part of the address to determine the actual sender.

[Note: the route-addr syntax is officially deprecated in RFC 1123 and should not be used.]

Many sites also support the "percent hack" for simplistic routing:

        user%hostc%hostb@hosta

is routed as indicated in the previous example.

Postmaster.

Every site is required to have a user or user alias designated "postmaster" to which problems with the mail system may be addressed.

Other Networks.

Some other networks can be reached by giving the name of the network as the last component of the domain. *This is not a standard feature* and may not be supported at all sites. For example, messages to CSNET or BITNET sites can often be sent to "user@host.CSNET" or "user@host.BITNET" respectively.

SEE ALSO
        mail(1), sendmail(8);
        Crocker, D. H., *Standard for the Format of Arpa Internet Text Messages,* RFC822.

HISTORY
        Mailaddr appeared in 4.2 BSD.

BUGS

The RFC822 group syntax ("group:user1,user2,user3;") is not supported except in the special case of "group:;" because of a conflict with old berknet-style addresses.

Route-Address syntax is grotty.

UUCP- and Internet-style addresses do not coexist politely.

NAME

man – (deprecated) macros to typeset manual

SYNOPSIS

nroff **–man** file ...

troff **–man** file ...

DESCRIPTION

These macros were used in the past to lay out pages of this manual. A skeleton page may be found in the file /usr/share/misc/man.template. The new macros are in mdoc(7).

Any text argument *t* may be zero to six words. Quotes may be used to include blanks in a 'word'. If *text* is empty, special treatment is applied to the next input line with text to be printed. In this way .I may be used to italicize a whole line, or .SM may be followed by .B to make small bold letters.

A prevailing indent distance is remembered between successive indented paragraphs, and is reset to default value upon reaching a non-indented paragraph. Default units for indents *i* are ens.

Type font and size are reset to default values before each paragraph, and after processing font and size setting macros.

These strings are predefined by **–man**:

*R   '®', '(Reg)' in *nroff*.

*S   Change to default type size.

FILES

/usr/share/tmac/tmac.an
/usr/man/man.template

SEE ALSO

man(1), troff(1)

BUGS

Relative indents don't nest.

REQUESTS

Request	Cause If no Break Argument		Explanation
.B *t*	no	*t*=n.t.l.*	Text *t* is bold.
.BI *t*	no	*t*=n.t.l.	Join words of *t* alternating bold and italic.
.BR *t*	no	*t*=n.t.l.	Join words of *t* alternating bold and Roman.
.DT	no	.5i 1i...	Restore default tabs.
.HP *i*	yes	*i*=p.i.*	Set prevailing indent to *i*. Begin paragraph with hanging indent.
.I *t*	no	*t*=n.t.l.	Text *t* is italic.
.IB *t*	no	*t*=n.t.l.	Join words of *t* alternating italic and bold.
.IP *x i*	yes	*x*=''''	Same as .TP with tag *x*.
.IR *t*	no	*t*=n.t.l.	Join words of *t* alternating italic and Roman.
.LP	yes	-	Same as .PP.
.PD *d*	no	*d*=.4v	Interparagraph distance is *d*.
.PP	yes	-	Begin paragraph. Set prevailing indent to .5i.
.RE	yes	-	End of relative indent. Set prevailing indent to amount of starting .RS.
.RB *t*	no	*t*=n.t.l.	Join words of *t* alternating Roman and bold.
.RI *t*	no	*t*=n.t.l.	Join words of *t* alternating Roman and italic.
.RS *i*	yes	*i*=p.i.	Start relative indent, move left margin in distance *i*. Set prevailing indent to .5i for nested indents.
.SH *t*	yes	*t*=n.t.l.	Subhead.
.SM *t*	no	*t*=n.t.l.	Text *t* is small.

.TH $n\ c\ x\ v\ m$ yes	-		Begin page named n of chapter c; x is extra commentary, e.g. 'local', for page foot center; v alters page foot left, e.g. '4th Berkeley Distribution'; m alters page head center, e.g. 'Brand X Programmer's Manual'. Set prevailing indent and tabs to .5i.
.TP i	yes	i=p.i.	Set prevailing indent to i. Begin indented paragraph with hanging tag given by next text line. If tag doesn't fit, place it on separate line.

* n.t.l. = next text line; p.i. = prevailing indent

NAME

mdoc – quick reference guide for the –**mdoc** macro package

SYNOPSIS

groff –m*doc files* ...

DESCRIPTION

The –**mdoc** package is a set of content-based and domain-based macros used to format the BSD man pages. The macro names and their meanings are listed below for quick reference; for a detailed explanation on using the package, see the tutorial sampler mdoc.samples(7).

The macros are described in two groups, the first includes the structural and physical page layout macros. The second contains the manual and general text domain macros which differentiate the -**mdoc** package from other troff formatting packages.

PAGE STRUCTURE DOMAIN

Title Macros

To create a valid manual page, these three macros, in this order, are required:

.Dd	*Month day, year*	Document date.
.Dt	*DOCUMENT_TITLE [section] [volume]*	Title, in upper case.
.Os	*OPERATING_SYSTEM [version/release]*	Operating system (BSD).

Page Layout Macros

Section headers, paragraph breaks, lists and displays.

.Sh   Section Headers. Valid headers, in the order of presentation:

NAME	Name section, should include the .Nm or .Fn and the .Nd macros.
SYNOPSIS	Usage.
DESCRIPTION	General description, should include options and parameters.
RETURN VALUES	Sections two and three function calls.
ENVIRONMENT	Describe environment variables.
FILES	Files associated with the subject.
EXAMPLES	Examples and suggestions.
DIAGNOSTICS	Normally used for section four device interface diagnostics.
ERRORS	Sections two and three error and signal handling.
SEE ALSO	Cross references and citations.
STANDARDS	Conformance to standards if applicable.
HISTORY	If a standard is not applicable, the history of the subject should be given.
BUGS	Gotchas and caveats.
other	Customized headers may be added at the authors discretion.

.Ss   Subsection Headers.
.Pp   Paragraph Break. Vertical space (one line).
.D1   (D-one) Display-one Indent and display one text line.
.Dl   (D-ell) Display-one literal. Indent and display one line of literal text.
.Bd   Begin-display block. Display options:

–**ragged**	Unjustified (ragged edges).
–**filled**	Justified.
–**literal**	Literal text or code.
–**file** *name*	Read in named *file* and display.

`-offset` *string*	Offset display. Acceptable *string* values:	
	left	Align block on left (default).
	center	Approximate center margin.
	indent	Six constant width spaces (a tab).
	indent-two	Two tabs.
	right	Left aligns block 2 inches from right.
	xxn	Where *xx* is a number from **4n** to **99n**.
	Aa	Where *Aa* is a callable macro name.
	string	The width of *string* is used.

`.Ed`   End-display (matches .Bd).
`.Bl`   Begin-list. Create lists or columns. Options:

    List-types

        `-bullet` Bullet Item List
        `-item` Unlabeled List
        `-enum` Enumerated List
        `-tag` Tag Labeled List
        `-diag` Diagnostic List
        `-hang` Hanging Labeled List
        `-ohang` Overhanging Labeled List
        `-inset` Inset or Run-on Labeled List

    List-parameters

        `-offset` (All lists.) See `.Bd` begin-display above.
        `-width` (`-tag` and `-hang` lists only.) See `.Bd`.
        `-compact` (All lists.) Suppresses blank lines.

`.El`   End-list.
`.It`   List item.

MANUAL AND GENERAL TEXT DOMAIN MACROS

The manual and general text domain macros are special in that most of them are parsed for callable macros for example:

    `.Op Fl s Ar file`   Produces [`-s` *file*]

In this example, the option enclosure macro `.Op` is parsed, and calls the callable content macro 'Fl' which operates on the argument 's' and then calls the callable content macro 'Ar' which operates on the argument `file`. Some macros may be callable, but are not parsed and vice versa. These macros are indicated in the *parsed* and *callable* columns below.

Unless stated, manual domain macros share a common syntax:

    `.Va argument [ . , ; : ( ) [ ] argument ... ]`

Note: Opening and closing punctuation characters are only recognized as such if they are presented one at a time. The string ') ,' is not recognized as punctuation and will be output with a leading white space and in what ever font the calling macro uses. The argument list]) , is recognized as three sequential closing punctuation characters and a leading white space is not output between the characters and the previous argument (if any). The special meaning of a punctuation character may be escaped with the string '\&'. For example the following string,

    `.Ar file1 , file2 , file3 ) .`   Produces *file1*, *file2*, *file3*).

Manual Domain Macros

Name	Parsed	Callable	Description
Ad	Yes	Yes	Address. (This macro may be deprecated.)
Ar	Yes	Yes	Command line argument.
Cd	No	No	Configuration declaration (section four only).
Cm	Yes	Yes	Command line argument modifier.
Dv	Yes	Yes	Defined variable (source code).
Er	Yes	Yes	Error number (source code).
Ev	Yes	Yes	Environment variable.
Fa	Yes	Yes	Function argument.
Fd	Yes	Yes	Function declaration.
Fn	Yes	Yes	Function call (also .Fo and .Fc).
Ic	Yes	Yes	Interactive command.
Li	Yes	Yes	Literal text.
Nm	Yes	Yes	Command name.
Op	Yes	Yes	Option (also .Oo and .Oc).
Ot	Yes	Yes	Old style function type (Fortran only).
Pa	Yes	Yes	Pathname or file name.
St	Yes	Yes	Standards (-p1003.2, -p1003.1 or -ansiC)
Va	Yes	Yes	Variable name.
Vt	Yes	Yes	Variable type (Fortran only).
Xr	Yes	Yes	Manual Page Cross Reference.

General Text Domain Macros

Name	Parsed	Callable	Description
%A	Yes	No	Reference author.
%B	Yes	Yes	Reference book title.
%C	No	No	Reference place of publishing (city).
%D	No	No	Reference date.
%J	Yes	Yes	Reference journal title.
%N	No	No	Reference issue number.
%O	No	No	Reference optional information.
%P	No	No	Reference page number(s).
%R	No	No	Reference report Name.
%T	Yes	Yes	Reference article title.
%V	No	No	Reference volume.
Ac	Yes	Yes	Angle close quote.
Ao	Yes	Yes	Angle open quote.
Aq	Yes	Yes	Angle quote.
At	No	No	AT&T UNIX
Bc	Yes	Yes	Bracket close quote.
Bf	No	No	Begin font mode.
Bo	Yes	Yes	Bracket open quote.
Bq	Yes	Yes	Bracket quote.
Bx	Yes	Yes	Bx.
Db	No	No	Debug (default is "off")
Dc	Yes	Yes	Double close quote.
Do	Yes	Yes	Double open quote.

Dq	Yes	Yes	Double quote.
Ec	Yes	Yes	Enclose string close quote.
Ef	No	No	End font mode.
Em	Yes	Yes	Emphasis (traditional English).
Eo	Yes	Yes	Enclose string open quote.
No	Yes	Yes	Normal text (no-op).
Ns	Yes	Yes	No space.
Pc	Yes	Yes	Parenthesis close quote.
Pf	Yes	No	Prefix string.
Po	Yes	Yes	Parenthesis open quote.
Pq	Yes	Yes	Parentheses quote.
Qc	Yes	Yes	Strait Double close quote.
Ql	Yes	Yes	Quoted literal.
Qo	Yes	Yes	Strait Double open quote.
Qq	Yes	Yes	Strait Double quote.
Re	No	No	Reference start.
Rs	No	No	Reference start.
Sc	Yes	Yes	Single close quote.
So	Yes	Yes	Single open quote.
Sq	Yes	Yes	Single quote.
Sm	No	No	Space mode (default is "on")
Sx	Yes	Yes	Section Cross Reference.
Sy	Yes	Yes	Symbolic (traditional English).
Tn	Yes	Yes	Trade or type name (small Caps).
Ux	Yes	Yes	Ux
Xc	Yes	Yes	Extend argument list close.
Xo	Yes	Yes	Extend argument list close.

Macro names ending in 'q' quote remaining items on the argument list. Macro names ending in 'o' begin a quote which may span more than one line of input and are close quoted with the matching macro name ending in 'c'. Enclosure macros may be nested and are limited to eight arguments.

Note: the extended argument list macros (.Xo, .Xc) and the function enclosure macros (.Fo, .Fc) are irregular. The extended list macros are used when the number of macro arguments would exceed the troff limitation of nine arguments.

CONFIGURATION

For site specific configuration of the macro package, see the file /usr/src/share/tmac/README.

FILES

tmac.doc	Manual and general text domain macros.
tmac.doc-common	Common structural macros and definitions.
tmac.doc-nroff	Site dependent nroff style file.
tmac.doc-ditroff	Site dependent troff style file.
tmac.doc-syms	Special defines (such as the standards macro).

SEE ALSO

mdoc.samples(7)

NAME

`mdoc.samples` – tutorial sampler for writing BSD manuals with –**mdoc**

SYNOPSIS

`man mdoc.samples`

DESCRIPTION

A tutorial sampler for writing BSD manual pages with the –**mdoc** macro package, a *content*–based and *domain*–based formatting package for `troff(1)`. Its predecessor, the –man(7) package, addressed page layout leaving the manipulation of fonts and other typesetting details to the individual author. In –**mdoc**, page layout macros make up the *page structure domain* which consists of macros for titles, section headers, displays and lists. Essentially items which affect the physical position of text on a formatted page. In addition to the page structure domain, there are two more domains, the manual domain and the general text domain. The general text domain is defined as macros which perform tasks such as quoting or emphasizing pieces of text. The manual domain is defined as macros that are a subset of the day to day informal language used to describe commands, routines and related BSD files. Macros in the manual domain handle command names, command line arguments and options, function names, function parameters, pathnames, variables, cross references to other manual pages, and so on. These domain items have value for both the author and the future user of the manual page. It is hoped the consistency gained across the manual set will provide easier translation to future documentation tools.

Throughout the UNIX manual pages, a manual entry is simply referred to as a man page, regardless of actual length and without sexist intention.

GETTING STARTED

Since a tutorial document is normally read when a person desires to use the material immediately, the assumption has been made that the user of this document may be impatient. The material presented in the remained of this document is outlined as follows:

1. TROFF IDIOSYNCRASIES
   Macro Usage.
   Passing Space Characters in an Argument.
   Trailing Blank Space Characters (a warning).
   Escaping Special Characters.

2. THE ANATOMY OF A MAN PAGE
   A manual page template.

3. INTRODUCTION OF TITLE MACROS.

4. INTRODUCTION OF MANUAL AND GENERAL TEXT DOMAINS.
   What's in a name....
   General Syntax.

5. MANUAL DOMAIN
   Addresses.
   Arguments.
   Configuration Declarations (section four only).
   Command Modifier .
   Defined Variables.
   Errno's (Section two only).

7

TROFF IDIOSYNCRASIES

The **−mdoc** package attempts to simplify the process of writing a man page. Theoretically, one should not have to learn the dirty details of troff(1) to use **−mdoc**; however, there are a few limitations which are unavoidable and best gotten out of the way. And, too, be forewarned, this package is *not* fast.

Macro Usage

As in troff(1), a macro is called by placing a '.' (dot character) at the beginning of a line followed by the two character name for the macro. Arguments may follow the macro separated by spaces. It is the dot character at the beginning of the line which causes troff(1) to interpret the next two characters as a macro name. To place a '.' (dot character) at the beginning of a line in some context other than a macro invocation, precede the '.' (dot) with the '\&' escape sequence. The '\&' translates literally to a zero width space, and is never displayed in the output.

In general, troff(1) macros accept up to nine arguments, any extra arguments are ignored. Most macros in **−mdoc** accept nine arguments and, in limited cases, arguments may be continued or extended on the next line (See Extensions). A few macros handle quoted arguments (see Passing Space Characters in an Argument below).

Most of the **−mdoc** general text domain and manual domain macros are special in that their argument lists are *parsed* for callable macro names. This means an argument on the argument list which matches a general text or manual domain macro name and is determined to be callable will be executed or called when it is processed. In this case the argument, although the name of a macro, is not preceded by a '.' (dot). It is in this manner that many macros are nested; for example the option macro, .Op, may *call* the flag and argument macros, 'Fl' and 'Ar', to specify an optional flag with an argument:

    [**−s** *bytes*]   is produced by .Op Fl s Ar bytes

To prevent a two character string from being interpreted as a macro name, precede the string with the escape sequence '\&':

    [Fl s Ar bytes]   is produced by .Op \&Fl s \&Ar bytes

Here the strings 'Fl' and 'Ar' are not interpreted as macros. Macros whose argument lists are parsed for callable arguments are referred to as parsed and macros which may be called from an argument list are referred to as callable throughout this document and in the companion quick reference manual mdoc(7). This is a technical *faux pas* as almost all of the macros in **−mdoc** are parsed, but as it was cumbersome to constantly refer to macros as being callable and being able to call other macros, the term parsed has been used.

Passing Space Characters in an Argument

Sometimes it is desirable to give as one argument a string containing one or more blank space characters. This may be necessary to defeat the nine argument limit or to specify arguments to macros which expect particular arrangement of items in the argument list. For example, the function macro .Fn expects the first argument to be the name of a function and any remaining arguments to be function parameters. As ANSI C stipulates the declaration of function parameters in the parenthesized parameter list, each parameter is guaranteed to be at minimum a two word string. For example, *int foo*.

There are two possible ways to pass an argument which contains an embedded space. *Implementation note*: Unfortunately, the most convenient way of passing spaces in between quotes by reassigning individual arguments before parsing was fairly expensive speed wise and space wise to implement in all the macros for AT&T troff. It is not expensive for groff but for the sake of portability, has been limited to the following macros which need it the most:

Cd	Configuration declaration (section 4 SYNOPSIS)
Bl	Begin list (for the width specifier).
Em	Emphasized text.
Fn	Functions (sections two and four).
It	List items.
Li	Literal text.
Sy	Symbolic text.
%B	Book titles.
%J	Journal names.
%O	Optional notes for a reference.
%R	Report title (in a reference).
%T	Title of article in a book or journal.

One way of passing a string containing blank spaces is to use the hard or unpaddable space character '\ ', that is, a blank space preceded by the escape character '\'. This method may be used with any macro but has the side effect of interfering with the adjustment of text over the length of a line. Troff sees the hard space as if it were any other printable character and cannot split the string into blank or newline separated pieces as one would expect. The method is useful for strings which are not expected to overlap a line boundary. For example:

fetch(*char *str*)   is created by   .Fn fetch char\ *str

fetch(*char *str*)   can also be created by   .Fn fetch "*char *str"

If the '\' or quotes were omitted, .Fn would see three arguments and the result would be:

fetch(*char, *str*)

For an example of what happens when the parameter list overlaps a newline boundary, see the BUGS section.

Trailing Blank Space Characters

Troff can be confused by blank space characters at the end of a line. It is a wise preventive measure to globally remove all blank spaces from <blank-space><end-of-line> character sequences. Should the need arise to force a blank character at the end of a line, it may be forced with an unpaddable space and the '\&' escape character. For example, string\ \&.

Escaping Special Characters

Special characters like the newline character '\n', are handled by replacing the '\' with '\e' (e.g. \en) to preserve the backslash.

THE ANATOMY OF A MAN PAGE

The body of a man page is easily constructed from a basic template found in the file:

```
.\" /usr/share/misc/man.template:
.\" The following six lines are required.
.Dd Month day, year
.Os OPERATING_SYSTEM [version/release]
.Dt DOCUMENT_TITLE [section number] [volume]
.Sh NAME
.Sh SYNOPSIS
.Sh DESCRIPTION
.\" The following requests should be uncommented and
.\" used where appropriate.  This next request is
.\" for sections 2 and 3 function return values only.
```

```
.\" .Sh RETURN VALUES
.\" This next request is for sections 1, 6, 7 & 8 only
.\" .Sh ENVIRONMENT
.\" .Sh FILES
.\" .Sh EXAMPLES
.\" This next request is for sections 1, 6, 7 & 8 only
.\"     (command return values (to shell) and
.\"       fprintf/stderr type diagnostics)
.\" .Sh DIAGNOSTICS
.\" The next request is for sections 2 and 3 error
.\" and signal handling only.
.\" .Sh ERRORS
.\" .Sh SEE ALSO
.\" .Sh STANDARDS
.\" .Sh HISTORY
.\" .Sh AUTHORS
.\" .Sh BUGS
```

The first items in the template are the macros (.Dd, .Os, .Dt); the document date, the operating system the man page or subject source is developed or modified for, and the man page title (*in upper case*) along with the section of the manual the page belongs in. These macros identify the page, and are discussed below in TITLE MACROS.

The remaining items in the template are section headers (.Sh); of which NAME, SYNOPSIS and DESCRIPTION are mandatory. The headers are discussed in PAGE STRUCTURE DOMAIN, after presentation of MANUAL DOMAIN. Several content macros are used to demonstrate page layout macros; reading about content macros before page layout macros is recommended.

TITLE MACROS

The title macros are the first portion of the page structure domain, but are presented first and separate for someone who wishes to start writing a man page yesterday. Three header macros designate the document title or manual page title, the operating system, and the date of authorship. These macros are one called once at the very beginning of the document and are used to construct the headers and footers only.

.Dt DOCUMENT_TITLE section# [volume]
> The document title is the subject of the man page and must be in CAPITALS due to troff limitations. The section number may be 1, ..., 8, and if it is specified, the volume title may be omitted. A volume title may be arbitrary or one of the following:

> AMD   UNIX Ancestral Manual Documents
> SMM   UNIX System Manager's Manual
> URM   UNIX Reference Manual
> PRM   UNIX Programmer's Manual

> The default volume labeling is URM for sections 1, 6, and 7; SMM for section 8; PRM for sections 2, 3, 4, and 5.

.Os operating_system release#
> The name of the operating system should be the common acronym, e.g. BSD or ATT. The release should be the standard release nomenclature for the system specified, e.g. 4.3, 4.3+Tahoe, V.3, V.4. Unrecognized arguments are displayed as given in the page footer. For instance, a typical footer might be:

> .Os BSD 4.3

or for a locally produced set

        .Os CS Department

The Berkeley default, .Os without an argument, has been defined as BSD Experimental in the site specific file /usr/src/share/tmac/doc-common. It really should default to LOCAL. Note, if the .Os macro is not present, the bottom left corner of the page will be ugly.

.Dd month day, year
        The date should be written formally:

        January 25, 1989

MANUAL DOMAIN
What's in a name...

The manual domain macro names are derived from the day to day informal language used to describe commands, subroutines and related files. Slightly different variations of this language are used to describe the three different aspects of writing a man page. First, there is the description of –mdoc macro request usage. Second is the description of a UNIX command *with* –mdoc macros and third, the description of a command to a user in the verbal sense; that is, discussion of a command in the text of a man page.

In the first case, troff(1) macros are themselves a type of command; the general syntax for a troff command is:

        .Va argument1 argument2 ... argument9

The .Va is a macro command or request, and anything following it is an argument to be processed. In the second case, the description of a UNIX command using the content macros is a bit more involved; a typical SYNOPSIS command line might be displayed as:

        filter [**–flag**] *infile outfile*

Here, **filter** is the command name and the bracketed string **–flag** is a *flag* argument designated as optional by the option brackets. In –mdoc terms, *infile* and *outfile* are called *arguments*. The macros which formatted the above example:

        .Nm filter
        .Op Fl flag
        .Ar infile outfile

In the third case, discussion of commands and command syntax includes both examples above, but may add more detail. The arguments *infile* and *outfile* from the example above might be referred to as *operands* or *file arguments*. Some command line argument lists are quite long:

        make [**–eiknqrstv**] [**–D** *variable*] [**–d** *flags*] [**–f** *makefile*] [**–I** *directory*]
                [**–j** *max_jobs*] [*variable=value*] [*target* ...]

Here one might talk about the command **make** and qualify the argument *makefile*, as an argument to the flag, **–f**, or discuss the optional file operand *target*. In the verbal context, such detail can prevent confusion, however the –mdoc package does not have a macro for an argument *to* a flag. Instead the 'Ar' argument macro is used for an operand or file argument like *target* as well as an argument to a flag like *variable*. The make command line was produced from:

        .Nm make
        .Op Fl eiknqrstv
        .Op Fl D Ar variable
        .Op Fl d Ar flags
        .Op Fl f Ar makefile
        .Op Fl I Ar directory

```
.Op Fl j Ar max_jobs
.Op Ar variable=value
.Bk -words
.Op Ar target ...
.Ek
```

The .Bk and .Ek macros are explained in Keeps.

General Syntax

The manual domain and general text domain macros share a similar syntax with a few minor deviations:
.Ar, .Fl, .Nm, and .Pa differ only when called without arguments; .Fn and .Xr impose an order on their argument lists and the .Op and .Fn macros have nesting limitations. All content macros are capable of recognizing and properly handling punctuation, provided each punctuation character is separated by a leading space. If an request is given:

```
.Li sptr, ptr),
```

The result is:

```
sptr, ptr),
```

The punctuation is not recognized and all is output in the literal font. If the punctuation is separated by a leading white space:

```
.Li sptr , ptr ) ,
```

The result is:

```
sptr, ptr),
```

The punctuation is now recognized and is output in the default font distinguishing it from the strings in literal font.

To remove the special meaning from a punctuation character escape it with '\&'. Troff is limited as a macro language, and has difficulty when presented with a string containing a member of the mathematical, logical or quotation set:

$$\{+,-,/,*,\%,<,>,<=,>=,=,==,\&,',',"\}$$

The problem is that troff may assume it is supposed to actually perform the operation or evaluation suggested by the characters. To prevent the accidental evaluation of these characters, escape them with '\&'. Typical syntax is shown in the first content macro displayed below, .Ad.

Address Macro

The address macro identifies an address construct of the form addr1[,addr2[,addr3]].

```
Usage: .Ad address ... {.,:;()[]}
       .Ad addr1             addr1
       .Ad addr1 .           addr1.
       .Ad addr1 , file2     addr1, file2
       .Ad f1 , f2 , f3 :    f1, f2, f3:
       .Ad addr ) ) ,        addr)),
```

It is an error to call .Ad without arguments. .Ad is callable by other macros and is parsed.

Argument Macro

The .Ar argument macro may be used whenever a command line argument is referenced.

```
Usage: .Ar argument ... {.,:;()[]}
       .Ar              file ...
       .Ar file1        file1
       .Ar file1 .      file1.
       .Ar file1 file2  file1 file2
       .Ar f1 f2 f3 :   f1 f2 f3:
       .Ar file ) ) ,   file)),
```

If .Ar is called without arguments '*file ...*' is assumed. The .Ar macro is parsed and is callable.

Configuration Declaration (section four only)

The .Cd macro is used to demonstrate a config(8) declaration for a device interface in a section four manual. This macro accepts quoted arguments (double quotes only).

device le0 at scode? produced by: .Cd device le0 at scode?.

Command Modifier

The command modifier is identical to the .Fl (flag) command with the exception the .Cm macro does not assert a dash in front of every argument. Traditionally flags are marked by the preceding dash, some commands or subsets of commands do not use them. Command modifiers may also be specified in conjunction with interactive commands such as editor commands. See Flags.

Defined Variables

A variable which is defined in an include file is specified by the macro .Dv.

```
Usage: .Dv defined_variable ... {.,:;()[]}
       .Dv MAXHOSTNAMELEN MAXHOSTNAMELEN
       .Dv TIOCGPGRP )    TIOCGPGRP)
```

It is an error to call .Dv without arguments. .Dv is parsed and is callable.

Errno's (Section two only)

The .Er errno macro specifies the error return value for section two library routines. The second example below shows .Er used with the .Bq general text domain macro, as it would be used in a section two manual page.

```
Usage: .Er ERRNOTYPE ... {.,:;()[]}
       .Er ENOENT        ENOENT
       .Er ENOENT ) ;    ENOENT);
       .Bq Er ENOTDIR    [ENOTDIR]
```

It is an error to call .Er without arguments. The .Er macro is parsed and is callable.

Environment Variables

The .Ev macro specifies an environment variable.

```
Usage: .Ev argument ... {.,:;()[]}
       .Ev DISPLAY        DISPLAY
       .Ev PATH .         PATH.
       .Ev PRINTER ) ) ,  PRINTER)),
```

It is an error to call .Ev without arguments. The .Ev macro is parsed and is callable.

Function Argument

The .Fa macro is used to refer to function arguments (parameters) outside of the SYNOPSIS section of the manual or inside the SYNOPSIS section should a parameter list be too long for the .Fn macro and the enclosure macros .Fo and .Fc must be used. .Fa may also be used to refer to structure members.

```
Usage: .Fa function_argument ... {.,:;()[]}
       .Fa d_namlen ) ) , d_namlen)),
       .Fa iov_len           iov_len
```

It is an error to call .Fa without arguments. .Fa is parsed and is callable.

Function Declaration

The .Fd macro is used in the SYNOPSIS section with section two or three functions. The .Fd macro does not call other macros and is not callable by other macros.

```
Usage: .Fd include_file (or defined variable)
```

In the SYNOPSIS section a .Fd request causes a line break if a function has already been presented and a break has not occurred. This leaves a nice vertical space in between the previous function call and the declaration for the next function.

Flags

The .Fl macro handles command line flags. It prepends a dash, '−', to the flag. For interactive command flags, which are not prepended with a dash, the .Cm (command modifier) macro is identical, but without the dash.

```
Usage: .Fl argument ... {.,:;()[]}
       .Fl            −
       .Fl cfv        −cfv
       .Fl cfv .      −cfv.
       .Fl s v t      −s −v −t
       .Fl - ,        −−,
       .Fl xyz ) ,    −xyz),
```

The .Fl macro without any arguments results in a dash representing stdin/stdout. Note that giving .Fl a single dash, will result in two dashes. The .Fl macro is parsed and is callable.

Functions (library routines)

The .Fn macro is modeled on ANSI C conventions.

```
Usage: .Fn [type] function [[type] parameters ... {.,:;()[]}]
.Fn getchar                          getchar()
.Fn strlen ) ,                       strlen()),
.Fn "int align" "const * char *sptrs",  int align(const * char *sptrs),
```

It is an error to call .Fn without any arguments. The .Fn macro is parsed and is callable, note that any call to another macro signals the end of the .Fn call (it will close-parenthesis at that point).

For functions that have more than eight parameters (and this is rare), the macros .Fo (function open) and .Fc (function close) may be used with .Fa (function argument) to get around the limitation. For example:

```
.Fo "int res_mkquery"
.Fa "int op"
.Fa "char *dname"
.Fa "int class"
.Fa "int type"
.Fa "char *data"
.Fa "int datalen"
.Fa "struct rrec *newrr"
.Fa "char *buf"
```

```
.Fa "int buflen"
.Fc
```

Produces:

int res_mkquery(*int op, char *dname, int class, int type, char *data, int datalen, struct rrec *newrr, char *buf, int buflen***)**

The .Fo and .Fc macros are parsed and are callable. In the SYNOPSIS section, the function will always begin at the beginning of line. If there is more than one function presented in the SYNOPSIS section and a function type has not been given, a line break will occur, leaving a nice vertical space between the current function name and the one prior. At the moment, .Fn does not check its word boundaries against troff line lengths and may split across a newline ungracefully. This will be fixed in the near future.

Function Type

This macro is intended for the SYNOPSIS section. It may be used anywhere else in the man page without problems, but its main purpose is to present the function type in kernel normal form for the SYNOPSIS of sections two and three (it causes a page break allowing the function name to appear on the next line).

```
Usage: .Ft type ... {.,:;()[]}
       .Ft struct stat  struct stat
```

The .Ft request is not callable by other macros.

Interactive Commands

The .Ic macro designates an interactive or internal command.

```
Usage: .Li argument ... {.,:;()[]}
       .Ic :wq                 :wq
       .Ic do while {...}       do while {...}
       .Ic setenv , unsetenv    setenv, unsetenv
```

It is an error to call .Ic without arguments. The .Ic macro is parsed and is callable.

Literals

The .Li literal macro may be used for special characters, variable constants, anything which should be displayed as it would be typed.

```
Usage: .Li argument ... {.,:;()[]}
       .Li \en           \n
       .Li M1 M2 M3 ;    M1 M2 M3;
       .Li cntrl-D ) ,   cntrl-D),
       .Li 1024 ...      1024 ...
```

The .Li macro is parsed and is callable.

Name Macro

The .Nm macro is used for the document title or subject name. It has the peculiarity of remembering the first argument it was called with, which should always be the subject name of the page. When called without arguments, .Nm regurgitates this initial name for the sole purpose of making less work for the author. Note: a section two or three document function name is addressed with the .Nm in the NAME section, and with .Fn in the SYNOPSIS and remaining sections. For interactive commands, such as the while command keyword in csh(1), the .Ic macro should be used. While the .Ic is nearly identical to .Nm, it can not recall the first argument it was invoked with.

```
Usage: .Nm argument ... {.,:;()[]}
       .Nm mdoc.sample    mdoc.sample
       .Nm \-mdoc         −mdoc.
       .Nm foo ) ) ,      foo)),
       .Nm                mdoc.samples
```

The .Nm macro is parsed and is callable.

Options

The .Op macro places option brackets around the any remaining arguments on the command line, and places any trailing punctuation outside the brackets. The macros .Oc and .Oo may be used across one or more lines.

```
Usage: .Op options ... {.,:;()[]}
.Op                              []
.Op Fl k                         [−k]
.Op Fl k ) .                     [−k]).
.Op Fl k Ar kookfile             [−k kookfile]
.Op Fl k Ar kookfile ,           [−k kookfile],
.Op Ar objfil Op Ar corfil       [objfil [corfil]]
.Op Fl c Ar objfil Op Ar corfil , [−c objfil [corfil]],
.Op word1 word2                  [word1 word2]
```

The .Oc and .Oo macros:

```
.Oo
.Op Fl k Ar kilobytes
.Op Fl i Ar interval
.Op Fl c Ar count
.Oc
```

Produce: [[−k kilobytes] [−i interval] [−c count]]

The macros .Op, .Oc and .Oo are parsed and are callable.

Pathnames

The .Pa macro formats path or file names.

```
Usage: .Pa pathname {.,:;()[]}
       .Pa /usr/share        /usr/share
       .Pa /tmp/fooXXXXX ) .  /tmp/fooXXXXX).
```

The .Pa macro is parsed and is callable.

Variables

Generic variable reference:

```
Usage: .Va variable ... {.,:;()[]}
       .Va count          count
       .Va settimer,      settimer,
       .Va int *prt ) :   int *prt):
       .Va char s ] ) ) , char s])),
```

It is an error to call .Va without any arguments. The .Va macro is parsed and is callable.

Manual Page Cross References

The .Xr macro expects the first argument to be a manual page name, and the second argument, if it exists, to be either a section page number or punctuation. Any remaining arguments are assumed to be punctuation.

```
Usage: .Xr man_page [1,...,8] {.,:;()[]}
       .Xr mdoc          mdoc
       .Xr mdoc ,         mdoc,
       .Xr mdoc 7         mdoc(7)
       .Xr mdoc 7 ) ) ,   mdoc(7)),
```

The .Xr macro is parsed and is callable. It is an error to call .Xr without any arguments.

GENERAL TEXT DOMAIN
AT&T Macro

```
Usage: .At [v6 | v7 | 32v | V.1 | V.4] ... {.,:;()[]}
       .At          AT&T UNIX
       .At v6 .      Version 6 AT&T UNIX.
```

The .At macro is *not* parsed and *not* callable. It accepts at most two arguments.

BSD Macro
```
Usage: .Bx [Version/release] ... {.,:;()[]}
       .Bx          BSD
       .Bx 4.3 .    4.3BSD.
```

The .Bx macro is parsed and is callable.

UNIX Macro
```
Usage: .Ux ... {.,:;()[]}
       .Ux          UNIX
```

The .Ux macro is parsed and is callable.

Emphasis Macro

Text may be stressed or emphasized with the .Em macro. The usual font for emphasis is italic.

```
Usage: .Em argument ... {.,:;()[]}
       .Em does not          does not
       .Em exceed 1024 .     exceed 1024.
       .Em vide infra ) ) ,  vide infra)),
```

The .Em macro is parsed and is callable. It is an error to call .Em without arguments.

Enclosure and Quoting Macros

The concept of enclosure is similar to quoting. The object being to enclose one or more strings between a pair of characters like quotes or parentheses. The terms quoting and enclosure are used interchangeably throughout this document. Most of the one line enclosure macros end in small letter 'q' to give a hint of quoting, but there are a few irregularities. For each enclosure macro there is also a pair of open and close macros which end in small letters 'o' and 'c' respectively. These can be used across one or more lines of text and while they have nesting limitations, the one line quote macros can be used inside of them.

Quote	Close	Open	Function	Result
.Aq	.Ac	.Ao	Angle Bracket Enclosure	<string>
.Bq	.Bc	.Bo	Bracket Enclosure	[string]
.Dq	.Dc	.Do	Double Quote	''string''
	.Ec	.Eo	Enclose String (in XX)	XXstringXX
.Pq	.Pc	.Po	Parenthesis Enclosure	(string)
.Ql			Quoted Literal	'st' or string
.Qq	.Qc	.Qo	Straight Double Quote	"string"
.Sq	.Sc	.So	Single Quote	'string'

Except for the irregular macros noted below, all of the quoting macros are parsed and callable. All handle punctuation properly, as long as it is presented one character at a time and separated by spaces. The quoting macros examine opening and closing punctuation to determine whether it comes before or after the enclosing string. This makes some nesting possible.

.Ec, .Eo   These macros expect the first argument to be the opening and closing strings respectively.

.Ql   The quoted literal macro behaves differently for troff than nroff. If formatted with nroff, a quoted literal is always quoted. If formatted with troff, an item is only quoted if the width of the item is less than three constant width characters. This is to make short strings more visible where the font change to literal (constant width) is less noticeable.

.Pf   The prefix macro is not callable, but it is parsed:

        .Pf (Fa name2
                becomes (*name2.*

      The .Ns (no space) macro performs the analogous suffix function.

Examples of quoting:

```
.Aq                             <>
.Aq Ar ctype.h ) ,              <ctype.h>),
.Bq                             []
.Bq Em Greek , French .         [Greek, French].
.Dq                             ''''
.Dq string abc .                ''string abc''.
.Dq ''[A-Z]'                    ''''[A-Z]''''
.Ql man mdoc                    man mdoc
.Qq                             ""
.Qq string ) ,                  "string"),
.Qq string Ns ),                "string),"
.Sq                             ''
.Sq string                      'string'
```

For a good example of nested enclosure macros, see the .Op option macro. It was created from the same underlying enclosure macros as those presented in the list above. The .Xo and .Xc extended argument list macros were also built from the same underlying routines and are a good example of −mdoc macro usage at its worst.

No−Op or Normal Text Macro

The macro .No is a hack for words in a macro command line which should *not* be formatted and follows the conventional syntax for content macros.

No Space Macro

The `.Ns` macro eliminates unwanted spaces in between macro requests. It is useful for old style argument lists where there is no space between the flag and argument:

`.Op Fl I Ns Ar directory`   produces [−I*directory*]

Note: the `.Ns` macro always invokes the `.No` macro after eliminating the space unless another macro name follows it. The macro `.Ns` is parsed and is callable.

Section Cross References

The `.Sx` macro designates a reference to a section header within the same document. It is parsed and is callable.

`.Sx FILES`   FILES

Symbolic

The symbolic emphasis macro is generally a boldface macro in either the symbolic sense or the traditional English usage.

`Usage: .Sy symbol ... {.,:;()[]}`
`       .Sy Important Notice`   **Important Notice**

The `.Sy` macro is parsed and is callable. Arguments to `.Sy` may be quoted.

References and Citations

The following macros make a modest attempt to handle references. At best, the macros make it convenient to manually drop in a subset of refer style references.

`.Rs`	Reference Start. Causes a line break and begins collection of reference information until the reference end macro is read.
`.Re`	Reference End. The reference is printed.
`.%A`	Reference author name, one name per invocation.
`.%B`	Book title.
`.%C`	City/place.
`.%D`	Date.
`.%J`	Journal name.
`.%N`	Issue number.
`.%O`	Optional information.
`.%P`	Page number.
`.%R`	Report name.
`.%T`	Title of article.
`.%V`	Volume(s).

The macros beginning with '%' are not callable, and are parsed only for the trade name macro which returns to its caller. (And not very predictably at the moment either.) The purpose is to allow trade names to be pretty printed in `troff/ditroff` output.

Trade Names (or Acronyms and Type Names)

The trade name macro is generally a small caps macro for all upper case words longer than two characters.

`Usage: .Tn symbol ... {.,:;()[]}`
`       .Tn DEC`   DEC
`       .Tn ASCII` ASCII

The `.Tn` macro is parsed and is callable by other macros.

Extended Arguments

The `.Xo` and `.Xc` macros allow one to extend an argument list on a macro boundary. Argument lists cannot be extended within a macro which expects all of its arguments on one line such as `.Op`.

Here is an example of `.Xo` using the space mode macro to turn spacing off:

```
.Sm off
.It Xo Sy I Ar operation
.No \en Ar count No \en
.Xc
.Sm on
```

Produces

I*operation*\n*count*\n

Another one:

```
.Sm off
.It Cm S No / Ar old_pattern Xo
.No / Ar new_pattern
.No / Op Cm g
.Xc
.Sm on
```

Produces

S/*old_pattern*/*new_pattern*/[**g**]

Another example of `.Xo` and using enclosure macros: Test the value of an variable.

```
.It Xo
.Ic .ifndef
.Oo \&! Oc Ns Ar variable
.Op Ar operator variable ...
.Xc
```

Produces

.ifndef [!]*variable* [*operator variable ...*]

All of the above examples have used the `.Xo` macro on the argument list of the `.It` (list-item) macro. The extend macros are not used very often, and when they are it is usually to extend the list-item argument list. Unfortunately, this is also where the extend macros are the most finicky. In the first two examples, spacing was turned off; in the third, spacing was desired in part of the output but not all of it. To make these macros work in this situation make sure the `.Xo` and `.Xc` macros are placed as shown in the third example. If the `.Xo` macro is not alone on the `.It` argument list, spacing will be unpredictable. The `.Ns` (no space macro) must not occur as the first or last macro on a line in this situation. Out of 900 manual pages (about 1500 actual pages) currently released with BSD only fifteen use the `.Xo` macro.

PAGE STRUCTURE DOMAIN
Section Headers

The first three `.Sh` section header macros list below are required in every man page. The remaining section headers are recommended at the discretion of the author writing the manual page. The `.Sh` macro can take up to nine arguments. It is parsed and but is not callable.

.Sh NAME   The `.Sh NAME` macro is mandatory. If not specified, the headers, footers and page layout defaults will not be set and things will be rather unpleasant. The NAME section consists of at least three items. The first is the `.Nm` name macro naming the subject of the man page. The second is the Name Description macro, .Nd, which separates the subject name from the third item, which is the description. The description should be the most terse and lucid possible, as the space available is small.

.Sh SYNOPSIS   The SYNOPSIS section describes the typical usage of the subject of a man page. The macros required are either .Nm, .Cd, .Fn, (and possibly .Fo, .Fc, .Fd, .Ft macros). The function name macro .Fn is required for manual page sections 2 and 3, the command and general name macro .Nm is required for sections 1, 5, 6, 7, 8. Section 4 manuals require a .Nm, .Fd or a .Cd configuration device usage macro. Several other macros may be necessary to produce the synopsis line as shown below:

> cat [–benstuv] [–] *file* ...

The following macros were used:

```
.Nm cat
.Op Fl benstuv
.Op Fl
.Ar
```

Note: The macros .Op, .Fl, and .Ar recognize the pipe bar character 'l', so a command line such as:

```
.Op Fl a | Fl b
```

will not go orbital. Troff normally interprets a l as a special operator. See PREDEFINED STRINGS for a usable l character in other situations.

.Sh DESCRIPTION

In most cases the first text in the DESCRIPTION section is a brief paragraph on the command, function or file, followed by a lexical list of options and respective explanations. To create such a list, the .Bl begin-list, .It list-item and .El end-list macros are used (see Lists and Columns below).

The following .Sh section headers are part of the preferred manual page layout and must be used appropriately to maintain consistency. They are listed in the order in which they would be used.

.Sh ENVIRONMENT

The ENVIRONMENT section should reveal any related environment variables and clues to their behavior and/or usage.

.Sh EXAMPLES

There are several ways to create examples. See the EXAMPLES section below for details.

.Sh FILES   Files which are used or created by the man page subject should be listed via the .Pa macro in the FILES section.

.Sh SEE ALSO

References to other material on the man page topic and cross references to other relevant man pages should be placed in the SEE ALSO section. Cross references are specified using the .Xr macro. At this time refer(1) style references are not accommodated.

.Sh STANDARDS

If the command, library function or file adheres to a specific implementation such as IEEE Std1003.2 (''POSIX'') or ANSI C X3.159-1989 (''ANSI C '') this should be noted here. If the command does not adhere to any standard, its history should be noted in the HISTORY section.

.Sh HISTORY

Any command which does not adhere to any specific standards should be outlined historically in this section.

.Sh AUTHORS

Credits, if need be, should be placed here.

.Sh DIAGNOSTICS

Diagnostics from a command should be placed in this section.

.Sh ERRORS

Specific error handling, especially from library functions (man page sections 2 and 3) should go here. The .Er macro is used to specify an errno.

.Sh BUGS　　Blatant problems with the topic go here...

User specified .Sh sections may be added, for example, this section was set with:

        .Sh PAGE LAYOUT MACROS

Paragraphs and Line Spacing.

.Pp　　　The .Pp paragraph command may be used to specify a line space where necessary. The macro is not necessary after a .Sh or .Ss macro or before a .Bl macro. (The .Bl macro asserts a vertical distance unless the -compact flag is given).

Keeps

The only keep that is implemented at this time is for words. The macros are .Bk (begin-keep) and .Ek (end-keep). The only option that .Bl accepts is **−words** and is useful for preventing line breaks in the middle of options. In the example for the make command line arguments (see What's in a name), the keep prevented nroff from placing up the flag and the argument on separate lines. (Actually, the option macro used to prevent this from occurring, but was dropped when the decision (religious) was made to force right justified margins in troff as options in general look atrocious when spread across a sparse line. More work needs to be done with the keep macros, a **−line** option needs to be added.)

Examples and Displays

There are five types of displays, a quickie one line indented display .D1, a quickie one line literal display .Dl, and a block literal, block filled and block ragged which use the .Bd begin-display and .Ed end-display macros.

.D1　　　(D-one) Display one line of indented text. This macro is parsed, but it is not callable.

        −ldghfstru

The above was produced by: .D1 **−ldghfstru**.

.Dl　　　(D-ell) Display one line of indented *literal* text. The .Dl example macro has been used throughout this file. It allows the indent (display) of one line of text. Its default font is set to constant width (literal) however it is parsed and will recognized other macros. It is not callable however.

        % ls -ldg /usr/local/bin

The above was produced by .Dl % ls -ldg /usr/local/bin.

.Bd　　　Begin-display. The .Bd display must be ended with the .Ed macro. Displays may be nested within displays and lists. .Bd has the following syntax:

```
.Bd display-type [-offset offset_value] [-compact]
```

The display-type must be one of the following four types and may have an offset specifier for indentation: .Bd.

−ragged   Display a block of text as typed, right (and left) margin edges are left ragged.

−filled   Display a filled (formatted) block. The block of text is formatted (the edges are filled – not left unjustified).

−literal   Display a literal block, useful for source code or simple tabbed or spaced text.

−file *file_name*   The file name following the **−file** flag is read and displayed. Literal mode is asserted and tabs are set at 8 constant width character intervals, however any troff/**−mdoc** commands in file will be processed.

−offset *string*   If **−offset** is specified with one of the following strings, the string is interpreted to indicate the level of indentation for the forthcoming block of text:

      left   Align block on the current left margin, this is the default mode of .Bd.

      center   Supposedly center the block. At this time unfortunately, the block merely gets left aligned about an imaginary center margin.

      indent   Indents by one default indent value or tab. The default indent value is also used for the .D1 display so one is guaranteed the two types of displays will line up. This indent is normally set to 6n or about two thirds of an inch (six constant width characters).

      indent-two Indents two times the default indent value.

      right   This *left* aligns the block about two inches from the right side of the page. This macro needs work and perhaps may never do the right thing by troff.

.Ed   End-display.

Tagged Lists and Columns

There are several types of lists which may be initiated with the .Bl begin-list macro. Items within the list are specified with the .It item macro and each list must end with the .El macro. Lists may be nested within themselves and within displays. Columns may be used inside of lists, but lists are unproven inside of columns.

In addition, several list attributes may be specified such as the width of a tag, the list offset, and compactness (blank lines between items allowed or disallowed). Most of this document has been formatted with a tag style list (**−tag**). For a change of pace, the list-type used to present the list-types is an over-hanging list (**−ohang**). This type of list is quite popular with TeX users, but might look a bit funny after having read many pages of tagged lists. The following list types are accepted by .Bl:

−bullet
−item
−enum

These three are the simplest types of lists. Once the .Bl macro has been given, items in the list are merely indicated by a line consisting solely of the .It macro. For example, the source text for a simple enumerated list would look like:

```
.Bl -enum -compact
.It
Item one goes here.
.It
And item two here.
.It
Lastly item three goes here.
.El
```

The results:

1.　Item one goes here.
2.　And item two here.
3.　Lastly item three goes here.

A simple bullet list construction:

```
.Bl -bullet -compact
.It
Bullet one goes here.
.It
Bullet two here.
.El
```

Produces:

- Bullet one goes here.
- Bullet two here.

−tag
−diag
−hang
−ohang
−inset

These list-types collect arguments specified with the `.It` macro and create a label which may be *inset* into the forthcoming text, *hanged* from the forthcoming text, *overhanged* from above and not indented or *tagged*. This list was constructed with the '**−ohang**' list-type. The `.It` macro is parsed only for the inset, hang and tag list-types and is not callable. Here is an example of inset labels:

Tag The tagged list (also called a tagged paragraph) is the most common type of list used in the Berkeley manuals.

Diag Diag lists create section four diagnostic lists and are similar to inset lists except callable macros are ignored.

Hang Hanged labels are a matter of taste.

Ohang Overhanging labels are nice when space is constrained.

Inset Inset labels are useful for controlling blocks of paragraphs and are valuable for converting **−mdoc** manuals to other formats.

Here is the source text which produced the above example:

```
.Bl -inset -offset indent
.It Em Tag
The tagged list (also called a tagged paragraph) is the
most common type of list used in the Berkeley manuals.
.It Em Diag
```

```
Diag lists create section four diagnostic lists
and are similar to inset lists except callable
macros are ignored.
.It Em Hang
Hanged labels are a matter of taste.
.It Em Ohang
Overhanging labels are nice when space is constrained.
.It Em Inset
Inset labels are useful for controlling blocks of
paragraphs and are valuable for converting
.Nm —mdoc
manuals to other formats.
.El
```

Here is a hanged list with just one item:

> *Hanged* labels appear similar to tagged lists when the label is smaller than the label width.

> *Longer hanged list labels* blend in to the paragraph unlike tagged paragraph labels.

And the unformatted text which created it:

```
.Bl -hang -offset indent
.It Em Hanged
labels appear similar to tagged lists when the
label is smaller than the label width.
.It Em Longer hanged list labels
blend in to the paragraph unlike
tagged paragraph labels.
.El
```

The tagged list which follows uses an optional width specifier to control the width of the tag.

SL   sleep time of the process (seconds blocked)
PAGEIN
         number of disk I/O's resulting from references by the process to pages not loaded in core.
UID   numerical user-id of process owner
PPID   numerical id of parent of process process priority (non-positive when in non-interruptible wait)

The raw text:

```
.Bl -tag -width "PAGEIN" -compact -offset indent
.It SL
sleep time of the process (seconds blocked)
.It PAGEIN
number of disk
.Tn I/O Ns 's
resulting from references
by the process to pages not loaded in core.
.It UID
numerical user-id of process owner
.It PPID
numerical id of parent of process process priority
(non-positive when in non-interruptible wait)
.El
```

Acceptable width specifiers:

–width *Fl*   sets the width to the default width for a flag. All callable macros have a default width value. The `.Fl`, value is presently set to ten constant width characters or about five sixth of an inch.

–width *24n*

sets the width to 24 constant width characters or about two inches. The 'n' is absolutely necessary for the scaling to work correctly.

–width *ENAMETOOLONG*

sets width to the constant width length of the string given.

–width *"int mkfifo"*

again, the width is set to the constant width of the string given.

If a width is not specified for the tag list type, the first time `.It` is invoked, an attempt is made to determine an appropriate width. If the first argument to `.It` is a callable macro, the default width for that macro will be used as if the macro name had been supplied as the width. However, if another item in the list is given with a different callable macro name, a new and nested list is assumed.

PREDEFINED STRINGS

The following strings are predefined as may be used by preceding with the troff string interpreting sequence `\*(`xx where *xx* is the name of the defined string or as `\*x` where *x* is the name of the string. The interpreting sequence may be used any where in the text.

String	Nroff	Troff
<=	<=	≤
>=	>=	≥
Rq	"	"
Lq	"	"
ua	^	↑
aa	'	
ga	`	`
q	"	"
Pi	pi	π
Ne	!=	≠
Le	<=	≤
Ge	>=	≥
Lt	<	>
Gt	>	<
Pm	+-	±
If	infinity	∞
Na	NaN	NaN
Ba	I	I

Note: The string named 'q' should be written as `\*q` since it is only one char.

DIAGNOSTICS

The debugging facilities for –mdoc are limited, but can help detect subtle errors such as the collision of an argument name with an internal register or macro name. (A what?) A register is an arithmetic storage class for `troff` with a one or two character name. All registers internal to –mdoc for `troff` and `ditroff` are two characters and of the form <upper_case><lower_case> such as 'Ar', <lower_case><upper_case> as 'aR' or <upper or lower letter><digit> as 'C1'. And adding to the muddle, `troff` has its own internal registers all of which are either two lower case characters or a dot plus a letter or meta-character character. In one of the introduction examples, it was shown how to prevent the interpretation of a macro name with the escape sequence '\&'. This is sufficient for the internal register names also.

If a non-escaped register name is given in the argument list of a request unpredictable behavior will occur. In general, any time huge portions of text do not appear where expected in the output, or small strings such as list tags disappear, chances are there is a misunderstanding about an argument type in the argument list. Your mother never intended for you to remember this evil stuff - so here is a way to find out whether or not your arguments are valid: The .Db (debug) macro displays the interpretation of the argument list for most macros. Macros such as the .Pp (paragraph) macro do not contain debugging information. All of the callable macros do, and it is strongly advised whenever in doubt, turn on the .Db macro.

```
Usage: .Db [on | off]
```

An example of a portion of text with the debug macro placed above and below an artificially created problem (a flag argument 'aC' which should be \&aC in order to work):

```
.Db on
.Op Fl aC Ar file )
.Db off
```

The resulting output:

```
DEBUGGING ON
DEBUG(argv) MACRO: '.Op'  Line #: 2
        Argc: 1  Argv: 'Fl'  Length: 2
        Space: ''  Class: Executable
        Argc: 2  Argv: 'aC'  Length: 2
        Space: ''  Class: Executable
        Argc: 3  Argv: 'Ar'  Length: 2
        Space: ''  Class: Executable
        Argc: 4  Argv: 'file'  Length: 4
        Space: ' '  Class: String
        Argc: 5  Argv: ')'  Length: 1
        Space: ' '  Class: Closing Punctuation or suffix
        MACRO REQUEST: .Op Fl aC Ar file )
DEBUGGING OFF
```

The first line of information tells the name of the calling macro, here .Op, and the line number it appears on. If one or more files are involved (especially if text from another file is included) the line number may be bogus. If there is only one file, it should be accurate. The second line gives the argument count, the argument ('Fl') and its length. If the length of an argument is two characters, the argument is tested to see if it is executable (unfortunately, any register which contains a non-zero value appears executable). The third line gives the space allotted for a class, and the class type. The problem here is the argument aC should not be executable. The four types of classes are string, executable, closing punctuation and opening punctuation. The last line shows the entire argument list as it was read. In this next example, the offending 'aC' is escaped:

```
.Db on
.Em An escaped \&aC
.Db off
```

```
            DEBUGGING ON
            DEBUG(fargv) MACRO: '.Em'  Line #: 2
                    Argc: 1  Argv: 'An'  Length: 2
                    Space: ' '  Class: String
                    Argc: 2  Argv: 'escaped'  Length: 7
                    Space: ' '  Class: String
                    Argc: 3  Argv: 'aC'  Length: 2
                    Space: ' '  Class: String
                    MACRO REQUEST: .Em An escaped &aC
            DEBUGGING OFF
```

The argument \&aC shows up with the same length of 2 as the '\&' sequence produces a zero width, but a register named \&aC was not found and the type classified as string.

Other diagnostics consist of usage statements and are self explanatory.

GROFF, TROFF AND NROFF

The —**mdoc** package does not need compatibility mode with groff.

The package inhibits page breaks, and the headers and footers which normally occur at those breaks with nroff, to make the manual more efficient for viewing on-line. At the moment, groff with —*Tascii* does eject the imaginary remainder of the page at end of file. The inhibiting of the page breaks makes nroff'd files unsuitable for hardcopy. There is a register named 'cR' which can be set to zero in the site dependent style file /usr/src/share/tmac/doc-nroff to restore the old style behavior.

FILES

```
/usr/share/tmac/tmac.doc      manual macro package
/usr/share/man0/template.doc  template for writing a man page
```

SEE ALSO

mdoc(7), man(1), troff(1)

BUGS

Undesirable hyphenation on the dash of a flag argument is not yet resolved, and causes occasional mishaps in the DESCRIPTION section. (line break on the hyphen).

Predefined strings are not declared in documentation.

Section 3f has not been added to the header routines.

. Nm font should be changed in NAME section.

. Fn needs to have a check to prevent splitting up if the line length is too short. Occasionally it separates the last parenthesis, and sometimes looks ridiculous if a line is in fill mode.

The method used to prevent header and footer page breaks (other than the initial header and footer) when using nroff occasionally places an unsightly partially filled line (blank) at the would be bottom of the page.

The list and display macros to not do any keeps and certainly should be able to.

NAME

me – macros for formatting papers

SYNOPSIS

nroff –me [options] file ...

troff –me [options] file ...

DESCRIPTION

This package of *nroff* and *troff* macro definitions provides a canned formatting facility for technical papers in various formats. When producing 2-column output on a terminal, filter the output through *col*(1).

The macro requests are defined below. Many *nroff* and *troff* requests are unsafe in conjunction with this package, however, these requests may be used with impunity after the first .pp:

.bp	begin new page
.br	break output line here
.sp n	insert n spacing lines
.ls n	(line spacing) n=1 single, n=2 double space
.na	no alignment of right margin
.ce n	center next n lines
.ul n	underline next n lines
.sz +n	add n to point size

Output of the *eqn, neqn, refer,* and *tbl*(1) preprocessors for equations and tables is acceptable as input.

FILES

/usr/lib/tmac/tmac.e

/usr/lib/me/*

SEE ALSO

eqn(1), troff(1), refer(1), tbl(1)

–me Reference Manual, Eric P. Allman

Writing Papers with Nroff Using –me

REQUESTS

In the following list, "initialization" refers to the first .pp, .lp, .ip, .np, .sh, or .uh macro. This list is incomplete; see *The –me Reference Manual* for interesting details.

Request	Initial Value	Cause Break	Explanation
.(c	-	yes	Begin centered block
.(d	-	no	Begin delayed text
.(f	-	no	Begin footnote
.(l	-	yes	Begin list
.(q	-	yes	Begin major quote
.(x *x*	-	no	Begin indexed item in index *x*
.(z	-	no	Begin floating keep
.)c	-	yes	End centered block
.)d	-	yes	End delayed text
.)f	-	yes	End footnote
.)l	-	yes	End list
.)q	-	yes	End major quote
.)x	-	yes	End index item
.)z	-	yes	End floating keep
.++ *m H*	-	no	Define paper section. *m* defines the part of the paper, and can be **C** (chapter), **A** (appendix), **P** (preliminary, e.g., abstract, table of contents, etc.), **B** (bibliography), **RC** (chapters renumbered from page one each chapter), or **RA** (appendix renumbered from page one).
.+c *T*	-	yes	Begin chapter (or appendix, etc., as set by .++). *T* is the chapter title.
.1c	1	yes	One column format on a new page.

.2c	1	yes	Two column format.
.EN	-	yes	Space after equation produced by *eqn* or *neqn*.
.EQ *x y*	-	yes	Precede equation; break out and add space. Equation number is *y*. The optional argument *x* may be *I* to indent equation (default), *L* to left-adjust the equation, or *C* to center the equation.
.GE	-	yes	End *gremlin* picture.
.GS	-	yes	Begin *gremlin* picture.
.PE	-	yes	End *pic* picture.
.PS	-	yes	Begin *pic* picture.
.TE	-	yes	End table.
.TH	-	yes	End heading section of table.
.TS *x*	-	yes	Begin table; if *x* is *H* table has repeated heading.
.ac *A N*	-	no	Set up for ACM style output. *A* is the Author's name(s), *N* is the total number of pages. Must be given before the first initialization.
.b *x*	no	no	Print *x* in boldface; if no argument switch to boldface.
.ba +*n*	0	yes	Augments the base indent by *n*. This indent is used to set the indent on regular text (like paragraphs).
.bc	no	yes	Begin new column
.bi *x*	no	no	Print *x* in bold italics (nofill only)
.bu	-	yes	Begin bulleted paragraph
.bx *x*	no	no	Print *x* in a box (nofill only).
.ef ´*x*´*y*´*z*´	´´´´	no	Set even footer to x y z
.eh ´*x*´*y*´*z*´	´´´´	no	Set even header to x y z
.fo ´*x*´*y*´*z*´	´´´´	no	Set footer to x y z
.hx	-	no	Suppress headers and footers on next page.
.he ´*x*´*y*´*z*´	´´´´	no	Set header to x y z
.hl	-	yes	Draw a horizontal line
.i *x*	no	no	Italicize *x;* if *x* missing, italic text follows.
.ip *x y*	no	yes	Start indented paragraph, with hanging tag *x*. Indentation is *y* ens (default 5).
.lp	yes	yes	Start left-blocked paragraph.
.lo	-	no	Read in a file of local macros of the form .*x*. Must be given before initialization.
.np	1	yes	Start numbered paragraph.
.of ´*x*´*y*´*z*´	´´´´	no	Set odd footer to x y z
.oh ´*x*´*y*´*z*´	´´´´	no	Set odd header to x y z
.pd	-	yes	Print delayed text.
.pp	no	yes	Begin paragraph. First line indented.
.r	yes	no	Roman text follows.
.re	-	no	Reset tabs to default values.
.sc	no	no	Read in a file of special characters and diacritical marks. Must be given before initialization.
.sh *n x*	-	yes	Section head follows, font automatically bold. *n* is level of section, *x* is title of section.
.sk	no	no	Leave the next page blank. Only one page is remembered ahead.
.sm *x*	-	no	Set *x* in a smaller pointsize.
.sz +*n*	10p	no	Augment the point size by *n* points.
.th	no	no	Produce the paper in thesis format. Must be given before initialization.
.tp	no	yes	Begin title page.
.u *x*	-	no	Underline argument (even in *troff*). (Nofill only).
.uh	-	yes	Like .sh but unnumbered.
.xp *x*	-	no	Print index *x*.

NAME
mm – groff mm macros

SYNOPSIS
groff –m/usr/share/tmac/tmac.m [*options.,.*] [*files...*]

DESCRIPTION
The groff mm macros are intended to be compatible with the DWB mm macros with the following limitations:

- no letter macros implemented (yet).

- no Bell Labs localisms implemented.

- the macros OK and PM is not implemented.

- groff mm does not support cut marks

m/usr/share/tmac/tmac.m is intended to be international. Therefore it is possible to write short national macrofiles which change all english text to the preferred language. Use **m/usr/share/tmac/tmac.mse** as an example.

Groff mm has several extensions:

APP name text
> Begin an appendix with name *name*. Automatic naming occurs if *name* is "". The appendixes starts with **A** if auto is used. An new page is ejected, and a header is also produced if the number variable **Aph** is non-zero. This is the default. The appendix always appear in the 'List of contents' with correct pagenumber. The name *APPENDIX* can be changed by setting the string **App** to the desired text.

APPSK name pages text
> Same as **.APP**, but the pagenr is incremented with *pages*. This is used when diagrams or other non-formatted documents are included as appendixes.

B1   Begin box (as the ms macro) Draws a box around the text.

B2   End box. Finish the box.

BVL   Start of broken variable-item list. As VL but text begins always at the next line

COVER [arg]
> **COVER** begins a coversheet definition. It is important that **.COVER** appears before any normal text. **.COVER** uses *arg* to build the filename /usr/share/tmac/*arg*.cov. Therefore it is possible to create unlimited types of coversheets. *ms.cov* is supposed to look like the **ms** coversheet. **.COVER** requires a **.COVEND** at the end of the coverdefinition. Always use this order of the covermacros:
> .COVER
> .TL
> .AF
> .AU
> .AT
> .AS
> .AE
> .COVEND
> However, only **.TL** and **.AU** are required.

COVEND
> This finishes the cover description and prints the cover-page. It is defined in the cover file.

GETHN refname [varname]
> Includes the headernumber where the corresponding **SETR** *refname* was placed. Will be X.X.X. in pass 1. See **INITR**. If varname is used, **GETHN** sets the stringvariable *varname* to the

headernumber.

GETPN refname [varname]
Includes the pagenumber where the corresponding **SETR** *refname* was placed. Will be 9999 in pass 1. See **INITR**. If varname is used, **GETPN** sets the stringvariable *varname* to the pagenumber.

GETR refname
Combines **GETHN** and **GETPN** with the text 'chapter' and ', page'. The string *Qrf* contains the text for reference:

.ds Qrf See chapter *[Qrfh], page *[Qrfp].

Qrf may be changed to support other languages. Strings *Qrfh* and *Qrfp* are set by **GETR** and contains the page and headernumber.

GETST refname [varname]
Includes the string saved with the second argument to **.SETR**. Will be dummystring in pass 1. If varname is used, **GETST** sets the stringvariable *varname* to the saved string. See **INITR**.

INITR filename
Initialize the refencemacros. References will be written to *filename.tmp* and *filename.qrf.* Requires two passes with groff. The first looks for references and the second includes them. **INITR** can be used several times, but it is only the first occurence of **INITR** that is active. See also **SETR**, **GETPN** and **GETHN**.

7

MC column-size [column-separation]
Begin multiple columns. Return to normal with 1C.

MT [arg [addressee]]
Memorandum type. The *arg* is part of a filename in */usr/share/tmac/*.MT*. Memorandum type 0 thru 5 are supported, including *"string"*. *Addresse* just sets a variable, used in the AT&T macros.

MOVE y-pos [x-pos [line-length]]
Move to a position, pageoffset set to *x-pos*. If *line-length* is not given, the difference between current and new pageoffset is used. Use **PGFORM** without arguments to return to normal.

MULB cw1 space1 [cw2 space2 [cw3 ...]]
Begin a special multi-column mode. Every columns width must be specified. Also the space between the columns must be specified. The last column does not need any space-definition. MULB starts a diversion and MULE ends the diversion and prints the columns. The unit for width and space is 'n', but MULB accepts all normal unitspecifications like 'c' and 'i'. MULB operates in a separate environment.

MULN Begin the next column. This is the only way to switch column.

MULE End the multi-column mode and print the columns.

PGFORM [linelength [pagelength [pageoffset]]]
Sets linelength, pagelength and/or pageoffset. This macro can be used for special formatting, like letterheads and other. **PGFORM** can be used without arguments to reset everything after a **MOVE**.

PGNH No header is printed on the next page. Used to get rid off the header in letters or other special texts This macro must be used before any text to inhibit the pageheader on the first page.

SETR refname [string]
Remember the current header and page-number as refname. Saves *string* if *string* is defined. *string* is retrieved with **.GETST**. See **INITR**.

TAB reset tabs to every 5n. Normally used to reset any previous tabpositions.

VERBON [flag [pointsize [font]]]
Begin verbatim output using courier font. Usually for printing programs. All character has equal width. The pointsize can be changed with the second argument. By specifying the font-argument

it is possible to use another font instead of courier. *flag* control several special features. It contains the sum of all wanted features.

Value   Description
1   Enable the escape-character (\). This is normally turned off during verbose output.
2   Add en empty line before the verbose text.
4   Add en empty line after the verbose text.
8   Print the verbose text with numbered lines. This adds four digitsized spaces in the beginning of each line. Finer control is available with the string-variable **Verbnm**. It contains all arguments to the **troff**-command **.nm**, normally '1'.
16   Indent the verbose text with five 'n':s. This is controlled by the number-variable **Verbin** (in units).

VERBOFF
End verbatim output.

New variables in m/usr/share/tmac/tmac.m:

App   A string containing the word "APPENDIX".

Aph   Print an appendix-page for every new appendix if this numbervariable is non-zero. No output will occur if **Aph** is zero, but there will always be an appendix-entry in the 'List of contents'.

Hps   Numbervariable with the heading pre-space level. If the heading-level is less than or equal to **Hps**, then two lines will precede the section heading instead of one. Default is first level only. The real amount of lines is controlled by the variables **Hps1** and **Hps2**.

Hps1   This is the number of lines preceding **.H** when the heading-level is greater than **Hps**. Value is in units, normally 0.5v.

Hps2   This is the number of lines preceding **.H** when the heading-level is less than or equal to **Hps**. Value is in units, normally 1v.

Lifg   String containing *Figure*.

Litb   String containing *TABLE*.

Liex   String containing *Exhibit*.

Liec   String containing *Equation*.

Licon String containing *CONTENTS*.

Lsp

The size of an empty line. Normally 0.5v, but it is 1v
if **n** is set (**.nroff**). **MO1 - MO12** Strings containing *January to December*.

Qrf   String containing "See chapter *[Qrfh], page \\n[Qrfp].".

Sectf Flag controlling "section-figures". A non-zero value enables this. Se also register N.

Sectp Flag controlling "section-page-numbers". A non-zero value enables this. Se also register N.

.mgm   Always 1.

A file called **locale** or *lang*_**locale** is read after the initiation of the global variables. It is therefore possible to localize the macros with companyname and so on.

The following standard macros are implemented:

1C   Begin one column processing

2C   Begin two column processing

AE   Abstract end

AF [name of firm]
Authors firm

AL [type [text-indent [1]]]]
Start autoincrement list

AS [arg [indent]]
Abstract start. Indent is specified in 'ens', but scaling is allowed.

AST [title]
Abstract title. Default is 'ABSTRACT'.

AT title1 [title2 ...]
Authors title

AU name [initials [loc [dept [ext [room [arg [arg [arg]]]]]]]]]
Author information

B [bold-text [prev-font-tex [...]]]
Begin boldface No limit on the number of arguments.

BE   End bottom block

BI [bold-text [italic-text [bold-text [...]]]
Bold-italic. No limit on the number of arguments.

BL [text-indent [1]]
Start bullet list

BR [bold-text [roman-text [bold-text [...]]]]
Bold-roman. No limit on the number of arguments.

BS   Bottom block start

DE   Display end

DF [format [fill [rindent]]]
Begin floating display (no nesting allowed)

DL [text-indent [1]]
Dash list start

DS [format [fill [rindent]]]
Static display start. Can now have unlimited nesting. Also right adjusted text and block may be used (R or RB as *format*).

EC [title [override [flag [refname]]]]
Equation title. If *refname* is used, then the equationnumber is saved with **.SETR,** and can be retrieved with **.GETST** *refname*.

EF [arg]
Even-page footer.

EH [arg]
Even-page header.

EN   Equation end.

EQ [label]
Equation start.

EX [title [override [flag [refname]]]]
Exhibit title. If *refname* is used, then the exhibitnumber is saved with **.SETR,** and can be

retrieved with **.GETST** *refname*.

FD [arg [1]]
Footnote default format.

FE   Footnote end.

FG [title [override [flag [refname]]]]
Figure title. If *refname* is used, then the figurenumber is saved with **.SETR**, and can be retrieved with **.GETST** *refname*.

FS   Footnote start. Footnotes in displays is now possible.

H level [heading-text [heading-suffix]]
Numbered heading.

HC [hyphenation-character]
Set hyphenation character.

HM [arg1 [arg2 [... [arg7]]]]
Heading mark style.

HU heading-text
Unnumbered header.

HX dlevel rlevel heading-text
Userdefined heading exit. Called just before printing the header.

HY dlevel rlevel heading-text
Userdefined heading exit. Called just before printing the header.

HZ dlevel rlevel heading-text
Userdefined heading exit. Called just after printing the header.

I [italic-text [prev-font-text [italic-text [...]]]]
Italic.

IB [italic-text [bold-text [italic-text [...]]]]
Italic-bold

IR [italic-text [roman-text [italic-text [...]]]]
Italic-roman

LB text-indent mark-indent pad type [mark [LI-space [LB-space]]]
List begin macro.

LC [list level]
List-status clear

LE   List end.

LI [mark [1]]
List item

ML mark [text-indent]
Marked list start

MT [arg [addressee]]
Memorandum type. See above note about MT.

ND new-date
New date.

OF [arg]
Odd-page footer

OH [arg]
　　　　Odd-page header

OP　　Skip to odd page.

P [type]
　　　　Begin new paragraph.

PE　　Picture end.

PF [arg]
　　　　Page footer

PH [arg]
　　　　Page header

PS　　Picture start (from pic)

PX　　Page-header user-defined exit.

R　　Roman.

RB [roman-text [bold-text [roman-text [...]]]
　　　　Roman-bold.

RD [prompt [diversion [string]]]
　　　　Read to diversion and/or string.

RF　　Reference end

RI [roman-text [italic-text [roman-text [...]]]
　　　　Roman-italic.

RL [text-indent [1]]
　　　　Reference list start

RP [arg [arg]]
　　　　Produce reference page.

RS [string-name]
　　　　Reference start.

S [size [spacing]]
　　　　Set point size and vertical spacing. If any argument is equal 'P', then the previous value is used. A 'C' means current value, and 'D' default value. If '+' or '-' is used before the value, then increment or decrement of the current value will be done.

SA [arg]
　　　　Set adjustment.

SK [pages]
　　　　Skip pages.

SM string1 [string2 [string3]]
　　　　Make a string smaller.

SP [lines]
　　　　Space vertically. *lines* can have any scalingfactor, like *3i* or *8v*.

TB [title [override [flag [refname]]]]
　　　　Table title. If *refname* is used, then the tablenumber is saved with **.SETR**, and can be retrieved with **.GETST** *refname*.

TC [slevel [spacing [tlevel [tab [h1 [h2 [h3 [h4 [h5]]]]]]]]]
　　　　Table of contents. All texts can be redefined, new stringvariables *Lifg*, *Litb*, *Liex*, *Liec* and *Licon* contains "Figure", "TABLE", "Exhibit", "Equation" and "CONTENTS". These can be redefined to other languages.

TE   Table end.

TH [N] Table header.

TL   Begin title of memorandum.

TM [num1 [num2 [...]]]
        Technical memorandumnumbers used in **.MT**. Unlimited number of arguments may be given.

TP   Top of page user-defined macro.

TS [H] Table start

TX   Userdefined table of contents exit.

TY   Userdefined table of contents exit (no "CONTENTS").

VL [text-indent [mark-indent [1]]]
        Variable-item list start

VM [top [bottom]]
        Vertical margin.

WC [format]
        Footnote and display width control.

Strings used in m/usr/share/tmac/tmac.m:

EM   Em dash string

HF   Fontlist for headings, normally "2 2 2 2 2 2 2". Nonnumeric fontnames may also be used.

HP   Pointsize list for headings. Normally "0 0 0 0 0 0 0" which is the same as "10 10 10 10 10 10 10".

Lf   Contains "LIST OF FIGURES".

Lt   Contains "LIST OF TABLES".

Lx   Contains "LIST OF EXHIBITS".

Le   Contains "LIST OF EQUATIONS".

Rp   Contains "REFERENCES".

Tm   Contains \(tm, trade mark.

Number variables used in m/usr/share/tmac/tmac.m:

Cl=2   Contents level [0:7], contents saved if heading level <= Cl

Cp=0   Eject page between LIST OF XXXX if Cp == 0

D=0   Debugflag, values >0 produces varying degree of debug. A value of 1 gives information about the progress of formatting.

De=0   Eject after floating display is output [0:1]

Df=5   Floating keep output [0:5]

Ds=1   space before and after display if == 1 [0:1]

Ej=0   Eject page

Eq=0   Equation label adjust 0=left, 1=right

Fs=1   Footnote spacing

H1-H7 Heading counters

7

Hb=2   Heading break level [0:7]

Hc=0   Heading centering level, [0:7]

Hi=1   Heading temporary indent [0:2] 0 -> 0 indent, left margin
1 -> indent to right , like .P 1
2 -> indent to line up with text part of preceding heading

Hs=2   Heading space level [0:7]

Ht=0   Heading numbering type 0 -> multiple (1.1.1 ...)
1 -> single

Hu=2   Unnumbered heading level

Hy=1   Hyphenation in body 0 -> no hyphenation
1 -> hyphenation 14 on

Lf=1, Lt=1, Lx=1, Le=0
Enables (1) or disables (0) the printing of List of figures, List of tables, List of exhibits and List of equations.

Li=6   List indent, used by .AL

Ls=99   List space, if current listlevel > Ls then no spacing will occur around lists.

N=0   Numbering style [0:5] 0 —— (default) normal header for all pages.
1 —— header replaces footer on first page, header is empty.
2 —— page header is removed on the first page.
3 —— "section-page" numbering enabled.
4 —— page header is removed on the first page.
5 —— "section-page" and "section-figure" numbering enabled. Se also the number-register Sectf and Sectp.

Np=0   Numbered paragraphs.
0 —— not numbered
1 —— numbered in first level headings.

Of=0   Format of figure,table,exhibit,equation titles.
0= ". "
1= " - "

P   Current page-number, normally the same as % unless "section-page" numbering is enabled.

Pi=5   paragraph indent

Ps=1   paragraph spacing

Pt=0   Paragraph type.
0 —— left-justified
1 —— indented .P
2 —— indented .P except after .H, .DE or .LE.

Si=5   Display indent.

AUTHOR
Jvrgen Hdgg, Lund Institute of Technology, Sweden <jh@efd.lth.se>

FILES
/usr/share/tmac/tmac./usr/share/tmac/tmac.m

/usr/share/tmac/*.cov

/usr/share/tmac/*.MT

/usr/share/tmac/locale

SEE ALSO

      groff(1), troff(1), tbl(1), pic(1), eqn(1)
      mm(7)

NAME

ms – text formatting macros

SYNOPSIS

nroff −**ms** [options] file ...
troff −**ms** [options] file ...

DESCRIPTION

This package of *nroff* and *troff* macro definitions provides a formatting facility for various styles of articles, theses, and books. When producing 2-column output on a terminal or lineprinter, or when reverse line motions are needed, filter the output through *col* (1). All external −ms macros are defined below. Many *nroff* and *troff* requests are unsafe in conjunction with this package. However, the first four requests below may be used with impunity after initialization, and the last two may be used even before initialization:

.bp	begin new page
.br	break output line
.sp n	insert n spacing lines
.ce n	center next n lines
.ls n	line spacing: n=1 single, n=2 double space
.na	no alignment of right margin

Font and point size changes with \f and \s are also allowed; for example, ''\fIword\fR'' will italicize *word*. Output of the *tbl, eqn,* and *refer* (1) preprocessors for equations, tables, and references is acceptable as input.

FILES

/usr/share/tmac/tmac.x
/usr/share/ms/x.???

SEE ALSO

eqn(1), refer(1), tbl(1), troff(1)

REQUESTS

Macro Name	Initial Value	Break? Reset?	Explanation
.AB *x*	–	y	begin abstract; if *x* =no don't label abstract
.AE	–	y	end abstract
.AI	–	y	author's institution
.AM	–	n	better accent mark definitions
.AU	–	y	author's name
.B *x*	–	n	embolden *x* ; if no *x*, switch to boldface
.B1	–	y	begin text to be enclosed in a box
.B2	–	y	end boxed text and print it
.BT	date	n	bottom title, printed at foot of page
.BX *x*	–	n	print word *x* in a box
.CM	if t	n	cut mark between pages
.CT	–	y,y	chapter title: page number moved to CF (TM only)
.DA *x*	if n	n	force date *x* at bottom of page; today if no *x*
.DE	–	y	end display (unfilled text) of any kind
.DS *x y*	I	y	begin display with keep; *x* =I,L,C,B; *y* =indent
.ID *y*	8n,.5i	y	indented display with no keep; *y* =indent
.LD	–	y	left display with no keep
.CD	–	y	centered display with no keep
.BD	–	y	block display; center entire block
.EF *x*	–	n	even page footer *x* (3 part as for .tl)
.EH *x*	–	n	even page header *x* (3 part as for .tl)
.EN	–	y	end displayed equation produced by *eqn*

.EQ x y	–	y	break out equation; x=L,I,C; y=equation number
.FE	–	n	end footnote to be placed at bottom of page
.FP	–	n	numbered footnote paragraph; may be redefined
.FS x	–	n	start footnote; x is optional footnote label
.HD	undef	n	optional page header below header margin
.I x	–	n	italicize x; if no x, switch to italics
.IP x y	–	y,y	indented paragraph, with hanging tag x; y=indent
.IX x y	–	y	index words x y and so on (up to 5 levels)
.KE	–	n	end keep of any kind
.KF	–	n	begin floating keep; text fills remainder of page
.KS	–	y	begin keep; unit kept together on a single page
.LG	–	n	larger; increase point size by 2
.LP	–	y,y	left (block) paragraph.
.MC x	–	y,y	multiple columns; x=column width
.ND x	if t	n	no date in page footer; x is date on cover
.NH x y	–	y,y	numbered header; x=level, x=0 resets, x=S sets to y
.NL	10p	n	set point size back to normal
.OF x	–	n	odd page footer x (3 part as for .tl)
.OH x	–	n	odd page header x (3 part as for .tl)
.P1	if TM	n	print header on 1st page
.PP	–	y,y	paragraph with first line indented
.PT	- % -	n	page title, printed at head of page
.PX x	–	y	print index (table of contents); x=no suppresses title
.QP	–	y,y	quote paragraph (indented and shorter)
.R	on	n	return to Roman font
.RE	5n	y,y	retreat: end level of relative indentation
.RP x	–	n	released paper format; x=no stops title on 1st page
.RS	5n	y,y	right shift: start level of relative indentation
.SH	–	y,y	section header, in boldface
.SM	–	n	smaller; decrease point size by 2
.TA	8n,5n	n	set tabs to 8n 16n ... (nroff) 5n 10n ... (troff)
.TC x	–	y	print table of contents at end; x=no suppresses title
.TE	–	y	end of table processed by *tbl*
.TH	–	y	end multi-page header of table
.TL	–	y	title in boldface and two points larger
.TM	off	n	UC Berkeley thesis mode
.TS x	–	y,y	begin table; if x=H table has multi-page header
.UL x	–	n	underline x, even in *troff*
.UX x	–	n	UNIX; trademark message first time; x appended
.XA x y	–	y	another index entry; x=page or no for none; y=indent
.XE	–	y	end index entry (or series of .IX entries)
.XP	–	y,y	paragraph with first line exdented, others indented
.XS x y	–	y	begin index entry; x=page or no for none; y=indent
.1C	on	y,y	one column format, on a new page
.2C	–	y,y	begin two column format
.]-	–	n	beginning of *refer* reference
.[0	–	n	end of unclassifiable type of reference
.[N	–	n	N= 1:journal-article, 2:book, 3:book-article, 4:report

REGISTERS

Formatting distances can be controlled in −ms by means of built-in number registers. For example, this sets the line length to 6.5 inches:

    .nr LL 6.5i

Here is a table of number registers and their default values:

Name	Register Controls	Takes Effect	Default
PS	point size	paragraph	10
VS	vertical spacing	paragraph	12
LL	line length	paragraph	6i
LT	title length	next page	same as LL
FL	footnote length	next .FS	5.5i
PD	paragraph distance	paragraph	1v (if n), .3v (if t)
DD	display distance	displays	1v (if n), .5v (if t)
PI	paragraph indent	paragraph	5n
QI	quote indent	next .QP	5n
FI	footnote indent	next .FS	2n
PO	page offset	next page	0 (if n), ~1i (if t)
HM	header margin	next page	1i
FM	footer margin	next page	1i
FF	footnote format	next .FS	0 (1, 2, 3 available)

When resetting these values, make sure to specify the appropriate units. Setting the line length to 7, for example, will result in output with one character per line. Setting FF to 1 suppresses footnote superscripting; setting it to 2 also suppresses indentation of the first line; and setting it to 3 produces an .IP-like footnote paragraph.

Here is a list of string registers available in −ms; they may be used anywhere in the text:

Name	String's Function
*Q	quote (" in *nroff*, `` in *troff*)
*U	unquote (" in *nroff*, '' in *troff*)
*−	dash (-- in *nroff*, — in *troff*)
*(MO	month (month of the year)
*(DY	day (current date)
**	automatically numbered footnote
*[	opening footnote string delimiter
*]	closing footnote string delimiter
*([.	opening reference tag delimiter
*(.]	closing reference tag delimiter
*´	acute accent (before letter)
*`	grave accent (before letter)
*^	circumflex (before letter)
*,	cedilla (before letter)
*:	umlaut (before letter)
*_	tilde (before letter)

The opening and closing delimiters for footnote numbers and reference tags may be changed by resetting the appropriate string. Both opening delimiters change to italics and superscript in *troff*, reverting to the previous font and the baseline at the closing delimiter. In *nroff*, square brackets are used as delimiters, with footnote numbers in italics.

When using the extended accent mark definitions available with .AM, these strings should come after, rather than before, the letter to be accented.

BUGS

Floating keeps and regular keeps are diverted to the same space, so they cannot be mixed together with predictable results.

NAME

    `operator` – C operator precedence and order of evaluation

DESCRIPTION

Operator	Associativity
--------	-------------
() [] -> .	left to right
! ~ ++ -- - (type) * & sizeof	right to left
* / %	left to right
+ -	left to right
<< >>	left to right
< <= > >=	left to right
== !=	left to right
&	left to right
^	left to right
|	left to right
&&	left to right
||	left to right
?:	right to left
= += -= etc.	right to left
,	left to right

FILES

    `/usr/share/misc/operator`

NAME

re_format – POSIX 1003.2 regular expressions

DESCRIPTION

Regular expressions ("RE"s), as defined in POSIX 1003.2, come in two forms: modern REs (roughly those of *egrep*; 1003.2 calls these "extended" REs) and obsolete REs (roughly those of *ed*; 1003.2 "basic" REs). Obsolete REs mostly exist for backward compatibility in some old programs; they will be discussed at the end. 1003.2 leaves some aspects of RE syntax and semantics open; '†' marks decisions on these aspects that may not be fully portable to other 1003.2 implementations.

A (modern) RE is one† or more non-empty† *branches*, separated by 'I'. It matches anything that matches one of the branches.

A branch is one† or more *pieces*, concatenated. It matches a match for the first, followed by a match for the second, etc.

A piece is an *atom* possibly followed by a single† '*', '+', '?', or *bound*. An atom followed by '*' matches a sequence of 0 or more matches of the atom. An atom followed by '+' matches a sequence of 1 or more matches of the atom. An atom followed by '?' matches a sequence of 0 or 1 matches of the atom.

A *bound* is '{' followed by an unsigned decimal integer, possibly followed by ',' possibly followed by another unsigned decimal integer, always followed by '}'. The integers must lie between 0 and RE_DUP_MAX (255†) inclusive, and if there are two of them, the first may not exceed the second. An atom followed by a bound containing one integer *i* and no comma matches a sequence of exactly *i* matches of the atom. An atom followed by a bound containing one integer *i* and a comma matches a sequence of *i* or more matches of the atom. An atom followed by a bound containing two integers *i* and *j* matches a sequence of *i* through *j* (inclusive) matches of the atom.

An atom is a regular expression enclosed in '()' (matching a match for the regular expression), an empty set of '()' (matching the null string)†, a *bracket expression* (see below), '.' (matching any single character), '^' (matching the null string at the beginning of a line), '$' (matching the null string at the end of a line), a '\' followed by one of the characters '^.[$()I*+?{\' (matching that character taken as an ordinary character), a '\' followed by any other character† (matching that character taken as an ordinary character, as if the '\' had not been present†), or a single character with no other significance (matching that character). A '{' followed by a character other than a digit is an ordinary character, not the beginning of a bound†. It is illegal to end an RE with '\'.

A *bracket expression* is a list of characters enclosed in '[]'. It normally matches any single character from the list (but see below). If the list begins with '^', it matches any single character (but see below) *not* from the rest of the list. If two characters in the list are separated by '−', this is shorthand for the full *range* of characters between those two (inclusive) in the collating sequence, e.g. '[0-9]' in ASCII matches any decimal digit. It is illegal† for two ranges to share an endpoint, e.g. 'a-c-e'. Ranges are very collating-sequence-dependent, and portable programs should avoid relying on them.

To include a literal ']' in the list, make it the first character (following a possible '^'). To include a literal '−', make it the first or last character, or the second endpoint of a range. To use a literal '−' as the first endpoint of a range, enclose it in '[.' and '.]' to make it a collating element (see below). With the exception of these and some combinations using '[' (see next paragraphs), all other special characters, including '\', lose their special significance within a bracket expression.

Within a bracket expression, a collating element (a character, a multi-character sequence that collates as if it were a single character, or a collating-sequence name for either) enclosed in '[.' and '.]' stands for the sequence of characters of that collating element. The sequence is a single element of the bracket expression's list. A bracket expression containing a multi-character collating element can thus match more than one character, e.g. if the collating sequence includes a 'ch' collating element, then the RE '[[.ch.]]*c' matches the first five characters of 'chchcc'.

Within a bracket expression, a collating element enclosed in '[=' and '=]' is an equivalence class, standing for the sequences of characters of all collating elements equivalent to that one, including itself. (If there are no other equivalent collating elements, the treatment is as if the enclosing delimiters were '[.' and '.]'.)

For example, if o and ô are the members of an equivalence class, then '[[=o=]]', '[[=ô=]]', and '[oô]' are all synonymous. An equivalence class may not† be an endpoint of a range.

Within a bracket expression, the name of a *character class* enclosed in '[:' and ':]' stands for the list of all characters belonging to that class. Standard character class names are:

alnum	digit	punct
alpha	graph	space
blank	lower	upper
cntrl	print	xdigit

These stand for the character classes defined in *ctype*(3). A locale may provide others. A character class may not be used as an endpoint of a range.

There are two special cases† of bracket expressions: the bracket expressions '[[:<:]]' and '[[:>:]]' match the null string at the beginning and end of a word respectively. A word is defined as a sequence of word characters which is neither preceded nor followed by word characters. A word character is an *alnum* character (as defined by *ctype*(3)) or an underscore. This is an extension, compatible with but not specified by POSIX 1003.2, and should be used with caution in software intended to be portable to other systems.

In the event that an RE could match more than one substring of a given string, the RE matches the one starting earliest in the string. If the RE could match more than one substring starting at that point, it matches the longest. Subexpressions also match the longest possible substrings, subject to the constraint that the whole match be as long as possible, with subexpressions starting earlier in the RE taking priority over ones starting later. Note that higher-level subexpressions thus take priority over their lower-level component subexpressions.

Match lengths are measured in characters, not collating elements. A null string is considered longer than no match at all. For example, 'bb*' matches the three middle characters of 'abbbc', '(weel|week)(knights|nights)' matches all ten characters of 'weeknights', when '(.*).*' is matched against 'abc' the parenthesized subexpression matches all three characters, and when '(a*)*' is matched against 'bc' both the whole RE and the parenthesized subexpression match the null string.

If case-independent matching is specified, the effect is much as if all case distinctions had vanished from the alphabet. When an alphabetic that exists in multiple cases appears as an ordinary character outside a bracket expression, it is effectively transformed into a bracket expression containing both cases, e.g. 'x' becomes '[xX]'. When it appears inside a bracket expression, all case counterparts of it are added to the bracket expression, so that (e.g.) '[x]' becomes '[xX]' and '[^x]' becomes '[^xX]'.

No particular limit is imposed on the length of REs†. Programs intended to be portable should not employ REs longer than 256 bytes, as an implementation can refuse to accept such REs and remain POSIX-compliant.

Obsolete ("basic") regular expressions differ in several respects. '|', '+', and '?' are ordinary characters and there is no equivalent for their functionality. The delimiters for bounds are '\{' and '\}', with '{' and '}' by themselves ordinary characters. The parentheses for nested subexpressions are '\(' and '\)', with '(' and ')' by themselves ordinary characters. '^' is an ordinary character except at the beginning of the RE or† the beginning of a parenthesized subexpression, '$' is an ordinary character except at the end of the RE or† the end of a parenthesized subexpression, and '*' is an ordinary character if it appears at the beginning of the RE or the beginning of a parenthesized subexpression (after a possible leading '^'). Finally, there is one new type of atom, a *back reference*: '\' followed by a non-zero decimal digit d matches the same sequence of characters matched by the dth parenthesized subexpression (numbering subexpressions by the positions of their opening parentheses, left to right), so that (e.g.) '\([bc]\)\1' matches 'bb' or 'cc' but not 'bc'.

SEE ALSO

    regex(3)

POSIX 1003.2, section 2.8 (Regular Expression Notation).

BUGS

Having two kinds of REs is a botch.

The current 1003.2 spec says that ')' is an ordinary character in the absence of an unmatched '('; this was an unintentional result of a wording error, and change is likely. Avoid relying on it.

Back references are a dreadful botch, posing major problems for efficient implementations. They are also somewhat vaguely defined (does 'a\(\(b\)*\2\)*d' match 'abbbd'?). Avoid using them.

1003.2's specification of case-independent matching is vague. The "one case implies all cases" definition given above is current consensus among implementors as to the right interpretation.

The syntax for word boundaries is incredibly ugly.

7

NAME

    `symlink` – symbolic link handling

SYMBOLIC LINK HANDLING

    Symbolic links are files that act as pointers to other files. To understand their behavior, you must first understand how hard links work. A hard link to a file is indistinguishable from the original file because it is a reference to the object underlying the original file name. Changes to a file are independent of the name used to reference the file. Hard links may not refer to directories and may not reference files on different file systems. A symbolic link contains the name of the file to which it is linked, i.e. it is a pointer to another name, and not to an underlying object. For this reason, symbolic links may reference directories and may span file systems.

    Because a symbolic link and its referenced object coexist in the filesystem name space, confusion can arise in distinguishing between the link itself and the referenced object. Historically, commands and system calls have adopted their own link following conventions in a somewhat ad-hoc fashion. Rules for more a uniform approach, as they are implemented in this system, are outlined here. It is important that local applications conform to these rules, too, so that the user interface can be as consistent as possible.

    Symbolic links are handled either by operating on the link itself, or by operating on the object referenced by the link. In the latter case, an application or system call is said to "follow" the link. Symbolic links may reference other symbolic links, in which case the links are dereferenced until an object that is not a symbolic link is found, a symbolic link which references a file which doesn't exist is found, or a loop is detected. (Loop detection is done by placing an upper limit on the number of links that may be followed, and an error results if this limit is exceeded.)

    There are three separate areas that need to be discussed. They are as follows:

        1.   Symbolic links used as file name arguments for system calls.
        2.   Symbolic links specified as command line arguments to utilities that are not traversing a file tree.
        3.   Symbolic links encountered by utilities that are traversing a file tree (either specified on the command line or encountered as part of the file hierarchy walk).

System calls.

    The first area is symbolic links used as file name arguments for system calls.

    Except as noted below, all system calls follow symbolic links. For example, if there were a symbolic link "`slink`" which pointed to a file named "`afile`", the system call "`open("slink" ...)`" would return a file descriptor to the file "afile".

    There are four system calls that do not follow links, and which operate on the symbolic link itself. They are: lstat(2), readlink(2), rename(2), and unlink(2). Because remove(3) is an alias for unlink(2), it also does not follow symbolic links.

    Unlike other filesystem objects, symbolic links do not have an owner, group, permissions, access and modification times, etc. The only attributes returned from an lstat(2) that refer to the symbolic link itself are the file type (S_IFLNK), size, blocks, and link count (always 1). The other attributes are filled in from the directory that contains the link. For portability reasons, you should be aware that other implementations (including historic implementations of 4BSD), implement symbolic links such that they have the same attributes as any other file.

    The 4.4BSD system differs from historical 4BSD systems in that the system call chown(2) has been changed to follow symbolic links.

Commands not traversing a file tree.

The second area is symbolic links, specified as command line file name arguments, to commands which are not traversing a file tree.

Except as noted below, commands follow symbolic links named as command line arguments. For example, if there were a symbolic link "`slink`" which pointed to a file named "`afile`", the command "`cat slink`" would display the contents of the file "`afile`".

It is important to realize that this rule includes commands which may optionally traverse file trees, e.g. the command "`chown file`" is included in this rule, while the command "`chown -R file`" is not. (The latter is described in the third area, below.)

If it is explicitly intended that the command operate on the symbolic link instead of following the symbolic link, e.g., it is desired that "`file slink`" display the type of file that "`slink`" is, whether it is a symbolic link or not, the −h option should be used. In the above example, "`file slink`" would report the type of the file referenced by "`slink`", while "`file -h slink`" would report that "`slink`" was a symbolic link.

There are three exceptions to this rule. The mv(1) and rm(1) commands do not follow symbolic links named as arguments, but respectively attempt to rename and delete them. (Note, if the symbolic link references a file via a relative path, moving it to another directory may very well cause it to stop working, since the path may no longer be correct.)

The ls(1) command is also an exception to this rule. For compatibility with historic systems (when ls is not doing a tree walk, i.e. the −R option is not specified), the ls command follows symbolic links named as arguments if the −L option is specified, or if the −F, −d or −l options are not specified. (If the −L option is specified, ls always follows symbolic links. Ls is the only command where the −L option affects its behavior even though it is not doing a walk of a file tree.)

The 4.4BSD system differs from historical 4BSD systems in that the **chown**, **chgrp** and **file** commands follow symbolic links specified on the command line.

Commands traversing a file tree.

The following commands either optionally or always traverse file trees: chflags(1), chgrp(1), chmod(1), cp(1), du(1), find(1), ls(1), pax(1), rm(1), tar(1) and chown(8).

It is important to realize that the following rules apply equally to symbolic links encountered during the file tree traversal and symbolic links listed as command line arguments.

The first rule applies to symbolic links that reference files that are not of type directory. Operations that apply to symbolic links are performed on the links themselves, but otherwise the links are ignored.

For example, the command "`chown -R user slink directory`" will ignore "`slink`", because symbolic links in this system do not have owners. Any symbolic links encountered during the tree traversal will also be ignored. The command "`rm -r slink directory`" will remove "`slink`", as well as any symbolic links encountered in the tree traversal of "`directory`", because symbolic links may be removed. In no case will either **chown** or **rm** affect the file which "`slink`" references in any way.

The second rule applies to symbolic links that reference files of type directory. Symbolic links which reference files of type directory are never "followed" by default. This is often referred to as a "physical" walk, as opposed to a "logical" walk (where symbolic links referencing directories are followed).

As consistently as possible, you can make commands doing a file tree walk follow any symbolic links named on the command line, regardless of the type of file they reference, by specifying the −H (for "half-logical") flag. This flag is intended to make the command line name space look like the logical name space. (Note, for commands that do not always do file tree traversals, the −H flag will be ignored if the −R flag is not also specified.)

For example, the command "chown -HR user slink" will traverse the file hierarchy rooted in the file pointed to by "slink". Note, the −H is not the same as the previously discussed −h flag. The −H flag causes symbolic links specified on the command line to be dereferenced both for the purposes of the action to be performed and the tree walk, and it is as if the user had specified the name of the file to which the symbolic link pointed.

As consistently as possible, you can make commands doing a file tree walk follow any symbolic links named on the command line, as well as any symbolic links encountered during the traversal, regardless of the type of file they reference, by specifying the −L (for "logical") flag. This flag is intended to make the entire name space look like the logical name space. (Note, for commands that do not always do file tree traversals, the −L flag will be ignored if the −R flag is not also specified.)

For example, the command "chown -LR user slink" will change the owner of the file referenced by "slink". If "slink" references a directory, **chown** will traverse the file hierarchy rooted in the directory that it references. In addition, if any symbolic links are encountered in any file tree that **chown** traverses, they will be treated in the same fashion as "slink".

As consistently as possible, you can specify the default behavior by specifying the −P (for "physical") flag. This flag is intended to make the entire name space look like the physical name space.

For commands that do not by default do file tree traversals, the −H, −L and −P flags are ignored if the −R flag is not also specified. In addition, you may specify the −H, −L and −P options more than once; the last one specified determines the command's behavior. This is intended to permit you to alias commands to behave one way or the other, and then override that behavior on the command line.

The ls(1) and rm(1) commands have exceptions to these rules. The **rm** command operates on the symbolic link, and not the file it references, and therefore never follows a symbolic link. The **rm** command does not support the −H, −L or −P options.

To maintain compatibility with historic systems, the **ls** command never follows symbolic links unless the −L flag is specified. If the −L flag is specified, **ls** follows all symbolic links, regardless of their type, whether specified on the command line or encountered in the tree walk. The **ls** command does not support the −H or −P options.

SEE ALSO

chflags(1), chgrp(1), chmod(1), cp(1), du(1), find(1), ln(1), ls(1), mv(1), pax(1), rm(1), tar(1), lstat(2), readlink(2), rename(2), unlink(2), fts(3), remove(3), chown(8)

NAME

term – conventional names for terminals

DESCRIPTION

Certain commands use these terminal names. They are maintained as part of the shell environment (see sh(1), environ(7)).

The list goes on and on. Consult /usr/share/misc/termcap (see termcap(5)) for an up-to-date and locally correct list.

Commands whose behavior may depend on the terminal either consult TERM in the environment, or accept arguments of the form −T*term*, where **term** is one of the names given above.

SEE ALSO

stty(1), tabs(1), plot(1) sh(1), environ(7) ex(1), clear(1), more(1), ul(1), tset(1), termcap(5), termcap(3), ttys(5) troff(1)

BUGS

The programs that ought to adhere to this nomenclature do so only fitfully.

HISTORY

Term appeared in Version 32 AT&T UNIX.

BERKELEY 4.4 SOFTWARE DISTRIBUTION

4.4BSD is the final release of what may be one of the most significant research projects in the history of computing. When Bell Labs originally released UNIX source code to the R&D community, brilliant researchers wrote their own software and added it to UNIX in a spree of creative anarchy that hasn't been equaled since. The Berkeley Software Distribution became the repository of much of that work.

In those years of creative ferment, source code was widely available, so programmers could build on the work of others. As UNIX became commercialized, access to source became increasingly curtailed and original development more difficult.

With this release of 4.4BSD-Lite, you need no longer work at a university or UNIX system development house to have access to UNIX source. The source code included on the 4.4BSD-Lite CD-ROM Companion will provide invaluable information on the design of any modern UNIX or UNIX-like system, and the source code for the utilities and support libraries will greatly enhance any programmer's toolkit. (Note that the 4.4BSD-Lite distribution does not include sources for the complete 4.4BSD system.

The source code for a small number of utilities and files, including a few from the operating system, were removed so that the system could be freely distributed.)

In addition to source code, the CD includes the manual pages, other documentation, and research papers from the University of California, Berkeley's 4.4BSD-Lite distribution.

This documentation is also available in printed form as a five-volume set.

—*Tim O'Reilly*

4.4BSD-Lite CD Companion

112 pages plus CD-ROM
CD Domestic ISBN 1-56592-081-3
CD International ISBN 1-56592-092-9

This CD is a copy of the University of California, Berkeley's 4.4BSD-Lite release, with additional documentation and enhancements. Access to the source code included here will provide invaluable information on the design of a modern UNIX-like system, and the source code for the utilities and support libraries will greatly enhance any programmer's toolkit. The CD is a source distribution, and does not contain program binaries for any architecture. It will not be possible to compile or run this software without a pre-existing system that is already installed and running. The 4.4BSD-Lite distribution did not include sources for the complete 4.4BSD system. The source code for a small number of utilities and files (including a few from the operating system) were removed so that the system could be freely distributed.

4.4BSD System Manager's Manual

646(est.) pages, ISBN 1-56592-080-5

Man pages for system administration commands and files, plus papers on system administration.

4.4BSD User's Reference Manual

909 pages, ISBN 1-56592-075-9

The famous "man pages" for over 500 utilities.

4.4BSD User's Supplementary Documents

686(est.) pages, ISBN 1-56592-076-7

Papers providing in-depth documentation of complex programs such as the shell, editors, and word processing utilities.

4.4BSD Programmer's Reference Manual

884 pages, ISBN 1-56592-078-3

Man pages for system calls, libraries, and file formats.

4.4BSD Programmer's Supplementary Documents

606(est.) pages, ISBN 1-56592-079-1

The original Bell and BSD research papers providing in-depth documentation of the programming environment.

GLOBAL NETWORK NAVIGATOR

The Global Network Navigator™ (GNN) is a unique kind of information service that makes the Internet easy and enjoyable to use. We organize access to the vast information resources of the Internet so that you can find what you want. We also help you understand the Internet and the many ways you can explore it.

Charting the Internet, the Ultimate Online Service

In GNN you'll find:

- **The Online Whole Internet Catalog**, an interactive card catalog for Internet resources that expands on the catalog in Ed Krol's bestselling book, *The Whole Internet User's Guide & Catalog*.

- **Newsnet**, a news service that keeps you up to date on what's happening on the Net.

- **The Netheads department**, which features profiles of interesting people on the Internet and commentary by Internet experts.

- **GNN Metacenters**, special-interest online magazines aimed at serving the needs of particular audiences. GNN Metacenters not only gather the best Internet resources together in one convenient place, they also introduce new material from a variety of sources. Each Metacenter contains new feature articles, as well as columns, subject-oriented reference guides for using the Internet, and topic-oriented discussion groups. Travel, music, education, and computers are some of the areas that we cover.

All in all, GNN helps you get more value for the time you spend on the Internet.

Subscribe Today

GNN is available over the Internet as a subscription service. To get complete information about subscribing to GNN, send email to **info@gnn.com**. If you have access to a World Wide Web browser such as Mosaic or Lynx, you can use the following URL to register online: **http://gnn.com/**

If you use a browser that does not support online forms, you can retrieve an email version of the registration form automatically by sending email to **form@gnn.com**. Fill this form out and send it back to us by email, and we will confirm your registration.

BOOK INFORMATION AT YOUR FINGERTIPS

O'Reilly & Associates offers extensive online information through a Gopher server (*gopher.ora.com*). Here you can find detailed information on our entire catalog of books, tapes, and much more.

The O'Reilly Online Catalog

Gopher is basically a hierarchy of menus and files that can easily lead you to a wealth of information. Gopher is also easy to navigate; helpful instructions appear at the bottom of each screen (notice the three prompts in the sample screen below). Another nice feature is that Gopher files can be downloaded, saved, or printed out for future reference. You can also search Gopher files and even email them.

To give you an idea of our Gopher, here's a look at the top, or root, menu:

```
O'Reilly & Associates (The public gopher server)

    1.  News Flash! -- New Products and Projects/

    2.  Feature Articles/

    3.  Product Descriptions/

    4.  Ordering Information/

    5.  Complete Listing of Titles

    6.  Errata for "Learning Perl"

    7.  FTP Archive and Email Information/

    8.  Bibliographies/


Press ? for Help, q to Quit, u to go up a menu
```

The heart of the O'Reilly Gopher service is the extensive information provided on all ORA products in menu item three, "Product Descriptions." For most books this usually includes title information, a long description, a short author bio, the table of contents, quotes and reviews, a gif image of the book's cover, and even some interesting information about the animal featured on the cover (one of the benefits of a Gopher database is the ability to pack a lot of information in an organized, easy-to-find place).

How to Order

Another important listing is "Ordering Information," where we supply information to those interested in buying our books. Here, you'll find instructions and an application for ordering O'Reilly products online, a listing of distributors (local and international), a listing of bookstores that carry our titles, and much more.

The item that follows, "Complete Listing of Titles," is helpful when it's time to order. This single file, with short one-line listings of all ORA products, quickly provides the essentials for easy ordering: title, ISBN, and price.

And More

One of the most widely read areas of the O'Reilly Gopher is "News Flash!," which focuses on important new products and projects of ORA. Here, you'll find entries on newly published books and audiotapes; announcements of exciting new projects and product lines from ORA; upcoming tradeshows, conferences, and exhibitions of interest; author appearances; contest winners; job openings; and anything else that's timely and topical.

"Feature Articles" contains just that—many of the articles and interviews found here are excerpted from the O'Reilly magazine/catalog *ora.com*.

The "Bibliographies" entries are also very popular with readers, providing critical, objective reviews on the important literature in the field.

"FTP Archive and Email Information" contains helpful ORA email addresses, information about our "ora-news" listproc server, and detailed instructions on how to download ORA book examples via FTP.

Other menu listings are often available. "Errata for 'Learning Perl,'" for example, apprised readers of errata found in the first edition of our book, and responses to this file greatly aided our campaign to ferret out errors and typos for the upcoming corrected edition (a nice example of the mutual benefits of online interactivity).

Come and Explore

Our Gopher is vibrant and constantly in flux. By the time you actually log onto this Gopher, the root menu may well have changed. The goal is to always improve, and to that end we welcome your input (email: **gopher@ora.com**). We invite you to come and explore.

Here are four basic ways to call up our Gopher online.

1) If you have a local Gopher client, type:
   ```
   gopher gopher.ora.com
   ```

2) For Xgopher:
   ```
   xgopher -xrm "xgopher.root\
   Server: gopher.ora.com"
   ```

3) To use telnet (for those without a Gopher client):
   ```
   telnet gopher.ora.com
   ```
   login: **gopher** (no password)

4) For a World Wide Web browser, use this URL:
   ```
   http://gopher.ora.com:70/
   ```

COMPLETE LISTING OF TITLES
from O'Reilly & Associates, Inc.

INTERNET
The Whole Internet User's Guide & Catalog
Connecting to the Internet: An O'Reilly Buyer's Guide
!%@:: A Directory of Electronic Mail Addressing & Networks
Smileys

USING UNIX AND X
UNIX Power Tools (with CD-ROM)
UNIX in a Nutshell: System V Edition
UNIX in a Nutshell: Berkeley Edition
SCO UNIX in a Nutshell
Learning the UNIX Operating System
Learning the vi Editor
Learning GNU Emacs
Learning the Korn Shell
Making TeX Work
sed & awk
MH & xmh: E-mail for Users & Programmers
Using UUCP and Usenet
X Window System User's Guide: Volume 3
X Window System User's Guide, Motif Edition: Volume 3M

SYSTEM ADMINISTRATION
Essential System Administration
sendmail
Computer Security Basics
Practical UNIX Security
System Performance Tuning
TCP/IP Network Administration
Learning Perl
Programming perl
Managing NFS and NIS
Managing UUCP and Usenet
DNS and BIND
termcap & terminfo
X Window System Administrator's Guide: Volume 8
    (available with or without CD-ROM)

UNIX AND C PROGRAMMING
ORACLE Performance Tuning
High Performance Computing
lex & yacc
POSIX Programmer's Guide
Power Programming with RPC
Programming with curses
Managing Projects with make
Software Portability with imake
Understanding and Using COFF
Migrating to Fortran 90
UNIX for FORTRAN Programmers
Using C on the UNIX System
Checking C Programs with lint
Practical C Programming
Understanding Japanese Information Processing

DCE (DISTRIBUTED COMPUTING ENVIRONMENT)
Distributing Applications Across DCE and Windows NT
Guide to Writing DCE Applications
Understanding DCE

BERKELEY 4.4 SOFTWARE DISTRIBUTION
4.4BSD System Manager's Manual
4.4BSD User's Reference Manual
4.4BSD User's Supplementary Documents
4.4BSD Programmer's Reference Manual
4.4BSD Programmer's Supplementary Documents
4.4BSD-Lite CD Companion

X PROGRAMMING
The X Window System in a Nutshell
X Protocol Reference Manual: Volume 0
Xlib Programming Manual: Volume 1
Xlib Reference Manual: Volume 2
X Toolkit Intrinsics Programming Manual: Volume 4
X Toolkit Intrinsics Programming Manual, Motif Edition: Volume 4M
X Toolkit Intrinsics Reference Manual: Volume 5
Motif Programming Manual: Volume 6A
Motif Reference Manual: Volume 6B
XView Programming Manual: Volume 7A
XView Reference Manual: Volume 7B
PEXlib Programming Manual
PEXlib Reference Manual
PHIGS Programming Manual (softcover or hardcover)
PHIGS Reference Manual
Programmer's Supplement for R5 of the X Window System

THE X RESOURCE
A quarterly working journal for X programmers
The X Resource: Issues 0 through 10

OTHER
Building a Successful Software Business
Love Your Job!

TRAVEL
Travelers' Tales Thailand

AUDIOTAPES
Internet Talk Radio's "Geek of the Week" Interviews
The Future of the Internet Protocol, 4 hours
Global Network Operations, 2 hours
Mobile IP Networking, 1 hour
Networked Information and Online Libraries, 1 hour
Security and Networks, 1 hour
European Networking, 1 hour

Notable Speeches of the Information Age
John Perry Barlow, 1.5 hours

INTERNATIONAL DISTRIBUTORS

Customers outside North America can now order O'Reilly & Associates' books through the following distributors. They offer our international customers faster order processing, more bookstores, increased representation at tradeshows worldwide, and the high-quality, responsive service our customers have come to expect.

EUROPE, MIDDLE EAST, AND AFRICA

except Germany, Switzerland, and Austria

INQUIRIES

International Thomson Publishing Europe
Berkshire House
168-173 High Holborn
London WC1V 7AA
United Kingdom
Telephone: 44-71-497-1422
Fax: 44-71-497-1426
Email: danni.dolbear@itpuk.co.uk

ORDERS

International Thomson Publishing Services, Ltd.
Cheriton House, North Way
Andover, Hampshire SP10 5BE
United Kingdom
Telephone: 44-264-342-832 (UK orders)
Telephone: 44-264-342-806 (outside UK)
Fax: 44-264-364418 (UK orders)
Fax: 44-264-342761 (outside UK)

GERMANY, SWITZERLAND, AND AUSTRIA

International Thomson Publishing GmbH
O'Reilly-International Thomson Verlag
Königswinterer Strasse 418
53227 Bonn
Germany
Telephone: 49-228-445171
Fax: 49-228-441342
Email (CompuServe): 100272,2422
Email (Internet): 100272.2422@compuserve.com

ASIA

except Japan

INQUIRIES

International Thomson Publishing Asia
221 Henderson Road
#05 10 Henderson Building
Singapore 0315
Telephone: 65-272-6496
Fax: 65-272-6498

ORDERS

Telephone: 65-268-7867
Fax: 65-268-6727

AUSTRALIA

WoodsLane Pty. Ltd.
Unit 8, 101 Darley Street (P.O. Box 935)
Mona Vale NSW 2103
Australia
Telephone: 61-2-9795944
Fax: 61-2-9973348
Email: woods@tmx.mhs.oz.au

NEW ZEALAND

WoodsLane New Zealand Ltd.
7 Purnell Street (P.O. Box 575)
Wanganui, New Zealand
Telephone: 64-6-3476543
Fax: 64-6-3454840
Email: woods@tmx.mhs.oz.au

THE AMERICAS, JAPAN, AND OCEANIA

O'Reilly & Associates, Inc.
103A Morris Street
Sebastopol, CA 95472 U.S.A.
Telephone: 707-829-0515
Telephone: 800-998-9938 (U.S. & Canada)
Fax: 707-829-0104
Email: order@ora.com